The Gospel of Accor █W9-CRC-545

The Gospel of According to St. John

THE SUNDAY SERMONS OF
THE GREAT FATHERS

VOLUME THREE

Semper redeundum ad divinae revelationis Fontes; quod depositum Divinus Redemptor concredidit authentice interpretandum soli Ecclesiae Magisterio.

Pope Pius XII,

Encyclical *Humani Generis*,

12 August 1950

THE
SUNDAY SERMONS
OF THE GREAT
FATHERS

VOLUME THREE

*From Pentecost to the
Tenth Sunday after Pentecost*

TRANSLATED AND EDITED BY
M. F. TOAL, D.D.

𝔓reseruation 𝔓ress

P.O. Box 612   Swedesboro, NJ 08085

Library of Congress Cataloging-in-Publication Data

Patristic homilies on the Gospels.
  The Sunday sermons of the great Fathers: a manual of preaching, spiritual reading,
and meditation / translated and edited by M. F. Toal.
      p.   cm.
  Originally published Patristic homilies on the Gospels. Chicago: Regnery, 1955-
1963.
  Contains Saint Thomas Aquinas' Catena aurea.
  Includes bibliographical references and indexes.
  Contents: v. 1. From the first Sunday of Advent to Quinquagesima—v. 2. From the
first Sunday in Lent to the Sunday after the Ascension—v. 3. From Pentecost to the
tenth Sunday after Pentecost—v. 4. From the eleventh Sunday after Pentecost to the
twenty-fourth and last Sunday after Pentecost.
  ISBN 1-886412-14-6 (set: alk. paper). — ISBN 1-886412-15-4 (v. 1: alk. paper). —
ISBN 1-886412-16-2 (v. 2: alk. paper). — ISBN 1-886412-17-0 (v. 3: alk. paper). —
ISBN 1-886412-18-9 (v. 4: alk paper)
    1. Bible. N.T. Gospels—Sermons. 2. Sermons, English. 3. Church year ser-
mons. 4. Bible. N.T. Gospels—Commentaries. 5. Fathers of the church. I. Toal,
M. F. II. Thomas, Aquinas. Saint, 1225?-1274. Catena aurea. English. III. Title.
BS2555.A2T6 1997
252'.011 —dc21   96-44004
                                                                            CIP

2   3   4   5   6   7   8   9   10   Printing/Year   00   99   98

For information write Preservation Press:
P.O. Box 612, Swedesboro, NJ 08085

FOREWORD
TO THE FIRST VOLUME

THE author of the present work has had as his purpose to put into the hands of his fellow priests material of incomparable value, in a form easy of access, with a view to aiding them in the sacred ministry of preaching. This apostolic ministry is the one on which all else depends in the mission of the Church for the salvation of souls.

A large portion of it will always consist in homilies on the Gospels of the Sundays and Principal Feasts. Father Toal, in this first volume, has in view this sector of the preacher's work. For the Gospel of each Sunday and Feast he has brought together from the most reliable sources, and translated, all that he thought to be best and most useful in the homilies and expositions of the Fathers and of the Angel of the Schools.

Nothing more suited to his noble purpose could be conceived. The word of God contained in Scripture, and especially in the Gospels, has been given to the Church for the instruction of men. Sacred Tradition guided by the Spirit of God has expounded it in the writings of the Holy Fathers and Doctors.

Father Toal has placed in the easiest possible reach of the busy priest this treasure house of sacred lore, this quintessence of the doctrine of Tradition on each Gospel. What he supplies may, of course, not be all that may be usefully known in relation to it, but it is, and by long odds, the most important thing. A sermon well prepared on the matter here supplied cannot fail to be learned, solid, simple and effective.

What more can be said in praise of the utility of Father Toal's contribution? We shall all be grateful to him, and *his reward will indeed be great* (Mt. v. 12).

MICHAEL BROWNE, O.P.

Master General of the Order of Preachers
formerly Master of the Sacred
Apostolic Palace

Vatican
24 *November* 1954

v

BIBLIOGRAPHY AND
ABBREVIATIONS

Bibliotheca Patrum Concionatoria of P. Francois Combefis
    O.P. Paris 1681   BPC

Migne's Patrologiae Cursus Completus
    Series Graeca. Edition Paris 1886. Vols. 161   PG
    Series Latina. Edition Paris 1844–66. Vols. 221   PL

Corpus Scriptorum Ecclesiasticorum Latinorum   CSEL

Catena Aurea Sancti Thomae
    Editio Joannis Nicolae O.P. Lyons 1686   CA
    (A complete edition in English of the Catena Aurea is in
    course of preparation.—Ed.)

Catena Sexaginta-quinque Graecorum Patrum in Lucam,
    Quae Quatuor simul Evangelistarum introduxit Ex-
    plicationem. Luce ac latinitate donata a Balthasare
    Corderio Soc. Jesu. Antwerp 1628   Catena GP

Catena Patrum Graecorum in S. Joannem, ex antiquissimo
    Graeco codice MS nuncprimum in lucem edita, a
    Balthasare Corderio Soc. Jesu. Antwerp 1630   Catena GP

Graffin, Patrologia Syriaca   GPS

Vossio, Sti Ephraem Syri Opera Omnia, Cologne 1616   Vossio S. Eph.

Graffin, Patrologia Orientalis   GPO

Denzinger, Enchiridion Symbolorum 1928   Denz.

Enchiridion Biblicum, 1954   EB

Dictionnaire de Theologie Catholique   DTC

Clavis Patrum Latinorum, Sacris Eruduri III, 1051   Clavis

Pour Revaloriser Migne, Tables Rectificatives, par Mgr.
    Glorieux, Lille 1952   PRM

Etude, Textes, G. Morin, Maredsous 1913
    Faure, Glossarium

A Glossary of Later Latin to A.D. 600, compiled by Alexander
    Souter, Oxford 1949   GLL

Mediaeval Latin Word List, Baxter and Johnson, Oxford 1947

Texts and Studies

Altaner, Patrologie, 1951

NOTE ON THE ARRANGEMENT OF THIS BOOK

For each Sunday or Feast Day in the book there is given the Gospel of the Day, and after that the parallel passages from other gospels where such passages exist. In every case these are followed by an exposition of the Gospel taken from the Catena Aurea of St Thomas Aquinas, which in turn is followed by a selection of sermons on the Gospel.

LIST OF DOCTORS AND FATHERS
IN THIS VOLUME

THE FOUR GREAT DOCTORS OF THE EAST

1. St Basil the Great, Confessor, Doctor of the Church, Archbishop of Cappadocia, Asia Minor. Born c. 330; died 379.
2. St Gregory Nazianzen, Confessor, Doctor of the Church, Archbishop of Constantinople 379. Born 329; died 390.
3. St John Chrysostom, Confessor, Doctor of the Church, Archbishop of Constantinople 397. Born 354; died 407.
4. St Cyril of Alexandria, Confessor, Doctor of the Church, Archbishop of Alexandria 412. Died 444.

THE FOUR GREAT DOCTORS OF THE WEST

1. St Ambrose, Confessor, Doctor of the Church, Archbishop of Milan 373. Born 339; died 397.
2. St Jerome, Confessor, Doctor of the Church, Priest. Born 347; died 420.
3. St Augustine, Confessor, Doctor of the Church, Bishop of Hippo 395. Born 354; baptized 387; died 28 August 430.
4. St Gregory the Great, Pope, Confessor, Doctor of the Church. Born 540; successor of St Peter 590; died 604.

FATHERS, DOCTORS, ECCLESIASTICAL WRITERS

1. St Clement, Pope, Martyr, early successor of St Peter. Fellow-labourer of St Paul (Phil. iv. 3).
2. St Justin Martyr. Born c. 100; martyred Rome 165.
3. St Irenaeus, Martyr, Father of the Church, Bishop of Lyons. Martyred c. 202.
4. Clement of Alexandria, learned and saintly Christian layman. Died 215.
5. Origen, Confessor, Priest. Born c. 185; died 253.
6. St Cyprian, Martyr, Father of the Church, Bishop of Carthage. Martyred 14 September 258.
7. St Hilary, Confessor, Doctor of the Church, Bishop of Poitiers from 350. Died 368.
8. St Ephraim, Confessor, Deacon, Doctor of the Church. Died 373.
9. St Gregory of Nyssa, Confessor, Doctor of the Church, Bishop of Nyssa 371. Died 394.
10. St Amphilocius of Iconium. Born 339; died c. 400.
11. St Gaudentius, Bishop of Brescia from 387. Died 410.

12. St Asherius, Bishop of Amasene, Metropolitan of Pontus. Died *c.* 410.
13. St Proclius, Archbishop of Constantinople 434. Died 446.
14. St Peter Chrysologus, Confessor, Doctor of the Church, Archbishop of Ravenna. Died 450.
15. St Leo the Great, Pope, Confessor, Doctor of the Church. Successor of St Peter A.D. 440. Died 461. The supreme witness and teacher of the Incarnation.
16. St Maximus, Bishop of Turin. Born 380; died 465.
17. The Venerable Bede, Priest, Confessor, Doctor of the Church, of Jarrow (Northumberland). Born 672; died 735.
18. Theophylactus, Patriarch of Bulgaria. Born 765; died 840.
19. Remigius, of Auxerre, ecclesiastical writer. Died 908.

CONTENTS

PENTECOST

THE GOSPEL OF THE SUNDAY

John xiv. 23–31

At that time: Jesus said to his disciples: If any one love me, he will keep my word, and my Father will love him, and we will come to him, and will make our abode with him. He that loveth me not, keepeth not my words. And the word which you have heard is not mine; but the Father's who sent me. These things have I spoken to you, abiding with you. But the Paraclete, the Holy Ghost, whom the Father will send in my name, he will teach you all things, and bring all things to your mind, whatsoever I shall have said to you.

Peace I leave with you, my peace I give unto you: not as the world giveth, do I give unto you. Let not your heart be troubled, nor let it be afraid. You have heard that I said to you: I go away, and I come unto you. If you loved me, you would indeed be glad, because I go to the Father: for the Father is greater than I.

And now I have told you before it come to pass: that when it shall come to pass, you may believe. I will not now speak many things with you, For the prince of this world cometh. and in me he hath not any thing.

But that the world may know, that I love the Father: and as the Father hath given me commandment, so do I.

Exposition from the Catena Aurea

V. 23. Jesus said: If any one love me, he will keep my word . . .

Gregory, *Hom.* 30 *in Gospel*: The proof of love is to do good. The love of God is never idle; where you find it, it is doing great things. If it does nothing, love is not there.

Augustine, *Tr.* 76 *in John* 2: It is love divides the sanctified from the world, and makes men dwell in peace in one house, and in this house the Father and the Son take up their abode: They Who give this love to those to whom they will finally give the Divine Wisdom. There is a certain inward vision of God of which the wicked know nothing; there is no vision of the Father and the Holy Spirit for them. Of the Son there could be, in the flesh; but this is not the same as the other: it is only for a little while, not for ever; for judgement, not for joy; for punishment, not as a reward.

And we will come to him. They come to us, when we go to Them. They come to us, helping us; we go to Them, by obedience. They come in light, we come in contemplation. They come filling us, we come receiving: so the vision given us is inward, not outward, and their abode in us is not fleeting but eternal. And so we have: *And will make our abode with them.*

Gregory, *as above*: For He comes into certain hearts, but does not make His abode there; for though through compunction they do in fact feel a love for God, in time of temptation they forget what moved them to repentance. He who truly loves God, into that heart God comes, and there makes His abode. For the love of God has so penetrated it, that in time of temptation it will not go back upon this love. For he truly loves whose soul is not conquered by consent to evil delight.

Augustine, *as above*, 4: Are we to suppose that the Holy Ghost is excluded from this mansion the Father and Son are making in the heart that loves Them? What then is the meaning of the words spoken earlier: *He shall abide with you, and shall be in you* (v. 17)? Unless there is anyone so foolish as to believe that when the Father and Son come the Holy Ghost departs; as giving place to superiors? Yet even to this carnal notion Holy Scripture has an answer, when it says: *That he may abide with you for ever* (v. 16). Therefore He shall be with Them for ever in this same mansion; for as He came not without Them, neither did They come without Him. For in the teaching of the Trinity certain acts are imputed to separately named Persons; yet by reason of the Substance (*nature*) of the same Trinity by this it is not to be understood that these are done separately from the Others.

Gregory: The more a man delights in earthly things, the more he is shut off from heavenly love. Hence:

V. 24. He that loveth me not, keepeth not my words.

So life, soul and tongue proclaim our love of the Creator.

CHRYSOSTOM, *Hom.* 74 *in John*: Or: Judas thought that they were to see Him as we see the dead in sleep, and so he asks Him: *How is it that thou wilt manifest thyself to us, and not to the world?* As though he were to say: Woe to us that you will die and appear to us as the dead appear. Lest they have this notion in mind He says: *I and the Father will come to him*; that is, as the Father reveals Himself, so shall I. *And will make our abode with him*; which is not the way of dreams. Then follows: *And the word you have heard is not mine; but the Father's who sent me*; that is, He who does not hear My words, not alone does he not love Me, but neither does he love the Father. He said this because He uttered nothing without the Father; or spoke that alone which was pleasing to Him.

AUGUSTINE, *as above*: And also, perhaps because of a certain distinction, where He speaks of His *words* He speaks of them in the plural; as when He says: *He that loveth me not, keepeth not my words.* But where He says the Word is not His, but the Father's, He means Himself. For He is not His own Word, but the Father's; as He is not His own image, but the Father's. Rightly then does He attribute what He does, as His Equal, to the Author from Whom comes the Attribute of being wholly His Equal.

V. 25. *These things have I spoken to you, abiding with you.*

CHRYSOSTOM: Since some of the things He said were clear and some they did not understand, that they

might not be troubled, He adds: *These things I have spoken etc.* AUGUSTINE: The promised *abode* is not the same as this abiding He here speaks of. The first is spiritual, and made known inwardly to souls; this other is of the body and made known by eyes and ears.

CHRYSOSTOM: That they might the more cheerfully bear the departure of His bodily presence from among them, He prepares them for this by promising that His bodily going from them would be the source of great blessings. For while He dwelt among them in His body, and until the Spirit had come, they could not come to the knowledge of great things. Hence:

V. 26. *But the Paraclete, the Holy Ghost, whom the Father will send . . .*

GREGORY: Paraclete means *Consoler* or *Advocate*. He is called Advocate when He intercedes with the Father for sinners; while those He fills He inspires to pray for themselves. The same Spirit is called Consoler (Comforter), because He uplifts with the hope of pardon those who grieve for the sins they have committed. CHRYSOSTOM: He constantly calls Him the *Paraclete* because of the afflictions that then surrounded them.

DIDYMUS, *On the Holy Spirit, Jerome II*: The Saviour declares that the Holy Spirit is sent by the Father in His, the Saviour's, Name: for the true name of the Saviour is Son; since by this word there is made known to us both community of Nature and, if I may say so, the distinction of Persons. Because of the relationship of Father to Son it is only the Son Who can come in the

Name of the Father. No one else comes in the Name of the Father, but only, for example, in the Name of God, or of the Lord, or of the Almighty. Just as servants who come in the name of a master, by the very fact of serving and obeying they proclaim their master (for servants mean a master); so the Son Who comes in the Name of the Father bears that Name for the reason that He is the acknowledged Only-Begotten Son of God.

That the Holy Spirit is sent in the Son's Name by the Father, shows He is joined in Oneness with the Son. For this He is called the Spirit of the Son; and through adoption by Him He makes sons of those who wish to receive Him. This Holy Spirit then, sent by the Father, comes in the Name of the Son, and will teach all things to those who have been confirmed in the faith of Christ: all spiritual things, all that can be understood of divine truth, and the secrets of holy wisdom. And He will teach, not as those who by industry and study have acquired a little knowledge, and a little wisdom, but, as though He were Himself Knowledge and Doctrine and Wisdom, the Spirit of Truth will make known, invisibly, to our mind the knowledge of divine things.

GREGORY: Unless the same Spirit is in the heart of the hearer the words of the teacher are in vain. Let no one then attribute to the man who is teaching that which he understands from the lips of his teacher; for, unless there is One within Who teaches, the tongue of the teacher without labours in vain. The Creator Himself does not speak for man's enlightenment, unless the Spirit, by His unction, also speaks to the man (I John ii. 27).

AUGUSTINE, *Tr.* 77, 2: Is it that the Son speaks, and the Holy Spirit teaches, so that when the Son speaks we hear the words, and when the Holy Spirit teaches we understand them? It is the whole Trinity that both speaks and teaches. But unless this mystery (of the Trinity) is placed before us, Person by Person, in no way could human infirmity grasp it.

GREGORY: Let us ask ourselves why is it said of the Spirit: *He will bring all things to your mind*; since to prompt is the office of an inferior? But as we use the word prompt sometimes to convey the meaning of secretly helping, the Spirit is here said to prompt us invisibly, not because He adds to our knowledge in a lowly manner, but in a secret manner.

AUGUSTINE: Or, that He adds, *He will bring all things to your mind* (that is, He will remind you) we should understand to mean what we are bidden not to forget, that His most salutary reminders refer to the grace by which the Spirit reminds us.[1]

THEOPHYLACTUS: The Holy Spirit then has both taught us and reminded us. He has taught whatever it was Christ did not teach His Disciples, because they were not able to bear it; He reminded them of whatever the Lord had said to them, but which they could not remember, either because of its obscurity, or because they were slow of mind.

V. 27. *Peace I leave with you, my peace I give unto you.*

CHRYSOSTOM: Because they were troubled at hearing of the hatred and strife they would meet when He was gone, He again comforts them by saying: *Peace I leave you etc.*

AUGUSTINE: He has left us peace in this world, abiding in which we shall overcome the enemy, and that also here below we may love one another. His own peace He will give us in the world to come: when we shall reign without an enemy, and where there can be no discord. But He is Himself our peace: both when we believe He is, and when we shall see Him as He is.

What does He mean when He says, *Peace I leave with you*, but does not add, *my*; but where He says, *I give unto you*, He there says *my*? Are we to understand that *my* is implied even where it is not said; or is there perhaps something hidden here? *His* peace, He wishes us to understand, is that which He has Himself. That peace which He has left us in this world, must be called ours rather than his: since He has nothing within Himself to combat, being wholly without sin, while we now possess but that peace in which we yet must say: *Forgive us our trespasses*. In like manner have we peace amongst ourselves; for we trust each other that we do love one another. But neither is this a perfect peace: for we do not see into the thoughts of each other's heart. I am aware just the same that these words of the Lord can be taken as a simple repetition of the same sentence.

That the Lord adds: *Not as the world giveth, do I give unto you*, what else does He imply but, not as men give who love the world? They give themselves peace: that they may enjoy the world untroubled. And even when they leave the just in peace, by not persecuting them, even this cannot be called true peace: for there is no true harmony, because their hearts are divided.

CHRYSOSTOM: Outward peace can also be an evil, and of no profit to those who enjoy it. AUGUSTINE, *Serm.* 59: Peace is serenity of mind, tranquillity of soul, simplicity of heart, the bond of love, the company of charity. No man can enter into the inheritance of the Lord who refuses to observe the covenant of peace; and neither can he live in peace with Christ who of his own will lives in conflict with a Christian. Then follows: *Let not your heart be troubled, nor let it be afraid.*

CHRYSOSTOM: As He had said, *Peace I leave you*, the speech of one who is departing, and as this could cause them sorrow, He then says: *Let not your heart be troubled, nor let it be afraid*; since they suffered one emotion through loving Him, the other because of fear.

V. 28. *You have heard that I said to you: I go away, and I come unto you.*

AUGUSTINE, *Tr.* 78 *in John*: Their hearts could be troubled and afraid because He was going from them, though He was to come to them again, for fear that in the absence of the Shepherd the wolf might then attack the flock. So there follows: *You have heard etc.*

He was going from them as man, and remaining with them as God. Why then should their hearts be troubled or afraid when He was going only from before their eyes, but not from their heart? To make them understand that it was as man that He said, *I go away, and I come unto you,* He goes on to say: *If you loved me you would indeed be glad, because I go to the Father; for the Father is greater than I.*

In that therefore wherein the Son is not equal to the Father, through this it is He goes to the Father: from Whom He will come again, to judge the living and the dead. In that wherein He is equal to the Father, at no time does He leave the Father, but is everywhere wholly One with Him in the Undivided Trinity, which no place confines. He then, the Son of God, equal to the Father in the Form of God (because He emptied Himself, not losing the Form of God, but taking the form of a servant), is greater even than Himself; for greater is the Form of God, which was not forfeited, than the form of a servant, which was assumed by Him. It is in this form of a servant, therefore, that the Son of God is less than the Holy Spirit, as well as less than the Father. In this form the Child Jesus was less even than His parents, when as a Child *He was subject to them,* as it is written.

Let us then acknowledge the twofold substance (*nature*) of Christ: the divine, namely, in which He is equal to the Father, and the human, than which the Father is greater. But both together are not two, but one Christ: lest God be believed to be a quaternity, not a Trinity. And so He says: If you loved me, you would indeed be glad, because I go to the Father. For human nature should rejoice at being taken up to heaven, by the Only-Begotten, and made immortal there: that what was of earth should become sublime, and that perishable dust should sit at the right hand of God. Who that loves Christ should not rejoice at this, seeing his own nature now immortal, and that he too has the hope of becoming the same, in Christ?

HILARY, *On the Trinity,* 9: Or, if the Father is greater than Me by virtue of giving, is the Son lesser through confessing the gift? Greater is the one giving, but He is not lesser to Whom is given Oneness with the Giver. CHRYSOSTOM: The Apostles did not yet know what this resurrection was which He had foretold, when He said: *I go away, and I come unto you,* nor what they were to think of it. The Father, they knew, was mighty. So He says to them: Although you fear for Me, that I cannot defend Myself, and you are not certain that I shall see you again after My Crucifixion, yet, at hearing that I go to the Father you ought to rejoice, since I am going to One Who is greater than Me, and able to scatter all such tribulations. All this He said because of the timidity of the Disciples; so He continues:

V. 29. *And now I have told you before it come to pass . . .*

AUGUSTINE, *Tr.* 79: Why does He say this? For if a thing is to be believed, it should be believed before it happens. Is it not the glory of faith that it believes what is not seen? For the one to whom it was said: *Because thou hast seen thou hast believed,* saw one thing, and believed another. He saw man, but believed Him God. But though belief is used of things seen, as when a man says he believes his own eyes, this is not the faith in which we are formed; but from what we see we are prepared to believe that which we do not see.

The words of our Lord then: *That when it shall come to pass*, that they shall see Him living, after His death, and ascending to the Father, mean, that when they see Him they will believe He is Christ the Son of God, able to do this, and to foretell He would do it. And they would believe this, not by a new faith, but by an increased one; or by a faith grown faint when He died, but renewed at His Resurrection.

V. 30. *I will not now speak many things with you. For the prince of* . . .

HILARY: He goes on then to speak of the re-assumption of His glory: *I will not now speak.* BEDE: He says this because the time was drawing near for His capture, and delivering up to death. *For the prince of this world cometh.* AUGUSTINE: Who is this but the devil? The devil is not a prince of creatures, but of sinners; as the Apostle explains when he says our warfare was *against the rulers of the world* (Eph. vi. 12); he further explains what *world* means when he adds: *of this darkness*: the world, that is, of evil doers. *And in me he hath not anything.* For God had come without stain of sin, nor had the Virgin brought forth His Body from a root of sin. And as though asked, why then do You die if you are without sin, of which death is the punishment, He goes on:

V. 31. *But that the world may know, that I love the Father* . . .

He had been sitting at table with them while He spoke. *Let us go,* He said: to that place from which He was to be delivered up to death, Who had not deserved death. But He had a commandment from the Father that He should die.

AUGUSTINE, *Contra serm. Arianorum,* 11: That the Son is obedient to the will and to the commandment of the Father does not, no more than among men, show a difference and an inequality of nature as between Father commanding and the Son obeying. And to this is to be added that Christ is not alone God, and in this Equal in Nature with the Father, but also man, in which He is by nature less than the Father.

CHRYSOSTOM: *Arise let us go hence.* This is the beginning of another discourse. The time and place had made the Disciples fearful; for they were now in the depth of night, and in the midst of the city, and so probably not paying full attention to what He was saying to them, but turning their eyes this way and that, imagining an attack at any moment, especially when they heard Him say: *Yet a little while I am with you,* and then, *the prince of this world cometh.* Frightened as they were at these and like words, He brings them to another place, where, thinking themselves safe, they would listen with attention. For now they were to hear great and sublime truths.

I. St Basil the Great, Bishop and Doctor

On the Holy Spirit[2]

Let us here consider what are common expressions for the Holy Spirit, both those we have gathered from Sacred Scripture concerning Him, and those we have received from the unwritten tradition of the Fathers. First we ask, who is not uplifted in his soul, raising his mind to that Nature on high, when he hears the titles of the Holy Spirit? For He is called *The Spirit of God*, and *The Spirit of Truth, Who proceeds from the Father* (Jn. xv. 26), the *Spirit of virtue*, a *Commanding Spirit* (Ps. l. 12, 14). His true and proper name however is *The Holy Spirit*; a name which above all others declares that He is wholly incorporeal, free of matter, indivisible. For this reason the Lord, teaching the woman who believed God must be adored in a given place, that the mind cannot know the incorporeal, said, *God is a spirit* (Jn. iv. 24).

When we hear of the Spirit the mind may not imagine to itself an image of some limited circumscribed nature, liable to change, or alteration, or at all like a created thing, but must go on in its conception to the very highest notions, and form to itself an idea of an intelligent Being, infinite in power, of greatness without measure, bounded neither by time nor by ages, bountiful of its own goodness, to whom all turn who need sanctification, to whom all aspire who live in holiness, as though watered and assisted by Its breath to arrive at their due perfection. A Being who perfects others, Itself needing nothing; existing as not needing to be renewed, yet giving life abundantly; enlarging through no addition, but at once complete; at rest within itself, yet in all places; the source of holiness, the light of the mind, and providing light from Itself to every faculty of the soul that searches for truth; by nature inaccessible, yet yielding to goodness; filling every need by Its power, but given only to those who are worthy of It, to whom It is not given in the same measure, but in the measure of each man's faith (Rom. xii. 6).

Simple in nature, manifold in powers, wholly present in each single one, and whole and entire in all places. Impassively divided, yet wholly bestowed, like the rays of the sun whose favour each enjoys as though it shone for him alone; yet it shines on land and sea and fills the air. So the Spirit, to each one who receives It, as though given to him alone, pours forth sufficient and perfect grace to each one, is enjoyed by each one, not in the measure of Its power, but of their capacity.

Now the Spirit is not united to the soul by drawing near to it in place (for how may what is corporeal draw near to what is incorporeal?), but through the withdrawal of the passions; which, drawing close to the soul, through its affection for the flesh, have drawn it away from its friendship with God. When a man becomes clean of the stain he received through sin, and has returned to his natural beauty, restoring to its former resemblance the royal image within him, only then may he draw near to the Paraclete. And He, like the sun, will shew thee, thy eye now made pure, the Image of the Invisible in Himself. And in the blessed contemplation of this Image thou shalt see the unspeakable beauty of the Archetype.

Through His aid hearts are lifted up, the weak led by the hand, those going forward are perfected. Shining upon those who have been purified of every stain, He makes them spiritual in heart, through union with Himself. For just as when the sunlight falls on clear transparent bodies, they too become resplendent, and begin to shine from another light within themselves, so the souls that contain the Spirit within them, become themselves spiritual, and their brightness shines forth on others.

From this comes knowledge of the future, the understanding of mysteries, the seeing of things hidden, the apportioning of gifts, heavenly association with the angelic choirs, joy without end, abiding with God, being made like to God, and, highest of all, that you are made God (*partaker of the divine nature*, II Pet. i. 4). These then are some of the notions we possess regarding the Holy Spirit, to speak of but a few; and which we have been taught concerning His greatness, His dignity, and His operations, from the very words of the Spirit Himself. Now we must reply to those who deny them; refute the objections brought forward in the name of so-called science.[3]

It is not right, they say, to make the Holy Spirit one with the Father and the Son, because He is of a different nature, and lesser in dignity. It is fitting that we answer this in the words of the Apostles: *We ought to obey God, rather than men* (Acts v. 29). For if the Lord in

bequeathing to us the baptism of salvation, clearly laid it upon His Disciples, that they were to baptize all nations, *In the name of the Father, and of the Son, and of the Holy Ghost* (Mt. xxviii. 19), not declining fellowship with Him, while these, on the contrary, assert that the Holy Spirit must not be associated with the Father and the Son, how can they be other than in open conflict with God's command? And if they say that association of this kind does not imply Communion, or Oneness of any kind, let them say why we must hold this belief, and to what kind of intimate union do they pretend?[4] And if the Lord did not unite the Holy Spirit with Himself and with the Father in baptism, let them not blame us for the conjunction:[5] for we neither put forward nor believe anything different. If He is there joined to the Father and there is no one so impudent as to say anything else, let no one blame us for following the Scriptures.

But all the sources of war are prepared against us, every kind of belief is imputed to us; and the tongues of blasphemers hit us more violently than the stones that once were flung at Stephen by the killers of Christ. And do not allow them to hide the fact that attacking us is but a ruse of war; for their real aim is higher up. They pretend that it is against us they prepare their artifices and their snares, and urge each other on, that each one may try his strength or skill against us. But it is against the Faith they make war. The common aim of all our adversaries, and of all *who are contrary to sound doctrine* (I Tim. i. 10), is to overthrow the foundations of the Faith of Christ, by levelling the

Apostolic traditions to the earth, and wholly destroying them. So like debtors, good debtors of course, they demand proof, written proof, from the Sacred Writings, and dismiss, as wholly unworthy of belief, the unwritten witness of the Fathers.

But we shall not falter in our defence of the truth; nor forsake its defence through cowardice. For the Lord has left us as a necessary and saving truth the conjunction of the Holy Spirit with the Father. For them it shall not be so; and they seek to separate and humiliate the Holy Spirit, and lower Him to the degree of one who serves. Is it not then true to say, that with them their own blasphemy has more authority than the Law laid down by our Lord? Let us put aside all contention and see what we have in hand.

Whence is it that we are Christians? Through faith, all will answer. How are we saved? By being born again in the grace of baptism. For how else could we be? Then, knowing that this salvation is confirmed by the Father, Son, and Holy Ghost, shall we cast aside this *form of doctrine* (Rom. vi. 17) handed down to us? Would this not be the cause of the greatest grief if we now found we were further off from salvation than when we first believed (Rom. xiii. 11); that we must now deny what before we believed? For it is the same loss for anyone to depart this life unbaptized, as to receive that baptism from which one thing of what has been handed down has been omitted. And whoever does not observe the profession we made on our first *entering in*, when, delivered *from idols*, we approached the living God, and does not hold fast to it throughout his life as his surest protection, makes himself a *stranger* from the *promises* of God (I Thess. i. 9); dishonouring the pledge (*handwriting*) he himself gave at his profession of faith.

For if for me my baptism was the beginning of my life, and that day of my rebirth the first of all days, then, plainly, the word I spoke on the day of my adoption is the one most of all to be honoured. Can I then, misled by the deceptions of such teachers as these, deny that tradition which brought me to the Light, guided me to the knowledge of my God, and made me a son of God who before was His enemy through sin? For myself I pray that I may depart to the Lord holding fast to this profession; and I exhort them also, to preserve the faith inviolate till the Day of Christ, to maintain the Spirit undivided from the Father, and from the Son, and observe the faith of their baptism, both in their profession of faith, and in giving praise to God, Father, Son, and Holy Ghost, to Whom be praise and glory, world without end.
Amen.

II. St Ambrose, Bishop and Doctor

The Names of the Holy Spirit[6]

Ambrose proves from Sacred Scripture that one is the name of the Three Divine Persons; and in the first place the unity of name of the Son and Holy Ghost, since they are both called Paraclete and Truth

1. Who will venture to deny Their unity of name when he sees Their unity in work? But why do I seek to establish Their unity of name,

since it is evident from the witness of the Divine Voice, that one is the name of Father, Son, and Holy Ghost? For it is written: *Going therefore, teach ye all nations, baptizing them in the name of the Father, and of the Son, and of the Holy Ghost.* In the *name*, He said; not in the names. Therefore, there is not one name for the Father, one for the Son, and another for the Holy Ghost. As God is One He has not many names; for there are not two gods, or three gods. *There is no God but one* (I Cor. viii. 4).

And that He might show One is the Divinity, One His power, since one is the name of Father, Son, and Holy Ghost, the Son does not come in any other name, nor the Holy Ghost in any other name, as the Lord Himself says: *I am come in the name of my Father, and you receive me not; if another shall come in his own name, him you will receive* (Jn. v. 43).

Scripture tells us that what the Father's name is this also is the Son's; for in the book of Exodus the Lord Himself says: *I shall call on thee in my name, O Lord; I shall invoke the name of the Lord before thee* (xxxiii. 19 Sept.). The Lord therefore has said that He will call upon the Lord in His own name. Lord is therefore the name of both the Father and the Son.

Since one is the name of the Father and of the Son, receive then that the same is also the name of the Holy Ghost, since the Holy Ghost likewise comes in the name of the Son, as it is written: *The Paraclete, the Holy Spirit, whom the Father will send in my name, he will teach you all things.* He Who comes in the name of the Son, truly comes in the name of the Father and the Son: for one is the name of the Father and the Son.

And so it is that one is the name of the Father and the Son and the Holy Ghost. For there is no other name under heaven given to men whereby we must be saved (Acts iv. 12).

It further teaches us that we are to believe the unity, not the dissimilarity, of the divine name; since Christ comes in oneness of name. Antichrist will come in his own name, as it is written: *I am come in the name of my Father, and you receive me not; if another shall come in his own name, him you will receive.* By this we are taught that between the Father and the Son and the Holy Paraclete there is no contradiction in name; likewise that what is the Son's name is also the name of the Holy Spirit: since the Son like the Holy Spirit is called Paraclete. And accordingly the Lord Jesus says in the Gospel: *I will ask my Father, and he will give you another Paraclete, the spirit of truth that he may abide with you forever* (Jn. xiv. 16). And for this reason He says, *another*; lest you understand that the Spirit is the Son: for the oneness is not of the Son and Holy Spirit—a Sabellian confusion—but of the name.

And so the Son is a Paraclete, the Holy Spirit another Paraclete; for John says the Son is a Paraclete, in the words: *But if any man sin, we have an advocate with the Father, Jesus Christ the Just* (I Jn. ii. 1). So just as there is oneness of name, there is also oneness of power: for where the Spirit Paraclete is, there also is the Son. For as here (Jn. xiv. 16) the Lord says that the Spirit shall be with the faithful for ever, so in another place He shows that He will be with His Apostles for ever: *Behold I am with you all days, even to the consummation of the world* (Mt. xxviii. 20).

One therefore are the Son and the Holy Spirit; one the name of the Trinity; and One its indivisible Presence.

But as we have shown the Son is also called Paraclete, so also have we shown that the Spirit is called Truth. Christ is Truth; that the Spirit is Truth, you may read in John's Epistle: *Since the Spirit is truth.*[7] He is then called not alone the Spirit of Truth, but Truth Itself; just as the Son is called Truth; He Who says: *I am the way, the truth, and the life* (Jn. xiv. 6).

That it is shown from the Sacred Books that the Persons of the Trinity are light.

2. Why do I seek to establish that as the Father is light, so also is the Son light, and the Holy Ghost light? Because this beyond doubt relates to the divine majesty; as John has told us: *God is light, and in him there is no darkness* (I Jn. i. 5). And the Son is light; for *the life was the light of men* (Jn. i. 4). And the Evangelist, that he might show that he was speaking of the Son of God, also says of John the Baptist: *He was not the light, but was to give testimony of the light. That was the true light which enlighteneth every man that cometh into this world* (vv. 8, 9). Therefore because God is light, the Son of God is *the true light*; for without doubt the Son of God is True God.

You may also read elsewhere that the Son is light: *The people that walked in darkness have seen a great light* (Is. ix. 2). What is more to the point are these words which say: *For with thee is the fountain of life; and in thy light we shall see light* (Ps. xxxv. 10); that is, with Thee, God the Father Almighty, Who is

the Fount of life, in Thy Son, Thy Light, we shall see the Light of the Holy Spirit. As the Lord Himself elsewhere says: *Receive ye the Holy Ghost* (Jn. xx. 22); and elsewhere: *Virtue went out from him* (Lk. vi. 19).

Who will doubt the Father is light, since we read of the Son, that He is the *Brightness of His Eternal Glory* (Heb. i. 3)? Of Whom save of the Eternal Father is the Son the Brightness, Who is forever with the Father? Nor does He shine forth from a different glory, but from the same.

That the Spirit is also Fire.

And Isaias makes known that the Holy Spirit is not alone Light, but Fire: *And the light of Israel shall be as a fire, and the Holy One thereof as a flame* (x. 17). And because of this the prophets call Him a burning fire; because we observe the power of the divinity very frequently under these three aspects: it is of the nature of the Divinity to *sanctify*; to give light is a property of *light* and *fire* equally; and it is the divine way to be seen, or to be described, under the appearance of fire: *The Lord thy God is a consuming fire*, as Moses declared (Deut. iv. 24).

For he had seen fire in the bush, and had heard the Lord when a voice spoke to him from the midst of the flames, saying: *I am the God of Abraham, the God of Isaac, and the God of Jacob* (Exod. iii. 15). The voice then came from the flames, and the flames enveloped the bush, yet the flames did not hurt it. The bush was on fire, yet it was not burnt; that the Lord might show us by this mystery, that He would come to cast light on the thorns of our body, that He would not consume the afflicted but would lighten our afflictions, that He would baptize in the Holy Spirit and in fire (Mt. iii. 11), that He would give us grace, and destroy our sins. And so the plan of God is laid bare to us under the figure of fire.

Also, in the Acts of the Apostles, when the Holy Ghost descended upon the faithful, He appeared under the image of fire. For we read: *And suddenly there came a sound from heaven, as of a mighty wind, and it filled the whole house where they were sitting; and there appeared to them parted tongues as it were of fire* (Acts ii. 2, 3). So was it when Gideon was about to defeat the Madianites, and commanded his three hundred men to take pitchers, and to carry burning torches in the pitchers, and a trumpet in their right hands (Jgs. vii. 16); so our Fathers cherished what they have received from the Apostles; because our bodies are pitchers, formed from the clay of the earth, which shall burn with the fire of spiritual grace, and shall bear witness with the voice of confession to the Passion of the Lord Jesus.

Who then may doubt of the divinity of the Holy Ghost, since where the Divinity appears in visible form, there the grace of the Spirit is found? From testimony such as this we arrive, not at diversity, but at the oneness of divine power. For how can there be division in the divine power, where the result of Their activity is the same in each One (i.e. *grace*)? Neither can there be any grace of sacraments, except where there has been forgiveness of sins.[8]

What therefore is this fire? Of a certainty it is not built up from a lowly bush; nor does it flame up from the burning brambles of the forest. This is a fire which, as with gold, makes what is good better, and devours sin as stubble. Here beyond doubt is the Holy Spirit, Who is called the Countenance of the Lord, and Fire, and Light: Light, because the countenance of the Lord is light, and it is the light of the Holy Spirit: *The light of thy countenance O Lord, is signed upon us* (Ps. iv. 7). And what is this light signed upon us, if not that of the spiritual sign, *believing in which you were signed with the holy Spirit of promise* (Eph. i. 13).

And as He is the Light of the Divine Countenance, so also is He the Fire that burns before the Face of God, as it is written: *A fire shall burn before thee* (Ps. xlix. 3). Grace shall shine forth on the Day of Judgement, that the forgiveness by which the obedience of the just shall be rewarded may follow. O great riches of the Scripture, which no mind can describe! O supreme witness of the Divine Oneness! How many things are made clear to us in these two verses!

3. *The Holy Spirit is Life.* We have said that the Father is light, that the Son is Light, that the Holy Ghost is Light. Let us believe also that the Father is Life, the Son Life, and the Holy Ghost Life. For John has said: *That which was from the beginning, which we have heard, which we have seen with our eyes, which we have looked upon, and our hands have handled, of the word of life: For the life was manifested; and we have seen and do bear witness, and declare unto you the life eternal, which was with the Father* (I Jn. i. 1, 2). And the Word of life He has also called Life; that the

Son, as well as the Father, might signify life. For what is the Word of God, but the Word of Life? And through this both God and the Word of God are Life. And as He is called *the Word of Life*, so is He also called the Spirit of life. For it is written: *And the Spirit of life was in the wheels* (Ezech. i. 20). And as *the Word of life* is Life, so also *the Spirit of life* is Life.

Let you therefore believe, that as the Father is the Fount of Life, so also, as many have stated, is the Son revealed to us as the Fount of Life: in that, *with thee*, as the psalmist says (xxxv. 10), *is the fountain of life*, thy Son, O Omnipotent God; that is, the Holy Spirit. For the Spirit is life, as the Lord tells us: *The words that I have spoken to you, are spirit and life* (Jn. vi. 24); for where the Spirit is, there also is life; and where is life, there also is the Holy Spirit.

Yet many believe that in this place in Scripture the Father alone is signified by the *fountain*; though it is plain that the Scripture says: *With thee is the fountain of life*; that is, that Son is with the Father: since the Word is with God, as He was in the beginning, with God. Whoever interprets these words to mean that it is the Father Who is the Fountain, or that it is the Son, in neither case do we mean a fountain of created water, but the Fountain of divine grace; that is, the Fountain of the Holy Ghost: for He is the Living Water. For it was of Him the Lord said: *If thou didst know the gift of God, and who he is that saith to thee: Give me to drink; thou perhaps wouldst have asked of him, and he would have given thee living water* (Jn. iv. 10).

The soul of David thirsted for this water. *As the hart panteth after the fountains of water; so my soul panteth after thee, O God* (Ps. xli. 1). The hart longs for the fountain of this water; it does not thirst for the poison of the serpent. For the water of grace is living, and by this it purifies the depths of the spirit, washes away all sin from the soul, and cleans us from the stains of pagan superstition.

4. *The Holy Spirit is a Great River.* Should anyone presume to say, that because the water flowing from it is but a limited part of the fountain, that consequently a diminution of the Spirit is implied, and so there is in Him a difference in dignity from that which belongs to the Father and the Son, let them suffer no harm from this comparison with created things, which are not adequate to illustrate the divinity. Let them understand that the Holy Spirit is called, not water alone, but also *rivers of water*. For we read, that: *Out of his belly shall flow rivers of living water. Now this he said of the Spirit which they should receive, who would believe in him* (Jn. vii. 38, 39).

The Holy Spirit is therefore a river, and the supreme river, which, according to the Hebrews, flowed from Jesus down to the earth; as was foretold by the mouth of the prophet Isaias: *Behold I will bring upon her as it were a river of peace, and as an overflowing torrent the glory of the Gentiles which you shall suck* (lxvi. 12). Mighty is this river, which flows for ever, and never grows less. And not alone the river, but also the rushing of the torrent, and its overflowing splendour, of which David has also said: *The stream of the river maketh the city of God joyful* (Ps. xlv. 5).

Nor is that Jerusalem, which is above, watered by the course of any earthly river, but by that flowing from the Fountain of Life, the Holy Ghost, of which we are filled at a single draught; that delights to pour out ever more abundantly upon the heavenly Thrones, Dominations, and Powers, upon the Angels and Archangels, rushing forth in the full stream of its sevenfold spiritual power. For if a river, overflowing the tops of its banks, spreads out, how much more will not the Spirit, overtopping every created thing, make joyful with a more abundant richness of grace the creatures of heaven, when it pours out over the as it were lowlier fields of our soul!

Do not be troubled that John has said *rivers* (vii. 38), and, in another place, *the seven spirits of God* (Apoc. v. 6). By these tokens of the sevenfold Spirit is meant the fulness of powers, as Isaias has said: the spirit of wisdom, and of understanding, the spirit of counsel, and of fortitude, the spirit of knowledge, and of godliness, the spirit of the fear of the Lord (xi. 2). One therefore is the river, but many the channels of its spiritual gifts. This then is the river that flows forth from the Fountain of Life.

And do not turn your mind aside towards inferior things, because there is an obvious difference between a fountain and a river. For the Divine Scripture provides for all things, so that the limited human mind may not be led into error by the poverty of human speech. For whatever be the river you imagine to yourself, it comes from a fountain; they are of the one substance, the one clarity, and the one beauty.

Let you then say, the Holy Spirit is one in substance with the Son of God, and with God the Father, one in brightness, and one in glory. Let me take an example of oneness of power, and here I have no fear of any question of degrees of divine dignity. In this example also the Scripture has provided for us. The Son of God says: *He who drinks of the water I shall give him, it shall become in him a fountain of water, springing up into life everlasting* (Jn. iv. 14). This fountain, spiritual grace, is beyond doubt a river flowing from a living fountain. The Holy Spirit therefore is also a Fountain of Life.

You see then that the Oneness of the Divine Majesty is made known to us from the very words of Christ; and it cannot be denied by the unbelieving, that Christ also is a fountain; since He as well as the Holy Spirit is spoken of as a fountain. *Behold I will bring upon her* (Jerusalem) *as it were a river of peace, and as an overflowing torrent the glory of the Gentiles* (Isa. lxvi. 12). Who can doubt that the Son of God is the river of life from Which have issued forth streams of life eternal?

Spiritual grace therefore is good water: who will give to my breast this fountain? Let it spring up in me; may He flow in me, the Giver of eternal life. May this fountain overflow upon us, not pass us by. For Wisdom says: *Drink water out of thy own vessel, and the streams of thy own well: let thy fountains be conveyed abroad, and in the streets divide thy waters* (Prov. v. 15, 16). How shall I hold this water, lest it vanish, lest it slip away? How shall I keep my vessel safe, that the water of eternal life may not trickle away, leaking through some crack of sin? Teach us, Lord Jesus, teach us as Thou didst teach Thine Apostles, saying to them: *Lay not up to yourselves treasures on earth; where the rust and moth consume, and where thieves break through and steal* (Mt. vi. 19).

He means that the unclean spirit is the thief, who cannot steal from those who walk in the light of good works. But if a man has taken his delight in the dark of earthly desires, or in the midst of earthly pleasures, he will strip him of every enduring flower of virtue. And it is because of this the Lord says: *Lay up to yourselves treasures in heaven: where neither the rust nor moth doth consume, and where thieves do not break through nor steal* (v. 20).

Our rust is wantonness, our rust is wilful passion, our rust is luxurious living, all things that darken the brightness of our soul with the stains of shameful living. Again, our rust is Arius, our rust is Photinus (*heresiarchs*), who by their impiety tear asunder the holy garment of the Church; and, eager to shatter the indivisible oneness of the Divine Power, they gnaw with blasphemous teeth at the precious veil of the Faith. Water is poured forth if by chance Arius' teeth make a rent; it flows away should Photinus thrust his dart through another's vessel.

We are but poor clay; quickly we give ear to evil. But let no one say to the Potter: *Why hast thou made me thus?* (Rom. ix. 20). For though lowly our vessel, yet it is one thing when held in honour, another when held in ignominy. Then leave not thy cistern uncovered; do not dig under it with the vices, and with evil doing, so that no one may say: *He hath opened a pit and dug it; and he is fallen into the hole he made* (Ps. vii. 16).

If you seek Jesus, forsake the old pits; for Christ sits not by a pit, but by a well. There the Samaritan woman found Him; she who believed, she who desired to draw water from the well (Jn. iv. 6). And though you ought to have come early, yet though it is late, still come; for even at the sixth hour you will find Jesus, weary from His journey. He is weary, but because of you, because He has long sought for you; it is your long unbelief has wearied Him. Yet He will not be offended should you come now; He asks that He may drink, Who will give you to drink. He drinks, but not of the stream that goes past, but of your salvation. He drinks of your love, He drinks of the chalice, that is, of that Passion which redeemed you from your sins; that the drink of His sacred blood may extinguish in you the thirst of this world.

So Abraham merited after he had dug the well (Gen. xxi. 30). So did Isaac merit as he walked to the well (xxiv. 62), receiving as his wife her who came there as a figure of the Church. The believer at the well; the unbeliever at the pit. And lastly Rebecca, at the well, as we read, found him who sought her; and harlots washed themselves in blood in the pool of Jezabel (III Kgs. xxii).[10]

III. St John Chrysostom, Bishop and Doctor

The Gifts of the Holy Ghost[11]

1. Great indeed, and beyond the power of man's tongue to describe, are the gifts this day bestowed on us by a most loving God. And because of this we all rejoice together, and rejoicing give praise to the Lord. For today we celebrate a great public festival as well as a feast day. For as in the course of the year the seasons and the solstices succeed each other, so in the Church one feast succeeds another, and brings us all together. But recently we celebrated the feast of the Cross, the Passion, the Resurrection, then the Ascension of our Lord Jesus Christ to heaven. Today we have reached the very summit, the capital (*metropolis*) itself of the feasts, to the very maturing of the promise of the Lord: *If I go not*, He said, *the Paraclete will not come to you; but if I go I will send him to you.*

Behold His solicitude for us. Consider His unspeakable kindness. Previous to these present days He had ascended into heaven, taking possession of His royal throne, and receiving back His place at the right hand of the Father. Today He bestows on us this Descent of the Holy Spirit, and through Him imparts to us a thousand other gifts of heaven. For of all the gifts which contain within them our soul's salvation, which of them has not been given us by the ministry of the Spirit? Through Him we are freed from slavery, called to freedom, made children of God through His adoption, and above all we have been, if I may say so, remade, putting off the heavy and fetid burthen of our sins. Through Him we see

before us the choirs of priests, through Him we have the help of our schools of instructors. From this source come the gifts of revelations, the graces of healing, and all the other gifts with which the Spirit adorns the Church of God.

This is what Paul proclaims in the words: *All these things one and the same Spirit worketh, distributing them to each one according as he wills* (I Cor. xii. 11). *According as he wills*, he says; not according as He is commanded. *Distributing*, not distributed; showing Himself the Author of these gifts, not as subject to another's authority. And the power which Paul testifies that the Father possesses, the same He attributes to the Holy Ghost. And as He says of the Father: *It is the same God who worketh all in all* (v. 6), so does he also say of the Holy Ghost: *All these things one and the same Spirit worketh, distributing to each one according as he wills* (v. 11). Behold here the fulness of authority. Where the Nature is one, there can be no doubt that the same also is the Dominion: and being equal in dignity, Their power and Authority is also one.

Through Him we obtain forgiveness of sin; through Him are we made clean of every stain. Through the gift of Him we have been changed from men into angels, those among us who co-operate with His grace: not actually changing our nature, but, what is more wonderful, while remaining in the nature of men we show forth a manner of life that is worthy of angels.

Such then is the power of the

Spirit. And just as material fire, applied to the soft clay, changes it to hard pottery, so the fire of the Holy Ghost, when it penetrates our soul, though it should find it softer than the clay, yet it will make it more unyielding than iron. And the soul that a little while ago was stained with the mire of sin, is all at once more splendid than the sun.

It is this that the blessed Paul teaches us, when he cries: *Do not err: Neither fornicators, nor idolaters, nor adulterers, nor the effeminate, nor liers with mankind, nor thieves, nor covetous, nor drunkards, nor railers, nor extortioners, shall possess the kingdom of God* (I Cor. vi. 9, 10). And when he had recounted almost every kind of unworthiness, and had taught us that those who made themselves the slaves of these would be strangers to the kingdom of heaven, he goes on to say: *And this some of you were; but you are washed, you are sanctified.* How? In what manner? For it is this we must know. *In the Name of our Lord Jesus Christ.* See here then, Beloved Brethren, the power of the Holy Ghost. See how it is the Spirit wipes away all this iniquity, and uplifts to the highest dignity those who before had been betrayed by their own sins.

2. Who is there then who does not rightly grieve over and deplore the blasphemy of those who seek to take away the dignity of the Holy Spirit, who like persons out of their mind are not restrained from this ingratitude by remembrance of the greatness of His gifts? Nay, they are not ashamed to work against all that relates to their own salvation, rejecting Him, endeavouring as far as they can to take from Him the dignity of

Lord, and reduce Him to the rank of creature. Of these I would like to ask one question. You, for what reason do you war so bitterly against the majesty of the Holy Spirit, or rather, against your own salvation? Do you not want your minds to take in what Christ said to His Disciples: *Going therefore, teach ye all nations; baptizing them in the name of the Father, and of the Son, and of the Holy Ghost?* (Mt. xxviii. 19).

Here you can behold equality in dignity; here you see the most perfect accord. Here you behold the Undivided Trinity. Do you see anywhere a difference, a diminution or change? What are you presuming to add to the words of the Lord? Do you not know that in human affairs anyone who should attempt this, who had gone so far in madness as to add or to detract something from the letters of a king, who is one of our own kind, and a sharer of our common nature, he would suffer the supreme penalty, and nothing could deliver him from his merited punishment? And if such danger threatens you in human affairs, what pardon will they receive who have gone so far in their presumption that they try to corrupt the words of the common Saviour of all mankind, and will not deign to listen to the words of Paul—in whom Christ Himself spoke—as he cries out to us in a clear voice: *That eye hath not seen, nor ear heard, nor hath it entered into the heart of man, what things God hath prepared for them that love him* (I Cor. ii. 9).

If then eye hath not seen, nor ear heard, nor hath it entered into the heart of man to imagine what good things are prepared for those who love God, from where, O Blessed

Paul, shall we be able to come to the knowledge of these things? Listen a moment and you will hear him answer. He goes on then to add: *But to us God hath revealed them, by his Spirit.* Nor does he stop there, but, so that he may show the greatness of the Spirit's power, and how He is of the same nature as the Father and the Son, he continues: *For the Spirit searcheth all things, yea, the deep things of God.* Then, desiring to implant in our souls a yet more precise knowledge, by means of human examples, he adds: *For what man knoweth the things of man, but the spirit of man that is in him? So the things also that are of God no man knoweth, but the Spirit of God.* You see here the most complete teaching. Just as the things that are in the mind of a man, he says, cannot be known by another, and he alone knows his own secrets, so the things which are in the mind of God no one knows but the Spirit of God: a perfect and wholly becoming illustration of the dignity of the Spirit. For the illustration he employs conveys to us, as it were, that it cannot happen that the things a man has in his mind are unknown to him, and so in exactly the same way the Holy Spirit knows the things of God.

But it cannot be denied that in these words the blessed Apostle comes down on those who, because of their own notion, and against their own salvation, show themselves as opposing the dignity of the Spirit, and striving as far as in them lies to lower Him to the rank of creature. But while these, led by the spirit of contumacy, show themselves as enemies of Sacred Scripture, we, accepting the divine teachings as coming down from heaven, offer them fitting reverence, and with upright faith proclaim the exact knowledge of the truth.

But what has been said will suffice against those who dare to teach what is contrary to the words of the Holy Spirit. But for our own part, it is our duty to say a few words to Your Charity with regard to the cause of these so precious gifts which the Lord bestowed on us, not immediately following His Ascension, but after allowing some days to pass, so that the Disciples might recover themselves, when He sent down the grace of the Spirit. Nor was this done lightly, and without reason. For mankind did not know how to value the wondrous good things in its hands, nor how to honour, sufficiently, what seemed so great and pleasing, unless they had first experienced their contraries. For example—for this must be put clearly—he who has a sound healthy body neither sees, nor can he know accurately, how great a good is the health he enjoys, unless through a sudden illness he also learns what sickness is. And he who sees the day again does not think anything of a lamp, until the dark of night comes on. So the experience of contrary things teaches us clearly the value of what we now enjoy.

And because of this, after His coming the Disciples began to enjoy countless good things, and while He was with them the time passed most pleasantly, for all the people of Palestine looked up to them, as to wondrous luminaries, when they began raising the dead to life, healing lepers, casting out devils, healing the sick, and doing many other wonderful things. Therefore because they were so admired, and so famous, for this reason He permits them to be deprived of the great power which had assisted them, so that when they were deprived of it they would then learn how much the presence of its goodness had bestowed on them; and when they had come to see how great was the grace they had enjoyed, they would then with greater eagerness receive the gift of the Holy Spirit. For He consoled them when they were grieving, and when they were filled with sorrow and mourning for the loss of their Master He shone down upon them with the beams of His own light; He raised up those who were almost prostrate, scattered the darkness of their grief, and ended their uncertainty.

For when they had heard the voice of the Lord saying: Go, *teach all nations*, they were at a loss and did not know whither each one should turn, and in what part of the world each one should preach the word of God. The Holy Ghost came in the form of tongues, and He assigned to each one of them the region of the world where each should teach, making known to them by means of the given tongue, as though by a written tablet, the limits of the realm entrusted to them, and of their teaching.

For this cause the Holy Spirit came in the form of tongues, but not for this cause alone, but to recall the past to our minds. For when of old men, filled with pride, had sought to build a tower to reach the heavens, through the division of their tongues God put an end to the evil purpose of their common speech (Gen. xi.). Because of this the Holy Spirit descends upon them now in the form of fiery tongues, that by

this means He may join together the divided world. So there then took place something new and wondrous: for as in times past tongues divided the world, and changed an evil accord into division, so now tongues join the world together, and bring together in harmony those that before were divided.

And so He appeared in the form of tongues, and of tongues of fire, because the thorn of sin in us has grown into a forest. For as land, which though rich and fertile is left uncultivated, will bring forth a large crop of thorns, so is our nature which, though created good, and suited to the cultivation of the crop of virtue, because it had never felt the plough of reverential love of God, nor received the seed of the knowledge of God, had brought forth impiety as though it were thorns and other useless growth. And as, as often happens, through the dense growth of thorns and unprofitable weeds the face of the earth is not even seen, so the purity and nobility of our soul did not appear until the husbandman of the nature of man had come, and, touching it with the fire of the Spirit, cleansed and prepared it, that it might be ready to receive the good seed.

3. Such as these and many more besides are the good things we have received through His Coming. And since this is so, I beseech you, because of the dignity of the good things that have been heaped upon us, let you celebrate this feast, not simply by adorning the city, but by beautifying your own souls; not by decking out the Forum in rich tapestries, but by making our own souls joyous with the garment of

virtue, that in this way we shall be enabled, both to receive the grace of the Holy Spirit, and thereafter to gather in Its fruits.

What is the fruit of the Holy Spirit?

What is the fruit of the Spirit? Let us hear Paul speaking. *The fruit of the Spirit is, charity, joy, peace* (Gal. v. 22). What precision of speech, what harmony of teaching! He places charity first; then recounts what follows. He establishes what is the root; then shows us the fruit. He lays down the foundation; then leads on to the edifice. He begins with the fountain; and at once goes on to the streams. For a foundation cannot be laid for joy, if we value our own health and happiness before that of others, our own welfare above that of our neighbour. This will not come to pass until the rule of charity prevails. Charity is the root, the fount, the mother of all good. And as a root she sends forth countless branches of virtues, as a fount she gives birth to many streams, and as a mother she embraces within her folds those who have recourse to her. And this the blessed Paul clearly understood, and called it the fulfilment of the Law: *Love, therefore, is the fulfilment of the law* (Rom. xiii. 10). Indeed the Lord of all has placed before us, as a true indication, and a sign worthy of belief, that a man has proved himself His disciple, no other token than that demanded by charity, when He said to us: *By this shall all men know you are my disciples, if you love one another* (Jn. xiii. 35).

Because of this, I beseech you, let us all fly to it, and hold fast to it, and with it let us celebrate this festival. For where there is charity

the worst faults come to nothing; where there is charity the unruly thoughts of the mind come to an end. *For charity*, he says, *dealeth not perversely, is not puffed up, is not ambitious* (I Cor. xiii. 4, 5). Charity works no evil against a neighbour; where charity rules there is no Cain slaying his brother. Take away the fount of envy, and you have taken away the river of all evil things. Cut off the root, and you cut off the fruit with it, at the same time.

I have spoken these words to you because I am more concerned with those who envy than with those who are envied. For it is they above all who suffer most; bringing disaster upon themselves. For those who suffer through envy it is a beginning of the crown of glory, if they will it. See with me how Abel the Just is remembered with honour; the manner of his death the occasion of his glory. Even after death he cried out by his blood, and with a clear voice denounces the one who was guilty of his death (Gen. iv. 10). But he who remained received the reward of his deed; living out his life on earth fearful and lamenting. But the other, slain and laid to rest, after his death gave forth even more perfect testimony of his justice (Heb. xi. 4). And just as the sin of Cain, even while he lived, made him more unhappy than the dead, so the justice of Abel rendered him more perfect after he was dead.

Because of this we too, that we may give greater testimony to ourselves both here and in heaven, that we may with greater joyfulness gather the fruits of this feast, let us cast from us the soiled garments of the soul, and especially let us strip ourselves of the cloak of envy. For though you may think to yourself that you have already gained countless merits, you will be deprived of all of them if this sharp and brutal taint should afflict us.

May it come to pass that we shall all escape it, especially those who this day through the grace of baptism have cast aside the ancient garment of their former sins, and now shine even more brightly than the sun. I exhort you, accordingly, you who this day have been enrolled as sons by adoption, who have clothed themselves in this shining garment, preserve with every care the bright-ness of soul in which you now stand clothed, and at every turn shut out the approach of the devil, that you may be able to gather the more abundantly the joys of the grace of the Spirit; one thirtyfold, another sixtyfold, and another a hundred-fold: that you may be made worthy to meet with confidence the King of Heaven when He shall come, and shall distribute the good things that are above all speech to those who have brought this present life to a just end, in Jesus Christ our Lord to Whom be praise and glory for ever and ever. Amen.

IV. St Augustine, Bishop and Doctor

Exposition of the Gospel[12]

1. When the Disciples question their Master Jesus, and when He answers their questions, we also, whenever we read or listen to the holy Gospel, are being instructed together with them. So when our Lord had said: *Yet a little while: and the world seeth me no more. But you shall see me,* Judas asked Him the meaning of these words; not that Judas who betrayed Him, who was surnamed Iscariotes, but the one whose Epistle is numbered among the canonical Scriptures. *Lord,* he said, *how is it, that thou wilt manifest thyself to us, and not to the world?* Let us be with them as disciples questioning Him, and let us also listen to the answer of our common Master. For the holy Judas, not the defiled one, not the betrayer, but the follower of our Lord, asked Him why He was to show Himself to His own, and not to the world, and why the world, in a little while, would not see Him, but they would see Him.

2. *Jesus answered and said to him: If any one love me, he will keep my word, and my Father will love him, and we will come to him, and will make our abode with him. He that loveth me not, keepeth not my words.* Here then is the reason why He will show Himself to His own, not to strangers, whom he calls by the name of *the world*; and the reason is, that the one love Him, and the others do not. This is the reason why the sacred psalm intones: *Judge me, O God, and distinguish my cause from the nation that is not holy* (xlii. 1). For they who love are chosen because they love; but they who do not love, though they speak in the tongues of angels and of men, become as sounding brass and as a tinkling cymbal. And if they had the gift of prophecy, and should they know all mysteries, and all knowledge, and if they had all faith, so that they could move mountains, and should they give away all they possess, and deliver up their bodies to be burned,

it will gain them nothing (I Cor. xiii).

It is love which distinguishes the sanctified from the world; love which makes men dwell together in peace in the same house (Ps. lxvii. 7). And it is in this house the Father and the Son make their abode; They Who give this love to those to whom They will also finally give the Vision of Themselves. It was concerning this last Vision the Disciple questioned his Master, so that not alone might they then hear the answer from His mouth, but that we also might come to know it through His Gospel. For he had asked about the seeing of Christ, and he learned about love and indwelling. There is therefore a certain inward vision of God of which the wicked know nothing; for them there is no vision of the Father and the Holy Ghost: of the Son there could be, but in the Flesh. But this is not the same as the other, and such as it is they cannot have it for ever, but only for a little while; and this for their judgement, not their delight; to receive punishment, not reward.

These things have I spoken to you, abiding with you. But the Paraclete, the Holy Ghost, whom the Father will send in my name, he will teach you all things, and bring all things to your mind, whatsoever I have said to you. Peace I leave you, my peace I give unto you: not as the world giveth, do I give unto you. In the words of the Holy Gospel which precede these just now recited the Lord Jesus had said, that He and the Father would come to those who loved Them, and would take up Their abode with them. And a little before this He said of the Holy Ghost: *But you shall know him; because he shall abide with you, and shall be in you* (v. 17); and from this we understand that God the Trinity dwells all together in the sanctified as in a temple.

Now He says: *These things have I spoken to you, abiding with you.* There is accordingly one *abiding* which He promises us is yet to come; this is another, which He declares is now present to them. The one is spiritual, made known inwardly to the soul; the other bodily, made known outwardly to their eyes and ears. The one will ever give joy to the delivered; this other now visits those to be delivered. In the first the Lord does not depart from those who love Him; in this other He comes, and He goes away. *These things,* He says, *have I spoken to you, abiding with you,* that is, abiding with you in the Body; which was visible to them as He was speaking to them.

But the Paraclete, He says, *the Holy Ghost, whom the Father will send in my name, he will teach you all things, and bring all things to your mind, whatsoever I shall have said to you.* Is it that the Son speaks, and the Holy Ghost teaches, so that when the Son speaks we hear the words, and when the Holy Ghost teaches we understand them? As though the Son speaks without the Holy Ghost, or the Holy Spirit teaches without the Son; or as though it is not the case that the Son also teaches, and the Holy Ghost also speaks, and that when God says or teaches something, it is the Trinity Itself that both speaks and teaches?

But since it is the Trinity, it was necessary to make known Its single Persons, that we should hear It in Its separate Persons, and understand Them as inseparable. Hear the Father speaking, where you read the words: *The Lord said to me; thou art my Son* (Ps. ii. 7). Hear Him again, where you read: *Every one that heard of the Father, and hath learned, cometh to me* (Jn. vi. 45). Just now you have heard the Son speaking, for He says of Himself: *Whatsoever I shall have said to you.* And should you wish to know Him as a Teacher, recall the Master saying: *One is your master, Christ* (Mt. xxiii. 10). Furthermore, the Holy Ghost, Whom just now you have heard of as teaching, where it was said that, *He will teach you all things,* hear Him also speaking, where you read in the Acts of the Apostles that the Holy Spirit said to the blessed Peter: *Go with them, for I have sent them* (x. 20).

The whole Trinity therefore both speaks and teaches, but unless It had been made known to us, Person by Person, in no way could the human mind have grasped It. Since It is wholly inseparable, if It were always spoken of inseparably, the Trinity would then never be known: for when we are speaking of the Father and of the Son and of the Holy Ghost, we do not speak of them together; though they cannot be other than together. Because He added: *He will bring all things to your mind,* we must also understand, that the most salutary monitions relate to God's favour, as the Spirit reminds us.

Peace I leave you, He says, *my peace I give unto you.* This is the peace we read of in the prophet, *Peace upon peace* (Is. lvii. 19, Sept.). Going away He leaves us peace; when He comes at the end He will give us His own peace. He leaves us peace in this world; His own peace He will give us in the world to come. He leaves us peace, abiding

in which we shall overcome the enemy; He will give us His own peace, when we shall reign without an enemy. He leaves us peace, so that even here we may love one another; He will give us His own peace, where we can no more be divided. He leaves us peace, that as long as we are in this world we may not judge one another in our secret faults; His own peace He will give us, when He makes manifest the counsels of the heart, when every man shall have his praise from God (I Cor. iv. 5).

Yet it is in Him, and from Him, we have peace, whether that which He leaves us as He goes to the Father, or that which He will give us when He brings us to the Father. What does He now leave us as He ascends to the Father but Himself, as long as He does not withdraw from us? *For He is our peace, who hath made both one* (Eph. ii. 14). He it is then Who is our peace; both while we believe that He is, as well as *when we shall see Him as He is* (I Jn. iii. 2). For if as long as we are in this corruptible body, which afflicts the soul, we walk by faith, and not by sight, He does not leave us journeying far from Him (II Cor. v. 6, 7), how much more will He not fill us of Himself, when we have come before His sight?

But what does it mean that, where He says, *Peace I leave you,* He does not also add the word *my,* while where He says, *peace I give you,* He says, *my peace?* Are we to think *my* is implied where it was not said; because what was said once, can also be referred to both? Or is there perhaps something hidden here, to be asked for, and sought after, to be opened to those who knock? What if He wishes us to understand as His peace that which He Himself possesses? This which He leaves us in this world is to be called ours rather than His. For within Him there is no conflict, for He is wholly without sin; while the peace we possess is such that we must still say, *forgive us our trespasses.*

We have then some peace, for within us we delight in the law of God; but it is not a complete peace, for we see another law in our members warring against the law in our minds (Rom. vii. 22, 23). And we have peace with one another; for we believe that we love one another. Yet neither is this perfect; for we see not the thoughts of each other's heart, and we believe certain things about one another, either for better or for worse, which are not in us. This then is *our* peace, though left to us by Him: for unless it were from Him we would not have even this. But this is not the peace He possesses. But if we keep to the end what we have received, what He has we also shall have; wherein nothing of ourselves shall war within us, and nothing shall be hidden in us from one another.

I know that these words of the Lord can also be so understood as to appear but a repetition of the same phrase: *Peace I leave with you, my peace I give unto you*; that when He had said *peace*, He repeated it saying,

my peace; and having said, *I leave with you*, He repeated this saying, *I give unto you.* Each may take it as he wishes. Nevertheless, it gives me great joy, and I believe you also, my beloved brethren, so to keep this first peace, wherein united we shall defeat the enemy, as yet to long for that other peace, wherein we shall have no enemy.

That the Lord goes on to say: *Not as the world giveth, do I give unto you*, what does this mean, but that not as men who love the world give peace do I give it to you? They so give peace to one another that without the distraction of wars and quarrels they may be able to enjoy, not God, but their friends in this world. And when they leave the just in peace, in that they do not persecute them, that cannot be a true peace, where there is no true accord: for their hearts are far from one another. For as he is called a partner who is joined with you in fortune, so must they be called partners who are united in heart.

Let us then, Brethren, to whom Christ has left peace, to whom He gives His own peace, not as the world gives it, but as He gives it by Whom the world was made, that we may be at peace one with another, let us be joined in heart to one another, and let us lift up our hearts, that they may not be corrupted on earth.

V. St Augustine, Bishop and Doctor

The Holy Spirit the Soul of the Church[13]

I. The Solemnity of this day brings to our minds remembrance of the great Lord God, and of the great grace that has been poured out on us. It is so that we may not suffer to be

wiped from our memory what has once taken place that a solemnity is held. A solemnity, as we know, receives its name from that which takes place once a year; just as a stream is called perennial which does not dry up in summer, but flows all the year round. So as what goes on all the year is perennial, what takes place but once in the year is solemn.

Today we celebrate the Coming of the Holy Ghost. For this day the Lord sent down the Holy Spirit Whom He had promised us while He was on earth. And as He had so promised that He was about to send Him from heaven, *for he cannot come,* He says, *unless I go; but when I go I will send him to you,* He then suffered, He died, He rose again, He ascended into heaven. There remained then that He should fulfil what He had promised.

Therefore, His Disciples, to the number of one hundred and twenty souls, as it is written, tenfold the number of the Apostles, for He had chosen twelve, and sent the Holy Spirit down on one hundred and twenty, persevered together in prayer, in one house, awaiting the fulfilment of His promise. Now they began to desire this with faith, with prayer, with eagerness of the spirit. They were the new wineskins, and they looked for the new wine from heaven. For the great Grape Cluster had been trodden out, and glorified. For we read in the Gospels: *The Spirit was not yet given, because Jesus was not yet glorified* (Jn. vii. 39).

II. *The Gift of Tongues.*

What great wonder followed you have already heard. All who were present in that assembly had learned but one tongue. The Holy Spirit came. They were filled with Him, and they began to speak in the tongues of different nations, which they neither knew before, nor had learnt. But He taught them Who had come. He entered into them, and they were all filled with Him. He transformed them. And this then was a sign of whoever had received the Holy Spirit, that of a sudden filled with the Spirit, they began to speak in the tongues of every nation; not these one hundred and twenty alone.

The Sacred Writings teach that after men had believed, were baptized, and received the Holy Ghost, they began to speak in the tongues of all nations. Those present were astonished, some wondering, some mocking, so that they said: *These men are full of new wine* (Acts ii. 1–13). They laughed, yet they said a true thing. For these skins were filled with new wine. You heard when the Gospel was being read, how, *no one puts new wine into old wineskins* (Mt. ix. 17): the carnal minded cannot grasp spiritual things. The carnal mind is age, grace is newness. To whatever degree a man is changed for the better, so much the more does he grasp the flavour of truth. The new wine bubbled up, and as the must boiled the tongues of the nations poured forth.

III. *Why the Gift of Tongues is not given now.*

Is the Holy Spirit not given now, Brethren? Whoever thinks this is not worthy to receive Him. He is given; even now. How is it then that no one speaks in the tongues of all nations, as they spoke who at that time were filled with the Holy Ghost? Why? Because what this wonder signified is now fulfilled. What is that? When we celebrated Quadragesima (*the fortieth day, i.e. the Ascension*) you remember that we told you, that the Lord Jesus

Christ had established His Church, and ascended into heaven. His Disciples had asked Him, *When shall the end of the world be?* He answered: *It is not for you to know the times or moments, which the Father had put in his own power.* Yet He promised them what He has this day fulfilled: *You shall receive the power of the Holy Ghost coming upon you, and you shall be witnesses unto me in Jerusalem, and in all Judea, and Samaria, and even to the uttermost part of the earth* (Acts i. 6–8).

The Church that was then within one house received the Holy Spirit: it was few in numbers, in tongues it represented the whole earth. Behold how far it has now spread. That this little Church spoke with the tongues of all nations, what does this mean but that this mighty Church, from the rising of the sun to its going down, speaks in the tongues of all nations? What was then promised, is now fulfilled. We have heard, and we have seen. *Hearken, O Daughter, and see* (Ps. xliv. 11). To the queen (*the Church*) was it said: *Hearken, O Daughter, and see.* Hear the promise; see the fulfilment. Thy God has not deceived thee; thy Spouse has not failed thee; He has not failed thee who endowed thee with His Blood. He has not failed thee who changed thee from ugliness to beauty, from a wanton to a virgin. Thou wert promised to thyself; promised to a few, but fulfilled in many.

IV. *The Holy Spirit the soul of the Church; Does not dwell outside It.*

Therefore, let no one say: I have received the Holy Spirit, why do I not speak in the tongues of every nation? If you wish to have the Holy Spirit, attend to what I say, my brethren. The spirit within us, by which a man lives, is called a soul; our spirit, by which each single one of us lives, is called the soul. Consider what the soul does within the body. It gives life to all the members. It sees through the eyes, hears through the ears, smells through the nostrils, speaks by the tongue, works by means of the hand, walks by means of the feet. It is present at the same time in all the members, that they may live. It gives life to all; to each it allots duties. The eye does not hear, the ear does not see, the tongue does not see, and neither does the eye speak, or the ear; and yet each lives. The ear lives, the tongue lives. The duties are diverse, but the life is one.

Such is the Church of God. In some of its saints it works miracles, in others of the saints it utters truth; in some saints it cherishes virginity, in others of the sanctified it upholds conjugal modesty; in others this, in others that. Each one does what belongs to him, but they live in the same manner. What the soul is to the body of man, the Holy Ghost is to the Body of Christ: which the Church is. What the soul does in all the members of one body, this the Holy Spirit does throughout the Church.

But see that you are on your guard, see that you are restrained, see that you fear God. It happens sometimes in the human body, that from this same body something is cut off, a hand, a finger, a foot. Do you think the soul follows the part cut thus off? While it belonged to the body it lived. Cut off it loses life. So likewise the

Christian Catholic man; while in the Body he lives, becoming a heretic he is cut off: for the Spirit follows no amputated member. If therefore you wish to live in the Holy Ghost, hold fast to the bond of charity, love the Truth, long for Unity, that you may attain to eternity.

Turning then to the Lord our God, the Father Almighty, let us as best we can give thanks with all our hearts, beseeching Him that in His Goodness He will mercifully hear our prayers, and by His grace drive evil from our thoughts and actions, increase our faith, guide our minds, grant us His holy inspirations, and bring us to joy without end, through His Son our Lord and Saviour Jesus Christ. Amen.

VI. St Augustine, Bishop and Doctor

The Holy Spirit the Unity of the Church[14]

1. The Coming of the Holy Ghost with the Gift of Tongues foretells the Unity of the Church throughout all peoples.

This is a solemn day for us, because of the Coming of the Holy Ghost; the fiftieth day from the Lord's Resurrection, seven days multiplied by seven. But multiplying seven by seven we have forty-nine. One is then added: that we may be reminded of unity.

What is the meaning of the Coming of the Holy Ghost? What did it accomplish? How did He tell us of His Presence; reveal It to us? By the fact that all spoke in the tongues of every nation. There were a hundred and twenty people gathered in one room; ten times twelve. The sacred number of the Apostles was multiplied ten times. What then, did each one upon whom the Holy Spirit descended speak in one of the tongues of each of the nations: to this man one language, to this man another, dividing as it were among themselves the tongues of all the nations? No, it was not so: but each man, singly, spoke in the tongue of every nation. One and the same man spoke the tongue of every nation: the unity of the Church amid the tongues of all the nations. See here how the unity of the Catholic Church spread throughout all nations is set before us.

2. The Holy Spirit not outside the Church.

He therefore who possesses the Holy Spirit is in the Church, which speaks in the tongues of all nations. Whosoever is without this Church, has not the Holy Spirit. For this reason the Holy Spirit deigned to reveal Himself in the tongues of all nations, that each may understand, that he possesses the Holy Spirit who is nourished within the unity of the Church, which speaks in every tongue. *One body*, says Paul the Apostle, *one body and one Spirit* (Eph. iv. 4).

Attend to this, you who are our members. A body is composed of many members, and one spirit gives life to all the members. By the human spirit, by which I am myself a man, I join together all my members: I command my members to move, I direct the eye to see, the ears to hear, the tongue to speak, the hand to work, the feet to walk. The duties of each member are different, but one soul joins all together. Many things are commanded, many done, but one commands, one is obeyed. What our spirit, that is, our soul, is to our own members, this the Holy Spirit is to the members of Christ, to the Body of Christ, which is the Church.

And so, where the Apostle speaks of it as *a body*, let us not think of it as a dead body without life. *One body*, he says. But, I ask you, is this a living body? It is living. By what does it live? By one spirit. *And one Spirit.* Be watchful therefore, brethren, within our own body; and grieve for those who are cut off from the Church. As long as we live, while we are in our senses, let all members fulfil their duties among our own members. Should one member suffer anything, let all the members suffer with it (I Cor. xii. 26). Yet, though it may suffer, because it is in the body, it cannot die. For what does *to die* mean but to lose the spirit? Now if a member be cut off from the body, does the soul follow it? It can still be seen what member it is: it is a finger, a hand, an arm, an ear; besides substance, it has form; but it has no life. So is it with a man separated from the Church. Seek if he has the sacrament. You learn he has. Look for baptism. You find it. The creed? You find it. This is the outward form; but unless inwardly you live by the Spirit, in vain do you glory in the outward form.

3. *Unity is put before us in the Creation, and in the Birth of Christ.*

Dearly Beloved, God greatly commends unity. Let you dwell upon this, that in the beginning of creation, when God established all things, He placed the stars in the heavens and trees and all green things upon the earth. He said: *Let the earth bring forth*, and trees and all living things were brought forth. He said: *Let the waters bring forth creeping things and flying things*; and it was done. *Let the earth bring forth the living creature in its kind and cattle and beasts of the earth*; and it was done. Did God make the other birds from one bird? Did He make all the fish from one fish? All horses from one horse? All beasts from one beast? Did the earth not produce many things at the same time? Did it not complete many created things with numerous offspring?

Then He came to the creation of man, and He created one man; and from one man the human race. Nor did He will to create two separate beings, male and female, but one man; and from this one man He made woman (Gen. i. 11). Why did He do this? Why did He begin the human race from one man, if not to commend unity to mankind? And the Lord Christ was born of one person. Virgin therefore is unity; let it hold fast to its integrity; let it preserve it uncorrupted.

4. *Christ commends to the Apostles the Unity of the Catholic Church.*

The Lord commends to the Apostles the unity of the Church. He shows Himself; and they think they are seeing a spirit. They are frightened. He gives them courage, when He says to them: *Why are you troubled, and why do thoughts arise in your hearts? See my hands: handle and see; for a spirit hath not flesh and bones, as you see me to have.* And see how as they wondered for joy He takes food; not from necessity, but for His purpose. He eats it before them. In the face of the unbelieving He commends to them the reality of His Body; He commends the Unity of the Church.

For what does He say? *Are not these the words I spoke to you, while I was with you, that all things must needs be fulfilled, which are written in the law of Moses, and in the prophets, and in the psalms, concerning me? Then he opened their understanding,* the Gospel says, *that they might understand the scriptures. And he said to them: thus it is written, and thus it behoved Christ to suffer, and to rise again from the dead the third day* (Lk. xxiv. 44). Behold our Head. Behold our Head; but where are the members? Behold the Bridegroom; where is the Bride? Read the marriage contract; listen to the Bridegroom. You seek the Bride? Learn from Him. No one takes away from Him His Bride; no one puts another in *Her* place. Learn from Him. Where do you seek Christ? Amid the fabrications of men, or in the truth of the Gospels? He suffered, He rose the third day, He showed Himself to His Disciples. We now have Him; we ask where She is? Let us ask Him. *It behoved Christ to suffer, and to rise again from the dead, the third day.*

Lo, this is now come to pass; already we have seen Him. Tell us, O Lord; tell us Thou, Lord, lest we fall into error. *And that penance and remission of sins should be preached in his name unto all nations, beginning at Jerusalem.* It began at Jerusalem, and it has reached unto us. It is there, and it is here. For it did not cease there to come to us. It has grown forth not changed places. He com-

mended this to us immediately after His Resurrection. He passed forty days with them. About to ascend to heaven, He commended the Church to them again. The Bridegroom now about to depart entrusted His Bride to the care of His friends: not that she should love one among them, but that She might love Him as Her Spouse, and them as friends of the Bridegroom; but none of them as the Bridegroom.

They are jealous for Him, the friends of the Bridegroom; and they will not suffer her to be corrupted by a wanton love. Men hate rather when they so love. Listen to the jealous *friend* of the Bridegroom, when he knew, through friends, that the Bride was in a way to being corrupted. He says: *I hear there are schisms among you; and in part I believe it* (I Cor. xi. 18). Also, *it hath been signified to me, my brethren, of you, by them that are of the house of Chloe, that there are contentions among you, that everyone of you says, I indeed am of Paul; and I am of Apollo; and I of Cephas; and I of Christ. Is Christ divided? Was Paul then crucified for you? Or were you baptized in the name of Paul?* (I Cor. i. 11–13.) O friend of the Bridegroom! He refuses for himself the love of Another's Spouse. He wills not to be loved in the place of the Bridegroom, that he may reign with the Bridegroom.

The Church therefore has been entrusted to them (the friends of the Bridegroom). And when He was about to ascend into heaven, He said so to those who thus asked Him about the end of the world: *Tell us when shall these things be? And when shall be the sign of thy coming?* And He said: *It is not for you to know the times which the Father hath put in his own power.* Hear, O disciple, what you have learned from your Master: *But you shall receive the power of the Holy Ghost coming upon you.* And it has come to pass. On the fortieth day He ascended into heaven, and behold, coming upon this day, all who were present are filled with the Holy Ghost, and speak in the tongues of all nations. Once more unity is commended; by the tongues of all nations. It is commended by the Lord rising from the dead; it is confirmed this day in the Coming of the Holy Ghost. Amen.

VII. St Augustine, Bishop and Doctor

The Meaning of Pentecost[15]

1. Since we are celebrating the Solemnity of a day so holy, the day upon which the Holy Spirit came down among us, such a joyful and blessed occasion as this moves us to speak to you concerning this very gift of God, the grace of God, and upon the abundance of His mercy towards us; that is, to say something to you concerning the Holy Ghost Himself. In the School of the Lord we are all fellow pupils. For we have one Master; in whom we are all one, and Who, for fear we might dare to pride ourselves upon being a master, has warned us, saying: *Be you not called Rabbi* (Master); *for one is your master, Christ* (Mt. xxiii. 8). So therefore, since we ought to be instructed in His Scriptures, pay heed to the few words I shall say to you, in the Presence of that Master whose Chair is heaven; He assisting my efforts Who has commanded me to speak.

Those who already know of these things, let them recall them to mind. And those who do not know of them, let them listen and learn. Oftentimes it puzzles the devoutly curious mind—if it be allowed that human lowliness and weakness of mind may search into such things, and this is allowed; for what is closed to us is still not so denied us that it will not be opened to us if we knock, as the Lord tells us: *Ask, and it shall be given to you; seek, and you shall find; knock, and it shall be opened to you*—oftentimes then it puzzles the devoutly curious mind of those who study these things, why was it that the Holy Ghost was sent to us on the Fiftieth day after the Lord's Passion and Resurrection?

2. *Why the Holy Ghost could not come till Christ was gone. The Humanity of Christ, to which human affection clung, needed to be taken away from before the eyes of the Disciples. The Rock on which the Church is founded is Christ Himself.*

If I go not, the Paraclete will not come to you (Jn. xvi. 7). In the first place I wish Your Charity to take the trouble to consider, why was it the Saviour then said: *If I go not, the Paraclete will not come to you?* As though the Lord Christ had, if we speak in human fashion, laid up something in heaven, and coming down from there He had placed this in the care of the Holy Spirit, and the Holy Spirit could not come down to us until He had given back what had been entrusted to Him; or as if we were not able to receive Them Both, and neither could we endure the Presence of Both. As though

One should be separated from the Other; or else, should they both come to us, either They would be incommoded, or we would need to be enlarged.

What then is the meaning of the words: *He cannot come unless I go?* For He says: *It is expedient to you that I go. For if I go not the Paraclete will not come to you.* What this means then let Your Charity now briefly take in with the ear of the mind, in as far as we are able to grasp it, or enter into it, or with His help understand it; or, because we are speaking of what we believe.

It appears to me that the Disciples were taken up with the human figure of the Lord Christ, and, as men, were held by their human love for Him as a man. He began now to wish them to have rather a divine love, and so change them from unspiritual men to spiritual: which a man does not become without the gift of the Holy Ghost. Therefore, this is what He says: I shall send you a gift whereby you will become spiritual men; namely, the gift of the Holy Ghost. But you cannot become spiritual men unless you cease to be unspiritual. You will cease to be unspiritual, if this human form is taken from before your eyes, so that the form of God may be grafted instead upon your hearts.

It was by this human form, the form that is of a servant, that the Lord *emptied himself, taking the form of a servant* (Phil. ii. 7). By this form of a servant the human affection of Peter was held, since He loved Him so greatly that he was in great fear lest He should die. For he loved the Lord Jesus Christ as man loves man, as one in the flesh

loves one in the flesh, not as the spiritual man loves the divine majesty. How do we prove this? Because when the Lord asked His Disciples Whom did men say He was, and when they said, telling the opinions of others, that some said He was John, others Elias, others Jeremiah, or one of the prophets, He said to them: *But whom do you say that I am?* And Peter as the leader of the others, one speaking for all of them, said: *Thou art Christ, the Son of the Living God* (Mt. xvi).

This he said perfectly; most truly. Rightly did such an answer deserve to hear: *Blessed art thou, Simon Bar-jona: because flesh and blood has not revealed it to thee, but my father who is in heaven. And I say to thee*, because thou hast said this to me; thou hast spoken: now listen; thou hast confessed: receive in turn a blessing. Therefore: *And I say to thee: Thou art Peter*: because I am the Rock, *thou art Peter*; for the Rock is not from Peter, but Peter is from the Rock; because Christ is not from Christian, but Christian is from Christ. *And upon this rock I will build my Church*: not upon Peter (*non supra Petrum*) who thou art, but upon the Rock (*sed supra petram*) Whom thou hast confessed. *I will build my church:* I will build *thee*, who in this answer are in yourself the figure of the Church. This fact and other things, because of which Peter had said, *Thou art Christ, the Son of the living God*, and so had heard, as you remember, *Flesh and blood hath not revealed it to thee*, that is, a human mind, human infirmity, human ignorance of the things of God did not reveal this to you, *but my Father who is in heaven.*

Then the Lord Jesus began to

foretell His Passion, and to reveal to them what He was now to suffer at the hands of impious men. This terrified Peter; and he feared lest Christ the Son of God should perish in death. But Christ the Son of the Living God, the Good from the Good, God of God, the Living from the Living, the Fount of Life, and True Life, had come to destroy death; not to perish in death. Nevertheless, Peter, a man in great fear, whose human love was, as I have said, centred around the physical person of Christ, said: *Lord, be it far from thee, that this shall not be unto thee.* And the Lord rejected such words with a worthy and fitting reply. Just as He bestowed merited praise on his confession of faith, so here He gave a fitting rebuke to his faltering. *Go behind me, Satan,* He said.

Of whom is it said, *Blessed art thou, Simon Bar-Jona?* Compare the words of praise, and the words of correction. Mark the reasons for both; the confession, and the faltering. The reason for the confession: *Flesh and blood hath not revealed it to thee, but my Father who is in heaven.* The reason for the fear: *Because thou savourest not the things that are of God, but the things that are of men* (Mt. xvi. 13–23). We will therefore that such words should not be uttered, *for it is expedient for you that I go: for if I go not the Paraclete will not come to you.* Unless this human form is taken away from your bodily eyes, you will be wholly unable to take in, to perceive, to think of anything divine. Let this suffice.

Hence it was necessary that after the Resurrection and Ascension of our Lord Jesus Christ, His promise of the Holy Spirit should be fulfilled. For so had John the Evangelist of

his own accord spoken, when Jesus, signifying the same Holy Spirit, had cried out, saying: *If any man thirst, let him come to me and drink; and out of his belly shall flow rivers of living water,* the Evangelist continued, saying: *This he said of the Spirit which they should receive, who believed in him; for as yet the Spirit was not given, because Jesus was not yet glorified* (Jn. vii. 37–9). Glorified therefore by His Resurrection and Ascension into heaven, our Lord Jesus Christ sent forth the Holy Ghost.

3. *Why the Holy Spirit came on the Tenth Day after the Fortieth Day from the Ascension. The mystery of the Number Forty, and of the Number Ten. The Holy Spirit comes on the Tenth Day to signify the Law is fulfilled through Grace. How without Grace the letter killeth. The Holy Spirit was sent to complete the Law.*

As we learn from the Sacred Scriptures, the Lord remained with His Disciples for forty days after His Resurrection, making clear to them the reality of His risen Body, lest they should believe it to be something fictitious; eating and drinking with them. On the fortieth day, which we celebrated ten days ago, before their eyes He ascended into heaven, and it was promised at the same time, that He would come again as He had departed (Acts i. 3–11); that is, in the human form in which He had suffered judgement, in that same form shall He come again to give judgement.

He willed to send the Holy Spirit on a day other than that on which He ascended; not after two or three days, but after ten. This question compels us to search into and to examine certain obscurities with regard to numbers. Ten by four give forty days. As far as I can see there is a divine mystery placed within this number. For we are speaking as men to men; and we are called rightly preachers of the Scriptures, not assertors of our own opinions. This quadragenary number, therefore, containing four tens, signifies, as it seems to me, this world through which we are now passing, and in which we now labour. We are borne along, and are troubled in the course of our years, by the uncertainty of things, by their recurring, and by their passing, by their fleeting rapacity, by as it were the stream of things that never stand still. This world therefore is signified, because of the four seasons of the year, also because of the four cardinal points of the earth, known to all, and frequently spoken of in the Sacred Scriptures: *From the east and the west and the north and the south* (Lk. xiii. 29). Throughout these fourfold seasons, and throughout this fourfold division of the world, the Law of God, as the number ten, is preached. For this reason also the Decalogue was first given to us. For the Law was built upon the Ten Commandments; because there seems to be a certain perfection in this denary number. For in counting a man goes up to this number, and then returns again, from one up to ten, and back again to one, and so on to hundreds, to thousands, which again multiplied by tens grow without end into a forest of numbers. The perfect law therefore is in the number ten, and the law, preached throughout the four parts of the world, ten multiplied by four, becomes forty.

And we are taught that while living in this world we should refrain ourselves from worldly desires: which the forty days' fast known to us all as Lent signifies. This the Law imposes on you, this the Prophets, this likewise the Gospel. Because of this the Law, Moses, fasted for forty days; because of this Prophecy, Elias, fasted for forty days; because of this the Gospel, the Lord Christ, fasted for forty days. Then after the forty days were ended, when another ten days had passed after the forty days, one set of ten, ten simply, not fourfold, the Holy Spirit came, that the Law might be completed through Grace. For the Law without Grace is a killing letter. *For if there had been a law given*, it says, *which could give life, verily justice should have been by the law. But the Scripture hath concluded all under sin, that the promise, by the faith of Jesus Christ, might be given to them that believe* (Gal. iii. 21, 22). And therefore, *The letter killeth, but the spirit quickeneth* (II Cor. iii. 6). Not that you should fulfil something other than what the letter lays down, but that the letter alone makes us guilty; Grace delivers us from sin, and enables us to fulfil the letter.

Hence is it that through Grace comes forgiveness of all sins, and the faith which works through charity. Do not therefore think that the letter is condemned, because it was said that the letter killeth. For this means that the letter puts us in peril of the law. A commandment is given, and you are not aided by grace. At once you find yourself, not alone not *a doer* of the law, but even guilty of a fault. *Where there is no law, neither is there transgression* (Rom. iv. 15). When therefore it was said that, *the letter killeth, but the*

Spirit quickeneth, the Law was not thereby condemned; as though the former was condemned, the Latter praised. But *the letter killeth*; the letter alone, without grace. Here is an example. In a certain sentence we are told that *knowledge puffeth up* (I Cor. viii. 1). What does this mean, *knowledge puffeth up*? Is he condemning knowledge? If it makes us puffed up, it is better to remain ignorant. But since he adds: *But charity edifieth*, as where he adds: *But the Spirit quickeneth*, the Apostle gives us to understand, that the letter without the Spirit kills, with the Spirit it gives life and enables the letter to be fulfilled; so knowledge without charity inflates, with charity it edifies. Therefore the Holy Spirit was sent so that the Law might be fulfilled, and that come to pass which the Lord Himself had said: *I am come, not to destroy the law, but to fulfil it* (Mt. v. 17). This gift He bestows on the believing; this grace He grants to the faithful; this He gives to those to whom He gives the Holy Ghost. The more capable a man becomes by means of it, the easier does it become for him to fulfil the law.

4. *The Law is fulfilled by Charity; not through fear of punishment. Charity is from the Holy Spirit.*

I shall tell you something, Beloved, which you can both readily see and readily reflect upon: that charity fulfils the law. Fear of punishment makes a man do what is good, but in a servile manner. For if you do good because you are afraid to suffer evil, or avoid doing what is evil, because you fear to suffer evil, should anyone promise you immunity from punishment you would soon put your hand to evil doing. Supposing it were said to you: Do not be afraid, you will not suffer any punishment, do as you wish. You would do it. You are held back only through the fear of punishment, not because of your love for justice. For charity has not begun to work in you.

See therefore how charity works. Let us so love Him Whom we fear, that we may fear Him with a chaste love. For a chaste wife fears her husband. But consider carefully these different fears. A chaste wife fears lest she should be forsaken by her absent husband. An adulterous wife fears lest her husband should find her out when he returns. Love therefore fulfils the law: for *perfect love casts out fear* (I John iv. 18), that is, servile fear; fear arising from sin. *The fear of the Lord is holy, enduring for ever and ever* (Ps. xviii. 10). Therefore, if love is the fulfilling of the law, from where does this love come? Reflect carefully, and note and understand, that Charity is the gift of the Holy Ghost. *The charity of God is poured forth in our hearts, by the Holy Ghost, Who is given to us* (Rom. v. 5). Rightly then at the end of ten days, by which number the perfection of the law is indicated, the Lord Jesus Christ sent the Holy Spirit; for Grace enables us to fulfil the law, which it came not to destroy but to fulfil.

5. *The Holy Spirit commended to us in the Number Seven. Sanctification, and the Rest of the Seventh Day.*

The Holy Spirit is commended to us in the number seven, not in the number ten: the law by the denary number, the Holy Ghost by the septenary. That the law relates

to the denary number we have seen;
why the Holy Ghost has affinity to
the septenary number let us now
relate. In the very first book, at the
beginning of the Book called
Genesis, the works of God are recounted to us. Light was made, the
heaven was made, which was called
the firmament between *the waters
and the waters*. The dry land appeared, the sea is separated from the
land, and to the earth is given the
fruitful bringing forth of all growing
things. And He created the greater
and the lesser lights, the sun, the
moon, and the other stars. The
waters bring forth their increase;
the earth also. Man is made in the
image of God. And on the sixth
day God completes all His work. In
no one of these so manifold works,
recounted and completed, is there
any mention of sanctification.

The Lord said: *Be light made; and
light was made; and God saw the light,
that it was good.* Yet it is not said that
God sanctified the light. *Let there
be a firmament made; and a firmament
was made; and God saw that it was
good.* Yet it is not said that He
sanctified the firmament. And, that
we may not linger too long here, so
on with the rest of creation, up to
those things which were made on
the sixth day, when man was made
to the image of God. All are recounted; but nothing is spoken of as
sanctified.

We come to the seventh day, on
which no work was done, but it is
made known that God rested, and
that God sanctified the seventh day.
Sanctification is spoken of for the
first time in the septenary number of
the days; searched for in every place
of Scripture, here first found. Where
God's rest is spoken of, our own rest

is also taught. For God did not need
a rest because He worked; so that
after toil He rejoiced in the holiday,
and sanctified that day on which He
was allowed to rest! This is an
earthly notion. But here it is made
known to us, that as God rested after
all His good works, so after all our
good works we too shall have rest.

*God made all things, and they were
good. And he rested on the seventh day
from all his work which he had done.*
Do you also wish to rest? Then first
do all your works well. Thus, in an
unspiritual way, the observance of
the sabbath was laid upon the Jews;
as were other things also, those
which signified the mysteries. For
a certain period of rest was commanded. Seek you then what this
rest implies. For tranquillity of soul
is spiritual rest. But tranquillity of
soul comes from a good conscience.
He then truly observes the sabbath
rest who does not sin. For it is this
they were commanded on whom the
sabbath rest was laid. *You shall do
no servile work therein* (Lev. xxiii. 7).
*Whosoever committeth sin is the
servant of sin* (Jn. viii. 34).

The septenary number is accordingly dedicated to the Holy Ghost,
as the denary is to the Law. This
Isaias also reveals to us where he
says: *The spirit of the Lord shall rest
on him: the spirit of wisdom, and of
understanding, the spirit of counsel, and
of fortitude, the spirit of knowledge and
of godliness, the spirit of the fear of the
Lord* (xi. 2). As though spiritual
grace coming down to us begins at
wisdom and ends at fear. But we,
ascending from below, striving upwards towards the highest things,
should begin with fear and end at
wisdom. For *the fear of the Lord is
the beginning of wisdom* (Ps. cx. 10).

It would take too long, and it would be beyond our powers though not our willingness, to recount to you all the testimonies there are regarding the number seven, as it relates to the Holy Spirit. Therefore let these suffice.

6. *In the number fifty the Law is commended to us in the ten, and the Holy Spirit in the seven.*

Let us consider now how, as the Law is perfected through grace, by this same grace of the Holy Spirit both the number ten, as we have shown, and the number seven were brought before our mind and commended to us. Christ commended to us, in the number ten, the law which He commanded to be fulfilled, when after ten days He sent us the Holy Spirit. Where shall we find in Scripture a commendation of the number seven that is specially connected with the Holy Spirit? In the Book of Tobias you will read, that this Festival, that is, Pentecost, consists of *weeks* (Tob. i. 2, *Sept.* rightly, II Mach. xii. 31). How is this? The septenary number multiplied by itself, that is, seven by seven, as we learn in school; seven times seven is forty-nine.

As to this form of the septenary number, seven by seven: since it is the Holy Spirit Himself who gathers us together, and unites us, it is for this reason He gives us this first sign of His Coming, that they who would receive Him would, each of them, speak in all tongues. For the unity of the Body of Christ is gathered together from all tongues, by means of all the peoples who are spread throughout the whole earth. And that one should then speak in the tongues of all, bore witness to

the unity that was to be between all peoples. But the Apostle says: *Supporting one another in charity*, which is love; *careful to keep the unity of the Spirit in the bond of peace* (Eph. ii. 2). Therefore, as the Holy Spirit gathers us together from many into one body, so unity is received into the mind through humility, and driven out through pride. For the heart that is humble is like water seeking a hollow place where it may come to rest. Driven out by the exaltation of pride, as by the swelling of a hill, it runs away. Because of this was it said: *God resisteth the proud, and giveth grace to the humble.* What does *giveth grace* mean? He gives the Holy Ghost. He fills the humble, because He finds them capable of receiving Him. Therefore, since these things are so, to the number forty-nine, made up of seven by seven, one is added; and unity is commended to us.

7. *Concerning the Two Fishings; and the 153 Great Fishes taken after the Resurrection.*

That the zeal of Your Charity may be a help to my own infirmity of mind before the Lord, receive with the ears of your own minds something that, as it seems to me, is as sweet after it has been explained, as it is obscure if it is not explained. The Lord, after He had chosen His Disciples, and before His Resurrection, bade them cast their nets into the sea. They cast them, and they took such an innumerable multitude of fishes that the nets broke, and the ships being overladen were near to sinking. He did not say to them on what side they should cast their nets; but only said: *Let down your nets* (Lk. v). For had He told them to let down their nets on the right-hand side, they would have caught only the good fish; if on the left, they would have caught only the bad. Because they cast at random, neither to the left nor the right, they caught both good and bad.

This is a figure of the Church of the present time, in this world. Likewise those servants sent out to those who were invited, going forth gathered all they found, both good and bad, and brought them in; and the marriage was filled with guests (Mt. xxii. 10). Good and bad therefore are now gathered in. And how do schisms happen, if not through the nets breaking? How are the ships overladen, if not when the Church is weighed down with the scandals of lustful disorders that wickedly disturb it?

This the Lord did before His Resurrection. But in like manner after His Resurrection He again found His Disciples fishing. He again bade them cast in their nets, but not anyhow, and at random; for now it is after the Resurrection. For after the Resurrection His Body, which is the Church, will no longer contain the bad. *Cast the net,* He says, *on the right side of the ship, and you shall find* (Jn. xxi. 6). They cast the net, as He told them, on the right-hand side of the ship, and they caught a certain number of fish. For those caught which were not numbered are those from that draught by which the Church is signified as it now is. *I have declared, and I have spoken: they are multiplied above number* (Ps. xxxix. 6). These are understood to be above the due number, and, in a measure, superfluous. Those however caught on the right-hand side are *great fishes,*

and *numbered. He that shall do and teach,* He says, *he shall be called great in the kingdom of heaven* (Mt. v. 19). And so there were taken *great fishes,* to the number of one hundred and fifty-three.

Who does not feel that this number was not mentioned without reason? And that neither was it without meaning that the Lord should say: *Let down your nets,* or that it should concern Him that they should be cast on the right-hand side of the ship. This number one hundred and fifty-three also signifies something. And the Evangelist had a purpose in telling this, as though he were looking back to that first draught, where the broken nets foreshadowed schisms—because in the Church of eternal life there will be no schisms, because there will be no division; and all shall be *great,* for all shall be filled with charity. Therefore, looking back as it were to what had happened the first time, as portending schisms, he was at pains to say of this second draught: *And although there were so many, the net was not broken* (Jn. xxi. 11).

And so what the right hand meant has been told us; namely, that they are all good. What their greatness signifies is also told; because, *he that shall do and teach, he shall be called great in the kingdom of heaven.* We are told what it means that *the net was not broken:* for in heaven there shall be no schisms. What then is the meaning of the number one hundred and fifty-three? This assuredly will not be the number of the blessed. The saints will not be limited to one hundred and fifty-three; for they alone *who were not defiled with women* are numbered *a hundred forty-four thousand* (Apoc.

xiv. 1–4). This number seems to grow like a tree from some seed. The seed of this great number is in a certain lesser number, which is ten and seven. Ten and seven make a hundred and fifty-three; if you count from one to seventeen, and add up all the numbers. If you do not add up the numbers from one to seventeen, all of which you counted, there will only be seventeen. But if you add them up this way, one, two, and three make six, six plus four and five make fifteen, and so on up to seventeen, you reach a total of one hundred and fifty-three.

Recall now what I reminded you of and commended to you a while ago, and think of what and Whom does ten and seven signify. Ten means the Law; seven the Holy Spirit. By this number what are we to understand, but those who will be the Church of the eternal Resurrection, where there shall be no schisms, where death shall no more be feared, for after the Resurrection it *shall be no more*; those therefore who shall live forever with God, who have fulfilled the law by the gift of God, the grace of the Holy Spirit, Whose feast we celebrate this day? Turning then etc.

VIII. St Augustine, Bishop and Doctor

What is Peace?[16]

John xiv. 27. It is the voice of the Lord, Dearly Beloved: *Peace I leave with you, my peace I give unto you.* As we are to speak of peace, let us learn first what are the rewards of peace. Peace is serenity of mind, tranquillity of soul, simplicity of heart, the bond of love, the fellowship of charity. This it is that takes away enmities, restrains wars, holds back anger, treads down pride, loves the humble, calms those who quarrel, reconciles those who are enemies, and is pleasing and acceptable to all. It seeks nothing that belongs to another; regards nothing as its own. It teaches a love that has never learned to hate. It knows not how to be lifted above itself. It knows not how to be puffed up.

He therefore who acquires this peace, let him hold fast to it. He who has broken it, let him strive to restore it again. He who has lost it, let him seek earnestly to find it again. For whosoever is found

without this peace is rejected by the Father, disinherited by the Son, and becomes a stranger to the Holy Ghost. He refuses a gift offered to him who despises the blessing of the law (of peace) that is given to us. Nor can any man attain to the inheritance of the Lord who refuses to accept his will. He cannot have the friendship of Christ who is deliberately at enmity with another Christian.

Therefore, it is the offence of stubbornness that we are to reject from us, that we are bidden to oppose, commanded to turn away from. What part have you with enmities, O Christian Soul? Why should you love rages and quarrellings which cannot be pleasing to the Author of peace? Why do you foster enmities whose consequences not even the devil could escape, who first invented them? For in the beginning, as a serpent, he practised enmities against the First Man, and destroyed him. And in bringing misfortune on Man he was himself brought down to the dust. While he was trying to entrap Adam, he was himself entrapped from the beginning in his own snares.

Therefore, O Christian, either you embrace the Charity of Christ, or else you must know and understand, that in following the likeness of the devil's works, you are yourself become like to the author of all enmity. Amen.

IX. St Augustine, Bishop and Doctor

Peace the Inheritance of Christ[17]

1. We read in the Gospel, dearest Brethren, that as the time of His Passion drew near, our Lord and Saviour began to make known to His Disciples His own *crossing over* from this world to the Father. And among other discourses which He bestowed on His beloved companions, as part of their remembrance of Him, He commended to them, as a special gift, the blessing of unity and peace, saying to them: *Peace I leave you, my peace I give unto you*; as though He said to them: In peace I leave you; in peace I shall find you. Going away from them, He wishes to give them what He desired to find in all men at His return. To His own He left this inheritance, and foretold all the good things of His Promise, and the rewards of keeping peace. And therefore, Brethren, if we wish to be heirs of Christ, we must possess and abide in His peace. Christ has given us peace, as you have heard. He has commanded us to be at peace, and to be of one mind with one another. He has laid it upon us that we keep unbroken and inviolate the bonds of peace and of love.

In another place He makes known to us the rewards of peace, where He says: *Blessed are the peacemakers: for they shall be called the children of God* (Mt. v. 9). And if a man begins to be called a child of God, who has

begun to be a peacemaker, he refuses to be a child of God, who is unwilling to embrace peace. He who scorns to be a peacemaker denies that God is his Father. The children of God must therefore be peacemakers, kind in heart, simple of speech, united in the peace of love, joined firmly one to another in the bonds of fellowship.

2. *With whom are we to be at peace. The effects of peace.* This peace is to be observed only with the good, and with those who keep the commandments of God; not with the wicked, or with evil doers; who are at peace with one another in their sins. The peace of Christ leads us to eternal salvation. The peace that belongs to the devil leads us to eternal damnation. We must ever be at peace with the just, and ever at war with evil: for we must for ever hate the evil doing of the wicked. For men themselves, even though they are wicked, must still be loved; for they are creatures of God. The peace therefore which is found in the good, joins brothers together in peace, neighbours in love for one another.

Peace brings us the Spirit of God in a special manner. Peace is the mother of love. Peace is a mark of holiness. The Lord, through His prophet, says of it: *Love ye truth and peace* (Zach. viii. 19). Peace is the healing of the people, the glory of the priesthood, the joy of our country, and the terror of our enemies, visible and invisible. Every man must be watchful of peace, Brothers; for he is always living in God who lives in holy peace, and shares with the saints the company of God.

3. *The Office of Priest. Without peace neither prayer nor gift is acceptable.* It is the duty of the priest to instruct his people that they must live in peace. It is the duty of the people to hear in obedience what the priest must teach them. It is the duty of the shepherd to forbid what is not lawful. It is the duty of the people to learn this teaching, and to follow it. And all, both priests and people, should in all circumstances keep *the bond of unity* in faith and love; for without peace neither the prayer of the priest nor the offering of the faithful is acceptable to God. So if we wish that God will speedily answer our prayers we must live in true peace. *If therefore thou offer thy gift at the altar, and there thou remember that thy brother hath anything against thee: leave there thy offering before the altar, and go first to be reconciled to thy brother: and then coming thou shalt offer thy gift* (Mt. v. 23, 24).

4. That God desires that we live in peace and in one mind towards each other our Saviour reveals to us, where He speaks in the Gospel to His heavenly Father. *Holy Father,* He says, *keep them in thy name whom thou hast given me; that they may be one as we also are* (Jn. xvii. 11). And because of this the Apostle exhorts

the faithful, saying to them: *I beseech you, brethren, that you all speak the same thing, that you be perfect in the same mind* (I Cor. i. 10). And again: *Let there be no contention and envy among you* (Rom. xiii. 13). *Let all bitterness, and anger, and indignation, and clamour, and blasphemy, be put away from you, with all malice* (Eph. iv. 31). And in another place he says: *Supporting one another in charity, careful to keep the unity of the Spirit in the bond of peace. One body and one spirit; as you are called in one hope of your calling* (Eph. iv. 4).

This unity of mind was therefore to be found among the Apostles. So the new people of those who believed in Christ, observing the commandments of the Lord, observed also His charity. The divine Scriptures prove this. *And the multitude of the believers had but one heart and one soul* (Acts iv. 32). And in another place we read: *All were persevering in one mind in prayer, with the women, and Mary the mother of Jesus, and with his brethren* (Acts i. 14). And so their prayers were heard: for they could ask with confidence for whatever it was they sought from the mercy of God.

5. *The diminution of Charity, the falling away of faith.* This unity of heart grows less in proportion as our generosity in good works falls away. The early Christians sold their houses and their lands, and laying up treasure for themselves in heaven, they gave to the Apostles, for the needs of the poor, the money they received (Acts ii. 45). But now we do not give even a tenth of what we possess. And where the Lord has bidden us to sell, we buy so as to increase what we have. So the strength of faith

has grown less in us; the power to believe has grown less. And because of this our Lord, having our days before His eyes, says to us in the Gospel: *The Son of man when he cometh, shall he find, think you, faith on earth?* (Lk. xviii. 8).

We are seeing what He foretold coming to pass. Faith consists of the fear of God, of the law of justice, of love, of good works. There is no one who thinks in fear of that which is to come. There is no one who thinks of the Day of the Lord, and of His Anger, of the punishments to come upon those who will not believe, of the eternal torments that have been decreed for the wicked. That which the conscience would fear if it believed, that it fears in no way, since it does not believe. For if the conscience believed it would be watchful. And if it was vigilant, it would escape punishment.

6. *Vigilance.* Let us stir up our hearts, as much as we can, Dearest brethren, and come out of the sleep of our past neglect, and let us, each one of us, be vigilant in keeping, in fulfilling, the commandments of the Lord. Let us be like those to whom he said: *Let your loins be girt, and lamps burning in your hands. And you yourselves like to men who wait for the Lord, when he shall return from the wedding; that when he cometh and knocketh, they may open to him immediately* (Lk. xii. 34, 35). We must stand ready with our loins girt; lest when the day of our setting forth comes, it may find us bound and encumbered. Let our light be shining with good works, and let it glow so brightly that it will lead us out of the night of this world into the day of eternal brightness, where with Christ the True Author of peace, and with His angels, we may come to enjoy peace without end, and joy without end, by the help of our Lord Jesus Christ, Who with the Father and the Son, reigns for ever and ever. Amen.

X. St Leo the Great, Pope and Doctor

The Work of the Holy Spirit[18]

Synopsis:

    I. The Christian Pentecost succeeds to the Mosaic.
    II. How speedily and wondrously the Disciples were taught by the Holy Ghost.
    III. The Perfect Equality of the Persons of the Most Holy Trinity.
    IV. Heresy of the Montanists against the Holy Ghost: the Fount and Cause of every good.
    V. That all things in the Church are sanctified by the Holy Ghost, and that by Him the Fasts also were instituted.

I. The hearts of all Catholics are fully aware that this day's Solemnity is to be venerated among the greatest of the Feasts. We have no uncertainty as to the reverence due to this day, made sacred by the Holy Spirit in the surpassing miracle of the gift of Himself. For this is the tenth day that has shone upon us from that on which the Lord *mounted above the heaven of heavens* (Ps. lxvii. 34), to sit at the right hand of God the Father, and the fiftieth from His Resurrection in Whom the day begins. And it holds within it great mysteries which relate both to the Old and the New Dispensations, wherein it is most clearly revealed to us, that grace was foretold by the law, and that the law is made perfect through grace.

For as of old on the fiftieth day after the Sacrifice of the Lamb, the Law was given on Mount Sinai to the Hebrew people, now delivered from the Egyptians, so, after the Passion of Christ, in which the True Lamb of God was slain, on the fiftieth day after His Resurrection, the Holy Spirit descended upon the Apostles and upon the people who believed (Acts ii. 3); so that an earnest Christian might know beyond any uncertainty, that the sacred rites of the Old Testament had served as foundations for the Gospel, and that by this same Spirit was the Second Covenant laid down, by Whom the first had been established.

II. For as the history of the Apostles bears witness, *when the days of the Pentecost were accomplished, they were all together in one place: and suddenly there came a sound from heaven, as of a mighty wind coming, and it filled the whole house where they were sitting. And there appeared to them parted tongues as it were of fire, and it sat upon every one of them. And they were all filled with the Holy Ghost, and they began to speak with divers tongues, according as the Holy Ghost gave them to speak* (Acts ii. 1–4). How swift the word of wisdom; and how quickly when the Lord is our instructor do we learn what He teaches! There was no need of an interpreter to understand, nor for

usage to give them facility, nor of time for study, for the Spirit of Truth, breathing where it willed, the particular tongues of every nation are shared together in the mouth of the Church.

From that day forth the trumpet of the preaching of the Gospel has sounded. From that day the rain of spiritual graces, the streams of blessings, have watered every desert, and the whole parched world; for *the Spirit of God moved over the waters* (Gen. i. 2) to renew the face of the earth, and the brightness of new light began to flash forth to scatter the old darkness, when, in the splendour of those ardent tongues, the shining word, the burning eloquence of the Lord was received; which holds within it both the power of making light, to give understanding, and the power of fire, to burn away all sin.

III. But, though truly wondrous, Dearly Beloved, was the manner in which all this took place, and though beyond doubt that in the midst of this joyous harmony of every human tongue the divine majesty of the Holy Spirit was present, yet let no one imagine that the divine substance showed itself in these things which were seen by bodily eyes. His Invisible Nature, which belonged also to the Father and to the Son, revealed the nature of His office and of His work, in the manner He willed, but the substance of His divine Being was contained within His divinity; for as the Father and the Son so likewise the Holy Ghost is inaccessible to human sight.

For in the Divine Trinity there is no dissimilarity, no inequality, and all that can be conceived of Its substance can be separated neither from Its power, nor Its glory, nor Its eternity. And though in Their separate Persons the Father is one Person, the Son another, the Holy Ghost another, yet there is no other Godhead and no other divine nature. For since the Son is the Only-Begotten of the Father, and the Holy Ghost the Spirit of both Father and Son, not as any creature whatever which belongs to the Father and the Son, but as possessing life and power with Them Both, and being eternally of that which the Father and Son are.

For this reason, when the Lord on the day before His Passion promised His Disciples the Holy Ghost would come, He said: *I have yet many things to say to you: but you cannot bear them now. But when he, the Spirit of Truth, is come, he will teach you all truth. For he shall not speak of himself; but what things soever he shall hear, he shall speak; and the things that are to come, he shall show you. All things whatsoever the Father hath are mine; therefore I said, that he shall receive of mine, and show it to you.* It is not therefore that some things belong to the Father, some to the Son, and some to the Holy Ghost, but that all that the Father has the Son has, and the Holy Ghost has also; nor has the Trinity ever been wanting in this communion, for in the Trinity to have all things is the same as to exist for ever.

There, let no times, no degrees, no differences be thought of; and if there is no one can explain what God is, let no one dare to affirm what He is not. For it is more to be pardoned that we say nothing worthy of His sublime nature, than that we say what is contrary to it. And so whatever pious hearts may understand of the eternal and unchangeable glory of the Father, let them understand the same of the Son and of the Holy Ghost, without distinction and without separation. For this reason do we confess that the Blessed Trinity is one God, because in these three Persons there is no difference either in substance, in power, in will or in operation.

IV. Therefore, as we detest Arians, whose desire it is to place a certain division between the Father and the Son, so do we likewise detest the Macedonians, who, though they admit equality between Father and Son, believe at the same time that the Holy Spirit is of a lower nature; not thinking that they are falling into that blasphemy which shall be forgiven neither in this world nor in the judgement to come, according to the words of the Lord: *He that shall speak against the Holy Ghost, it shall not be forgiven him, neither in this world, nor in the world to come* (Mt. xii. 32). Whosoever continues in this heresy is unpardonable: for he has cut himself off from Him through Whom He could confess God; nor can he ever attain to the remedy of forgiveness who no longer has an Advocate (Paraclete) to intercede for him. For it is through Him we call upon the Father, from Him come the tears of repentance, from Him the groans of those who kneel in supplication; *no man can say the Lord Jesus, but by the Holy Ghost* (I Cor. xii. 3), Whose Omnipotence and Unity with the Father and the Son the Apostle most clearly proclaims: *There are diversi-*

ties *of graces, but the same Spirit;
and there are diversities of ministries,
but the same Lord; and there are
diversities of operations, but the same
God, who worketh all in all* (ib. 4–6).

V. Let us one and all be encouraged by these and innumerable
other testimonies, in which the
authority of the divine eloquence
shines forth, to the highest venera-
tion of Pentecost, rejoicing in
honour of the Holy Spirit, by
Whom the whole Catholic Church
is sanctified, and every rational being
instructed, Who is the Inspirer of
Faith, the Teacher of knowledge,
the Fount of love, the Seal of chastity, the Cause of all virtue. Let
the souls of all who believe rejoice,
that in all the world One God,
Father, Son, and Holy Ghost is
praised in the confession of every
tongue; and that this Sign which
appeared in the form of fire has
steadfastly continued both in power
and in deed.

For it is the Spirit of Truth Himself which causes the house of His
glory to shine with the splendour of
His own light, and in this temple He
wills that there shall be nothing unworthy, nothing wanting in fervour.
It is also by His teaching and assistance that the purification of fast and
almsdeeds has been imposed on us.
For this venerable day is followed
by the most salutary practise of
abstinence; which all holy men have
ever found most profitable to themselves, and which we exhort you,
with all pastoral solicitude, that you
carefully observe, so that should you
in these days have acquired any stain
through heedless neglect, then let the
correction of fasting cleanse it, and
the devotion of your piety amend it.

Accordingly, let us fast on the
fourth and sixth day of the week.
On the sabbath (Saturday) we shall
celebrate the same with the customary devotion of the vigil.
Through Jesus Christ our Lord,
Who with the Father and the Holy
Ghost livest and reignest world
without end. Amen.

XI. St Leo the Great, Pope and Doctor

The Redemption the Work of the Trinity[19]

Synopsis:

    I. That the Holy Spirit did not make a beginning of His gifts at Pente-
cost, but increased them; when the Trinity indivisibly wrought.

    II. It is a consequence of sin, that the Persons of the Trinity would share
amongst Them the work of our reparation; in what manner?

    III. That this sharing is in no way contrary to Their Equality and Con-
substantiality.

    IV. We should not think regarding the Trinity, Which is wholly Equal,
as we do of created, visible things.

    V. Why Christ wished His Disciples to rejoice at His Ascension.

    VI. The Three Persons have but one Being and one Power of Operation.

I. The Coming of the Holy Ghost,
Dearly Beloved, Who, on the fiftieth
day after the Resurrection of the
Lord, flowed down upon the
Apostles and the Faithful, has con-
secrated the Festival that is reverenced

this day throughout the whole world. They had awaited it in hope, for the Lord Jesus had promised He would come (Acts i. 8); not that He would then begin to dwell within the sanctified, but that He would then fill more abundantly, inflame more ardently, the breasts that were consecrated to Himself; increasing, not beginning, His gifts to them; not new in operation, but now more abounding in richness.

For never was the divine majesty of the Holy Spirit separated from the Omnipotence of the Father and of the Son, and whatever the divine dispensation has done in the ordering of all things proceeded from the Providence of the Whole Trinity. One is the mildness of divine mercy, and one the correction of Its justice; and there can be no separateness in Their work in Whom there is no separateness in their willing. Whom the Father enlightens, the Son enlightens, the Holy Ghost enlightens; and since one is the Person Sent, Another the Sender, and another the Promiser, their Unity and Trinity is together revealed to us: since being equal in essence, yet including separateness of Person, this may be understood of the one Substance, but not of one and the same Person.

II. Allowing therefore for the indivisible operation of the Divinity, such is the Plan of our Redemption, the Design of our salvation, that the Father in Person does certain things, the Son likewise yet other things, the Holy Ghost the same. For had man, made to the image and likeness of God, continued in the dignity of his own nature, and had not been deceived by the fraud of the devil,

he would not have turned aside through evil desires from the law laid down for him, and the Creator of the world would not have become a creature, the Eternal subject to time, nor would God the Son, the Equal of God the Father, have taken upon Himself the form of a servant, and the likeness of our sinful flesh. But because *by the envy of the devil, death came into the world* (Wisd. ii. 4), and because human bondage could be undone in no other way, unless He took our cause upon Him Who without loss of His divine majesty could become both true man and the One only free of the infection of sin, the Merciful Trinity shared among Them the work of our redemption: so that expiation might be offered to the Father, the Son might offer expiation, and the Holy Ghost purify by fire.

There was need that they also who were to be saved should do something for themselves, and, turning in heart to their Redeemer, turn away from the domination of the devil; for as Paul says, *God hath sent the Spirit of His Son into your hearts, crying: Abba, Father* (Gal. iv. 6). *Now the Lord is a Spirit. And where the Spirit of the Lord is, there is liberty* (II Cor. iii. 17). And also: *No man sayeth the Lord Jesus, but by the Holy Ghost* (I Cor. xii. 3).

III. If therefore, Dearly Beloved, guided by grace, we come in faith and wisdom to know what, in the work of restoration, is proper to the Father, to the Son, and what to the Holy Ghost, and what they do in common, let us without any doubt so receive what was done for us in a lowly and bodily manner as not to think unworthily of the glory of the

One and Undivided Trinity. For though no human mind is able to conceive of God, as He is, and no human tongue to speak of Him, nevertheless, whatever the human understanding comes to see of the nature of the Godhead of the Father, unless it is one and the same with that which we conceive, either of His Only-begotten Son, or of the Holy Spirit, such a human mind is not spiritually enlightened, rather is it carnally darkened, and that which it seems to conceive rightly of the Father profits it nothing. For we separate ourselves from the Trinity, if we do not hold fast to Its Unity: for in no way is that truly one with the divine nature which is contrary to it through some inequality.

IV. When therefore we turn the understanding of our soul to the praise and confession of the Father and the Son and the Holy Ghost, let us put away from our minds the outward appearances of visible things, the ages of temporal things, and the places which bodies occupy. Put out of your mind what is extended through space, enclosed within boundaries, or whatever is not always and everywhere complete and perfect.

Let the notion we form in our mind of the divinity of the Trinity understand nothing of differences, and seek for no degrees. And if the mind has come to think of what is worthy of God, let it not dare to deny this to any Person: as though it would attribute to the Father, as the more worthy, what it does not attribute to the Son, or to the Holy Ghost. There is no reverence for God in preferring the Father to the Son. An affront to the Son is an offence to the Father. What is denied to the One is withheld from Them Both. The Father is not believed Omnipotent and Unchanging, if He should beget One Who is inferior to Himself, or made greater by having One Whom He before had not, since Divinity and Eternity is common to Them Both.

V. The Lord Jesus, as we read in the Gospel, said indeed to His Disciples: *If you loved me, you would indeed be glad because I go to the Father: for the Father is greater than I* (Jn. xiv. 28). But those ears which had often heard: *I and the Father are one* (Jn. x. 30); and, *He that seeth me, seeth the Father also* (xiv. 9), do not receive these words as implying a difference within the Divinity, nor do they understand them of that Being they came to learn was of the same nature and everlasting with the Father. It is the exaltation of man's nature, through the Incarnation of the Word, that is being placed before the Holy Apostles. And they who were troubled when told of the Lord's going from them, are heartened onwards towards eternal joy by this enlargement of their own dignity. *If you loved me; you would indeed be glad, because I go to the Father;* that is, could you see with perfect understanding what honour is given you, that I, Begotten of God the Father, am also born of a human mother; that I the Lord of all ages have willed to become one of mortal men; that I the Invisible have visibly revealed Myself; that I Eternal in the Form of God have taken upon Me the form of a servant: *you would indeed be glad, because I go to the Father.*

For it is to you the Ascension is

given; it is your lowliness that is exalted in Me above all the heavens, and placed at the right hand of God! But I, Who with the Father am what the Father is, remain Inseparable with Him Who has begotten Me. And as in coming to you I do not go from Him, so, returning to Him, I do not leave you. Rejoice therefore, *because I go to the Father: for the Father is greater than I.* For I have united you to Myself; and become a Son of man that you may be children of God.

And so, though I am the same Person in either nature, yet in that in which I am made like to you, I am less than the Father. But in that nature in which I am not separated from the Father, I am greater even than Myself. Therefore, let the nature that is lower than the Father go to the Father, that where the Word is, there always the Flesh may be; and let the one Faith of the Catholic Church, which doubts not that as man He is less than the . Father, believe that He is Equal with Him as God.

VI. Therefore, let the blind and foolish subtlety of heretical impiety be despised, Dearly Beloved, which flatters itself with a perverted interpretation of this sentence—*for the Father is greater than I*—and even with the Lord saying: *All things whatsoever the Father hath are mine*

(Jn. xv. 16), it will not understand that it takes from the Father whatever it dares to deny the Son. And it is so foolish in what relates to His humanity, that it thinks that, because the Son of man took our nature upon Him, He lost what was His Father's!

In God mercy does not lessen power; nor is the restoration to God of the creature He loves a lessening of His own eternal glory. What belongs to the Father belongs to the Son, and what belongs to the Father and the Son belongs also to the Holy Ghost; for the Whole Trinity together is One God. And this belief is no discovery of earthly wisdom, and neither has human opinion convinced us, but the Only Begotten has taught it to us; the Holy Spirit has established us in it: that Spirit in Whom we must believe in no other way than we believe in the Father and the Son.

For though He is neither the Father nor the Son, He is yet not separate either from the Father or from the Son. And He is a Person of the Trinity; therefore through His Divinity He shares in the Substance of both the Father and the Son, filling all things, containing all things, and, together with the Father and the Son, disposing all things. To Whom be honour, praise, and glory, for ever and ever. Amen.

XII. St Gregory the Great, Pope and Doctor

Given to the People in the Basilica of St Peter the Apostle on the Holy Day of Pentecost

Explanation of the Gospel[20]

1. We shall, if it is agreeable to you, Dearest Brethren, go briefly over

the words of the Gospel lesson, so that afterwards there may be more time to dwell in contemplation on this so great Solemnity. For on this day the Holy Spirit, with the sound of a mighty wind, descended upon the Apostles, transformed their souls from the love of earthly things to the love of Him, and by outward visible tongues of fire set their own inward hearts aflame; for as they receive God in the vision of fire, they begin to burn with the sweet fire of His love. For the Holy Spirit is love. And so John tells us: *God is love* (I Jn. iv. 8, 16). He therefore who desires God with his whole soul, possesses Him he loves. For no one could love God unless he does indeed possess Him Whom he loves.

But should any one of you be asked whether he loves God, he will answer with confidence and a sure mind, I do love Him. Now at the beginning of this Gospel you heard what Truth has said: *If any one love me, he will keep my word.* The proof of love then is to show it in deed. On this question the same John says in his Epistle: *If any man say, I love God, and hateth his brother, he is a liar* (I Jn. iv. 20). For we truly love God if we keep His commandments, if we restrain ourselves from pleasures. For he who has given himself up to unlawful desires does not of a surety love God; for he contradicts Him in the pursuit of his own pleasures.

2. *And my Father will love him, and we will come to him, and make our abode with him.* Reflect, Dearly Beloved, how great a dignity this is: to have the Lord come and abide in our heart. Should some rich and powerful friend enter your home you would make haste to clean the whole house, lest there be anything to displease the eye of the one who is coming. Let you then cleanse the stains of evil doing from the house of your soul, in preparation for the coming of God.

But note what Truth says: *We shall come and make our abode with him.* For He comes into the hearts of some, but does not make His abode there; for though because of their remorse God may turn towards them, yet in time of temptation they forget even what it was they repented of, and turn back to continue their evil doing as if they had never repented. He therefore who truly loves God, who keeps His commandments, the Lord enters his heart, and there takes up His abode; because the love of the Divinity has so penetrated him, that in time of temptation he will not turn his back on that love.

He therefore truly loves God whose soul, not consenting to evil delight, is not overcome by it. For the more a man gives himself to the love of the baser things, the more does he cut himself off from the love of God. For this reason He goes on to say: *He that loveth me not, keepeth not my words.* Turn your minds inwards upon yourselves, Dearly Beloved Brethren. See whether you do indeed love God. And let no one believe himself, whatever his mind may say, unless it is confirmed by deeds. Let us ask of our life, our soul, our tongue, whether we love our Creator? The love of God is never idle. It works *great things*, if it is present; if it refuses to bring forth good works, it is not love.

And the word which you have heard is not mine; but the Father's who sent me. You know, Dearest Brethren,

that He Who speaks is the Word, the
Only-Begotten Son of the Father,
and because of this the words the
Son speaks are not the Son's but the
Father's: for the Son is Himself the
Word of the Father. *These things
have I spoken to you, abiding with you.*
When He was no longer to be with
them, being now about to ascend to
heaven, He promised them: *Behold
I am with you all days, even to the
consummation of the world* (Mt. xxviii.
20). But the Word Incarnate both
abides with us, and departs from us;
He departs in His Body, He abides
in His Divinity. He says therefore
that he was then abiding with them:
because He was about to depart
from before their bodily eyes, Who
was ever present in invisible power.

3. *But the Paraclete, the Holy Ghost,
whom the Father will send in my name,
he will teach you all things, and bring
all things to your mind, whatsoever I
shall have said to you.* Most of you
know, my brethren, that the Greek
word *Paraclete* is rendered by the
word *Advocate*, or *Comforter*. He is
called *Advocate* because He pleads
with the mercy of the Father on
behalf of sinners. He Who is one in
nature with the Father and the Son
is said to obtain pardon for sinners,
because those whom He fills (with
His Spirit) He inspires to pray for
themselves. Because of this Paul
says: *The Spirit himself asks for us
with unspeakable groanings.* But he
who pleads is lesser in dignity
than he to whom he pleads; how
then is the Spirit said to ask Who
is not lesser in dignity than Him to
Whom he prays? But the Spirit
prays for us in that He rouses those
He fills to pray for themselves.

The same Spirit is also called
Comforter, because He uplifts the
soul in its dejection, giving hope of
pardon to those who grieve because
of the sins they have committed.
Rightly was it promised of Him:
He will teach you all things. Because
unless the same Spirit is in the heart
of the one who learns, unprofitable
is the word of the teacher. Let no
one then attribute to the man who
instructs him, that which he understands from the mouth of his teacher;
for unless He is within Who *will
teach us*, the tongue of the teacher
labours in vain. All alike hear the
voice of the speaker, yet all do not
understand alike the meaning of the
words they hear. Since the word is
the same, why do your hearts not
understand alike, if not for the
reason that, although the voice of
the speaker is directed towards all,
it is the Master within us Who teaches
us what is said, and some more than
others.

Of this anointing of the Spirit
John again speaks, where he says:
His unction teacheth you all things
(I Jn. ii. 27). We are not therefore
instructed by the voice when the
mind is not anointed at the same time
by the Spirit. But why do we say
this of the teaching of men when
even the Creator does not speak for
any man's instruction, unless He
speaks to him through the unction of
the Spirit? Cain, before he had slain
his brother, heard the words: *Thou
hast sinned, be at peace* (Gen. iv. 6
Sept.). Because of his sins he was
admonished by a voice, but not
anointed by the Spirit; he could hear
the words of God, but he refused
to hearken to them.

Let us ask ourselves why is it said
of the same Spirit: *He will bring all
things to your mind*; since to bring to

another is the task of an inferior? But as the word to bring is also sometimes used by us in the sense of to supply secretly, the Invisible Spirit is said to bring things to our minds, not servilely, but secretly. *Peace I leave you, my peace I give unto you.* Here I leave it; there I shall give it. I leave it for those who come after Me; I shall give it to those who shall attain to the possession of Me.

4. We have so far, dearest brethren, spoken to you, briefly, on the words of today's Gospel. Let us now turn our hearts to the contemplation of this so great Feast. As there was also read, together with the Gospel, a Lesson from the Acts of the Apostles, let us also draw something from this to assist us in our meditation. You have heard that the Holy Spirit appeared above each of the Apostles, in the form of tongues of fire, and that He gave them knowledge of all tongues. What is revealed to us by this sign if not that the Holy Church, filled by this Spirit, shall speak with the voice of every nation? They who long ago strove to build a tower against God (Gen. xi. 6) lost the tongue they had then in common. But in those who humbly fear God all tongues are made one. Here lowliness has merited power; there pride brought down confusion.

5. But we must also ask ourselves why did the Holy Spirit, Who is Co-eternal with the Father and the Son, appear in the form of fire? Why did He appear in the form of fire, and at the same time in the form of tongues? Why is He sometimes made known to us in the form of a dove, and sometimes as fire? Why did He appear above the Only-begotten in the form of a dove, and above the Disciples in the form of fire, and did not descend upon the Lord in the form of fire, nor appear above the Disciples in the form of a dove?

Let us return and explain these four points as we have mentioned them. The Spirit that is Co-eternal with the Father and the Son is shown under the form of fire because God is invisible, ineffable, and incorporeal fire, as Paul testifies: *For our God is a consuming fire* (Heb. xii. 29). God is called fire because by Him the rust of sin is consumed. It is of this fire that Truth has said: *I am come to cast fire on the earth; and what will I but that it be kindled* (Lk. xii. 49). And by *the earth* is meant earthly hearts, which as they at all times heap up evil thoughts within them, are trodden on by the spirits of evil. But the Lord sends fire on earth when, by the breath of His Holy Spirit, He sets fire to the hearts of unspiritual men. And the earth catches fire when the heart of flesh, indifferent to its own evil pleasures, puts away the lusts of the present life, and becomes inflamed with the love of God. Fittingly then did the Spirit appear in fire; because in every heart that He enters into He drives out the torpor of coldness, and kindles there the desire of His own Eternity.

He is shown in the form of *tongues* of fire, because the Spirit is Co-eternal with the Son, and the tongue has the closest connection with the word. The Son is the Word of the Father. And since one is the substance of the Son and the Spirit, the Spirit should be shown in the form of a tongue. And because a word proceeds from the tongue, the Spirit appears in the form of tongues; because whosoever is touched by the Holy Spirit confesses the Word of God, that is, the Only-begotten Son, and is unable to deny the Word of God, since he now has in him the tongue of the Holy Spirit.

The Spirit appeared in the form of *fiery* tongues, because all whom He has filled He has made both ardent and eloquent. The Doctors of the Church have tongues of fire; for while they preach that God must be loved, they inflame the hearts of their hearers. For unprofitable is the word of the teacher, if it is unable to kindle the fire of the divine love. This fire of doctrine they laid hold of from the mouth of Truth Itself who declared: *Was not our heart burning within us, whilst he spoke in the way, and opened to us the Scriptures* (Lk. xxiv. 32)?

At the hearing of a sermon the soul is enkindled, the cold of mental listlessness departs from the heart, the mind becomes anxious with longing for heavenly things, and a stranger to earthly desires. The true love that fills it torments it with tears; yet tormented by this flame it is nourished by its very sufferings. It delights in hearing heavenly things; and the precepts that instruct it are like so many torches to inflame it; and where before it was chilled by its natural desires, hearing the words it presently grows warm. Well was it said through Moses: *In his right hand a fiery law* (Deut. xxxiii. 2). For the left hand signifies the reprobate, who shall be on the left-hand side. But the elect are called the right hand of God. In the right hand of God, therefore, there is a fiery law; for the elect

never hear the words of God with a cold heart, but loving with all their hearts they burn like torches at hearing them. As the word reaches their ear, their mind, angry with itself, is consumed by the flame of its own inner affection.

The Holy Spirit was represented in the form of a dove, and as fire, because He makes those He fills both simple and ardent; simple in purity, ardent in zeal. For simplicity without zeal, or zeal without simplicity cannot please God. Because of this the Truth has said: *Be ye wise as serpents and simple as doves* (Mt. x. 16). And we must note that the Lord willed not to admonish His Disciples by the figure of a dove without that of the serpent, or of a serpent without that of the dove; in that the cunning of the serpent should sharpen the simplicity of the dove, and the simplicity of the dove temper the sharpness of the serpent.

For this reason Paul says: *Do not become children in sense* (I Cor. xiv. 20). Here we listened to the guile of the serpent; next we are taught the simplicity of a dove: *But in malice be children.* Likewise of Job was it said that, *he was a simple and upright man* (Job i. 1). What is uprightness without simplicity, and simplicity without uprightness? Therefore, since the Spirit teaches us both uprightness and simplicity it was to be shown to us under the figure of fire, and under that of a dove; in order that every heart that is touched by His grace may become tranquil in the mildness of His clemency, and inflamed with the zeal of His justice.

6. Lastly, we must ask ourselves why He appeared above our Redeemer, the Mediator of God and

man, in the form of a *dove*, and above the Apostles in the form of *tongues of fire*? The Only-begotten Son of God is in truth the judge of all mankind. But who could bear His justice if, before drawing us to Himself in mildness, He had willed to search with harsh exactness into our offences? So for man He became man, revealing Himself to man as gentle. He willed not to crush sinners, but to gather them to Himself. He desired to correct with mildness at first, that there might then be those whom afterwards He would save when He came to judge. And so it was fitting that the Spirit should appear as a dove above Him Who came, not now to punish sinners in His zeal, but that He might bear with them yet a while in mildness.

But above the Disciples it was fitting He should be shown in the form of fire; that spiritual fervour might inflame them against themselves, so that these who were but men, and therefore sinners, would themselves punish, through penance, the sins God has spared through patience. For not even they who followed so closely after the heavenly Master could be without sin; as John bears witness when he says: *If we say that we have no sin, we deceive ourselves, and the truth is not in us* (I Jn. i. 8).

He came therefore in fire above men, in the form of a dove above the Lord, because we should through zeal for justice search out our own sins, which the Lord had mildly borne in patience, and consume them in the fire of penance. The Spirit is therefore shown as a dove over the Redeemer, as fire over men, because the more the severity

of our Judge is tempered with mildness, the more should our own feebleness be enkindled against itself. So, having explained these fourfold reasons, we now pass on to the consideration of the gifts of the same Spirit.

7. Of this Spirit it was written: *His Spirit hath adorned the heavens* (Job xxvi. 13). For the adornments of the heavens are the virtues of those who preach; and these adornments Paul recounts to us, saying: *To one indeed, by the Spirit, is given the word of wisdom: and to another the word of knowledge, according to the same Spirit. To another faith in the same Spirit; to another grace of healing in one Spirit; to another the working of miracles; to another, prophecy; to another the discerning of tongues; to another the interpretation of speeches. But all these things one and the same Spirit worketh, dividing to every one according to his will* (I Cor. xii. 8). As many as are the gifts of those who preach the Gospel, so many are the adornments of the heavens. For this reason again was it written: *By the word of the Lord the heavens were established* (Ps. xxxii). For the Word of the Lord is the Son of the Father. That it might be shown that the whole Trinity together had wrought these heavens, namely, the holy Apostles, there is immediately added, of the divinity of the Holy Spirit: *and all the power of them by the Spirit of his mouth*. Therefore the power of *the heavens* (*the Apostles*) is derived from the Spirit: for they would not have dared to withstand the rulers of this world, had not the power of the Holy Spirit sustained them. What the Teachers of the holy Church were like before the

Coming of the Holy Ghost we know; what their courage became after His Coming we shall now see.

8. What fear, what weakness, the very Pastor of the Church, close to whose most holy body we are sitting, showed before the Coming of the Holy Ghost, the maid who was doorkeeper will tell us, should we ask her. Terrified at the voice of a woman, fearful of death, he denied Life (John xviii. 7). And Peter denied Him on the ground at the very time when the Thief would confess Him upon the cross. But let us hear what was the courage of this man after the Coming of the Holy Ghost. There was an assembly of the Council and of the Ancients, and, after they had been scourged, the Apostles were charged that they must speak no more in the name of Jesus. Peter with firm decision replied: *We ought to obey God, rather than men* (Acts v. 29). And again: *If it be just in the sight of God, to hear you rather than God, judge ye. For we cannot but speak the things which we have seen and heard* (iv. 19, 20). *And they indeed went from the presence of the Council, rejoicing that they were accounted worthy to suffer reproach for the name of Jesus* (v. 41). Behold Peter, rejoicing at being scourged, who before had trembled at a word. And he who, when she questioned him, was terrified by the voice of a serving maid, after the Coming of the Holy Spirit, though scourged, stands firm against the power of princes.

It is my delight to lift up eyes of faith to the wonders of our Creator; and here and there to dwell upon the Fathers of both the Old and New Testament. I behold with these same eyes, that were opened by faith, David and Amos and Daniel and Peter and Paul and Matthew, and I am moved to consider how great, as Creator, is the Holy Spirit, but in my reflection I fall far short. For it is He Who inspires the youthful harpist, and He Who has created the psalmist (I Kings xvi. 18). He moves the soul of *the herdsman plucking wild figs*, and makes him a prophet (Amos vii. 14). He enters into a young boy, disciplined in spirit, and makes him a judge (Dan. xiii. 46). He enters into a fisherman, and makes of him a preacher of the Gospel (Mt. iv. 19). He fills a persecutor of the Church, and makes him the Doctor of the Gentiles (Acts ix). He fills a publican, and makes of him an Evangelist (Lk. v. 27, 28). What power of creation has this Spirit! In all that He willed there is no pause to learn. As He touches a soul He teaches it; and simply to have touched is to have taught it. For as His Light illumines it, the human spirit of a sudden changes; it rejects on the instant what it was, and shows itself at once as it was not.

9. Let us reflect on what kind of men did this day find the holy Apostles to be, and what kind of men it made them. It is certain, that of those who had remained together for fear of the Jews, each of them had known his own native tongue, yet, even in the tongue they knew, they had not dared to speak openly of Christ. The Spirit came, and as He endows their lips with the gift of diverse tongues He strengthens their minds with firmness. They begin to speak openly of Christ, and in a

strange tongue; they who before had feared to speak of Him even in their own tongue. For their hearts were on fire, and the bodily torments they had dreaded before, they now despise. The love of their Creator defeats the power of their bodily fear. And they who had yielded to the dread of their enemies, now dominate them by their authority. He then Who has raised them to such heights, what shall I say of Him, but that He has made *heavens* of the minds of earthly men?

Reflect, Dearest Brethren, how this day's solemnity has a significance that is next to that of the Incarnation of the Only-begotten Son of God. For this solemnity is held in equal honour with that. In the one God, while remaining God, takes to Himself the nature of man; in the other, men have received God within them as He descends upon them. In the one case, God became man by nature; in the other, men became gods by adoption. If then, Brethren, we do not wish to linger on in death as carnal men, let us love this Life-giving Spirit.

10. But since flesh knows not spirit, someone from his own unspiritual thinking will say to himself: How can I love someone whom I know not? To this we agree; for the mind that is taken up with visible things cannot see what is invisible. For it only thinks of visible things; and even when not actually engaged in them, the mind follows them from within itself, and while thus held fast by bodily things is unable to rise to what is incorporeal. And as a consequence, the more closely it is linked in thought to the earthly creation, the

more imperfectly will it know its Creator.

But since we cannot see God in Himself, there is something we may do, through which the eye of our understanding may approach Him. Since we can in no way see Him in Himself, we may yet see Him in His servants. For when we see them do that which is above the ordinary nature of things, we know for certain that God dwells within their souls. In this spiritual matter let us take an example from things that are not spiritual. There is not one of us can look directly at the orb of our sun as it mounts up in splendour to the heavens: for our eyes weakened by its rays are beaten down. But we can see the mountains glistening in the sunrise, and know from them that the sun has risen. We then, who cannot of ourselves look upon the Sun of Justice, let us look up to the mountains that shine in Its splendour: the Holy Apostles, who shine so clearly by their virtues, who glitter with miracles, who are flooded with the radiance of the Risen Sun, Which, Invisible in Himself, as it were makes Himself visible to us in these sunlit mountains.

For the perfection of the Divinity is as the sun in the heavens. The power of the Divinity revealed in men is as the sunlight upon the earth. Let us then here on earth so look upon the Sun of Justice Whom we cannot look upon in heaven; and walking securely in good works by this light on earth, we may come in time to lift up our eyes and behold It in heaven. And we shall accomplish our earthly journey without stumbling, if we love God, and our neighbour, with all our heart. For we cannot love God unless we love our neighbour; nor love our neighbour without loving God.

For it was to this end that, as we said in another sermon (xxvi. III), the Spirit was given a second time to the Disciples: the first time, it was given by the Lord Himself while still on earth; afterwards by the Lord reigning in heaven. It was given on earth that we might love our neighbour. It was given from heaven that we might love God. Why was it given first here on earth, and afterwards from heaven, if not that we might clearly understand that which John has said to us: *He that loveth not his brother, whom he seeth, how can he love God, whom he seeth not?* (I Jn. iv. 20).

Let us then, dearest brethren, love our neighbour. Let us love him who is close beside us, that we may then come to love Him Who is far above us. Let the soul practise towards its neighbour, what it may offer up to God: so that it may merit to enjoy both God and its neighbour for ever.

Then shall we reach to that joy of the heavenly throng, of which we now receive a pledge in the Holy Spirit. Let us press forward with all our heart to that end in which we shall have joy without end. There we shall rejoice in the holy company of the Blessed. There secure happiness, there untroubled rest, there true peace, shall no more be *left with us*, but shall be *given to us* by our Lord and Saviour Jesus Christ Who with the Father and the Holy Ghost liveth and reigneth for ever. Amen.

NOTES

[1] All editions of the *Catena Aurea*, one presumably following the other, have: Which Christ recalls to our mind—*quae nos commemorat Christus*. But the text in Migne has: *quam nos commemorat Spiritus*: which is what the holy commentator must have cited in the beginning.

[2] PG 31, Liber De Spiritu Sancto. This discourse is made up of chapters nine and ten of the saint's book on *The Holy Spirit*; on the notions regarding the Holy Spirit which conform with the Scriptures, and also on the equality of the Spirit with the Father and the Son. There is a homily on the Holy Spirit attributed to St Basil, but it is not authentic.

[3] St Basil was one of the greatest defenders of the Divine Tradition of the Consubstantiality of the Holy Spirit with the Father and the Son

against the Arians and Semi-Arians, of whom Eunomius and Macedonius were leaders. This latter gave his name to the faction who were defective in their notions regarding the Third Person of the Bl. Trinity.

[4] The word used is *sunapheia*; which later became a key word in the heresies that arose concerning the union of the Divine and human natures in Jesus Christ. Subsequently, in the third anathema of Cyril against Nestorius, the notion expressed by *sunapheia* was condemned, and the term *sunodos*—union or *natural unity* as against connection, or association, in rank or authority or power—was there formally adopted (Den. 115).

[5] The words of Scripture either confess or deny that the Holy Ghost is truly united with the Father and

the Son. If they must find fault with the union, as there described, then they must not fault Basil.

⁶ PL 16. This discourse is made up of chapters 13, 14, 15, and 16 of St Ambrose's Book I on the Holy Spirit, and treats of the names of the Holy Spirit: God, Light, Fire, Life, River.

⁷ The *Vetus Itala* version, with which many other versions agree here. Many however have St Jerome's later Vulgate version: *And it is the Spirit which bears witness that Christ is the truth.*

⁸ *Gratia sacramentorum.* The holy Doctor is not of course using these two terms in their later defined form, but as simply expressing the living truth of Divine Tradition, which later when defined by the Church became known as *dogma*; for what we know as *dogma* are the living truths of sacred Divine Tradition which have formed part of the faith and practice of the faithful from the beginning and which were received from Christ through the Apostles.

⁹ In which the holy Doctor, with a great number (*plerique*) of others, teaches the *procession* of the Holy Ghost from the Son.

¹⁰ This reference cannot be verified. The pool is probably *the pool of Samaria*, which was then Jezabel's also, as queen of Samaria (III Kings

xxii. 38). The substitution of *meretrices* for dogs is, possibly, derived from the reference in Deuteronomy xxiii. 18.

¹¹ PG 50, col. 463. De S. Pent. II.

¹² PL 35, Tr. 76. The Gospel citations appear to be still from the *Vetus Itala* version.

¹³ PL 38, Sermo 267.

¹⁴ PL 38, Sermo 268.

¹⁵ PL 38, Sermo 270.

¹⁶ PL 39, Appendix, Sermo 97. The style is not of Augustine, but rather of St Peter Chrysologus, to whom it has been ascribed. It is also attributed to St Ambrose. It is included here because of its evident antiquity and authority.

¹⁷ PL 39, Appendix, Sermo 98. This sermon is certainly not St Augustine's. The reference says some of it is from St Cyprian; actually, with the exception of a few phrases from Alcuin on De Virtutibus, it is taken almost verbatim from the last three chapters of St Cyprian's book on *The Unity of the Church.* It is included here for its venerable authority, and antiquity, on this sacred theme (St Cyprian, PL 4, pp. 517–18).

¹⁸ PL 54, Sermo 75, Pentecost I, col. 400.

¹⁹ PL 54, Sermo 77, Pentecost III, col. 411.

²⁰ PL Sermo 30. In Evangelia.

TRINITY SUNDAY

I. St Basil the Great: Sacred Tradition a Divine Guide

II. St Gregory Nazianzen: The Holy Trinity

III. St Augustine: The Trinity in the Baptism of Christ

THE GOSPEL OF THE SUNDAY

Matthew xxviii. 18–20

At that time: Jesus said to his disciples: All power is given to me in heaven and in earth. Going therefore, teach ye all nations; baptizing them in the name of the Father, and of the Son, and of the Holy Ghost. Teaching them to observe all things whatsoever I have commanded you: and behold I am with you all days, even to the consummation of the world.

Exposition from the Catena Aurea

V. 18. *And Jesus coming, spoke to them, saying: All power is given . . .*

BEDE: After the blessed Matthew had stated that an angel had announced the Lord's Resurrection, he then relates the vision of the Lord seen by the Disciples, telling us that *the eleven Disciples went into Galilee, unto the mountains where Jesus had appointed them.* For when going towards His Passion the Lord had said to His Disciples, *But after I shall be risen again, I will go before you into Galilee* (xxvi. 23). This the angels also told the holy women. And so the Disciples obey the command of the Master. But only eleven go to adore Him. For one had perished: he who had betrayed his Lord and Master.

JEROME: And so after His Resurrection Jesus is seen on the mountain in Galilee, and there adored; and though some were doubting, their doubt but increases our faith: *And seeing him they adored: but some doubted.*

REMIGIUS: The Evangelist Luke relates this more fully. For he tells us how when the Lord, rising from the dead, appeared to His Disciples, they were terrified and believed they were seeing a ghost.

RHABANUS MAURUS (or BEDE): The Lord appeared to them upon the mountain to signify that the Body which in His birth He had taken from the common earth of the human race, He had now in His

Resurrection exalted above all earthly things. And that He might teach the faithful that if they desired co see the supreme glory of the Resurrection they must be earnest in passing from earthly delights to heavenly ones. And Jesus goes before His Disciples into Galilee, because *Christ is now risen from the dead, the first fruits of them that sleep* (I Cor. xv. 20). And they who are Christ's follow Him and in their order pass over from death to life; to behold the Divinity in visible form. And that Galilee is interpreted to mean, *revelation*, fittingly agrees with this.

AUGUSTINE, *Harmony of the Four Gospels* 3, 25, 81: Let us consider in what manner the Lord was seen bodily in Galilee. For it is evident that He was not seen on the day of His resurrection. For on that day He was seen in Jerusalem at nightfall, as Luke and John plainly agree. Neither was it during the eight following days, after which, John tells us, the Lord appeared to His Disciples when Thomas, who had not seen Him on the day of the Resurrection, saw Him for the first time. Unless it be said that these were not *the eleven* (who were now spoken of as the Apostles) but eleven out of the great number of His Disciples. But (par. 82) there is another difficulty against this. For when John had related that the Lord was seen, not by the eleven on the mountain, but by seven of them who were fishing by the lake of Tiberias, he adds: *This is now the third time that Jesus was manifested to his disciples, after he was risen from the dead* (xxi. 14). We must here understand him as referring to the number of days,

not to the number of manifestations. If however we take it that the Lord was seen by the eleven within those eight days before Thomas had seen Him, this manifestation by the lake of Galilee will be the fourth, not the third. Because of this we are forced to believe that He was seen last by the eleven on the mountain in Galilee.

We find therefore (par. 82) in the four Evangelists, that there were ten separate manifestations of the Lord after His Resurrection.

1. To the women by the sepulchre.
2. To the same women as they are returning from the sepulchre.
3. To Peter.
4. To the two Disciples going to the village.
5. To many in Jerusalem when Thomas was not there.
6. When Thomas saw Him.
7. By the lake of Tiberias.
8. On the mountain of Galilee of which Matthew speaks.
9. To the eleven *as they were at table*, as told by Mark; as they were not again to eat with Him on earth.
10. On the same day, no longer upon the earth, but lifted up in a cloud as He was taken up to heaven, which Mark and Luke relate (par. 84). But as John confesses all were not written down (xxi. 25). For He had frequent conversations with them throughout the forty days which preceded His Ascension into heaven (Acts i. 3).

REMIGIUS: The Disciples seeing Him knew it was the Lord, and casting themselves with their faces to the ground they adored Him. And for this their kind and tender Master, to take all doubt from their hearts, draws near and confirms them in their belief. Hence there follows: *And Jesus coming, spoke to them, saying: All power is given to me in heaven and in earth.*

JEROME: Power is given to Him Who a little while before was crucified and buried in the sepulchre; Who afterwards rose again. RHABANUS (or BEDE): He does not say this of His Divinity Co-eternal with the Father, but of the humanity He assumed, in which *he was made a little lower than the angels* (Heb. ii. 9).

CHRYSOLOGUS, *Serm.* 80: The Son of God brought to the son of the Virgin, God brought to man, Divinity to flesh, that which He possessed forever with the Father. JEROME: Power is given in heaven and on earth, so that He Who before reigned in heaven might now reign on earth through the faith of those who believed in Him.

REMIGIUS: That which the psalmist says of the Lord rising again from the dead: *Thou hast set him over all the works of thy hands* (viii. 7), this the Lord now says of Himself: *All power is given to me in heaven and on earth.* And here we should note, that even before His Resurrection the angels knew they were the subjects of the Man Christ. Willing therefore that it should be known to all men, that He was given all power in heaven and on earth, He sent preachers who would make known the Word of Life to all nations. Hence follows:

V. 19. *Going therefore, teach ye all nations; baptizing them in the* . . .

BEDE: He Who before His Passion had said: *Go ye not into the way of the Gentiles* (Mt. x. 5), now risen from the dead, says: *Go teach all nations.* By this the Jews are confounded, who say that the Christ is to come for their salvation only. And let the Donatists blush for shame who, wishing to limit Christ to one locality, assert that He is only in Africa, and not in any other places.

JEROME: Therefore, they first teach all nations, and when they are taught they are baptized in water. For it may not happen that the body receives baptism before the soul has received the truth of faith. *In the name of the Father, and of the Son, and of the Holy Ghost*; so that one shall be Their gift Whose Divinity is one; and the name of the Trinity is One God.

CHRYSOLOGUS: Therefore, the One and the Same Power who made them re-creates all nations unto salvation. DIDYMUS, *On the Holy Spirit*, 1, 2 (in Jerome): And though there may be someone of so perverted soul that he will attempt to baptize omitting one or other of these Names, and this in disobedience to Christ who laid down the law of baptism; nevertheless he will baptize without effect; or rather, he could not deliver from their sins those he thinks he has baptized.

From these words we may understand how undivided is the nature of the Trinity, that the Father is truly the Father of the Son, and the Son indeed the Son of the Father, and that the Holy Ghost is in truth the Spirit of both the Father and of the Son of God; and that He is also the Spirit of Wisdom and Truth, that is, of the Son of God. This then is the baptism of believers, and in this Trinity the divine plan of the Church's obedience is perfected.

HILARY: For what that relates to human salvation is not contained within this mystery? In it all things are complete and perfect as uttered by Him Who is complete and perfect. For the basis of Their relationship is in the name *Father*. But He is the sole Father; He has not as among men derived from yet another source that He is a Father: for He is Un-begotten, Eternal, possessing ever within Himself the source of His own Being; known only to the Son etc. The Son is the Offspring of the Un-begotten, One of the One, The True from the True, the Living from the Living, the Perfect from the Perfect, the Strength of Strength, Wisdom of Wisdom, Glory of Glory, the Image of the Invisible God, the Form of the Un-begotten Father.

Nor can we separate the Holy Spirit from our confession of the Father and the Son. And this Consolation of our expectation is nowhere wanting. In the fruits of His gifts is the pledge of our hope. He is the Light of our minds; the Brightness of our souls. And since the heretics cannot change things, they place their own interpretation on them; like Sabellius, who would have it that Father and Son are one, separate one from the other in name only, not in reality, and proposing the Father and the Son as one and the same Person. Like Ebion, who contending that He began with Mary, had dared to assert that He was not Man from God, but God made from man. Like the Arians, who would bring forth

the wisdom and power and form of God from nothing, and in time. What wonder men hold such varying beliefs of the Holy Ghost, when they are thus the presumptuous authors of the Son, creating and altering Him Who bestows the Spirit?

JEROME: Consider the order there is here commanded. First He commands the Apostles to teach all nations; then to baptize them in the sacrament of faith, and after faith and baptism to teach them what they must do.

V. 20. *Teaching them to observe all things whatsoever I have commanded ...*

RHABANUS (or BEDE): For as the body without the spirit is dead, so also faith without good works is dead (I John ii. 26).

CHRYSOSTOM: And because He had imposed a great task upon them, to raise their spirits, He says: *And behold I am with you all days, even to the consummation of the world*; as though to say: Do not say that the task laid on you is difficult, for I Who can make all things light am with you. He did not say that He would be with these alone, but with all who believe after them; for the Apostles were not to live until the consummation of the world: but He is speaking to all who shall believe, as though to one body.

RHABANUS: From this we may understand that, until the end of the world, there shall not be wanting those who are worthy of being a divine abode and place of habitation.

CHRYSOSTOM: He places before them the end of the world, that He may draw them onwards, and lest they too should look only to the things of the present, and not rather towards the good things to come, which shall last without end. As though to say: The afflictions you will endure will pass with this present life, since the whole world will come to a consummation. But the good things which you shall enjoy will be without end.

BEDE: It may be asked: Why did He say those words: *I am with you*, since we read elsewhere that He said: *I go to him that sent me* (John xvi. 5)? But what is spoken of His humanity is one thing; what is spoken of His Divinity another. In His humanity he will go to the Father; He will abide with His Disciples in the form in which He is equal to the Father. When He said: *Unto the consummation of the world*, He makes use of the finite for the infinite. For He Who remains with His elect in this world, protecting them, the Same will continue with them after the end of the world, rewarding them.

JEROME: He therefore Who promises He will be with His Disciples unto the end of the world, reveals to them that He will live for ever, and likewise that He will never abandon those who believe in Him.

LEO THE GREAT, *Sermon on the Passion*: Ascending into heaven He does not abandon His adopted, but from above strengthens those to endure whom He is inviting upwards to glory; of which glory may He make us partakers Who is Christ the King of Glory, God Blessed for ever. Amen.

I. St Basil the Great, Bishop and Doctor

Sacred Tradition a Divine Guide[1]

Tradition as Guide to the right understanding of Holy Scripture. Of the beliefs and public doctrines entrusted to the care of the Church, there are some which are based on Scriptural teaching, others which we have received handed down *in mystery*[2] by the tradition of the Apostles; and in relation to the true religion they both have the same force. Nor is there anyone will contradict them; no one certainly who has the least acquaintance with the established laws of the Church.

For were we to attempt to reject the unwritten practices of the Church, as being without great importance, we would unknowingly inflict mortal wounds on the Gospel, or rather, we would make of our public teaching a mere pretence and nothing more.[3] For example, if I may cite in the first place what are the first and most common practices of Tradition, who is it has taught us in writing to sign with the sign of the Cross those who place their trust in Jesus Christ our Lord? What is written has taught us to turn towards the East when we pray? The words of invocation at the consecration of the Eucharistic Bread and the Chalice of Blessing, which of the saints has left them to us in writing? For we are not content with the words both the Gospel and the Apostle have recorded, but have added some others, both before these and after them, as having great significance in relation to the *mystery*, and which have been received from unwritten tradition.

We also bless the water for baptism, and also the oil of chrism, and even the person baptized. On the authority of what writings? Is it not rather on the authority of secret mystic tradition? And the anointing with oil, what written words tell us to do this? And the threefold immersion, where does it come from? And the other practices at baptism, the renouncing of Satan, and his angels? Do these not come from that veiled and secret doctrine which our Fathers have safeguarded in unquestioning and simple silence? For they had learned to guard the sacredness of the mysteries in silence. For doctrine that was withheld even from the uninitiated (*catechumens*) was not to be made known to all and sundry in writing. What did the great Moses mean by not making known to all the sacred things of the Sanctuary (Num. iv. 20)? He decreed that those not dedicated to the service of the altar should stay without the gates, the first court to be accessible only to the purified, and only the Levites were to be held worthy of being servants of the Divinity (xviii. 21, 22); sacrifices and burnt offerings and the remainder of the sacred ritual he allotted to the priests (Num. vii), one chosen from the rest he admitted to the innermost part, and this one not at all times, but only on one day in the year, and it was lawful to enter only at a certain hour of the day, when because of its wonder and strangeness he might look with awe at the Holy of Holies. For Moses in his wisdom knew that what becomes accessible to all is then exposed to irreverence, while what is unseen

and withheld tends, because of our nature, to be held in reverence.

In the same way the Apostles and the Fathers, when they were establishing the order of things at the beginning, guarded the sanctity of the mysteries with silence and secrecy. For that is not a mystery at all which is divulged to the ears of everyone. This is the reason of the *handing down* of what was not written, so that the knowledge of our doctrines might not be neglected by the people because of too great familiarity. Public and private teaching are two distinct things;[4] the one is retained in silence, the other made known to all. A form of this silence is seen in Sacred Scripture, which makes certain truths difficult to understand, and this for the advantage of the reader.

Tradition and The Confession of Faith at Baptism. Time will run short if I go on to recall the unwritten mysteries of the Church. Of all the rest I shall be silent, but of the Confession of Faith itself, in the Father, Son, and Holy Ghost. From what written sources does it come? For if, in accord with the tradition of baptism, and of true reverence for God, as we are baptized so also should we believe, and our profession of faith should be in accord with our baptism, then let our adversaries grant us, that we should also give praise to God in accord with our faith. And if they reject the form in which we give praise to God (the *doxology*), as not given in the Scriptures, let them also give us from the Scriptures the proofs for the Confession of faith and the other things we spoke of.

We believe that He Who is named in the giving of baptism should also be named in the Profession of faith. For we have made the Profession of faith the beginning, the mother as it were, of our giving praise to God (*doxologia*). What then must we do? Now, they must teach us, either not to baptize in the manner handed down to us, or not to believe in accordance with our baptism, or not to give glory to God in accordance with our belief. Let any man disprove if he can the logical relationship of these propositions to one another, or that any innovation in regard to these things does not mean the undoing of the whole structure of faith. Yet high and low they never cease from shouting that the praise of God *with* the Holy Spirit is without authority and unscriptural, and so on. We have told you that it makes no difference to the meaning whether you say, Glory be to the Father and to the Son and *to* the Holy Ghost, or say, Glory be to the Father and to the Son together *with* the Holy Ghost. The syllable *and*, which comes from our Lord's own mouth, we can neither cancel nor reject; neither are we forbidden to reject its equivalent (*with*): their similarity we have already proved to you. And our opinion is confirmed by the Apostle who uses either the one or the other, as when he says: *In the name of our Lord Jesus Christ, and the Spirit of our God* (I Cor. vi. 11). And again: *You being gathered together, and my Spirit, with the power of our Lord Jesus* (I Cor. v. 4); holding it as of no importance whether you use the conjunction or the preposition.

Confirmation from Tradition. In reply to those who say that in the formula used in giving praise to God the preposition *with* the Spirit

has no authority in Scripture we answer: If no other unwritten teaching is received, then neither must this be. But if the greatest number of our mystical truths have come to us through unwritten tradition, then let us receive this together with these so many others. For I hold it to be an apostolic practice to adhere also to unwritten tradition. For the Apostle says: *I praise you, that in all things you are mindful of me; and keep my ordinances as I have delivered them to you* (I Cor. xi. 2). And again: *Hold the traditions which you have learned, whether by word, or by our epistle* (II Thess. ii. 14).

One of these traditions is the practice of which we now speak, which they who established things in the beginning rooted by long custom firmly in the Church, and handed down from one to the other, the practice advancing ever with time and usage. If in a court of law, in default of written proof, we could bring forward many witnesses would we not secure a verdict of dismissal? For my part I think we would. *In the mouth of two or three witnesses every word shall stand* (Deut. xix. 15). And if we show clearly to you that a long period of time was also in our favour, would it not seem probable to you that this charge should not be made against us? For these ancient teachings must be held in reverence, and should be revered even for their hoary antiquity.

I shall therefore recount to you the champions of this belief (and time too must be taken into account in regard to what has continued unchallenged). For it did not begin with us. How could it? *For we are but of yesterday*, as Job says (Job viii.

9), at least in comparison with the history of this custom. For my own part, if I may speak of myself, I cherish this usage as a sort of inheritance come down to me from the Fathers, delivered to me by one who had long laboured in God's service,[5] by whom I was baptized, and admitted to the service of the Church. While searching as far as I was able to see if any of the blessed ancients made use of these words which are now called into question, I found many; who possess great authority, both because of their antiquity, and because of the accuracy of their knowledge (unlike these others). Of these some joined together the words of the doxology by means of the preposition, others by the conjunction; neither thinking they were doing anything different, that is, contrary to the true mind of religion.

There is Irenaeus,[6] and Clement of Rome,[7] and Dionysius of Rome,[8] and, strange to say, Dionysius of Alexandria,[9] in his second letter to his namesake; *On Accusations and Defences*—I shall give you his very words: *With all these we too, giving thanks, and with the same words which they used who lived before us, and in the form and in the order received by them, end our letter to you: To God the Father, and to the Son our Lord Jesus Christ, together with the Holy Ghost, glory and empire for ever and ever. Amen.* Nor can any one say these words have been altered. He would not have so emphatically said he had *received* a form and an order had he said '*in* the Spirit'. For of this phrase there was frequent use; it was the other phrase needed to be defended.

And in the middle of his letter he

writes, against the Sabellians: *If, because the hypostases are three they say they are divided, they are three, even if they do not wish it; or else let them abolish the Trinity altogether.* And again: *Because of this, after the Unity, most divine is the Trinity.* And likewise Clement, who writes simply: *God lives, and the Lord Jesus and the Holy Spirit.*[10] But let us hear how Irenaeus, who lived close to the days of the Apostles, speaks of the Holy Spirit in his work, *Against Heresies*: *Rightly does the Apostle call carnal those who, unbridled and urged on by their own desires, have no love for the Holy Spirit.*[11] And elsewhere he says the same: *The Apostle cries out to us that flesh and blood cannot enter into the kingdom of heaven, lest we fail to reach the kingdom of heaven, through having no part in the Divine Spirit.*[12]

And if anyone should consider Eusebius of Palestine as being also worthy of credit, because of his wide experience, I shall put before you certain words of his concerning polygamy among the ancients; he speaks in this way, leading up to the question: *Calling upon the God of the Prophets, Who gives light through our Saviour Jesus Christ, together with the Holy Spirit.*

We find Origen also, in so many of his expositions of the psalms, giving glory to God, *together with the Holy Spirit*, and though he is not altogether sound in all his notions concerning the Holy Spirit, nevertheless he also, in many places, accepting with reverence the authority of custom, uses phrases concerning the Holy Spirit which are in accord with true belief. It is, if I do not err, in the sixth book of his *Commentary on John*, that he clearly says the Spirit is to be adored, in these very words: *As the washing with water is a symbol of the purification of the soul, now washed clean of every filth of evil doing, nevertheless it is also, and of itself, to the one who gives himself up to the Divinity of the adorable Trinity, a source and beginning of blessings.*[14] And again, in his *Exposition of the Epistle to the Romans*, he says: *The holy Powers are able to comprehend the Divinity of the Only-begotten and of the Holy Spirit.* Thus it seems to me that the authority of tradition often compels men to speak in a manner contrary to their own notions.[15]

How then am I an innovator, and a maker of new phrases, when I have set before you, as the beginners, the champions, of this word, whole nations, peoples, and usage that is older than the memory of man, as well as men who were pillars of the Church, renowned both for knowledge and spiritual authority? Yet because of this a whole host of enemies have attacked me, and every village and town and even remote places are full of those who calumniate me. Painful indeed are such things to one whose desire is peace, but great is the reward of patience,

and surpassing afflictions endured for the faith. Charitable readers will find my defence in what I have said: that we have received a word that was found worthy and acceptable by holy men, and confirmed by long usage. For from the time of the proclaiming of the Gospel until now, it is shown to have been used in the churches, and, what is more, as having a significance that is in accord with what is sacred, and with true religion.

For the rest, what defence have we prepared for ourselves before the Supreme Tribunal? This: that in the first place we were led to give glory to the Spirit because of the honour given to Him by the Lord, uniting Him to the Father and to Himself in the giving of baptism. And then because of this: that each one of us is established in the knowledge of God through this initiation in the divine mysteries. And lastly, by the fear above all of the threatened punishment, which drives from us all thought of indignity and unworthy belief concerning the Holy Spirit, to Whom, with the Father and the Son, be honour, praise, and glory, for ever and ever. Amen.

II. St Gregory Nazianzen, Bishop and Doctor

The Holy Trinity[16]

In those who dwell on high I note two states of existence; namely, that of ruling, and that of serving. This division is not of the same kind as that which we find among us, which either tyranny has driven between us, or poverty has made, but that which nature makes, if it is right to use this word. For the first of these is also above nature. Of the two this latter is creative, ruling,

unmoving; the other created, subject to rule and subject to change. Or, to speak more precisely, the One is above time, the other subject to time. The first is called God, and subsists in the Three Greatest; namely, The Cause, the Maker, the Perfecter, that is, in the Father, the Son, and the Holy Ghost. But they are not so separate from each other that they are divided in nature; and neither are they so confined in Their nature as to be restricted to one Person: the one alternative is the madness of the Arians, the other of the Godless Sabellians. But It is yet more single than what is completely divided, and yet richer than what is wholly undivided. The other kind is round about us, and is called creature; though among created beings one may be raised above the other, according to the degree of its nearness to God.

And since this is so, *if any man be on the Lord's side, let him join with us* (Exod. xxxii. 26), and let us adore the one Godhead in Three Persons; not attributing a title of humiliation to The Unapproachable Glory, but having ever on our lips *the high praise of the One God* in three Persons (Ps. cxlix. 6). For since to speak of its Greatness, of its Nature, Infinite and Undefined, is beyond us, how can we attribute lowliness to It? But if anyone be a stranger to God, and because of this divide the One and Supreme Being into different natures, it is a wonder that such a man is not sundered by the sword, *and his portion appointed with unbelievers* (Lk. xii. 46); reaping both now and hereafter the evil fruit of his evil mind.

And of the Father, what shall we say, Whom all who are ruled by natural reason by common consent forbear to affront, although He has endured the beginnings of an affront through being divided as it were into two: the Good and the Creator (*demiourgos*),[17] by earlier innovators? Of the Son and Holy Ghost you will see how simply and briefly we shall speak. If any one can say of Either of These, that He was subject to change, or changeable, or that He was subject to limitations, either of time or place or of power or action, or that He was not Good by nature, or not Self-moved, or not free, or that He was but a minister of God, or that He sang before Him, or was subject to fear, that He was *given* freedom, or that He was not to be numbered with the Father, let him prove this and we shall bear with it, and we shall endure it that we are glorified by the dignity of our fellow servants; though we suffer the loss of One Who is God.

But if all the Father has belongs also to the Son, save being Unbegotten, and all the Son has belongs to the Holy Ghost, save Sonship, as well as what is said of Him through being made man, for my salvation, so that taking what was mine He might give me what was His, through this new union, then make an end of your babbling, O ye makers of empty phrases, that at once fall to the ground. *Why will you die, O house of Israel* (Ezech. xviii. 31), if I may mourn for you from the Scriptures!

For my part I hold in reverence all the titles of the Word, so many, so great, and so exalted, that even the demons revere them. I reverence the equal majesty of the Holy Ghost, and I am fearful of the punishment threatened those who blaspheme Him (Mt. xii. 31). And the blasphemy is not in speaking of Him as God, but in the taking away of His Divinity. And here we must note that He Who is blasphemed is the Lord. He that is to be avenged, the Holy Spirit, is manifestly avenged as Lord. After my Illumination (i.e. *baptism*) I cannot suffer darkness with patience, forging another stamp than that of the Three in Whom I was baptized; thus to be truly buried in water, not indeed to new life, but unto very death.

O Trinity, I rashly dare to proclaim something, and may I be forgiven for my rashness, for the danger to my soul. I also am an image of God, of the Glory that is on high, though I dwell on earth. And I cannot be persuaded that I am redeemed by my equal. If the Holy Ghost is not God, let Him first be made God, and let Him then make me His equal.

What now is this manipulation of grace, or rather of Those Who communicate grace, to make as it were a profession of believing God, and come away without God? To profess one thing, to be taught another? What sort of juggling with words is this, asking and receiving the confession of one thing, and teaching something else? Alas for this Enlightenment (baptism), if after my baptism I have become black again, if I am to see those who are not yet washed whiter than myself, if I am to be endangered by the false belief of my baptizer; if I am to seek a mightier Spirit, and not find Him! Give me a different baptism, and think as you will of this first. Why should you begrudge me a perfect regeneration? Why do you change me, who am a temple of the Holy Spirit, into the dwelling place of something that was created? Why do you partly honour, partly dishonour, what belongs to me, judging falsely of the Divinity, that you may cut off the divine gift, or rather, cut me off from the divine gift? Either give honour to the whole Divinity, O new teacher of divine truth, or deny honour to It, so that if you must be blasphemous, you

may also be consistent: you who set forth unequally a Nature that is to be held in equal honour in each Who shares it.

To sum up my discourse to you; Give praise to God with the Cherubim, who join the Three Most Holy into one Lordship (Is. vi. 3), and reveal to us the First Being in the measure that they open their wings to men of good will. With David be enlightened, who said to the Light: *In thy light we shall see light* (Ps. xxxv. 10), that is, in the Spirit we shall see the Son, than Whom who can be more far-shining? Thunder with John, *the son of thunder* (Mk. iii. 17), giving forth no sound that is mean or earthly, but only what is of heaven and exalted regarding the majesty of God, namely, the Word that was in the beginning, and was with God, and was God (Jn. i. 1), knowing God, True God from the True Father; and not a good fellow-servant honoured with the name of Son. And the other Comforter, Other, I mean, from the One Who spoke: for it was the Word of God spoke, and when you hear His words: *I and the Father are one* (John x. 30), understand and keep before your mind unity of nature (*substance*). And when you read: *We will come and make our abode with him* (John xiv. 23), think then of the distinction of Persons. And when you hear the names of Father, Son, and Holy Ghost, think of Three Separate Persons.

As you read the Acts of the Apostles let you with Luke be also inspired. Why should you associate yourself with Ananias and Saphira, with this new kind of thieves (for stealing what is your own is new indeed), and this by stealing, not money, or any other thing of small value, as a golden tongue (Jos. vii. 21), a soldier's cloak, like a certain greedy soldier, but stealing the Divinity Itself; and lying, *not to men, but to God,* as you have heard (Acts v. 4)? Who does not revere the authority of the Holy Spirit, Who breathes upon whom He wills, and when and where He wills (John iii. 8)? He came down upon Cornelius before baptism, to others when they were baptized by the Apostles (Acts x. 44; xix. 2), that testimony might be given to the Divinity of the Spirit, in that He enters as Lord, and not as servant, and in that He is sought for unto perfection.

Speak with Paul of the things of God, with one who was caught up to the third heaven (II Cor. xii. 2), who frequently numbers for us the Three Persons, and this in various ways, not keeping to the same order, but placing the same Person now first, then second, and again third. Why? To make plain to us Their equality of nature. Sometimes he speaks of Three Persons, sometimes of Two, sometimes of One; as though the Others are wholly inseparable.

And sometimes he attributes a work of God to the Spirit of God (I Cor. xii. 11), as though He were in no way different from Him. Sometimes in place of the Spirit he speaks of Christ (Rom. viii.9). And when he distinguishes one Person from another, he uses such words as these: *One God, from whom are all things, and we unto him; and one Lord Jesus Christ, by whom are all things, and we by him* (I Cor. viii. 6). At another time he unites the Divinity in Oneness, as when he says: *For of him, and by him, and in him, are all things* (Rom. xi. 36); that is, through the Holy Ghost, as is proved from many places in Scripture. To Him be glory for ever and ever. Amen.

III. St Augustine, Bishop and Doctor

The Trinity in the Baptism of Christ[18]

Matthew iii. 13

I—1. *God the Trinity placed before us in Christ's Baptism.* This Gospel places before us that on which we shall speak to Your Charity as though the Lord had commanded us, and He has truly commanded us. For my heart has waited as it were for His command to speak, that by this I might understand that He wills me to speak on that which He has also willed should be read to you. Therefore let you listen with earnestness and with devotion; and may God our Lord Himself help me in my task.

For here by the river Jordan we behold, and we contemplate as in a divine scene set before us, Our God made known to us as a Trinity. For when Jesus came, and had been baptized by John, the Lord by the servant—and this He did as an example of humility: for He showed us that it was in humility charity was made perfect; and when John said to Him: *I ought to be baptized by thee, and thou comest to me,* He answered: *Suffer it to be so now. For so it becometh us to fulfil all justice*— when then He had been baptized, the heavens opened, and the Holy Spirit descended upon Him in the form of a Dove. Then a Voice followed from heaven, saying: *This is my beloved Son, in whom I am well pleased.*

Here then we have the Trinity, brought before us as it were separately: the Father in the Voice, the Son in the Man, the Holy Ghost in the form of a Dove. There was need to bring it to our mind in this way: for to see is the easiest thing to do. For clearly, and beyond any shadow of doubt, the Trinity is here placed before us. For the Lord Christ Himself, coming in the form of a servant to John, is truly the Son: for it cannot be said He is the Father, nor can it be said He is the Holy Ghost. *Jesus*, it says, *came*; that is, the Son of God. And who can doubt about the Dove; or who can say, What does the Dove mean, since the Gospel itself tells us most clearly: *The Spirit of God descended upon Him in the form of a dove?* And likewise, who can doubt that it is the Father's, since it reads: *This is my beloved Son?* Here then we have the Trinity distinguished One from the Other.

II—2. *A difficulty concerning the Inseparable Trinity.* And if we consider one place with another, I shall venture to say (and though I say it with diffidence, I shall venture to say it) that the Trinity is as it were separable, the one from the other. When Jesus came to the river, He came from one place to another. The Dove descended from heaven to earth: from one place to another. Even the Voice of the Father sounded neither from the earth, nor from the waters, but from heaven. The

three are as it were separate in place, in purpose, and in work.

Some one will say to me: 'Show the Trinity to be inseparable. Remember, you who speak to us, that you are a Catholic, that you are speaking to Catholics. For this is our faith, that is, the true faith, the right faith, the Catholic faith, which comes, not from private judgement (*opinione praesumptionis*), but from the testimony of the Scriptures, not based on faltering heretical rashness, but on Apostolic Truth. This we know; this we believe. And although we do not see it with our eyes, nor yet with the heart, while being purified by faith, yet by this very faith we most truly and most strongly hold that the Father and the Son and the Holy Spirit are an inseparable Trinity: One God, not three Gods. They are One God, yet so that the Son is not the Father, that the Father is not the Son, that the Holy Spirit is neither the Father nor the Son, but the Spirit of the Father and of the Son. We know that this ineffable Divinity, abiding within Itself, renewing all things, creating, re-creating, sending, recalling, judging, delivering, this Trinity is, we know, ineffable and inseparable.'

3. What then are *we* to do? Here is the Son comes separately in His humanity, the Holy Spirit descends separately in the form of a Dove, the Voice of the Father sounds separately from heaven, saying: *This is my beloved Son.* Where then is your inseparable Trinity? God has made you attentive, through my words. Pray for me, and open your own hearts, that He may give to me to fill what you have opened. Let us work together. For you see what

we have undertaken; and you see not alone what I am but who I am, and of what it is I desire to speak, and how I am situated, how I dwell within *a corruptible body that is a load upon the soul,* and in an *earthly habitation that presses upon the mind as it muses on many things* (Wisd. ix. 15). When therefore I withdraw this mind from the *many things,* and apply it to the One God, the Inseparable Trinity, that I may understand something so as to speak of it, do you think that in this body which weighs upon the soul I shall be able to speak, so as to say something worthy of this sublime theme? *To thee, O Lord, I have lifted up my soul* (Ps. lxxxv. 5). May He help me, may He lift it up with me. For I am weak before Him, and a burthen to myself.

III—4. *The Works of Father and Son Inseparable.* This is a question that is wont to be propounded by learned brethren, and spoken of in the conversation of the lovers of God's word; for this there is much knocking at God's door, with men saying: Does the Father do anything which the Son does not do; or does the Son do something the Father does not do? For the present let us speak of the Father and the Son. And when He to Whom we say, *Be thou my helper, forsake me not* (Ps. xxvi. 9), shall have helped our effort, then shall we understand that the Holy Ghost also is in no way excluded from the work of the Father and the Son. Hearken then, Brethren, to what we have to say of the Father and the Son. Does the Father do anything without the Son? We answer, No. Do you doubt this? For what does He do without Him,

by whom all things are made? *All things,* says the Scripture, *were made by him.* And impressing this to repletion upon the slow of mind, upon the unlearned, upon the disputatious, it added, *And without him was made nothing that was made.*

5. *The Father makes and rules all things by the Son.* What then do we mean, Brethren, by *All things were made by Him?* We understand that the whole Creation made by the Son, the Father made by His Word, God wrought through His power and Wisdom. Are we then to say that *all things,* when they were made, were made by Him, but that the Father does not now make all things by Him? By no means. Far from the hearts of the faithful be such a thought, let it be banished from devoted souls, from pious minds! It cannot happen that He created through Him, and will not govern through Him. Let it be far from our minds that the Father should rule creation without Him, when, that it might be, He made it.

But let us show you, and this by the testimony of Scripture, that not alone were all things made by Him, as we recalled from Scripture—*All things were made by him, and without him was made nothing that was made*—but that all that was made, is ordered and governed by Him. You confess that Christ is the Power and the Wisdom of God. You know what is said of Wisdom: *She reacheth from end to end mightily, and ordereth all things sweetly* (viii. 1). Let us not doubt that by Him all things are ruled, by Whom all things were made. Accordingly, the Father does nothing without the Son, the Son nothing without the Father.

6. *Is the Son's Birth and Passion also the Father's? Heresy of the Patripassiani.* A question then arises which we shall take upon ourselves to answer in the Lord's Name, and by His permission. If the Father does nothing without the Son, and the Son nothing without the Father, does it not follow that we must say that the Father also was born of the Virgin Mary, that the Father suffered under Pontius Pilate, that the Father rose from the dead, and ascended into heaven? Far from it. We do not say this, because we do not believe it. *I have believed, therefore have I spoken; we believe also, for which cause we speak also* (Ps. cxv. 10; II Cor. iv. 13). What does the Creed say? That the Son, not the Father, was born of the Virgin. Again what does the Creed say? That the Son, not the Father, suffered under Pontius Pilate, and that He died. Have we forgotten that there are certain persons, misunderstanding this, called Patripassiani, who say that the Father was born of a woman, that the Father suffered, that the Father and the Son are the same: they are two names, not two things? And these persons the Church has cut off from the Communion of Saints, that they may deceive no one, but, apart from Her, may dispute among themselves.

7. *The Difficulty.* Let us bring before your minds the difficulty of this question. Someone may say to me: You have said that the Father does nothing without the Son, nor the Son without the Father, and you have proved from Holy Scripture the Father does nothing without the Son because all things were made by Him, and that what was made is not

ruled without the Son, since He is the Wisdom of the Father, reaching from end to end mightily, and ordering all things sweetly. Now you tell me, contrary as it were to what you are saying, that the Son, not the Father, was born of the Virgin; that the Son, not the Father, died; that the Son, not the Father, rose from the dead? Here then I behold the Son doing something which the Father does not do. Then you must confess, either that the Son does something without the Father, or that the Father was born, suffered, died, rose again. Say either one thing or the other: choose which of the two.

I choose neither. I shall say neither the one nor the other. I shall neither say the Son does something without the Father: for should I say that I would lie; nor say that the Father was born, suffered, rose again; for were I to say this I should again lie. How then, he will say, will you free yourself from this contradiction?

IV—8. *Christ alone born of the Virgin; but This was wrought by both Father and Son.* The question placed before you pleases you. May God assist me so that its answer may also please you. See what I am saying: that He may free both you and me! For we stand together in the one faith in the Name of Christ, and we dwell in One House under One Lord, and we are members of One Body, under One Head, and we live by One Spirit. And this I say; so that the Lord may deliver from the entanglement of this most tedious question, both me who am speaking to you, and you who listen to me: The Son it was, and not the

Father, that was born of the Virgin Mary; but this very birth of the Son, not of the Father, from the Virgin Mary, was wrought by the Father and the Son. It was not the Father Who suffered; the Son did. Yet both the Father and the Son wrought the Passion of the Son. The Father did not rise; the Son did. But the Resurrection of the Son was the work of both Father and Son. We seem then to be delivered from the difficulty; but perhaps only from my words. Let us see if this be so from the divine words also.

Now it rests on me to prove to you, from the testimonies of the Holy Books, that the Birth of the Son was the work of both the Father and the Son; and the same with regard to the Passion; likewise the Resurrection: that while it is the Son's Birth, Passion, and Resurrection, yet these three works, which relate to the Son alone, were the work, not of the Father alone, nor of the Son alone, but in every way of both Father and Son.

Let us prove each point singly; you listen as judges; the case has been stated; let the witnesses come forward. Let your court say to me what is wont to be declared by those who handle causes: Make good what you allege. This with God's help I shall clearly show you; and I shall quote for you from the written books of the law of heaven. You have listened carefully as I set out the matter; listen more carefully while I prove it.

9. *The Nativity of the Son made by the Father; Paul an authority on Divine Law.* We must first show you with regard to the Birth of Christ, how the Father wrought it,

and the Son wrought it, though what both Father and Son wrought related only to the Son. I shall quote Paul, a fitting authority on Divine Law. For advocates have today a Paul who is an authority on the laws of litigants as well as of Christians. I shall quote for you, I say, Paul, who is an authority on the laws of peace, not of strife. Let the holy Apostle show us how the Father has wrought the Nativity of the Son. *But when*, he says, *the fulness of time was come, God sent His Son, made of a woman, made under the law: That he might redeem them who were under the law: that we might receive the adoption of sons* (Gal. iv. 4, 5). You have heard, and because what was said is clear and direct, you have understood. Behold how the Father made the Son to be born of a Virgin. For when the fulness of time had come, God sent his son; the Father truly sends Christ. How did He send him? *Made of woman, made under the law.* The Father therefore made Him from a woman, under the Law.

10. This puzzles you perhaps: That I said, of a Virgin, and Paul said, *of a woman*? Let it not trouble you. We shall not stop at this point; and neither am I speaking to the uninstructed. The Holy Spirit says both; both from a Virgin, and from a woman. When from a Virgin? *Behold a Virgin shall conceive, and bear a Son* (Is. vii. 14). And, *of a woman*, you have already heard: there is no contradiction. For the Hebrew tongue gives the name *woman*, not merely to non-virgins, but to all females. You have proof of this in Genesis, when Eve herself was first made: *The rib he took from*

Adam he formed into a woman (Gen. ii. 23). In another place Holy Scripture says also that God bade the women be set apart who had not known the bed of a man (Num. xxxi. 18; Jgs. xxi. 11). This should be known to you already, and need not detain us, so that we may with God's help explain other things which deserve to be explained.

11. *The Son's Nativity also made by the Son.* We have therefore proved that the Birth of the Son was wrought by the Father; let us prove that it was also wrought by the Son. Now what is the Birth of the Son from the Virgin Mary? Is it not simply the taking of the form of a servant in the womb of the Virgin? Is the Birth of the Son anything other than the taking of the form of a servant in the womb of the Virgin? Hear then how this is also the work of the Son: *Who being in the form of God, thought it not robbery to be equal to God: but emptied himself, taking the form of a servant* (Phil. ii. 5, 6). *But when the fulness of the time was come, God sent his son, made of a woman; who was made to him of the seed of David, according to the flesh* (Gal. iv. 4; Rom. i. 3). We see therefore that the Birth of the Son was wrought by the Father, but since the Son emptied Himself, *receiving the form of a servant*, we see that the Birth of the Son was also the work of the Son. This then is proved. Let us go on from here. Give your attention now to another question which comes next in order.

12. Let us prove that the Passion of the Son was made by the Father, and made by the Son. That the Father wrought the Passion is evi-

dent: *He that spared not even his own Son, but delivered him up for us all* (Rom. viii. 32). That the Son also wrought the Passion: *Who loved me, and delivered himself for me* (Gal. ii. 20). The Father delivered up the Son; the Son delivered Himself up. The Passion was wrought for One, but it was the work of both. As the Birth was not wrought by the Father without the Son, so likewise the Passion. What did Judas work in it but his own sin? Let us pass on from here also and come to the Resurrection.

13. *The Same is shown of the Resurrection of Christ.* We shall see the Son, not the Father, rising from the dead, but both Father and Son accomplishing the Resurrection of the Son. The Father works the Resurrection of the Son: *For which cause God also hath exalted him, and hath given him a name which is above all names* (Phil. ii. 9). The Father therefore has raised up the Son, exalting Him, and *quickening Him* from among the dead. But has the Son not raised Himself? He has truly raised Himself. For He said of the Temple, as of the figure of His own Body: *Destroy this temple, and in three days I will raise it up* (Jn. ii. 19).

Next, as the laying down of His life refers to the Passion, so the taking it up again relates to the Resurrection, let us see if the Son truly laid down His life, and if the Father truly restored it to Him, not He to Himself? That the Father restored it to Him is evident. For of this the psalmist says: *But, Thou, O Lord, have mercy on me, and raise me up again* (Ps. xl. 11). But what need to look to me for a proof that the Son likewise restored to Himself

His own life? Let Him tell us: *I have power to lay down my life.* I have not yet, I know, made good what I promised. I said *laying down life;* already you are shouting it out, because you are ahead of me. Well taught in the school of the Heavenly Master, listening attentively to the lessons, devoutly reciting them, you are not unacquainted with what follows: *I have power,* He says, *to lay down my life: and I have power to take it up again. No man taketh it away from me: but I lay it down of myself* (Jn. x. 18).

V—14. We have made good what we promised. We have proved our assertions with, I think, the solidest documentary proof. Hold firmly to what you have heard. I shall briefly sum it up, and commit it to you, to be retained carefully in your mind as something, in my opinion, supremely profitable.

The Father was not born of the Virgin; nevertheless this Birth of the Son from the Virgin was the work of both the Father and the Son. The Father did not suffer on the Cross; yet the Passion of the Son was the work of both Father and Son. The Father did not rise from the dead; yet the Resurrection of the Son was wrought by both Father and Son.

You have then both a distinguishing of Persons, and Their inseparableness in work. Therefore let us not say that the Father does something without the Son, or the Son something without the Father. But perhaps the miracles Jesus wrought give you anxiety, lest perhaps He wrought some the Father did not? And then what of His words: *The Father who abideth in me, he doth the works?* (Jn. xiv. 10). All we have said was

plain to you, only needing to be repeated. We had not to labour to make you understand; but we had to take care it should be brought to your remembrance.

15. *We must not think of God as occupying space like a body.* I would like to speak of another point, and here I earnestly ask for your very close attention, and for recollection of the Presence of God. Only material bodies fill or occupy material space. The Godhead is beyond all space; let no one seek It as though it were in space. Everywhere It is Invisible and indivisibly present. Not greater in one direction, lesser in another; but whole and entire in all places, and no where divided.

Who can see this? Who can comprehend it? Let us humble ourselves; keep in mind who we are, of Whom we speak. Let this truth or that truth, or whatever it is that God is, be devoutly believed, piously meditated on, and, as far as it is given us, as well as we can, understood in silence. Let words cease, let the tongue be at rest, but let the heart be enkindled, let the heart be uplifted. For It is not such as enters into the heart of man, but whither the heart of man may ascend. Let us turn our minds towards creation. *For the invisible things of him, from the creation of the world, are clearly seen, being understood by the things that are made* (Rom. i. 20), to see if perhaps we may find there, in the things God has made, and with which we have a certain measure of intimacy, some similitude, by means of which we may show that there are three things which reveal themselves to us as separate, and which are yet inseparable in operation.

VI—16. *God is Incomprehensible.*
Come then, Brethren, attend with
all your mind. Consider first what
I am putting before you: to see if I
may find this in creation; for the
Creator is remote above us. And it
may be that one among us, whose
mind the lightning of truth has as
it were blinded with its brilliance,
may cry out the words: *I said in the
excess of my mind*—what said you in
the excess of your mind? *I am cast
away from before thy eyes* (Ps. xxx. 23).
For it seems to me that he who said
this had uplifted his soul to God,
had *poured out his soul* within him,
while they said to him day by day:
Where is thy God (Ps. xli. 4, 11)?—
that he had by some touching of the
Spirit attained to that Unchangeable
Light, and in his infirmity could not
bear to look upon It,[19] and had
fallen back again as it were into his
own languor and weakness, and had
compared himself with It, and saw
that the eye of his soul could not yet
be adjusted to the light of the Wisdom of God.

And because he had done this in
ecstasy, while caught up from the
body's senses, brought unawares before God, when recalled in a manner
from God to man, he cried: *I said
in the excess of my soul.* For in my
ecstasy I saw I know not what,
which I could not long endure, and
returning to my mortal members,
and to *the many thoughts of mortal men*
(Ps. xix. 21), from this body that
weighs upon the soul, I cried. What
did you cry? *I am cast away from
before thy eyes.* Thou art far above;
I am far below.

What then, Brethren, are we to
say of God? For if you have grasped
what you wish to say, it is not God.
If you had been able to compre-

hend it, you would have comprehended something else in the place
of God. If you had been *almost*
able to comprehend it, your mind
has deceived you. That then is
not He, if you have understood It.
But if it is He, you have not understood It. What therefore would you
say of that which you could not
understand?

17. *The Similitude of God to be
looked for in Us.* Let us see then if
we may find in created things something by means of which we may
prove that there are three things
which may be both shown to us as
separate and which are inseparable
in operation. Whither shall we
turn? To the heavens, that we may
consider the sun, the moon, and the
stars? To earth, to speak perhaps of
its fruits, of the trees and the living
things that fill the earth? Or shall
we speak of both heaven and earth
which contain all things that are in
heaven and earth? How long, man,
will you wander through creation?
Turn back to yourself; look at yourself; consider yourself; speak of
yourself! You are searching throughout creation for three things which
must be shown to be separate, and
are yet inseparable in operation. If
you search among creatures, first
search within yourself. For are you
not a creature? You are searching
for a similitude. Will you search
among cattle? For it was of God
you were speaking, when you were
searching for a similitude. You were
speaking of the Ineffable Majesty of
the Trinity; and since you availed
nothing in divine things, and with
fitting humility have confessed your
own infirmity, you have come to
man. Try there. Look among cattle,

seek in the sun, search among the stars! Which of these is made in the *image and likeness* of God? Look then within yourself to see whether the image of the Trinity may not possess some imprint of the Trinity.

And what kind of *image* is it? A created image, though one far removed. A *likeness* nevertheless, and an image, however far removed. Not such an Image as the Son is, Who is What the Father is. One is the image in a son, another that we find in a mirror. They are far apart. In a son your image is yourself; for by nature your son is what you are. In substance the same as you, in person different. Man therefore is not an image like the Only-begotten Son, but is made in a certain image and in a certain likeness. Let him seek whether he can find some things within himself which may be made known as separate and which are yet inseparable in operation. I shall search; let you seek with me. I shall not seek it in you, but I seek it in myself, and you in yourselves. Let us seek for it together, and let us together examine our common nature and our common substance.

VII—18. *Our Soul was made in God's Image.* Reflect, O Man, and consider if what I say be true. Have you a body, have you flesh? I have, you say. For how else am I here, how am I in one place, how do I move from place to place? How do I hear the words of someone who is speaking to me, except through the ears of my body? How do I see the mouth of the speaker, unless with the eyes of my body? You have a body, it is plain; nor need we trouble further about something so evident.

Reflect on something else; consider what it is that is acting through the body. For you hear by the ear, but it is not the ear hears. Within is someone who hears by the ear. You see by the eye: look at it. Do you see the house, and pay no heed to the occupant? Does an eye see by itself? Is there not someone within who sees by the eye? I do not say that the eye of a dead man, from whose body it is apparent the occupant has departed, does not see, but that the eye of a man thinking of something else does not see the face of someone in front of him.

Look then at your interior man. It is there rather the similitude is to be looked for, of three things that are to be shown to be separate, and which are inseparable in their operation. What are the properties of your mind? Should I search I may find many things there. But there is something of great import, readily known. What is it your soul possesses? Recall it to mind; remember. I am not asking you to believe me in what I am going to say. Do not accept what I say, if you do not find this thing within you. Look inward then; but first let us see something we overlooked; namely, whether man is not the image of the Son only or of the Father only, but of both Father and Son, and then of the Holy Ghost likewise? Genesis tells us. *Let us*, it says, *make man to our image and likeness* (i. 26). The Father therefore did not make him without the Son, nor the Son without the Father. *Let us make man to our image and likeness.* It says, *Let us make*, not, I shall make; or, make; or, let him make; but, *Let us make man to our image*; not to your image, or to mine; but, *to our image*.

19. *The Similitude of the Trinity in Man.* I am enquiring into, I am speaking now of something dissimilar to ourselves. Let no one say: Look, he is comparing us with God. I have said this already, I began by saying it; I cautioned you, and I have myself been cautious. They *are* far removed, the one from the other: as the lowest is from the highest, the changeable from the Unchangeable, the created from Those Who are creating, the human from the Divine. I am drawing your attention to this from the start, so that no one may speak against me, because that of which I am about to speak is so remotely different. Since therefore, while I am asking for your ears, someone else may be getting ready his teeth (i.e., *to attack him*), take note that I promise but this: to show you, that there are three things in us, which are known to be separate, which work inseparably. I am not considering now how like or how unlike they may be to the Omnipotent Trinity; but in this lowest of creatures, in this changeable creature, we find three certain things, which can be shown, to be separate and yet work inseparably.

O unspiritual of mind! O obstinate and unbelieving mentality! Why do you doubt in this Ineffable Majesty of what you could discover within your own self? Here now I say to you, I now ask you. Man, have you a memory? If you have not, how do you keep in your mind what I said to you? But perhaps you have already forgotten what I said to you a moment ago. Even these two words, *I said*, you could not keep in your mind except by the aid of memory. How would you know they were two, if while the

second is sounding in your ears you had forgotten the first? Why do I linger so long on this? Why do I insist so much? Why am I striving to make this clear? It is manifest why. Because you have a memory.

I wish to know something else. Have you an understanding? I have, you will say. If you had not a memory, you could not retain what I said. If you had not an understanding, you would not know what it was you retained. So you have this also. You apply your understanding to what you hold in your mind, and you reflect upon it, and perceiving it you are instructed, so that you are said to know. I wish to know a third thing. You have a memory, by which you retain what is said to you. You have an understanding, by which you grasp what you retain. But as to these two, I ask you: was it not through willing that you both retained and understood? Of course it was by willing, you will say. You have a will then. These therefore are the three things which I undertook to make known to your ears and to your minds. These are the three things within you which you can number, but cannot separate. These three: memory, understanding, and will. Observe, I say, that these three are made known to us separately, and are yet inseparable in operation.

VIII—20. *Memory, intellect, and Will are proved separate, yet are inseparable in operation.* The Lord will aid me, and I know He is near at hand. From your understanding I perceive that He is present. For from your very voices (i.e. *acclamations!*) I can see in what measure you have understood me; and it is my hope He will continue to assist you, that you may understand all that I say. I have undertaken to place before you three things that are known to us separately, which operate inseparably.

Now I knew not what was in your mind, but you revealed it to me by saying, 'Memory'. This word, this sound, this utterance, came forth from your mind to my ears. For this 'memory' you were wont to think of to yourself only; you did not speak of it. It was within you, but it had not yet come forth to me. But that what was in you might be communicated to me, you told me its name, namely, Memory (*Memoria*). I heard it. In the name, Memory, I heard these three syllables. It is a word, a noun of three (four) syllables; it sounded, it proceeded to my ear, it made known something to my mind. The sound by which it was made known has passed away; what was made known remains.

But let me ask you this: when you spoke this name of memory, you are no doubt aware that this name refers only to memory. For the other two faculties have their own names. For one is called, understanding (*intellectus*), the other, will (*voluntas*), not memory: this other faculty is alone called memory. But that you should say this, that you should give utterance to these three (four) syllables, from what source has it come that you should do this? This word, which relates but to memory alone, was wrought within you, by the memory, that you might retain what you said, by the understanding, that you might know what you retained, by the will, that you might communicate what you knew.

Thanks be to the Lord our God!

He has helped us; He has been near at hand both in you and in me. I declare truly to Your Charity that it was with the greatest trepidation that I undertook to discuss and make this known to you. I feared I might please only those of larger understanding, and greatly weary those whose minds were slower. Now I see, as well by the attention with which you listened to me as by the quickness of your understanding, that you have not alone grasped what I said, but that you have been ahead of me, in what I was about to say. Thanks be to God!

IX—21. *By these three things the Mystery of the Trinity is explained.* You see then that it is with an untroubled mind I now put before you that which you have already understood. I have not taught something that was unknown to you, but am recalling to your minds what you already knew. Now one thing is referred to by these three; the name used refers but to one thing. Memory is the name of one of these three things; yet it was these three made the name of this one of the three. It could not be named by memory alone, unless through the work of will, memory and understanding. Understanding by itself could not be named unless through memory, will and understanding working together. Will of itself could not be named will, unless by the common action of will, memory and understanding.

I think I have explained what I undertook to explain: that what I made known to you as separate, I have employed inseparably in my mind. The three together have made one thing of all of them. Yet this one thing the three made does not relate to the three, but to one of them. The three made the name, memory. But this name relates solely to memory. The three made the name, understanding; but it relates only to the understanding. The three made the name, will; but this belongs solely to the will. So the Trinity made the Flesh of Christ; but this belongs to Christ alone. The Trinity made the Dove from heaven; but this refers to the Spirit alone. The Trinity made the Voice from heaven; but the Voice itself belongs only to the Father.

22. *Which of these relates to the Father, which to the Son and Holy Ghost is left to recollection.* Now let no one say to me, let no bothersome person try to pin down my poor self, saying: Which then of the three things you show are in our mind or soul, which of these relates to the Father, that is, has it were the *likeness* of the Father, and which has the likeness of the Son, and which of them is made in the likeness of the Holy Ghost? I cannot tell you, I cannot find out. Let us leave something to those who meditate; and let us yield something to silence. Enter into yourself, and withdraw yourself from all strife. Look within you; see if you possess there some sweet inner sanctuary of the soul's awareness, where there is no disquiet, no strife, no contest, where you give no thought to harshness or discord. There, *be meek to hear the word, that thou mayst understand* (Ecclus. v. 13). It may be that then you will say: *To my hearing thou wilt give joy and gladness: and the bones that have been humbled shall rejoice* (Ps. l. 10); the bones that have been humbled, not exalted.

X—23. *By this it can be sufficiently understood, that the Persons of the Trinity can be shown as separate but that they work together inseparably.* It is enough then that we have shown that there are three things known to us separately, that are inseparable in work. If you have found this within you, if you have found it in man, if you have found it in any person walking this earth, bearing about a *frail body that is a load upon the soul* (Wisd. ix. 15), believe then that the Father and the Son and the Holy Ghost may, through certain single perceivable things, by means of certain images borrowed from a creature, be shown as separate, and as inseparable in operation.

Let this suffice. I do not say, the Father is Memory, the Son is Understanding, the Spirit is will. This I do not say. Let each one understand it as he pleases; I do not presume to say. Let us leave the greater questions to those who are capable of them; but we who are weak, to the weak we make known what we can. I do not say that these things are to be compared with the Trinity, in a sort of proportion (*ad analogiam*); that is, that they are to be considered as a ground of comparison. This I do not say. But what do I say? I say this: that I have found within you three things shown to be separate, yet inseparable in operation. And that of these three, each single name was made by the three together; but would yet belong, not to the three, but to some one of the three.

Believe there (i.e. in the Trinity) what you are unable to see, if here you have learned of it, have seen it, and have understood it. For what is in yourself, you may know;

but what is in Him Who made you what you are, whatever you are, how can you know? And if you ever shall be able, you are not yet able. And even when you will be able, will you, do you think, be able so to know God as He knows Himself? Let this suffice Your Charity. All we could say we have said. I have made good my promises to those who required them of me. As to what remains to be added, so that you may *grow* in knowledge, seek it from the Lord.

May then the power of His mercy strengthen our heart in His truth. May it confirm and calm our souls. May His grace abound in us, may He have pity on us, and remove obstacles from before us, and from before the Church, and from before all those who are dear to us, and may He by His power, and in the abundance of His mercy, enable us to please Him for ever, through Jesus Christ His Son our Lord, Who with Him and with the Holy Ghost lives and reigns world without end. Amen.[20]

NOTES

[1] Any sermon or homily on the Blessed Trinity is inevitably an exposition of the Mystery of the Trinity, together with praise and adoration. And any exposition is inevitably a defence of the Second Person and the Third Person from the errors that seek to deprive them of their Divine Dignity. From instincts of reason, as St Gregory Nazianzen says, men have, for the most part, forborne to affront the Father. This sermon is a discourse on the evidence, part of it, for the Divinity of the Holy Ghost, and is taken from Chapter 27 of St Basil's *Book on the Holy Spirit*, and includes paragraphs 66, 67, 68, 71, 72, 73, 74, and part of 75. The error of Arius assailed the dignity of the Holy Ghost as well as that of the Son. But while the Nicene definition (A.D. 325) made clear our belief with regard to the Second Person it left that of the Third Person comparatively open as it were, as this aspect of the Arian apostasy was not greatly to the fore. Macedonius made it so. Because of his errors he was expelled from the See of Con-

stantinople in 360. St Athanasius began then to defend the Holy Spirit; principally from the Commission to baptize in the name of the Trinity (Matthew xxviii. 19). Later, at the urgent request of his cousin, St Amphilocius of Iconium, Basil took up the same theme; followed by St Gregory Nazianzen, and by St Ambrose. The errors of Macedonius (*Pneumotomachius*) were condemned at the Council of Constantinople 381. In this portion of his work Basil defends, from Sacred Tradition, the use of the preposition *with*, joining the Holy Ghost in dignity and equality to the Father and the Son. The striking part of this selection is the living force and conservatism of Tradition; how it is weighed and guarded, how it must always be deferred to as a divinely given guide. The due place of the doxology as a Confession of Faith and of Praise is made clear; something we tend to neglect in individual cases, but which the Church in her formal prayer, as well as true piety, employs with due honour and reverence.

² This is possibly a reference to I Cor. ii. 7, and probably has in mind the practice of withholding certain higher divine truths from all except those ready and prepared for them.

³ i. 2. If nothing has force but what is written, there is no need to proclaim or define what is *already* expressed in writing, i.e. Scripture.

⁴ St Basil uses the word *dogma* (*dogmata*) with reference to doctrines and practices privately taught, while employing *kerugmata* for what is *now* understood by dogma: what has been publicly defined, such as the *Kerugma* of Nicaea. This is confirmed by Eulogius, Patriarch of Alexandria, 579–607, of whom Photius says (Migne, PG 103, p. 1027: 'In his (Eulogius) work he says of the doctrines *handed down* (*didagmaton*) in the Church by the ministers of the word, some are *dogmata*, and others *kerugmata*. The distinction is that *dogmata* are announced with concealment and prudence, and are often designedly compassed with obscurity, in order that holy things may not be exposed to profane persons nor pearls cast before swine. *Kerugmata*, on the other hand, are announced without any concealment. Dogma now is the formal expression, generally against the attack of some error, of any one of the body of truths which the whole divine tradition of the Church has agreed comes down to us from revelation, either written, or that given to us orally by the Redeemer, our Lord Jesus Christ, True God and True Man.'

⁵ Dianius, Bishop of Caesarea of Cappadocia, who, about the year 357, baptized Basil, then aged twenty-seven, and admitted him to

his first sacred order, that of Reader.

⁶ Died *c*. A.D. 200.

⁷ Died *c*. A.D. 100.

⁸ Died *c*. A.D. 269.

⁹ Dionysius was patriarch of Alexandria A.D. 247–65. The remark 'strange to say', is due apparently to a suspicion of his orthodoxy, due to limited acquaintance with his writings. In his Epistle 188 he later speaks of him as 'the great Dionysius'.

¹⁰ St Clement, Pope. Epis. ad Cor. 58.

¹¹ Adversus Haereses IV, 38, 2.

¹² Ibid., V, 9, 1.

¹³ Eusebius of Caeserea, the historian, so called to distinguish him from Eusebius of Nicomedia. This work is not extant.

¹⁴ 185–254. Priest and Confessor, 'who, among the Easterns, holds chief place, in the liveliness of his mental powers, and the wondrous constancy of his labours, from whose manifold writings almost all have since drawn'; Encyclical, *Providentissimus Deus* 1893.

¹⁵ The question regarding Origen is obscured for many reasons. His mind and his teaching ranged over a vast and profound field; uncharted as yet by the as it were divinely appointed pilots. In view of his influence and significance, as recognized by such authority (see preceding note), it would have been a great victory for the powers of darkness to have discredited this channel of divine tradition. The attempt to do so, it appears, began early. The impression one gathers of his character from his homilies is of a very holy and humble mind.

¹⁶ PG 36, Oratio 34. A discourse preached to the crews of a fleet of ships arriving with corn from Egypt.

The crews passed by all the great churches, then held by the Arians, and came to his little church, the *Anastasia*, which had become the tiny centre of the Catholic Faith in the city now almost wholly Arian and heretical. His constant theme here was the worship of the Trinity. St Jerome has left on record his pleasure at listening to, and conversing with, the great defender of the Faith, called the Divine, because of the sublimity of his five great Theological Orations. The opening part of this sermon, which is called *On the Arrival of the Egyptians*, is devoted to praise of Egypt, its faith, its loyalty, and defence of orthodoxy; and this in tribute to their devotion in coming there. He then begins his discourse proper; given here from Chapter VIII to the end. *Note:* At this time Baptism was spoken of among Easterns as *Illumination*, or *Enlightenment* (*Photismos*).

[17] The Two Principles of the earlier heresies, especially of the Marcionites; one Good, the other Evil. By the Evil principle was understood the Maker of things, *Demiourgon*. PG 36, col. 250 (87).

[18] PL 38, Sermones de Scripturis 52. This is one of the most significant sermons ever delivered. It is also a masterpiece of the didactic art; making clear, exact, precise (and human), a theme of the utmost sublimity, while at the same time arousing (and holding) interest and attention, and, it would seem, clamorous appreciation.

[19] Cf. *Confessions*, Book 9, Ch. 10.

[20] This concluding prayer is from Sermo II of those edited by Michael Denis; Sancti Augustini Sermones Reperti, G. Morin, O.S.B., Rome 1930. It is found in no other place in Augustine's works. At the close of a sermon in the vigil of the Pasch we find: *Conversi ad Dominum et oratio: Virtus misericordiae Ejus* etc. It is added here as a fitting close to this striking exposition of the supreme truth of the Trinity.

FIRST SUNDAY AFTER PENTECOST

I. St Ambrose: The Character of a Just Judge

II. St John Chrysostom: On Rash Judgement

III. St Augustine: On Correcting One Anotehr

THE GOSPEL OF THE SUNDAY

Luke vi. 36–42

At that time: Jesus said to his disciples: Be ye merciful, as your Father also is merciful. Judge not, and you shall not be judged. Condemn not, and you shall not be condemned. Forgive, and you shall be forgiven. Give, and it shall be given to you: good measure and pressed down and shaken together and running over shall they give into your bosom. For with the same measure that you shall mete withal, it shall be measured to you again.

And he spoke also to them a similitude: Can the blind lead the blind? Do they not both fall into the ditch? The disciple is not above his master: but every one shall be perfect, if he be as his master. And why seest thou the mote in thy brother's eye: but the beam that is in thy own eye thou considerest not? Or how canst thou say to thy brother: Brother, let me pull the mote out of thy eye, when thou thyself seest not the beam in thy own eye? Hypocrite, cast first the beam out of thy own eye; and then shalt thou see clearly to take out the mote from thy brother's eye.

Exposition from the Catena Aurea

V. 36. *Be ye therefore merciful, as your Father also is merciful.*

Cyril: Great indeed is the praise of mercy. For this virtue makes us like to God, and impresses on our souls the mark as it were of a sublime nature; hence there follows: *Be ye merciful* etc. Athanasius: That is, keeping before our eyes His mercies, whatever good we may do, let us not do it for the eyes of men but for His; seeing that it is from God and not from men that we shall receive our reward.

V. 37. *Judge not, and you shall not be judged . . .*

Ambrose: The Lord added, that we should not lightly judge, lest you may be compelled to condemn in another a crime of which you are yourself conscious.[1] Chrysostom,

Hom. 24 *in Matt*: Do not judge your superiors; that is, a disciple must not judge his master, nor a sinner one who is innocent. Do not reproach, but advise and correct with love. Nor should we ever judge in things that are uncertain, or in those which have no resemblance to sin, or which are not grave, or forbidden.

CYRIL: He here checks the worst evil of our thoughts; the source and the beginning of the proud man's contempt. For though there are some men who should be watchful of themselves, and live justly before God, this they fail to do, devoting their attention rather to the lives of others. And if they see others weak, unmindful of their own infirmities, they make these an object of slander.

CHRYSOSTOM: You will not easily find anyone who is free of this fault; not even a member of the cloister, or the father of a family. But such things are the snares of the tempter. For they who search sharply into the faults of others will never merit forgiveness of their own. And so we have: *And you shall not be judged.* For he who is mild and forbearing lessens the fear his own sins cause him, while the harsh and the cruel but add to their offences.

GREGORY NYSSA: Be not rash then, harshly condemning those who serve you, lest you suffer in the same way. For so to judge, calls down on yourself a harsher condemnation. Hence follows: *Condemn not, and you shall not be condemned.*

BEDE: He concludes, summing up in one short sentence all that He had laid upon them as to how they were

to treat their enemies, saying: *Forgive, and thou shall be forgiven.* Here He bids us forgive injuries, and show kindness to others, that our own sins may be forgiven, and that we may receive life eternal.

V. 38. *Give, and it shall be given to you: good measure and pressed down.*

CYRIL: He goes on to show that we shall so receive a more generous recompense from God, Who gives bountifully to those who love Him, saying: *Good measure and pressed down and running over shall they give into your bosom.* THEOPHYLACTUS: As much as to say: Just as when you go to measure out meal unsparingly, you press it down, you shake it together, and you let it overflow generously, so will the Lord give into your heart in generous and overflowing measure.

AUGUSTINE, *Gospel Questions II*, 8: But He says *they* shall give; because they shall merit to receive a heavenly reward because of the merits of those (*these little ones* of Mt. x. 42) to whom they have given even a cup of cold water (if only, *tantum*), in the name of a disciple. *For with the same measure that you shall mete withal, it shall be measured to you again.*

BASIL, *Catena GP*: For according to the measure each one of you uses in doing good, or in doing evil, in that same measure shall you receive punishment or reward. THEOPHYLACTUS: But someone may very subtly enquire: If the return is made overabundantly, how is it made in the same measure? To this we answer, that, He did not say, 'in just as great measure', but, *with the same measure.* For he who has done good, good will be done to him: which is to measure back with the same measure. But He spoke of the measure *running over*; because to such a one will He show mercy a thousand times. So also in judging. For he that judges, and then afterwards is judged, he will receive the same measure of justice. Because he judged another severely, yet more severely shall he be judged, the measure *running over*.

CYRIL: This the Apostle explains when he says: *He who soweth sparingly* (that is, lightly, and with a sparing hand) *shall also reap sparingly* (II Cor. ix. 6); that is, not in abundance; *and he who soweth in blessings, shall also reap blessings*; that is, bountifully. But if a man has nothing he is not held guilty if he does nothing; for a man is held accountable for what he has, not for what he has not.

V. 39. *And he spoke also to them a similitude: Can the blind etc.?*

CYRIL: To what He had just said the Lord adds a very needful parable. For His Disciples were the future Teachers of the world. So it was fitting they should know the way of virtuous living, and have their minds illuminated by the Divine Brightness; that they might not as blind lead the blind. And so He goes on: *Can the blind lead the blind? Do they not both fall into the ditch?* And should it happen that some attain to the same degree of virtue as their Teachers, let them prove themselves worthy of the name of their Teachers, and follow in their footsteps. Thence follows:

V. 40. *The disciple is not above his master . . .*

Because of this Paul also says: *Be ye followers of me, as I also am of Christ* (I Cor. iv. 16). If Christ does not judge, why do you judge? He came, not to judge, but to shew mercy.

THEOPHYLACTUS: Or again: If you judge another, and commit the same sin yourself, are you not as the blind leading the blind? For how can you lead them to good, since you also are committing sin? For the disciple is not above his master. If you who hold yourself to be a Teacher and a Guide go on sinning, where will he come to who is taught and led by you? *For every one shall be perfect, if he be as his master.*

BEDE: Or: the meaning of this sentence depends on those which precede it, where we are bidden to give alms and forgive injuries against us. If, He says, anger has blinded you against the violent, and greed has blinded you against the avaricious, how can you with your own soul corrupted cure his corruption? If even Christ our Master, Who as God could have punished injuries against Him, chose rather by suffering them to make His tormentors milder, then should His Disciples, who are but men, follow His rule of perfection.

AUGUSTINE, *Gospel Quest. II*, 9: Or it may be that the Lord's saying: *Can the blind lead the blind etc.*, was added here that they might not look to receive from the Levites this *measure* of which He said, *they shall give into your bosom.* For they gave them tithes. It is these He calls blind, because they would not receive the Gospel. He said this so that the people would now rather begin to look for this repayment from the Lord's Disciples. Wanting to point them out as His imitators, He added: *The disciple is not above his master.*

V. 41. *And why seest thou the mote in thy brother's eye . . .?*

THEOPHYLACTUS: The Lord spoke another parable also on the same theme, going on: *And why seest thou the mote,* that is, the little fault, *in thy brother's eye, but the beam* (that is, your own grievous fault) *that is in thy own thou considerest not?* BEDE: This refers to the earlier sentence where He warns them that the blind cannot lead the blind; that is, the sinner cannot be corrected by the sinner. Hence was added:

V. 42. *Or how canst thou say to thy brother: brother, let me . . .*

CYRIL: As though He said: How can he who is guilty of grievous sin (which he describes as a *beam*) condemn him who has committed but small offences, and sometimes has not even committed sin: for this is what the mote means?

THEOPHYLACTUS: This parable applies to all men, but especially to preachers, who, while they castigate the small sins of those subject to them, leave their own sins uncorrected. Because of this the Lord calls them *hypocrites*; because they condemn others' sins to make themselves appear as just. And so we have: *Hypocrite, cast first the beam out of thy own eye; and then shalt thou see clearly to take out the mote from thy brother's eye.*

CYRIL: That is, first show thyself free of grievous sin. Then afterwards think of the little faults of your neighbour. BASIL: It seems that self-knowledge is the most important of all things. For not alone does the eye that is taken up with outward things fail to turn its glance inwardly, but even our very mind, while swift to note another's fault, is slow at seeing its own defects.

I. ST AMBROSE, BISHOP AND DOCTOR

The Character of a Just Judge[2]

Be ye therefore Merciful. How great the reward of mercy we receive under the law of Divine adoption! Walk in the way of mercy that you may merit this divine blessing. The kindness of God spreads far and wide. It rains upon *the unthankful*; and the fruitful earth does not deny its yield even to the wicked. The same light of the world shines on impious and God-fearing alike. Or that we may consider these things mystically, the Lord watered the people of Israel with prophetic rains, and shone upon them in the rays of His Eternal Sun; even upon those who were not deserving. But because they became drenched with the dew of earth the Church of God is now received into that celestial Light, that believing they may also attain to the rewards of mercy. *Judge not, and you shall not be judged.*

He also laid down that you must not judge rashly lest, should you be conscious of the same offence, you find you are thus made to pass sentence on yourself.[3] For it is a grave thing to judge another. Because of this was it written: *Judge not, that you may not be judged* (Mt. vii. 1). For if each one is conscious of his own sins, how can he judge the sin of another? Let him judge of another's sin who has not on his conscience that which condemns himself. Let him judge who does not himself do what he judges must be punished in another; lest while judging the other he passes sentence upon himself. Let him give judgement on another's sin who is not led to deliver it by any hate, by dislike, or by foolish levity. You have heard what the True and Just Judge has said: *I cannot of myself do anything* (Jn. v. 30).

There are certain heretics who try to make a difficulty out of this sentence, as if the Son were without power, and could do nothing of Himself; that in relation to the Godhead He was as an inferior, subject to the authority of the Father. They do not perceive that by these words also the unity of the Divine dominion is proved the more; where they think there is a difference between the power of the Father and the Son. The Son does nothing of Himself, because through the unity of Their operation the Son does nothing without the Father, nor the Father without the Son. In consequence of this the Father said to the Son: *Let us make man to our image and likeness* (Gen. i. 26), showing that there is common action where there is common purpose. What does He do without Wisdom Who has made all things in Wisdom, as we read: *Thou hast made all things in wisdom* (Ps. ciii. 24)?

And then Wisdom has said: *When he prepared the heavens I was present. I was with him forming all things* (Prov. viii. 27, 30). And the Evangelist says: *All things were made by him, and without him was made nothing that was made* (John i. 3), that He might teach us that not alone is the Son the Producer (*Operator*) of all things, but that He is also an equal Partner of the Paternal action.

I however think that these words (*I cannot of myself do anything*) seem to refer to the manner of giving judgement. For the Gospel is not alone the teaching of faith, it is also the School of our laws and conduct, and the Mirror of our manner of life. I find in the Gospel that the Lord Jesus took upon Himself the condition and the duties of many men, that He might teach us how we ought to conduct ourselves with respect to these duties. He took upon Himself the character of a shepherd, and He says: *The good shepherd giveth his life for his sheep* (Jn. x. 11). And because of this He refused not the passion of His Body on behalf of His rational flock, so that He might raise up the weary sheep upon the shoulders of His Cross, and restore it to life by the discharge of that blessed payment.

He took upon Him the character of an advocate: *We have an advocate with the Father, Jesus Christ the Just* (I Jn. ii. 1). For us He *passed the night in prayer* (Lk. vi. 12), that He might teach us by example how we should implore the pardon of our sins. For He did not pass the night in this way because He was unable by any other means to return us to the friendship of the Father, but that He might show us what an advocate ought to be; what a priest should be, that he should take his stand as intercessor for the flock of Christ not alone by day but also by night. Did He need the assistance of prayer Who could Himself do what He prayed for, as He Himself has said: *I go to the Father: and whatsoever you shall ask the Father in my name, that will I do* (Jn. xiv. 13).

And then elsewhere He says: when He raised Lazarus: *I knew thou hearest me always* (Jn. xi. 42). Here, as though He were a mere man, He passed the night Who knew that He was always heard, and He cried: *Lazarus, come forth.* He Who is the Resurrection spoke; and death withdrew.

He took upon Himself the condition of a criminal, and stood as one guilty before a judge; nor did the Lord of all reject the judge because of his baseness. Questioned, *He gave no answer* (Jn. xix. 9), showing that the defence of innocence lies not in the outcry of protest, nor in the formal defence of our advocate, but in purity of conscience: that what we must safeguard is not the health of the body, but the health of the soul. And He Who delivered the silent Susanna (Dan. xiii. 40), offered Himself to death. In her case He showed that we must never despair; in this that He would not renounce the sacrifice of universal redemption. When struck, He did not revile, nor strike back; and the Lord of heaven and earth put aside the desire of revenge, and said in the voice of humility: *If I have spoken evil, give testimony of the evil; but if well, why strikest thou me?* As though like some poor creature He grieved because of the unjust blow; and when He could avenge, He preferred to complain than take vengeance.

And for this reason here also He takes upon Himself the character and the duty of a judge, saying: *I cannot of myself do anything.* For a good judge does nothing of his own authority, by the resolve of his own private will, but will give sentence in accord with what is decreed and with law, and will conform to the law as he knows it, and will not indulge his own personal inclination. He will bring nothing prepared and thought out from his house, but as he hears, so will he judge, and he will settle the matter in accord with its nature. He obeys the laws; he will not oppose them. He examines the rights and the wrongs of the case; he does not alter them.

Let you learn, you who are judges in this world, to what dispositions you must hold fast in judging, to what sobriety of mind, to what sincerity. The Lord of all says: *I cannot of myself do anything.* I read elsewhere: *He cannot deny himself* (II Tim. ii. 13). He cannot, not because of weakness, but because of integrity of soul; not because it is impossible to Him, but out of reverence for the office of giving judgement. What can He not do Who can do all things save what He wills *He cannot do?* He wills that *He cannot do* what He condemns. He wills that *He cannot do* what is against faith. He wills that *He cannot do* what is against truth.

Hear Him then, as He goes on to say why He cannot of Himself do anything. *As I hear*, He says, *so I judge* (Jn. v. 30); that is, I do not judge as I will, because of the power given to me, but with reverence for the duty of giving judgement; in accordance with what is just. And therefore my judgement is true, because in it I conform, not with my own will, but with justice. Hear what the heavenly judge says to us: *I cannot of myself do anything. As I hear, so I judge.*

And Pilate also said to the Lord Jesus: *I have power to crucify thee, and I have power to release thee* (Jn. xix. 10). You usurp, O man, power that does not belong to you; since the Lord Who has power over all things says that He has not this power. Hear what Justice says: *I cannot of myself do anything.* Hear what the Impartial Judge says: *As I hear, so I judge.* Hear what the iniquitous judge says: *I have power to crucify thee, and I have power to release thee.*

Pilate, by your own voice, you are bound with fetters, by your own decision you are condemned. Because of your power, not because justice demanded it, you delivered the Lord to be crucified. By your power, you let a murderer go free; but the Author of life you killed (Acts iii. 15). But not from yourself have you that power you claim to possess. For then did the Lord say to you: *Thou shouldst not have any power against me, unless it were given thee from above.* Evil power, to make lawful what is not lawful. Power such as this is from darkness: to see what is true, and to spurn it.

Hear what the True Judge says: *I seek not my own will, but the will of him that sent me* (Jn. v. 30). He speaks as man; He teaches as a judge: since he who judges should not obey his own will, but hold fast to what is of the law. Take a judge of this world; will he go against the imperial constitution? Will he overstep the precedent of an imperial decision? How much the more

ought we to observe the pattern of the Divine Judge!

Christ says: *I seek not my own will*; that is, My will as man, which is guided by hate, or biased through affection, or swayed by interest, or perverted by the falsehood of others: for *every man is a liar* (Ps. cxv. 2). *But*, He says, *the will of him that sent me*; that is, I have come to teach the pattern of the divine manner of trial: that in judging the safeguarding of truth may be closer to your heart than obedience to your own will. Here there is no inconstancy of human authority, but the clear form of justice.

And so just is the judgement of the Son of God; because it is in accord with the Will of God, not with the desires of man. For God is full of mercy, and there is mercy in His judgement, and judgement with His mercy. For He neither shows mercy without judgement, nor will He give judgement without mercy. And it is written: *I will set judgement in weight, and justice in measure* (Is. xxviii. 17). But, *The sons of men are liars in the balances, that they may deceive* (Ps. lxi. 10). God examines and weighs the merits of each one in turn, and gives His grace in accordance with measure, lest it exceed due measure; so likewise does He give mercy in due measure. And because of this He says: *Good measure and pressed down and running over shall they give to your bosom. For with the same measure that you shall mete withal, it shall be measured to you again.*

So also are the works of each in turn weighed in the balance, and should the good works outweigh the bad payment of a reward shall be made. But should our sins outweigh our virtues a very grievous compensation is exacted from the guilty one, as is clear from what you read in the words of Paul the Apostle to Timothy: *Some men's sins are manifest, going before to judgement: and some men they follow after* (I Tim. v. 24). So likewise are our good works manifest; and those which are far from being so cannot be hidden.

The Lord our God therefore will do all things in accord with due weight and measure. *Who hath weighed the mountains on scales, and the hills in a balance* (Is. xl. 13); and, before this, *Who hath measured the waters in the hollow of his hand, and weighed the heavens with his palms?* He Who weighs our actions, and upon due examination judges all things, and in due measure bestows His rewards. He has weighed His mercy, He has weighed His justice; and in both there is a certain weight, a just measure. Because of this David cries: *How long wilt thou give us for our drink tears in measure* (Ps. lxxix. 6), lest, without the moderation of this measure, we should be weighed down by the burthen of our expiation, and unable to bear it?

And elsewhere the same prophet says: *In the hand of the Lord there is a cup of strong wine, full of mixture. And he hath poured it out from this to that: but the dregs thereof are not emptied: all the sinners of the earth shall drink* (Ps. lxxiv. 9). And Jeremiah says: *Babylon hath been a golden cup in the hand of the Lord, that made all the earth drunk* (Jer. li. 7); that is, the nations shall be chastised

lest they mock too long, for with most bitter spoliation have they afflicted the people of God. Accordingly, the meaning of David's verse is this: Complete and ready is the chastisement due to the impious, which the Lord pours out to the unbelieving; yet in the exercise of His mercy He does not pour it out to the dregs, lest they be unable to endure the full measure of His justice. He therefore pours from the cup, and does not empty it. What he pours out relates to His judgement; that He does not empty it relates to His mercy.

The Lord our God therefore tempers His justice with His mercy. For who among us could stand without the divine mercy? What could we do that would be worthy of heavenly rewards? Who amongst us could so rise up in this body of ours so as to uplift his own soul to where it might for ever cleave to Christ? How far would the good men do avail them, that this corruptible body might put on incorruption, and this mortal put on immortality (I Cor. xv. 53)? By what labours of ours, by what sufferings, could we wash clean our own sins? *The sufferings of this time are not to be compared to the glory to come* (Rom. viii. 18). It is not therefore in accordance with our merits that the nature of the divine decrees concerning man reveals itself, but in accordance with the mercy of God, to Whom be honour and glory for ever and ever. Amen.

II. St John Chrysostom, Bishop and Doctor

On Rash Judgement[4]

Judge not, that you may not be judged. What does this mean? Are we not to denounce those who are committing sin? And Paul too says this same thing; or rather Christ says it through Paul: *But thou, why judgest thou thy brother?* (Rom. xiv. 10). And again later he says: *Therefore judge not before the time, until the Lord come* (I Cor. iv. 5).

Why then does he elsewhere say: *Reprove, entreat, rebuke* (II Tim. iv. 2)? And in another place: *Them that sin reprove them before all* (I Tim. v. 20)? And Christ also, saying to Peter: *Go, and rebuke him between thee and him alone. If he shall hear thee, thou shalt gain thy brother; and if he will not hear thee take with thee one or two more. And if he will not hear them, tell the Church* (Mt. xviii. 15–17)? And why has He set up so many to reprove, and not alone to reprove, but to punish? For He has commanded that he who will not hear any of these is to be looked upon as the heathen and the sinner.

Why then did He give them the power of the keys? For if they are not to judge, they are without authority, and in vain have they received the power of binding and loosing. And besides, if this were to be the case, everything would come to an end, in the churches, in the cities, in homes; for if the master did not correct the servant, and the mistress the maid, the father the son, the friend his friend, everything would go to the bad. And did I say unless friend should correct friend? Unless we correct our enemies also, we shall never put an end to enmity, and everything would be turned upside down. Let us then carefully study the meaning of what is said here, so that no one may think that the remedies of our salvation, and the laws of peace are really laws of disorder and confusion. For He has, in what follows, made as clear as

possible to those who have understanding, the perfection of this law, saying to us: *And why seest thou the mote in thy brother's eye, and seest not the beam in thy own?*

But if it still seems obscure to many of the more unreflecting I shall try to explain it from the beginning. It seems to me that in these words He does not absolutely command us not to judge any sins, neither does He wholly forbid us to do this, but that He is here speaking to those who, laden with countless sins, trample on others because of their misfortunes. He seems to be referring to certain Jews who, though bitter denouncers of the small and trifling sins of their neighbour, were themselves carelessly committing the gravest sins. And in fact, towards the end, rebuking them, He says to them: *They bind heavy and insupportable burdens, but with a finger of their own they will not move them*; and again: *You tithe mint, and cummin, and have left the weightier things of the law; judgement, and mercy, and faith* (Mt. xxiii. 4, 23).

It seems to me then that it was these He had in mind, seeking to restrain them beforehand, because of the things they were to say of His Disciples. For though the Disciples had not been guilty of sin, yet by these men certain things were held to be faults; such as, not to observe the sabbath, not to wash the hands before eating, to eat with publicans. And of these men He said in another place that, *they strain at a gnat and swallow a camel* (Mt. xxiii. 24). However, in regard to such matters He here lays down a universal law.

Paul also, writing to the Corinthians (I. iv. 5), does not simply command them not to judge, but not to judge those placed over them, and in matters which are not clear; but he does not wholly forbid them to correct sinners. And neither was he reproving all without distinction, but only those disciples who were doing this very thing to their own teachers, and those also who were guilty of countless sins and were at the same time slandering those who were without sin.

It is to this therefore that Christ is referring, and not alone does He refer to it, but He makes it a matter of grave anxiety and inexorable punishment: *For with what judgement you judge, you shall be judged.* For it is not the other person that you condemn, He says, but your own self. You are preparing a dreadful judgement for yourself, and your punishment shall be severe. For as with the forgiveness of our sins we begin with ourselves, so likewise in this judgement, the measure of our own condemnation is fixed by ourselves. For we ought not to condemn, or insult, but to admonish; we ought not to slander, but to counsel; not to attack in arrogance, but to correct with gentleness and affection. For it is not this other person that you are giving over to severe punishment, not sparing him when there was need to pass sentence on his faults, but your own self.

You see that these two precepts are both of them light, and that they are the cause of great good to those who fulfil them, as they are also the cause of great evils to those who disregard them? For he who forgives his neighbour, without any effort on his own part frees himself rather than his neighbour from reproach. And he who inquires into the faults of his neighbour, with forbearance and fellow feeling, great is the store of forgiveness he has laid up for himself, by this manner of practising forbearance.

What then, you will say, if he has committed fornication; am I not to say that fornication is a wicked thing, am I not to correct his evil conduct? Correct him, yes; but not like a foe, an enemy, one out for vengeance, but like a physician administering healing remedies. For the Lord did not say: Do not restrain the sinner from his sins, but, *Do not judge,* that is, Do not be a harsh judge. And besides, it was not of great faults or of things forbidden He said this, but of things that do not appear to have been sins at all. And that was why He said: *Why seest thou the mote in thy brother's eye?* And this is what many are doing even now. For if they see, for example, a monk wearing some extra covering, they invoke the law of the Lord against him, although they themselves are grabbing at everything, cheating day after day. And if they see him eat a bit more than he is accustomed to, they criticize him bitterly, though every single day they are themselves eating and drinking to excess; not caring that together with their own sins, because of this rash judging, they are building up for themselves a still bigger fire, leaving for themselves no grounds for God's mercy. For when you sit in judgement on your neighbour in this way, you are yourself laying down the law according to which your own sins shall be examined. You must not think it severe if it is you yourself who will inflict the penalties.

Thou hypocrite, cast out first the beam out of thy own eye. Here He wills to make clear to us the great anger He feels against those who do such things. For wherever He wishes to show us that a sin is grievous, or that the punishment prepared for it is grievous, He begins with a reproach. Just as He said to the man who demanded back the debt of a hundred pence: *Thou wicked servant, I forgave thee all the debt* (Mt. xviii. 32), so here also He says, *Thou hypocrite.* For judgement of that kind does not spring from concern for, but from bitterness towards your fellow man, and while it may put on the mask of benevolence, such a one is only giving vent to his own ill will, making up the worst possible accusations against his neighbours, taking upon himself the rank of a teacher, when he is not fit to be even a pupil. It is because of this he is called a hypocrite. For you, you who are so bitter over what other people do, watching even for trifles, how is it you do not attend to your own faults; for there, even the gravest sins seem to escape your notice!

First cast the beam out of thy own eye. You see how He does not forbid us to judge, but commands us first to remove the beam from our own eyes, and only then should we correct the faults of others. For every one knows his own faults better than those of others, and sees big ones more easily than little ones; and loves himself more than he loves his neighbour. And so if you do this out of care for him, have a care first for yourself; where the sin is nearer to you, and greater. But if you have no care for yourself, it is very plain indeed that you judge your brother, not out of care for him, but out of hate, and because you want to defame him. And if he must be judged, then let him be judged, but not by thee, but by One Who does no wrong, to Whom be honour, praise, and glory, for ever and ever. Amen.

III. St Augustine, Bishop and Doctor

On Correcting One Another[5]

I. *The mote is anger; The beam is hate.* Our Lord counsels us that we are not to be indifferent to the sins of one another; not however by searching for what you may find fault with, but by seeing only what you may help to amend. For his eye is sharp to cast a mote from his brother's eye who has no beam in his own. What this means I shall briefly make clear to Your Charity.

A mote in the eye is anger; a beam in the eye is hatred. When therefore some one who hates rebukes some one who is angry, he wishes to take a mote out of the eye of his brother, but he is prevented by the beam he has in his own eye. A mote is the beginning of a beam. For a beam when it begins is first a mote. By watering the mote you bring it on to become a beam; and by nourishing anger, with evil suspicions, you lead it on to hate.

II—2. *The sin of anger; The cruelty of hate.* But there is a great difference between the sin of anger, and the cruelty of one who hates. For though we are angry even with our children, whom do you find hating his children? Even among cattle a young cow will be angry with her growing calf, will drive it away from her, but none the less she will cherish it with the love of a mother. She butts at it when she is annoyed with it, but when it is missing she will go searching for it. Nor do we discipline our children otherwise than by a certain amount of anger, and indignation; but we would not discipline them at all unless we loved them. So everyone who is angry is yet far from hating, so much so that at times a man might be thought to hate if he did not show some anger. For suppose a child wishes to play in the water of a stream, where he may drown in the current. If you see this, and let him, you hate him; your indulgence is the cause of his death. How much better be angry with him, and correct him, than let him drown by not being angry with him?

Hate then is to be shunned above everything; we must cast the beam from our eye. Great is the difference between a man being angry, going beyond what is right in some word or other, and keeping treachery locked up in his heart. And there is a great difference between these words of Scripture: *My eye is troubled through indignation* (Ps. vi. 8), and those said of the other evil, of which we read: *Whosoever hateth his brother is a murderer* (I Jn. iii. 15). Great the difference between a troubled eye, and one that is destroyed. A mote troubles it; a beam destroys it.

3. *Hate injures more gravely the one who hates, than the one hated.* So that we may worthily do and fulfil what

we have been taught this day, let us first convince ourselves that above all things we must not hate. For only when there is no beam in your own eye, may you then clearly see whatever there may be in your brother's eye; and you will be unhappy till you cast out from your brother's eye what you know is injuring it. The Light that is in you does not suffer you to be indifferent to your brother's light. For if you hate him, and wish to correct him, how can you restore his light when you have lost your own? For the Scripture which said to us: *Whosoever hateth his brother is a murderer,* also tells us plainly that, *he that hateth his brother is in darkness even until now* (I Jn. ii. 9).

Hatred then is darkness. And it cannot happen that one who hates another will not first injure himself. Outwardly he is trying to injure another; inwardly he is destroying himself. The more our soul is above our body, the more should we guard it so that it does not hurt itself. But he is wounding his own soul who cherishes hate for another. And what will he do to the one he hates? What does he do to him? He steals his money. Does he steal his faith? He injures his good name. Does he injure his conscience? However he may harm him, he only harms him outwardly. But look how he harms himself.

He who hates another man becomes the enemy of his own soul. But it is because he does not see the harm he does himself that he rages against another; and all the more dangerously for himself, because he does not see what he is doing to himself: for, raging against another he has lost the power of discretion.

96

First Sunday after Pentecost

You raged against your enemy, and raging you robbed him; but you have become evil. There is a great difference between a person robbed and one who is evil. He has lost his money; you have lost your integrity of soul. See if you can find out which has suffered the greater loss. He lost something that will perish; you have become someone who will perish.

III—4. *In what spirit we should correct a brother.* We are therefore to correct with charity; not with the desire to hurt him, but with the wish to help him. If this is our intention, we shall do very well what this day we have been admonished to do. *If thy brother offend thee, rebuke him between thee and him alone.* And why do you rebuke him? Is it because you suffer through his injury against you? Far from it. If you do this from self-love, you do nothing. If you do it out of love for him, then you have done well. See in the words themselves for love of whom you should do it; for love of him or love of yourself? *If he shall hear thee,* He says, *thou shalt gain thy brother.* Therefore do it for his sake: to gain him. Doing it, you gain him who would have been lost had you not done it. Why is it then that many men take little notice of these sins, and say of them, 'What great harm am I doing? I only sinned against a man.' Do not take these sins lightly. You have sinned against a man. Do you know that in sinning against a man you are lost? If he against whom you offended rebuked you, between him and you alone, and you listen to him, he has gained you. And what does this mean, *he has gained you,* if not that you were lost

had he not gained you? For unless you were lost, how could he have gained you? Let no man therefore regard it as a small thing to sin against a brother. For the Apostle says in a certain place: *When you sin against the brethren, and wound their weak conscience, you sin against Christ* (I Cor. viii. 12); and this because we have all been made members of Christ. And how can you not sin against Christ when you sin against a member of Christ?

5. *The Remedy of this sin.* Therefore let no one say, I did not sin against God, I sinned against a brother, I sinned against man, a light sin, or no sin at all. Perhaps you call it a light sin for this reason, because it is quickly healed. You have sinned against a brother. Then give satisfaction and you are safe again. You did in a moment what could destroy you; but as quickly you found a remedy. Which of us, my brethren, can hope for the kingdom of God, when the Gospel says: *Whosoever shall say to his brother, Thou fool, shall be in danger of hell fire?* What dread! But see there also is the remedy: *If therefore thou offer thy gift at the altar, and there thou remember that thy brother hath anything against thee; leave there thy offering before the altar.* God is not angered because you put your gift aside for a while: God waits for you, rather than for your gift. For if with evil in your heart against your brother you draw near to God with a gift, He will say to you: You are lost; why bring a gift to Me? You offer a gift, and you are not yourself a gift worthy of God. Christ looks more for you, whom He redeemed with His Blood, than for that which you found in your gar-

den. Therefore: *leave there thy offering before the altar, and go first to be reconciled to thy brother; and then coming thou shalt offer thy gift.* See how swiftly the dread of hell is banished. Unreconciled to your brother, you were in danger of hell; reconciled, with a mind at peace, you offer your gift at the altar.

IV—6. *What he must do who has suffered injury.* But men are quick to inflict injuries, slow to be reconciled to peace. Ask pardon, He says, of the one you offend, of the man you have offended. He answers: I will not humble myself. Then, if you despise your brother, at least pay heed to God's words: *He that humbleth himself shall be exalted* (Lk. xiv. 11). You who have fallen, will you not humble yourself? There is a great difference between one who humbles himself, and one who is lying on the ground. You already lie fallen; and yet you will not humble yourself? You might well say, I shall not lower myself, had you already refused to fall.

7. He who has inflicted an injury, let him do this. But he who has suffered injury, what must he do? What have we heard this day? *If thy brother shall offend against thee, go, and rebuke him between thee and him alone.* If you disregard this word, then you are worse than he is. He has done wrong, and doing wrong has gravely injured his own soul. Do you care nothing for your brother's injury? Will you look on while he perishes, or is lost; and you remain indifferent? You do worse remaining silent than he does by his abuse. Therefore, when anyone sins against us, we should be greatly

concerned, but not for ourselves; for it is a glorious thing to be unmindful of injuries. Be unmindful then of your own injuries, but not of your brother's wound. *Rebuke him,* therefore, *between thee and him alone,* desiring that he shall be made better, yet without putting him to shame.

For it may happen that from a natural feeling of shame he will begin to make excuses for his fault, and he whom you wish to make better you make worse. *Rebuke him,* therefore, *between thee and him alone. If he shall hear thee, thou shalt gain thy brother;* for he would have been lost had you not done this. But *if he will not hear thee;* that is, should he defend himself as though what he did was right, *take with thee one or two more; that in the mouth of two or three witnesses every word may stand. And if he will not hear them, tell the Church. And if he will not hear the Church, let him be to thee as the heathen and the publican.* Do not consider him as any more one of your brethren; nevertheless you must not be indifferent to his salvation. For even though we do not consider the heathens, that is, the Gentiles and Pagans, as numbered among our brethren, we are yet ever seeking their salvation.

This is what we have heard, the Lord so warning us, and teaching us with such care, so that He goes on to add this also: *Amen I say to you, whatsoever you shall bind upon earth, shall be bound also in heaven; and whatsoever you shall loose upon earth, shall be loosed also in heaven.* When you have begun to treat your brother as a heathen, you bind him on earth;[6] but see that you bind him justly. For justice will undo unjust

bonds. But when you have corrected him, and have been reconciled to your brother, you have
loosed him on earth. And when you
have loosed him on earth, he will be
loosed also in heaven. You do a
great thing, not for yourself but for
him; because he was doing grave
injury, not to you but to himself.

V—8. *The Gospel in accord with
Solomon.* But if this be so what does
Solomon mean in the words we
heard earlier, in another lesson: *He
that winketh with the eye brings sorrow
to men; but he who reproves openly
makes peace?*[7] If then he who
openly reproves *makes peace,* why
rebuke him between thee and him alone?
That the divine words are contrary
to each other is not to be thought of.
Let us understand that here there is
complete accord, and, unlike certain conceited minds (Manicheans),
not hold the notion according to
which they erroneously imagine that
the two Testaments of the Old and
the New Books are contrary to each
other, so that we are to believe that
here we have a contradiction, since
the one teaching is in the Book of
Solomon, the other in the Gospel.
For if anyone, unskilled in the
Scriptures, and a perverter of them,
were to say: Here we have a contradiction between the Two Testaments; the Lord says, Correct him
between thee and him alone; Solomon
says, He who *reproves openly makes
peace.* Does the Lord then not know
what He commanded? Solomon
would crush the hard brow of the
one who sins; Christ would spare
the modesty of the one who is
ashamed.

Now in the one place is written:
He who reproves openly makes peace;

in the other: *Rebuke him between thee
and him alone*; not openly, but apart,
and in secret. But do you wish to
know, you who imagine such things,
that the Two Testaments are not
opposed to each other, because the
first saying is found in Solomon and
the other in the Gospel? Listen to
the Apostle. And the Apostle is
beyond doubt a minister of the New
Testament. Listen then to Paul the
Apostle speaking to Timothy, and
instructing him: *Them that sin
reprove before all: that the rest also may
have fear* (I. v. 20). The Book of
Solomon seems to disagree now,
not with the Gospel, but with
the Epistle of Paul the Apostle. Let
us without discourtesy put Solomon aside for a moment, and let us
pay attention to the Lord Christ and
to His servant Paul.

What sayest thou, O Lord? *If
thy brother shall offend against thee, go,
and rebuke him between thee and him
alone.* What sayest thou, O Apostle?
*Them that sin reprove before all: that
the rest also may have fear.* What are
we doing; are we listening to this
debate as though we were judges?
Far from it. Rather as subject to
judgement, let us knock, let us seek
to obtain that this door may be
opened to us. Let us fly under the
wings of the Lord our God, for He
has not spoken against His own
Apostle, because He it is has spoken
in him, as the Apostle says: *Do you
seek a proof of Christ that speaketh in
me* (II Cor. xiii. 3)? Christ is in the
Gospel, Christ is in the Apostle;
Christ therefore has said both things:
one by His own mouth, the other
by the mouth of His Herald. For
when a herald announces something
from the tribunal, it is not inscribed
in the records that the herald said

this; but it is written that he said it who told the herald what to say.

VI—9. *Correction should sometimes be secret, sometimes public.* Let us pay heed to these precepts, Brethren, that we may understand them; and let us put our minds at rest with regard to both of them. Let us be of one heart within ourselves, and Holy Scripture will nowhere contradict itself. It is wholly true; and each is right, but now we do one thing, now another. Sometimes a brother is to be rebuked between thee and him alone; sometimes rebuked before all: *that the rest also may have fear.* If we sometimes do the one, and sometimes the other, we shall preserve the concord of the Scriptures; and in fulfilling them, and in obeying them, we shall not err. But someone will say to me: When shall I do one thing, and when the other, so that I shall not rebuke someone between me and him alone, when I ought to rebuke him before all; or reprove him before all, when I ought to reprove him in secret?

VII—10. *When the rebuke should be secret, when public.* Your Charity will quickly perceive when and what we should do: would that we may not be slow to do it! Attend carefully and learn. *If thy brother,* He says, *shall offend against thee, go, and rebuke him between thee and him alone.* Why? Because he has sinned *against thee.* What does that mean: he has sinned *against thee?* You alone know he has sinned. When it is not known that he sinned against you, seek for a secret place when you correct him who sinned against you. For if you alone know he has

offended you, and you wish to reprove him before all, you are not his corrector but his betrayer.

Recall to mind how that *just man* Joseph spared his wife with such tenderness, and this in regard to the crime he had suspected her of before he knew whence she had conceived; for he had perceived she was with child, and he knew he had not approached her. So there remained a lawful suspicion of adultery; and yet because he alone had seen this, he alone knew, what does the Gospel relate of him? *But Joseph being a just man, and not willing to expose her* (Mt. i. 19). The grief of a husband desired no revenge; he wished to be of help to the sinner, not to punish her. *Not willing to expose her, he was minded to put her away privately.* And while he reflected on this, behold an angel of the Lord appeared to him in his sleep, and showed him what this meant, that she had not violated her husband's bed, because she had conceived of the Holy Ghost the Lord of them both.

If your brother therefore has sinned against you; if you alone know this, then in truth he has sinned against you alone. For had he injured you in the presence of many, he would also have sinned against those he made witness of his evil doing. For I shall tell you, most Dearly beloved brethren, something you may well know from your own hearts. When in my hearing someone does injury to my brother, far be it from me to think that this injury is no concern of mine. For he did it to me also; rather he did more to me, had he thought to please me in what he did. And so those faults should be corrected before all, which have been committed before all; and those must be corrected in secret which were committed in secret. Choose the times, and the Scripture will then be in agreement.

VIII—11. *The Manner of correction. Sins of the flesh are deadly.* So must we act, and so let us act; not alone when someone sins against us, but whenever it is not known that another has sinned. We should argue with him in secret, correct him in secret; lest accusing him in public we betray the man. We wish to rebuke him and to reform him; what if an enemy wants to know about it, to have revenge on him? Suppose that a bishop knows that someone is a murderer, and no one else knows of it. I wish to rebuke him; but you wish to indict him. I shall neither betray him, nor disregard him; I shall rebuke him in secret. I shall place before his eyes the judgement of God. I shall terrify his blood-stained conscience. I shall move him to repentance. We should be filled with this charity. On this account men sometimes complain of us, because we do not rebuke; or because they think we know what we do not know, or because they think we hide what we know. But perhaps what I know you know also. But I shall not correct him in your presence; for my desire is to correct him, not to denounce him.

There are men who commit adultery in their own homes; they sin in secret. Sometimes they are betrayed to us by their wives; generally from jealousy, but sometimes out of anxiety for the salvation of their husbands. We do not make this publicly known; but we censure them in private. Where the evil happens let the evil die. Neverthe-

less we do not treat this wound with indifference, but strive above all to show the man who is living in such sin, and bearing about with him a wounded conscience, that this wound is a mortal one: which they sometimes think little of who commit this sin; from what perversity I know not. And they bring together all kinds of empty foolish arguments to show that God does not take much notice of the sins of the flesh.[8] What then becomes of the words we heard today: *Fornicators and adulterers God will judge* (Heb. xiii. 4)? Let him beware who is afflicted with such an injury. Hear what God says; not what your own mind, indulgent to its own sins, may say to you, or what your friend, your enemy rather, bound with you to the same chain of evil doing, will tell you. Hear then what the Apostle says: *Marriage honourable in all, and the bed undefiled. For fornicators and adulterers God will judge.*

IX—12. *Life must be quickly amended.* Come then, Brethren, be reformed in your life! You dread lest an enemy should bring you before a court; and you have no fear that God will judge you? Where is your faith? Fear while you have time to fear. The Day of Judgement is indeed far off; but the last day of every individual man cannot be far away: for life is short. And since even this brief span is uncertain, you know not when your last day will be.

Because of tomorrow correct your life today. Let the reproof in secret profit you now. I speak openly, but I am rebuking you in secret. I knock at the ears of all; but I address myself to the consciences of some in particular. Were I to say,

You, adulterer, mend your ways, I would in the first place say what I did not know, or maybe only suspect from something chance heard. But I do not say, You, adulterer, mend your ways; but what I do say is this: Let each one of you in this congregation who is an adulterer mend his ways. The rebuke is public; amendment is in secret. He who fears God will, I know, amend his life.

X—13. *Sins of the flesh are not to be regarded lightly.*

Let no one say in his heart: God does not concern himself with the sins of the flesh. *Know you not,* says the Apostle, *that you are the temple of God, and that the Spirit of God dwelleth in you? But if any man violate the temple of God, him shall God destroy* (I Cor. iii. 16, 17). Let no man deceive himself. It may be that someone will say: My soul is the temple of God, but not my body; and he will bring forward this testimony: *All flesh is as grass, and all the glory thereof as the flower of grass* (I Pet. i. 24). Unhappy interpretation! Notion that deserves to be punished. Flesh is called grass because it dies; but let not that which dies in time rise again to accuse you! Would you like to hear a clear decision on this also? *Know you not,* says the Apostle, *that your members are the temple of the Holy Ghost, who is in you, whom you have from God?* (I Cor. vi. 19). Do not now think lightly of the sins of the flesh; for see that, *your members are the temple of the Holy Ghost who is in you, whom you have from God.*

If you have been thinking lightly of carnal sin, do you think lightly of the profanation of a temple? Your own body within you is a temple of God. Take care then what you make of a temple of God. What could be more wicked than that you should choose to commit adultery within these walls? But you are now yourself a temple of God. Going in you are a temple, going out you are a temple; you pass the night a temple, you rise at day a temple. Take care then of what you are doing. Beware lest you offend Him Who dwells in that temple, lest He abandon you, and you then fall to ruin. *Know you not,* he says, *that your bodies* (and in this the Apostle was speaking of fornication, lest they should think lightly of the sins of the body) *are the temple of the Holy Ghost, who is in you, whom you have from God: and you are not your own? For you are bought with a great price.* If you think little of your own body, reflect upon the price that was paid for you.

XI—14. *Amendment not to be put off. The Voice of the Crow. Men desire all goods save Life.*

I have come to know, and with me so will any man who has reflected even a little, that there is no man who fears God who will not amend his life at His word, unless the man who thinks he has a longer time to live. It is this brings death to so many, as they keep saying, 'tomorrow, tomorrow' (*crās, crās*); and of a sudden the door is closed. He remains without, with his raven's croak,[9] because his voice was not the grieving voice of the dove. Tomorrow, tomorrow (*Crās, crās*): the voice of the raven. Mourn like the dove, and beat your breast; but as you beat your breast, let what you beat amend itself, lest you seem not so much to be beating your conscience as ramming it hard with blows; making a bad conscience more unyielding instead of more obedient. Mourn, but not in fruitless grieving.

It may be that you say to yourself: God has promised me forgiveness, whenever I reform; so I am safe. I read in the Holy Scriptures: *If the wicked do penance for his sins which he hath committed, and shall do justice, I will not remember all his iniquities* (Ezech. xviii. 21, 22). I am safe; tomorrow, when I amend my life, God will pardon me my sins. And what am I to say? Am I to cry out against God? Am I to say to God: Do *not* give him pardon? Am I to say that this is *not* written in the Scriptures, that God has *not* made this promise? If I were to say that, I would say what was false. You are right; what you say is true. That God has promised you pardon when you amend your life, I cannot deny. But tell me, pray: I agree and I grant you and I know that God has promised you forgiveness. But who has promised you tomorrow? Where you read that you will receive forgiveness, when you do penance, read for me also how much longer you have to live. It is not there, you say. Therefore you do *not* know how long more you have to live. Then reform your life, and be always prepared.

Do not live in fear of the last day, as though it were a thief coming to wreck your house while you sleep; but keep watch, and amend your life this day. Why put it off till tomorrow? If your life is to be long, let it be happy as well as long. No one puts off a good long dinner; and you would like a long evil life! If it is to be long, it will be all the better for being good. If it is to be short, it is as well that its fruits should last. Men so neglect their own life that,

in it, they will have nothing bad except the life itself. You buy a house, you look for a good one. You marry a wife, you choose a good one. You desire children, and you hope they will be good. You buy shoes, and you will not have bad ones. But you love a bad life! What has life done to you that you will only have it bad; that among all the good things that are yours, your life alone is bad?

XII—15. *The Duty of the Pastor not to be put aside.* And so, Brethren, should I wish to correct one among you in private, it may be that he will listen to me. In public I correct many among you. All approve; would that some might do as I say! I do not care for the man who approves of me with his voice, and scorns me in his heart. For when you approve of what I say, and yet do not amend your life, you are a witness against yourself. If your life is bad, and what I say pleases you, then be displeased with yourself; because if your life is bad, and you are displeased with it, once you amend it you will be pleased with yourself; as, if I mistake not, I said the day before yesterday.

In all that I am saying to you now, I am but placing a mirror before you. These are not my words. I speak to you only at the command of the Lord; for fear of Whom I dare not be silent. Who would not rather be silent, and not have to render an account because of you? But we have already assumed a burthen which we cannot, and ought not, throw off our shoulders. When the Epistle to the Hebrews was being read, my brethren, you heard these words: *Obey your pre-*

lates, and be subject to them. For they watch as being to render an account of your souls; that they may do this with joy, and not with grief. For this is not expedient for you (xiii. 17).

When do we do this with joy? When we see men draw fruit from God's words. When does the labourer work *with joy* in his field? When he looks at the tree, and sees the fruit; when he looks at his crop, and looks forward to an abundant yield on the threshing floor; when he has not laboured in vain, nor bent his back in vain, nor worn his hands in fruitless toil, nor borne in vain both heat and cold. It is for this he says: *That they may do this with joy, and not with grief; For this is not expedient for you.* Did he say, Not profitable for them? No; he said: *Not expedient for you.* For when those

placed over you are saddened by your wickedness it is profitable to them; their sadness is profitable to them; but it is not expedient for you. It is our desire that nothing shall profit us that does not profit you. Let us then, brethren, labour together in doing good in God's field; that together we may enjoy His reward.

Turning then to the Lord our God, the Father Almighty, let us, as best we can, give thanks with all our hearts, beseeching Him that in His goodness He will in mercy hear our prayers, and by His grace drive evil from our thoughts and actions, increase our faith, guide our minds, grant us His holy inspirations, and bring us to joy without end, through His Son our Lord and Saviour Jesus Christ. Amen.

NOTES

[1] The meaning of this passage in the *Catena Aurea* appears somewhat indecisive or uncertain. The saintly writer later makes the same point more clearly in his *Exposition in Ps. cxviii*, Ch. 10, par. 31. Here the text says: 'Let him judge who does not do what he judges must be punished in another; lest, while judging the other, he passes sentence on himself.' The meaning in this citation in the *Catena Aurea*, which corresponds to the text in Migne (PG 15, col. 1658), seems to call for *on oneself*, not for *on another*; namely: that you should not rashly judge lest, when conscious of this offence yourself, you are (by the fact of your rash judgement, together with the fact of the sin in your conscience) thereby compelled

to give sentence on yourself—a *seipsum* for *alterum*.

[2] PL 15. This homily is made up of an opening paragraph from the saint's Book Von Lk. lxxviii–lxxx, and paragraphs 31–42 of his *Exposition in Ps. cxviii*, Ch. 20.

[3] From this point to the end the homily is taken from the *Exposition in Ps. cxviii*.

[4] PG 57. Homily 24 in Matthew.

[5] PL 38, Sermo 82.

[6] Cf. St Hilary of Poitiers, PL 9, Comment. in Mt., Ch. 18, par. 8: 'Those he has bound on earth, that is, those he has left entangled in the bonds of their sins, and those he has loosed, that is, received unto salvation by granting them forgiveness.'

⁷ Prov. x. 10, Septuagint Version. The Vulgate has for the second part of the sentence: *And the foolish in lips shall be beaten.*

⁸ Cf. Easter sermon, Vol. II, page 225, II.

⁹ Cf. Easter sermon, Vol. II, page 227, IV.

CORPUS CHRISTI

THE GOSPEL OF THE FEAST

John vi. 56–9

At that time: Jesus said to the multitude of the Jews: My flesh is meat indeed: and my blood is drink indeed. He that eateth my flesh, and drinketh my blood, abideth in me, and I in him. As the living Father hath sent me, and I live by the Father; so he that eateth me, the same also shall live by me. This is the bread that came down from heaven. Not as your fathers did eat manna, and are dead. He that eateth this bread, shall live for ever.

Exposition from the Catena Aurea

V. 56. *For my flesh is meat indeed: and my blood is drink indeed.*

Bede *in John*: He had just said: *He that eateth my flesh, and drinketh my blood, hath everlasting life*, and that He might reveal to them how great was the distance between bodily food and drink and the spiritual mystery of His Body and Blood, He goes on to say: *For my flesh is meat . . .*

Chrysostom, *Hom.* 46 *in John*: He said this, either that they might believe what had been said (that is, that they might not think it an enigma or some riddle, but that they might know that it was wholly necessary to eat the Body of Christ) or, He desired to tell them that the true food is This Which has power to save the soul.

Augustine, *Tr.* 26 *in John*: Or again: As to food and drink, men seek it that they may not hunger or thirst, but this that Food alone truly causes which makes them both immortal and incorruptible: that is, the society of the Blessed, where there is peace in full and perfect unity. For this reason our Lord has given us His Body and Blood under those appearances which are made into one thing from many. For bread is something made from a number of grains of wheat. Wine something else, which flows forth from the juice of many grapes. Then He explains what it means to eat His Body and drink His Blood, saying:

V. 57. *He that eateth my flesh, and drinketh my blood, hath . . .*

This it is therefore to eat this Food and drink this Drink: To abide in Christ, and to have Christ within us. And in consequence, he who does not dwell in Christ, and in whom Christ does not dwell, beyond any doubt neither eats His Flesh nor drinks His Blood; rather he eats the Sacrament (i.e. the Sacred Elements) of This so great Thing unto his own condemnation.

Chrysostom: Or again: Because He had promised life everlasting to those who ate Him, as it were confirming this promise He says: *He that eateth my flesh etc.*

Augustine, *Serm.* 11: There are many who eat This Bread and drink This Wine with a wicked heart, or, when they have eaten it become apostates; do they abide in Christ, and Christ in them? But there is a certain perfect way of eating This Bread and of drinking This Blood, so that he who has eaten and he who has drunk abides in Christ and Christ in him.

Augustine, *City of God*, 21, 27: As they observe who eat the Body of Christ and drink the Blood of Christ, not alone in the Sacrament, but in reality.

V. 58. *As the living Father hath sent me, and I live by the Father.*

Chrysostom: Since I live, it is plain he too will live. And to make this clear He adds: *As the living Father hath sent me, and I live by the Father, so he that eateth me, the same also shall live by me.* As though to say: As the Father lives, so do I. And lest He should appear as Unbegotten He adds: *By the Father*; conveying that the Father is His beginning. That He goes on to say: *So he that eateth me, the same also shall live by me*, does not refer to life in the simple sense, but that Life which has been commended to us. For even unbelievers live; though not eating of This Flesh. Neither is He referring to the general resurrection of the dead; for all will rise from the dead. He is speaking of that glorious resurrection which is a reward.

AUGUSTINE, *Tr. 26 in John*: But He does not say: As I eat of the Father, and so live by the Father, so he who eats Me, the same also shall live by Me. For the Son is not made more perfect by partaking of the Father, as we are made better by partaking of the Son: through the unity of His Body and Blood, which this eating and drinking signifies. If then He does say, *I live by the Father*: since He is from Him: it is said without prejudice to His equality with Him. Neither does this mean that our equality with Him is the same as His with the Father. He is simply revealing to us His state as Mediator.

But if we take the words, *I live by the Father*, in the light of what He says elsewhere: *The Father is greater than I* (Jn. xiv. 28), He spoke the words: *As the living Father hath sent me*, as though saying: That I live by the Father, that is, refer my life to Him as to My Superior, is brought about by My emptying of Myself, My being sent. That anyone should *live by Me*, is brought about by that partaking in which he eats of Me.

HILARY, *The Trinity VIII*, 14: Of the truth of the Body and Blood of Christ there remains no grounds for doubt. For we have now, first the declaration [*words*][1] of the Lord Himself, and then our faith [*the Church's teaching*], that it is truly Flesh and truly Blood. [He therefore lives by the Father, and as He lives by the Father, so do we live by His Flesh.] He then is the cause of our Life: that we have Christ abiding in us, by means of His Flesh, while we are ourselves in the flesh; and that we shall live by Him in the same way as He lives by the Father. If we therefore live by Him in a manner which accords with our nature; that is, partaking of Him according to the flesh, does He not then, since He lives by the Father, dwell in Him in a natural manner according to the spiritual nature? He lives by the Father since His Birth did not bring Him a strange or different nature.

AUGUSTINE, *Tr. 26 in John*: That we who of ourselves cannot have life eternal may Live, by eating this Bread, He came down from heaven. Hence we have:

V. 59. *This is the bread that came down from heaven. Not as . . .*

HILARY, 10, 1: Here He calls Himself Bread: for He is the source of His own Body. And lest we should think that the power and the nature of the Word have left Him, and dissolved into flesh, He said the Bread is His own Flesh; that by this, the Bread coming down from heaven, it might be known that the source of the Body was not a human conception; since He reveals that it is a heavenly Body. To say the Bread is *His*, is a declaration of the taking of a body by the Word.

THEOPHYLACTUS: For we do not simply eat God: since He is incorporeal and impalpable; and neither do we simply eat the flesh of a man: which would profit us nothing. But since God joined flesh to Himself, This Flesh becomes Life-giving; not that it changes us into the nature of God, but that just as heated iron remains iron yet gives forth heat, so the Flesh of the Lord is Life giving, as the Flesh of the Word of God.

BEDE: And to show how far apart are the Shadow and the Light, the Figure and the Reality, He adds: *Not as your fathers did eat manna, and are dead. He that eateth this bread, shall live for ever.*

AUGUSTINE, *Tr. 26 in John*: That they *are dead* must be understood to mean that they have not *Life everlasting*;

for even they who eat Christ in this life will suffer death: but they *shall live for ever*: because Christ is Life Eternal.

CHRYSOSTOM: For if it was possible to preserve the life of the Israelites for forty years in the desert, without harvests, without grain, much more can He do this by means of Spiritual Food: of which these other foods were but the Figures. He repeats often this promise of Life; knowing that nothing is more desired by men. For this reason He was wont in the Old Testament to promise men long life. Here he promises Life without end. He wishes to reveal to them, at the same time, that He has now undone the sentence that imposed death on us, and that in its place He gives us the promise of everlasting life.

I. ST JUSTIN MARTYR

The Faith of Christians[2]

1. *Administration of the Sacraments.* It is our practice that, after we have baptized the one who has become convinced, and has assented to our teaching, to bring him to where those who are called the *brethren* are assembled, that we may offer common prayers, both for ourselves and for the one who has been enlightened, and for all others everywhere, that because of this grace also we may be accounted worthy, now that we have attained to the Truth, by good works, by living a just life, and as keepers of the divine commandments, to attain to eternal salvation. When the prayers are ended we salute each other with a kiss.[3] Then bread, and a cup of wine, mingled with water, is brought to

the one presiding over the brethren, and he, taking them, gives praise and glory to the Father of all things, together with the Son and the Holy Ghost, and also offers prolonged thanks on behalf of those who are found worthy to receive these Gifts at his hands.

And when the prayers and thanksgiving come to an end all the people present express their assent by saying, *Amen.* This word *Amen* corresponds in the Hebrew language to, *be it so.*[4] And when the President has given thanks, and all the people have expressed their assent, those who are called by us *deacons* give to each one present to partake of the bread and wine mixed with water over which thanks had been pronounced, and to those who are absent they carry a portion.

2. *The Eucharist.*

And among us this food is called the Eucharist; of which no one is allowed to partake but the one who believes that the things we teach are true, and who has also been washed with the washing that is for the forgiveness of sins, and unto regeneration, and who is living as Christ has taught us. For not as common bread and common drink do we receive these; but as Jesus Christ our Saviour, made Flesh by the Word of God, took flesh and blood for our salvation, so likewise have we been taught, that the food which is consecrated by the prayer of His words, and by which our own flesh and blood by transmutation is nourished, is the Flesh and Blood of that Jesus Who became Flesh and Blood.

For the Apostles, in the Memories composed by them, and which are called Gospels, have thus delivered to us what Jesus delivered to them: That Jesus took bread, and, when He had given thanks, said, *This do ye in remembrance of me, this is my body* (Lk. xxii. 19). And that in the same manner, having taken the chalice, and given thanks, He said, *This is my blood*; and He gave it them only. And this the evil demons have imitated in the rites of Mithras, commanding that the same things be done. For that bread and a cup of water, together with certain words, have been added to their rites of initiation you either already know or can learn.

3. *Their common charity.*

And from then on we continually remind each other of these things. And the wealthy among us help those who are in need. And we always keep together. And for all that we receive we bless the Maker of all things, through His Son Jesus Christ, and the Holy Spirit. And on the day called Sunday all who live in cities or in the country come together at one place, and the Memories of the Apostles, or the writings of the Prophets, are read, for as long as time permits. Then when the Reader has ceased he who presides instructs us by word and exhorts us to the imitation of these beautiful things. Then we rise together and pray, and, as we said before, when our prayer is ended, bread and wine is brought, and he who presides, with all fervour, offers up prayers and thanksgiving, and the people present say, *Amen.* And then there is a distribution to each one, and a partaking of That over which thanks have been given, and to those who are absent a portion is sent by the deacons.

And they who have wealth, and are of good will, give what each one thinks fit, and what is collected is deposited with the one who presides, who cares for widows and orphans and those who through sickness or any other cause are in want, and for those who are in prison, and for strangers sojourning amongst us, and in a word takes care of all who are in need.

Sunday is the day on which we all hold our common meeting, because it is the First Day, upon which God, banishing darkness from the primal matter, created the world. And on the same day Jesus Christ arose from the dead. For He was crucified on the day before that of Saturn (Saturday), and on the day after Saturday, which is the day of the Sun, appearing to His Apostles and Disciples, He taught them those truths which we have now delivered to you for your consideration.

II. St Justin Martyr

The Figure of the Lamb[5]

The mystery of the lamb which God commanded should be sacrificed at the Passover was a Figure of Christ, with Whose Blood, in accord with their faith in His word, they who believe in Him anoint their houses, that is, themselves: for that that creature whom God made, namely Adam, was created as a house for the Spirit that proceeds from God you can all also understand. But that this command was given only for a time I shall prove to you.

God did not permit that the lamb of the Passover should be sacrificed in any other place than where His Name was named: knowing that the days would come, after the Passion of Christ, in which the City of Jerusalem would be delivered up to your enemies, and all your sacrifices would come to an end. And this lamb which was commanded to be roasted whole was a symbol of the suffering on the Cross which Christ was to undergo. For the lamb which is eaten is dressed and roasted in the form of a cross: one spit is transfixed right through from the lower part to the head, and one across the back, to which the forelegs of the lamb are attached.

And the two goats, which it was commanded should be offered during the fast, of which one was sent into the desert bearing as it were others' sins upon it (*scapegoat*), and the other sacrificed, were also Figures of the twofold appearances of Christ: The first, in which the Elders of your people, and the priests, having laid hands on Him, and put Him to death, sent Him away bearing their sins upon Him. The other, when in the same place, in Jerusalem, you would look upon Him Whom you had dishonoured, and Who was an Offering for all sinners who wish to repent of their sins, and who observe the fast of which Isaias speaks, undoing the bonds of oppressive obligations, and observing all the other good counsels he mentions (lviii. 5) and which, as I have said elsewhere,[6] are observed by those who believe in Jesus.

The offering of fine flour was a figure of the Eucharist. And the offering of fine flour (Lev. xiv. 10, 21), which, as I said elsewhere, was prescribed to be offered by those who were purified from leprosy, was also a Figure of the Eucharistic Bread Which Our Lord Jesus Christ prescribed should be eaten in memory of His passion by those whose souls are purified from all iniquity, that we may at the same time thank God for having created the world, with all that is in it, for man's benefit, for delivering us from the evil in which we were held fast, and for casting down to nothing the Principalities and Powers, through Him Who of His own will became subject to suffering.

For this same reason God, by the mouth of Malachy, one of the twelve Prophets, as I said before (par. 28) says of the sacrifices which were then offered by your people: *I have no pleasure in you, saith the Lord of hosts: and I will not receive a gift of your hand. For from the rising of the sun even to the going down, my name is great among the Gentiles, and in every place there is sacrifice, and there is offered to my name a clean oblation: for my name is great among the Gentiles, saith the Lord of hosts. But you have profaned it* (i. 10–12).

So does He there foretell us of the Gentiles, who in every place offer sacrifices to Him: the Sacrifice, namely, of the Eucharistic Bread, and of the Eucharistic Cup, foretelling also that His Name is glorified among us, but that you profane it.

III. St Irenaeus, Bishop and Martyr

The Eucharist in Prophecy[7]

From the witness of the Old Testament[8] it is made plain to us, that God was not seeking from men sacrifices and burnt offerings, but faith and obedience, and living in justice and truth that they may be saved. So God, speaking by the mouth of the prophet Osee, teaches them His will, saying to them: *I desire mercy, and not sacrifice: and the knowledge of God more than holocausts* (vi. 6). And the Lord taught them the same when He said: *And if you knew what this meaneth:* I will have mercy and not sacrifice: *you would never have condemned the innocent* (Mt. xii. 7); giving testimony to the prophets by these words, that they had been preaching the truth, and reproving those for their evil doing who had acted foolishly.

And when instructing His own Disciples, that they should offer Firstfruits to God from the things He has created, and that they were not to offer them as to one who needed them, and that neither should they so offer that they themselves become fruitless and ungrateful, He took that creature which is bread, and, giving thanks, He said: *This is my body* (Mt. xxvi. 26). And in like manner He declared that the chalice,

which is from that creation of which we also are a part, was His Blood; teaching us also that it was the New Oblation of the New Testament, which the Church, receiving It from the Apostles, offers to God throughout the whole world; offering to Him who gives us our food the Firstfruits of His own gifts to us in the new covenant between God and man. Of this sacrifice Malachy, one of twelve prophets, foretold: *I have no pleasure in you, saith the Omnipotent God, and I will not receive sacrifice from your hands. For from the rising of the sun to its going down my name is glorified among the Gentiles, and in every place incense is offered to my name, and a pure sacrifice; for great is my name among the Gentiles, saith the Lord Almighty* (i. 10, 11), clearly foreshadowing by these words that His former people will cease to offer sacrifice to God; but that in every place a Sacrifice will be offered Him, and this a Pure Sacrifice; and that among the Gentiles His Name will be glorified.

What other name is there that is glorified among the Gentiles but that of Our Lord, through Whom God is glorified, and man is glorified? And since it is His Son's Name, and

He was made man by Him, He therefore calls it His. As a king who had painted the likeness of his son might say it was his own likeness, and for two reasons: since it is of his son, and he made it, so also does the Father say that the name of Jesus, which is glorified in the Church throughout all the world, is His name, since it is the name of His Son, and writing it down He gave it for the salvation of men. Since the name of the Son is the name of the Father, and the Church offers sacrifice to the Omnipotent God through Jesus Christ, rightly does He say of both: *And in every place incense is offered in my name, and a pure sacrifice.* And John, in the Apocalypse, says that *incense is, the prayers of saints* (v. 8).

In the Catholic Church alone is the True and Pure Sacrifice to be offered; in justice and simplicity of heart; namely, the Eucharist, Which is the very Body and Blood of Christ.

And so the Oblation of the Church, Which the Lord has taught us is to be offered throughout the whole world, is held by God to be a pure sacrifice, and acceptable to Him: not because He needs sacrifice from us, but because he who offers it is glorified in that which he offers, if his offering is accepted. For love and honour are shown to a king through a gift. As the Lord wills that we offer sacrifice with true faith and a clean heart, He declared to us: *If therefore thou offer thy gift at the altar, and there thou remember that thy brother hath anything against thee; leave there thy offering before the altar, and go first to be reconciled to thy brother; and then coming thou shalt offer thy gift* (Mt. v. 23, 24).

We are therefore to offer to God the firstfruits of His creation, as Moses tells us: *No one shall appear before the Lord with empty hands* (Deut. xvi. 16); so that in the things with which man is blessed he may be held as blessed in them, and receive the reward that is from God.

But the whole order of oblations has not been changed. For there are offerings for this occasion, and offerings for that; sacrifices among the people, sacrifices in the Church. Only the appearance is changed: since it is now offered not by slaves, but by children. One and the same however is the Lord; but one is the sacrifice of slaves, and another the sacrifice of free men; so that even by our offerings is our freedom made known. With God there is nothing without purpose, nothing without a sign, nothing without proof. And because of this the Jews dedicated tithes of their goods to Him. But they who have received freedom have set aside all that is theirs for the Lord's purposes; giving joyfully and freely, and not a small part: for they have the hope of greater things. Such was she who though poor and a widow cast all that she had into the treasury of God.

It is not therefore sacrifices which sanctify a man; for God has no need of your sacrifices. It is the pure conscience of the offerer that sanctifies the sacrifice. Since it is pure it moves God to accept your sacrifice, as though from a friend. *But a sinner,* He says, *who sacrifices a calf, is to me as though he had slain a dog* (Is. lxvi. 3). Since therefore it is in simplicity of soul that the Church offers sacrifice, rightly does God look on Her offering as a *Pure Sacrifice.* As Paul says to the Philippians: *I am filled, having received from Epaphroditus the things you sent, an odour of sweetness, an acceptable sacrifice, pleasing to God* (iv. 18).

We must therefore offer ourselves as an offering to God, and in all things be found pleasing to God our Maker, with an upright heart, with sincere faith, well grounded in hope, fervent in charity, offering Him the firstfruits of His own creation. This Pure Oblation the Church alone offers to the Creator; offering it to Him from His own creation, with giving of thanks. This the Jews do not offer: for *their hands are full of blood* (Is. i. 2, 15); for they would not receive the Word Which is offered to God. And neither do all the synagogues of the heretics. For some of them, by declaring that the Father is different from the Maker of the world, and so, sacrificing to Him what belongs to this creation of ours, they exhibit Him as seeking what is another's right, desiring what is not his own. How can it appear to them that this bread, over which thanks have been given, is the Body of their Lord, and the chalice His

Blood, if they say He is not the Son of the Creator of the world; that is, His Word, through Whom the tree bears fruit, the fountains spring up, *and the earth itself bringeth forth, first the blade, then the ear, and afterwards the full corn in the ear* (Mk. iv. 28)?

And how again can they say that the flesh which is nourished with the Body of the Lord, and with His Blood, will go down to corruption [not to rise again], and not partake of eternal life? Let them change their beliefs, or cease from offering what we have spoken of. Our own thought is in harmony with the Eucharist, and the Eucharist in turn establishes our belief. For we offer to Him what is His, correctly proclaiming the fellowship and union of body and spirit. For as the bread which is produced from the earth, upon receiving the invocation of God, is now no longer bread, but the Eucharist, consisting of two things, one of the earth and one of heaven, so also our bodies, when they receive the Eucharist, are no longer corruptible, having now the hope of resurrection, unto life eternal.

IV. ST IRENAEUS, BISHOP AND MARTYR

Christ's Blood the Source of our Resurrection[9]

Christ Redeemed us by His Blood. They are false and deceivers who pretend to despise the whole divine covenant between God and man, who deny the salvation of the flesh, and scorn the notion of its return to life, declaring it incapable of immortality. For if this be not saved, then neither has the Lord redeemed us by His Blood, and neither is the chalice of the Eucharist the participation of His Blood, nor is the

Bread Which we break the participation of His Body (cf. I Cor. x. 16). For it is not Blood unless it comes from Flesh, and from veins, and from the rest of man's substance, which the Word of God truly became. By this Blood He redeemed us, as the Apostle also tells us: *In whom we have redemption, through his blood, the remission of sins* (Col. i. 14).

And since we are His members,

and are nourished by what He has created—for it is He who gives us creation, and causes the sun to rise, and sends down the rain as He so wills (Mt. v. 45)—He has declared that this Chalice, which is His creature, is His Blood, by which our own blood is renewed, and that this Bread, Which is His creature, is His Body, by which He makes our own bodies flourish.

When therefore the mingled cup and the bread that is broken, receive the word of God, and become the Eucharist of the Body and Blood of Christ, by Which the substance of our flesh is nourished and made strong, how can they say that that body is incapable of receiving that gift of God, eternal life, which is nourished on the Flesh and Blood of Christ, and a member of His Body? As the blessed Apostle says in his Epistle to the Ephesians: *For we are members of his body, of his flesh, of his bones* (v. 30). He did not say these words of some ghostly disembodied man: *For a spirit hath not flesh and bones, as you see me to have*; but of that arrangement which is in accord with the disposition of a true man, consisting of flesh and of bone and of nerves, which is nourished by the chalice, His Blood, and by the Bread, Which is His Body.

And as the vine tree planted in the earth will in due time yield fruit, and a grain of wheat falling to the ground, and there perishing, will rise again, multiplied by the Spirit of God that sustains all things, then through the Wisdom of God goes on to serve the needs of man, and, receiving the word of God, they both become the Eucharist, Which is the Body and Blood of Christ, so also our bodies, which are nourished by It, are placed in the earth, and dissolve there, shall in due time rise again, the Word of God bestowing on them an awakening unto the glory of God the Father Who freely clothes this mortal body with immortality, and gives to this corruptible flesh incorruptibility (I Cor. xv. 53): for the power of God is made perfect in infirmity (II Cor. xii. 9).

Reflecting on this we shall not as it were be puffed up within ourselves, as though we drew life from ourselves, and not cut ourselves off from God, permitting our minds to become ungrateful. Rather, let us learn from experience, that it is only by His supreme power, and not of our own nature, that we shall endure for ever: lest we fail to attain to the glory that surrounds the Divinity, and fail to come to know even our own nature. Let us seek to know what God can do, what goodness He has shown to man, so that we may not at any time fall into error concerning the relations that exist between God and man. And, as we have said elsewhere, may it not be, that it is for this purpose God permits our dissolution in the earth, that taught in all ways we may in the future know all things clearly, and be not in ignorance either of God or of ourselves? Amen.

V. St Cyprian, Bishop and Martyr

On the Sacrament of the Chalice of the Lord[10]

1. You must know, that we have been clearly taught, that when we offer the chalice we must observe what the Lord has handed down to

us, and that we must do nothing other than what the Lord first did for us, namely: That the chalice, which is offered up in commemoration of Him, is to be offered mingled with wine. For since Christ says, *I am the true wine* (Jn. xv. 1), the blood of Christ is then assuredly not water, but wine. And neither can it be *seen* that His Blood, by which we have been redeemed, and revivified, is in the chalice, when, in the chalice, the wine is missing whereby His Blood is *shown*: as the mystic rite, and the testimony of all the Scriptures, proclaim.

2. For in the Book of Genesis (ix. 21), where it relates the mystery of Noah, we find this same thing there foreshadowed, standing as a Figure of the Lord's Passion: that he drank wine and was inebriated, that he was uncovered in his own house, that he lay with his thighs naked and exposed, that the nakedness of his father was discovered by his second son and told of outside, but that it was covered by his two sons, his eldest and his youngest, and the other details about which we need not continue, since this alone suffices to complete what we are saying, that Noah, standing as a Figure of the Truth to come, drank, not water, but wine, and in this way placed before us a symbol of the Lord's Passion.

3. Again, in the High Priest Melchisedech (xiv. 18), we have another Figure of the mystery of the Lord's sacrifice, as divine Scripture testifies, where it says: *And Melchisedech the king of Salem brought forth bread and wine.* He was the Priest of the Most High God, and he blessed Abraham.

And that Melchisedech was a Figure of Christ the Holy Ghost reveals in the psalms, speaking as from the Father to the Son: *Before the day star I begot thee. Thou art a priest for ever according to the order of Melchisedech* (cix. 4, 5). This order was assuredly that deriving from this sacrifice, and from there descending to us; and so Melchisedech was the Priest of the Most High God, in that he offered up bread and wine, and in that he blessed Abraham.

For who is more the Priest of the Most High God than Jesus Christ our Lord, Who offered a Sacrifice to God the Father, and offered this same that Melchisedech had offered, namely: Bread and Wine, that is, His own Body and Blood? And the blessing that was given to Abraham has continued on to our Christian people. For if Abraham believed God, *and it was reputed to him unto justice* (Gen. xv. 6), then whoever believes in God, and *lives by faith*, is reputed as just, and long ago was declared to be blessed and justified in the faithful Abraham, as the blessed Apostle Paul makes known to us, saying: *Abraham believed God, and it was reputed to him unto justice.* Know ye therefore, that they who are of the faith, they are the children of Abraham. And the Scriptures, foreseeing that God will justify the Gentiles by faith, foretold to Abraham that in him all nations would be blessed (Gal. iii. 6–8).

Because of this we find in the Gospel, that the children of Abraham are raised up from stones, that is, they are gathered in from the Gentiles (Mt. iii. 9). And when the Lord praised Zacheus, He declared that, *this day is salvation come to this house, because he also is a son of*

Abraham (Lk. xix. 9). Therefore, that the blessing of Abraham by the Priest Melchisedech in Genesis might be rightly imparted, there preceded it the Figure of Christ's Sacrifice, composed of bread and wine. And the Lord, perfecting and bringing this Figure to fulfilment, offered bread, and the chalice mingled from wine. And He Who is the Fulness of Truth fulfilled the image of the truth that had been prefigured.

4. And the Holy Spirit also made known beforehand, through Solomon, a Figure of the Lord's Sacrifice: speaking of a slain victim, and of bread and wine, and of an altar, and of the Apostles. *Wisdom hath built herself a house*, He says, *she hath hewn her out seven pillars. She hath slain her victims, mingled her wine, and set forth her table. She hath sent her maids to invite to the tower, and to the walls of the city: Whosoever is a little one, let him come to me. And to the unwise she said: Come, eat my bread, and drink the wine which I have mingled for you* (Prov. ix. 1). He makes clear to us that it is mingled wine; that is, with prophetic voice He foretells that the chalice of the Lord shall be mingled of wine and water, so that it might be seen that what had been foretold had come to pass in the Lord's Passion.

5. This is also signified in the blessing of Juda, where here again a Figure of Christ is put before us: that He should receive praise and adoration from His brethren, that He would bend down the necks of His enemies, who would yield and fly before Him, that He would do this with the hands by which He bore the Cross, and conquered death, that He is the Lion of the Tribe of Juda, and would be the hope of the Gentiles. To this the divine Scripture adds, and says: *He shall wash his robe in wine, and his garment in the blood of the grapes* (Gen. xlix. 8–11). And when the blood of the grape is spoken of, what is it He is revealing to us but the wine of the Chalice of the Lord's Blood?

6. And again in the Book of Isaias, the Holy Spirit testifies to the same thing with regard to the Lord's Passion, saying: *Why then is thy apparel red, and thy garments like theirs that tread in the winepress?* (lxiii. 2). Can water make garments red? And is it water that is treaded with the feet, or pressed out with the wine-press? The reference undoubtedly is to wine, and it is introduced so that by the wine the Blood of the Lord might be understood; and so that what was afterwards made visible in the Chalice of the Lord, might be foretold by the heralding voices of the prophets. The treading of the grapes and the pressure of the wine press is also spoken of, for as we cannot have wine to drink unless the grape be treaded and pressed out, so neither could we drink the Blood of Christ if Christ had not first been treaded on and crushed, and had not first drunk of the chalice that He would give those who believed in Him to drink.

7. As often as water alone is spoken of in Holy Scripture Baptism is foretold; as we may see pointed out in Isaias. *Remember not*, he says, *former things, and look not on things of old. Behold I do new things, and now*

they shall spring forth, verily you shall know them: I will make a way in the wilderness, and rivers in the desert, to give drink to my people, to my chosen. This people have I formed for myself, they shall show forth my praise (xliii. 18–21). Here God has foretold by His prophet that in later times rivers would flow forth among the Gentiles, in places that before had been waterless, and that they would give water to the chosen children of God, that is, to those who by the rebirth of Baptism have become children of God.

And again it was prophesied and foretold that the Jews, should they thirst for and seek Christ, would be given water to drink among us; that is, they would attain to the grace of Baptism. *If they thirst,* he says, *he shall lead them through deserts, he shall bring forth water out of the rock, the rock shall be cleft, and my people shall drink* (Is. xlviii. 21 Sept.). And this is fulfilled in the Gospel when Christ, Who is the Rock, is cleft by the thrust of a lance in His Passion. And He also, bringing to our minds what had been foretold by the prophet, cries out to us, saying: *If any man thirst, let him come to me, and drink. He that believeth in me, as the Scripture tells, Out of his belly shall flow rivers of running water* (Jn. viii. 37–9).

And that it might be yet more manifest that the Lord is here speaking, not of the chalice, but of Baptism, the Scripture adds this, saying: *Now this he said of the Scripture which they should receive who believed in him: for as yet the Spirit was not given, because Jesus was not yet glorified.* For the Holy Spirit is received by Baptism, and so they who are baptized, and have received the Holy Spirit, may come to the drinking of the Lord's Chalice. And let it disturb no one that when the divine Scripture speaks of Baptism it speaks of us as thirsting and drinking, since in the Gospel the Lord also says: *Blessed are they that hunger and thirst after justice* (Mt. v. 6); because what is received with eager and thirsty desire is drained more copiously and more abundantly. As in another place the Lord speaks to the Samaritan woman, saying: *Whosoever drinketh of this water shall thirst again; but he that shall drink of the water that I shall give him shall not thirst for ever* (Jn. iv. 13). By this the saving waters of Baptism are referred to, which of course is received once, and not repeated again.

8. There is no need of many arguments, Dearly Beloved, to prove that by the naming of water Baptism is always signified, and that we ought to understand it in this way, since the Lord at His Coming has revealed to us the truth of both Baptism and the Chalice, and commanded that the water of faith, the water of eternal life, should be given by Baptism, to those who believe, but by His own example He taught us that we were to mingle the chalice by a union of water and wine.

For on the eve of His Passion, taking the chalice, He blessed it, and gave it to His Disciples, saying: *Drink ye all of this. For this is my blood of the new testament, which shall be shed for many unto remission of sins. And I say to you, I will not drink from henceforth of this fruit of the vine, until that day when I shall drink it with you new in the kingdom of my Father* (Mt. xxvi. 27–9). And here we find that the chalice the Lord offered was mingled, and that He called His own

Blood *wine*. From which it is made clear to us, that the Blood of Christ is not offered up if there was first no wine in the chalice, and that the Lord's Sacrifice is not commemorated by a true consecration if our offering and sacrifice does not correspond to His Passion. For how shall we drink the new wine, the fruit of the vine, with Christ in the kingdom of the Father, if in the Sacrifice of God the Father and of Christ we offer no wine, and do not mingle the Chalice of the Lord in accord with what the Lord has delivered to us?

9. And the blessed Apostle Paul, who was chosen and sent forth by the Lord Himself, and appointed a preacher of the Truth of the Gospel, lays down this same teaching in his epistle, saying to us: *The Lord Jesus, the same night in which he was betrayed, took bread, and giving thanks, broke, and said: Take ye, and eat: This is my body, which shall be delivered for you: This do for the commemoration of me. In like manner also the chalice, after he had supped, saying: This chalice is the new testament: This do ye, as often as you shall drink, for the commemoration of me. For as often as you shall eat this bread, and drink the chalice, you shall shew the death of the Lord, until he come* (I Cor. xi. 23–6). Now if it was delivered to us by the Lord, and this is confirmed and handed on to us by the Apostle, that as often as we shall drink, we shall do in commemoration of the Lord that which the Lord also did, we shall find that we are not doing what was commanded, unless we also do the same as the Lord did; and for this reason when we mingle the chalice let us not depart from the divine teaching.

In another place the blessed Apostle firmly and repeatedly teaches us, that we must never in any way depart from the Gospel precepts, and that these very things which the Master did and taught, the disciples must also do and observe. *I wonder*, he says, *that you are so soon removed from him that called you into the grace of Christ, unto another Gospel. Which is not another, only there are some that trouble you, and would pervert the Gospel of Christ. But though we, or an angel from heaven, preach a Gospel besides that which we have preached to you, let him be anathema. As we have said before, so now I say again: If anyone preach to you a Gospel, besides that which you have received, let him be anathema* (Gal. i).

10. Therefore, since neither the Apostle himself, nor an Angel from heaven, can make known to you or teach anything other than that which Christ taught once and for all and which His Apostles have announced, I wonder greatly from what source has it come that, contrary to the Gospel and to Apostolic practice, in certain places water is offered up in the Lord's chalice, which of itself cannot represent Christ's Blood. Even as to the mystery of this sacrament the Holy Spirit is not silent; making mention in the Psalms of the Lord's chalice, saying: *Thy chalice which inebriates me, how good it is?* (Ps. xxii. 6). Now a chalice which inebriates is assuredly mixed with wine; for water cannot inebriate anyone. And the chalice of the Lord inebriates, as Noah in Genesis was inebriated, drinking wine. But as the inebriety of the Lord's Chalice and Blood is not the inebriety of this earth's wine, when the Holy

Spirit said in the psalm, *Thy chalice which inebriates me*, He added, *how good it is*; because the Lord's Chalice so inebriates those who drink It, that It makes them sober: so that their minds are brought to spiritual wisdom, so that each one turns from the flavour of this world to the understanding of God. And just as the mind is loosened by ordinary wine, and the soul is relaxed, and all care laid aside, so when we have drunk the saving Cup of the Lord's Blood, the memory of the former man in us is put aside, and there comes a forgetfulness of our former worldly way of life, and the breast that was heavy and sad and oppressed by its tormenting sins is set free in the joy of the divine compassion: for if that which he drinks contains the Reality of the Lord, he may then indeed rejoice, drinking *in the midst of the Church of the Lord* (Ps. xxi. 23).

11. How perverse and contradictory it is that we should make water of wine, when the Lord at the wedding feast made wine of water, since even the sacred rite of this action should warn us, and teach us, that in the Lord's Sacrifices we ought rather to offer wine. For as among the Jews there had been a want of spiritual grace, wine was also wanting. For the house of Israel was the Lord's vineyard (Is. v. 7). But Christ, teaching us and making clear to us, that the people of the nations would soon succeed and, because of their faith, take the place the Jews had lost, made wine from water; that is, He shows us, that at the nuptials of Christ and the Church, since the Jews had failed Him, it was rather the people of the Gentiles who would assemble and come to the Wedding.

For the divine Scripture in the Apocalypse declares, that waters stand for peoples, saying: *The waters which thou sawest, where the harlot sitteth, are peoples, and nations, and tongues* (xvii. 15). On which account, manifestly, do we see that it [water] also is contained in the mystery of the Chalice.

12. For as Christ has borne us all, because He bore our sins, we perceive that by the water we are to understand the Christian people, but that by the wine the Blood of Christ is shown. But when in the chalice water is mingled with the wine, the people are united to Christ; the multitude of the believing is joined to, and made one, with Him in Whom they believe. And this joining together and union of water and wine is so blended in the Lord's chalice, that what has been mingled can never be separated again. Because of this there is nothing that can separate the Church from Christ, so that Her undivided love shall endure and hold to Him forever; and by the Church I mean the people in the Church, who faithfully and firmly persevere in that in which they believe.

And so it is that in the consecration of the chalice of the Lord water alone is not to be offered; even as wine alone may not be. For should anyone offer wine only the Blood of Christ begins to be present without us; but if water alone is offered, the people are present without Christ. But when both are mingled and joined one to the other in perfect union, then the heavenly and spiritual mystery is complete. So the chalice of the Lord is not water alone, or wine alone; the one must be mingled with the other; just as the Body of the Lord cannot be from flour alone or water alone, unless the one has been added to the other, and united and made firm in the substance of one bread. And in this mystery our people are also shown as made one; in that, as many grains of wheat gathered together, and ground and mixed, make one bread, so let us learn that in Christ, Who is the Bread of heaven, there is one Body, in which the multitude of us are all united, and make One.

13. There are then, Dearly Beloved, no grounds for thinking that what certain persons put forward should be believed; those who presume to think that water alone is to be offered in the Lord's chalice. We should ask who they are following. For if in the sacrifice Christ offered no one is to be imitated but Christ, we must beyond doubt obey and do what Christ did, and what He commanded to be done; since in the Gospel He tells us: *You are my friends if you do the things that I command you* (Jn. xv. 14). And that only Christ is to be listened to, the Father also testifies from heaven, saying: *This is my beloved Son, in whom I am well pleased: hear ye him* (Mt. xvii. 5).

So if Christ alone is to be listened to, we must pay no attention to what another thinks is to be done, but do what Christ Who is above all first did. We are not to follow after the notions of men, but the truth of God; since God says to us by His prophet Isaias: *In vain do they worship me, teaching the doctrines and the commands of men* (xxix. 13). And in the Gospel He says this same thing: *Making void the word of God by your own tradition, which you have given forth* (Mk. iv.

13). And He lays it down again, in another place, and says: *He therefore that shall break one of these least commandments, and shall so teach men, shall be called the least in the kingdom of heaven* (Mt. v. 19).

And if it is not lawful to undo even the least of the Lord's commandments, how much more is it unlawful to break those that are so grave, so serious, so closely related to the mystery of the Lord's Passion, and to our own Redemption, or to change into something else, because of some human notion, that which has been divinely handed down to us? For if Jesus Christ, our Lord and our God, is Himself the High Priest of God the Father, and has offered Himself in sacrifice to the Father, and has commanded that this be done in commemoration of Him, then that priest truly fulfils the office of Christ who does the same as Christ did; and he then offers to God in the Church the true and perfect sacrifice, when he proceeds to offer it as he sees that Christ Himself has offered it.

It is therefore becoming to our Rule (belief), to holy fear, to the sacred place, and to the office of our priesthood, Dearly Beloved, that we safeguard the truth of the Lord's Tradition when we mingle and offer the chalice of the Lord, and, in accord with the warning of the Lord, correct early among certain people what is seen to be erroneous; so that when He shall arise to come in His heavenly splendour and majesty, He may find that we hold fast to what He told us, observe what he taught us, do what He did, Who with the Father and the Holy Ghost liveth and reigneth world without end. Amen.

VI. St Ephraim, Confessor and Doctor

The Mystery of the Eucharist[11]

You have learned, Dearest Brethren, that God the Father sent His Only-begotten Son into the world for your salvation. Believe this with firm and undoubting faith: for God the Holy speaks only Truth. You have also heard that the Only-begotten Himself took flesh from the womb of the Holy Virgin, that He was truly born of Her, and conceived of the Holy Ghost. Keep these truths within your heart as most certain; and let nothing whatsoever incline you to doubt concerning that of which the Holy Gospel speaks daily to you. Rather let you receive all its teaching with fullest faith; ever contemplating the divine truths with the unclouded eyes of faith. And contemplate the Lord with the eyes of the soul; embracing Him with all your faith. Follow Him whithersoever He goes, and from the great love within your own heart bring light into each single place.

Let your soul rejoice when you behold the Lord, curing *all sick people* by His grace (Mt. iv. 8, 9; Lk. v. 6, 10), and casting out unclean spirits from the possessed, by His divine power and by His word only. Go with Him, as His inseparable companion, to the wedding Feast of Cana, and drink of the wine of His blessing. Let you have ever before you the Face of the Lord, and look upon His beauty, and let your earnest gaze turn nowhere away from His most sweet countenance. Go before Him into a desert place and see the wonder of His works, where He multiplied in His own

Holy Hands the bread that sufficed to feed a great multitude. Go, my brother, go forward, and with all the love of your soul follow Christ wheresoever He may go. For if you so follow Him, and if you keep Him company, walking in love and faith, *there shall no evil come to thee,* and the wicked one *shall not come nigh to thee* (Ps. xc. 10, 7).

And follow Him to the Last Supper, in which He bequeathed, and to His Disciples, the Holy Mysteries, and ponder earnestly why it was that He there washed the feet of His Disciples, and, moved within you by the profound reflection of untroubled faith, with fear and wonder exclaim: God the Creator of all things, who of His grace made man from the dust has washed the feet of His own image, of His own creation! Ponder earnestly within you, O Brethren, and praise and adore His infinite goodness.

And lovingly behold Him as taking bread into His Hands, He blesses it, and breaks it, as the outward form of His own Immaculate Body; and the chalice which He blessed as the outward form of His Precious Blood, and gave to His Disciples; and be you also a partaker of His Sacraments.

And going from there, and descending to the court of the impious and unjust Caiphas, enter in with your Lord, and stand there firmly, so that you may witness the insults He suffers for you, that you may then become a more perfect lover of your Lord. Follow Him still further, and stand at the place of His

Cross, as a faithful servant by his Lord. Behold how blood flowed from His side, and water, for the redemption of your soul, O my Brother! And also look carefully where they laid Him, when taken down from the Cross. And go in the morning early; go with the women to His tomb, and see the stone rolled back from above Him, and see the Angels standing there. Listen to what the Angels say to the women: *The Lord is truly risen: as he told you.*

All these things let you prudently, fully, faithfully, and without faltering consider; and believe most fervently that all these things are true, as are the accounts set down concerning them. For unless you look upon all these things with the understanding eyes of faith you cannot be uplifted from earth to heaven, and behold the sufferings of Christ with spiritual understanding. For the eye of faith, when it shines clear and bright as light in the heart of any man, shall also clearly and openly behold the Lamb of God, Who for us was slain and sacrificed, and Who gave us His Holy and Immaculate Body that we eat of it for ever, and partake of it unto the forgiveness of our sins. (Cf. I Cor. v; Apoc. v.)

He who possesses this eye of faith shall clearly and openly look upon the Lord, and with sure and perfect faith eat of the Most Holy Body of the Immaculate Lamb, the Only-begotten Son of the heavenly Father, and drink of His Blood; a faith that is far from presuming to scrutinize the divine and holy nature. For faith is a gift of God; and it is faith which works within us, and looks to the things to come; and it is ever called faith, and not curiosity.

Do you believe, Dearly Beloved, in Christ Jesus, the Only-begotten Son, and that for you He was born as man on earth? What need then have you to search into the Unsearchable, or to trace the Untraceable? For if you pry curiously into these things you shall be called curious rather than a believer. Be therefore a believer, and without blame.

Partake of the Immaculate Body and Blood of Your Lord with fullest faith; certain that you are receiving wholly the Lamb Itself. The mysteries of Christ are an immortal fire. Take care you do not rashly search into them, lest you be burned partaking of them. Abraham the Patriarch placed earthly food before the heavenly angels, and they ate of it. A truly great wonder: to behold incorporeal spirits on earth eating the food of corporeal men. But this surpasses all wonder, all understanding, all speech: what Jesus Christ our Saviour, the Only-begotten Son, has done for us. For He has given us who are clothed in flesh fire and spirit to eat and to drink; namely, His own Body and Blood.

For my part, Brethren, since I am unable with my mind to comprehend the sacraments (divine signs) of Christ, I do not dare to go on to the things beyond them, nor even to draw near to these secret and most sacred mysteries. And even if I had the presumption to speak of them, I should still be unable to comprehend these mysteries of God. Indeed I should be imprudent as well as presuming, and grasping at the air in my foolish attempt: for because of its rarity no one can grasp hold of air. And so do these holy, adorable, and tremendous mysteries surpass all my powers. Rather I shall praise and glorify God and the Father, because through His Only-begotten and Beloved Son He has deigned to save me, an unworthy sinner, yet believing in Him with a simple heart: for I have ever detested, hated, fled from, such unlawful questionings, and from every notion that is displeasing to God.

I am mortal, and earthy of the earth, fashioned through God's favour from the substance of earth. I cheerfully acknowledge the weakness of my state, and I desire in no way to investigate my Creator. For He is *terrible*, and His nature is wholly incomprehensible. And therefore let me bless and adore His most excellent power and glory for ever and ever. Amen.

VII. ST GREGORY OF NYSSA, BISHOP AND DOCTOR

The Mystic Wine[12]

Let my beloved come into his garden, and eat the fruit of his apple trees.

I am come into my garden, O my sister, my spouse, I have gathered my myrrh, with my aromatical spices: I have eaten the honeycomb with my honey, I have drunk my wine with my milk: Eat, O Friends, and drink, and be inebriated, my dearly beloved. Canticle of Canticles v. 1.

You see how the Bridegroom goes beyond the prayer of His Spouse in the greatness of His gift? For the Spouse had prayed Him to come to the fountains of the aromatical spices, to the trees in her garden, refreshed by the wind that blows from the south, and that the Husbandman should eat of the fruit of his apple trees. All fragrant odours please the senses, as each one knows. But apples as food for the nourishment of the body have not the strength of bread. And when He came down to His garden, and had changed the nature of its fruits into something better, something more precious, He gathered myrrh from among His aromatical spices. For whatever is beautiful is His, wherever it may be found, the prophetic voice has said. In place of apples He

makes the trees bring forth bread as food, to be mixed with His honey. And in this is made clear the saying of the prophet, that He has honey and all the rest of the good things mentioned (iv. 11), and that He has drunk wine mingled with honey: *For of him, and by him, and in him are all things* (Rom. xi. 35; Exod. xvi. 31).

O blessed are those gardens whose trees we are told bear such fruits as may be changed into every kind of food, having in it *the sweetness of every taste* (Wisd. xvi. 21)! To the one who delights in sweet odours it becomes as myrrh, distilled of a pure and sweet-smelling life, through the mortification of our earthly members, and blended from the manifold and contrasting perfumes of virtue. To the one who seeks a more perfect food it becomes bread, and bread that need no longer be eaten *with wild* (bitter) *lettuce* (Exod. xii. 8) as the law laid down. It tastes bitter now, but it will become as honey to him when, in due time, the fruits of virtue sweeten the faculties of his soul; of which we have a proof in the Bread, sweetened with a honeycomb, that appeared to the Disciples on the evening of the Resurrection (Lk. xxiv. 35, 42). To the one who thirsts it becomes as a cup of wine, mixed with milk; not with gall, not a sponge soaked in vinegar, such as the Jews held up on a reed to their Benefactor: to show their gratitude (Lk. xxiii. 36).

We are not wholly without understanding of the meanings hidden in what has here been said. How Paul is a tree bearing myrrh, dying daily, inflicting on himself the sentence of death, and through the purity and self-denial of his life giving forth a good odour, and becoming a sweet odour to them that are saved (I Cor. xv. 31; II Cor. ii. 15). How the trees of the garden are breadmakers to the Lord of the garden; as He will testify, sitting upon a throne, saying: *I was hungry and you gave me to eat* (Mt. xxv. 35): for charity is the joy of the soul made sweet by the honey of precept. How the plants that have grown in His garden pour out wine for the Bridegroom; to whom He will say: *I was thirsty, and you gave me to drink*, wine mingled with milk, not water, as the winesellers mix it. Milk is the first food of man's nature; it is pure and simple, and like the child is without guile, and free of every source of evil.

The Word saying these things to the Spouse is setting before His neighbours the mysteries of the Gospel, saying: *Eat, O friends, and drink, and be inebriated, my dearly beloved* (or *brothers*). For to the one acquainted with the mystical tones of the Gospel, there seems no difference between what is said here, and what was revealed there in the mystical initiation of the Disciples. For here as well as there the Scripture says: *Eat ye, and drink ye.* But the encouragement to inebriety which the Word here makes to His *beloved*, seems to many to contain something more than the Gospel invitation. But if the words we treat of be carefully reflected on they will be found in agreement with the words of the Gospel. For here He encourages His friends with words, there He does this by deeds: for each kind of inebriation causes the mind that is overcome with the wine to fall into a trance (*ekstasis*).

Therefore, what is here encouraged now happens through this divine food and this divine drink, and happens always, as often as there is a change in our food and drink together with a turning away from what is inferior to what is better. So they are *inebriated*, as the prophecy says, *who drink of the plenty of the house; and thou shalt make them drink of the torrent of thy pleasure* (Ps. xxxv. 9). So even the great David was inebriated at times, who, going out of himself, and falling into ecstasy, beheld an unseen Beauty and cried out in that renowned saying: *Every man is a liar* (Ps. cxv. 11); giving us by a word a sort of hint of unguessed at treasures. So also was our Paul, the new Benjamin, inebriated, who cried out in ecstasy: *Whether we be transported in mind* (for this did ecstasy do to him), *whether we are sober in mind, it is for you* (II Cor. v. 13); as when he said he was not mad in respect of what he said to Festus, but that *He spoke words of truth and soberness* (Acts xxvi. 24).

I know that the blessed Peter also was caught up in this kind of inebriety, hungering and thirsting at one and the same time. For before his bodily food had been set down before him, when he was hungry and *desired to taste something*, and as they were preparing it, there came upon him a divine and wineless intoxication, in which he went out of himself, and beheld the Evangelical *great linen sheet, let down by the four corners from heaven to the earth*, holding within it men of every race, in the myriad forms of birds and of four-footed and creeping things, according to the multifold varieties of worship men had fashioned for themselves. And a voice commanded Peter to sacrifice one from the beasts, that was without reason, and these being purified the rest would become eatable; and seeing that the pure teaching of religion is here being given, not once only does the divine voice declare, *That which God hath cleansed, do not thou call common* (Acts x. 15). Three times was this teaching given: so that through the first voice we might learn what God the Father has made clean; by the second likewise that God making clean is God the Only-begotten Son; and similarly by the third voice that God making clean all that is unclean is the Holy Spirit.

Since inebriety of this kind arises from the wine the Lord sets before His guests, through which there arises a going out of the soul towards divine things, rightly does He bid those who are neighbours to Him through their virtues, not those who are far from Him: *Eat, O friends, and drink, and be inebriated, my dearly beloved*. For he who eats and drinks unworthily eats and drinks damnation to himself (I Cor. xi. 27). And rightly does He call those who are found worthy to eat his *brothers*

(or *beloved*): for he who does the will of His Father is by the Word called, *my brother, and sister, and mother* (Mt. xii. 50).

After inebriety comes sleep, that through good digestion His guests may receive the gift of wellbeing. And so following this banquet the Spouse falls into a sleep. It is a new sleep this, one strange to our natural habit. For in our accustomed sleep he who sleeps does not watch, and he who watches does not sleep, but each state ends the order; that is, sleeping and watching give place one to the other. But here a strange and wondrous mingling and joining of contraries is seen. For *I sleep*, He says, *and my heart watches*. What therefore are we to understand by these words? Sleep is an image of death. In it all activity of the senses comes to rest; since in the time of sleep neither sight nor hearing nor smell nor taste nor touch fulfil their office. On the contrary all tension of body is undone. It brings forgetfulness of the cares that trouble men, puts fear to rest, soothes anger, eases the strain of bitter feelings; and as long as the soul has the mastery of the body it makes it insensible to every evil.

Through what has been said we therefore learn, that the soul is so raised above itself that, becoming boastful, it exclaims: *I sleep, and my heart watches*. For as long as the soul lives within itself alone, untroubled by the senses, the nature of the body becomes relaxed in a kind of sleep or stupor, so that it may be truly said that sight being powerless is asleep; heedless of such sights as bring wonder to the eyes of children. And heedless not alone of such things as are formed from this earth, as gold and silver and precious stones, which by their beauty and colour arouse within us the concupiscence of the eyes, but even of the wonders seen throughout the heavens, the splendour of the stars, the motion of the sun, the varying forms of the moon, and whatever changing beauty may bring pleasure to our eyes: since there is nothing that is ever at rest, and not moved and wheeled about, in the motion and at the measure of time.

All such things being rejected for the contemplation of the true and supreme Good, the body's eye is now listless, for the things that it sees have no attraction for the more perfect soul: because of the things seen above, beheld by the mind alone. And hearing too is as it were listless and dead: the soul being held by that which is far above the power of human speech. Of the more animal senses we need not speak, as being remote from the soul, and giving off as it were a certain flavour of death. For the sense of smell gathers in odours at the nostrils, taste is given to the service of the stomach, and touch is the blind and servile minister of sense; which nature has perhaps made only for the sake of the blind. And all these being held, through inaction, in a sort of sleep, the activity of the soul is undimmed, and reason dwelling in soundless quiet, and free of every movement of the senses, fixes its gaze on high.

For in man's nature pleasure is of two kinds: one has place in the soul through calm, and one in the body through passion. And whichever of the two the will may choose this has dominion over the other. For if one turns towards the senses, choosing the pleasure that has its root in the body itself, such a one will pass through life without tasting of the divine delights: for the more perfect joys will have been shut out by the baser. But to those in whom the desire for God is strong, from these the True God does not remain hidden; provided that they shun whatever is wont to bewitch the senses.

Because of this the soul, as it takes its delight in the sole contemplation of Him Who Is, will be stirred by none of the things that awaken pleasure through the senses. Rather, every bodily motion now put to sleep, the soul through holy vigilance, with pure unclouded reason, receives the vision of God. To this may we also be found worthy to attain, by means of that sleep we have spoken of, and through steadfast vigilance of soul, in Christ Jesus, to Whom be praise and glory for ever and ever. Amen.

VIII. St Ambrose, Bishop and Doctor

The Sacrifice of Melchisedech[13]

The Christian Sacraments are older than the Jewish. You have come to the altar of God, you have seen the sacraments placed there, and you wonder to see there a created thing; nevertheless it is a solemn and an unusual created thing. Someone has said perhaps: God showed great favour to the Jews. He rained manna on them from heaven (Exod. xvi. 15). What more has He given His own faithful; what more has He given to those to whom He promised more?

Take in what I now say. The mysteries of the Christians were before those of the Jews; and more sacred are the sacraments of the Christians than those of the Jews. How can this be? Pay heed to this. Where did the Jews begin? From Judah, the great-grandson of Abraham; or, if you wish to understand it that way, from the Law; that is, when the Jews merited to receive the Law. So they are called Jews from the great-grandson of Abraham, or from the time of the saintly Moses. And if God then rained manna from heaven on the Jews, murmuring against Him, the figure of these holy sacraments preceded this: in Abraham's time, when he collected three hundred and eighteen well-appointed men, and pursued his enemies, and brought his grandchild back from captivity. Then, returning a victor, there met him Melchisedech the priest, and he offered *bread and wine* (Gen. xiv. 18).

Who had the bread and wine? Abraham did not have it. But who had it? Melchisedech. He then is the author of the sacraments (Heb. vii. 1 *seq.*). Who is Melchisedech? He who is made known to us as the King of Justice, the King of Peace. Who is the King of Justice? Can any man be King of Justice? Who then is King of Justice if not the Justice of God, Who is also the Peace of God, the Wisdom of God? Who could say: *Peace I leave with you, my peace I give unto you?* (Jn. xiv. 27.)

Let you then grasp, that these sacraments which you receive are prior in time to those of the Law of Moses; whatever the Jews may have to say. And that the Christian people had begun before the Jewish people

had begun: we through predestination, they in name.

Melchisedech therefore offered a sacrifice of bread and wine. Who is Melchisedech? *He was*, says the Apostle, *without father, without mother, without genealogy, having neither beginning of days nor end of life, but likened unto the Son of God, continueth a priest for ever*; and this we read in the Epistle to the Hebrews (vii). *Without father*, he says, and *without mother*. In this whom does he resemble? The Son of God. For the Son of God, in His heavenly generation, was born *without a mother*: He was born of the Father alone. And again when He was born of the Virgin, He was born *without father*: for He was not begotten of the seed of man, but born of the Holy Ghost (Mt. i. 20) and of the Virgin Mary, and brought forth from Her virginal womb, in all things as the Son of God.

Melchisedech was also a priest, as Christ is a priest; to Whom it was said: *Thou art a priest for ever according to the order of Melchisedech* (Ps. cix. 4). Who therefore is the author of the sacraments if not the Lord Jesus? These sacraments have come down from heaven; from whence all counsel comes. It was a truly great and divine miracle that God should rain manna from heaven on His people; and that the people should eat though they did not work.

But perhaps you will say: My bread is ordinary bread. On the contrary, this bread is bread only before the words of the sacred rite. When the consecration has been added, from being bread it becomes the Body of Christ. Let us therefore prove this. How can that which is bread be the Body of Christ? By consecration. Consecration by what words; by whose words? Those of the Lord Jesus. For all the other words which are said previous to this are said by the priest: the praises that are offered to God, the prayer that is offered for the congregation, for rulers, and for others. But when the moment comes to consecrate the venerable sacrament, the priest will no longer use his own words, but will use the words of Christ. It is therefore the Word of Christ that consecrates this sacrament.

Who is the Word of Christ? Who but He by Whom all things were made. The Lord commanded, and the heavens were made. The Lord commanded, and the earth was made. The Lord commanded, and the seas were made. The Lord commanded, and every creature was brought forth (Gen. i). You see then how wondrous in work is the Word of Christ.

If then there is such power in the Word of the Lord Jesus, so that the things that were not by It began to be, how much the more can It change what is into another thing? The heavens did not exist, nor the sea, nor the land, yet hearken to David speaking: *He spoke, and they were made. He commanded, and they were created* (Ps. cxlviii. 5). And accordingly I answer you; that the bread was not the Body of Christ before the consecration. But I say to you that after the consecration it is now Christ's Body. He spoke, and It was made. He commanded, and It was created. You were yourself; but you were your old self. After you were consecrated[14] you began to be *a new creature*. Do you wish to know what sort of new

creature? *Everyone*, says the Scripture, *in Christ is a new creature* (I Cor. v. 17).

Understand therefore how the words of Christ have changed every creature; and now change, when He wills, the order of nature. You wish to know in what manner? Listen then; and first let us take an example from His own Birth. It is the rule of nature that a man is born only from the conjugal relation of man and woman. But because the Lord willed it, because He chose this sacred means (*sacramentum*), Christ, that is, the one Mediator of God and men, the Man Jesus Christ (I Tim. ii. 5), was born of the Holy Ghost, and the Virgin Mary. You see then how, contrary to the order and custom of nature, a Man was born of a Virgin?

Consider another example. The Jewish people were hemmed in by the Egyptians, and behind them was the sea. By divine command Moses struck the waters with a rod, and the waves were divided; not certainly in accord with nature's laws, but in accord with the grace of the heavenly command (Exod. xiv). And consider another example. The people were thirsty, and they came upon a well. But it was a bitter well. So the saintly Moses cast a certain tree into the well, and the fountain that was bitter was made sweet; that is, it changed the quality of its nature, and was *turned into sweetness* (Exod. xv. 23). Consider a fourth example. An iron axe had fallen into the water, and since it was iron it sank. And Elisaeus cast in a piece of wood, and the iron swam upon the surface of the water; and this surely is contrary to the nature of iron (IV Kgs. vi. 6), which is a far heavier element than water.

From these examples therefore you may understand how great is the power of the heavenly word? If it can work a wonder in an earthly well, if the heavenly word can work wonders in other things, will it not work similarly in the heavenly Sacraments? And so you have learned that the Body of Christ is made from bread; and that wine and water are mingled in the chalice, but that this becomes Blood by the consecration of the heavenly words. But perhaps you will say: 'I see no appearance of blood.' But it posesses a likeness to it. For as you have taken on *the likeness of his death*, so do you also drink *the likeness* of His Precious Blood:[15] that there may be no horror of spilt blood, and yet that the price of our Redemption may be efficacious. You have therefore learned that what you receive is the Body of Christ.

The words of the Lord make and consecrate His own Body and Blood.

And would you know by what heavenly words It is consecrated? Here then are the words. The Priest says: Grant us, he says, that this oblation may be attributed to us, confirmed, an offering of our reason, acceptable to Thee, as the figure of the Body and Blood of our Lord Jesus Christ, Who, on the day before He suffered, took bread in His holy hands, looked up to heaven to Thee, Holy Father Almighty, Eternal God, and giving thanks He blessed, broke it, and gave what was broken to His Apostles and to His Disciples, saying: *Take ye, and eat ye all of this; for this is my body, which shall be broken for many* (Lk. xxii. 19 V.I.).

In like manner also, on the day before He suffered, after He had supped, He took the chalice, looked up to heaven to Thee, Holy Father Almighty Eternal God, and giving thanks He blessed it and gave to His Apostles and Disciples, saying: *Take ye, and drink ye all of this; for this is my blood* (Mt. xxvi. 27). Consider all this. These are the words of the Evangelist up to *Take ye*, whether of the Body or the Blood. From there on they are the words of Christ: *Take ye, and drink ye all of this; for this is my blood.* Consider each word.

Who, he says, *on the day before He suffered took bread in His holy hands.* Before it is consecrated it is bread. When the words of consecration have been added, it is the Body of Christ. Then listen to Him saying: *Take ye, and eat ye all of this; for this is my body.* Again, before the words of consecration, it is a chalice filled with wine and water. Where the words of Christ have wrought, there the Blood of Christ, Which has redeemed His people, is made. You see then in how many ways the words of Christ are able to change all things. Lastly, the Lord Jesus Himself testifies to us that we receive His Body and Blood. Are we to doubt His honesty and His testimony?

Now return with me to the main subject of my sermon. It was a great and venerable sign that manna rained from heaven upon the Hebrews (Exod. xvi. 13). But reflect. Which is the greater wonder: the manna from heaven, or the Body of Christ? The Body of Christ, the Creator of heaven. Then again he who ate manna is dead; but he that will eat of This Body his sins will be forgiven him, and he shall not die for ever.

So not without meaning do you say: *Amen*; in that moment confessing in spirit that you receive the Body of Christ. The priest says to you: *The Body of Christ*; and you answer: *Amen*; that is: It is truly. What the tongue confesses, let the heart hold fast.

Perfection of This Sacrament; It renews Christ's Passion.

That you may know that this is a divine mystery, its Figure preceded it. Learn then how great is this sacrament. Consider what He says: As often as you shall do this, do it in commemoration of Me, until I come again (cf. I Cor. xi. 26). And the Priest says: Mindful therefore of His most glorious passion, and of His Resurrection from the dead, and of His Ascension into heaven, we offer Thee this immaculate Host, this reasoning victim, this unbloody sacrifice, this holy Bread, and the Chalice of eternal life; and we beg and pray that by the hands of the Angels thou wilt receive this Offering upon Thy heavenly altar, as Thou didst deign to receive the gifts of Thy servant, Abel the Just, and the sacrifice of Abraham our father, and that which the High Priest Melchisedech offered to Thee.

So then, *as often as you shall receive*, what does the Apostle say to you? As often as you shall receive, you shall announce the death of the Lord. It we announce His death, we announce the forgiveness of sins. If as often as His Blood is shed, it is shed unto the remission of sins, I ought to receive It always; that my sins may always be forgiven. I who am always sinning ought always to have what heals me.

Today we have made clear to you what we could. Tomorrow (on the Sabbath day) we shall speak to you as best we can on the Lord's Prayer. May the Lord our God preserve you in the grace He has given you, and may He deign to enlighten yet more the eyes He has opened, through His only Son, the Lord God our King and Saviour, through Whom and with Whom be there to Him, together with the Holy Spirit, praise, honour, glory, magnificence, from all ages, and now, and for ever and ever, world without end. Amen.

IX. St Ambrose, Bishop and Doctor

The Sacrament of the Altar[16]

I. Our sermon yesterday brought us to the mysteries of the holy altar. And we learned that in Abraham's days a Figure preceded them: when the holy Melchisedech offered sacrifice; he who had, as the Apostle Paul says in the Epistle to the Hebrews, neither beginning nor end of days. Who are they who say the Son of God is of time; and of Melchisedech that he has neither beginning nor end of days?[17] If Melchise-dech has not beginning nor end of days: could Christ not have it? But the Figure is not greater than the Reality. You see then that *He is the beginning* and *the end* (Apoc. i. 1); *the beginning*, because He is the Author of all things; *the end*, not that He comes to an end, but because He contains the universe.

We have said then that the chalice and the bread are placed upon the altar. What is put in the chalice?

Wine. And what else? Water.[18] But you will say to me: How then, did not Melchisedech offer bread and wine? What is the meaning of the addition of water? Here is the reason.

First of all, what was the meaning of that Figure which preceded this, in the time of Moses? That when the Jewish people thirsted, and they murmured because they could find no water, God commanded Moses to strike the rock with a rod. He struck the rock, and *water came forth in abundance* (Num. xx. 11); and, as the Apostle says: *They drank of the spiritual rock that followed them, and the rock was Christ* (I Cor. x. 4). For that was not an unmoving rock which followed the people. And let you also drink, that Christ may follow you. Behold a mystery. Moses, that is, a prophet. A rod, that is, the word of God. The priest touches the rock with the word of God, and water flows forth, and the people drink. The priest therefore strikes, the water flows into the chalice, *springing up into life everlasting* (Jn. iv. 14); and the people of God drink; they who have attained to the grace of God. This then you have now learned.

Now learn another truth. At the time of our Lord's Passion, when the *great Sabbath* was drawing near, as our Lord Jesus Christ and the thieves still lived, soldiers were sent to kill them. But when they came they found the Lord Jesus Christ dead. Then one of the soldiers struck His side with a lance, and from His side blood flowed out, and water (Jn. xix. 33). Why water? Why blood? Water, that it might cleanse; blood, that it might redeem. And why from His side? Because from whence guilt came, from there grace also

comes. Guilt came through the woman; grace through the Lord Jesus Christ.

II. *Mystical Meanings.* You have drawn near to the altar; the Lord Jesus invites you, or your soul, and also the Church, and He says: *Let him kiss me with the kiss of his mouth* (Cant. i. 1). Do you wish to meet Christ? Nothing could be more joyful. Do you wish Him to come to your soul? Nothing could be more pleasing. *Let him kiss me.* See that you are free from all sin; that your offences are washed away, that He may judge you worthy of His heavenly mysteries, and invite you to His heavenly banquet. *Let him kiss me with the kiss of his mouth.* And then, because of what follows, your soul, or mankind, or the Church, seeing itself free from all sin, and worthy to draw near to the altar of Christ (and what is the altar if not the likeness of Christ's Body?) beholds the sacramental wonders, and exclaims: *Let him kiss me with the kiss of his mouth*; that is, may Christ place His kiss upon me.

Why? *Because thy breasts are better than wine* (Cant. i. 1); that is, better Thy affection, better Thy sacraments than wine. Better than that wine which though it possesses sweetness, and has joy and flavour in it, is yet the joy of this world. But in Thee the joy is of the spirit. So even then Solomon was drawing us to the nuptials of Christ with the Church, or to the nuptials of the spirit and flesh and the soul. And he added: *Thy name is as oil poured out: therefore young maidens have loved thee* (ib. 2). Who are the young maidens, but the souls of each one who has put away the old age of this body,

which has been renewed again by
the Holy Spirit?
*Draw me: we will run after thee to
the odour of thy ointments* (ib. 3).
Consider what He says. You cannot
follow after Christ, unless He draws
you. And then, that you may understand this, He says: *If I shall be
lifted up, I will draw all things to
myself* (Jn. xii. 32).
*The king has brought me into his
chambers.* The Greek[19] has, *into his
storeroom,* and into *his wine-cellar,*
where the bounteous gifts are; the
good odours, the sweet Mella;[20]
where the different fruits are; the
diversities of dishes, so that the banquet may be seasoned from His
manifold spiritual delights.

III. You have then drawn near to
the altar; you have received the
Body of Christ. Listen again to
what sacred mysteries you have attained. Listen to the holy David
speaking; he who foresaw these
mysteries in the Spirit, and rejoiced,
and declared that he *wanted for
nothing* (Ps. xxii). And why? Because he who receives the Body of
Christ shall not hunger for ever.
How often have you listened to the
twenty-second psalm without comprehending its meaning? See how
it is linked with the heavenly sacraments: *The Lord is my Shepherd;
and I shall want for nothing. He hath
set me in a place of pasture. He hath
brought me up on the water of refreshment: he hath converted my soul. He
hath led me along the ways of justice,
for his own name's sake. For though I
should walk in the midst of the shadow
of death, I will fear no evils, for thou
art with me. Thy rod and thy staff,
they have comforted me.*
The *staff* stands for His authority;

the *rod* for His sufferings: that is,
for the eternal divinity of Christ, and
also for His Bodily Passion. The one
created me; the other redeemed me.
*Thou hast prepared a table before me,
against them that afflict me. Thou hast
anointed my head with oil; and my
chalice which inebriates me, how precious it is.*

You have come then to the altar,[21]
you have received the grace of
Christ, you have attained to the
heavenly mysteries. The Church
rejoices in the Redemption of many,
and exults in spiritual gladness because of the white-robed family that
stands around her. You may read
this in the Canticle of Canticles.
Rejoicing, She invites Christ, having
prepared a banquet that seems
worthy of heavenly eating. And
She says: *Let my brother* (alternatively,
beloved) *come into his garden, and eat
the fruit of his apple trees* (v. 1).
What are those apple trees? You
became *a dry tree* in Adam; but now,
through the grace of Christ, as apple-
bearing trees you put forth fruit.

Freely the Lord Jesus accepts, and
with heavenly condescension He
replies to His Church: *I am come,* He
says, *into my garden. I have gathered
myrrh with my aromatical spices. I
have eaten my bread with my honey,
and I have drunk my wine with my
milk. Partake,* He says, *my brothers*
(or, *beloved*), *and be inebriated.*

*I have gathered myrrh with my
aromatical spices.* What is this har-
vesting? Know the vineyard, and
you will know what is harvested.
Thou hast brought, it is said, *a vineyard out of Egypt* (Ps. lxxix. 9); that
is, the people of God. You are this
vineyard; you are His harvest of
grapes. Planted as a vineyard, you
have borne fruit like the grape

harvest. *I have gathered myrrh with my aromatical spices,* that is, in the odour (of sweetness) *which you have accepted* (Ezech. xx. 41).

I have eaten my bread with my honey. You see that in this bread there is no bitterness; but that all is sweetness? *I have drunk my wine with my milk.* You see what that joy is which is undefiled by the sordidness of sin? For as often as you shall drink you shall receive forgiveness of sin, and be inebriated in your soul. Because of this the Apostle says: *Be not drunk with wine . . . but be ye filled with the Holy Spirit.* He who is made drunk with wine staggers and reels about; but he who is inebriated with the Spirit is *rooted in Christ.* Precious therefore is this inebriety; and making for sobriety of mind.

IV. *The Lord's Prayer.* We have gone briefly with you through the sacred mysteries. What remains then but the Prayer? And do not think it a matter of little moment to know how to pray. The holy Apostles said to the Lord Jesus: *Lord, teach us to pray, as John also taught his disciples.* The Lord then spoke the Prayer. *Our Father who art in heaven; hallowed be thy name. Thy kingdom come. Thy will be done on earth as it is in heaven. Give us this day our daily bread. And forgive us our debts, as we forgive them who are indebted to us, and suffer us not to be led into temptation, but deliver us from evil.* See how short this prayer is, and how full of every excellence? What beauty there is in the first prayer!

O Man! You who did not dare to look up to heaven, who turned your eyes to the ground, and of a sudden received the grace of Christ, and all your sins were forgiven. From being a wicked servant, you became a good son. Presume then, not on your own action, but on the grace of Christ; for *by his grace you are saved* (Eph. ii. 5), the Apostle says. Let there be no arrogance here; only faith. And to make known what you have received is not pride, but devotion. Therefore lift up your eyes to the Father, Who has begotten you through Baptism; to the Father Who redeemed you through His Son; and say: *Our Father.* A good presumption, but a tempered one. As a son you call Him Father; but do not because of this presume to any particular degree. Of Christ alone is He the individual Father; to all of us He is the common Father: He begot Him alone; us He created. Say therefore, and you say it through grace: *Our Father;* so that you may merit to be a son. Place yourself under the care and protection of the Church.

Our Father who art in heaven. What does *in heaven* mean? Hear what the Scripture says: *The Lord is high above all nations; and his glory above the heavens*(Ps. cxii.4).And in every place the Lord is high above the *heavens* of heaven; as though the Angels are not in heaven, as though Dominations are not in heaven, but in those *heavens* of which it was said: *The heavens show forth the glory of God* (Ps. xviii. 2). Heaven is where disorder has ceased; heaven is where shameful evils have received their death blow; where there is no wound of death, there is heaven.

Our Father who art in heaven; hallowed be thy name. What does *hallowed* mean? Is it that we desire that He be made holy Who says: *Be ye holy, because I am holy* (Ps.

xviii. 2): as though something of sanctity might be added to Him from our prayer? No. But we pray that His Name may be sanctified in us, that Its sanctifying power may reach us.

Our Father who art in heaven; hallowed be thy name. Thy kingdom come. As though the kingdom of God is not eternal? Jesus says Himself: *For this was I born* (Jn. xviii. 37); and you say to the Father: *Thy kingdom come*; as though it had not come? The kingdom of God comes, when we have attained to His grace. For He has also said: *The kingdom of God is within you* (Lk. xvii. 21).

Thy kingdom come. Thy will be done on earth as it is in heaven. Give us this day our daily bread. By the blood of Christ all things are reconciled, whether in heaven or on earth (Col. i. 20). Heaven is sanctified; the devil cast forth (cf. Habacuc iii. 5). Where does he now hover? Where is the man whom he deceived? *Thy will be done*; that is, let there be peace on earth as there is in heaven.

Give us this day our daily bread. Recall to mind the words I spoke to you yesterday, when I was explaining the Sacraments. I said to you, that before the words of Christ are spoken, what is offered is bread. When the words of Christ have been uttered, it is no longer called bread, it is called a Body. Why then, in the part of the Lord's prayer that follows, does He say: *Our bread?* He says *bread*, but ἐπιούσιον, that is, superstantial. This is not the bread which goes into the body; but Bread of eternal life, Which sustains the substance of our soul. For this reason, in Greek it is called ἐπιούσιος. But the Latin calls *daily bread*, what

the Greeks call *bread for the coming day*. For the Greeks say, τὴν ἐπιοῦσαν ἡμέραν, *the coming day*. So what the Latin as well as the Greek says is equally fitting: the Greek says both in one phrase, the Latin says, *daily*.

It it be daily bread why do you receive it after a year, as the Greeks do in the East?[22] Receive daily what profits you each day. So live, that each day you may be worthy to receive: he who is not worthy to receive each day, is not worthy to receive after a year. As the saintly Job each day offered sacrifice for his children, lest they should have sinned in their heart, or by word (Job i. 1). Let you understand, therefore, that as often as the sacrifice is offered, the death of the Lord, the Resurrection of the Lord, the Ascension of the Lord, is signified, and likewise the forgiveness of sins, and that *this* Bread, which you receive, is the Bread of eternal life, not daily bread (I Cor. xi. 26). He that has a sickness needs medicine. It is a sickness that we are subject to sin. The medicine is the heavenly and venerable sacrament.

Give us this day our daily bread. If you receive daily, daily you have *this day.* If you have Christ this day, He rises daily for you. In what way? *Thou art my son, this day have I begotten thee* (Ps. ii. 7). When Christ rises it is therefore *this day. Yesterday, and today*, the apostle Paul says (Heb. xiii. 8). But elsewhere he says: *The night is passed, and the day is at hand* (Rom. xiii. 12). Yesterday's night has passed; today's day is at hand.

Then follows: *Forgive us our debts, as we forgive them who are indebted to us.* This debt, what is it if not sin? Therefore had you not incurred another's debt, you would not be poor; and so it is imputed as sin to you. You had wealth, with which you were born rich. When you were made in the image and likeness of God you were rich (Gen. i. 26). You have lost what you possessed; aspiring to what was not yours. When Adam was made naked, you lost your riches. You incurred a debt with the devil; of which you had no need. And so you who were free in Christ, became a debtor to the devil. The enemy held your bond; but the Lord fastened it to the Cross, and with His own Blood blotted out the decree against you (Col. ii. 14). He has taken away your debt, and set you at liberty.

Rightly then does He say: *And forgive us our debts, as we forgive them who are indebted to us.* See what this means. As I forgive you, so do you also forgive me. If you forgive, you

then justly deserve to be forgiven. If you do not forgive, how is it right that He should forgive you?

And suffer us not to be led into temptation, but deliver us from evil. See what this says: *Suffer us not to be led into temptation,* which we cannot bear. It does not say: Do not lead us into temptation, but, like an athlete, desires trial, yet such as human nature can bear; and that each one may be delivered from evil; that is, from the enemy, from sin.

For the Lord Who has taken away your sin, and pardoned your offences, is able to guard and defend you against the snares of your adversary the devil, that the enemy, who it is is wont to beget sin, may not catch you unawares. He who puts his trust in God need not fear the devil; for *if God be for us, who is against us?* So to Him be praise and glory from all ages, and now, and always, and throughout all ages. Amen.

X. St John Chrysostom, Bishop and Doctor

The Eucharist the Memorial of Christ's Passion[23]

And while they were at supper, Jesus took bread, and blessed, and broke: and gave to his disciples, and said: Take ye, and eat. This is my body. And taking the chalice, he gave thanks, and gave to them, saying: Drink ye all of this. For this is my blood of the new testament, which shall be shed for many unto remission of sins (Mt. xxvi. 26–8).

And while they were at supper. Why did the Lord ordain this Mystery in the time of the Pasch? That you might learn in many ways that He was the Lawgiver of the Old Testament, and that the mysteries contained in it were only Figures of This. And because of this, where the Figure was, there also should the

Reality be found. And in the evening time; because evening is a symbol of the end of these times: that these rites were now at an end.

He gave thanks. And He gives thanks, teaching us how we also are to celebrate this mystery, and showing us that He is not approaching His Passion against His will; in this also teaching us, that whatever we too may have to suffer, let us suffer with giving of thanks; in this also laying a foundation for just expectations. For if the Figure (of the Lamb) could deliver from such slavery (i.e. that of the Hebrews, from bondage to the Egyptians), how much more will the Reality set free the world, when it is offered for the deliverance of the race of men?

Because of this, He did not give us the Mystery before this time, but only when the practices of the Law were to come to an end. And He brings to an end the head and chief of their Feasts; leading them to another and most awesome Table, and saying: *Take ye, and eat. This is my body.* And how was it that they were not amazed at hearing these words? Because He had already taught them many things, and great things, with regard to it. And so He does not prepare them further; for they had been prepared sufficiently. But He speaks to them of the cause of His Passion; namely, the taking upon Him of our sins. And He calls His Blood *the blood of the new testament*; that is, the blood of the Promise, of the Fulfilment, of the New Law: for This had been promised of old, and This the New Law contains. As in the Old Law they had sheep and oxen; so in the New they have the Blood of the Lord. And by this also He conveys to them that He is about to die, and so He speaks of a testament; reminding them of the former one, for that also was dedicated in blood.

And again He speaks of the cause of His death: *Which shall be shed for many unto remission of sins.* And He says: *Do this in commemoration of me.* You see here how He is drawing them away from, and separating them from, the Jewish observances? For as you celebrated this Pasch in memory of the wonders that were done in Egypt, so now let you do this in remembrance of Me. That blood (of the lamb) was shed for the salvation of the firstborn; This for the forgiveness of the sins of the

world. *For this is my blood,* He says, *which shall be shed for many unto the remission of sins.*

He said this furthermore to show us that His Cross and Passion were a mystery; and also so as to encourage His Disciples. And as Moses said: *And this day shall be for a memorial to you* (Exod. xii. 14), so likewise the Lord says: *Do this for a commemoration of me* (Lk. xxii. 19), until I come. And for the same reason He says also: *With desire I have desired to eat this pasch with you* (ib. 15), that is, that I might bestow on you the new things, and give you a Pasch by means of which I might make you eager for the things of the Spirit.

And He Himself drank of It; that they on hearing what He had said might not exclaim: What? Are we to eat flesh and drink blood, and then be gravely troubled? (For when He first began to speak of these things many were scandalized at His words; Jn. vi. 61.) And so that they might not be troubled, He first did this; leading them calmly to the participation of the mysteries. So He therefore drank His own Blood.

Someone may say: What then of the old Pasch, must we celebrate that also? Far from it. For when He says: *Do this,* He says, *this* that He may lead them away from it. For if *This* our Pasch brings about the forgiveness of sins, and it truly does, then that other Pasch is superfluous. And as formerly among the Jews, so here also, He unites the memory of the benefit received to the sacred mysteries: in this closing the mouth of heretics. For should they say: Where is it shown that Christ was sacrificed, we close their mouths by means of the sacred mystery, as well as by other proofs. For if Jesus was not put to death, to whom do these symbols of death refer that are set before us?

You see then what care He has taken, that we might ever be mindful of what He did for us? For since there would be many who would deny this Dispensation of Redemption, even in the Mysteries He reminds us of His Passion; so that no one may lead us away from the Truth: thus both delivering us and teaching us at the same time, by means of the Sacred Table. For this is the Head and Chief of all our graces; as the blessed Paul is at all times reminding us.

Let us then everywhere obey God; and never contradict Him, even though what He may say seems contrary to our own reason, or to our power to see. Rather let His word prevail over our understanding and our power to see. And let us do this in the sacred mysteries also; looking not alone to what we see before us, but also holding firmly to His words. For His words do not deceive, while our senses are easily deceived. His word never fails; but our mind fails in many things.

Since therefore He has said: *This is my body,* let us trust Him, let us believe Him, and let us look upon Him with the eyes of our soul. For Christ has given us nothing that the senses can perceive. For though they are under sensible forms, yet they are all things of the mind. So it is in Baptism, where a gift is bestowed on us by means of the visible substance of water; yet what is done is something spiritual, namely, birth and regeneration. For if you had no body, He would have given you these spiritual gifts as it were un-

veiled. But since your soul is united to a body, He gives you His spiritual gifts within things you can see.

How many are there who now say: Would that I could see Him in human form, see the print of His feet, His garments? But you do see him, you do touch Him, you eat of Him. You long to see even His garments; but He gives Himself to you, and not merely to see, but to be touched by you, to eat, to be received within you. But let no one on that account draw near with a sense of nausea, no one with indifference, but all eager and fervent. For if the Jews ate the Paschal lamb *in haste,* standing, their feet shod, staff in hand (Exod. xii), how much the more ought we to eat it with sober watchfulness? They were about to journey forth to Palestine, and for this they were dressed as travellers. You are soon to go to heaven. And so because of this we must be vigilant on all sides: for not light is the punishment of those who eat the Pasch unworthily.

The Evil of Unworthy Communions. Think how strong is your own anger against His betrayer, against those who crucified Him. Take care lest you yourself should become guilty of the Body and Blood of Christ. They put that Sacred Body to death; but you, and this after so many kindnesses received from Him, receive this Body into an evil soul. It was not enough that He became man, that He was struck in the face, that He was slaughtered, but He also commingles Himself with us; and this not alone through faith. He has in very deed made us His own Body. Who should be more free from sin than one who partakes of such a sacrifice? As spotless as the sunbeam should be the hand that breaks that Body, the mouth that is to be filled with this spiritual Fire, the tongue that is stained by this awesome Blood! Consider with what honour you have been honoured; at what Table you feast. That which the Angels tremble to behold, and dare not gaze upon because of Its flashing brightness. It is with This we are nourished, to This we are joined; made one Body and One Flesh with Christ.

Who shall declare the powers of the Lord? Who shall set forth all His praises? (Ps. cv. 2). What shepherd nourishes his flock with his own members? What shepherd do I say? There are many mothers who, after their maternal sufferings, will hand over their child to another to nurse. He does not endure to do this, but nourishes us Himself, and with His own Blood, binding us to Him by every means.

Reflect on this truth: He was born of our nature. But, you may say, this is not a matter that concerns all men. And yet it does concern all men. For if He came because of our nature, it is plain that He came for all men. And if He came for all, He came for each one. And how is it all have not been enriched by His coming? This is not His fault, Who of His own will did this for all men, but rather the fault of those who have no will to profit by Him. By this Mystery He unites Himself to each believing soul; and those to whom He has given life He nourished from Himself—not giving to others to nourish—by this also proving to you that He has taken your flesh.

Let us then not hold this honour lightly: we who have been held worthy of such honour. You see how eager infants are for the maternal breast, how thirstily they drink from it? Let us with a like eagerness approach this Table, and to the breast of the Spiritual Chalice. Let us with even more eagerness drink deep, like infants at the breast, of the love of the Spirit; and let it be our one grief that we should be deprived of this Food. These gifts set before us do not come from human power. He Who then made them at that Supper, the Same now makes what is here before us. We who minister, hold but the place of servants; it is He who consecrates, He who changes them.

Therefore let there be no Judas present; no lover of silver. If there be any one who is not a disciple, let him withdraw; the Table does not receive such as these. For He says: *I make the pasch with my disciples.* And This is the same Table, and upon it there is no less than there was upon That. It is not as though Christ had wrought at that Table, and man at This. It is He has prepared this Table also. This church is that *Upper Room* where they then were; it was from here they went forth to the Mount of Olives. Let us go forth, to the hands of the poor; for there is the Mount of Olives: the multitude of the poor are as olive trees planted in the House of God, from which drops the oil that is profitable to us Above; which five virgins had, and the five others who had it not perished for want of it. Having it, we too may enter in, so that with our lamps burning brightly we may draw near to the Bridegroom. Receiving it let us go forth from here. Let no one who is inhuman be present, no one who is cruel and without mercy, no one at all that is unclean.

What I am saying, I say to you also who minister, as well as to you who are ministered to. For it is necessary that I also address myself to you; that you may distribute the sacred gifts with great caution. For your punishment is not light should you, knowingly, admit anyone to the Communion of this Table whom you know to be unworthy of it. *His blood will be required at thy hand* (Ezech. xxxiii. 8). And even though he were a general, or a governor, or even he who wears the crown, should he draw near unworthy, forbid him: for higher is your authority than his. For if a spring of pure water were placed in your care for your flock, and you saw a sheep coming, with its mouth smeared with mud, you would not let it put down its mouth to dirty the well. Now you have been given charge of a well, not of water, but of Blood and the Spirit; and should you see some one draw near who is soiled with sin, a more grievous thing than clay or mud, and you are not moved to wrath, and you do not drive him away, how do you deserve to be forgiven? It was for this God honoured you with this dignity: that you might exercise judgement in these things. This is your office; this is your own security; this is your whole crown: not that you may go about clothed in a shining white habit.

And how, you may ask me, can I know about this person or that person? I am not speaking of those you do not know, but of those you do know. And shall I say something more serious? It is not as dreadful

to be possessed by evil spirits, such as those of whom Paul speaks, as to tread Christ under foot, and to *hold the blood of the testament unclean*, and *offer an affront to the Spirit of grace* (Heb. x. 29). He who has sinned, and comes to Holy Communion, is lower than one possessed by a demon. For those who are afflicted by an evil spirit are not on that account punished. But these others, should they come, unworthy, to the altar, they are handed over to ever-lasting punishment.

Let us drive away not these only, but all without exception whom we see draw near who are unworthy. Let no Judas receive, lest he suffer as Judas did. This Gathering is also the Body of Christ. Watch therefore, you who fulfil the office of deacon in these Sacred Mysteries, that you do not provoke the anger of the Lord by not purifying His Body: that you do not give a sword in place of food. And though such a one should approach the altar out of ignorance, exclude him, and be unafraid. Be in fear of God, not of man. For if you fear a man, you will be laughed at, even by him. But if you fear God, you will have the respect of men. Yet, if you do not dare to do this, then bring them to me. I shall not suffer that this be even attempted. I would lay down my life first, before I would present the Lord's Blood to one who was unworthy of It; and pour out my own blood rather than give this Fearful Blood contrary to what is fitting.

But if you do not know who is unworthy, though exercising much care, then there is no fault on your part. For what I am saying is about those who are well known. If we correct those, God will soon disclose those we do not know. But if we do not disturb those who are known to be unworthy, why should God make the others known to us? I say these things to you, not to drive these away, not simply to cut them off, but that we may lead them to do what is right, that we may take care of them. For by doing this God

will be gracious to us, and we shall find many who will then receive worthily. And for our own zeal, and because of our care for the souls of others, our *reward shall be very great*. And to this may we all attain, by the grace and mercy of our Lord Jesus Christ, to Whom be honour and glory for ever and ever. Amen.

XI. St John Chrysostom, Bishop and Doctor

The Body of Christ[24]

Because of these things I also, hearing of your faith that is in the Lord Jesus, and of your love towards all the saints, never cease to give thanks for you, making commemoration of you in my prayers, that the God of our Lord Jesus Christ, the Father of glory, may give unto you the spirit of wisdom and of revelation, in the knowledge of him: the eyes of your heart enlightened, that you may know what the hope is of his calling, and what riches of glory is in the inheritance of his saints, and what is the exceeding greatness of his power towards us, who believe in accord with the work of the power of his greatness, which he wrought in Christ, raising him from the dead (Eph. i. 15–20).

Expositional Part.

There was never anything equal to the tender affection of the Apostle; never anything like the sympathy and kindness of the heart of the blessed Paul, who was wont to pour out all his prayers for his cities and people; writing to all of them: *I never cease to give thanks for you, making mention of you in my prayers.* Think of how many he had in mind; it was a task even to remember them. Of how many he remembered in his prayers; giving thanks to God

on behalf of them all, as though he had himself received the greatest blessings.

Because of these things, he says; that is, because of what is to come, because of the good things that are laid up for those who live and believe justly. For it is right and just to give thanks to God, for all the things He has given to men, both before the present time, and in the hereafter. *Hearing of your faith that is in the Lord Jesus, and of your love towards all the nations.* Everywhere he links faith and love; admirable yoke-fellows. And he does not speak simply of those who belong there, but of all who are there. *I never cease to give thanks for you, making mention of you in my prayers.* And what is your prayer, Paul; what is it you ask for? *That the God of our Lord Jesus Christ may give you the spirit of wisdom and revelation.*

He wishes them to learn two things, and as they should learn them. Why they are called; and how they have been delivered from their former state of slavery. He says himself there are three things. How three? We must also learn of the things that are to come. For it is from the things that are laid up for us, that we shall come to understand God's ineffable and abounding richness. And learning who we are, and how we have come to believe, we shall also come to know of His power and omnipotence: converting those who were so long His enemies.

For *the weakness of God is stronger than men* (I Cor. i. 25). It is by that same power by which He raised Christ from the dead, that He draws us to Himself. Nor does His power stop at Christ's Resurrection. *Raising him up from the dead, and setting him on his right hand, he hath subjected all things to his feet, and hath made him head over all the Church, which is his body, and the fulness of him who is filled all in all* (20–3).

Great indeed are the mysteries and secrets He has made known to us; nor could we learn of them save through partaking of His Holy Spirit, and by receiving much grace. And it is for this Paul prays for us; that *the Father of glory may give you the spirit of wisdom and of revelation*; that is, that He may lift up your mind and give it wings; for otherwise it is not possible to learn of these things. *For the unspiritual man perceiveth not the things that are of the spirit of God* (I Cor. ii. 14).

We therefore stand in need of spiritual wisdom, that we may come to know spiritual things, that we may see things hidden. For it is the Spirit reveals all things (ib. 14). He stands ready to make known to us the mysteries of God: *even the deep things of God.* No angel or archangel or any other created power can give us this; that is, spiritual gifts. And if this understanding is given to us, then the searching for proofs is futile: for he who learns of God, he who knows God, has no longer

room for doubt. Such a man will not say: This cannot be, that cannot be; and how does this come to be? If we learn of God, as He should be known; if we learn of God from Him from Whom we ought to learn, from the Spirit of God, we can no longer be in doubt about anything. It is for this reason he says: *The eyes of your heart enlightened, in the knowledge of Him.*

And he hath subjected all things under his feet. He has not placed Him above the rest in honour, nor by way of contrast; but He has placed Him over them as His servants. O wondrous thing! Each created Power is made subject, has become the servant of a Man, because of the indwelling God the Word (Jn. i. 14). It is possible for a man to be above others; not as higher than them, but as being the more honoured. Here it is not so; for all things are made subject to Him, and not merely subject, but in total subjection: *Under his feet.*

And hath made him head over all the Church. Where He has upraised the Church; as though by some instrument He has raised it to the heights, and set it upon That Throne. For where the Head is, there also is the Body. No interval separates the Head from the Body. For were they separate, then there would no longer be a Body, and no longer a Head. *Which is his body, and the fulness of him who is filled all in all.* So that when you hear He is the Head of the Church you may not think of His power only, but also of His stability; that not alone does He rule, but also that He is the Head of a Body.

Christ is the Fulness of the Church. As though this did not suffice to show their closeness and relationship, what does he add? That *the fulness of Christ is the Church.* For the body completes, fills out, the head, and the head completes the body. Note the order Paul makes use of; how he leaves out no words which may serve to bring the glory of God before our minds. The *fulness,* he says; that is, as a head is completed by a body: for a body is made up of all its members, and has need of each one. Observe how He brings Him before us as having need of all His members. For unless we are many, and unless one is the hand, another the foot, and another some other member, the whole is not made full. It is therefore by means of all the members together that His Body is made full. Then shall the Head be made complete, then shall the Body be perfect, when we shall all be united and joined one to another.

Moral Part. Let us then fittingly reverence our Head. Let us keep in mind of Whose Head we are the Body; the Head to whom *all things are subject.* To be in accord with this enlightenment of our minds we should be better even than the Angels, more worthy than the Archangels, as being honoured above them all. God did not *take hold of the angels,* as Paul says, writing to the Hebrews, but *He took hold of the seed of Abraham* (ii. 16). He did not take upon Him the nature of a Principality, or of a Power, or of a Dominion, or of any other Greatness, but He took our nature, and set it in honour on high. What am I saying, 'set it in honour'? He made it His own garment; not alone this, He has placed all things at its feet. The Resurrection itself is not great when I consider these things.

These things he says, not of God the Word, but of *the God of our Lord Jesus Christ.*

Let us revere in wonder the closeness of our relation to Him. Let us be fearful lest anyone should cut us off from this Body; lest anyone perish from it, lest there be anyone unworthy of It. If someone were to place a diadem upon our brow, a crown of gold, would we not do all we could to appear worthy of these lifeless stones? Here a diadem is not placed upon our head, but Christ Himself becomes our Head, something far greater, and we make nothing of it. Yet the Angels reverence Him, and the Archangels, and all the Powers of heaven. And we who are His Body, if we do not do Him honour, either for the one reason or the other: then what hope of salvation have we?

Dwell in mind upon the kingly Throne; reflect upon this supreme dignity. This, rather than hell, might serve to strike fear into us. For if there were no hell, that we who have been given such honour should be found unworthy, what punishment, what pain would this not deserve? Remember near Whom our Head is seated. That thought alone should be enough for us; at Whose right hand He sits. He our Head is above all Principality and Power and Virtue: is His Body to be trampled on by devils? God forbid! If this should happen it would no longer be His Body. Good servants will reverence your own head; and should you submit your body to those who dishonour it, what punishments would you not deserve? If a man were to tie the king by the feet to the public pillory, would he not deserve the extreme punishment? You expose the whole Body to ravening beasts, and feel no horror?

Since we are speaking to you of the Body of Christ, come then, let us turn our minds to That, to the Body that was crucified, the Body that was fastened with nails, to That which was sacrificed. If you are the Body of Christ, bear the Cross; for He bore it. Suffer to be spat upon, bear with the blows, bear with the nails. Such things did it endure; the Body that was sinless. His Body *who did no sin, neither was guile found in his mouth* (I Pet. ii. 22). His hands that did everything for those who were in need; from His mouth came nothing that was unseemly. He heard them say: *Thou hast a devil,* and He answered nothing.

And since we are speaking of this Body, whoever among us shall partake of this Body and drink of this Blood, let them bear in mind that in nothing does it differ from that Body which sits on high, Which is adored by the Angels, seated close to the Unclouded Glory: it is of This we taste. Oh, how many are the ways of salvation open to us! He has made us His own Body. He has bestowed on us His own Body; yet there is nothing keeps us from evil. O what darkness, as of a deep abyss! O what senselessness! *Mind the things that are above,* says Scripture, *where Christ is sitting at the right hand of God* (Col. iii. 1). And with all this, there are those whose hearts are set on riches, and others who have been defeated by their passions!

I have noticed that there are many who partake of the Body of Christ in a careless manner, unreflectingly, rather from custom than because it is the law, rather for a purpose than from belief. When the season of Lent comes round, you say, every man, whoever he is, will partake of the Holy Mysteries, or when Epiphany comes round.[25] It should not depend on the circumstance of time; for it is not the Epiphany, it is not Lent, which makes us worthy to approach to Communion, but the purity and sincerity of our soul. With this you may approach always; without it you should never approach. *For as often as you do this, you shall shew the death of the Lord* (I Cor. xi. 26); that is, you will recall to mind your own salvation, and what I have done for you.

Recall to mind the austerity of those who were to partake of the ancient sacrifice; what they abstained from, what they did not do. They were ever purifying themselves; but you, you who come to that Sacrifice before Which the Angels tremble, do you arrange the matter by the time of the year? And how will you face the judgement seat of Christ; you who force yourself so boldly upon His Body, with hands and lips that are defiled? You would not dare to kiss a king with an evil-smelling mouth, but you kiss the King of heaven with a stained and evil soul? Such a deed is an outrage. Tell me, would you of your own accord come to the holy Sacrifice with dirty hands? I think not. You would rather not come at all than come with dirty hands. And correct as you are in such a little thing, you dare to receive with a soul that is soiled. And yet your hands touch It but for a moment; while It is received wholly within your soul. You see the sacred vessels, how clean and burnished they are? Our souls should be cleaner than they are, more holy, more shining. And why? Because these vessels are made only for us. They do not partake of Him; they do not perceive Him. But we do; we do indeed. You would not use a dirty cup, and yet you come to the altar with a dirty soul? There is great inconsistency here. At other times of the year you will not come: even though you are often clean: but at Easter you dare to come, no matter what evil you have done. O these customs, this presumption! In vain do we offer the holy Sacrifice; in vain do we stand at the Altar. There is no one receiving. I say this to you, not to lead you on to receive any way; but that you make yourselves worthy to receive.

The apostle Paul prayed for us that we may be given the spirit of wisdom and revelation. That you may know what is the hope of His calling. It is hidden now, he means, but not to those who believe in Him. And also that we may know *what are the riches of the glory of his inheritance in the saints*; that is, His indescribable glory: for what words can describe that glory of which the saints shall be sharers? There are none. We have need of grace that the mind may learn of it, and grasp even one small ray of it. To this grace of knowing and loving the glory of God may we all come, through the grace and love of our Lord Jesus Christ, to Whom with the Father and the Holy Ghost be there glory and honour now and for ever. Amen.

XII. St Augustine, Bishop and Doctor

Explanation of the Gospel[26]

I am, He says, *the Bread of life*. And what was it the Pharisees boasted of? *Your fathers*, He said, *did eat manna in the desert, and are dead*. Why then do you boast? They ate manna, and they are dead. What does this mean; they ate manna, and are now dead? Because they believed in what they saw; what they did not see, they had no idea of. So they are your fathers, because you are like them. For, my brethren, as to this visible and bodily death, do we not die, we who do eat this Bread that comes down from heaven? As they died so shall we die; that is, as I said, as regards the visible, carnal death of our body. But as to that other death, from which the Lord frightens us, of which their fathers died, Moses ate manna, Aaron ate manna, Phineas ate manna, many there who were

pleasing to the Lord ate manna, and they did not die. How is this? Because they thought of that visible food in a spiritual way, they desired it spiritually, they tasted of it spiritually, that they might be filled spiritually.

And we too this day receive spiritual Food; but the Sacrament is one thing, the virtue of the Sacrament another. How many there are who partake of the Altar, and they die; and they die of partaking? Because of this the Apostle says, that such a one *eateth and drinketh judgement to himself* (I Cor. xi. 29). It was not the piece of dipped bread that was poison to Judas. Yet he received it, and when he received it, *the enemy entered into him* (Jn. xiii. 27): not that he had received an evil thing, but because he being evil

wickedly received what was good.
See then, brethren, that you eat the
heavenly Bread in a spiritual manner; bring an innocent soul to the
altar. Let your sins not be mortal,
though they are *daily* (Heb. vii. 27).
Before you come to the altar remember what you are wont to say:
*Forgive us our trespasses as we forgive
them who trespass against us.* If you
forgive, you shall be forgiven. Draw
near in confidence; it is Bread, not
poison. But see that you forgive.
For if you do not forgive, you are
lying; and you are lying to Him
Whom you cannot deceive. You can
lie to God; you cannot deceive God.
He knows what you do. He sees
within you, He searches within you,
He looks within you, He judges
within you, within you He either
condemns you or crowns you.

*This is the bread that came down
from Heaven.* The *manna* was a
Figure of This Bread; *the altar of God*
was a Figure of This Bread. They
were mystical symbols; they differed
as *signs* but in what they signified
they were alike. Hear what the
Apostle says: *I would not have you
ignorant, brethren, that our fathers were
all under the cloud, and all passed
through the sea. And all in Moses were
baptized, in the cloud, and in the sea,
and did all eat the same spiritual food*
(I Cor. x. 1-4). The same food
spiritually, for corporally it was
different; because they ate manna,
we eat something else. They ate
spiritually, as we do. *Our* fathers
however, not their fathers; they
whom we are like, not they whom
these (the *pharisees*) resemble.

And he adds: *And all drank the
same spiritual drink.* They drank one
thing; we drink another: another
only as to its visible form, but sig-

nifying the same thing as to its
spiritual power. How was it *the
same drink*? *They drank*, he says, *of
the spiritual rock that followed them,
and the rock was Christ.* Where the
Bread came from, the Drink has
come. The *rock* was Christ in
Figure; the True Christ is in the
Word and in the Flesh. And how
did they drink? The rock was struck
twice with a rod. The two blows
signify the two beams of the Cross.
This then *is the bread which cometh
down from heaven; that if any man eat
of it he may not die*; in what belongs
to the virtue of the Sacrament, not
as to what belongs to the visible
Sacrament: if any man eats of it
inwardly, not outwardly: any man
who eats it with his heart, not the
one who encloses it within his teeth.

I am the living bread. Living
Bread, because I came down from
heaven. But the manna also came
down from heaven. The manna was
a shadow; This is the Reality. *If any
man eat of this bread, he shall live for
ever; and the bread that I will give is
my flesh for the life of the world.* When
would flesh receive this Bread which
He called His flesh? It is called flesh,
because flesh does not receive it; and
because it is called flesh, all the more
does flesh not receive it. It was this
had frightened them; this they said
was too much, this they had believed
impossible: *My flesh*, He says, *for
the life of the world.* The baptized
come to know the Body of Christ,
if they fail not to be the Body of
Christ. Let them become the Body
of Christ, if they wish to live by the
Spirit of Christ.

My brethren, understand what I
am saying to you. You are a man.
You have a spirit, and a body: by
spirit I mean what we call soul, and

by which it is that you are a man;
for you are composed of body and
soul. So you have an invisible
spirit; a visible body. Tell me:
Which lives by the other; does your
spirit live by your body, or your
body live by your spirit? Every
living man will answer me—he who
cannot answer I doubt if he is alive
—what will every living man answer
me? That my body lives by my
spirit beyond a doubt. Do you then
also wish to live by the Spirit of
Christ? Belong then to the Body of
Christ. Does my body live by your
spirit? My body lives by my spirit,
and yours by your spirit. The Body
of Christ can only live by the Spirit
of Christ. It is because of this that
Paul the Apostle, explaining this
Bread to us, says: *We, being many,
are one body, one bread* (I Cor. x. 17).
O Mystery of compassion! O Sign
of unity! O Bond of charity! He
who would live, has where he may
live, has what he may live by. Let
him draw near. Let him believe;
let him be made one with that
Body, so that he may live by It.
Let him not fear to be united to Its
members. Let him not be a decaying member, that deserves to be cut
off. Let him not be a deformed
member, of which It is ashamed.
Let him be a pleasing member,
sound and healthy. Let him adhere
firmly to the Body. Let him live of
God, unto God. Let him labour
now on earth, that afterwards he
may reign in heaven.

*The Jews therefore strove among them-
selves, saying: How can this man give
us his flesh to eat?* Beyond doubt
they strove among themselves; for
they did not understand the Bread
of Peace, nor did they wish to partake of It. For they who eat this
Bread do not strive among themselves; for *we, being many, are one
bread, one body.* And by means of
this, God makes us *to dwell in unity*
(Ps. lxvii. 7).

But what they are asking as they
strive among themselves, that is,
how the Lord could give us His flesh
to eat, they do not at once learn.
But they are told: *Amen, amen, I say
unto you: Except you eat of the flesh of
the Son of man, and drink his blood,
you shall not have life in you.* How it is
eaten, and what is the manner in
which it must be eaten, you know
not. Nevertheless, *unless you eat of
the flesh of the son of man, and drink
His blood, you shall not have life in you.*
Here He was speaking, not to the
dead, but to living men, and so lest
they should, thinking He was speaking of this life, begin to strive among
themselves about this too, He goes
on to add: *He that eateth my flesh,
and drinketh my blood, hath everlasting
life.* He therefore who does not eat
this Bread, and drink this Blood, has
not this life: without it a man may
have temporal life, but in no way
can he possess eternal life. He therefore who does not eat His Flesh, and
drink His Blood, has not life in him;
and he who eats His Flesh, and drinks
His Blood, has life. In either case
this means *eternal* life.

It is not so in the case of the food
we take to sustain our temporal life.
For he who does not take this will
not live; yet neither does he live
who does take it. For it can happen
that many take it and die of old age,
or of illness, or of some other cause.
But in this True Food, that is, in the
Body and Blood of the Lord, this is
not so. For as he who does not eat
of It has not life, so he who does eat
of it has life, and this is eternal life.

And so He wills that this Food and Drink is to be understood as the fellowship of His Body and of His members, which is the Holy Church in the predestined, the called, in the justified, in His glorified saints and faithful. Of these the first has taken place, that is, predestination; the second and third, that is, calling and justification, now go on, and will go on; the fourth, that is, glorification, is now laid up in hope, but shall have place in the future. The Sacrament of this, that is, of the unity of the Body and Blood is prepared and partaken of from the Lord's Table, in some places daily, in others at intervals of days: to some unto life, to some to their destruction. But the Reality (*res vero ipsa*), of which it is a sacrament, is for every man unto life, and for no man unto death, whosoever shall partake of it.[27]

But lest they should think that they who were promised eternal life through partaking of this Food and Drink would not now, through receiving it, die in the body, He deigned to anticipate this thought. For when He had said: He that eateth my flesh, and drinketh my blood, hath everlasting life, He went on to say: *And I will raise him up on the last day*: so that, as regards the spirit, it may at once have eternal life in the rest which the spirits of the saints receive. As to the body, it too will receive eternal life; but on the last day, in the resurrection of the dead.

For my flesh, He says, *is meat indeed; and my blood is drink indeed.* By food and drink men seek to be free of hunger and thirst; and this that Food and Drink alone causes, which makes those who receive it

both incorruptible and immortal: namely, the company of the blessed, where there shall be full and perfect peace and unity. For this reason, as men of God have understood before us, our Lord Jesus Christ has given us His Body and Blood under those appearances which are made into one thing from many. For the one, bread, is made into one thing from many grains of wheat; the other, wine, from many grapes.

Finally, He here expounds how this happens of which he is speaking, and what it means to eat His Body, and to drink His Blood. *He that eateth my flesh, and drinketh my blood, abideth in me, and I in him.* This therefore is what it means to eat this Food, and drink this Drink: To live in Christ, and to have Him dwell within us. For He who does not live in Christ, and in whom Christ does not dwell, assuredly does not, spiritually, eat His Flesh, nor drink His Blood: though he may in a bodily and visible manner enclose within his teeth the Sacrament of the Body and Blood of Christ: rather he eats and drinks the Sacrament (the Sacred Elements) of this so great Thing unto his own condemnation; because, though unworthy, he dares to approach to the Sacraments of Christ, which no one worthily receives unless he that is clean from sin; of whom it is said: *Blessed are the clean of heart: for they shall see God* (Mt. v. 8).

As the living Father hath sent me, and I live by the Father; so he that eateth me, the same also shall live by me. He does not say: As I eat of the Father, and I live by the Father; so he that eateth Me, the same also shall live by Me. For since He is born equal to Him, the Son is not made more perfect by partaking of the Father: as we are made better by partaking of the Son, through the communion of His Body and Blood, which this eating and drinking signifies. We therefore live by Him when we eat Him; that is, receiving Him as that Eternal Life which of ourselves we had not. He Himself lives by the Father, being sent by Him: for He emptied Himself, becoming obedient even to the death of the Cross (Phil. ii. 8).

For if we take the words: *I live by the Father*, in conjunction with what He says elsewhere: *The Father is greater than I* (Jn. xiv. 28); so do we also live by Him, Who is greater than us. His being sent was His emptying of Himself, and taking the form of a servant; which may be understood in its strict sense, provided we keep before us the equality of nature of both the Father and the Son. For the Father is greater than the Son as man; but His Son is equal to Himself: for the same Jesus Christ is both God and man, the Son of God and the Son of man. In this sense, if we rightly understand the words, He declared that: *As the living Father hath sent me, and I live by the Father; so he that eateth me, the same also shall live by me*, as meaning,

that I live by the Father, that is, my emptying Myself in My Incarnation is the reason I refer My life to Him, as to My source; that another should live by Me, this he does by his participation of Me in the Eucharist. I being made lowly live by the Father. He being raised up lives by Me.

If He said *I live by the Father* as meaning, that He is from the Father, and not the Father from Him, it was said without prejudice to His equality with the Father. Nevertheless, when He said: *He that eateth me, the same also shall live by me*, He does not mean by these words that the equality between Him and the Father, and between Him and us, is the same; He was making known to us His state of Mediator.

This is the Bread that came down from heaven, so that eating it we may live; because of ourselves we could not possess eternal life. *Not, however*, He says, *as your fathers did eat manna and are dead; he that eateth this bread shall live for ever.* That they are dead must be understood to mean, that they do not live for ever. For as to this present life, even they die who eat of Christ. But they live for ever: for Christ is Life Everlasting. Amen.

XIII. St Augustine, Bishop and Doctor

Explanation of Holy Communion[28]

We have heard the words of the Gospel that follow the previous sermon. On this a sermon is due to your ears and to your minds, and it is not unfitting to this present day: for it concerns the Body of the Lord, Which He said He gives us to eat, to gain eternal life. But He explained to us the manner of this

giving and the measure of the gift, how He would give us His Flesh to eat, by saying: *He that eateth my flesh, and drinketh my blood, abideth in me, and I in him.* The sign that a man has eaten and drunk is this: If He abides in Him, and is abided in; if He dwells in us, and He is dwelt in; if He adheres to us, and we to Him.

It is this then that He has taught us, and put into our minds by mystic words, that we are in His Body among His members, under Him as our Head, eating of His Flesh, not departing from union with Him. But many of those who were present, not understanding Him, were scandalized: for when they heard Him say this they thought He was speaking of simple flesh, such as they were themselves. The Apostle however says, and says truly, that *to know by means of the flesh is death* (Rom. viii. 6). The Lord gives us His Flesh to eat, and to know with the flesh is death; seeing that He says of This Flesh, that in It is Eternal Life. So therefore we should not understand This Flesh, *according to the flesh*; as in the words that follow:

Many therefore, not of His enemies, *but of his disciples, hearing it, said: This saying is hard, and who can bear it?* If His Disciples found this saying hard, what of His enemies? And yet it was fitting that it should be so spoken of, that it might not be understood by all. The secret of God should make us eager, not hostile. But these men, when they heard the Lord Jesus saying these things, promptly forsook Him: they did not consider that He might be giving utterance to some great truth, and that His words cloaked some great divine favour. But just as they were themselves inclined, so did they understand Him; and from the point of view of men, namely, that Jesus would, or that Jesus intended this: to distribute in fragments, to those who believed in Him, the Flesh with which the Word was clothed. *This saying*, they say, *is hard; who can believe in it?*

But Jesus, knowing in himself, that

his disciples murmured at this, said to them. For they had said this amongst themselves so that He would not hear them. But He Who knew them within themselves, hearing them within Himself, answers them, and He says: *Doth this scandalize you, that I said I shall give you My Flesh to eat, and My Blood to drink; this scandalizes you? If then you shall see the Son of man ascend up where he was before?* What does He mean by this? Is there an answer here to the question that had troubled them? Has He made clear by this that which had scandalized them before? Yes, if they understand Him. For they had been thinking that He was about to give them His own Body. But He says that He is now about to ascend up to heaven, and of course in His present state. *When you shall see the Son of man ascend up where he was before*, then will you see beyond doubt, that He is not giving His Body in the way that you are thinking: then certainly you will understand that His Gift is not eaten in mouthfuls at a time.

And He says: *It is the Spirit that quickeneth: the flesh profiteth nothing.* Before we explain these words, as the Lord may give us His light, we cannot pass over lightly what is here said: *If then you shall see the Son of man ascend up where He was before?* For Christ is the Son of man from the Virgin Mary. The Son of man therefore had a beginning here on earth, where He took flesh from the earth. And because of this the prophet had said: *Truth is sprung out of the earth* (Ps. lxxxiv. 12). What then does He mean when He says: *When you shall see the Son of man ascend up where He was before?* There would be no difficulty had He said: *When you shall see the Son of God ascend up where He was before?* But since He said *the Son of man* ascending up where He was before, was the Son of man in heaven before, seeing that He began to be on earth? In another place He says: *No man hath ascended into heaven, but He that descended from heaven, the Son of man who is in heaven* (Jn. iii. 13). He did not say the Son of man Who *was* in heaven, but *the Son of man*, He says, *who is in heaven.*

He was speaking on earth, and He said that He was in heaven. And He did not say: *No man hath ascended into heaven, but He that descended from heaven,* the Son of God *who is in heaven.* To what does this point, but that we are to understand what I have commended to Your Charity in a former sermon, that Christ God and man is one Person, not two: that the object of our faith is not a quaternity, but a Trinity? Christ is therefore one: The Word, soul and Body, are one Christ; the Son of God and the Son of man are one Christ. The Son of God always, the Son of man in time; yet one Christ by means of the oneness of His Person. He was in heaven while He was speaking on earth. The Son of man was in heaven as the Son of God was on earth. The Son of God was on earth in the Flesh He had assumed; the Son of man was in heaven in the unity of the Person.

But what is the meaning of what He here adds: *It is the Spirit quickeneth; the flesh profiteth nothing?* Let us say to Him—for He endures us who, not contradicting Him, are but eager to know—O Lord, good Master, how can it be that the Flesh profits us nothing, since You have told us that, *unless a man shall eat my*

flesh, and drink my blood, he shall not have life in him? Does Life profit us nothing? And why are we what we are, if not to gain that Eternal Life You promise us by means of Your Flesh? What then is the meaning of the words: *The flesh profiteth nothing?*

It *profiteth nothing*, as they understood it: they had understood His Body as though He were speaking of a carcase, to be cut into small pieces, or as sold in the meatshops; not as made living by the Spirit. He said, *the flesh profiteth nothing*, just as it is said that *knowledge puffeth up* (I Cor. viii. 1). Are we then to hate knowledge? Far from it. And what does *knowledge puffeth up* mean? Knowledge by itself, without charity. And so he adds: *But charity edifieth.* Therefore add charity to knowledge, and knowledge will be profitable; not of itself, but because of charity. So here also, *flesh profiteth nothing*, that is, simply flesh. Let the Spirit be added to the Flesh, as charity to knowledge, and it does indeed profit us. For if the Flesh was of no profit to us, the Word would not have become Flesh, that He might dwell among us. If by the Flesh Christ has brought great profit to us, how does the flesh profit nothing? But it was by means of the Flesh the Spirit wrought much for our salvation. The Flesh was a vessel. Consider what it contained; not what it was. The Apostles were sent; did their flesh profit us nothing? If the flesh of the Apostles has been a gain to us, does the Flesh of the Lord profit us nothing? How did the sound of the Word come to us, except through the voice of the flesh? Whence came the pen of the writer, and the writing? All these are the works of the flesh: but through the Spirit working in them, as through an instrument. *It is the Spirit that quickeneth; the flesh profiteth nothing.* Not as they understood flesh, do I give My Body to be eaten.

Furthermore He says: *The words that I have spoken to you are spirit and life.* We said, Brethren, that the Lord had commended to us, in the eating of His Flesh and the drinking of His Blood, that we abide in Him, and He in us. We are in Him, when we are His members; He abides in us, when we are His temple. Unity joins us to Him that we may be His members. But what can bring us together in unity save charity? And where does the charity of God come from? Ask the Apostle. He answers: *The charity of God is poured forth in our hearts by the Holy Ghost* (Rom. v. 5). Therefore, *it is the Spirit that quickeneth.*

For it is the spirit gives life to the members. But the spirit gives life only to the members it finds in the body it vivifies. For the spirit in you, O man, and by which you are a man, will it give life to a member it finds cut off from your body? I am calling your soul your spirit: your soul gives life only to the members that belong to your body. If one is removed, it no longer draws life from your soul; for it no longer belongs to the unity of your

body. These things are said so that we may love unity, and that we may fear division. For there is nothing a Christian should dread more than to be separated from the Body of Christ. For if he is separated from the Body of Christ he is not one of His members. If He is not a member of Christ, then he does not live by His Spirit. *If any man have not the Spirit of Christ,* says the Apostle, *he is none of his* (Rom. viii. 9). Therefore, *it is the Spirit that quickeneth; the flesh profiteth nothing. The words that I have spoken to you are spirit and life.* What does, *are spirit and life,* mean? That the words are to be understood in a spiritual manner. If you understand them spiritually, they are spirit and life to you. If you understand them in a non-spiritual way, they are still spirit and life; but not to you.

May then the power of His mercy strengthen our hearts in His truth. May it confirm and calm our souls. May His grace abound in us. May He have pity on us, and remove obstacles from before us, and from before the Church, and from before all who are dear to us. And may He by His power, and in the abundance of His mercy, enable us to please Him for ever, through Jesus Christ His Son our Lord, Who with Him and with the Holy Ghost lives and reigns world without end. Amen.

XIV. St Augustine, Bishop and Doctor

Chaste Living[29]

John vi. 56, 57

Chapter I. *The Catechumens are invited to the grace of Regeneration.* As we heard, while the holy Gospel was being read, the Lord Jesus Christ exhorts us, with the promise of eternal life, to eat His Flesh and drink His Blood. You have heard these words, but not all of you have understood them. You who are baptized and believing, you have come to know the meaning of what He said. But those among you who are called Catechumens, or Hearers, could be Hearers while it was being read, but could you also understand?[30] And so our sermon will be directed to both the one and the other. They who now eat the Flesh of the Lord and drink His Blood, let them reflect on what it is they eat, and what they drink: lest, as the Apostle says, they eat and drink damnation to themselves. They who do not yet eat, and who do not yet drink, let them as invited guests hasten to taste these delights.

During these days the instructors give you to eat, Christ feeds you daily; His Table is this which is placed in your midst. What is the reason, Hearers, that while you may see the Table, you may not draw near to the Feast? And perhaps even while the Gospel was being read you said in your own heart: What are we to think of this saying: *My flesh is food indeed and my blood is drink*? How is the Lord's Flesh eaten, and how do we drink His Blood? What must we think He means?

Who has shut you out from this that you may not know? It is hidden from you; but if you wish it shall be revealed to you. Come and make your (baptismal) profession, and the question is solved for you. What the Lord Jesus said, the faithful already know. But you, you are called a Catechumen, you are called a Hearer, and you are deaf! The ears of your body are open, for you hear words spoken; but the ears of your heart are still shut, for what is said you do not understand. I am merely speaking of this with you;

not teaching you. Give in your name for Baptism. If the festivity will not rouse you, then let curiosity lead you along: that you may come to know what is the meaning of the words: *He that eateth my flesh and drinketh my blood abideth in me, and I in Him.* That with me you may learn what is meant by, Knock, and it shall be opened to you. And as I say to you, Knock, and it shall be opened to you, so do I also knock. Open to me! When I speak to your ears, I knock at your breast.

Chapter II. *Married Christians, already partaking of the Body of Christ, are instructed regarding the observance of chastity.* But if Catechumens are exhorted, my Brethren, that they are not to delay in drawing near to this so great grace of regeneration, what must be our care in building up the faithful, so that that may profit them to which they draw near; that is, that they may not eat and drink This Food to their own damnation?

That they may not eat and drink unto judgement, let them live justly. Let you be exhorters, not in words, but in your deeds; so that they who are not baptized may so follow you that they will not perish by imitating you. You who are married, keep faith with your wives. Do that which you demand of them. You as a husband demand chastity of your wife; teach this by example, not by mere talk. You are the leader; look where you are going. For you should not go where she may not follow without danger; more, the way in which you would have her walk, you ought also travel. It is of the weaker sex you demand fortitude; though the concupiscence of the flesh is in you both. Let the one who is stronger, first obtain the mastery.

But it is a grievous thing that in this women surpass many men. Women observe the chastity men will not observe; and men desire to appear as men through not observing it: as though it was for this man was the stronger sex, that the enemy may the more easily overcome him. It is a struggle, a war, a battle. The man is stronger than the woman; the husband is the head of the wife (Eph. v. 23). Your wife struggles, and overcomes; do you give in to the enemy? The body stands firm; but the head falls down?

You who are yet without wives, and who still come to the Lord's Table, and eat of the Flesh of Christ and drink of His Blood, if you intend to marry, preserve yourselves chaste for your wives. Such as you would have them come to you, such let them also find you. What young man is there who does not wish to marry a chaste wife? And if he were to take to himself a virgin, who is there would not desire that she should be undefiled? You seek for a pure wife; be yourself unstained. It is not as though she can be, but you cannot be. If it is impossible, then it is impossible for her. But since it is possible to her, then let this teach you that it can be done. And the Lord has a care for her, that she may do this. Should you, however, also do this, you are the more to be honoured. Why the more to be honoured? Because in her case the vigilance of her parents protects her; the very modesty of the weaker sex is itself a restraint. And then she fears laws you do not fear. So if you do this you are the

more to be honoured: for should you achieve this, it is because you fear God. She has much else to fear besides God: You have God alone to fear. But He you fear is greater than all others. He is to be feared in public; He is to be feared in private. Go out from your house; you are seen. Enter in; you are seen. The lamp shines; He sees you. The lamp goes out; He sees you. You enter your room; He sees you. You reflect within your own heart; He sees you. Fear Him; for *He hath care of you*, that He may see you (I Pet. v. 7); and, fearing Him, be chaste. Or else, if you wish to sin, seek a place where He cannot see you, and then do what you will.

Chapter III. *Those bound by a vow of chastity.* You who are already vowed to God, let you restrict your body more severely, and do not allow it to relax the restraints of concupiscence, even in what is permitted; so that not alone do you turn away from unlawful intercourse, but so that you will forego even a lawful glance. Bear in mind, whichever sex you belong to, whether male or female, that you are to lead the life of the angels while you are here on earth. For Angels neither marry, nor are given in marriage; so shall we be, when we have risen from the dead (Mt. xxii. 30). How much better are you who begin before death to be that which men shall be after the resurrection? Cherish your state: for your rewards God lays up for you. The resurrection of the dead is compared to the stars in the heavens. For *star from star differeth in glory*, the Apostle says; *so also is the resurrection of the dead* (I Cor. xv. 42). For there virginity shall shine in one way; there married chastity shall shine another way; there holy widowhood shall shine another way. They shall shine one different from another; but all shall be there. The splendour will vary; but they will possess heaven in common.

Chapter IV. *Each should cherish his own state.* Reflecting therefore, each one of us, on his own state of life, and mindful of what you have each promised, draw near to the Body of the Lord, draw near to the Blood of the Lord. He who knows that he is other than he should be, let him not draw near. And let you repent yet more at my words. And they will feel joy at my words, who know that they observe for their spouses' sake what they demand from their spouses; and they too who have learned to observe chastity in every way, if they have vowed this to God. They grieve who hear me saying: Whosoever does not observe chastity, let him not draw near to This Bread. Would that I need not say this to them! But what am I to do? Shall I fear man, and hide the truth? If those wicked servants did not fear the Lord, am I also not to fear Him? As though I did not know that it was said: *Wicked and slothful servant,* you should have given my money to the bankers, that I might exact it with interest.

See O Lord, My God, I have given it. Behold, in Thy sight, and before all Thy Angels, and before all Thy people, I have laid out Your money: for I walk in fear of Thy judgement. I have given it; Do Thou exact it back! Even had I not spoken, Thou wouldst still exact it. So therefore I say instead: I have given it; Do Thou change us, and spare us! Those who were unchaste, make them chaste, so that when You come to judge us, we may all rejoice together before Thy face; both he who now gives out Your money, and he to whom it is given. Does this comfort you? May it be so! Whosoever you are who live unchastely, change your way of life, while you have life. I can speak the word of God to you; but the unchaste who continue in their evil way of life I cannot deliver from the judgement, and from the damnation of God.

Let us give then thanks to our Lord and Saviour Jesus Christ, Who, without any merit of ours, has healed our wounds, made us His friends who were His enemies, delivered us from the servitude of evil, led us from darkness into light, and recalled us from death to life. And humbly confessing our own weakness, let us implore His mercy, that, with the psalmist, His mercy may go before His Face, that He may deign to preserve us in the gifts and graces He has given us, and may also deign to increase them, Who with the Father and the Holy Ghost lives and reigns world without end. Amen.

XV. St Cyril of Alexandria, Bishop and Doctor

Meditation on the Mystical Supper, and on the Washing of the Feet[31]

What could be more joyful and more precious to men of good will, and to those who are desirous of True Life, than to enjoy God for ever, and be wholly at rest within the shelter of His divine Providence?

For if those who are well nourished with food and drink, and take their share in other fleeting delights, come to possess a tall and vigorous body, how much the more shall they not be glorified, *with gilded clothing, surrounded with variety* (Ps. xliv. 10), who are brought up *on the waters of refreshment,* that is, upon divine revelation? As the prophet says, *They shall take wings like the eagles; they shall run and not be weary, they shall walk and not faint* (Is. xl. 31).

Come then, and follow after the riches of secret places, as partakers of a heavenly vocation, in faith unfeigned, and having on a wedding garment, and let us hasten to the mystical Supper.[32] This day Christ receives us as His guests. This day Christ waits upon us; Christ the lover of all mankind gives us refreshment. Awesome what has been spoken; fearful what has here been wrought. The fattened calf is slaughtered. The Lamb of God Who takes away the sins of the world is slain. The Father rejoices. Of His own will the Son is sacrificed; not by the enemies of God today, but by Himself, that by this He may show that His sufferings were freely borne, and for our salvation.

Would you have me place before you the highest testimony to the truth of what has been said? Pay no heed to the poverty of my speech, nor to my unworthiness, but to the words and to the greatness of those who have foretold these things. For it is not the testimony of ordinary persons, insignificant, such as are taken in by the idle chatter of the market place, but the testimony of the great Solomon, sent as the Herald of the King of Kings, Who rules from His Throne on high.

It is he who foretold the secrets of the Most High; he, clothed in the royal purple, and crowned with the diadem, has proclaimed the edict of the King Who raises up and puts down kings. You see how great is the dignity of the Herald. Hear then what he has announced.

Wisdom hath built herself a house; she hath hewn her out seven pillars. She hath slain her victims, mingled her wine, and set forth her table. She hath sent her maids to invite to the tower, and to the walls of the city: Whosoever is a little one, let him come to me. And to the unwise she said: Come, eat my bread, and drink the wine which I have mingled for you. Forsake childishness, and live, and walk by the ways of prudence (Proverbs ix. 1-6).

These words, Beloved, are for you symbols of things now fulfilled. These words speak to you of the pleasures of this banquet now prepared. The Giver of gifts is at hand. The divine gifts are set before us. The mystical Table is prepared. The Life-giving Chalice is mingled. The King of glory invites us. The Son of God receives us. God the Word Incarnate entertains us. She who has built herself a house, not made with hands, the substantial (*Person*) Wisdom of God the Father, distributes His Body as *Her bread*, and gives His Blood as *Her wine* to us to drink.

O Fearful Mystery! O Ineffable work of the Divine Wisdom! O Incomprehensible Goodness! O Sublime Condescension! The Creator gives Himself to His creatures, for their delight. Life bestows Itself on mortal men, as food and drink. Come, eat My Body, He exhorts us, and drink the wine I have mingled for you. I have prepared Myself as

Food. I have mingled Myself for those who desire Me. Of My own will I became Flesh; I Who am Life Itself. I have become a partaker of your flesh and blood; I Who am the Word and the Substantial Image of the Father. *O taste and see that I the Lord am sweet* (Ps. xxxiii. 9).

You have tasted the fruit of disobedience. You have learned how bitter the food of that bitter counsellor. Taste now the Food of obedience, Which keeps evil away; and then you will learn that it is sweet and profitable to obey God. You ate fruit out of *due season*, and you died; eat now in a seasonable time, and you shall live. By trial you have come to know the consequences of disobedience; by trial let you now learn how profitable obedience is. *Taste and see that I the Lord am sweet.* Weigh one trial against the other. You have learned of evil, you have come to know what disobedience is. Through knowledge of evil you have gained an understanding of what disobedience means; through knowing goodness, learn how different is obedience. *Taste and see that I the Lord am sweet!*

Adam to his own hurt stretched forth his hand; having no reverence for My commandment of salvation. Since he would not acknowledge the commandment of the Lord, and the obedience of a servant; since he would not, trusting in God, turn away from the apostasy of his mistrust, he put forth his hand. There he made an evil bargain. He sold the life of happiness he held within his hands, and in exchange received a miserable death. He inflicted on himself the death of which he had been forewarned (Gen. ii. 17): which until now had not been: in place

of that immortality with which through divine favour he was to be clothed. Of his own will he put on corruption. Of his own will He was made subject to death. In his condemnation he learned to distinguish between the commandment of Me His Lord, and the counsel of the evil tempter. Judging rashly of the command that was true, He wounds himself by his want of faith, and is brought to nothing.

Because of all these things once more I place the fruits of obedience before those who died through disobedience. Taste and see that I the Lord am most truthful in all things. Truth cannot bring forth falsehood; nor is the flower of death found growing from life: for things contrary to one another cannot join together as one. Eat of Me Who am Life, and live. For this is what I desire. Eat of life which never comes to an end. For this I came: *That you may have life, and may have it abundantly* (Jn. x. 10). Eat My Bread: for I am the Life-giving grain of the wheat, and I am the Bread of Life. Drink the Wine I have mingled for you; for I am the Draught of immortality. Put away the folly of sin, and live. Learn once more by trial of them what things are good; and through obedience make yours once more, what you lost through the disobedience of your first parent. He was driven from Paradise through unbelief; let you enter in again through faith. Put away his impiety, and in its place receive love of Me your Maker. Seek after Wisdom, that you may live; and perfect your understanding in the knowledge of Me.

If there is any one who is unwise,

let him turn to Me, and he shall see the light of truth. I God am First, and I am afterwards, and beside Me there is no other God born of God the Father. *I am in the Father, and the Father in me* (Jn. x. 30). And: *he that seeth me, seeth the Father also* (Jn. xiv. 9). *I am the resurrection and the life* (Jn. xi. 25). *I am the bread of life which cometh down from heaven, and giveth life to the world* (Jn. vi. 33). Receive Me as the ferment in your dough, that you may become partakers of that unfailing Life which is Mine. *I am the true vine* (Jn. xv. 1). Drink of my delight, *drink the wine which I have mingled for you* (Prov. ix. 5). For *my chalice which inebriates me*, as a most potent remedy, and one that inebriates me, has burst forth in gladness from the sorrow that was in Adam. See, *I have prepared a table before thee, against them that afflict thee* (Ps. xxii. 5). I placed a guard before Eden against Adam who had violated that wondrous place, that even through his eyes he might suffer on in grief for the now withdrawn happiness. But against those that oppress you, I have prepared for you a life-giving table, and a joyful one; exchanging your sorrow for a joy that is unspeakable.

Eat the Bread that restores your nature. Drink the wine that is the Brightness of immortality. Eat the Bread that will purify you of the ancient bitterness; and drink the Wine that will heal the ancient wound. This is the Medicine of nature; this is the Punishment of the one who inflicted the wound. For your sake have I become like you, while My own nature I have not changed; so that you through Me might become of My divine nature. So let you be changed, and changed

to what is good, as to fruits in due season, and be changed from the world to God, from the flesh to the Spirit. I have become the True Vine among you; that in Me you may bring forth sweet-smelling fruits. Suck the fatness of My divine Food, and grow fat.

I am the Lord, *Who giveth food to all flesh* (Ps. cxxxv. 25); especially to those who fear Me, as David foretold in the words: *Being a merciful and gracious Lord, he hath given food to them that fear him* (cx. 5). In times past I rained manna on Israel, sending down bread from heaven that was prepared without labour (Wisd. xvi. 20). But the people whom I loved despised this wonder, and held it as nothing. *Israel hath not known me, and my people have not understood* (Is. i. 3). But not as to those, who ate manna in the desert and are dead, do I give you My Body. He that eateth this bread shall live for ever.

Have you grasped these things, Beloved? Have I made clear to you *the concealed riches of the secret places* of the Lord's words for this most holy day? Or do you wish me to dwell at length upon their glories? Most willingly shall we unfold them before you, to place them in a clear light before the eyes of the friends of Truth: that *upon which angels desire to look* (I Pet. i. 12): not however as putting aside the divinely revealed texts, or as making little account of them, but as striving to make clear the things with which they have relationship, as from an earlier source.

So therefore, as kind children, I beseech you to pray for me, that the Lord may grant me, who now am old and weary from living, and worn and stooped from a long and uphill journey, to ponder deeply and worthily upon the words that have been delivered to us, and to speak to you with judgement. Sustain me, O beloved, as those of Israel long ago bore Him Who was born amongst us, so that together we may go unto that most glorious Sion, and in spirit contemplate that sublime Citadel, and how He Who rules the ends of the earth has prepared Himself as a Mystic Supper, how He Who is seated upon the Cherubim reclines at a table, how He Who was eaten in Figure in Egypt here sacrifices Himself of His own will, and, eating of the Figure, as the Fulfiller of the Figures shows Himself as their Reality, and forthwith places Himself before His guests as the Food of Life; fulfilling the divine prophecies that came from Himself, framing anew the foundations of the things all-wisely decreed by Him, *flowing forth ever in a continuous stream* to all mankind, that He may bestow on every state and condition of men the divine gifts of His Love. Here then is the Gospel narrative of these events:

And while they were at supper, Jesus took bread, and blessed, and broke; and gave to his disciples, and said: Take ye, and eat. This is my body. And taking the chalice, he gave thanks, and gave to them, saying: Drink ye all of this. For this is my blood of the new testament, which shall be shed for many unto remission of sins (Mt. xxvi. 26–8).

O wondrous happening! O divine beginning of mysteries! He shows the way by the Letter; He fulfils through the Spirit. He prepared us by Types and Figures; He has shown favour to us in His Sacrifice. In Sion He fulfilled the law of

the Letter. From Sion He proclaims the law of Grace. Let us now see what things were done during the Supper; of what kind they were, and how great?

He riseth from the supper, and layeth aside his garments, and having taken a towel, girded himself. After that he putteth water into a basin, and began to wash the feet of the disciples, and to wipe them with the towel wherewith he was girded (Jn. xiii. 4, 5).

What could be stranger than this? What more awesome? He Who is *clothed with light as with a garment* (Ps. ciii. 2) is girded with a towel. He Who *binds up the waters in his clouds* (Job xxvi. 8), Who sealed the abyss by His fearful Name, is bound with a girdle. He Who *gathers together the waters of the sea as in a vessel* (Ps. xxxii. 7) now pours water into a basin. He Who *covers the tops of the heavens with water* (Ps. ciii. 3) washes in water the feet of His Disciples; and He Who *hath weighed the heavens with his palm, and the earth with three fingers* (Is. xl. 12) now wipes with undefiled palms the soles of His servants. He before Whom *every knee should bow, of those that are in heaven, on earth, and under the earth* (Phil. ii. 10) now kneels before His servants.

The Angels beheld Him, and wondered. Heaven saw it, and was afraid. Creation looked, and trembled. *He cometh therefore to Simon Peter. And Peter saith to him: Lord, dost thou wash my feet?* Have I not already declared I am unworthy even to be in your Presence, when I said: *Depart from me, O Lord, for I am a sinful man* (Lk. v. 8)? And now who am I that I should presume to this? Should I let You, this miserable nature of mine will die of shame and confusion. Everyone will find fault with me for my presumption, should I be so bold. Do not grieve Your servant, O Lord! I am not worthy to be called Your servant. Never in all eternity shall You wash my feet. I would shudder to see it; I am numbed even at the thought of it. God acting as a servant to a man! A king doing obedience to a slave! A master made subject to his servant! Spare me, I beseech You, for fear any one under heaven should come to hear of the presumption of Peter.

And what did the All-wise Dispenser of the Sacred Mysteries say to this? *What I am doing you do not now understand, Peter; but afterwards you will know. Let Me then do this holy service for you also. If you do not, you shall have no part with Me.* When he heard this the Chief of the Apostles began instead to listen, and did not know what answer to make. Alas, Lord, he says, I am straitened on every side. To be stubborn, would grieve me. To contradict You, would cause me pain. To refuse, would bring punishment on me. And to consent, would be the worst of all. So let the word of God prevail; not the arrogance of a slave. Let Divine wisdom prevail; not the stupidity of a servant. But I beg pardon for my presumption. Do You bear with me, and bid me to receive this service from You. Do as You will, Lord. Fulfil what is in Your Mind, Lord. And that I may attain to this inheritance with You, wash not alone my feet, but also my hands and my head. I now implore You, I most earnestly entreat You, that I may receive this divine washing, so that I may not be deprived of Your divine favour. May it be given to me to obtain the request of Your adorable will, lest I be deprived of Your great joy. I shall spread out my feet to You, I shall stretch out my hands to You, I shall bow my head, that I may not be cut off from the inheritance of my Lord. That I may not lose joy beyond all telling, I shall not hold to my own will, resisting God. Let every creature know that by a washing I, Peter, this day gain a heavenly kingdom.

After He had washed their feet the Lord sat down again, and He said to them: *Know you what I have done to you? You call me Master, and Lord; and you say well, for so I am. If I then being your Lord and Master, have washed your feet; you ought also to wash one another's feet. For I have given you an example, that as I have done to you, so you do also.* Therefore, imitate Me, your Lord, so that through this sacred action of Mine you may become partakers of the divine nature. I lay upon you this perfect way of exaltation. In time past I came down to this earth, when I was preparing for your race that first state of happiness. And taking the slime of the earth I formed man, and created spirit also upon the earth. And now it is My will to bend down again among you, that I may strengthen the foundations, the bases of my creation that have fallen.

I placed enmity and execration between the one who deceived, and the one deceived; his head lying in wait for her heel (Gen. iii. 15; xlix. 17). And now I arm that wounded heel against the dragon, that it may no longer limp along the right way. I have restored your feet that you may have *power to tread on serpents and scorpions, and upon all the power of*

the enemy, and nothing shall hurt you
(Lk. x. 19). The whisperer humbled
the pride of the first man formed of
the earth; wipe out that pride by a
cheerful humility, one with another.
Seek for this with your whole heart.
I am the Lord, Who gives grace to
the humble, detesting pride. *Every
one that exalteth himself shall be
humbled; and he that humbleth himself
shall be exalted* (Lk xviii. 14). Because of this I lay it upon you, that
you love one another: *By this shall
all men know that you are my disciples,
if you have love one for another.*

Again I say to you, Beloved, how
great is the dignity of this glorious
day, to which the Festivity itself,
the Presence of God, the Sacrifice
of this tremendous Victim, the gift
of immortality, and the pledge of
eternal life, all invite you.

And therefore, my beloved, and
sharers with me of the heavenly
vocation, imitate in this respect the
Author and the Perfecter of our
salvation, Jesus. Let us long for the
uplifting of our lowliness, for the
love that unites us to God, and for
a pure sincere faith in the Divine
Mysteries. Fly from all division;
avoid all discord; put far from you
all profane and idle tales, especially
such as are made up by empty-
mouthed and deceiving servants of
the devil: such as those who have
clothed themselves with the monas-
tic habit, though not with the mon-
astic silence, of the new wisdom;[33]
against whom the Lord has strongly
warned us to be watchful, as they
are difficult to guard against, because of the sheep's clothing they
have assumed; they who have armed
our spiritual brotherhood and our
much loved peace, and have grie-
vously disrupted our God-guarded

city. Their impious clamour He
will put down Who quelled the sea
by a word. And these very men,
while they themselves have but a
perverted understanding of Christ
our True God, strive to overthrow
our own hope of salvation in
Christ, and by this I mean our resurrection.

Where are they now, the solitary
wolves who have put on the clothing of sheep, who deny God, and
deny His power; those impious
pseudo-Christians, who because of
the Incarnation deny that Christ is
of the same Substance as the Father?
Let them tell us, these babbling
foolish praters, on Whose Body are
the Sheep of the Church pastured;
on what waters are the children of
the Church refreshed? For if the
Body of God is given to them, then
Christ the Lord is True God, and
not a simple man, nor as they say,
an angel, a minister of God, and one
of the incorporeal beings. And if
the Chalice is the Blood of God,
then it is not simply God, one of the
Adorable Trinity, the Son of God,
but God the Word made man. If
the Body of Christ is Food, and the
Blood of Christ is Drink, and so, as
they say, He is a mere man, how then
is eternal life promised to those who
approach the Sacred Table? How
is it He is shared among us here,
there, and everywhere, yet never
grows less? A mere body by no
means gives life to those who partake of it? Or do they call us false
witnesses of God, and in the Presence
of the Truth-loving God, because
we openly proclaim the Truth,
and teach the Mysteries that were
divinely bestowed on us?

May the divine mercy be gracious
to us, for making mention of these

things in the midst of the festive celebration of the most sacred Mysteries! Let us therefore receive the Body of Life Itself, Who because of us has taken up his abode in a body like ours, as the divine John says: *For the life was manifested* (I Jn. i. 2). And again: *And the word was made flesh, and dwelt amongst us* (Jn. i. 14); *Who is Christ, the Son of the living God* (Mt. xvi. 16), one of the Holy Trinity.

And let us drink His Sacred Blood unto the forgiveness of our sins, and unto the sharing with Him of life everlasting: believing that He is at the same time both Priest and Victim: He Who is offered and He Who offers, He Who gives and He Who is given: not dividing between two persons the divine, unbroken, and likewise uncommingled unity of the All Adorable Trinity. To Him be praise and adoration, with the Father and the Holy Spirit, for ever and ever. Amen.

NOTES

[1] PL 10, On the Trinity 8, 14. A very striking witness.

[2] PG 6, *First Apologia*, to the Emperor Titus and the People of Rome, on behalf of the Christians. Pars. 65–7. A Witness, and Martyr, of the Second Century (*c.* A.D. 100–65), to the Faith, life, and worship of the Church in his time.

[3] The peace, $\dot{\eta}$ $\epsilon\dot{\iota}\rho\dot{\eta}\nu\eta$, enjoined by St Paul on Corinthians, Thessalonians and Romans.

[4] $\gamma\dot{\epsilon}\nu o\iota\tau o$.

[5] From the *Dialogue with the Hebrew Trypho*. PG 6, pars. 40, 41.

[6] Ch. 15: Fast and almsdeeds.

[7] PG 7, *Against Heresies*, Book 4, Ch. 17, par. 4 *seq.*, Ch. 18, par. 1–5. St Irenaeus, Bishop of Lyons, and Father of the Church, is linked, through his acquaintance with St Polycarp, friend and disciple of St John, to the Apostolic age.

[8] Jer. ix. 24; Is. xliii. 23, 21; lxvi. 2; Jer. xi. 15; Zach. viii. 9, 10, 16, 17; Ps. xxxiii. 13, 4.

[9] PG 7, *Against Heresies*, Book 5, Ch. 2.

[10] PL 4, Epistle 63, *To Cecilius*. In opposition to those who used water (in place of wine) in the Chalice in the Lord's Supper. Although a letter, it was intended for public reading, being in fact an exposition and witness of Christian belief on the Eucharist and the Sacrifice of the Mass; it is a work of great mystical discernment.

[11] Vossio S. Ephraim, Tome 3, Oratio 17. This is the second half of the Sermon (*Oratio*), which is, *Against Those Who endeavour to scrutinize too closely the mysteries of the Son of God.*

[12] PG 44, On the Canticles, Homily X, col. 987.

[13] PL 16, On the Sacraments, Book 4, Ch. III–VI.

[14] Dedicate, bless, consecrate, celebrate, were used interchangeably at this time: their application deriving from the text; GLL 29, 73.

[15] Rom. vi. 3, 5. As Christ died, so you also died by the sacrament of Baptism, and you rose again through the grace of Christ. Death therefore there is; but not in the reality of bodily death, but in its likeness: for when you are dipped you put on the likeness of death and burial. St Ambrose, On the Sacraments, Book II, Ch. VII, 23.

[16] PL 16, On the Sacraments, Book V.

[17] The silence of Scripture regarding Melchisedech, as to the details of his life, where he came from, where he went, was part of the divine plan to foreshadow perfectly the Mystery of Christ's Eternal Generation and Priesthood, and its outward form. Abraham paid tithes to him, and received his blessing, and so acknowledges (and in Abraham Levi and the Priestly tribe) his superiority; and so the excellence of his, and therefore of the Church's, Priesthood. Cf. Genesis xiv. 8. There is also a reference to one of the innumerable heresies of the day: the Melchisedechians.

[18] PL 16, col. 445, footnote *c*. 'Many Fathers indicate that the mingling of water with the wine in the chalice was instituted by Christ Himself; as SS. Irenaeus, Book 4, Ch. 57; Cyprian, Epist. 63; Augustine, Bk. De Doctr. Christ., 21; to which may be added various liturgies, those of James, Mark, Basil, Chrysostom. In the Oriental Church water is poured into the chalice twice; cold water before the consecration, and warm just before Communion. There were heretics who believed water alone should be offered; concerning which, see Homily V.

[19] The Septuagint Version i. 3. τὸ ταμίειον ἀυτοῦ, His storeroom.

[20] *Mella suavia*, possibly a local allusion, to the wines of Mella, a river of Upper Italy, now Mela.

[21] Note *a*, col. 449, PL 16. From this, and a later, Ch. 6 de Myst., it is noted that the recently baptized were accustomed to receive Communion at the Altar. This was not everywhere observed as regards the rest of the faithful. In Constantinople the more notable laity, after bringing the *oblata* to the Priests at the Altar, remained in the choir, where they received the *Sacramenta*. In Milan these however, on presenting the *oblata*, withdrew outside the choir, but communicated at the Altar: Ambrose on one occasion ordering the Emperor Theodosius, following the oblation, to withdraw from the choir, and was immediately obeyed.

[22] Ambrose finds fault with their negligence in failing to receive Holy Communion frequently, and hints that some abstain from Communion on the pretext of being excluded by penance (which would imply private confession of sins); but this abstinence does not appear either frequent or continuous. But yet in this century the pristine fervour regarding daily Communion seemed to lessen, as Jerome also hints, Ep. 50, Adv. Jovin. Chrysostom castigates his people for the same negligence; but here again the negligence does not appear to be common. Daily Communion rather appears to be the rule; as Ambrose lays down.

[23] PG 58, Hom. 82–3, par. 4, *On Matthew*, col. 743.

[24] PG 62, Hom. 3 in Ephesians.

[25] The great festival of the Greek Church, when also the Lord's Baptism was commemorated.

[26] PL 35, Tr. 26 in John, par. 11 *seq.*, col. 1611.

[27] This close passage seems to mean, that of those partaking in this Sacred Rite, some, by reason solely of their *unworthy* partaking, are lost: so it is they, by their own will, who inflict death; not the Reality of the Sacrament.

28 PL 35, Tr. 27 in John.

29 PL 38, Sermon 132.

30 The Mystery of the Eucharist had been withheld from them till now.

31 PG 77, *Homiliae Diversae*, Hom. 10.

32 This whole discourse of the great Alexandrine Doctor is a mosaic of Scriptural phraseology. His mind seems to have been impregnated with the Scriptures, to such an extent that he thought and spoke only in their language, or with their words. It would be tedious, therefore, to trace out, and follow the source, of each single phrase or sentence; e.g., in this sentence, the five phrases are drawn respectively from: I Thess. v. 15; Is. xlv. 3; I Tim. i. 5; Mt. xxii. 11; Lk. xiv. 16.

33 The text here is a play on words, τὸ ἐρημικὸν καὶ οὐκ ἤρεμον κολόβιον. He is here referring to the bellicose Monophysite and Arian monks.

SECOND SUNDAY AFTER PENTECOST

I. CLEMENT OF ALEXANDRIA: THE CHRISTIAN USE OF FOOD

II. ST AUGUSTINE: THE THREE EXCUSES FROM THE SUPPER

III. ST GREGORY THE GREAT: THE SUPPER OF GOD AND THE SOUL

THE GOSPEL OF THE SUNDAY

LUKE xiv. 16–24

At that time Jesus spoke this parable to the Pharisees: A certain man made a great supper, and invited many. And he sent his servant at the hour of supper to say to them that were invited, that they should come, for now all things are ready. And they began all at once to make excuse. The first said to him: I have bought a farm, and I needs must go out and see it: I pray thee, hold me excused. And another said: I have bought five yoke of oxen, and I go to try them: I pray thee, hold me excused. And another said: I have married a wife, and therefore I cannot come.

And the servant returning, told these things to his lord. Then the master of the house, being angry, said to his servant: Go out quickly into the streets and lanes of the city, and bring in hither the poor, and the feeble, and the blind, and the lame. And the servant said: Lord, it is done as thou hast commanded, and yet there is room. And the Lord said to the servant: Go out into the highways and hedges, and compel them to come in, that my house may be filled. But I say unto you, that none of these men that were invited, shall taste of my supper.

EXPOSITION FROM THE CATENA AUREA

V. 16. *A certain man made a great supper, and invited many.*

CYRIL, *in Cat. GP*: This man is God the Father; as similitudes are formed in the likeness of reality. CHRYSOSTOM: For when God wills to manifest his power to punish He is spoken of as a bear, a leopard, a lion, and such like. When however He wishes

to reveal His mercy, He is spoken of as a man.

CYRIL: He therefore Who is the Creator of all things, and the Father of glory, made a great supper, that was made complete in Christ. For in these last times, and as it were in the evening of the world, the Son

164

of God shone upon us, and, suffering death for us, He gave us His own Body to eat. And because of this the lamb was slain at evening, according to the Mosaic law. Rightly then was the banquet prepared for us called a *supper*.

GREGORY, *Hom.* 36 *on the Gospels*: Or *He made a great supper* in that He has prepared for us the fulness of eternal delight. He invited many, but few came; for oftentimes those who are subject to Him in faith, refuse His eternal supper in their way of living. And this is the simple difference between the delights of the body, and those of the soul. Bodily delights, when we do not possess them, awaken in us a great desire for them. But when they are ours, and we taste them, our delight soon turns to distaste, through satiety. Spiritual delights on the other hand, when we do not possess them, are distasteful to us; but desired the more once we possess them. And the heavenly kindness recalls those delights to the eyes of our memory, and invites us so as to dispel our distaste. Hence:

V. 17. *And he sent his servant at the hour of supper to say . . .*

CYRIL, *as above*: This servant who is sent is Christ Himself, Who though by nature God, and True Son of God (cf. Is. xlii. 1), emptied Himself, taking the form of a servant. He was sent towards the hour of supper. For the Word of God did not take our nature from the beginning, but in these last times. And He adds: *For now all things are ready*. For in His Son the Father has prepared the good things given to the

world through Him: the taking away of sins, the partaking of the Holy Spirit, the dignity of adoption. To these Christ has called us, through the teaching of the Gospel.

AUGUSTINE, *Serm.* 112, I: Or again, the Man is the Mediator between God and man: the Man Jesus Christ. He sent so that they who were invited might come; that is, those whom He had called through the prophets He had sent, and who had in times past invited men to Christ's supper. They had been sent often to the people of Israel; often they had invited them to come at the hour of supper. And they, though they received those who invited them, refused the supper. They read the prophets, but they put Christ to death. *All things are ready*; that is, Christ now immolated, the Apostles are sent to those to whom the prophets were sent before.

GREGORY: By this servant, who is sent by the head of the family to summon those who were invited, is typified the company of those who are to preach the Gospel. It will sometimes happen that a great person may have a servant who is looked down upon. When the Lord commands something through him, the person of the one who speaks in His Name is not then to be despised; but let respect for the Lord Who sent him be observed in the heart of those who hear him.

The Lord is offering what should be asked for; He should not have to ask. He desires to give what could scarcely be hoped for; and yet they all begin at once to make excuses. For there follows:

V. 18. *And they began all at once to make excuses.*

When a rich man invites the poor to a banquet, how they hasten to come. We are invited to the divine banquet, and we make excuses. AUGUSTINE, *Serm.* 112: The excuses were three in number: *The first said, I have bought a farm, and I must needs go out and see it.* In the farm dominion is signified; and so the pride of dominion is the first vice to be castigated: for the first man wished to rule, and wished to serve no master.

GREGORY: Or by the farm is meant earthly substance. So he goes out to it who for the purpose of gain thinks only of worldly things. AMBROSE: Just as to a veteran is allotted the pay of a despised calling, so he who, intent on lesser things, purchases for himself but earthly goods, cannot obtain the kingdom of heaven; since the Lord says: *Sell all whatever thou hast, and come follow me* (Lk. xviii. 22).

V. 19. *And another said: I have bought five yoke of oxen . . .*

AUGUSTINE, *Serm.* 112: The *five yoke* of oxen mean the five senses of the body, which are, in the eyes sight, hearing in the ears, smell in the nostrils, taste in the mouth, touch in all the members. But the figure of the *yoke* is more easily seen in the three first: two eyes, two ears, two nostrils. Here are three yoke. In the mouth, that is, in the sense of taste, we find a sort of yoke: for nothing is tasted unless what is touched by both tongue and palate. The pleasure of the flesh, which belongs to touch, is doubled in a con-

cealed manner. It is both inward and outward.

They are called yoke *of oxen*, because it is through these bodily senses that earthly things are sought for. For *oxen* till the earth; and men without faith, given over to earthly things, refuse to believe in anything unless what they can examine with the fivefold perception of the body. For, says such a one, I believe only what I see. If such are our sentiments we too shall be kept from the supper by five yoke of oxen. But that you should know it is not the delights of these five senses that seduce him, and press their joys upon him, that was meant, but a certain curiosity, He does not say, *I have bought five yoke of oxen*, and I go to feed them; but, *I go to try them.*

GREGORY: And aptly is curiosity signified by the bodily senses, for they cannot see the things of the mind, but only outward things. And as it seeks to search into the lives of others, and is incapable of knowing its own inward life, it is ever eager to know of outward things. But we must note that each who excuses himself from the supper of the Inviter, the one because of his farm, the other because he must prove his five yoke of oxen, mingles with his reply some words of humility; for when he says, *I pray thee*, there is humility in his words; but pride in the deed.

V. 20. *And another said: I have married a wife, and therefore . . .*

AUGUSTINE, *as above*: That is, the pleasures of the body, which ensnare many; would that it were outward, not inward. For he who said, *I have married a wife*, is charmed by the delights of the flesh, so he too excuses himself from the supper. Let him take care he does not die of inward hunger. BASIL, *Cat. GP*: He says, *I cannot* come; for the reason that the human mind, inclining towards earthly seductions, becomes feeble in doing what relates to God.

GREGORY: For though marriage is good, and established by divine providence, for the begetting of human kind, yet some there are who seek it, not for children, but for bodily pleasure. And so by means of a just thing that which is unjust is aptly made clear to us.

AMBROSE: Or, marriage is not blamed, but virginity is called to greater honour; since *the unmarried woman thinketh on the things of the Lord, that she may be holy both in body and in spirit* (I Cor. vii. 34). But she that is married thinks about the things of the world.

AUGUSTINE: John, when he said: *All that is in the world, is the concupiscence of the flesh, and the concupiscence of the eyes, and the pride of life*, begins at the point where the Gospel ends. The concupiscence of the flesh: *I have married a wife*. The concupiscence of the eyes: *I have bought five yoke of oxen*. The pride of life: *I have bought a farm*. A part standing for the whole, the five senses have been commemorated by the eyes alone; which hold the chief place among the senses: for sight, though properly of the eye alone, is wont to be used of all five senses.

CYRIL, *in Luke*: Whom are we to think these are, who refused to come

for the causes mentioned, if not the rulers of the Jews, whom we see, throughout the sacred pages, rebuked for such things?

ORIGEN: Or, they who bought a farm, and declined the supper, are they who have taken to themselves other teaching concerning the divinity, and have not made trial of the doctrines they had. He who bought the five yoke of oxen is he who thinks little of his intellectual nature, and runs after the things of the senses alone; and so he is unable to comprehend the world of the spirit. He who married a wife, is he who is wedded to the flesh; a lover of pleasure rather than of God.

AMBROSE: Let us suppose there are three classes of men shut out from that supper: Gentiles, Jews, and heretics. The Jews by a corporeal ritual impose upon themselves the yoke of the Law; for the five yoke are *the ten words*, of which it is said: *God showed you his covenant, which he commanded you to do, and the ten words that he wrote in two tables of stone* (Deut. iv. 13, that is, the Commandments of the Decalogue etc.). Or the five yoke are the Five Books of the Law (of Moses). But heresy, like Eve, with feminine rashness, makes trial of the nature of faith. And the Apostle (Eph. v; Col. iii) tells us that avarice must be shunned, for fear that caught in the ways of the Gentiles we may be unable to reach Christ's Kingdom. So he who has bought a farm is a stranger to His Kingdom; and likewise is he who has chosen the yoke of the Law, rather than the gift of Grace; as he also who excuses himself because he has married a wife.

V. 21. *And the servant returning told these things to his lord* . . .

AUGUSTINE, *on Genesis* v. 19: God does not need messengers to know his lesser creature, as though through them He would know more. He knows all things for ever and without change. He uses messengers for our sake; and for theirs. For it is the happiness of their nature to stand before God, and serve him in this way, to care for those lower than themselves, and to obey His commands.

CYRIL: But the Master of the house is angry with the rulers of the Jews; in that they merited His indignation for rejecting their vocation; as they themselves bear witness: *Hath any one of the rulers believed in him?* So there follows: *Then the master of the house, being angry* . . .

BASIL, *in Psalm* xxxvii: Not that the passion of anger touches the Divine Nature, but an activity which in us is called anger and indignation is called the anger of God. CYRIL: In this way the Master of the house is said to be angry with the rulers of the Jews, and in their place were called many simple persons from the Jewish people; such as were without authority. For when Peter spoke to the multitude, at first three thousand believed, then five thousand, and afterwards many from among them. So there follows: *Go out quickly into the streets and lanes of the city, and bring in hither the poor, and the feeble, and the blind, and the lame.*

AMBROSE: He invites the poor and the feeble and the blind to show us that no imperfection of the body excludes us from the Kingdom; rather such as they sin more rarely, since they have not the same incitement to sin as the sound; or that the infirmity of sin is taken away through the mercy of the Lord. So he sends them into the streets, that they may come from the broad ways *to the narrow way.*

GREGORY: Since the proud refuse to come, the poor are then chosen. They are called *the poor and the feeble* who in their own estimate of themselves are weak. For there are *poor* who are strong; who though they live in poverty are yet proud. The *blind* are those who have no brightness in their minds. The *lame* those who do not follow the upright path in their journey through life. But just as their defects are symbolized by the infirmities of their bodily members, as those were sinners who being invited refused to come, so also were they sinners who were invited and came; but the proud sinners are rejected, the humble chosen.

So God chooses those whom the world despises, for it often happens that this very contempt will call a man to himself; and the less they have in the world to delight them, the more promptly will many hearken to the voice of God. When therefore the Lord calls certain persons from the streets and lanes to His supper, He is pointing to those who, dwelling in the city, had learned to observe the law. But the number that believed from the people of Israel did not suffice to fill the place of the heavenly supper. Hence we have:

V. 22. *And the servant said: Lord it is done as thou hast commanded* . . .

Already a great number of Jews had entered; but there was yet room in the kingdom: where the multitude of the Gentiles was yet to be received. So there is added:

V. 23. *And the Lord said to the servant: Go out into the highways . . .*

When He commands that His guests be brought in from *the highways and hedges*, He is seeking the people of the world, that is, the Gentiles.

AMBROSE: Or, He sends to the highways, and round about the hedges, because they are fit for the kingdom of heaven who are not taken up with the desires of the present life; and walking as it were along the narrow way of good will, they are hastening on to the things of the future life. And they also who, in the manner of a hedge, separate the cultivated from the untilled ground, and oppose the incursions of the beasts, know how to distinguish good from evil, and maintain a defence against the temptations of spiritual evil.

AUGUSTINE: The Gentiles came from *the streets and the lanes*; heretics from *the hedges*. For they who make a hedge make a division. Let them be withdrawn from the hedges; rooted out from the thorns. They refuse to be *compelled*; of their own will, they say, shall we enter. *Compel them to come in*, He says; outside they will find but want, and from that good will has its beginning.

GREGORY: They therefore who broken by the misfortunes of this world return to God's love are compelled to enter. But truly fearful is the sentence that follows:

V. 24. *But I say to you, that none of these men that were invited shall taste of my supper.*

Let no man then take this invitation lightly, lest through making excuses when he is invited, he may find when he has the desire to enter, that he is now unable.

I. CLEMENT OF ALEXANDRIA

The Christian Use of Food[1]

There are some who live to eat; which is no doubt also true of the dumb beasts, 'for whom life is but a stomach'. But the Master has taught us that we are to eat to live. For us eating is not a necessity, neither is pleasure our end. But because of our sojourn here below, we whom the Word is leading on to immortality, we choose to eat. It is simple and natural our food, not rare in kind, but such as is prepared for simple incurious children, adapted rather to maintain life than to provide pleasure.

For life depends on two things; namely, health and strength, and plain food contributes to this; as being good for the digestion, and also for the liveliness of the body. From this comes health, and reasonable strength; not strength beyond measure, excessive, painful, like the athletes'; because of their necessity to eat. There are very many detestable kinds of foods, which cause a variety of troubles: they weaken health, they upset the stomach, the sense of taste is spoiled by an evil skill in cooking, as well as by the useless art of pastry making.

And some men presume to call eating the refinement of delight; which then slips down into hurtful pleasures. Antiphanes, the physician of Delios, said that this is the sole cause of disease: the variety of dishes. For those who cannot endure truth reject, for I know not what vanity, a plain and moderate way of living, and make a great fuss over foreign foods. To me this folly is deplorable; but they are not ashamed to sing about their delights. They seek anxiously for eels from the Straits of Sicily, and other kinds of eels from the Meander, and for kids from Melos, and mullet from Sciathos, shellfish from Pelorus, oysters from Abydenus, Daphinian turtles, and Chelidonian figs; because of which the unhappy Persian with a countless host invaded Attica. And they buy birds from Phasis, Egyptian waterfowl, peacocks from Thrace. Exchanging these delicacies the gluttons open wide their mouths with relish; and whatsoever the earth provides, or the depths of Pontus, or the vast spread of the heavens, exists but to serve their gluttony.

To me it seems that a man of this kind is nothing more than a mouth. *Be not desirous of the food of rich men,* says the Scriptures (Prov. xxiii. 3 Sept.), for this goes with a life that is false and shameless. For they are devoted to dainties; which soon change into excrement. But we who seek the food of heaven have need to control our earthly stomach, and especially the things that are pleasing to it; since *God shall destroy*

both it and them (I Cor. vi. 13), says the Apostle, justly execrating those given to gluttony. For *meats are for the belly,* on which this carnal and deadly life depends; which some with unbridled tongue dare to call *agapes:*[2] these festive convivialities reeking of soup and the steam of cooking, dishonouring the sacred *agape,* beautiful and salutary work of the Word, with I know not what sort of stew, and going on to disgrace the name with the flow of wine, with carousals, with wantonness, and the reek of smoke. They are deceived in their notion if they expect what God has promised from such suppers as these.

Christian Frugality. But those gatherings which take place through joyfulness, and which we, following the example of our Lord, would call a gathering, a dinner, or also a supper, these the Lord did not call *agapes.* He says in one place: *When thou art invited to a wedding, sit not down in the first place. But when thou art invited, go sit down in the lowest place* (Lk. xiv. 8–10). And in another place He says: *When thou makest a dinner or a supper, call the poor:* for whom the meal is especially to be prepared. And later: *A certain man made a great supper.*

But I think I know from what source this beautiful name for such suppers has come. From the gluttons, and from gluttony, and 'from those infatuated with the love of such repasts', as the Comic says. But it is true to say that, 'the most of the dinner is dear to the most'; for they have not yet learned, that it is God Who has prepared for His masterpiece, which is man, both food and drink: for his life, not for his delight. For it is not in accord with the nature of our bodies that they are helped by luxuries. On the contrary they who eat the plainest food are the most robust, the healthiest, and superior to the rest; like servants as compared with their masters, labourers compared with the owners of the soil. And not alone are they stronger, but they have a better understanding; like philosophers as compared with rich men. For they do not bury their mind in nourishment, nor soften it with delights.

But the food that comes from heaven is charity, the rational feast. *It beareth all things, believeth all things, hopeth all things; charity never falleth away* (I Cor. xiii. 7, 8). And, *Blessed is he that shall eat bread in the kingdom of heaven* (Lk. xiv. 15). But it is the gravest misfortune should charity, which cannot fall away, be thrown down into the midst of earthly messes. And would you wish me to think that *this* supper is brought to an end? *If I should distribute all my goods to feed the poor, and have not charity, I am nothing* (I Cor. xiii. 3). On this charity depends *all the law and the prophets* (Mt. xxii. 40). If you love the Lord thy God and thy neighbour you shall have this celestial banquet in heaven; on earth it is called a supper, as we see from the Scripture. The supper takes place because of charity; but the supper is not charity; only a token of common good will, lightly bestowed. *Let not then our good be evil spoken of. For the kingdom of God is not meat and drink* (Rom. xiv. 16, 17), says the Apostle; lest it be thought to be but a casual meal, and not *justice and peace, and joy in the Holy Ghost.* He who eats of this supper, the most

perfect of all, shall obtain the Kingdom of God, beholding there the company of charity, the heavenly Church.

Charity therefore is something pure, worthy of God, and its mission a communion one with another. *The thought that moves us in the care of the child is love,* says holy Wisdom (vi. 19), and *love is the keeping of her laws.* These festive gatherings have some glimmer of charity, from a common way of life, a disposing together towards the delight that is forever. The supper therefore is not charity (*agape*); the festivity may prepare the way for charity. *May thy children, whom thou hast loved, learn, O Lord, that not bread alone doth nourish man, but thy word that cherishes those who believe in thee* (Deut. viii. 6 Sept.). For not in bread alone doth the just man live.

Let our supper then be light and digestible, suited to keeping vigil,[3] not mingled with a variety of flavours; nor is this something outside the scope of the Pedagogue. For charity is the nurse of fraternal love, being plentifully endowed, giving out in due measure, healthfully ministering to the body, sharing its goods with its neighbours. Food that exceeds a just measure is harmful to man, and makes the soul dull, the body unhealthy and prone to disease. And the voluptuaries who torment themselves and grieve and even utter blasphemies over sauces are branded with names such as, greedy, glutton, voracious, insatiable and such like. Rightly are they also called gadflies, weasels, parasites, gladiators in contests of voracity, selling their honour, friendships, even life itself, for the gratification of their stomach, crawling on their bellies, beasts in the likeness of men, and made in the likeness of their father, a devouring wild beast.

And those whom they call 'the abandoned' (ἀσώτους) seem to me to show clearly what their end will be; those who shall not be saved (with the letter *s* omitted). For are they not of those who are absorbed in pots, and in the manifold and precise use of condiments, of low and abject soul, children indeed of earth, who seek food day after day, and yet shall not be fed? Does not the Holy Scripture grieve over them by the mouth of Isaias, withholding from them the name love-feast (*agápe*), as their feasting was not in accord with reason? *They however gave themselves to joy and gladness, killing calves and slaying rams, saying: Let us eat and drink; for tomorrow we shall die* (xxii. 13). And that He holds such revelling sinful is then revealed. *This iniquity shall not be forgiven you till you die*, meaning, not that that death which takes from us all feeling brings us forgiveness of sin, but brings rather the death of salvation, as a consequence of sin. *Take no pleasure in their wanton revellings*, says Wisdom, *be they ever so small* (Ecclus. xviii. 32).

Things Sacrificed to Idols. Here we must also speak of things sacrificed to idols, since we are told that we must abstain from them (I Cor. viii). To me they seem foul and abominable, whose blood flies 'Towards souls in Erebos now void of light.' *I would not that you should be partakers with devils*, says the Apostle (I Cor. x. 20). Diverse is the food of those who are saved from those who perish. From this last we must abstain; not that we greatly fear them (for they are without power),

but because of our own conscience which is holy, and out of detestation of the demons, whom we abhor, and to whom this food has been sacrificed; and also because of the weak character of those who are easily led astray, *and their conscience, being weak, is defiled. But meat doth not commend us to God.* For, says the Gospel, *Not that which goeth into the mouth defileth a man, but that which cometh out of the mouth* (Mt. xv. 11). The natural use of food is in itself an indifferent thing: *For neither, if we eat, shall we have the more; nor if we eat not, shall we have the less.* But it is not fitting that those who are held worthy of divine food should be *partakers with devils.* For, says the Apostle, *Have we not the power to eat and to drink, and to carry about a woman*, but yet, keeping power over pleasures, let us keep our desires under control. *But*, he says, *take heed lest perhaps this your liberty become a stumbling block to the weak* (v. 9).

It is not becoming that, living wantonly and prodigally, we should, like the figure of the son in the Gospel, waste the gifts of the Father, but should rather use them worthily, as we are commanded; since we have received power to use them as we will, not to be slaves to them. It is therefore an admirable thing, and one to be striven for, raising our eyes upwards to the Truth, to keep to that Divine Food which is from above, and be filled with Its truly inexhaustible Vision, tasting of this unchanging, abiding and unclouded delight. For the food of Christ shows us that this is the *agape* we are to look for.

It is abhorrent to reason, and useless, and not even human, that we should be fattened like the beasts for slaughter, with our eyes ever towards the earth, like those who spend their time reclining at tables, pursuing a life dedicated to gluttony, burying what is good in this life which soon shall be no more, concerned only with the enticements of eating, because of which cooks are held in greater regard than those who till the earth.

Christian Conduct. We are not doing away with simple hospitality, but we consider the breaking down of our common life as a calamity. So gluttony must be avoided; partaking of but few things, and these according as we need them, *and if any of them that believe not invite you, and you be willing to go,* but it is better not to mix with those who are given to excess, *eat of anything that is set before you, asking no question for conscience's sake* (I Cor. x. 27). Similarly the Apostle tells us that, *whatever is sold in the shambles,* buy it, asking no question about it. It is not therefore wholly forbidden to use various kinds of foods, but we should not be eager for them. Whatever is put before us we should eat of it, in a Christian manner, honouring the community by the blamelessness and moderation of our conduct among others; and let us partake of whatever rich foods may be brought in, and placed before all, not touching however the seasoned dainties, that soon will not be.

Let not him that eateth, despise him that eateth not: and he that eateth not, let him not judge him that eateth (Rom. xiv. 3). Paul continuing gives us the reason for this precept: *He who eateth,* he says, *eateth to the Lord, and gives thanks to God. And he that eateth not, to the Lord he eateth not, and gives thanks to God* (v. 6); as to give thanks is fitting nourishment. And furthermore, he who always gives thanks to God is not carried away by pleasures. And where we also, for courtesy's sake, invite a few friends, much the more should we abstain from sumptuous and seasoned foods, giving in our own conduct an example of restrained living, as we ourselves have Christ's example. *For if food of any kind scandalize my brother, I will never eat flesh, lest I should scandalize my brother* (I Cor. viii. 13). With a little continence I can gain a man. For, *have we not power to eat and to drink?* And we know the truth, he says, *that an idol is nothing in the world, and that there is no God but one, and one Lord Jesus Christ, by whom are all things; but* he says, *through thy knowledge shall the weak brother perish, for whom Christ died?* They who so wound the weak conscience of the brethren sin against Christ.

For this reason the Apostle, warning us, decides concerning associations of this kind, bidding us not *to keep company with them. If any man that is named a brother, be a fornicator, or covetous, or a server of idols, with such a one not so much as to eat* (I Cor. v. 11); neither in word nor in dainties, fearing that for us from this source would come defilement, just as from the tables of evil spirits. *It is good not to eat flesh, and not to drink wine,* as he himself confesses (Rom. xiv. 21), and as do the Pythagoreans. For this is rather the food of the wild beast, and the fumes that rise thick and heavy from them darken the soul. And though a man does not sin by taking these things, partaking of them let him partake in moderation; being neither given over to them, nor depending on them, nor with mouth open longing for them. For then a voice will whisper to him: *Destroy not the work of God for meat* (Rom. xiv. 20).

Christian Moderation. Although all things are lawful for me, all things do not edify (I Cor. x. 23); for they who do all that is lawful, soon come down to doing what is not lawful. As justice is not acquired by greed, so neither is moderation through intemperance, nor the manner of life of a Christian by luxury. Far from the table of truth the foods that provoke to evil. For though all things were made purely for men's use, it is good nevertheless not to use all, nor is this ever expedient; for time and circumstances and place, the presence of someone, will give him who is being formed some indication as to what is profitable to him. And what is fitting has great power to put an end to a way of life that is given over to the stomach. No one is poor in what is necessary; no man has been overlooked. For it is the same God who feeds the birds and fishes, in a word, all dumb creatures (Mt. vi. 25). We as their masters are much more important than they; and closer to God, the more we are moderate in all things. For we were made that we might know God, not that we might eat and drink. *The just eateth and filleth his soul; but the belly of the wicked is never to be filled* (Prov. xiii. 25); in that their appetites never cease from desiring.

Abundance is to be used, not alone for ourselves, but also for social communion. So we must be careful of those foods which, though we are not hungry, we are forced to eat, and which serve to stimulate the appetite. For is there not in simple fare a great variety of healthy things to eat: onions, olives, certain greens, milk, cheese, ripe fruits, whatever is cooked without fat; and if meat is desired let some be provided, either roast or boiled. *Have you here anything to eat,* said the Lord (Lk. xxiv. 41) to His Disciples, after He had risen from the dead? And they who had learned frugality from Him, *offered him a piece of broiled fish.* And when He had eaten it before them, Luke tells us, He said to them the things He had said earlier.

They should not be concerned about sweets and dainties who eat after the manner of the Word. Of foods those are most fitting which may be eaten at once, without the use of fire, since they are already prepared for us. Then those which are simple and plain, as we have said. It is well known that happiness is found in the practice of virtue. Matthew the Apostle lived on seeds, fruit and vegetables, and went without meat. John went further in his austerity, *his food was locusts and wild honey* (Mt. iii. 4). Peter did not eat the flesh of swine. But, as we read in chapter ten of the Acts of the Apostles, on one occasion, being hungry, he desired to taste something. And as they were preparing it *there came upon him an ecstasy of mind. And he saw the heaven opened, and a certain vessel descending, as it were a great linen sheet let down by the four corners from heaven to earth: wherein were all manner of fourfooted beasts, and creeping things of the earth, and fowls of the air. And there came a voice to him. Arise, Peter: kill, and eat. But Peter said: Far be it from me;*

for I never did eat any thing that is common and unclean. And the voice spoke to him again the second time: That which God hath cleansed, do not call common.

And so for us the kind of food is neither good nor bad. *Not that which goeth into the mouth defileth a man,* but the follies of intemperance. For when God made man He said to him, *all things shall be food for you* (Gen. ix. 3). Nevertheless, *it is better to be invited to herbs with love, than to a fatted calf with hatred* (Prov. xv. 17). And this brings us once

more to what we said earlier, that herbs of themselves do not make a love feast, but that we should partake of our meals in brotherly love; using moderation in all things, but especially in the preparation of what we are to eat. For extremes are dangerous; the just mean is good. Those others, of whom we have spoken, *whose God is their belly; and whose glory is in their shame; who mind earthly things,* of those the Apostle has foretold nothing that is good; for he says of them: *Their end is destruction* (Phil. iii. 19).

II. St Augustine, Bishop and Doctor

The Three Excuses from the Supper[4]

Luke xiv. 16–24

I. *The Jews were invited to the Supper; we are brought there and compelled to enter.* The holy Lessons have been read out to us, and we have listened to them, and we now propose with God's help to say something to you concerning them. In the Apostolic lesson thanks are offered to God for the faith of the Gentiles, and this because He it was that wrought it. In the psalm we say: *O God of hosts, convert us; and show thy face, and we shall be saved* (lxxix. 8). In the Gospel we are invited to a supper; or rather, some were invited; we were not invited, but brought there, and not alone brought there, but compelled to enter. For this is what we have heard; that, *A certain man made a great supper.*

Who is this man, if not the Mediator between God and man, the Man Jesus Christ? He it was that sent word that those who were invited should now come; for the hour had

arrived for them to come. Who are the invited, but those who had been called by the prophets, who had been sent before this. When were they invited? Of old, when the prophets who were sent invited them to the supper of Christ. They were sent therefore to the people of Israel. They were sent often, and often they called to men to come at the hour of the Supper. They received those who invited them; but the invitation they rejected. They read the prophets; but they put Christ to death. And when they killed Him, unknowingly, they prepared the Supper for us. Christ being offered up, and the Supper now ready, the Supper of the Lord, commended to us and confirmed by His hands and by His mouth, as the faithful have learned, the Apostles are sent to those to whom the prophets had been sent before. *Come ye to the supper.*

II. *The Three Excuses*. They who would not come made excuses. How did they excuse themselves? One said: I have bought a farm; I must go and see it. Another said: I have bought five yoke of oxen, and I go to try them. I pray thee, hold me excused. The third said: I have married a wife; hold me excused, I cannot come. Are not these the excuses that serve all men who decline to come to this supper? Let us consider them, examine them, and find out: but to the end that we may be put on our guard.

In the purchase of the farm the pride of dominion is signified; so pride is castigated. For to have a farm, to hold it as their possession, to occupy it, to have it subject to them, to rule it, delights men. A bad fault; the first fault. For the first man wished to rule, and wished no one to have dominion over him. And what does having dominion mean but taking delight in one's own power? *I have bought a farm; pray hold me excused*. Having acquired power he refused to come.

III. *The Five Yoke of Oxen, the curiosity of the five senses*. Did it not suffice to say, I have bought oxen? There is no doubt something hidden here which because of its obscurity tempts us to look for it, to understand it; and because it is closed to us we are exhorted to knock. The five yoke of oxen are the senses of this body. The senses of the body as we all know are five in number; and they who have not noted this fact will no doubt recognize it when told it. We find therefore five senses in the body. In the eyes sight, hearing in the ears, smell in the nostrils, taste in the mouth, touch

in all the members. By seeing we perceive black and white, and things coloured in any way, dark or bright. By hearing we perceive harsh sounds and musical sounds. By smelling we perceive that things have sweet odours or unpleasant odours. By taste we perceive that things are sweet or bitter. By touching we perceive that things are hard or soft, rough or smooth, hot or cold.

They are five in number, and they are pairs. That they are pairs is seen easiest in the first three senses. We have two eyes, two ears, two nostrils: so we have three yoke. In the mouth, that is, in the sense of taste, we find pairing of a kind: for nothing can be tasted in the mouth unless when tongue and palate touch. The pleasure of the body which relates to the sense of touch is as it were paired in a concealed manner. For it is both internal and external. So it too is doubled.

And why are they spoken of as five yoke of *oxen*? Because it is through these senses of the body that earthly things are sought for. For oxen till the earth. There are men without faith, given over to earthly things, taken up with the things of the body, and they will not believe anything unless what they can discover by the fivefold perception of the body. They regard these five senses as the sole norm of their decisions. I do not believe, such a man will say, except what I can see. Here is what I know; I am sure of this: This is white, this is black, this is round, this is square, it is this colour or that colour; I know this, I perceive this, I understand this. Nature itself teaches me. I am not forced to believe what you cannot show me. Here is a voice; I hear it, that it is a voice: it sings, well or badly, or sweetly or hoarsely. I know, I have learned this, it comes to me. A thing smells well, or smells unpleasantly; I know this, I perceive it. This is sweet, this is bitter, this is salty, this is tasteless. What more can *you* tell me? By touch I know what is hard, what is soft, what is rough, what is smooth, what warms, what cools. What more can *you* show me?

IV. *What hinders faith. The Supper consecrated by the Lord's hands.* The Apostle, our Thomas, who would not believe even what his own eyes told him of Christ the Lord, that is, of the Resurrection of Christ, was held back by this difficulty. *Except I shall see in his hands the print of the nails, and put my hand into his side, I will not believe* (Jn. xx. 25). And the Lord, Who could have risen from the dead without any trace of a wound, had retained the scars that the Apostle might touch them, and be healed of the wounds in his own heart. And yet, about to call man to His supper, despite the excuse of the five yoke of oxen, He said: *Blessed are they that have not seen, and have believed.*

We, my brethren, we who are called to the supper, are not kept back by these five yoke. For in this time we have not aspired to see the face of the Lord in the flesh, or desired to listen with our ears to the voice proceeding from His mouth of flesh; nor sought for any earthly odour of Him. A certain woman anointed him with most precious ointment, and *the house was filled with the odour of it* (Jn. xii. 3). But we were not there. We did not

smell Him; yet we believe. The Supper He consecrated with His own hands, He gave to His Disciples. But we did not sit down with Him at that feast; yet daily we partake of that Supper through faith. Do not regard it as a strange thing that at that Supper, which He gave with His own hands, one who was without faith was present. Better the faith that came after that than the treachery of that hour. Paul was not there, who came to believe; Judas was there who betrayed. How many are there, even now, at this same Supper, who, though they have not seen that Table, nor tasted with their mouths, nor beheld with their eyes the Bread Which the Lord then took into His hands, yet since this is the Same that is now consecrated, how many are there, even now, in this same Supper, who *eat and drink judgement to themselves* (I Cor. xi. 29)?

V. *Curiosity of the senses no help to salvation.* How did it come about that the Lord spoke of this supper? It was because one of those who sat at table with Him, at a feast to which He had been invited, had said: *Blessed is he that shall eat bread in the kingdom of God.* This man was as it were sighing for what was afar off, and the Bread Itself sat there before him. Who is the Bread of the Kingdom of God if not He Who says: *I am the living bread which came down from heaven* (Jn. vi. 41)? Prepare then not thy mouth but thy heart. It was in this circumstance then that the supper was spoken of.

Now we believe in Christ when we receive Him in faith. In receiving Him we have learned what we are to think. We have received a little, and we are nourished, in our heart. So it is not what is seen but what is believed that feeds us. We have not therefore also looked for that outward seeing, nor have we said: They may have believed who with their eyes saw the Risen Lord and with their hands have felt Him, if what they said is true; but we have not touched Him, why should we believe? Were we to think such thoughts we would be kept from the supper by those five yoke of oxen.

That you may know, brethren, that it was not the gratification of these five senses, which seduce man and press their delights on him, that was signified, but a certain curiosity, He does not say: *I have bought five yoke of oxen*, and I go to feed them; but *I go to try them.* He who wishes to try, by the pairs of oxen, does not wish to be in doubt, as the holy Thomas, by means of his pairs, did not wish to be left in doubt. I wish to see, I wish to touch, I wish to put in my hand, he says. *Put thy fingers into my side*, says the Lord, *and be not faithless.* For you have I been put to death. Through the place you wish to touch I have poured out My blood, that I might redeem you. And yet you doubt of Me, until you touch Me? Then this too I shall give you; this also I shall reveal. Touch and believe. Look upon the place of My wound, and heal the wound of your own doubt.

VI. *The wife signifies the pleasures of the flesh.* It is this pleasure of the flesh that ensnares many; would that it were outward, and not inward also. There are those who say: A man cannot be happy unless he enjoys the pleasures of the body. It

is these to whom the Apostle refers, who say: *Let us eat and drink for tomorrow we shall die* (I Cor. xv. 32). Who has returned to this life from there? Who has told us what happens there?

He who says this is he who has married a wife, who has embraced flesh, who takes his delight in the pleasures of flesh, and excuses himself from the supper. Let him take care he does not die of inward hunger. Give ear to John, the holy Apostle and Evangelist: *Love not the world, nor the things which are in the world* (I Jn. ii. 15). O you who come to the Supper of the Lord, *Love not the world, nor the things which are in the world!* He did not say, Have not, but, *Love not.* You have had, you have possessed, you have loved. The love of earthly things is the bird-lime of the soul's wings. You have desired the things of earth, and you have been held fast. Who will give me the wings of a dove? When will you fly, and where will you truly be at rest, since here, where you have wilfully chosen to rest, you are unhappily held fast?

Love not the world. It is a divine trumpet speaking. By the words of this trumpet is it proclaimed without ceasing to the earth and to all the world: *Love not the world, nor the things that are in the world. If any man love the world, the charity of the Father is not in him. For all that is in the world is the concupiscence of the flesh, and the concupiscence of the eyes, and the pride of life.* He begins from the point where the Gospel leaves off: *I have married a wife*, is the concupiscence of the flesh; *five yoke of oxen*, the concupiscence of the eyes. *I have bought a farm*, the pride of life.

VII. *By the eyes are also meant the other senses.* As the whole may be represented by a part, so do the eyes signify the other senses also: for the eyes hold the first place among the five. And so we use the word *see* in speaking of the other senses, though sight pertains strictly to the eyes only. How is this? First, as to what refers to the eyes, you say: See how white it is. Look, see how white it is! This is the work of the eyes. Listen, and see how musical it is! Could we, do you think, say: Hear, and see how white it is? The word *see* is used for all the senses; whereas the distinguishing word of the other senses is not so used. Look and see how musical it is! Smell and see how pleasant it is! Taste and see how sweet it is! Touch and see how soft it is! Since they are all equally senses, we should also say: Hear and feel how musical it is! Smell and feel how soft! Taste and feel how sweet! Touch and feel how soft it is! But we do not use such phrases.

For the Lord also, when He appeared to His Disciples after His Resurrection, seeing them wavering in faith, thinking it was a ghost they saw, said to them: *Why are you troubled? And why do thoughts arise in your heart? See my hands and feet, that it is I Myself.* And a little later: *See,* He says, *Handle and see!* Look and see; handle and see. See with the eyes only; see with all the senses. Seeking the inward sense of faith He draws near to the outward senses of the body. We gather nothing of the Lord by these outward senses. We hear with the ears; but we have believed with the heart. We have heard, but not from His mouth, but from the mouth of His preachers; from the mouths of those who then

sat at table with Him, and in what they have poured forth, they invite us.

VII. *Let no one delay in coming to the Supper.* Let us put aside all idle wicked excuses, and come to the Supper in which our souls are fed. Let no swelling of pride keep us back, or lift us above ourselves; and neither let unlawful superstition frighten us, or turn us away from God. Let not the delights of the senses keep us from the delights of the soul. Let us come, and let us be feasted. And who have come but the poor and the feeble and the lame and the blind? But the rich have not come there, nor the healthy, who as it were could walk well, and see clearly, sure of themselves, and the more arrogant were they, the more endangered.

Let the poor come, for He Who invites us, though rich, became poor for our sakes, that by His poverty we might be made rich (II Cor. viii. 9).

Let the feeble come, for they who are in health need not the physician, but they that are ill (Mt. ix. 12).

Let the lame come, who say to Him: *Perfect thou my goings in thy paths* (Ps. xvi. 5).

Let the blind come, who say: *Enlighten my eyes that I may never sleep in death* (Ps. xii. 4).

Such as these came at the hour; those first called being rejected, because of their excuses. They came at the hour, and they came from the streets and the lanes of the city. *And the servant, who was sent, said: Lord, it is done as thou hast commanded, and yet there is room. Go,* he says, *out into the highways and hedges, and compel those you find to come in.* Those whom you find worthy, do not delay, compel them to come in. I have prepared a great Supper, a great house; I shall suffer no place there to remain empty.

The Gentiles came from the streets and the lanes. Let the heretics come from the hedges; here they will find peace. For they who make hedges are seeking to bring about divisions. Let them be drawn from the hedges; let them be plucked free of the thorns. They refuse to be compelled, and they cling to their hedges. Let us, they say, come in of our own will. But this is not what the Lord commanded. *Compel them,* He says, *to come in.* Outside they

find want. From that the will is born.[5]

May then the power of His mercy strengthen our heart in His Truth. May it confirm and calm our souls. May His grace abound in us, may He have pity on us, and remove obstacles from before us, from before His Church, and from before all those who are dear to us, and may He by His power and by the abundance of His mercy enable us to please Him for ever, through Jesus Christ His Son our Lord, Who with Him and with the Holy Ghost lives and reigns world without end. Amen.

III. St Gregory the Great, Pope and Doctor

Given to the People in the Basilica of the Blessed Apostles Philip and James on the Second Sunday after Pentecost

The Supper of God and the Soul[6]

Luke xiv. 16–24

1. There is this difference, Dearly Beloved Brethren, between the delights of the body and those of the soul, that the delights of the body, when we do not possess them, awaken in us a great desire for them; but when we possess them and enjoy them to the full they straightaway awaken in us a feeling of aversion. But spiritual delights work in the opposite way. While we do not possess them we regard them with dislike and aversion; but once we partake of them we begin to desire them, and the more we partake of them, the more do we hunger for them. In one case the appetite pleases, the reality brings displeasure; in the other it is the appetite displeases, the reality delights us more and more. In the one case appetite

leads to fulness, and fulness to disgust; in the other appetite begets fulness, and fulness in turn begets appetite. For spiritual delights, when they fill the soul, increase in us the desire of them; and the more we savour them, the more do we come to know what we should eagerly love.

And so we do not know these delights, because we have not come to savour them. For who can love what he does not know? Because of this the Psalmist speaks to us, and exhorts us, saying: *O taste and see that the Lord is sweet* (Ps. xxxiii. 9)! As though he were saying: You know not His sweetness if you have not tasted it. But try this Food on the palate of your heart, so that when you see how sweet it is then you will love it. Man lost this delight when he sinned in Paradise (Gen. iii. 6); he went forth from there when he closed his mouth against the sweetness of the eternal Food. And we too who are born into the sadness of this earthly pilgrimage, we arrive already soured against It, without knowing what we ought to desire, and the longer the soul puts off tasting this Food, the more the malady of our aversion increases. And in our aversion we waste away, and grow weak from the prolonged curse of our abstinence. And while inwardly refusing the delights prepared for us, outwardly we love to bemoan our hunger. But heavenly pity will not neglect us, even though we neglect ourselves.

2. For it will recall these delights to the eyes of our memory, and make them known to us, and rouse us from our torpor by the promise of them, and call to us that we must put away our aversion. For He says: *A certain man made a great supper, and invited many.* Who is this man, if not He of Whom it was said by the prophet: *And he is a man, and who knows him?* (Jer. xvii. 9 Sept.). He has made a great Supper, for He has prepared for us the fulness of inward delight. He has invited many, but few come; for oftentimes those who are subject to Him in faith, are hostile to the eternal Supper He has prepared because of their evil way of life.

Then follows: *And he sent his servant at the hour of supper to say to them that were invited, that they should come.* What is the hour of the Supper but the end of the world, in which we now are, as Paul has for a long time testified: *These things are written for our correction, upon whom*

the ends of the world are come (I Cor. x. 11). If therefore it is already the hour of Supper when we are called, the more we see that the end of the world has already drawn near, the less should we excuse ourselves from the Supper of God. For the more we realize that the time left is as nothing, the more fearful should we be of wasting the time of grace that remains.

Because of this the banquet of God is called a Supper, not a dinner; for after the dinner there is yet the supper, but after the supper there is no further meal. And because the eternal banquet of God is the last that will be prepared for us, it is fitting that it be called a supper and not a dinner.

And who is meant by the servant who is sent by the Father of the family to invite, if not the company of those who preach the word of God? And in these days to this company do we also belong, unworthy though we are, and laden with the burthen of our own sins, and when I speak to you for your edification this is what I am doing; for I am the servant of the Father of the family. And when I exhort you to despise the world, I come to invite you to God's supper. Let no one in this place despise me for myself. And if I appear to you far from worthy to invite you, nevertheless great are the joys which I promise you.

What I am saying to you, Brethren, often takes place; that a great person will have an unworthy servant. And when he sends the servant on business, to his friends or even to strangers, the person of the servant who speaks for him is not held in contempt, out of respect for the master who sent him. They who listen are thinking of *what* it is they hear, and *from* whom they hear; not *through* whom they hear. So let you also; and if perhaps you have reason to depise us, yet always keep reverence in your heart for the Lord Who is inviting you. Accept with readiness, and become the guests of the Supreme Father of the family. Search into your own hearts and drive out from them this deadly aversion. For now all things are prepared for driving away your aversion. But if you are still earthly minded, you will perhaps be seeking for earthly food. Behold how even earthly food has been changed for you into spiritual nourishment. To take away this distaste from your soul, the matchless Lamb has been slain for you in the Supper of the Lord.

3. But what are we to do, we who see that which follows happening with so many? *And they began all at once to make excuse.* What we should seek for in prayer, God offers, desires to give us unasked; something scarcely to be hoped for, seeing that when asked, what He deigned to give is nevertheless despised. He makes known to us that the joys of the eternal Supper are ready, yet all begin at once to excuse themselves. Let us imagine what happens on lesser occasions, so that we can reflect worthily upon greater ones.

If some great person should send word inviting a poor man to a banquet, what, I ask you, brethren, would this poor man feel but delight at this invitation, and send back a grateful acceptance, and change his clothes, and hurry off as quickly as possible, so that there might be no one before him at the great man's banquet? Let a rich man invite him, and a poor man hastens to come; we are invited to the banquet of God, and we excuse ourselves. But here I can imagine what your own hearts will answer. For in the depths of your thoughts they say to you: We do not wish to make excuses; we are grateful to be invited to come to that banquet of eternal delight.

4. Your hearts speaking to you in this way say what is true, if they do not love earthly things more than heavenly, if they are not more taken up with the things of the body than with the things of the soul. It is because of this last that the reason of the excuses is given, when straightaway there is added: *The first said: I have bought a farm, and I must needs go out and see it; I pray thee, hold me excused.* What is meant by the farm, if not earthly things? So he goes out to his farm who, with a view to gain, thinks only of earthly things.

Another says: *I have bought five yoke of oxen, and I go to try them; I pray thee, hold me excused.* What must we understand by the five yoke of oxen, but the five senses of the body? And they are rightly called *yoke*, because they are in pairs in either sex. These bodily senses, unable to see inward things, know only what is outward and, paying no heed to what is deepest in us, consider only what is superficial, fittingly symbolize human curiosity; which, seeking to pry into the lives of others, and ignoring its own deep inward needs, devotes itself wholly to outward things. For it is the

great fault of curiosity that while it
leads a man's mind to search into his
neighbour's life, it seeks always to
hide from him his own inward life,
so that while knowing his neighbour's business, he is ignorant of
himself; and the more the mind of
the curious knows of his neighbour's state, the less it knows of its
own.[7]

Because of this, of these same five
yoke of oxen is it said: *I go to try
them; I pray thee, hold me excused.*
The words of excuse are not at
variance with the showing up of his
moral fault, as he says: *I go to try
them,* for often testing goes with
curiosity. But note that he who
excuses himself from the supper of
the host because of his farm, and he
who excuses himself because of trying out his yoke of oxen, both
mingle words of humility with their
excuse, saying: *I pray thee, hold me
excused.* For when he says, *I pray
thee,* and at the same time refuses to
come, there is humility in his words,
but pride in his action. Any single
perverse person will condemn this,
when he hears of it, yet he will not
himself cease from doing the thing
he condemns. For when we say to
any person acting perversely, 'Change
your way of life, Seek for God,
Leave the world', whither are we
inviting him but to the Lord's Supper? And when he answers: 'Pray
for me; for I am a sinner, I am not
able to do that', what else is he doing
but praying to be excused? Saying,
I am a sinner, he implies he is
humble; but when he adds, I cannot
change my life, he shows he is
proud. Therefore, by praying to be
excused, he pretends to humility in
his words, but in what he does he
discloses his pride.

5. *And another said: I have married
a wife.* What is signified by the wife,
but the pleasures of the flesh? For
though marriage is good, and established by divine providence for the
getting of offspring, some there are
who do not seek it for the sake of
children, but for bodily pleasure;
and so by means of a just thing, that
which is unjust is aptly made clear to
us. The Supreme Father therefore
is inviting you to the Supper of
eternal joy, but while one man is
given over to greed, another to
curiosity, another to the delight of
the flesh, all the reprobate alike
make excuses. While one man is
held back by earthly cares, this other
by acute anxiety over somebody
else's business, and the mind of yet
another is given over to bodily lust,
each in turn contemptuous hastens
not to the feast of eternal life.

6. Then follows: *And the servant
returning told these things to his lord.
Then the master of the house, being
angry, said to his servants: Go out
quickly to the streets and lanes of the
city, and bring in hither the poor, and
the feeble, and the blind and the lame.*
See how he who is attached beyond
due measure to the things of this
world refuses to come to the Lord's
Supper. And how he who is given
over to curiosity[8] turns away in
disgust from the food of Life prepared for him. And how he who
obeys only his body's desires rejects
the banquet of spiritual delights.

And so because the proud refuse
to come the poor are chosen. And
why this? Because, according to
the words of Paul: *The weak things
of the world hath God chosen, that he
may confound the strong* (I Cor. i. 27).
But let us see how they are described

who are invited to the supper and come. *The poor and the feeble.* They are called the *poor* and the *feeble* who in their own esteem are of no importance. For there are the poor and the strong; those who even in poverty are proud. *The blind* are they who have no brightness of understanding. *The lame* those who do not follow the ways of virtue in their actions. But as the defects of their conduct is shown to us by the infirmity of their members, it is plain that just as they were sinners who were invited and refused to come, so these also were sinners who were invited and came. The sinners who were proud are rejected, just as the humble sinners are chosen.

7. So God chose those whom the world despises; because oftentimes the very contempt of the world will bring a man to himself. For he who had gone forth from his father, and had *squandered the portion of his inheritance*, began afterwards to be in want, and returning to himself, he said: *How many hired servants in my father's house abound in bread* (Lk. xv. 17)? He had gone far from himself when he began to sin. Had he not been in want, he would by no means have returned to himself; for when the sinner begins to want for bodily things, he begins then to think of the spiritual things he has lost.

The poor therefore and the feeble, the blind and the lame, are all invited and come; for the poor in general, and the despised of this world, will often more readily listen to the voice of God, the less they have to delight them in this world. And this the story of the young Egyptian of the Amalecites illus-trates (I Kgs. xxx. 11), who was left sick on the road by the Amalecites as they hastened onwards, pillaging as they went, while he lay perishing of hunger and thirst. David found him, and gave him food and drink, and when he was well again he became David's guide. He led them upon the feasting Amalecites, and they who had abandoned him in his weakness he prostrated in his strength. Amalecites means, the licking people. And what is meant by licking people if not the minds of worldlings? For these seeking for everything of the earth, and while delighting in them alone, are said as it were to lick them. As the licking people take booty, so those loving earthly things heap gain to themselves from others' misfortunes.

The Egyptian servant is aban-doned sick by the road, for every sinner growing weary of this world is at once despised by those whose minds are wholly of this world. David found him and gave him food and drink; for the Lord, Strong in hand, does not despise the weak things of the world, and will often convert to His love those who, no longer able to follow the ways of the world, are left by the way. And He gives them the food and drink of His word, and as it were chooses them as guides on the way when He also makes them His preachers. For when they bring Christ to the hearts of sinners, they as it were lead David upon the enemy. And like David they smite with the sword the feast-ing Amalecites; for they by the power of the Lord cast down the proud who despised them in the world. The Egyptian servant there-fore who had remained by the way slew the Amalecites; for often those souls overcome the world by preaching, who before were unable to keep up with the heathens of this world.

8. But having brought the poor into the supper, let us hear what the servant has then to say. And the servant said: *Lord, it is done as thou hast commanded, and yet there is room.* Many such as these were gathered in from Judea to the Lord's supper. But the multitude that believed from the people of Israel did not suffice to fill the places at the heavenly feast. Great numbers of the Jews had entered, but there was still vacant room in the kingdom, where the multitude of the Gentiles would be received. And so he said to the same servant: *Go out into the highways and hedges, and compel them to come in, that my house may be filled.*

When from the streets and the lanes the Lord invites some to His Supper, He had in mind those who dwelling in the city had learned the observance of the Law. When He commands that His guests be brought in from the highways and hedges, He is seeking the people of the outside world, that is, the Gentiles. And in regard to this figure the Psalmist says: *Then shall all the trees of the woods rejoice before the face of the Lord* (Ps. xcv. 13). The Gentiles are called *the trees of the woods*, because in their unbelief they were at all times twisted and fruitless. They therefore who are converted from this wild manner of life are they who have come as it were from the hedges to the Supper of the Lord.

9. We should note that in this third invitation He does not say,

Invite them, but, *Compel them to come in.* Some are called, and scorn the invitation. Others are called, and they come. Of yet others it is said that they were not even invited, but were compelled to come in. They are called, and refuse to come, who receive the gift of understanding, but do not go on to add good works to this understanding.[9] They are invited, and come who, having received the grace of understanding, perfect it with good works. Some are called in such a manner as to be compelled to enter. For there are some who understand the good they must do, but neglect to do it; they see the good works they ought to do, but are without desire to follow after them.

To these it will sometimes happen, as we said a moment ago, that the misfortunes of this world wound them in their worldly desires. They strive to attain to earthly glory and fail; and as they seek to cross the high seas to come as it were to the higher dignities of the world, they are forever thrown back by adverse winds to the shores of their own lowly state. And when they see themselves defeated in their ambitions by the opposition of the world, they are brought to remember what they owe to their Maker, so that in their shame they turn to Him Whom, in their pride, they had abandoned for the glory of this world.

And indeed oftentimes many who are eager to attain temporal honour will either suffer through wasting away in some prolonged illness, or fall and be afflicted by some injury, or be stricken with grievous losses, and so by means of the sufferings of this world they are forced to see they should place no trust in the joys it holds out, and, reproaching themselves for their desires, they turn to God with all their hearts. It was of these the Lord said through His prophet: *Behold I will hedge up thy way with thorns, and I will stop it up with a wall, and she shall not find her paths. And she shall follow after her lovers, and shall not overtake them; and she shall seek them, and shall not find, and she shall say: I will go, and return to my first husband, because it was better with me then, than now* (Os. ii. 6, 7).

The husband of every Christian soul is God; for she is joined to Him by faith. But that soul which has been joined to God follows after her lovers, when the mind that has already believed through faith submits itself in work to the unclean spirits, when it looks for the glory of this world, feasts on carnal delights, and nourishes itself with the choicest pleasures. But frequently Almighty God looks mercifully upon such a soul, and commingles bitterness with her delight. It is with this in mind He says: *I will hedge up thy way with thorns.* Our ways are hedged with thorns when we find the stings of pain in that which we have wickedly desired. *And I will stop it up with a wall, and she shall not find her paths.* Our ways are stopped up with a wall, when in this world the hardness of those who oppose us stands in the way of our desires. And we cannot find our paths, because we are hindered from obtaining what we have striven for in wickedness. *And she shall follow after her lovers, and shall not overtake them; and she shall seek them, and shall not find*; for the soul will never embrace, to fulfil her desires, the

evil spirits to which in her desires she has subjected herself.

But how great the profit that arises from this salutary misfortune He goes on to show, when there is added: *I will go, and return to my first husband, because it was better with me then, than now.* After she finds that her ways are hedged in, and that she cannot overtake her lovers, she returns to the love of her first husband; for often after we fail to obtain what we wish for in this world, after we have grown weary of earthly desires, because of our inability to attain them, we then recall God to our minds, then He Who displeased us begins to please us, and He, Whose commands had been bitter, of a sudden grows sweet in our memory; and the sinful soul that had tried to be adulterous, and had manifestly failed, decides to be a faithful spouse. And so they who are broken by the enmity of this world, and who return to the love of God, and are made free of the desires of this life, who are they, my brethren, if not those who are compelled to come in?

10. But truly fearful is the sentence that follows: with all the concern of your heart pay heed to this, my brethren and my masters: inasmuch as you are sinners, my brethren; as just men, my masters. Pay heed to it with all anxiety, so that the more fearfully you receive it in this sermon, the less fearfully shall you hear it at the last judgement. For He says: *But I say unto you, that none of these men that were invited, shall taste of my supper.* See how He invites us of Himself, He invites us through His angels, He invites us through the Patriarchs, He invites us through the prophets, He invites

us through the Apostles, He invites us through our pastors, He invites us through ourselves, He invites us sometimes through miracles, He invites us sometimes by means of scourges, He invites us sometimes by means of good fortune in this world, and sometimes He invites us through bad. Let no one refuse, lest, excusing himself when invited, he may find when he desires to enter, that he cannot.

Hear what Wisdom says through Solomon: *Then shall they call upon me, and I will not hear; they shall rise in the morning and shall not find me* (Prov. xi. 28). It was because of this that *the foolish virgins, coming late,* cry out, saying: *Lord, Lord, open to us* (Mt. xxv. 11). But even then was it said to those seeking to come in: *Amen I say to you: I know you not.* What must we do in the face of such warnings, dearest brethren, *but leave all things,* disregard the concerns of the world, and long only for the things of eternity? But to few is it given to do this.

11. I desire to exhort you to leave all things, but I do not dare to. If you cannot, then, abandon all that is of the world, so hold what you have of this world, that you are not held fast to the world because of it; that you so possess earthly things that they do not possess you; that what you possess is subject to the rule of your mind, lest your soul, overcome by love of earthly things, be rather possessed by them. Therefore let earthly things be for use; eternal things the object of our desires. Let temporal things be for the journey; eternal for our arrival there. Let us be as it were spectators in this world. Let the eyes of

our mind be directed straight before us, as with all earnestness they look towards the things to which we are drawing near.

Let our defects be wholly rooted out, not alone from our actions, but from the very thoughts of our hearts. Let neither the lusts of the body, nor the unrest of curiosity, nor the fever of ambition, keep us from the Supper of the Lord; and even that which we do justly in the world, let us undertake it with as it were one side of our mind, so that the things of this earth shall so serve our bodies as not to hinder our souls. We do not then dare to say to you, brethren, to leave all things; nevertheless, if you will it, you may leave all things while still retaining them, if you so use temporal things that you are still with all your heart striving towards the things of eternity.

12. It is with this in mind that Paul says: The time is short: *it remaineth that they who have wives be as if they had none; and they that weep as though they wept not; and they that rejoiced as if they rejoiced not; and they that buy, as though they possessed not; and they that use this world, as if they used it not; for the fashion of this world passeth away* (I Cor. vii. 29–31). He has a wife as though he had none who renders the debt of the body, yet so that he is not through this compelled to attach himself to the world with all his heart. For since the same illustrious preacher says: *But he that is with a wife is solicitous for the things of the world, how he may please his wife,* that man is one who has a wife as though not having one, who so is at pains to please his wife that he yet does not displease his Maker.

And likewise he weeps as though he wept not, who so grieves over his temporal losses, that his soul will still draw comfort from the thought of his eternal gains. He rejoices as if he rejoiced not, who is happy in his temporal possessions, while still mindful of the torments that do not end; and when his mind is uplifted through joy, he will restrain it with the counterweight of prudent fear. He buys as though he possessed not, who provides what is needed, and yet with wise reflection is aware that soon these too will be left behind. And he uses this world as if he used it not, who gathers what is needed for his daily needs in this world, yet not permitting that such things shall rule his life; that as subject to him they serve him outwardly, never hindering the end of his soul, in its striving towards the things that are above. Whoever therefore are of such mind, they do indeed possess all earthly things, not for their desires, but for their daily use; for they use what is needed, and desire not to possess anything through sin. They also gain a reward daily from the things they possess; but they rejoice more in a good work than in a good property.

13. And so that such things may not appear difficult to any of you, I shall relate something to you concerning a person whom many of you will have known, and which I myself learned of about three years ago from trustworthy persons of the city of Centumcelli. Not so long ago there was a certain count named Theophanius in this same city, a man greatly given to works of mercy, active in every good work, and particularly zealous in hospi-

tality. While occupied with the affairs of his command he had much to do with worldly and temporal things; more, as we shall see presently, out of duty than ambition. For as the hour of his death arrived a most dreadful storm arose so that it would not be possible to bring him to the cemetery, and his wife in great distress said to him: 'What shall I do? How shall I bring you to the cemetery when I cannot set foot outside the house because of this storm?' He then said to her: 'Do not grieve, for as soon as I die the storm will cease.' And after he had spoken he there and then died, and there came a great calm.

His poor hands and feet were swollen with the gout, and had broken out into sores. But when as is customary they uncovered the body to wash it, they found the hands and feet without any trace whatever of sores. He was then brought to the cemetery and buried. And there his wife decided that on the fourth day following his burial the marble placed over his tomb would have to be changed. When the marble placed over his body had been lifted off, such a fragrance arose from the body as though sweet odours instead of worms had multiplied from the decaying flesh. I tell you this to show you by a recent example, that there are many who wear a worldly dress, but beneath it have not a worldly soul. For they whom necessity binds to the world, so that they can in no way escape from it, should so possess the things of this world, as not at any time to surrender to them, out of weariness of spirit.

Reflect therefore on these things, and though you may be unable to leave all things which are of this world, use outward things justly, but inwardly hasten eagerly towards the things that are eternal. Let there be nothing which holds back the desires of your soul; let not the love of any single thing entangle you in this world. If you love good, let your mind delight in the better things, that is, in heavenly things. If you fear evil, put before your mind the eternal evils, so that be-

holding there that which you most love, and most fear, you will cling to nothing in this life.

And to enable us to do this we have as our Helper the Mediator of God and man, through Whom we shall the more speedily obtain all things, if we burn with a true love of Him, Who liveth and reigneth with the Father and the Holy Ghost God for ever and ever. Amen.

NOTES

[1] PG 8, Pedagogi, Book II, Ch. 1.

[2] The *agape* (love-feasts) began as suppers eaten in common because of the communion and friendship among early Christians, as also for the sustenance of the clergy, and the poor, and were held after the Lord's Supper. In the time of Clement it seems as if any convivial gathering of Christians had come to be called an *agape*, and it is such as these he is here reproving. Later, because of drunkenness and brawls and rivalries, and even because, through them, Judaism and paganism began to creep in, they were gradually abandoned.

[3] A reference to the night watches, or stations, as distinguished from the *day stations*, which the Christians of early times were wont to practise in obedience to the counsel, *to watch and pray.*

[4] PL 38, Sermo 112. Given in the Restored Basilica.

[5] The reference here to *compulsion* is to laws made against the Donatists by the Emperors; decreed again under Honorius in A.D. 408 and 410. Here it was not a case of prosecution for religious reasons, but simply of the protection of life and property, the safety and freedom of Catholics, because of the frequent murders of

priests and bishops by the Donatists. See also St Augustine, Epistle 185, n. 24. The supper (*convivium*) of the Lord is the unity of the Body of Christ, not alone in the sacrament of the Altar, but also in the bond of peace. The reference to *freedom* is to that of *the sons of God* by adoption, which we receive at baptism.

[6] PL 76, Sermo 36.

[7] At first sight it is hard to understand the holy Doctor's severity with regard to curiosity. But when we consider that the sating of this appetite is possibly the greatest single industry of our own time it is easier to understand. This natural appetite is now more than adequately provided for; where it could not be, then, among a restless, active-minded, and in great part corrupt people, it could understandably be a great and disturbing vice.

[8] The saint is speaking here not wholly of simple curiosity, but also possibly of superstitious practices, with all that they would imply in the light of faith and morals, especially in that age, not yet fully emerged from pagan darkness.

[9] In the sense of the gift of the Holy Ghost. Cf. Col. ii. 2; II Tim. ii. 7; Col. i. 9.

THIRD SUNDAY AFTER PENTECOST

I. St Ambrose: Exposition of the Gospel

II. St Cyril of Alexandria: On the Gospel

III. St Peter Chrysologus: The Parable of the Lost Drachma

IV. St Gregory the Great: The Angelic Choirs

THE GOSPEL OF THE SUNDAY

Luke xv. 1–10

At that time: The publicans and sinners drew near unto Jesus to hear him. And the Pharisees and the scribes murmured, saying: This man receiveth sinners, and eateth with them. And he spoke to them this parable, saying: What man of you hath an hundred sheep: and if he shall lose one of them, doth he not leave the ninety-nine in the desert, and go after that which was lost, until he find it? And when he hath found it, lay it upon his shoulders, rejoicing: and coming home, call together his friends and neighbours, saying to them: Rejoice with me, because I have found my sheep that was lost? I say to you, that even so there shall be joy in heaven upon one sinner that doth penance, more than upon ninety-nine just that need not penance.

Or what woman having ten pieces of silver, if she lose one piece, doth not light a lamp, and sweep the house, and seek diligently until she find it? And when she hath found it, call together her friends and neighbours, saying: Rejoice with me, because I have found the silver piece which I had lost. So I say to you, there shall be joy before the angels of God upon one sinner doing penance.

Exposition from the Catena Aurea

V. 1. *The publicans and sinners drew near unto Jesus to hear him.* . . .

Ambrose, *in Luke*: From what was said in the preceding verses you learned that you must not be held fast by earthly things; that you are not to place fleeting things before those that last for ever. But since human frailty cannot maintain a firm footing in this so uncertain world, the Good Physician shows you a remedy even against error. The Merciful Judge does not deny us the hope of pardon; so we have, *they drew near to hear Jesus.*

190

GLOSS: *Publicans*, that is, they who exacted, or farmed, the public taxes and who make a business of worldly gain.

THEOPHYLACTUS: It was for this He had taken flesh, to receive sinners as a physician receives the sick. But the real sinners, the Pharisees, repaid His kindness by murmuring against Him. Hence:

V. 2. *And the Pharisees and scribes murmured against him, saying . . .*

GREGORY, *Hom.* 34 *on the Gospel*: From which we may gather that true justice feels compassion, the false only scorn; though the just are also wont to feel angry with sinners, and rightly so. But what is done through zeal for the divine law is one thing, what is done through the swelling of pride another. For the just, outwardly, heap up reproaches against sinners, but out of devotion to the divine law, while inwardly they retain the bond of charity. In their own minds they place those they correct above themselves. They correct those subject to them, because of discipline, but through humility they keep a watch on themselves.

They however who pride themselves on a righteousness that is hollow despise everyone else, and are without any compassion for the weak. And the more they believe they are not sinners, the worse sinners they become. The Pharisees were undoubtedly of these; murmuring against the Lord because He received sinners, and from their own dried-up hearts rebuking the Fount of compassion. But because they were sick, and so sick that they did not know they were sick, the

Heavenly Physician treats them as with soothing foments; saying to them:

V. 3. *And he spoke to them this parable, saying:*

He gave them a similitude which a man could understand from within himself, but which however referred to the Author of all men. For as the *hundred* is a perfect number He Himself possessed a hundred sheep; since He possessed the natures of both angels and of men.

V. 4. *What man of you hath an hundred sheep: and if he shall lose one . . .*

CYRIL, *Catena PG*: From this we learn the extent of our Saviour's kingdom. For He says that there are a hundred sheep; bringing to a perfect number the sum of the rational creatures subject to him. For the *hundred* is a perfect number, being made of ten decades. But one from this number went astray, namely, the race of men who inhabited the earth. AMBROSE: A Rich Shepherd, of whom all we are but the hundredth part of what is His.

GREGORY, *as above*: One was lost when man through sin forsook the pastures of true life. But ninety-nine remained in the desert; for the number of the rational creatures, that is, of Angels and of men, who were created to know God, was lessened by the fall of man. Hence there follows: *Doth he not leave the ninety-nine in the desert?* For the angelic choirs remained in heaven. For then did man abandon heaven, when he sinned. And so that the perfect sum of the sheep might once more be made full in heaven fallen man was sought for on earth. Hence follows: *And go after that which was lost till he find it.*

CYRIL: Was He then displeased with the rest, but moved with compassion towards but one? Far from it. For they are safe; the Right Hand of the Most High encompasses them. But He needs must have compassion on the one perishing, that the remaining number might not be imperfect (incomplete). For this one brought back to safety the hundred will once more have its due perfection.

AUGUSTINE, *Questions on the Gospels*, II, 32: Or, He spoke of the ninety-nine whom He left in the desert as signifying the proud, having solitude as it were in their souls; in that they wish to be regarded as singular: to these unity is lacking for perfection. For when anyone withdraws from unity he withdraws through pride: desiring to be his own master, he does not follow that Master Who is God. With Him God numbers all who are reconciled through repentance, which in turn is gained through humility.

GREGORY NYSSA: But when the Shepherd found the sheep He did not punish it, He did not bring it back to the flock by driving it before Him, but, placing it on His own shoulders, and bearing it with gentleness, He restored it to the flock. Hence:

V. 5. *And when he hath found it, lay it upon his shoulders, rejoicing.*

GREGORY: He laid the sheep upon His shoulders in that taking upon Him our nature He bore the burthen of our sins. Finding the sheep He returns home; for our Shepherd, man now redeemed, has returned to His heavenly kingdom. Hence follows:

V. 6. *And coming home, call together his friends and neighbours . . .*

He calls the choirs of heaven His friends and neighbours, and they are His friends, because in their steadfastness they unceasingly uphold His will. They are His neighbours also, since being forever in His Presence He gives them the perfect enjoyment of the vision of His glory.

THEOPHYLACTUS: The heavenly powers are spoken of as sheep, in that every created nature in comparison with God Himself is as the beasts. In that they are rational they are called His friends and neighbours. GREGORY: And we must note that He did not say: Rejoice with the sheep that has been found, but, *Rejoice with me*; for our life is in truth His joy, and when we are restored to heaven we shall complete the feast of His rejoicing.

AMBROSE: Now the angels since they are rational do fittingly rejoice in the redemption of man. So there follows:

V. 7. *I say to you, that even so there shall be joy in heaven . . .*

Let this incite us to a just and upright life, that each man believes that his own conversion to God is pleasing to the angelic choirs; whose protection he should seek, and whose good will he should fear to lose.

GREGORY: The Lord confesses that there is more rejoicing in heaven over converted sinners than over those who remained faithful. For these oftentimes knowing themselves free of the burthen of grave sin stand indeed in the way of divine justice, yet they do not long for and sigh for the heavenly kingdom; and not infrequently they are reluctant to give themselves to the practice of the higher virtues, content in the knowledge that they do not commit any of the more grievous sins.

On the other hand it will often happen that those who are mindful of having committed certain grave sins, being moved to sorrow by this remembrance, the love of God is then kindled in their heart. And because they recognize that they had strayed from God, they make good the losses that went before with the gains that now follow. Greater therefore is the rejoicing in heaven. A leader in battle will have a warmer regard for the soldier who had first yielded and run away, and then had fought bravely back, than over the soldier who had never yielded, yet had never thrust bravely forward. So does the farmer love more the fields that now cleaned of weeds bear a fruitful crop, than the land which had never grown thorns, yet neither had it ever yielded a bountiful crop.

But with this we should also know, that there are many just in whose life there is joy so great that the repentance of no sinner whatever can awaken a greater joy. From this we may gather how pleasing to God is the humbled and afflicted heart of the just, if there is such rejoicing in heaven when the unjust through repentance rejects the evil he has done.

V. 8. *Or what woman having ten pieces of silver, if she lose one ...*

CYRIL: By the preceding parable, in which the human race is spoken of as a wandering sheep, we are taught that we are creatures of the Most High God, *who made us, and not we ourselves, and we are the sheep of his pasture* (Ps. ix. 7). Here another parable is added in which the human race is compared to a piece of silver that was lost. By this He makes known to us that we have been made in the image and likeness of God. For the piece of silver (*drachma*) is a coin upon which the royal image is stamped. Hence we have: *Or what woman etc.*

GREGORY: He who is signified by the shepherd is also signified by the woman. For it is God Himself; Himself together with the Wisdom of God. The Lord created the nature of both angels and men, to the end that they might know Him, and He created it in His own likeness. The woman then had ten pieces of silver; for nine are the orders of the angels. But to make perfect the number of the elect man the tenth was created.

AUGUSTINE, *as above*: Or, by the nine pieces of silver, as also by the ninety-nine sheep, He means those who trusting in themselves place themselves above sinners who are turning to salvation. For *One thing is wanting* to the nine to make it ten, and to the ninety-nine that they may be a hundred. To That One He assigns all who are reconciled through penance.

GREGORY: And since there is an image stamped upon the silver piece, the woman lost the piece of silver when man who had been made to the image of God lost by sin the likeness of His Maker. And this is what is added: *If she lose one, doth not light a lamp.* The woman lit a lamp; for the Wisdom of God appeared in human form. A lamp is a light in an earthen vessel: the divinity in human flesh is truly a light in an earthen vessel.

And the lamp being lit there follows: *And turns the house upside down,*[1] for as soon as His Divinity shines forth in our flesh the conscience of every man is shaken up. And the word, turned upside down (*evertit*) is not different in meaning from the word we read in other versions, namely, cleaned (*emundat*); for an evil soul is not made clean from its habits of sin unless it is first turned upside down through fear.

The house turned upside down the piece of silver is found. For there follows: *And seek diligently until she find it*; for when the conscience of man is greatly disturbed the likeness of His Maker is recovered within him.

GREGORY NAZIANZEN, *Or.* 42: The silver piece found, the heavenly Powers whom He had employed as ministers in the plan of man's Redemption are now made sharers of His joy. And so follows:

V. 9. *And when she hath found it, call together her friends . . .*

GREGORY: For the heavenly powers, the closer they approach Him through the grace of His unceasing Vision, the closer they are to His Divine Wisdom. THEOPHYLACTUS: Either they are His *friends*, as upholding His Will, and His *neighbours*, as spiritual beings, or, they are

His *friends*, since such are all the heavenly powers, and His *neighbours*, as being nearest Him, such as are the Thrones, Cherubim and Seraphim.

GREGORY OF NYSSA, *On Virginity* 12: Or again: This I think is what the Lord is proposing to us in the searching for the lost *piece of silver*: that we gain nothing through the possession of the other virtues which He calls pieces of silver: for though all the others are present to it the soul is widowed if that one alone is wanting through which the splendour of the divine likeness is acquired.[2] So He bids us light a lamp, that is, His Divine Word, which *makes manifest things hidden*, or even the torch of repentance.

But it is in his own house, that is, within himself, and within his own conscience, that he must seek for the lost piece of silver, that is, for the royal image; which however is not wholly lost, but hidden in the dust: meaning the infections that derive from the flesh. These wiped carefully away, that is, removed by the vigilance of our life, that which we are searching for will shine out.

And let him who finds it rejoice, and call together his neighbours to share his joy; that is, the companion powers of the soul, namely, that of reason, that of desiring, and that innate disposition towards anger, and whatever other powers are observed about the soul, which it teaches to rejoice in the Lord. Then concluding the parable He adds:

V. 10. *So I say to you, there shall be joy before the angels of God . . .*

GREGORY: For to repent means both to lament the sins we have committed, and not to commit again what we lament. For he who grieves over some sins, while he continues to commit others, either does not yet know how to repent, or but pretends to repent. He must especially have this in mind: that he is to make satisfaction to his Creator; that he who has done forbidden things should now forbid himself in what is lawful to him; and he who knows he has sinned in great things, let him restrain himself now from the least offences.

I. St Ambrose, Bishop and Doctor

Exposition of the Gospel[3]

Luke xv. 1–10

In the teaching of our Lord which preceded this Gospel reading you learned that we are to put away all carelessness, to avoid conceit, to begin to be earnest in religion, not to be held fast to the things of this world, not to place fleeting things before those that endure for ever. But though human frailty finds it hard to maintain a firm foothold in this so uncertain world, the Merciful Judge does not withhold the hope of His forgiveness, and has as a Good Physician made known to you the remedies even against going astray.

And so it was not without design that the holy Luke places in order before us three parables: that of the sheep that strayed and was found, that of the silver piece that was lost and also was found, that of the son who was dead (through sin) and who returned to life; so that sustained by this threefold cure we may seek to cure our own wounds: for a triple rope does not break.

Who are these three persons: the shepherd, the woman, the father? Is not Christ the Shepherd, the Church the woman, and God the Father? Christ Who took upon Himself your sins bears you upon His own Body; the Church searches for you; the Father receives you back. As a shepherd He brings us back, as a mother He looks for us, as a father He clothes us. First, mercy, second, intercession, third, reconciliation; each to each; the Redeemer comes to our aid, the Church intercedes for us, the Creator restores us to Himself. It is the same divine mercy in each operation; but grace varies according to our merits.

The sheep that strayed is brought back by the Shepherd. The silver piece that was lost is found. The son turns back fully repentant from his sinful wanderings, and retraces his footsteps to his father. Because of this was it fittingly said: *Men and beasts thou wilt preserve, O Lord* (Ps. xxxv. 7). Who are those beasts? The prophet tells us: *I will sow the house of Israel and the house of Juda with the seed of men, and with the seed of beasts* (Jer. xxxi. 27). And so Israel is saved as a man; Juda is gathered in as though it were a sheep. I would prefer to be a son than a sheep; for a sheep is brought back by a shepherd, the son is honoured by the Father.

Let us therefore rejoice because that sheep which had fallen by the way in Adam is uplifted in Christ. The shoulders of Christ are the arms of His Cross. There have I laid down my sins; upon the neck of that sublime yoke of torment have I found rest. This sheep is one in kind, but not one in outward appearance. For we are all one body, but many members; and so it was written: *Now you are the body of Christ and members of member* (I Cor. xii. 27). So therefore *the Son of man is come to seek and to save that which was lost* (Lk. xix. 10); that is, all men: for *as in Adam all die, so also in Christ all shall be made alive* (I Cor. xv. 22).

Rich then is that Shepherd of whose portion all we are but a hundredth part. For He has besides the innumerable flocks of the Archangels, of the Dominations, of the Powers, of the Thrones and all the rest whom He left upon the mountains. And since they are rational flocks, they not unfittingly rejoice because of the redemption of men. Let this also incite us to a just and up-

right life, that each one shall believe that his own conversion to God is pleasing to the angelic choirs, whose protection he should seek, and whose good will he should fear to lose. Be ye therefore a joy to the angels; let them have cause for rejoicing in your own return.

Neither is it without significance that the woman rejoices because of the silver piece that was found. For this is no ordinary piece of silver, upon which is the figure of the Prince. And because of this, the Image of the King is the wealth of the Church. We are His sheep; let us pray that He will place us amid *the waters of His refreshment* (Ps. xxii. 2). We are, I say, His sheep; let us seek of Him *a place of pasture.* We are pieces of silver; let us jealously cherish our value. We are children; let us hasten to our Father, Who with the Son and Holy Ghost liveth and reigneth world without end.

Amen.

II. St Cyril of Alexandria, Bishop and Doctor

On the Gospel[4]

God sent not his son into the world, to judge the world, as the Son tells us, *but that the world may be saved by him* (Jn. iii. 17). But how could the world be saved, caught as it was in the net of sin? By exacting punishment of it, or rather, by showing it kindness, so that, God being merciful and forbearing, man's past sins were forgotten, and those who had not been living worthily began a purer way of life? Why then, tell me, O Pharisee, do you murmur because Christ does not disdain to consort with publicans and sinners, prudently preparing the way for their conversion?

It was for this *He emptied himself,*

and became like to us. Do you then presume to question the wisdom of the Only-Begotten? The blessed prophets praised the wisdom of the divine Secret. The prophet David sings of it: *Sing ye wisely, God shall reign over the nations* (Ps. xlvi. 8). Habacuc says, *he has heard God's hearing,* beheld *his works,* and *was afraid* (iii. 2). How do you presume to question His works which you ought rather to praise?

The race of man wandered upon the face of the earth; it had slipped away from the hand of the Supreme Shepherd. Because of this He came to us Who feeds His heavenly flocks above, that He might lead us also into His fold, that He might unite us to those who had not wandered, that He might drive away the wild beast that works evil, and frustrate the unholy robber band of the unclean spirits of evil. He came therefore seeking the one that was lost, and He showed how foolish and vain were the murmurings of the Jews against Him.

And now reflect together with me, Beloved, upon the extent of the Kingdom of our Saviour, and upon the wondrous wisdom of His divine purposes. For, He says, the number of the sheep is a hundred; here referring to the full and perfect number of the rational beings subject to Him. The number hundred is ever the perfect number, made up of ten decades. From the inspired Scripture we learn that a thousand thousands minister to Him, and ten thousand times a hundred thousand surround His throne (Dan. vii. 10).

A hundred therefore is the number of His sheep, of whom one wandered from the flock, namely, the race of men, and for which the Supreme Pastor of all goes searching, leaving the rest, that is, the remaining ninety-nine, in the desert; that is, in a remote and lofty place that is full of peace. Was He then neglecting the greater number, and concerned only for this one? He was far from neglecting them. How is this? Because they remain in total security, sheltered within the right hand of the Almighty. But it was becoming that He should have compassion on the one that was lost, in order that nothing might appear wanting to the remaining multitude: for when this one was brought back He had then once more a hundred, the perfect number.

Let us explain this by another example, that we may the better explain the incomparable tenderness of Christ the Saviour of all mankind. Let us suppose that in the one house there are many persons, and that one of them falls sick. For whom will the physician be called? Will it not be for the one who is ill? And because the need and the circumstances call for it, the physician, without implying any neglect of the rest by this, will bestow all the assistance of his skill on the one who alone is sick.

He therefore, the God Who rules over all things, must stretch out a saving hand to the wandering sheep, whom the Supreme Shepherd has now in fact redeemed. For He looked for it as it wandered afar, and He has placed it in a secure sheepfold, safe against thieves and wild beasts: namely, His Church. And praising Him let us because of this say with the prophet: *Sion the city of our strength: a saviour, a wall and a bulwark shall be set therein* (Is. xxvi.1).

The parable which follows has the same meaning, that of the woman who had ten pieces of silver, and who we are told lost one, and who thereupon lit a lamp, greatly rejoicing when she finds the piece of silver. And this joy He compares to the supreme joy of heaven. From the previous parable, in which the wandering sheep was a figure of the earthly race of men, we learn that we are a creature of the most High God Who has created the things that before were not. *He made us, and not we ourselves,* as it is written (Ps. xcix. 3). And *he is the Lord our God, and we are the people of his pasture, and the sheep of his hand* (Ps. xciv. 7).

But in the second parable, in which the thing lost is compared to a piece of silver, of which there were ten, that is, a perfect number, or one which makes a complete total (for ten is a complete enumeration, counting from one upwards), we are shown clearly that we have been created in conformity with a royal image and likeness, that, namely, of the Most High God. For the drachma, the piece of silver, is a coin upon which is stamped a royal image. Who is there doubts that we had fallen and were lost, and that we have been found by Christ, and through His grace, and a just way of life, have been again made like unto Him?

Of this the Blessed Paul writes: *But we all beholding the glory of the Lord with open face are transformed into the same image from glory to glory, as by the spirit of the Lord* (II Cor. iii. 18). In his Epistle to the Galatians he also writes: *My little children, of whom I am in labour again, until Christ be formed in you* (iv. 19).

The woman lighting a lamp, a search was made for the thing that was lost. For we were found by the Wisdom of God the Father, Which is His Son, kindling again in us the light of the divine and rational Day Star, when the Sun of Justice rose, and the day dawned, as it is written (II Pet. i. 19). And elsewhere God through one of the holy prophets says of Christ the Saviour of all men: *Speedily my justice draws near, and soon my mercy shall be made known, and my salvation as a lamp shall be lit* (Is. lxii. 1 Sept.). Of Himself He says: *I am the Light of the world.* And again: *I am come a light into the world. He that followeth me walketh not in darkness, but shall have the light of life* (Jn. viii. 12; xii. 46).

Therefore was it in *the Light* that that which was lost was saved; and this has filled the heavenly powers with joy. For they rejoice even over one sinner doing penance, as He teaches us Who knows all things. And if these heavenly beings, ever seeking the fulfilling of the divine will, and given to the unending praise of the most tender divine compassion, rejoice over one sinner saved, what are we to say of their joy at the salvation of the whole world, called to the knowledge of truth, through faith in Christ, to Whom with the Father and the Holy Ghost be honour and glory for ever and ever. Amen.

III. St Peter Chrysologus, Bishop and Doctor

The Parable of the Lost Drachma[5]

They know, and they alone know, who receive the grace of the Holy Spirit, that throughout all the Gospel readings the secrets of the Divine Mind await us, and mystical meanings lie hidden there. For see how the Heavenly Shepherd after He has sought for the sheep that was lost from His flock of a hundred, and finds it, and brings it back to the sheepfold, to the joy of the whole heavenly host of angels, brings before us the figure of the Woman in the Gospel, who, lighting a lamp, so searches for the one of her ten pieces of silver which she had lost, that finding it, to her gain and to her joy, she gives joy to the heavenly host. For it says: *Or what woman having ten pieces of silver, if she lose one piece, doth not light a lamp, and sweep diligently till she find it? And when she hath found it call together her friends and neighbours, saying: Rejoice with me, because I have found the silver piece which I had lost. So I say to you, there shall be joy before the angels of God upon one sinner doing penance.*

Do you think that this is an ordinary woman, or one that is believed to have had ten pieces of silver in the ordinary sense, or that she is believed to have lost it by some earthly mischance, or that it simply happened without design that she looked for it in the night, or that she lit a lamp after our fashion, or that she lost it and found it within an ordinary house, or that she called together to rejoice with her neighbours and friends in the familiar sense of the words, and whom we do not read she called together to grieve with her when she lost it? He makes clear to us that this is a special kind of loss, that the silver piece was not stolen, but that it had disappeared; and He tells us that it is not artfully concealed by some deceit from without, but lying in some obscure place within the house.

See how unusual the whole account is, how it goes beyond, how it far exceeds, the human order of things, how it breathes and smells of divine meanings, how it lifts the mind towards heaven, how it begins to enlighten us about heavenly things, how it compels us to light the lantern of a heart seeking upwards, and like the woman of the Gospel search for this silver piece of saving knowledge amid the obscure places of the Lord's words. Before Christ had come for the wandering sheep, and after seeking here and there had raised it worn out upon

the shoulders of His mercy, and laden with the gentle sheep had arrived at the sheepfold that was inaccessible to the wolves, the Woman who had ten pieces of silver had long waited in darkness, and not alone did she grieve for the silver piece she had lost, she was unable to see the other nine that remained to her. For her it was a long night, and a darkness profound, and enduring; and without the divine fire her lamp gave no light to relieve the night.

But after the heavenly fire, the fire of the Holy Ghost, had poured down in a heavenly rain upon the Apostles, and warmed with its fire the no less cold as well as dark hearts of mortal men, the Woman, that is, the Church, lit her lamp, that is, the power of vision of her soul, *the enlightened eyes of your heart* (Eph. i. 18). She therefore lit her lamp and through the subsequent labour of the Apostles *turned upside down*[6] that Judaic house that was blind with the darkness of ignorance, until she finds in Christ the silver piece that was lost from the ten; that is, from the Decalogue of the Law. Christ is the coin of the divinity in full. Christ is the *drachma* of our Redemption, and of our purchase. Christ it is Who was both in the Law of the Decalogue, and concealed by it. Christ it is Whom the Synagogue both possessed, and yet did not see, because of the darkness that warred against her.

We have called the ten words of the Law ten pieces of silver, of which the Synagogue lost one. Which one? That one which John first found in the Church (because *he* was a burning light, as the Lord says: *He was a burning light* (Jn. v. 35), as the Evangelist tells us, saying: *In the* beginning was the Word, and the Word was with God, and the Word was God. That He was in the Decalogue is already plain to us. *Hear*, it says, *O Israel: The Lord thy God is one God* (Mk. xii. 9). This word the Synagogue, since it did not see it in Christ, loses in the Father; and since it did not believe in Christ, it put Christ to death upon the Cross; to whom in consequence is it rightly said through the Decalogue: *Thou shalt not kill.*

For the Jew, when he cut off the head of the whole series of the Decalogue, was the slayer of Christ before being the slayer of the Law;[7] whence is it that he threw back upon Christ the whole body of the Decalogue. *Thou shalt not kill: thou shalt not commit adultery;* the Synagogue was condemned, which, joined adulterously to the gods of the Gentiles, rejected Christ, Who, putting down the power of her oppressor, came down to her with the affection of a spouse. *Thou shalt not steal.* She stole the Lord's Resurrection who gave money to the soldiers that they might bury and conceal the truth of the Resurrection (Mt. xxviii. 12). *Thou shalt not bear false witness.* For she it was who found many witnesses, that the words might be fulfilled: *Unjust witnesses rising up have asked me things I knew not* (Ps. xxxiv. 11).

And indeed in no other way could they deliver up the Author of truth; because falsehood is ever the enemy of the Truth. So he runs on to disaster, so he falls, step by step, whosoever falls from the head of the steps of the commandments, and tumbles down. For had they believed in the One Lord God they would never have come down to this abyss of disaster.

But we now follow after the lamp of Mother Church, and walking in the light of the Lord's countenance we shall come upon the silver piece of Christ; and we shall call together our friends and neighbours, that is, the Church of the Gentiles, lest they may not know that our Mother has found her silver piece, and let us say with the prophet: *I have prepared a lamp for my anointed* (Ps. cxxxi. 17). And what help it will be to us, let us hear: *Behold we have heard of it in Ephrata; we have found it in the fields of the wood. We will go into his tabernacle: we will adore in the place where his feet stood* (vv. 6 and 7).

Behold what we have been seeking through far wide fields and through scattered woods, this let us find in the Lord, this let us find by the lamp of our Mother. For this heaven too rejoices, because in one sinner doing penance the multitude of all the Christian people becomes glorious, and the whole character of Christ's divinity shines forth in our silver piece.

IV. St Gregory the Great, Pope and Doctor

Given to the People in the Basilica of the Blessed John and Paul on the Third Sunday after Pentecost

The Angelic Choirs[8]

1. The summer, which is very hard on me, has not for a long time permitted me to speak to you on the Gospel. But because our tongue

may be silent, does charity cease to warm our heart towards you? May I say something to you which each one of you will of himself readily understand? It will happen often that charity, distracted by other cares, will still glow within the heart, though it is not revealed by any outward work; just as the sun veiled in clouds may not be seen upon the earth, yet it still continues to burn in the heavens. And this is how charity is when its attention is directed elsewhere: so that though inwardly it gives forth the power of its ardour, without it gives no sign of the flame of its activity. But now that a suitable time has come for me to speak to you, let you increase your attention to what I have to say, so that the more eagerly your minds desire it, the more I shall be disposed to speak to you.

2. In the reading of the Gospel, My Brethren, you have heard that publicans and sinners drew near to our Redeemer, and that they were received not alone in conversation, but that He ate with them. And that the Pharisees seeing this were scornful. From this you may infer that true justice of life will have compassion and false justice only scorn; though the just are wont also to be angry with sinners, and rightly so. But what is done out of zeal for the law of God is one thing, what is done through the swelling of pride another. For the just scorn, but not as scornful; they despair, but not as despairing; they stir up trouble, but because they love: for though outwardly, and out of zeal for the law of God, they will heap up rebukes, yet inwardly they hold fast to charity. Oftentimes, within their own

souls, they place those they are correcting above themselves, and regard them as better than those that have to judge them. And in doing this they both correct their subjects for discipline's sake, and guard themselves by humility. While on the contrary those who pride themselves because of a righteousness that is false despise all others, and are void of all compassion for the weak. And the more they believe that they themselves are not sinners, the worse sinners they become. And without doubt of this number were the Pharisees, murmuring against the Lord because He received sinners, and from their own dried-up hearts rebuking the Fountain of all compassion.

3. But because they were sick, so sick that they did not know they were sick, the Heavenly Physician treats them as with soothing foments, and seeks to check the swelling of the wound of pride in their hearts. He says to them: *What man of you that hath an hundred sheep: and if he shall lose one of them, doth he not leave the ninety-nine in the desert, and go after that which was lost, until he find it?* See how by this wondrous divine design Truth places before us a similitude of the tenderness a man might see within himself, but which however relates to the Author of all men.

Since a hundred is the perfect number, He possessed a hundred sheep when He created angels and men. But soon after one was lost, when man through sin forsook the pastures of true life. But the Lord left the ninety-nine in the desert; for these supreme angelic choirs remained in heaven. But why is

heaven spoken of as a desert, unless
it is because we call that place a
desert which is abandoned? For
when man sinned he abandoned
heaven.

The ninety-nine sheep remained
in the desert while the Lord searched
for the lost one on earth; because the
number of the rational creation, that
is, of angels and of men, who were
made to know God, was lessened by
the fall of man, and so that the perfect sum of the sheep might again be
made full in heaven fallen man was
sought for on earth. Where this
Evangelist says, *in the desert*, another
says, *in the mountains* (Mt. xviii. 12),
which means, *on high*, because the
sheep which had not gone astray
remained in their exalted place.

*And when he hath found it, lay it
upon his shoulders, rejoicing.* He
places the sheep upon His shoulders
in that taking upon Himself our
nature He bore the burthen of our
sins. *And coming home, call together
his friends and neighbours, saying: Rejoice with me because I have found my
sheep that was lost.* Having found the
sheep he returns home; for our
Shepherd, man now redeemed, has
returned to His heavenly kingdom.
There He finds His friends and
neighbours, that is, the choirs of
angels who are His friends, because
in their steadfastness they uphold His
Will unceasingly. They are His
neighbours also, because being forever in His Presence, to them is
given the perfect enjoyment of the
Vision of His eternal glory. And let
us note that He does not say, Rejoice with the sheep that has been
found, but, *Rejoice with me*; for our
life is His joy, and when we are
brought back to heaven we shall
complete the feast of His rejoicing.

*4. I say to you, that even so there shall
be joy in heaven upon one sinner that
doth penance, more than upon ninety-
nine just who need not penance.*

We must here consider, My
Brethren, why is it the Lord confesses that there is more rejoicing in
heaven over converted sinners than
over those who remained just? But
we already know this from daily experience. For oftentimes those who
know themselves to be free of the
burthen of grave sins stand indeed in
the way of justice, they do no evil,
yet neither do they sigh and long for
the heavenly kingdom; and aware
that they have committed no grievous offences against justice they, in
due measure, permit themselves the
use of things lawful. And frequently
they are reluctant to give themselves
to the practice of the higher virtues,
content in the knowledge that they
have not committed any of the more
grievous sins.

On the other hand it will sometimes happen that those who are
mindful of having committed certain sins, being moved to sorrow by
this remembrance, the love of God is
enkindled within them, and they begin to give themselves to the practice
of great virtue. They are eager for all
the hardships of this holy contest,
they abandon all that is of this world,
they fly from honours, they rejoice
in humiliations, they are consumed
with longing for their heavenly
home; and recognizing that they
have strayed from God, they make
good the losses that went before
with the gains that now follow.
Greater therefore is the rejoicing of
heaven over the sinner converted
than upon the soul that remained
just. A captain in battle will feel a
warmer regard for the soldier who

at first faltered and ran, and then had bravely fought back, than over the one who had never yielded yet had never thrust bravely forward. So will the farmer love more the fields that cleaned of their weeds now bear a fruitful yield, than the land which had never known thorns, yet had never yielded a bountiful crop.

5. But while we do know this we should also know that there are many just in whose life there is joy so great that the repentance of no sinner whatever gives a greater joy. For there are many who though not conscious of any evil within them nevertheless give themselves to such anguish of love as if they were burthened with all sin. They give up even what is lawful, ready in loftiness of soul to despise the world. They will that whatever pleases them shall not be lawful to them. They cut themselves off even from the good things allowed them. They hold as nothing things visible, and are on fire for the Unseen. They joy in tears, they humble themselves in all things; and as some grieve over sins of deed, they will grieve over sins of thought.

What then shall I call those if not the Just and the Repentant; they who humble themselves in penance for the sins of the mind, and persevere ever upright in deed? From this we may gather how pleasing to God is the humble affliction of the just, if there is such rejoicing in heaven when the unjust through repentance rejects the evil he has done.

6. *Or what woman having ten pieces of silver; if she lose one, doth not light a lamp, and turn the house upside down,* *and seek diligently until she find the silver piece she had lost?*

He Who is signified by *the shepherd* is also signified by *the woman.* For it is God Himself; Himself together with the wisdom of God. And since there is an image stamped upon the silver piece, the woman lost the silver piece when man who had been made in the image of God abandoned through sin the image of his Maker. The woman lit a lamp; for the wisdom of God has appeared in human form. A lamp is a light in an earthen vessel: the divinity in human flesh is truly a Light in an earthen vessel. And of this vessel of His Body Wisdom declares: *My strength is dried up like a potsherd* (Ps. xxi. 16). For as a vessel is made firm by fire, His strength is dried up like the potsherd; because through the fire of His Passion He has strengthened unto the glory of His own Resurrection the flesh He had taken upon Him.

And the woman lighting the lamp turns the house upside down, for as soon as His Divinity shone forth in flesh the conscience of every man is shaken. For the house is turned upside down when man's conscience is troubled at the thought of his sins. And the word, *turned upside down,* (*evertit*) is not different in meaning from the word we find in other versions, *cleaned* (*emundat*); for an evil soul is not made clean from its habits of sin unless it is turned upside down by the fear of God.

The house turned upside down the silver piece is found; for when the conscience of man is turned upside down the image of his Maker is again found within him. *And when she hath found it, call together her friends and neighbours, saying: Rejoice with me, because I have found the silver piece I had lost.* Who are these friends and neighbours but those heavenly Powers spoken of already, who, the closer they approach to God through the favour of His unceasing Vision, the closer they come to His heavenly wisdom?

But we must by no means carelessly pass over the question why this woman, who symbolizes the wisdom of God, is said to have *ten* pieces of silver, of which she lost *one*, and then searched diligently till she found it. Since the Lord created the natures of both men and angels to the end that they might know Himself, and willed that they should endure for ever, He made them without doubt to His own Image. The woman had ten pieces; for nine are the orders of the angels. To make perfect the number of the elect, man as the tenth was made: who, even after his sin, was yet not destroyed by his Maker; for the Eternal Wisdom, shining forth in wonders from the light of an earthen vessel, redeemed him by His Body.

7. We have said that there are nine orders of angels, because we know from the testimony of Holy Scriptures that there are Angels, Archangels, Virtues, Powers, Principalities, Dominations, Thrones, Cherubim and Seraphim. That there are Angels and Archangels all the pages of Sacred Scripture bear witness. The prophetical books speak often of the Seraphim and the Cherubim, as we know. Also Paul the Apostle mentions the names of four orders, where he says to the Ephesians: *Above all principality and power, and virtue and dominion* (i. 21). And again, writing to the Colossians, he

says: *Whether thrones, or dominations, or principalities, or powers* (i. 16). Speaking to the Ephesians, he had already mentioned *Dominions, Principalities,* and *Powers;* but being about to speak of these to the Colossians also he mentions first, *Thrones,* of whom he had not spoken to the Ephesians. Therefore, adding, *Thrones* to the four orders he had spoken of to the Ephesians, that is, to *Principalities, Powers, Virtues,* and *Dominations,* five orders are expressly mentioned. Adding to these the *Angels, Archangels, Cherubim,* and *Seraphim,* we find that there are certainly nine orders of angels.

Because of this the prophet says to the angel who was first created: *Thou wast the seal of resemblance, full of wisdom, and perfect in beauty* (Ezech. xxviii. 12). And let us take note that he does not call him, 'made to the likeness of God', but, *the seal of resemblance;* so that it may be made clear to him that the purer his nature, the more clearly is the image of God stamped on him. And immediately there follows: *Every precious stone was thy covering: the sardius, the topaz, and the jasper, the chrysolite, and the onyx, and the beryl, the sapphire, and the carbuncle, and the emerald.*

Here nine names are given of precious stones, because they are without doubt the nine orders of angels. Among these orders he the first stood forth, clothed and adorned with beauty; for as he was placed over all the angelic host in comparison with the others he was the more gloriously endowed.

8. The Ministry of Angels

But why have we touched thus briefly upon these enduring heavenly orders if not so that we may also say something however brief concerning the ministry they fulfil? Messengers, in the Greek tongue, are called *angels*; and the chief messengers are called *archangels*. We must also know that the name *angel* refers rather to their office, and not to their own nature. For these holy spirits of our heavenly fatherland are indeed always spirits, but cannot always be called *angels*; for then only are they *angels* when by means of them certain things are announced. Accordingly, through the Psalmist is it said: *Who makes his spirits angels* (Ps. ciii. 4), as though saying: Who when He wills makes angels (*messengers*) of those spirits who stand for ever in His Presence.

They who announce things of lesser significance are called *Angels*, and they who announce the greater things are called *Archangels*. Hence it was not any Angel that was sent to the Virgin Mary, but the Archangel Gabriel (Lk. i. 26). It was fitting that for this task the highest order of angel should come, to announce the One Who is above all things. Because of this they are thought to have also particular names, so that by them may be indicated their power and their ministry. That they have proper names is not for the sake of the inhabitants of the Holy City, lest they should not be known without them—for there because of the Vision of God they each enjoy perfect knowledge—but for our sake; for when they come to us on some mission they take their names from the task they fulfil.

9. Accordingly, Michael is called, *Who is like to God?* Gabriel is, *The Strength of God*. Raphael is called,

The Medicine of God. And when something of striking power is to be done Michael is said to be sent, so that by his name and action it may be shown that no one can do what God can do. Because of this that ancient enemy who through pride desired to be like to God declared: *I will ascend into heaven, I will exhalt my throne above the stars of God, I will sit in the mountain of the covenant, in the sides of the north. I will ascend above the height of the cloud. I will be like to the most high* (Is. xiv. 13), is left with his strength until the end of the world, when he is to be punished with extreme torment, when, it is said, he will meet Michael the Archangel in combat; as it is told by John: *And there was a great battle in heaven, Michael fought with the dragon* (Apoc. xii. 7), so that he who in pride had exalted himself to the likeness of God, cast down by Michael learns that by the way of pride no one ascends to the likeness of God.

To Mary was sent Gabriel, who is called *The Strength of God*. For he came to announce Him Who, that He might cast down the powers of brass, deigned to appear among us as one lowly. Of Him the Psalmist sings: *Lift up your gates, O ye princes, and be ye lifted up, O eternal gates: and the King of Glory shall enter in. Who is this King of Glory? The Lord who is strong and mighty: the Lord mighty in battle.* And again: *The Lord of hosts, he is the King of glory* (Ps. xxiii. 7, 8, 10). He therefore was announced by the *Strength of God* Who is the *Lord of hosts*, and *mighty in battle,* Who came to war against the Powers of brass.

Raphael also, who is as we have said *The Medicine of God*, in as it were the exercise of his mission anointed the eyes of Tobias and wiped away the darkness of his blindness (Tob. xi. 15). He therefore who is sent to heal is rightly called *the Medicine of God.* As we have limited ourselves to explaining the particular names of the angels, there remains for us to explain also briefly the words which describe their office.

10. Those spirits are called *Virtues* through whom signs and wonders are wrought from time to time. They are called *Powers* who, in their order, have received this gift more powerfully than the rest received it, so that the hostile Virtues, whose powers are curbed, are subject to their word, so that they shall not tempt the hearts of men as they will. They are called *Principalities* who are placed over the good angels, order the tasks to be done by those subject to them, and rule them in the fulfilling of their offices.

They are called *Dominations* whose powers surpass those of the *Principalities*, by reason of a special distinction. For to be a *Principality* means to stand first among the rest; but to be a *Dominion* means to have all the rest as subjects. That order of angels therefore to whom all the rest are subject, since they surpass them all in wondrous power, are called *Dominations.* *Thrones* they are called upon whom the Omnipotent God is ever seated to give judgement. For the Greek word *tronos* means a seat, and so we say that they are called the *Thrones of God* who are so filled with the grace of the Divinity that the Lord is seated upon them, and through them makes known His judgements. Hence the Psalmist

says: *Thou dost sit upon a throne who judges justice* (ix. 5).

Again, Cherubim means the fulness of knowledge. And these sublime spirits are called Cherubim for the reason that, contemplating more closely the glory of God, they are filled with a more perfect knowledge of Him; so that the closer, by reason of their rank, they draw near to the Vision of their Creator the more they, in due measure as creatures, know all things. And these choirs of holy spirits who because of their special closeness to the Creator burn with an incomparable love are called Seraphim. For since they are so close to God that no other spirits stand between them and God, the more closely they behold Him the more ardently they love Him. And their love is a flame: for the more vivid their perception of the glory of the Divinity, the more ardently do they burn with His love.

11. But of what use is it to speak of these angelic spirits unless we seek through fitting reflection upon them to derive some profit from them for ourselves? For since we believe that the heavenly city is made up of both angels and men, whither we believe men shall ascend to the number of the chosen angels who remained there, as it is written: *He appointed the limits of people according to the number of the angels of God* (Deut. xxxii. 8), we too should draw something from our earthly contemplation of these different orders of the heavenly citizens for the perfecting of the manner of our own life, and by means of our own zealous devotion excite ourselves to the increase of virtue within us. And since we believe that as great will be the mul-

titude of men who will ascend there as the multitude of the angels who remained there, it remains that those among men who are going back to the heavenly fatherland should seek in some measure to resemble the company to which they are returning.

For the manner of life of different men clearly corresponds to the diverse orders of the heavenly host, and they are assigned to their order each in accord with the similarity of their devotion. For there are many who have understanding in small measure, yet they cease not from devoutly announcing these same small matters to their brethren. They accordingly associate with the ranks of Angels. And there are some who are filled with the favour of the divine bounty, and able to comprehend and to speak of the highest heavenly secrets. Where shall these be placed if not among the number of the Archangels?

And there are others who perform miracles, and work great signs and wonders. To whom do they correspond but to the rank and number of the heavenly Virtues? And there are those who drive out evil spirits from the bodies that are possessed by them, and they cast them forth by virtue of their prayers and of the power they have received. Where shall they have place if not among the celestial Powers? And there are some who because of the graces they have received surpass in merit even the elect, and being better than the good are even placed over their elect brethren. Where are they received if not among the number of the Principalities? And there are some who have so overcome within themselves all the vices and all desires that

by merit of their purity they are called gods among men: for this was it said to Moses: *Behold I have appointed thee the god of Pharaoh* (Exod. vii. 1). With whom will they associate if not with the order of Dominations?

And there are some who rule themselves with watchful care, and while examining themselves with anxious zeal, holding fast to the fear of God, receive as the reward of their virtues that they are able to judge others justly. Their minds being ever held in divine contemplation God rests upon them as upon a throne while He examines the actions of other men, and from His seat orders all things wondrously. Who are these but the Thrones of the Creator? And with whom shall they be numbered but with the number of the Heavenly Thrones? By these, as long as the Holy Church is subject to rule, even the elect are sometimes judged regarding certain imperfect acts of theirs.

And there are some men who are so filled with the love of God and of their neighbour that they are rightly called cherubim. And since, as we have said above, cherubim means the fulness of knowledge, and as we have learned from the words of Paul that *love is the fulfilling of the law* (Rom. xiii. 10), all who are more filled than the rest with the love of God and of their neighbour shall receive the reward of their merits among the ranks of the Cherubim.

And there are some who set on fire by the perfections of the heavenly contemplation breathe only in the love of their Creator, desire nothing more of this world, are nourished solely by this eternal love, cast away whatever is of this earth, pass in their minds above all temporal things, they love and they are on fire, they take their rest but in this love, loving they burn, speaking they inflame others, and whom they touch by word they straightaway make them begin to burn with the love of God. What shall I call these if not seraphim; these whose hearts transformed to fire burn and give light: for they enlighten the eyes of our mind regarding heavenly things, and moving them to tears they clean away the blight of evil? These then so inflamed with the love of their Creator, among whom are they to receive the reward of their calling if not amid the company of the Seraphim?

12. But while I, Dearest Brethren, am speaking to you of these things, let you turn your minds inwards to yourselves, and examine the faults and secret thoughts of your own hearts. See if there be now within you anything of good, whether you shall receive the reward of your calling among the ranks of these angelic choirs of whom we have briefly spoken to you? Woe to the soul who finds nothing within it, however little, of those good things of which we have just been speaking; and yet greater woe threatens it should it see itself empty of these graces, and yet not grieve because of it. Whosoever therefore this soul may be, My Brethren, he is greatly to be grieved over in that he does not himself grieve.

Let us then reflect upon the gifts received by the elect, and let us with all our heart long for a share of such love as they possess. Let him grieve who sees in himself nothing of the grace of these gifts. He who discerns

within him a little let him not envy others who may possess more: for these degrees among the blessed spirits were so ordered that some might be placed over others.

It is related that Dionysius, an ancient and venerable Father,[9] said that angels are sent forth from the lesser choirs to fulfil certain tasks, visibly or invisibly; namely that they are sent as Angels or Archangels for the comfort of men. For the higher choirs of the heavenly host never depart from the inmost depths; and so those above these two ranks are never employed in outward missions. This appears contrary to what Isaias says: *And one of the seraphim flew to me, and in his hand was a live coal, which he had taken with the tongs off the altar, and he touched my mouth* (vi. 6, 7).

But in this sentence of the prophet we are able to understand that those spirits who are *sent* receive their name from the office they perform. For the angel who bore a live coal from the altar, to purge by fire the sins of speech, is called a Seraphim, which means fire. This meaning agrees we may well believe with what was said by Daniel: *Thousands of thousands ministered to him, and ten times a hundred thousand stood before him* (vii. 10). To minister is one thing, to stand before Him another. For they who minister to God come to us as His messengers. They who stand before Him take their joy in His close contemplation, so that they are not at any time sent outwards to fulfil another ministry.

13. But we learn from certain places in holy Scripture that certain things are done by the Seraphim and certain other things by the Cheru-

bim—but as to whether they do these things of themselves, or whether they are done by their subject choirs, which, as is said, in that they come from the greater spirits, take their name from them, we do not wish to say what we cannot confirm with clear testimonies. But this we know with certitude, that to fulfil a mission from on high some spirits send other spirits, as Zacharias the prophet bears witness where he says: *Behold the angel that spoke in me went forth, and another angel went out to meet him. And he said to him: Run, speak to this young man, saying: Jerusalem shall be inhabited without walls* (Zach. ii. 3, 4). When one angel says to another, *Run, speak,* there is no doubt but that one sends the other. But they who send are higher in degree than those they send.

And this also we firmly hold regarding the angels who are sent to us, that when they come they so outwardly fulfil their mission that never for a moment are they inwardly withdrawn from the divine contemplation. They are therefore sent, and at the same time they assist before God's Throne; for though the angelic spirit is circumscribed, the Supreme Spirit Who is God is not. The angels therefore are both sent and they stand before Him; for wherever being sent they come, they yet stand within His Presence.

14. We must also know that oftentimes these orders of blessed spirits take the names of the orders nearest them. Thrones, for example, the seat of God, are as we have said a special order of the blessed spirits, and yet is it said by the Psalmist: *Thou that sittest upon the Cherubims, shine forth* (lxxix. 3); because within the ranks of the heavenly court the Cherubim are joined to the Thrones, the Lord is said to be also seated upon the Cherubim, because of their proximity to the order next them. For in that supreme abode there are things that belong to certain orders of spirits which are yet common to all, and that which each order has in part, this some one order possesses fully. But not because of this are they one and all called by the same name; so each order is to be called by the particular name of whatever thing it is it receives more fully as its special office.

We have spoken of the Seraphim as a flame, yet all together burn with the love of their Creator; Cherubim, the fulness of knowledge, yet who among them is unknowing when all together see God the Fount of all knowledge? Likewise they are called Thrones seated upon whom the Creator rules all things, but who would be blessed if the Creator did not rule from within his soul? These gifts therefore which all share in part are given, together with a special name, to those who have received them more abundantly for their special office. And though there are some possess a certain quality others do not possess, as that for which Dominations and Principalities receive a particular name, yet all things there are possessed by each single one: because through charity of mind (*spiritus*) they are possessed by each one in the others.

15. But while we have been exploring the secrets of the heavenly citizens we have wandered far from the subject of our Gospel exposition. We long for those of whom we have been speaking, but we must return

to ourselves. We have to remember we are flesh and blood. Let us then be silent regarding the secrets of heaven, but let us, before the eyes of the Lord, and with the hands of repentance, wipe away the stains of our dust. For the Divine Mercy promises us that: *That there shall be joy in heaven upon one sinner that doth penance.* And yet the Lord says by His prophet: *In whatsoever day the just shall sin, all his justices shall be forgotten* (Ezech. xxxiii. 12). Let us reflect then and see if we can understand the plan of the heavenly justice.

To the upright it threatens punishment should they fall; to sinners it promises mercy, that they may struggle to rise. The one it frightens, lest they presume on their justice; the others it cherishes, that they may not despair in their wickedness. If you are a just man, fear His anger if you should fall; you are a sinner: presume on His mercy that you may rise up from sin.

But we have already fallen, and we have no will to rise; we lie prone in our evil desires. But He Who made us just still waits, and calls to us to rise. He opens wide the bosom of His compassion, and He seeks to regain us through repentance. But we cannot do fitting penance unless we also know the measure of this same repentance. For to repent means both to lament the sins we have committed, and to refrain from the sins we lament. For the one who grieves over some sins, yet continues to commit others, either does not know how to repent, or but pretends to repent. What good is it for a man to cease from committing the sins of the flesh, and still continue to be consumed by the fever of avarice? Or how does it

help him if he repents of his sins of anger, while at the same time he is being devoured by envy?

16. Far better to do that which we tell you: that he who grieves over his sins, let him cease from what he grieves for, and he who weeps for his crimes, let him be fearful of committing them again. But we should have this especially in our mind, that whosoever is aware he has done what is unlawful, let him be at pains to deny himself in lawful things, that in this way he may offer satisfaction to his Creator. For he who has done forbidden things should forbid himself in what is allowed him. And he who knows he has sinned in great things, let him now restrain himself from offending in small things.

What I tell you matters little unless I am able to declare it together with the testimony of Sacred Scripture. The Law of the Old Testament does indeed forbid a man to covet his neighbour's wife (Exod. xx. 17), but it does not forbid under penalty that soldiers be commanded by their king to do heroic things, or that water be thirsted for. And we all know that David, pierced by the sharp edge of lust, desired another man's wife, and abducted her (II Kgs. xi. 4). His guilt was chastised with scourges, and with tears of repentance he made amends for the evil he had done.

Long after when he was besieging some of his enemies, and had a great longing for a drink out of the cistern that was in Bethlehem (xxiii. 14), some of his best soldiers broke through the camp of the enemy and returned safely with the water the king desired. But this man, humbled by chastisements, of a sudden rebukes himself for desiring to drink water at the peril of his men's lives, and he sacrificed it to the Lord, as it is written: *He offered it to the Lord* (I Par. xi. 18). The water was poured out in sacrifice to the Lord, in that he punished the fault of his concupiscence by the penance of his self-rebuke. He therefore who before had not feared to desire the wife of another later feared greatly to drink of the water he had desired. And remembering that he had done forbidden things, severe with himself he abstains even from what is not forbidden him. Let us repent in this way, if we truly repent of the sins we have committed. Let us keep before us the generosity of our Creator. He sees us sin, and He bears with us.

17. He Who before our offence forbids us to sin, after our offence ceases not from waiting for us to repent. He Whom we have rejected calls after us. We have turned away from Him, but He has not turned from us. Well does Isaias say: *And thy eyes shall see thy teacher, and thy ears shall hear the word of one admonishing thee behind thy back* (xxx. 20, 21). Man is as it were warned to his face when, being created unto justice, he receives the commandments of uprightness. But when he despises these very commandments he as it were turns the back of his mind on the face of his Maker.

But He still follows behind our back, warning us; for though we have rejected Him He does not cease from calling us. We as it were turn our backs to Him Whose words we despise, Whose commandments we tread under foot. But standing behind our averted backs He recalls us. He sees us as we despise Him, yet He still calls us by His commandments, and waits for us in patience.

Reflect, therefore, Dearest Brethren, how, should a servant of yours, while you are speaking to him, of a sudden become proud and turn his back on you, would not his affronted master beat down his pride, and inflict severe punishment to chastise him? Just so do we turn our back to our Maker when we sin, yet we are suffered in patience. Those turned from Him in pride He calls back in mildness; and where He could afflict us, as we turn from Him, He promises us a reward that we may turn back of ourselves. Therefore let the tenderness of our Creator soften the hardness of our sin; if one man through being beaten could learn the evil he had one, another who is awaited with longing should at least feel ashamed.

18. I shall relate to you very briefly, Brethren, something I came to know from the venerable Maximianus, who at the time was a priest and abbot of my own monastery and is now bishop of Syracuse. Listen to it carefully, for I believe it will be no little encouragement to Your Charity. In our time there was a certain Victorinus, also known by the name Aemilianus, of no small substance in a modest way, but, as will often happen, in the midst of abundance the unchastity of the flesh ruled him, and he fell into a certain wickedness, because of which he began to be afraid and to think deeply of the fearfulness of his own death.

And so greatly moved by the remembrance of his own evil doing, he roused himself against himself, abandoned everything of this world, and entered our monastery. In the monastery he gave himself to a life of such humility and austerity that all his brethren, who had themselves grown up in the love of the Divinity, seeing his penance were brought to think little of their own life. For he strove with all the earnestness of his soul to chastise his body, to break with his own desires, to seek with longing after quiet prayer, bathed continually in tears, seeking to be despised, and fearful of the reverence shown to him by his own brethren.

He would therefore rise before the hour of the night watch of the brethren; and as there is a more retired spot at one side of the hill upon which the monastery is situated he used to go out there before the night watch, that he might the more freely, as the more secretly, offer to God the tears of his repentance. His mind dwelt upon the severity of his future Judge, and being already of one mind with this same Judge he chastised with tears the guilt of his own past offences.

On a certain night the abbot of the monastery keeping vigil saw this monk go quietly out, and followed him. When he saw him prostrate himself in prayer, in a retired part of the mount, he resolved to wait till he would get up again, to learn for himself how steadfast was his prayer. And then suddenly a light from heaven flooded the man lying prone upon the ground, and its brilliance was diffused in every direction, so that the whole mount was illuminated by this same light. The abbot when he saw this was frightened and fled back to the monastery.

And when after a good hour the monk returned to the monastery the abbot, to find out if he too knew of the splendid light that had shone down upon him, began to question him. 'Where were you, Brother?' he said. The brother, believing that he had not been seen, replied that he had been in the monastery. At this answer the abbot was compelled to tell what he had seen. The monk seeing he was found out told the abbot something else he did not know. 'When you saw that light', he said, 'which descended upon me from heaven, a voice also came to me with it, and said: "Your sin is forgiven."'

The Omnipotent God could have forgiven his sin in silence, but, speaking with a voice, and shining with a great light, He willed by this manifestation of His mercy to move our hearts to repentance. Let us not wonder, Dearest Brethren, that the Lord should cast His persecutor Saul to the ground and speak to him from on high. For here in our own days a repentant sinner hears a voice from heaven. To the one was said: *Why persecutest thou me* (Acts ix. 5)? This man merited to hear: 'Your sin is forgiven.' Far lower than Paul in merit is this poor sinner. But as we are here speaking of *Saul, breathing threats and slaughter*, we may say that Saul heard the words of rebuke because of his pride, this man because of his humility merited to hear words of consolation. He whom humility had laid prostrate divine compassion had uplifted, and he whom pride had exalted the divine severity had thrown to the ground.

Therefore, My Brethren, have confidence in the compassion of our

Creator. Reflect well on what you are now doing, and keep before you the things you have done. Lift up your eyes towards the overflowing compassion of heaven, and while He waits for you, let you draw near in tears to our merciful Judge. Having before your mind that He is a Just Judge, do not take your sins lightly; and having also in mind that He is compassionate, do not despair. The God-Man gives man confidence before God. For those who do penance there is a great hope; for then our Judge becomes our Advocate, Who with the Father and the Holy Ghost liveth and reigneth world without end. Amen.

NOTES

[1] St Gregory uses the verb *evertit*, which we have rendered *turned upside down*; his context rests on this verb. St Peter Chrysologus also uses it in the same way. *Evertit* is found in many of the older Latin books; also *emundat. At mendose* is the comment in PL 52, 643, note *a*. The Vulgate has *everrit* (sweep); as the Greek, *saroi*.

[2] And, more explicitly, the lost virtue regained, without which the rest are valueless, might well be, in the light of 1 Cor. xiii, that of *charity*; though earlier the holy father tells us that it is wisdom; often interchangeable in meaning with charity.

[3] PL 15, in Luke.

[4] PG 72, in Luke.

[5] PL 52, Sermo 169.

[6] See note 1.

[7] This is an obscure passage. It seems that the Jews, by turning to false gods, slew, in purpose, Christ in God, and therefore as it were cut off the head or the first commandment, which is: *I am the Lord thy God, thou shalt not have strange gods before me*. And so they were slayers of Christ before being slayers of the Law; becoming rejectors of the Law, so that its observance fell to Christ, or to the Church in Christ.

[8] PL 76, Homily 34. It is homilies such as this that have formed and taught the Christian mind; full of a simplicity that covers a divine depth of wisdom. The mind is ever held and directed upwards towards the supreme and perfect end of each creature; and for our comfort we are shown that perfection is the hope and the possibility of each soul, and not simply of the more abstrusely guided or informed. The great and holy Doctor takes occasion here to give a simple, popular if you will, instruction on the angelic choirs, who are for him always our fellow citizens; so that we may learn and imitate the virtues of those among whom we are to share the blessedness of heaven, and the glory of the Divine Presence. Ed.

[9] *On the Celestial Hierarchy*, 7, 9, 13. It is disputed whether or not this work is authentic. The saintly Pontiff does not decide the question, saying merely *it is related* (*fertur*).

FOURTH SUNDAY AFTER PENTECOST

I. St Ambrose: Explanation of the Gospel

II. St Ambrose: The Two Ships

THE GOSPEL OF THE SUNDAY

Luke v. 1–11

At that time: When the multitude pressed upon Jesus to hear the word of God, he stood by the lake of Genesareth, and saw two ships standing by the lake: but the fishermen were gone out of them, and were washing their nets. And going into one of the ships that was Simon's, he desired them to draw back a little from the land. And sitting he taught the multitudes out of the ship. Now when he had ceased to speak, he said to Simon: Launch out into the deep, and let down your nets for a draught. And Simon answering said to him: Master, we have laboured all the night, and have taken nothing: but at thy word we will let down the net. And when they had done this, they enclosed a very great multitude of fishes, and their net broke.

And they beckoned to their partners that were in the other ship, that they should come and help them. And they came, and filled both the ships, so that they were almost sinking. Which when Simon Peter saw, he fell down at Jesus' knees saying: Depart from me, for I am a sinful man, O Lord. For he was wholly astonished, and all that were with him, at the draught of fishes which they had taken. And so were also James and John the sons of Zebedee, who were Simon's partners. And Jesus saith to Simon: Fear not: from henceforth thou shalt catch men. And having brought their ships to land, leaving all things, they followed him.

Exposition from the Catena Aurea

V. 1. *And it came to pass that when the multitudes pressed on Jesus.*

Ambrose *in Luke*: After the Lord had healed many and various kinds of sicknesses the multitude began to be oblivious of time and place in their eagerness to be healed. Even-

ing comes on, they still follow Him. They come to a lake, and the crowds press in on Him. *And the multitudes pressed on him.*

Chrysostom, *Hom. 25 in Matt*: For they clung to Him, loving Him, and marvelling at Him, and longing to stay with Him. And who would leave while He was working such wonders? Who was there but wished simply to look upon His Face, and at the mouth that spoke such things? For He was wondrous not alone in His miracles; His countenance overflowed with grace. And so while He spoke to them they listened in silence, not interrupting the flow of His words. For it is said that: *They pressed on him to hear the word of God.*

BEDE: It is said that the Lake of Genesareth is that which is also called the Sea of Galilee, or the Sea of Tiberias. It is called the Sea of Galilee from the adjacent province; the Sea of Tiberias from the city close to it; but Genesareth from the lake itself, which from its tossing waves is said to create a breeze upon itself: the name being a Greek expression meaning, to make a breeze for itself. For the water is never still as in a lake, but stirred by frequent breezes moving over it. It is sweet to taste, and wholesome to drink. In the Hebrew tongue however every large body of water, whether fresh or salt, is called a sea.

THEOPHYLACTUS: The more the Lord flees from glory, the more it presses upon Him. And because of this He entered a ship; cutting Himself off from the multitude.

V. 2. *And saw two ships standing by the lake; but the fishermen . . .*

CHRYSOSTOM: This was a sign that they were not in use. But according to Matthew (iv. 21) they were mending their nets: for such was their poverty they must repair what was torn, unable to buy new nets. Jesus, desiring to bring together His audience, and so that there would be none behind Him, but that all should face Him, went up into a ship. Hence:

V. 3. *And going into one of the ships that was Simon's . . .*

THEOPHYLACTUS: Note the simplicity of Christ, how He asks Peter; and the promptness of Peter, how obedient he is in all things. CHRYSOSTOM: After He had worked many miracles He begins again to teach; and being on the sea He fishes for those who are on the land. *And sitting he taught the multitudes out of the ship.*

GREGORY NAZIANZEN, *Orat.* 37: Condescending to all men, that He might draw fish from the deep, i.e. man, swimming amid the moving things and bitter storms of this life. BEDE: The two ships mystically signify the two dispensations; Circumcision and Uncircumcision, because among either people He knows who are His, and seeing them, that is, visiting them in mercy, He carries them on to the shore, that is, to the peace of the life to come. The fishermen are the Teachers of the Church, who catch us in the net of faith, and as it were bring us to the shore: to the land of the living. But these nets are now launched for catching fish, now washed and folded up; for not every occasion is suited to teaching: now the tongue of the Teacher should be made use of, and now he should give care to himself. The ship of Simon is the primitive Church; of which Paul says: *He wrought in Peter to the apostleship of the circumcision* (Gal. ii. 8). Well does he say *one ship*, for *the multitude of the believers had but one heart and one soul* (Acts iv. 32).

AUGUSTINE, *Questions on the Gospel* (of Luke), ii. 2: And from this ship He taught the multitudes as by the authority of the Church He teaches the Gentiles. That the Lord asks Peter, *to draw back a little from the land*, signifies to us that we must deliver the word to the people with moderation; that they are not to be taught earthly things, nor are they to come suddenly from things earthly to the profundities of the mysteries. And also that He commands that they preach first to the neighbouring peoples, so that, as appears from His next words: *Launch out into the deep*, afterwards they shall preach to the remoter Gentiles.

CYRIL: After He had taught the people sufficiently, He returns again to the wonders that marked Him, and from a fishing boat He fishes for disciples. Hence there follows:

V. 4. *Now when he had ceased to speak, he said to Simon . . .*

CHRYSOSTOM: For condescending to men He calls the wise by a star; the fishermen by their fishing. THEOPHYLACTUS: And Peter did not delay. Hence:

V. 5. *And Simon answering said to him: Master, we have laboured . . .*

He did not add: 'I am not going to listen to you, and go out again to labour in vain.' Rather he says: *At thy word I will let down the net.* Be-

cause the Lord had taught the people from his ship, He did not let the master of the ship go without a reward, but doubly rewarded him; first with a multitude of fish, and then by making him a Disciple. Hence:

V. 6. *And when they had done this, they enclosed a very great . . .*

He netted so many fishes that he could not draw them out, so he asks for help from his companions. Hence: . . . *and their net broke.*

V. 7. *And they beckoned to their partners that were in the other ship.*

Unable to speak with astonishment at the haul of fish, he calls them with a sign. Their help is then spoken of. *And they came, and filled both the ships.*

AUGUSTINE, *Harmony of the Gospels*, 4, 9: John is seen to narrate a similar miracle. But it is a far different one, taking place long after, following the Lord's Resurrection, by the sea of Tiberias (Jn. xxi. 1–11). In this second account not only is the time widely different, but the event is also. For there the net was cast *on the right side of the ship*, and they caught a definite number, *one hundred and fifty-three fishes*; also they were *great fishes*. And the Evangelist was careful to say that though they caught so many, *yet the net was not broken*: making reference in this way to the former time when, as Luke relates, *because of the multitude of the fishes their net broke.*

AMBROSE: Mystically, the ship of Peter, according to Matthew, is tossed about by the waves; and according to Luke, is filled with fishes: That you may know that the beginnings of the Church are tempestuous, and know also of her later abundance. This ship which belongs to Peter is not tossed about; but that ship which holds Judas is. Peter is in both; but he who is secure through his own merits is endangered because of others.[1] Let us beware of a traitor, lest through one among us many be threatened by the waves. Where there is little faith there is confusion and distress; where love is perfect there is peace. Lastly, while the others were bidden to cast their nets, only to Peter is it said to, *Launch out into the deep.*

What is so deep as to know the Son of God? What are the nets of the Apostles which He commands them to let down, if not the forms of words, and as it were certain inflections of speech, and the subtleties of argument, by which they hold those that come to their nets. And aptly is it said that the Apostles use nets in their fishing, since these do not injure but retain the fish they catch. And they bring upwards to heavenly things those who before were tossing about in the depths. And Peter says: *Master, we have laboured all night, and have taken nothing.* For this is not a task for human eloquence; but the work of a divine vocation. They who before had caught nothing, at the word of the Lord take a great multitude of fishes.

CYRIL: This event was a figure of the future. For they shall not labour in vain who let down the net of the Gospel preaching, but shall gather in the peoples of the Gentiles. AUGUSTINE, *Questions on the Gospels* II, 2: That the nets broke, and the ships

filled with a multitude of fishes, so that *they were almost sinking* signifies, that so great will be the numbers of carnal men in the Church, that it would be torn by the disruption of Her peace through heresies and schisms.

BEDE: The net was broken, but the fish do not escape: for the Lord preserves His own amid the trials of persecution. AMBROSE: The other ship is Judaea, from out of which James and John are chosen. These therefore come from the Synagogue to the ship of Peter, that is, to the Church, that they may fill both ships; for all, whether Jew or Greek, bend the knee at the Name of Jesus.

BEDE: Or, the other ship is the Church of the Gentiles, and it also is filled with the fish of the elect; one ship not being enough. For *the Lord knoweth who are his* (II Tim. ii. 19); and with Him the number of the elect is a certain number. And when He does not find in Judaea as many believers as He knows are predestined to eternal life, seeking another ship as a receptacle as it were for His fish, He fills the hearts of the Gentiles also with His grace. And well do they call to the neighbouring ship when the net broke, since Judas the traitor, Simon Magus, Ananias and Sapphira, and many of the disciples went away. And later Paul and Barnabas were set apart for work among the Gentiles.

AMBROSE: We may well understand by the other ship another church; since from one church many others are founded. CYRIL: He beckons to his companions to help him. For many succeed to the labours of the

Apostles; first those who have brought out the writings of the Gospels; next the other bishops and pastors; and then those who are skilled in the teaching of the Truth.

BEDE: The filling of these ships goes on to the end of the world. The fact that when filled they are almost sinking, are, that is, low in the water (for they are not sunk but endangered), the Apostle explains when he says: *In the last days there shall be perilous times, and men shall be lovers of themselves* (II Tim. iii. 1). For ships sink when men fall back into the world from which they have been called by faith, and this because of their evil way of life.

AMBROSE: Peter was astonished at the divine gifts; and the more he merited, the more diffident of himself he became. Hence is said:

V. 8. *Which when Simon Peter saw, he fell down at Jesus' knees . . .*

CYRIL: For mindful of the sins he has committed he is in fear and trembling, and thinks that, stained as he is, he cannot endure the presence of the Pure: for he had learned through the Law to distinguish between what was holy and what was defiled.

GREGORY OF NYSSA: For when He commanded them to lower the nets, the number of fishes taken was as great as the Lord of the sea and land willed. For the Voice of the Word is the Voice of Power, at Whose command light and all other creatures came forth at the beginning of the world. Peter is astonished at this miracle; for we read hat:

VV. 9, 10. *He was wholly astonished, and all that were with him, at the draught of the fishes they had taken. And so were also James and John . . .*

AUGUSTINE, *Harmony of the Gospels,* 2, 17, 37: Luke does not mention Andrew by name; nevertheless, from the accounts of both Matthew and Mark he is understood to be in the ship. *And Jesus said to Simon: fear not: from henceforth thou shalt catch men.* AMBROSE: Let you also say: *Depart from me, O Lord, for I am a sinful man,* so that the Lord may say to you also: *Fear not;* for the Lord is forgiving, to those who confess their sin. See how good the Lord is, Who gives so much to men that they too have the power of giving life. For from this we have what follows: *From henceforth you shall catch men.*

BEDE: This relates especially to Peter. For it is to him the Lord explains what this capture of fish signifies: that as he now takes fish by the net, so henceforth shall he catch them by the word. And the whole order of this event shows what takes place daily in the Church, of which Peter is the symbol.

V. 11. *And having brought their ships to land, leaving all things, they . . .*

CHRYSOSTOM: Consider their faith and obedience. For though they have their own pleasant calling of fishing, as soon as they hear His command they do not hesitate, but, leaving all things, they follow Him. Such is the obedience Christ requires of us. Let us not refuse it; even though something else that is necessary may press upon us.

AUGUSTINE, *Harmony of the Gospels*, 2, 17, 37: Matthew and Mark give us a briefer account of this event, and how it took place. Luke relates it more fully. They seem to differ in this: that he states that only to Peter was it said, *from henceforth thou shalt catch men*, whereas they relate it as being said to both of the brothers (Peter and Andrew, cf. Mt. iv. 19; Mk. i. 17). But it could be that this was first said to Peter, when he was astonished at the great haul of fishes, which Luke describes, and said afterwards to them both, as the other two Evangelists relate.

And we are also to understand by this, that what Luke relates took place first, and that the others were not then yet called by the Lord, and to Peter only was it foretold that he would be a fisher of men; not however that he would not catch fish again. Hence we have ground for believing that they did return to their usual fishing, so that what Matthew and Mark relate might afterwards happen. For then they did not follow Him, leaving the ships drawn up, as if with the intention of returning to them, but they follow Him as though He were calling or commanding them to follow.

But if, according to John, Peter and Andrew followed Him somewhere in the neighbourhood of the Jordan (Jn. i. 37), how do the other Evangelists say that He found them fishing in Galilee, and called them to be disciples? (Mt. iv. 18; Mk. i. 16; Lk. v. 2). How can these accounts be reconciled unless we understand that these two men did not find Him out and speak to Him with a view to attaching themselves permanently to Him, but only so as to know Who

He was, and wondering at Him they then return to their own way of life?

AMBROSE: But, mystically, those whom Peter caught by word he denies are his gain, his doing. Depart from me, he says, O Lord. Let you not be afraid to attribute also to the Lord what is yours: for what is His He has given us.

AUGUSTINE, *Questions of the Gospel*, 2, 2: Or again. Peter speaks in the person of the Church, filled with unspiritual men, *Depart from me, O Lord, for I am a sinful man.* As though the Church, laden with carnal-minded men, and almost submerged by their evil way of life, rejects as it were the rule of spiritual men, in whom especially the life of Christ shines forth. For it is not merely by the word of the tongue that men tell the worthy servants of God to depart from them; but also by the voice of their deeds and evil living do they persuade them to depart from them: so as not to have good men over them. And this they do the more earnestly by honouring them; as Peter signifies their doing honour, falling at the feet of the Lord; but he signifies their conduct by saying: depart from me.

BEDE: The Lord soothes the fears of unspiritual men so that no man need be fearful in his conscience because of his own past guilt; or, confounded at sight of the innocence of others, be discouraged in setting out himself on the road to sanctity.

AUGUSTINE, *as above*: But the Lord did not depart from them; showing by this that men who are good and spiritual should not wish, when troubled by the evil lives of others, to give up their own tasks in the Church, that they may as it were live more safely and more peacefully. That they, bringing their ships to land, and leaving all things, followed Him, can be a Figure of the end of time, when they who have adhered to Christ will wholly retire from the sea of this world.

I. ST AMBROSE, BISHOP AND DOCTOR

Explanation of the Gospel[2]

1. When the Lord had healed many and various kinds of illnesses the multitudes began to be oblivious of time and place, in their eagerness to be healed. Evening comes on, they still follow Him. They come to a lake; they press upon Him. And so He goes up into the ship of Peter. This is that ship which, according to Matthew, had lately been tossed about by the waves (Mt. viii. 24), and which, according to Luke, is filled with fishes: that you may know that though the beginnings of the Church were stormy, Her later times shall be abounding. For they are fish who traverse this life. Then He slept amid His Disciples. Here He teaches. He sleeps amid the frightened; He watches with the steadfast. But hear the Prophet (Cant. v. 2) telling us how Christ sleeps: *I sleep, and my heart watcheth.*

2. And the holy Matthew rightly believed we must not lightly pass over this evidence of divine power, where He commands the winds. For here we have not human authority; for as you have heard, the Jews declare (Lk. iv. 36) that with a word, *He commands the unclean spirits and they go out.* Here is a sign of heavenly power. That the troubled sea is made calm, that the elements are obedient to the command of the divine voice, that things without sense receive an understanding of obedience: here a mystery of divine power is revealed to us. That the waves of the world grow still, that an unclean spirit is quieted; the one happening does not contradict the other, but both the one and the other is brought about. You have before you in the elements a miracle; in the mysteries you have a proof.

3. Therefore, that ship which the holy Matthew had anticipated, this the holy Luke chose for himself, namely, that from which Peter would fish. That ship is not tossed about which has Peter aboard, but that which has Judas. Although many meritorious Disciples sailed in it, nevertheless the perfidy of the traitor tossed it up and down. Peter was in both the one and the other; but one who is safe through his own good life is endangered by the crimes of others. Let us beware then of the unbelieving; let us be on our guard against a traitor; lest because of one person many of us be threatened by the waves. So that ship will not be tossed about in which prudence navigates, where there is no treachery, where the wind of faith blows. For how could that be troubled where He is present Who is the stability of the Church? Where there is little faith there is trouble and unrest; where there is perfect love there is calm.

4. Accordingly, though He commanded the others to let down their nets, only to Peter was it said: *Launch out into the deep,* that is, into the deeps of preaching. For what is so deep as to look upon the depths of the riches of God, to know the Son of God, and to take upon oneself to declare the Divine Generation; which though the human mind cannot with the full power of reason comprehend, yet the fulness of faith can. For though I may not know how He was born; yet I may not *not* know that He *is* born. I know not the line of His generation, but I confess the Author of His Birth. We were not present when the Son of God was born of the Father; but we were present when He was called Son of God by the Father. If we cannot believe in God, in whom shall we believe? For all that we believe, we either believe by sight or by hearing. Sight is often deceived; hearing is based on faith. Is the character of one who lays claim to another searched into? If good men should speak, we would think it a crime not to believe them. God lays claim to the Son; the Son confirms this; the sun hiding its light confesses it; the trembling earth bears witness to it. Into this deep of investigation the Church is led by Peter; that it may see here the Son of God rising from the dead, and there the Holy Spirit pouring forth.

5. What are the nets of the Apostles which they are commanded to let down, if not the forms of words, and as it were certain profundities of speech, and the subtleties of discussion, which do not let go those that come to their nets? And well is it said that the Apostles

use nets in their fishing, since they do not destroy those they catch, but save them, and draw them upwards from the depths to the light; bringing those who are wavering, from the knowledge of the lowest things to the knowledge of the highest.

6. There is another, apostolic, kind of fishing, and in this kind the Lord commanded Peter only to go fishing, saying: *Cast in a hook, and that fish which shall first come up, take* (Mt. xvii. 26). This is indeed a great and spiritual lesson; Christian men are taught that they are to be subject to the higher authorities, so that no one may think that the decree of an earthly king is to be set at naught. For if the Son of God pays the tribute to authority who are you to think it must not be paid? And He paid the tribute Who had nothing; but you who follow after the gain of this world, why do you not acknowledge the authority of this world? Why, through a sort of obstinacy of mind, do you hold yourself above the world, seeing you are subject to the world through your own miserable greed?

7. The didrachma, which was the price of our soul and body, is therefore paid; promised under the Law (Exod. xxx. 32), it was paid under the Gospel; and not without purpose is it found in the mouth of a fish: *For from out thy own mouth shalt thou be justified* (Mt. xii. 37). Truly is it said that our confession of faith is the price of our immortality; for it is written that, *with the mouth confession is made unto salvation* (Rom. x. 10).

8. And perhaps this first fish is the first martyr (*witness*); holding in its

mouth the didrachma, that is, the price of the tribute. Christ is our didrachma. That first martyr, Stephen namely, therefore held a treasure in his mouth, when in his passion he spoke to Christ. But let us return to our original subject, and learn humility from the Apostle.

9. *Master*, he says, *we have laboured all the night, and have taken nothing; but at thy word I will let down the net.* And I, O Lord, know that it is night to me when you do not command me. No one has yet given in his name;³ it is still night. I have cast the net of my voice all through Epiphany, and I have caught nothing. I cast it through the day; I wait for your command: *at thy word I will let down the net.* O vain presumption, O fruitful humility!⁴ He who before had taken nothing, at the word of the Lord encloses a very great multitude of fish. For this is not a work of human skill; it is the fruit of the divine calling. The arguments of men pass away; it is by their own faith the people believe.

10. The nets are broken, but the fish do not escape. Companions are called to help, that is, those in the other ship. What is this other ship if not Judea, from which James and John were chosen? *Judea was made his sanctuary* (Ps. cxiii. 2). They come therefore from the Synagogue to the ship of Peter, that is, to the Church: that they may fill both

ships. For in the name of Jesus every knee shall bend, whether of Jew or of Greek; *Christ is all in all* (Col. iii. 11). In me this over-fulness awakens mistrust, lest by their fulness the ships come close to sinking; for it must be that heresies come, that the good may be confirmed.

11. We can also consider the other ship as another church; for from one church many others are derived. Here is another task for Peter: for whom his catch of fishes is already an anxiety. But *the man of God who is perfect* (II Tim. iii. 17), just as he knows how to gather in those that were dispersed, can also safeguard those that are gathered in. Those Peter catches by his word, these he credits to the Word: he denies they are his catch, his work.

Depart from me, O Lord, he says, *for I am a sinful man.* For he is struck with fear at the divine blessings: and the more he had merited them, the less does he presume on this. Let you also say: *Depart from me, O Lord, for I am a sinful man*, so that the Lord may answer you also: *Fear not.* For the Lord is kind to those who confess their sins. Fear not also to attribute what is yours to the Lord: for what is His He has made over to us. He knows nothing of envy; He does not snatch away from us; He does not rob us. See how good the Lord is, Who has given so much to men; so that they even have power to give Life.

II. St Ambrose, Bishop and Doctor

The Two Ships⁵

1. How great were the wonders the Lord worked we can learn from this Gospel reading, wherein he describes the many divine favours He bestowed upon the people, so that the multitudes of men, now stirred

up, pressed upon him, to hear Him, rather than to ask Him questions. And they sought to obtain the healing of salvation, not through the grace of humility, but through the violence of their importunity, so that, as the Gospel says, *they press upon him,* that the desert should not separate the multitudes from the Lord Jesus, nor the Synagogue hold them back, nor reverence for the Divinity keep them at a distance. For this is the way they act who are sick, that when they have a hope of being healed of their infirmities, they are not held back from imploring it by any importunity of time or place or shame: so that the more he heals who treats them, the more importunate they become who suffer.

2. And so because Jesus could not on land be apart from the people, seeing two ships upon the sea He hastens to go into one of them, that which belonged to Peter, so that with the water between them He might be free of the violence of their importunity. For the reverence that was due to a Teacher was far from restraining them. And then from the little ship He begins to speak to men the words of His Teaching. Consider the kindness of our Saviour; separated in Body from men, He is united to them in the profit of His teaching. Everywhere He is compassionate, everywhere He helps us. On the land He heals the infirmities of their bodies, by His touch; on the sea He heals the wounds of the soul, by His teaching.

3. Let us see what is this little ship of Simon Peter, which the Lord judged the more suitable of the two

to teach from, which keeps the Saviour safe from injury, and from which He bestows His words on men of faith. For we have learned that the Lord sailed in another ship, and was provoked by many injuries. For He sailed with Moses in the Red Sea, when He carried the people of Israel through the midst of the waves. But He suffered many affronts, as He Himself says in the Gospel to the Jews: *If you did believe Moses, you would believe me also* (Jn. v. 46). The faithlessness of the Synagogue is an insult to the Saviour. Therefore He chose the bark of Peter, and deserted that of Moses; that is, He rejected the faithless Synagogue, and adopts the believing Church.

4. For there are as it were two ships which were destined by God, which were to fish in this world, as in the sea, for the salvation of men, as the Lord said to His Apostles: *Come, and I will make you to be fishers of men* (Mt. iv. 19). And of these two ships one is left at the land, idle and empty; the other, laden or filled, is launched upon the deep. For the Synagogue is left idle on the beach; because of its own fault it has lost Christ together with the warnings of the prophets. But the freighted Church is taken out into the deep, because it received the Lord together with the teaching of the Apostles. The Synagogue, I say, remains by the land, holding fast as it were to earthly things. The Church is called forth to the deep, as though to search into the profound mysteries of heaven: into that deep of which the Apostle says: *O the depths of the riches of the wisdom and knowledge of God!* (Romans xi. 33).

For this end is it said to Peter, *Launch out into the deep*; that is, into the deep of teaching the Divine Generation. For what is so profound as that which Peter says to the Lord: *Thou art the Christ the Son of the living God?* What so earthly as that which the Jews said of the Lord: *Is not this the Son of Joseph the carpenter?* (Lk. iv. 22). The one inspired with wisdom from on high confesses the divine birth of Christ; these others, with minds like vipers, speak carnally of the Heavenly-Born. For this the Saviour said to Peter: *Because flesh and blood hath not revealed it to thee, but my Father who is in heaven.* But to the Pharisees He says: *O Generation of vipers, how can you speak good things, whereas you are evil?* (Mt. xii. 34).

5. The Lord Jesus therefore goes up only into the bark of the Church, of which Peter is the appointed Master, the Lord saying to him: *Upon this rock I will build my Church.* This ship so floats upon the deep of this world, that as it sails across this present time it keeps safe from harm all it carries within it. We have a true Figure of this in the Old Testament. For as all whom Noah took with him in the Ark were saved in the shipwreck of the world, so when the world shall be destroyed by fire the Church of Peter will keep safe within her all whom she cherishes as her own. And as when the Flood had ceased a dove carried a token of peace to the Ark, so also when the judgement is over Christ will bring to the Church of Peter the joy of peace: for He is Himself the Dove or Peace: as He promised us, saying: *I will see you again, and your heart shall rejoice* (Jn. xvi. 22).

6. But since we read in Matthew that this same little ship of Peter, from which the Lord now makes known the mysteries of His heavenly doctrine, that while the Lord slept in it it was tossed about by the winds that arose, so that all the Apostles began to be in fear of the danger of death, let us see then why it was that from the one and the same vessel He here imparts His holy teaching to the people, while there He inflicts on His Disciples the fear of death: especially since Simon Peter was also there with the other Apostles? This is the cause of their danger. Simon Peter was there; but also the traitor Judas was there. Though Peter's faith could steady the ship, the faithlessness of the other could bring it to disaster. Where Peter alone sails there is calm; where Judas is added to the company there is storm. Though Peter would be safe by reason of his own merits, he is endangered through the wickedness of the traitor.

The Lord therefore sat sleeping, Peter was anxious, and the Disciples were in fear. It may seem hard perhaps that He should sleep while Peter was in anxiety. He slept for Peter, lest He should keep watch for Judas; and so by the crime of one the merits of all are placed in danger. The Lord has fallen asleep, and violence of the wind increases; for whoever sins, immediately he causes the Lord to fall asleep within him, and raises within himself a storm of unclean spirits. When the calm weather of the Lord has sunk to sleep, it must be that a diabolic tempest will rise up instead.

7. If therefore, by the sin of Judas, all the Apostles were placed in

danger, let us by this warning be on our guard against the faithless, be on our guard against the traitor: lest through one many are put in danger of the waves. And let us also drive such a one forth from our little ship, that the Lord may not fall asleep among us, but that He may keep watch in us, and while He keeps watch no storm of iniquity shall strike us.

For where faith is pure, there the Saviour teaches, watches, and rejoices; there is rest, there is peace, there is healing for all men. But where heresy becomes mingled with faith, there Christ grows drowsy, He sleeps, and is inactive. There you will have fear, and there storm, and there is danger for all. For it depends on us whether Christ sleeps in us, or keeps watch. Amen.

NOTES

[1] In Mt. viii. 23 we read: *And when he went into the boat, his disciples followed him*, among whom was Judas. Here in Luke there were only fishermen; which Judas was not. Peter was in both; but it was the first which contained Judas.

[2] PL 15, col. 1633. Book IV in Luke, pars. 68–79, and also text of Roman Breviary.

[3] The holy Doctor is addressing himself here to catechumens, among whom it was the custom to hand in their names for Baptism during Epiphany, in preparation for the solemn Baptisms at Easter. Many delayed in this; including such persons as St Basil. Their names were then entered in the book or album of the Catechumens. The net of his voice referred to is a short net thrown like a javelin, for game or fish.

[4] The exclamations seem contradictory; the first may refer to his own fishing, the second to Peter's.

[5] PL 17, col. 675. Sermo 37. Attributed to St Ambrose, but certainly not his, though containing ideas derived from him. It is commonly held as being the work of St Maximus, Bishop of Tours (A.D. 380–465). The sermon, while not striking in other respects, stresses a belief found generally among the Fathers, that Christ as it were sleeps in the sinner, is awake and vigilant in those free from heresy and evil. And also that the evil living of those about us is a danger to ourselves; that we should not associate with such people, especially those who err in matters of faith; or we are likely to share their chastisements.

FIFTH SUNDAY AFTER PENTECOST

I. St Ephraim: Charity and Forgiveness

II. St John Chrysostom: The Christian Manner of Life

III. St John Chrysostom: Let Us Consider One Another

IV. St Gregory the Great: The Folly of Anger

THE GOSPEL OF THE SUNDAY

Matthew v. 20–4

At that time: Jesus said to His Disciples: Unless your justice abound more than that of the Scribes and Pharisees, you shall not enter into the kingdom of heaven. You have heard that it was said to them of old: Thou shalt not kill. And whosoever shall kill shall be in danger of the judgement. But I say to you, that whosoever is angry with his brother, shall be in danger of the judgement. And whosoever shall say to his brother, Raca, shall be in danger of the council. And whosoever shall say, Thou fool, shall be in danger of hell fire.

If therefore thou offer thy gift at the altar, and there thou remember that thy brother hath anything against thee; leave there thy offering before the altar, and go first to be reconciled to thy brother; and then coming thou shalt offer thy gift.

EXPOSITION FROM THE CATENA AUREA

V. 20. *For I tell you that unless your justice abound more than* . . .

Hilary, *in Matt. Can.* 4: Declaring to the Apostles that there shall be for them no entering the kingdom of heaven unless they surpass the Pharisees in justice, with this most apt beginning He here commences to advance beyond the works of the Law. And this is what He means when He says: *I tell you.*

Chrysostom, *Hom.* 16 *in Matt*: By *in justice* He here means in every virtue. But note the increase of grace. For He now wills that His own Disciples, who were as yet untaught men, shall be better than the teachers of the Old Testament. He is not saying the Scribes and Pharisees are wicked: for otherwise He would not have said that they had a certain degree of justice. See how by these words He confirms the truth

226

of the Old Testament, comparing it with the New; for they are the more and the less of the same thing.

CHRYSOSTOM, *Opus Imperfectum, Hom.* 11:[1] The justice of the Scribes and Pharisees is the commandments of Moses; their perfect fulfilment is through the commandments of Christ. This then is what He means. Unless that over and above the commandments of the Law you also fulfil My precepts, which among them were held as *the least commandments*, you shall not enter into the kingdom of heaven. The observance of the first does deliver us from punishment, that, namely, which is due to the transgressors of the Law, but they do not lead us into the kingdom of heaven. But My commandments both deliver you from punishment and lead you into heaven. But since it is the same thing to break *the least of the commandments* as not to observe them, why does He say above (v. 19) of the one who breaks one of these least commandments that he shall be called the *least in the kingdom of heaven*?

But understand that to be the least in the kingdom of heaven is the same as not to enter it. For anyone to be in the kingdom does not mean that he reigns with Christ, but only that he is among the people of Christ: as though saying of the one breaking them that he will be indeed among Christians, yet the least among them. He however who enters into the kingdom becomes with Christ a partaker of His kingdom. And so he who does not enter into the kingdom of heaven shall not have glory with Christ, yet he will be in the kingdom of heaven; that is, among the number of those over whom the King of heaven reigns.

AUGUSTINE, *City of God*, 20, 9: Or again: Unless your justice abound more than that of the Scribes and Pharisees, that is, more than theirs who break what they teach; for elsewhere He said of them: *For they say, and do not* (Mt. xxiii. 3); just as though He says: Unless your justice so abounds that you do not break, but rather do, what you teach, you shall not enter into the kingdom of heaven. We are to understand the kingdom of heaven here in another sense, where both these are: They who break, and they who observe, what they both teach; but one is called *the least*, the other *is called great*: as the Church here present. And it is called the kingdom of heaven in yet another way; as that into which no one enters unless *he who does*; and this is the Church as it shall be in heaven.

AUGUSTINE, *Contra Faustum, Bk.* 19, *ch.* 31: This phrase of *the kingdom of heaven*, which the Lord so frequently uses, I know not if anyone has found it in the books of the Old Testament. For it belongs rightly to the revelation of the New Testament, and it was reserved to be uttered by His mouth Whom the Old Testament foreshadowed would reign as King over His servants. This end therefore, to which the commandments are to be related, was concealed in the Old Testament; although even then there were those who, living according to it became saints, looked to the revelation to come.

GLOSS: Or, that He says, *Unless your justice abound*, applies, not to what the Law itself contains, but to what the Scribes and Pharisees understand by it.

AUGUSTINE, *Contra Faustum*, *Bk.* 19, *ch.* 28: For almost everything that the Lord taught at the time that He added: *But I say to you*, is found also in these ancient books. But because they alone regarded as murder the killing of a human body, the Lord made known to them that every evil impulse to the hurt of a brother must be regarded as partaking of the nature of murder. For this reason He goes on:

V. 21. *You have heard that it was said to them of old: Thou shalt not kill.* CHRYSOSTOM, *Op. Imp. Hom.* 11: Christ willing to make known, that He is the God Who of old spoke in the Law, and Who now announces the dispensation of Grace, also places in the beginning of His own commandments that commandment which in the Old Law is placed before all the rest; that is, forbidding whatever is injurious to our neighbour.

AUGUSTINE, *City of God*, I, 19, 20 We do not think it a sin to kill a twig, because we have heard it declared that, *Thou shalt not kill*, as the Manichean folly imagines; nor do we understand that it was said of irrational animals. For by the most just law of the Creator their life and death is made subject to us. Accordingly, the commandment, *Thou shalt not kill*, is to be understood only with reference to men. Not another man other than yourself. For he who kills himself, kills none other than a man.

They however who by God's authority wage war do not act contrary to this precept; and neither do they who in the fulfilment of public office punish criminals with death, in strict accord with reason and justice.

And not alone was Abraham not charged with the crime of cruelty, he was praised in the name of piety, because he was ready through obedience to God to sacrifice his son. These then are examples of those whom God commands to kill, either by a law He has given, or by an express command to some person. For he does not commit murder who renders obedience to the one commanding him, as the hilt to the one using a sword. Otherwise Samson could not be excused, for pulling down the house upon himself and his enemies, had he not been secretly commanded by the Spirit, Which had wrought wonders through him.

CHRYSOSTOM, *Hom.* 16 *in Matt*: In saying, *Of old it was said*, He points out that it is a long time since they received this commandment. This He says in order to rouse His dulled hearers to the more sublime commandments; as a teacher might say to a dull boy, to urge him on, 'you have wasted sufficient time in learning to spell'. And accordingly He continues:

V. 22. *But I say to you, that whosoever is angry with his brother.*

See in this sentence the power of the Law-Giver. For none of the ancients spoke in this way. They said instead: *Thus saith the Lord*. For it was as servants that they proclaimed the commands of their Lord. Here He proclaims as Son the things that are His Father's, and which are also His. They proclaimed His words to their fellow servants; but He here gives the Law to His servants.

AUGUSTINE, *City of God*, IX, 5, 5: There are two opinions among the philosophers with regard to the passions of the soul. For to the Stoics it is not acceptable that such emotions afflict a wise man. The Peripatetics however say they do happen to a wise man, but to a moderate degree, and subject to the mind's control; as when mercy is shown, yet in such a way that justice is upheld. But in the Christian belief we do not ask whether a worthy soul is angered or saddened, but why is he?

CHRYSOSTOM, *Op. Imp*: For he who is angry without cause must answer for it. He who is so with cause has not to answer for it. For if this were not so teaching would be without profit, and crime could not be controlled. So he who with due cause is not roused to anger sins by this: for patience with things that are against reason breeds evil, fosters neglect, and becomes an invitation to wrong doing, not alone to the wicked, but also to the good.

JEROME: In certain copies (of the Scriptures) the words, *without cause*, are added. However in authentic copies the meaning is definite, and anger wholly forbidden: for if we are told to pray for those that persecute us, every excuse for anger is taken away. We must then erase, *without cause*; for *the anger of man worketh not the justice of God* (Jas. i. 20).

CHRYSOSTOM, *as above*: But that anger which has cause is not anger, but a criticism. For anger strictly means a commotion of feeling. He who with cause becomes angry, his anger does not derive from emotion; and so he is said to condemn rather than to be angry.

AUGUSTINE, *Book of Retractions*, XIV, 9: We affirm that this also is to be considered: What does it mean to be *angry with his brother*, since a man is not made angry by his brother, but by the offence of his brother. He therefore who is angry, not with the offence, but with his brother, is angry without cause.

AUGUSTINE, *City of God*, Bk. XIV, 9: No person of sane mind will fault being angry with a brother in order to correct him: for this impulse arises from the love of good. Such an emotion, coming from holy charity, since it is in accord with reason, is not to be called evil.

CHRYSOSTOM, *as above*: I believe however that Christ is speaking, not of the anger of the body, but of the anger of the soul: for the body cannot so obey as not to feel emotion. So when a man is angered, but will not do what his body urges, his flesh is angered, but his soul is not.

V. 22. *But I say to you, that whosoever is angry with his brother . . .*

AUGUSTINE, *Sermon on the Mount*, i. 9, 24: In this first sentence, therefore, there is but one thing spoken of, that is, anger only. In the second there are two: anger, and the voice of anger. Hence there follows: *Whosoever shall say to his brother, Raca, shall be in danger of the council.* Some wished to base the interpretation of this word on a Greek word meaning ragged (ῥάκος, a rag). More likely it is not a word with any particular meaning, but a mere sound expressive of resentment of mind: such as grammarians call an interjection, as when someone exclaims, Alas!

CHRYSOSTOM, *Hom.* 16 *in Matt*: Or; this word, *Raca*, is an expression of contempt or one conveying a slight. For as we when we speak to servants or inferiors say: 'Go, you', or, 'Tell him, you', so in Syriac they would say *Raca*, for *you* (*tu*). For the Lord comes down to the least things with us; and He is commanding us to treat one another with respect.

JEROME: Or; *Raca* is a Hebrew word, and means a foolish or empty person, one whom the vulgar offensive phrase would describe as *brainless*. Significantly He adds: *Whosoever shall say to his brother.* For no one is our brother unless he has the same Father as ourselves.

CHRYSOSTOM, *Op. Imp*: It is an unbecoming thing to call a person *empty* who has the Holy Ghost within him.

AUGUSTINE, *as above*: In the third sentence three things are spoken of: anger, the voice of anger, and the expression of insult in speech. And so He goes on to say: *And whosoever shall say, Thou fool, shall be in danger of hell fire.* There are then three degrees in these sins. The first when one is angry, but gives no sign of the anger within him. Should he give utterance to any sound, which may mean nothing, yet indicating by this outburst the inward commotion of his nature, this is more grievous than if he had repressed the rising emotion in silence. It is yet more grievous should he utter any word of definite abuse.

CHRYSOSTOM, *Op. Imp*: As no one is empty who has the Holy Spirit within him, so no one is a fool who

has come to know Christ. But if *Raca* means empty, it is one and the same thing, as far as meaning goes, to say, *you empty-head*, as to say, *you fool.* They differ however in the intention of the speaker. For *Raca* was a common phrase with the Jews, and was spoken, not out of anger or hatred, but from any slight impulse whatever, and arose out of familiarity rather than from a feeling of anger. But if it was not said out of anger, where is the sin? Because it arose out of contention, and not edification. For if we should say what is good, only *to the edification of faith*, how much more should we not use *speech* which is naturally *evil* (Eph. iv. 29)?

AUGUSTINE, *as above*: Here we have three degrees of liability: The Judgement, the Council, Hell fire: the degrees going from the less to the more serious. In the judgement there is still possibility of defence. In the Council there appears to be simply a delay of sentence, while the judges confer among themselves as to the penalty to be imposed. In the Gehenna of fire there is but condemnation, and the punishment is certain. So it is very plain what difference lies between the justice of the Scribes and Pharisees, and that of Christ. In the one, killing makes a man liable to the Judgement; in the other, anger places a man in danger of the Judgement; and this is the least of the three sins.

RHABANUS: Here the Saviour calls the torments of hell Gehenna: a name believed to be derived from the name of a valley dedicated to idols. It is close to Jerusalem, and was formerly filled with the bodies of the dead. Josia, as we read in the Book of Kings, ended its reproach (cf. III Kgs. xiii. 2; II Paral. xxxiv. 33).

CHRYSOSTOM, *Hom.* 16 *in Matt*: Here He makes the first mention of hell, after He had already spoken of the kingdom of heaven: showing that the gift of the latter is from His love towards us, but that the former is the consequence of our own neglect. To many it seems grievous that we should suffer a great punishment for a word, and so claim that He is speaking figuratively. But I fear that by deceiving ourselves here with words, we shall there suffer in deed this extreme punishment. Do not then think this severe; for many are the sins and crimes that had their beginning from a word. For often has a slight word led to murder, and to disaster for many a state. Neither let you regard it as a trivial thing to call your brother a fool, denying him that mind and understanding by which we are men, and differ from creatures without reason.

CHRYSOSTOM, *Op. Imp*: Or, *shall be in danger of the council*, means that he may be one of that Council which was against Christ; as the Apostles interpreted it in their constitutions.[2]

HILARY: Or, that he who reproaches with emptiness one who is filled with the Holy Ghost is liable to the Council of the saints, and by the judgement of the saints shall make reparation for the insult to the Holy Spirit.

AUGUSTINE, *Sermon on the Mount*, i. 9: Should anyone ask, what is the punishment of murder if insult is punished by hell, this will lead us to understand that there are degrees of hell.

CHRYSOSTOM, *Hom.* 16 *in Matt*: Or, Judgement and Council mean the punishment of the present life; the fire of Gehenna, that to come. He laid it down that anger shall be punished, that He may show that it is not possible for man to be wholly free of the passions, but that it is possible to restrain them. Accordingly He does not appoint any determined punishment, lest it might appear as if He wholly forbids anger. *Council* here stands for the Tribunal of the Jews: lest He seem to be always introducing novelties.

AUGUSTINE, *as above*: In these three phrases certain words are implied. The first sentence has all the needed words, so nothing is implied. Whoever is angry with his brother, He says: *without cause*, is added in some versions. But in the second, when He says: *whosoever shall say to his brother, Raca*, the words, *without cause*, are implied. For in the third, where He says: *whosoever shall say, Thou fool*, there are two phrases implied: 'to his brother', and, 'without cause'. And in this lies Paul's defence, when he calls the Galatians *fools*, though he also calls them *brothers*; for he says this not without cause.

V. 23. *If therefore thou offer thy gift at the altar . . .*

AUGUSTINE, *as above*: If it is not lawful to be angry with a brother, or to say, *Raca*, or, *Thou fool*, much less is it lawful to hold back in the mind what might change resentment into hate.

JEROME: He did not say: If you have anything against your brother; but: *If thy brother hath anything against thee*: that He may place on you the more disagreeable necessity of reconciliation.

AUGUSTINE, *Sermon on the Mount*, i. 10, 27: For he has something against us, if we have wounded him in anything; and we against him, when he has wronged us: where there is no obligation on us to seek to be reconciled. For you do not ask pardon of one who has wronged you. You forgive him, as you desire that the Lord may forgive you what you have committed against Him.

CHRYSOSTOM, *Op. Imp*: Should he injure you, and you first seek to be reconciled, great will be your reward.

CHRYSOSTOM, *Hom.* 16 in *Matt*: Should anyone be not disposed to be reconciled to his neighbour out of true charity, let this at least move him to be reconciled: lest his offering remain fruitless, and especially at that sacred place. Hence He says:

V. 24. *Leave therefore thy offering before the altar . . .*

GREGORY, *Hom.* 8 *in Ezech.*: See how He wills not to accept sacrifice from those who are in discord one with another. See then how great an evil is contention; because of which that is lost through which sin is forgiven.

CHRYSOSTOM, *Op. Imp*: Observe the mercy of God, how He cares for the profit of man above His own honour; He loves peace and goodwill among the faithful more than offerings. For as long as there is any discord among men who are of the faith, their gift is not received, their prayer is unheard. No one between two enemies can be the faithful friend of both. Nor does God wish to be a friend to such as are enemies to one another. We are not faithful to God if we love His enemies, and hate His friends. Such as was the offence, such should be the reconcilement. If you have offended in thought, in thought be reconciled. If you offended in words, be reconciled in words. If you offended in deeds, be reconciled in deeds. In the manner that any sin is committed, in that way let penance be done for it.

HILARY: He bids us, when human peace has been restored, to return to divine peace; that we are to pass from the love of men to the love of God. And so there follows: *And then coming thou shalt offer thy gift.*

AUGUSTINE, *as above*: If what is said here is taken literally, some one may think that this is to be done if your brother is present: for no long interval can be meant when we are bidden to leave our gift before the altar. For if he is not present, and is in fact, beyond the seas, and we then remember something, it is absurd to believe that we must leave our gift before the altar, and having crossed over sea or land then come and offer our gift to God. And so we are absolutely compelled to have recourse to a spiritual interpretation, so that what is said may be understood without absurdity.

And so we may interpret the altar spiritually, as being faith. For whatever gift we offer to God, whether teaching or prayer or whatever else

I. Ephraim

it may be, it cannot be offered to God unless it rests on faith. If therefore we have injured our brother in anything, we must go and be reconciled to him, not on the feet of our body, but with the impulses of the soul, where you may cast yourself in humble regret before him, in His sight to Whom you are offering your gift. And just as if he were present you may with a sincere heart dispose him towards you by asking his forgiveness, and then coming, that is, turning your mind back to that which you had begun to do, offer your gift.

I. St Ephraim, Confessor and Doctor

Charity and Forgiveness[3]

Matthew xi. 29, 30

Well did the Lord say that *My burden is light.* For what burden is it, what labour, to forgive a brother his offences against us? It is light indeed, it is as nothing, that we should of our own will pardon and forget, and be ourselves immediately held as just. He has not said to us: Offer me riches, or calves, or kids, or a fast, or a vigil, so that you may not be able to say, I have not such things, I cannot do such things. But that which is light and easy, and quickly done; this He commands us to do, saying to us: Let you forgive your brother his faults against you, and I shall forgive you yours against Me. You condone small offences, little debts, a few pence, a few shillings: but I am forgiving you to the extent of six hundred talents of silver. And you only forgive something; you give away nothing that is yours. But I both grant you forgiveness, and at the same time give you healing of soul, and a kingdom. And then I accept your gift, as soon as you have become reconciled to your enemy, when you cherish no hatred against anyone, when the sun has not gone down upon your wrath, when there is peace and charity in you towards all men, then your prayer is heard, then your offering is pleasing and acceptable to God, your house is blessed, and you are blessed.

If however you will not be reconciled to your brother, how can you seek forgiveness and pardon from Me? You let My words fall to the ground as it were, and you look for forgiveness? And I Who am your Lord, I command you and you do not listen to Me; and you who are a servant, how can you dare to come and offer prayer to Me, to offer sacrifices and first-fruits, while you are cherishing enmity in your heart against another? For just as you turn away your face from your brother, so shall I turn away My eyes from your prayers and from your offerings.

Again I ask of you, Brethren, since God is love, and since what is done without love is not pleasing to God, how then shall God receive the prayers, the offerings, the first-fruits, or the good works of a murderer, unless he repents as he should? But you will say: I am no murderer. I shall show that you are, or rather John the Divine will put it clearly to you; for he says: *Whosoever hateth his brother is a murderer* (I Jn. iii. 15).

It remains therefore that we are to hold nothing above charity; that nothing whatsoever is to be preferred before the possession of charity. And let us have nothing against another, nor render evil for evil, nor let the sun go down upon our anger. But let us forgive everything that has been done against us, and let us procure for ourselves that *charity which covereth a multitude of sins* (I Pet. iv. 8).

For what does it profit us, My Sons, to possess all things, and to be without this life-giving and saving charity? It would be just as if you had prepared a great feast, and had invited kings and great persons, and had omitted nothing that was wanting to the feast; but there was no salt: could anyone be pleased with a meal of that kind? Far from it. And what is more you will have suffered loss because of it: for you lose not alone your toil and trouble, but you have been shamed in the presence of those you invited. And this is how it is here; for all your labour is in vain and without profit, if you have not charity, without which whatever the good work or deed you do maybe remains unsanctified; even though the one who does them may lay claim to virginity, even though he fasts, or keeps watch in the night, though he gives shelter to the poor, though he is seen to offer gifts to God, or first-fruits, or to do good works, even though he should build a church, or do any other kind of good work short of possessing charity, all these will be held as nothing to Him by God: for without charity there is nothing in them that is pleasing to the Lord.

Hear the Apostle speaking of this: *If I should speak with the tongues of men and of angels, if I should have prophecy and should know all mysteries, and if I should have all faith, so that I could remove mountains, and have not charity, it profiteth me nothing* (I Cor. xiii). For he who nourishes enmity against a brother, and nevertheless is seen to offer something to God, it is as though he were *sacrificing a dog*, or offering *the price of a harlot* (cf. Is. lxvi. 1; Prov. vi. 26). Beware then of ever offering anything to God without charity; since charity covereth a multitude of sins.

O! of how many good things, of what joy are we deprived when we are without charity? Judas scorned it, and he left the company of the Apostles. Abandoning the True Light, His own Master, hating his brethren, he walked out into the darkness. Because of this Peter, the Prince of the Apostles, says: *Judas hath by transgression fallen, that he might go to his own place* (Acts i. 25). And again John the Divine: *He that hateth his brother, he says, is in darkness, and walketh in darkness, and knoweth not where he goeth; because the darkness hath blinded his eyes* (I Jn. ii. 11).

But should you say: Even though I do not love my neighbour, I do love God, the same John will contradict you, where he says: *If any man say, I love God, and hateth his brother; he is a liar. For he that loveth not his brother, whom he seeth, how can he love God, whom he seeth not* (I Jn. iv. 20)? He therefore who loves his neighbour, and is at enmity with no one, if he fulfils the words of the Apostle, *Let not the sun go down upon your anger*, he truly loves God, and is a true disciple of Christ; Who has said: *By this shall all men know that you are my disciples, if you have love one for another* (Jn. xiii. 35).

It is very clear, therefore, that in no other way are you seen to be disciples of Christ except by the practice of true charity. For he who hates his brother, and thinks to himself that he loves Christ, is a liar, and deceives himself. For the Apostle John tells us: *And this commandment we have from God, that he who loveth God, love also his brother* (I Jn. iv. 21). And again the Lord says: *Thou shalt love the Lord thy God, and thy neighbour as thyself* (Mt. xxii. 37, 39). And desiring to show us the power of this love He declares: *On these two commandments dependeth the whole law and the prophets.*

O rare and wondrous thing! That he who has true charity fulfils the whole of the Law; for *love is the fulfilling of the law* (Rom. xiii. 10) according to the Apostle. O incomparable power of charity! O immense power of charity! There is nothing in heaven or on earth that surpasses charity. And because of this Paul the Apostle, since he had learned that there is nothing more perfect than charity, instructing us, declares: *Brethren, owe no man anything, but to love one another* (Rom. xiii. 8); and lay down your lives for one another; for it is in this that charity consists, the chief of all the virtues, and their salt.

Charity is the fulfilment of the Law; charity is certain salvation. It dwelt in the heart of Abel from the beginning. It ruled in Noah's heart. It clothed the patriarchs as with a garment. Charity made of David a dwelling place of the Holy Spirit. Charity placed a tabernacle in the midst of the prophets (Lev. xxvi. 11). It was charity sustained Job.

And why should I not speak of greater things? It is this that compelled the Son of God to come down to us from heaven: He Who though free of flesh took upon Him our body. He Who is above time became subject to it for us; Who while Son of God became Son of man. Through charity all things serve for our salvation. Through charity death was overcome, the power of hell broken, Adam recalled to life, and Eve restored to freedom. Through God's love there has been made one Fold of men and angels. Through this charity the curse has been taken away, paradise reopened, Life revealed to us, and the Kingdom of heaven proclaimed. It has changed those who fished for fish into fishers of men. It was love gave strength and courage to the Martyrs in their agony. It has built cities in the wilderness, and filled mountains and caves with the sweet harmony of the Psalms.

Charity has changed men into angels. It has taught men and women alike to enter in by the narrow way. But why need I keep on spinning the thread of my discourse, keeping on about things that surpass human understanding? For who can speak the praises of charity? Not even the angels in their power, I believe, can do this. O blessed charity that has given us every good thing! O blessed charity that makes all who desire thee blessed also! Blessed and thrice blessed is the man *who in a pure heart, and with a good conscience,* possesses *charity*! (I Tim. i. 5).

But when you hear of this love take care that you do not understand it in an earthy bodily sense, as that which has place with feasting and revelling among those *whose God is their belly, and whose glory is in their shame* (Phil. iii. 19);[4] whose charity is confined within the limits of a single table, and whose love is an insult to God. Here friends are invited; not guests. Here the poor have no part. Here is laughter and revelry and noise; drunkenness and shame. Of these the Apostle James says: *Whoever therefore will be a friend of this world, becometh an enemy of God* (Jas. iv. 4). Of this charity, or mockery rather, and, let me add, which God turns away from, the Lord says that the Gentiles do the same: *For if you love them that love you, what thanks will be given to you, what reward shall you have?* (Mt. v. 46).

But we are not speaking of this love, we do not preach it or praise it, but that love rather which is without dissimulation, love that is blameless and free of every fault, unstained, incomparable. This charity, I say, contains within it all things, and is contained in every good work, as our Lord has taught us, saying, *that a man lay down his life for his friends.* For the Lord Himself has both taught this and done this, and has laid down His life for us; and not alone for his friends, but also for his enemies. *For God so loved the world, as to give His only-begotten Son for us* (Jn. iii. 16).

And Paul the Apostle, inflamed with this love, having this divine charity within him, has told us: *The love of our neighbour worketh no evil* (Rom. xiii. 10). Charity does not render evil for evil, nor give back cursing for cursing, but is ever *patient*, ever *long-suffering*, ever *kind. Charity envieth not, is not provoked to anger, thinketh no evil, rejoiceth not in iniquity, but rejoiceth with the truth. Beareth all things, believeth all things, hopeth all things, endureth all things. Charity* of this kind *never falleth away.* He who is endowed with this charity is blessed: blessed in this life, and shall be blessed in the life to come.

Blessed the soul that is adorned with charity, that is not *puffed up,* that *does not envy,* that hates no one at any time, that is not repelled by the poor, that does not turn away from those in want, that does not despise the widow nor the orphan nor the stranger. He that has this charity in his soul loves not alone those who love him: for this even the heathens do: but those also who afflict him. Clothed in this charity the first martyr Stephen prayed for those who stoned him; saying, *Lord, lay not this sin to their charge* (Acts vii. 59). Again I say, and I shall not cease to say it: Blessed is the man who despises all things that are of the earth, and subject to corruption, and who possesses charity. The profits of charity increase with him day by day. His reward and his crown is prepared for him, paradise is opened to him, and the kingdom of heaven is bestowed on him as a gift. All the Angels proclaim him blessed. The Heavens and all Powers together praise him. The choirs of the Archangels receive him with joy and gladness. For him the heavenly gates are opened wide, and through them he enters to be brought before the throne of God, to be crowned at the right hand of God, with Whom he shall reign for ever. Who is more blessed than this man? Who more uplifted? Who more honoured? Look upwards and behold to what heights charity raises those who possess her. As the Apostle has rightly declared: we ought to owe no man anything save this alone, that we love one another (Rom. xiii. 8). For *God is charity, and he that abideth in charity, abideth in God, and God in him* (I Jn. iv. 16) for ever and ever. Amen.

II. St John Chrysostom, Bishop and Doctor

The Christian Manner of Life[5]

Be angry, and sin not. Let not the sun go down upon your anger. Give not place to the devil. He that stole let him now steal no more. Let no evil speech proceed from your mouth; but that which is good, to the edification of faith, that it may administer grace to the hearers. And grieve not the Holy Spirit of God: whereby you are sealed unto the day of redemption (Eph.iv. 26–30).

Be ye angry, and sin not. It would be a good thing never to yield to anger. But should this feeling come upon one, let it be brief. *Let not the sun go down upon your anger.* Would you have your fill of anger? An hour of it is enough, or two, or three; but do not let the sun go down and leave you at enmity. It rose out of God's goodness to you; let it not now depart, having given light to those who were not worthy of it. But if the Lord sent it out of His great goodness, and has forgiven you your sins, and you will not forgive your neighbour, do you not see how great an evil is this?

And together with this there is yet another evil. For the blessed Paul is fearful lest the night should find him alone who was injured, and may set him on fire while he is still smouldering with resentment. For throughout the day there were many things to distract anger, and you might let it smoulder. But as the night draws on, be reconciled, put out this flame while it is still fresh. For should night overtake it the day that follows will not be able to put out the evil that has been added to it in the night. And even if you could cut off the greater part of it you cannot cut off the whole, and what is left will supply enough for the night that follows, to make a yet greater blaze. And just as when the sun cannot during the heat of the day dissolve and scatter the clouds that formed in the night, so when night overtakes the remainder it adds yet more to them, and so the storm is built up, so is it also with anger.

Give not place to the devil. And so to be at war with each other is to give place to the devil. For where we should stand together and unite against him, our enmity against him has weakened, and we turn on one another instead. For nothing gives so much place to the devil as enmities. So long as we are united one to another he cannot insert his evil devices to create enmity among us; but the moment a rift is made he pours in like a torrent. He needs only a beginning, and this it is that is difficult for him; but this opening made, he makes place for himself on all sides. Now he opens ears only to slanders; and they who speak lies are listened to: for enmity is their advocate, not truth which reasons and judges. And as where there is friendship evils which are true seem untrue, so where there is enmity what is false will now seem true. There is now a different mind, a different judgement; which no longer listens justly, but only with bitterness and one-sidedness.

So therefore let us, I beseech you, do all we can before the sun goes down to put an end to enmity and anger. For if you fail to overcome it on the first day, or on the second day, often you will keep it going for a year, and by then the enmity will nourish itself, and need no help to keep going; making us suspect of one meaning words spoken in a wholly different sense; even gestures and manner and anything whatever will serve to fan the flames, changing men into what is worse than being mad, not enduring in their fury either to hear or to speak some name, and speaking only out of hatred and evil.

How then shall we soften this anger? How extinguish a flame like this? By turning over in your mind the remembrance of our own sins, and of how much we ourselves have to answer for, before God. By reflecting that we are wreaking vengeance, but upon ourselves, not on our enemy. By thinking of how we are delighting the devil, our enemy, who is truly our enemy, and because of whom we are inflicting injury on our own members. Do you wish to be both an enemy, and forgiving at the same time? Then be an enemy, but of the devil; not with a member of your own body. It was for this God armed us with anger; not to drive a sword into our own bodies, but to plunge it into the heart of the devil. To the hilt, if you wish: hilt and all, and do not draw it out, but add another. This takes place when we spare one another; when we are at peace with one another.

He that stole, let him now steal no more. See of what kind were the members of *our old man*: our former selves: Falsehood, revenge, theft. Why does he not say, let him that stole be punished, be tormented? *Rather,* he says, *let him labour, working with his hands the thing which is good, that he may have something to give to him that suffereth need.* They stole: that is to commit sin. They steal no more: this is not to commit sin. How shall they do this? If they work with their hands, and give to others: this is to undo their sins. He does not wish us merely to labour, but to labour so that we may give to others. For even he who stole worked; but he worked that which was evil.

Let no evil speech proceed from your mouth. What is evil speech? It is what is also called idle talk, foul-mouthedness, ridicule, foolish talking. You see how here the Apostle is cutting at the very roots of anger: lying, theft, unfitting conversation. When he says, *let him steal no more,* he does not say this as though he were condoning the theft, so much as seeking to render kind and forbearing those who have suffered injury, persuading them not to be angry, and that they will not suffer such things again. And very rightly does he warn us regarding evil conversation. For we must suffer punishment for our words as well as our evil deeds.

But let us speak that which is good, to the edification of faith. That is, to speak only what will help to build up our neighbour in virtue; nothing more than that. For this has God given you a tongue, and a mouth: that you might give thanks to God, that you might help to build up your neighbour in virtue. Far better be silent, and not to speak at all, than destroy that building. For if the hands of a builder, which were meant to build up walls, had learned only to destroy them, they would justly deserve to be cut off. And this the psalmist also says: *May the Lord destroy all deceitful lips* (xi. 4). Here is the source of all evil, the mouth. Or rather, not the mouth, but those who make evil use of it. From the mouth come insults, cursings, blasphemies, incitements to lust, to murder, to adultery, to robbery. How, you will say, does murder come from it? Because insult leads to anger, anger to blows, blows to murder. And to adultery? Because some one will say: This or that woman loves you; she said such and such things of you. He weakens your steadfastness, and then desire enters into you also.

And so because of this Paul tells us to speak only *that which is good*. Since there is such a profusion of words he rightly speaks of this in general terms, and simply bids us speak of things of this kind, giving us at the same time an indication of what he has in mind. How does he do this? By saying, If a man has anything good to say, anything that serves to build up his neighbour in virtue, or says that which brings grace to the one who hears him. As for example: a brother has fallen into fornication. Do not disgrace him because of his fault; neither let you laugh at it. You will do no good to whoever hears you; rather what is more likely you will do him harm, goading him further. But if you advise him as to what he should do, you will do him a great favour: if you teach him to use speech fittingly,

and guide him so that he will abuse no one, you will teach him exceedingly well, and you will have brought him grace. If you speak with him about repentance, of the love of God, of giving to the poor, all these things will heal his soul. For all this he will be grateful to you. But if you laugh at him, or speak hurtfully to him, you will provoke him instead. If you show any approval of his evil doing, you will undo him and destroy him. This then is his meaning.

Or he may mean this: that you should so speak that those who hear you may be pleased. For as sweet ointments make those pleasant who use them, so likewise does good and pleasant conversation. Because of this it was once said: *Thy name is as oil poured out* (Cant. i. 2); which enabled those present to breathe of the sweet odour. You see then he is saying here what he commends to us at all times; bidding each one of us, as best we can, do what is in us to edify our neighbour. You then who commend such things to others, much more let you commend them to yourself.

And grieve not the Holy Spirit of God. This is something more fearful, something to be dreaded. And he says the same in the Epistle to the Thessalonians. For to them he says: *He that despiseth these things, despiseth not man, but God* (I Thess. iv. 8). So is it here also. If you use offensive words, if you strike a brother, you are not striking him, you are grieving the Holy Ghost. And then, to make it more serious, he speaks of the good the Spirit has done to us. *Grieve not the Holy Spirit of God, in whom you are sealed unto the day of redemption.* It is the Holy Spirit that marks us as the flock of the King. He it is Who has led us away from all the things of our former life. He it is Who does not leave us to lie among those who are subject to the anger of God. And you grieve Him? Take note of how fearfully he here warns us: *He that despiseth, despiseth not man, but God*; and how sharp his words here are: *Grieve not the holy Spirit of God, whereby you are sealed.*

Keep His seal upon your mouth; and do not remove the signs of it. A mouth that belongs to the Spirit does not speak such things. Do not then say: It makes no difference should I say something wicked, should I say something offensive to another. Because it seems of no importance, for this reason it is a great evil. For things that seem to be as nothing are easily thought nothing of. And what is held as nothing will become more frequent. And what becomes more and more frequent will in time become incurable.

You have a mouth sealed by the Spirit? When you are speaking, think first of what you are saying, of what words are fitting for a mouth such as yours. You call God Father, and straightaway you insult your brother. Think of why it is you call God your Father? By nature? No, you cannot for that reason. Because

of your virtue? No, nor for this reason either. Why then is it? Solely because of His love towards man, because of His kindness, because of His mercy. So when you call God Father remember this, that not alone do you do what is unworthy of your dignity when you insult another, but remember also that it is only from His kindness and mercy that you possess this dignity. Do not dishonour it; receiving it as you do out of His love and kindness: by using cruelty and unkindness against your brethren. You call God Father and you insult them? But such things are not *doing the things* that the Son of God does (Lk. vi. 46). The work of the Son of God is, to forgive His enemies, to pray for those who crucified Him, to shed His Blood for those that hated Him. Works such as these are worthy of the Son of God: to make brothers of those who are His enemies, of the ungrateful, of robbers, the shameless, the treacherous, and make them heirs with Him also; not to treat those that are now your brothers as though they were slaves.

May the God of peace guard your minds and your tongue, and surround you with His fear as with a firm wall, in Christ Jesus our Lord, to Whom with the Father and the Holy Ghost be there glory for ever. Amen.

III. St John Chrysostom, Bishop and Doctor

Let Us Consider One Another[6]

Let us consider one another, to provoke unto charity and to good works. Not forsaking our assembly, as some are accustomed; but comforting one another, and so much the more as you see the day approaching (Heb. x. 24, 25).

And in another place he says: *The Lord is nigh; be not anxious* (Phil. iv. 5, 6). *For now our salvation is nearer than when we believed* (Rom. xiii. 11); and again: *The time is short* (I Cor. vii. 29). And what is the meaning of, *not forsaking our assembly?* He knew that there is great strength in being together, and in gathering together. *For where,* says the Lord, *there are two or three gathered together in my name, there am I in the midst of them* (Mt. xviii. 20). And again, He prayed, *that they may be one, as we also are* (Jn. xvii. 11). And again: *And the multitude of believers had but one heart and one soul* (Acts iv. 32).

And not alone because of this, but because the things that arise from charity are increased by our coming together; and charity increasing, the things of God will also increase. *And prayer was made without ceasing by the Church for him* (Acts xii. 5).

As some are accustomed. Here the Apostle not alone exhorts, but reproves. *And let us consider one another, to provoke unto charity and to good works.* He knew that this also happens through their coming together in a common assembly. For as *iron sharpeneth iron* (Prov. xxvii. 17), so also being together increases love. For if a stone rubbed against a stone sends forth flame, how much more will not soul mingled with soul!

Let us consider one another, but not so as to cause rivalry between one another, but provoking one another *unto charity.* What is the meaning of, *to provoke unto charity?* Unto loving each other more and more. And he adds, *and to good works;* that they might acquire zeal one from another. For if doing has greater power to teach than mere speaking, you have many teachers among you in the congregation who teach by doing good works.

And a little before this he says: *Let us draw near with a true heart.*

What is the meaning of, *let us draw near with a true heart?* That is, without hypocrisy and pretence. For, *Woe to them that are o a double heart, and to wicked lips, and to the hands that do evil* (Ecclus. ii. 14). Let there be, he says, no falsehood among us. Let us not say one thing, and think another: for this is falsehood. And neither let us be faint-hearted: for this is not the sign of *a true heart.* For not to believe with a true heart is to become weak of soul. And how do we do this (*Draw near with a true heart*)? When we come in the fulness of faith. *Having our hearts sprinkled from an evil conscience?* Why does he not say: *having our hearts purified?* He says, having our hearts sprinkled, not purified, because He wills to show us the excellence of the sprinkling: that the one is from God, the other is our own. For to sprinkle and to wash the conscience is the work of God; but to draw near with a *true heart* and the *fulness of faith* is our own work. He then gives strength to faith, from the truth He has promised us. *And having our bodies washed with pure water.* What does this mean? With water which makes us pure, or water which has no blood.

Then he adds what is perfect, namely, charity. *Not forsaking our assembly,* which some, he says, are *accustomed to do,* dividing our assemblies. This he forbids them to do. *For a brother that is helped by his brother, is like a strong city* (Prov. xviii. 19). But let us consider one another, to provoke unto charity. What does, *let us consider one another,* mean? For example. If a man is virtuous; let us imitate him; let us look upon him so as to love him, and be loved by him; for it is from charity that good works come forth. This coming together is a great good; for this it is which makes charity more fervent, and from charity all good things are born; for nothing is good except what is done because of charity.

Let us strengthen this love amongst us; for *love is the fulfilling of the Law*. We have no need to labour and to sweat if we love one another. It is a road that leads of itself towards a virtuous life. For as when a man journeys along a highway, if he but finds the beginning of it, he is guided by it, and has no need of anyone to show him the way. So is it with regard to love. Only take hold of the beginning, and at once you are guided and directed from within yourself.

Charity, he says, *is patient, is kind, thinketh no evil*. Let a man consider himself, how he is disposed towards himself, then let him be so disposed towards his neighbour. For no one envies himself; he prays for all good things for himself, he prefers himself to all others, he is prepared to do all things for himself. If we are thus disposed towards others, all evils come to an end: there are no more enmities, no more greed; for who would wish to be covetous of himself? No one; rather much to the contrary.

Let us therefore possess all things in common; neither let us cease from assembling together. And if we do this, remembrance of injuries will have no place in us; for who would choose to remember injuries against himself by himself? Who would be angry against himself? Do we not make allowances for ourselves most of all? If we were thus disposed against our neighbours also, there would never be any remembrance of injuries.

And how is it possible, you will say, for any man so to love his neighbour as himself? Had others never done this you might well think it is impossible. But if others have done this, then it is evident that it is because of neglect that it has no place amongst us. And besides, Christ imposes nothing that is impossible; seeing that many have even surpassed what He commanded of us. Who has done this? Paul, Peter, all the company of the saints. If I say that they loved their neighbours, I would be saying no great thing. They so loved their enemies as no one has ever loved those who were of one mind with himself. For who would choose to go down into hell for the sake of those who were of one mind with himself, when he was about to depart for a kingdom? No man. But Paul chose to do this for his enemies, for those who had tried to stone him to death, for those who had scourged him. What forgiveness shall we have, what excuse, if we never show to our friends the very least part of that love which Paul showed his enemies? And before him the blessed Moses had prayed to be struck out from the book of God (Exod. xxxii. 32). David also seeing those who had resisted him put to the slaughter said to the Lord: *It is I the shepherd have sinned; these the sheep, what have they done* (II Kgs. xxiv. 17)? And when he had Saul in his power, he refused to kill him, and saved his life even though his own was then endangered.

If these things were done in the Old Testament what plea have we who live in the New, and yet have not reached to that degree of charity they possessed? *Unless your justice abound more than that of the scribes and Pharisees, you shall not enter into the kingdom of heaven* (Mt. v. 20). But since we have less, how are we to enter? The Lord Himself tells us: *Love your enemies: do good to them that hate you: and pray for them that persecute and calumniate you, that you may be the children of your Father who is in heaven* (xliv, 45). Therefore, love your enemy: for so you are doing good, not to him, but to yourself. How is this? Doing this you become like to God. Your enemy, should he be loved by you, has gained nothing very great; for he is but loved by a fellow servant. But you, should you love a fellow servant, you have gained much; for you have become like to God. See then how you do a favour, not to him, but to yourself. For it is to you, not to him, that God gives a reward.

And what if my enemy is evil? So much the greater your reward. Even for his wickedness you should feel thankful to him. Even should he be still evil after receiving innumerable kindnesses. For if he were not so evil, your reward would not be so great. And so the reason you have for not loving him, because

you say he is evil, this is the very reason for loving him. Take away the contestant and you take away the occasion of gaining a crown. You have seen how athletes toughen themselves with bags of sand? But you have no need to resort to such means. Life is full of things that test you, and make you strong. Look at the trees. The more they are shaken by the wind the more tough and unyielding they become. And we also, if we are patient, we also shall become strong, *For he that is patient is governed with much wisdom; but he that is impatient, exalteth his folly* (Prov. xiv. 29). See how great is the praise of one, and the condemnation of the other? Exalteth his folly, that is, is foolish beyond measure.

Let us then not be little-minded towards one another. For this impatience does not arise because of enmity, but through having a little soul. For if the soul is strong it can bear all things with ease, and nothing will submerge it, and it will make steadily for home, towards the harbour of salvation, to which may we all at length arrive, by the grace and loving mercy of our Lord Jesus Christ, to Whom with the Father and the Holy Ghost glory and honour, now and for ever. Amen.

IV. St Gregory the Great, Pope and Doctor

The Folly of Anger[7]

Anger killeth the foolish, and envy slayeth the little one (Job v. 2).

1. *The evils of anger.* And this is a true saying; but it is not true as spoken against the patience of so great a man (as Job). But let us weigh well what is said, though it is confuted by the virtue of his lis-

tener, that we may show how true is that which was said: though spoken unjustly against the blessed Job: since it is written: *But thou, being master of power, judgest with tranquillity* (Wisd. xii. 18). We should know above all things, that as often as we subdue the stormy impulses of the soul through the virtue of mildness, we are striving to recover within us the likeness of our Creator. For when anger has shattered your peace of mind, and, torn and rent as it were, it is thrown into confusion, so that it is no longer in harmony with itself, it loses the essence of that inward likeness.

Let us consider therefore how great a sin is anger, through which, when we let go of mildness, the likeness of the heavenly image is marred in us. Through anger wisdom is lost, so that we no longer know what we are to do, or in what manner we should do it; as it is written: *For anger resteth in the bosom of a fool* (Eccles. vii. 10), because it takes away the light of the understanding when it confuses the mind by stirring it up. Through anger true life is lost, though wisdom appears to be retained; for it is written: *Anger destroys even the wise* (Prov. xv. 1 Sept.). For the mind is confused and cannot fulfil its office, though it may still retain the power to understand intelligently.

Through anger justice is abandoned; as it is written: *For the anger of man worketh not the justice of God* (Jas. i. 20). When the mind is thrown into disorder this blunts the judgement of the reason, so that whatever rage may suggest is considered right. Through anger the pleasantness of social life is lost; as it is written: *Be not a friend to an angry man, and do not walk with a furious man, lest perhaps thou learn his ways, and take scandal to thy soul.* And the same inspired writer says to us: *A spirit that is easily angered, who can bear* (Prov. xxii. 24; xviii. 14)? For the man who will not moderate his feelings in accord with human

reason needs must, like a wild beast, live alone.

Through anger peace and mutual concord is broken up; as it is written: *A passionate man stirreth up strifes, but an angry man diggeth up sins* (xv. 18). An angry man *diggeth up sins*, for he makes even the wicked worse than they were, provoking them to strife. Through anger the light of Truth is lost; as it is written: *Let not the sun go down upon your anger* (Eph. iv. 26). For when anger brings the darkness of confusion upon the mind God hides from it the ray of our knowledge of Him.

Through anger the brightness of the Holy Ghost is shut out from the soul; and of the contrary to this was it written, according to the ancient translation: *Upon whom shall my Spirit rest, but upon him who is humble and peaceful, and that trembleth at my words?* (Is. lxvi. 2 Sept.). When he said an *humble* man, he added immediately, *and peaceful*. If therefore anger should deprive us of our peace of mind, it closes His own dwelling place to the Holy Spirit, and the soul left empty by His absence is soon led on to open folly, and its thoughts become disordered from top to bottom.

2. *The picture of an angry man.*

For the heart that is excited by the stings of its own anger begins to throb, the body begins to shake, the tongue to stammer, the face becomes inflamed, the eyes fierce, and persons who are well known to us become unrecognizable. He utters sounds with his mouth, but he has no knowledge of what he is saying. A man who does not know what he is doing, in what way is he different from a madman? And so often it happens that anger leaps into action, and the more the reason has gone away, the wilder anger grows. The soul has no longer the power to control itself: for it is now in the power of a stranger. And frenzy, the more it holds captive the mind, the mistress of our bodily members, the more will it use them to inflict violence.

Sometimes it will not make use of the hands; but it will turn the tongue into a dart of malediction. With prayers it will implore the destruction of a brother; it will demand of God that He shall do what the evil heart dares not do, or is ashamed to do. And doing this in word and in will it has committed murder: though it hold its hand from doing violence to a neighbour.

Sometimes when the soul is disturbed anger will as it were impose silence on itself; and the less it reveals itself by word of mouth, the more fiercely will it inwardly burn. So the angry man, withholding himself from ordinary speech with his neighbour, saying nothing, declares how great is his aversion to him. There are times when this restriction of silence serves for the purposes of discipline, and the service of God, provided it is used with discretion, and in regard to those with whom we are intimate.

Sometimes however it happens, that when the angry mind withholds itself from normal conversation, there comes a time when it is wholly cut off from the love of its neighbour; then sharper stings will come into the mind, and further pretexts arise there, to goad its anger still more; and in the eye of the angry man a mote changes into a beam, and anger itself is changed to hatred.

And at times it will happen that anger pent up in the heart through silence will then burn the more fiercely, and make clamorous conversation with itself, and taunt itself with words that provoke it still more, and then as it were giving judgement will answer itself still more fiercely; which Solomon hinted at very briefly where he says: *The expectation of the wicked is indignation* (xi. 23). And so it comes to pass that the tormented spirit suffers a greater clamour because of his silence, and the flame of his concealed anger burns him the more severely. Because of this long ago a certain wise man remarked: The thoughts of an angry man are a brood of vipers, that devour the mind that is their mother.

3. We should know that there are those whom anger quickly inflames, and as quickly leaves. Others it is slow to arouse, but slow also to leave. For some men are *like reeds* set on fire; when they make an outcry they sound like reeds crackling as they kindle: they leap quickly into flame, and as quickly cool down in ashes. And some are like the heavier and harder kinds of wood; slow to take fire, but once kindled they are with difficulty extinguished: rousing slowly to fierceness, they hold the longer to the fire of their rage. There are yet others, and the conduct of these is the worst, who are both quick to catch fire in anger, and slow to put it down. Then there are those who are slow to take anger, but quick to let it go. In these four kinds the reader will easily see, that the last rather than the first comes nearest to the blessing of peace of

mind; and that the third exceeds the second in evil. But what good will it do simply to describe how anger grips the mind, if we do not also describe how anger should be restrained?

4. *Two means of restraining anger.*

There are two ways by which anger is subdued, and abandons its hold on the mind. The first way is, that a cautious mind, before it begins to do anything, considers what possible affronts it is likely to meet, and, mindful of the insults offered our Redeemer, prepares itself for contradictions. And should these come its way, the more prudently it arms itself beforehand, the more courageously it meets them. For one caught unprepared by adversity is like a man caught asleep by the enemy; he is slain the more easily in that the enemy strikes an unresisting man. He who has carefully considered the evils that threaten him, waits as in ambush for the enemy to attack; strongly armed for victory where he was expected to be caught unawares.

So before undertaking any action the mind should carefully dwell upon the contradictions it may meet, that bearing them in mind at all times, and at all times fronting them with the breastplate of patience, it may through caution both overcome what it meets, and count as a gain what it does not meet.

The second way of safeguarding our peace of mind is, that when we regard the faults of others, let us reflect upon our own sins, in which we have done injury to others. For when we look at our own frailty it moves us to excuse the ills that are done to us by others. For he will bear patiently with others who injure him, if he duly remembers that there may be something in his own conduct which calls for patience in others. It is as though fire were put out with water when, should rage spring up in us, each one recalls his own faults to mind: for a man is ashamed not to spare others who often remembers that he has himself committed sins against God and his neighbour which must yet be forgiven.

5. *One anger arises from impatience, another from zeal. The first blinds the eye, the other so disturbs it that it sees more clearly.*

But we should carefully note that one kind of anger arises from impatience, another is that which zeal causes. The one arises from evil, the other from good. For if anger had never arisen from virtue, Phineas would never have allayed the force of the divine anger *with a dagger* (Num. xxv. 7; I Cor. x. 8). Because Heli was wanting in this anger, He roused against himself the force of the divine vengeance (I Kgs. iii. 11). For the more he was neglectful of the evil of those under his charge, the more severely the justice of the Eternal Ruler burned against himself. Of this anger the Psalmist says: *Be ye angry, and sin not* (iv. 5). This they interpret wrongly who would have us angry only with ourselves, and not with our neighbours who commit evil. For if we are commanded to love our neighbours as ourselves, it follows that we are to be angry with them for their offences as we are with ourselves for our own.

Of this anger it was said by Solomon: *Anger is better than laughter:*

because by the sadness of the countenance the mind of the offender is corrected (Eccles. vii. 4). And the Psalmist also says of it: *My eye is troubled through indignation* (vi. 8). Anger that comes of evil blinds the eye of the mind, but anger that comes of zeal troubles it; for in the measure that it is agitated by zeal for virtue, that image is disturbed which can only be perceived by a heart at rest. For even zeal for rectitude, because it disturbs the mind through unrest, will for a time obscure its vision; so that in its troubled state it no longer sees the higher things it had beheld clearly when at rest. But it is restored again to the vision of the higher things, and to a more acute vision, by that same power which so disturbed it that it could not see.

For this eternal zeal for justice, in a little while, opens to a wider vision in tranquillity of soul, closed to it by this passing unrest, and from the source that troubled it, so that it was unable to see, it now grows clear and goes on to see with yet greater truth. Just as when eye-salve is placed upon an ailing eye the light must then for a while be wholly shut out from it, and in this way it soon recovers the vision that for a little while it had profitably lost. For contemplation will never be joined to unrest, nor will the troubled mind ever attain to that vision to which a soul in peace is scarce able to desire; for not even the sun's bright ray is seen when storm clouds obscure the face of the heavens, nor will the troubled fountain give back the image it reflects when at rest: for that which moves its quiet face also obscures the image of the beholder.

6. *Just anger must not come to dominate the mind.*

But when the spirit is aroused by zeal we should take great care that the same anger which is used in the service of virtue does not come to dominate the mind, nor rule it as mistress, but like a handmaid ever at hand to render service, let it never depart from its place behind reason. For it is then uplifted the more strongly against evil when its service is rendered subject to reason. For however great the anger may be that is aroused by zeal for justice, if it is immoderate it has gained the mastery over the mind, and straightaway it scorns the service of reason; and the more it holds the vice of impatience to be a virtue, the more impudently will it begin to spread itself.

Because of this it is above all things necessary, that he who is moved by a zeal for justice should be careful of this; that his anger must never pass beyond the mind's control, that in punishing evil he should be careful both as to the time and the measure; to control the rising agitation of his mind by using it with precise care; to restrain his indignation, and subject the warmth of his own feelings to the rule of moderation and courtesy, so that the more he is master of himself, the more is he fit to judge of another's chastisement. For since he is to correct the faults of wrongdoers, let him who is to correct first enlarge his own mind through forbearance, and let him judge the matter by rising above his own resentment, lest through being provoked immoderately by his own zeal for what is right he may himself deviate far from what is right.

For, as we have said, even praise-worthy zeal for what is good may cloud the eye of the mind, as it is now here said: *Anger indeed killeth the foolish.* This is to say: Anger because of zeal troubles the wise, but anger that arises through evil destroys foolish men: for the one is subject to reason; but the other blindly rules the mind it has enslaved.

NOTES

[1] An incomplete commentary on Matthew — *Opus Imperfectum* — which appears under the name of Chrysostom. Cf. note 25, vol. I, 3rd Sunday after Epiphany.

[2] Apostolic Constitutions ii. 32.

[3] Vossio S. Eph., Tome I, Sermo 5, on Matt. xi. 29.

[4] Apparently a reference to the *agape*, or love feast of the early Christians, which as a custom had progressively degenerated, and was finally ended.

[5] PG 62, Homily 14 on Epistle to Ephesians.

[6] PG 63, Homily 19 on Epistle to Hebrews.

[7] PL 75, Pars Prima, Book V, Ch. 45, pars. 78–83 incl.

THE FEAST OF
SAINTS PETER AND PAUL

I. St Gaudentius: On Peter and Paul

II. St Augustine: On the Natal Day of the Apostles Peter and Paul

III. St Leo the Great: The Natal Day of the Apostles Peter and Paul

IV. St Leo the Great: The Natal Day of St Peter the Apostle

V. St Maximus of Turin: On the Same Natal Day of the Holy Apostles Peter and Paul

VI. The Venerable Bede: The Birthdays of the Blessed Apostles Peter and Paul

THE GOSPEL OF THE FEAST

Matthew xvi. 13–19

At that time: Jesus came into the neighbourhood of Cesarea Philippi: and he asked his disciples, saying: Whom do men say that the Son of man is? But they said: Some John the Baptist, and other some Elias, and others Jeremias, or one of the prophets. Jesus saith to them: But whom do you say that I am? Simon answered and said: Thou art Christ, the Son of the living God.

And Jesus answering, said to him: Blessed art thou, Simon Bar-Jona: because flesh and blood hath not revealed it to thee, but my Father who is in heaven. And I say to thee: That thou art Peter; and upon this rock I will build my church, and the gates of hell shall not prevail against it. And I will give to thee the keys of the kingdom of heaven. And whatsoever thou shalt bind upon earth, it shall be bound also in heaven: and whatsoever thou shalt loose on earth, it shall be loosed also in heaven.

Exposition from the Catena Aurea

V. 13. *And Jesus came into the neighbourhood of Cesarea Philippi* . . .

Gloss: After the Lord had drawn the Disciples away from the teaching of the Pharisees, He fittingly strengthens in them the foundations of the Gospel teaching, and to indicate greater solemnity the actual place is spoken of, where it is said: *Jesus came into the neighbourhood etc.*

249

CHRYSOSTOM, *Hom.* 54 *in Matthew*: It was called, not simply Cesarea, but Cesarea Philippi; because there is another place called Cesarea Stratonis. It was at the first, not this latter, place He questioned His Disciples; having led them a long way from the Jews, so that being unafraid they might say freely what was in their minds.

JEROME: This Philip, the brother of Herod, was Tetrarch of Iturea and Trachonitis, and he had called the city, now Paneas, Cesarea, in honour of Tiberius Caesar. GLOSS: About to confirm the Disciples in their faith He wills first to remove the errors and false notions of others. Hence we have: *And he asked his disciples, saying: Whom do men say that the Son of man is?*

ORIGEN, *Tr.* 1 *in Matthew* 16: Christ questions His Disciples so that we may learn from the Apostles' answers, that among the Jews there were various beliefs about Christ, and that we also may examine into the opinions men may have regarding us: so that if anything ill be said of us we may cut off what occasions it, and if anything of good we may increase what occasions it. GLOSS: And the disciples of bishops are taught by this example of the Apostles, that as often as they hear from outside opinions regarding their bishops, they are to relate them.

JEROME: The question is perfectly posed: *Whom do men say that the Son of man is?* For they who are speaking about the Son of man are men; but they who discern His Divinity are not men but Gods.

CHRYSOSTOM, *as above*: He does not say: Whom do the Scribes and Pharisees say I am, but, *Whom do men say?* He seeks to know the mind of the people, which was not degraded and inclined to evil. Their notion about Christ was below what it ought to be, yet it was free of malice. The mind of the Pharisees about Him was steeped in such malice.

HILARY, *Canon* 10 *in Matthew*: Therefore, by saying: *Whom do men say that the Son of man is,* He makes known to them that there is something further to be known regarding Him besides what He appeared to be; for He was the Son of man. What opinion regarding Himself did He seek? Not that, we believe, which He had himself confessed. What He was seeking for was something concealed, something to which the faith of those who believe in Him must reach. It is the kind of confession that must be held when we remember that as He is the Son of God so is He also the Son of man: for the one without the other offers us no hope of salvation. And so He said very clearly: *Whom do men say that the Son of man is?*

JEROME: He did not say: Whom do men say I am, but, Whom do men say *the Son of man is?* This was lest He should appear to speak boastfully about Himself. And note, that wherever in the Old Testament the Son of man is written, the Hebrew has *Son of Adam.* ORIGEN: The Disciples recount the various opinions concerning Christ. Hence:

V. 14. *But they said: Some John the Baptist . . .*

This was following Herod's notion. *Other some Elias*; that is, either thinking that Elias had had a second birth, or that as he was still living he had then appeared; *others Jeremias*, whom the Lord had made a prophet *unto the nations* (i. 5), and because they did not understand that Jeremias was a Figure of Christ. *Or one of the prophets.* For a similar reason; because of the things God had said to them by the prophets, fulfilled in Christ, not in them.

JEROME: But the people could easily be in error about Him, thinking He was Elias and Jeremias, just as Herod thought He was John. Because of this I am surprised that many interpreters go looking for reasons for each single error.

CHRYSOSTOM: As the Disciples had related what the people were saying, by a second question He calls upon them to give some higher opinion regarding Himself. And so there follows:

V. 15. *Jesus saith to them: but whom do you say that I am?*

You who have been at all times with Me; you have seen greater wonders than the people, so you should not be of the same opinion as the multitude. For this reason He asked them, not at the beginning of His preaching, but after He had wrought many miracles, and had said many things to them regarding His divinity.

JEROME: Observe that from the wording of this remark He here calls the Apostles not men but Gods. For when He had said: *Whom do men say the Son of man is*, He then

goes on to say: *Whom do you say that I am?* As though He said to them: They as men think human things; but you as Gods, Whom do you think I am?

RHABANUS (BEDE):[1] He seeks for the opinions of the Disciples, and of those outside, not as not knowing what He asks, but asks what they think of Him that He may bestow on them a reward worthy of a right faith. And so He asks what others think of Him, so that, the false notions being first set out, it might be seen that the Disciples had received the truth of their confession, not out of the common error, but from the mystery of the divine revelation.

CHRYSOSTOM: When the Lord asks about the opinions of the people, all the Disciples answer. But when all the Disciples are asked, Peter, as the Head and mouth of the Apostles, answers for all the rest. Hence:

V. 16. *Simon Peter answered and said: Thou art Christ . . .*

ORIGEN: By this confession Peter denies that Jesus was any one of those whom the Jews thought Him to be. But he confessed: *Thou art the Christ*: something the Jews did not know: and He added what was yet greater: *The Son of the living God*: He Who had said through the prophets: *I am the living God, saith the Lord* (Is. xlix. 18; Ez. v. 11). And he said, *living*, but in a transcendent degree, as transcending all things that live, since He alone has immortality, and is the fount of life, and so is rightly called Father: for He is life as it were flowing from a fountain Who said, *I am the life* (Jn. xi).

JEROME: He also calls Him *the living God*, in contrast to those who are thought to be Gods, but are dead: I mean, Saturn, Jove, Venus, Hercules, and the other monstrosities among the idols.

HILARY, *as above*: This is the true and inviolable faith: That God the Son has come forth from God, and that He has eternity from the eternity of the Father. That this God took a body and became man is a perfect confession. He has therefore comprehended all that the nature and the name express; in which is the sum of all His Powers.

RHABANUS (BEDE): And by a wondrous discrimination it happens, that the Lord Himself makes public confession of the lowliness of His assumed humanity; His Disciple the supreme perfection of His eternal Divinity.

HILARY: For having seen the Son of God in a man, the reward he received was worthy of his confession of faith. Because of this there follows:

V. 17. *And Jesus answering, said to him: Blessed art thou . . .*

JEROME: Christ returns testimony for testimony. Because Peter had said: *Thou art the Christ, the Son of the living God,* the Lord said to him: *Blessed art thou, Simon Bar-Jona.* For what reason? Because *flesh and blood hath not revealed it to thee, but my Father who is in heaven.* What flesh and blood could not reveal is revealed by the grace of the Holy Spirit. And because of this He

receives a name that means he has received a revelation from the Holy Spirit. For in our tongue Bar-Jona means, *son of the dove* (*filius columbae*). Others understand it simply that Simon, namely, Peter, is *the son of John* (cf. Jn. xxi. 15), and say that this first is a copyist's error: writing Bar-Jona for Bar-Joanna, leaving out a syllable. Now John is interpreted as, *the grace of God.* Either name therefore can be mystically interpreted: that the *dove* signifies the Holy Spirit, and *the grace of God* the gift of the Spirit.

CHRYSOSTOM: It would be idle to say, Thou art the son of Jona (or of Joanna), unless He wished to show, that Christ is as naturally the Son of God, as Peter is the son of Jona: of the same substance as He Who begot Him.

JEROME: Compare the words, *because flesh and blood hath not revealed it to thee*, to the Apostolic narration, where he says: *Immediately, I condescended not to flesh and blood* (Gal. i. 16). Flesh and blood here mean the Jews; so that here also in another discourse is it shown, that, not through the teaching of the Pharisees, but through the grace of God, was Christ revealed to him as the Son of God.

HILARY: Or again: Blessed is he who is praised for perceiving and comprehending beyond what human eyes see; seeing not that which is from flesh and blood, but beholding the Son of God, through the revelation of His heavenly Father; and who was held worthy of being the first to confess the Divinity that was in Christ.

ORIGEN: We must ask in this place, if the Disciples, when they were first sent out, already knew He was the Christ? For this speech shows that Peter, then for the first time, confessed that He was the Christ the Son of the living God. See can you answer this by saying: To believe Jesus is the Christ is less than to know Him. So that we may say that when they were sent to preach they did indeed believe Jesus was the Christ, but it was afterwards, as they advanced in the knowledge of Him, that they also came to know Who He was. Or are we to answer so as to say that the Apostles had then (*when first sent*) the beginnings of a knowledge of Christ, and had begun to know a little concerning Him; and that after this, advancing in the knowledge of Him, they were able to grasp the significance of Christ as revealed by the Father; they as well as Peter: who was declared *blessed*, not alone because he had said, *Thou art the Christ*, but yet more in that he added: *The Son of the living God* (PG 13, t. xii, V.I. 1, 15).

CHRYSOSTOM: There is no doubt that had Peter not confessed that Christ was in the real sense born of God this would have been no effect of revelation; nor would he be worthy of being declared blessed for thinking that Christ was but one among many adopted sons. For before this those who were in the ship had said: *Indeed thou art the Son of God* (Mt. xiv. 33). Nathaniel also said: *Rabbi, thou art the Son of God* (Jn. i. 49). Yet they were not called *blessed*, because they did not confess the Sonship Peter confessed, but considered Him as but one among many, and not His True Son; or if indeed as the First among many, yet not of the substance of the Father.

See how the Father makes known the Son, and the Son reveals the Father. From no one do we learn of the Son save from the Father; from no one of the Father, but from the Son. So that here also is it made known to us, that the Son is consubstantial with the Father, and equally to be adored with Him. Christ then shows us that from henceforward many shall believe what Peter has confessed. So there follows:

V. 18. *And I say to thee: That thou art Peter; and upon this rock . . .*

JEROME: As though He says: Because thou hast said to me, *Thou art Christ, the Son of the living God*, I also say to you, and not in idle words, which avail nothing, but I say to you, and for Me to say is to accomplish, that, *Thou art Peter*. For as He Who is the Light gave to the Apostles that they should be called *the light of the world*, and the other names which they obtained from the Lord, so also He gave to Simon, Who believed in the Rock Christ, the name of *Peter* (*rock*).

AUGUSTINE, *Harmony of the Gospels*, 2, 53: Let no one believe that it was here Peter received the name. For he received this name then only when John records that it was said to him: *Thou shalt be called Cephas, which is interpreted Peter* (Jn. i. 42).

JEROME: Continuing the metaphor of the *Rock*, rightly is it said to him: I will build My Church upon thee. And this is what follows: *And upon this rock I will build my church.*

CHRYSOSTOM: That is, on this faith and confession I will build My Church. Here He shows that many are to believe what Peter has confessed. And He raises up his spirit, and makes him a pastor.

AUGUSTINE, *Book of Retractions*, I, 21: In a certain place I said of the Apostle Peter, that upon him, as upon a rock, the Church was built. But I know that very frequently afterwards I explained that the words spoken by the Lord: *Thou art Peter; and upon this rock I will build my Church*, may be understood as upon Him Whom Peter had confessed when he said: *Thou art the Christ, the Son of the living God*; as if Peter, named from *this* rock, represented the Church, which is built upon *this* rock. For it was not said to him that, Thou art a rock (*tu es petra*), but, Thou art Peter (*Tu es Petrus*). *The rock was Christ* (I Cor. x. 4), Whom Simon having confessed, as the whole Church confesses Him, he was called Peter. The reader may choose whichever of these two opinions may seem to him the more probable.

HILARY, *as above*: This giving of a new name is a happy foundation for the Church, and a rock fitting for the edifice which would break down the rule of hell, the gates of Tartarus, and all the barriers of death. And so to show the stability of the Church built upon the *rock*, He goes on: *And the gates of hell shall not prevail against it.*

JEROME: I believe *the gates of hell* are sins and the vices; and especially the teachings of heretics, through which men are seduced and led down to Tartarus. ORIGEN, *as above*: But in heavenly things all spiritual evils are *the gates of hell*; to which are opposed *the gates of justice* (Ps. cxvii. 19).

RHABANUS (BEDE): *Gates of hell* are also the torments, the blandishments, of persecutors. And the evil works of unbelievers, and their foolish talk, are also *gates of hell*: because they open the way to perdition.

ORIGEN: He does not say whether *they shall not prevail* against the rock upon which Christ built His Church, or, *shall not prevail* against the Church which Christ built upon the rock. Nevertheless it is very clear to us, that the gates of hell shall prevail neither against *the rock*, nor against *the Church*.

CYRIL, *from the Book of the Treasure*: According to this promise of the Lord, the Apostolic Church of Peter in its Pontiffs, and in the full faith and authority of Peter, remains free of all heretical taint or deceit, above all heads and bishops, and above all primates of churches and peoples. And while other churches are shamed by the errors of certain members among them, it reigns the sole Church unshakably established, imposing silence, and closing the mouths of heretics. And we, not deceived by pride, not intoxicated by the wine of pride, necessarily, because of our salvation, proclaim and confess together with it, this pattern of holy Apostolic Tradition.[2]

JEROME: *And the gates* etc. Let no one think this was said of death; meaning that the Apostles would not be subject to death: they whose martyrdoms shine so brightly.

ORIGEN: So if we also confess that Jesus Christ is the Son of the living God, the Father Who is in heaven revealing it to us, that is, when our conversation is in heaven (Phil. iii. 20), to us also will it be said: *Thou art Peter* etc. For each one is a rock who is an imitator of Christ: He against whom the *gates of hell* do prevail is not to be called *the rock* upon which Christ built His Church, nor yet the Church, nor a portion of the Church which Christ builds upon *the rock*.

CHRYSOSTOM: Then He speaks of another reward bestowed on Peter, when He goes on to say:

V. 19. *And I will give to thee the keys of the kingdom of heaven etc.*

As though He said: As the Father has given to you to know Me, so I also shall give you something: The keys of the Kingdom of heaven. RHABANUS (BEDE): For as he had proclaimed, with a devotion surpassing the rest, the King of heaven, fittingly, before others, to him were entrusted the Keys of the heavenly kingdom: That it might be clear to all men, that without this confession, without this faith, no one can enter the kingdom of heaven. *The keys of the kingdom of heaven* designate this very discernment and power: power by which he binds and looses; discernment, by which he judges who are worthy, and who unworthy.

GLOSS (interlinear): Hence there follows: *And whatsoever thou shalt bind upon earth* etc.; that is, whomsoever among the living you shall judge unworthy of pardon shall be held as unworthy before God. *And whatsoever thou shalt loose upon earth* etc.; that is, whomsoever among the living you shall judge is to be pardoned, they shall obtain from God the remission of their sins.

ORIGEN: See how great is the power of the rock upon which Christ builds His Church; so that its judgements stand firm, as though God were judging by means of it.

CHRYSOSTOM: See how Christ leads Peter up to a lofty understanding of Himself. For He promises He will give him powers that belong to God alone; namely, the power to forgive sin, the power to maintain the Church immutable amid the storms of so many trials and persecutions.

RHABANUS (BEDE): The power of binding and loosing, though it seems to be given by the Lord to Peter only, is nevertheless given also to the other Apostles (Mt. xviii. 18), and is given now also to Bishops and Priests in every church. But Peter more particularly receives *the keys* of the kingdom of heaven, and the supremacy of the power of judging, to the end that all who would believe throughout the world might understand, that whosoever shall cut themselves off in any way from the unity of his faith, or his fellowship, can neither be loosed from the bonds of their sin, nor enter the gates of the kingdom of heaven.

GLOSS (from Anselm): He gave this power more particularly to Peter so as to invite us to unity. For this He made him the Prince of the Apostles, that the Church might have a chief Vicar of Christ, to whom opposed members of the Church should recur in case a difference might by chance arise among them; should there be differing heads within the Church the bond of union would be broken. Some say that He said *on earth* for this reason: That power is not given to men to bind and loose the dead but the living. Whoever would bind or loose the dead would not do this *on earth*.

SECOND COUNCIL OF CONSTANTI- NOPLE (Fifth Oecumenical): How do some presume to assert that these things were said only with regard to the living? Do they not know that the sentence of anathema is nothing else than a separation? They are to be shunned who are held fast in their most wicked offences; whether they be among the living or not. For we must ever fly from one who is wicked. And the various letters of Augustine, of holy memory, he who shone out among the bishops of Africa, are appealed to as notify- ing that we should anathematize heretics even after their death (Ep. clxxxv. 4). And other African bishops have maintained a similar tradition. And the Holy Roman Church has also anathematized cer- tain bishops after their death; even though no accusation has been made against their faith while they were alive.

JEROME: Bishops and priests, not understanding this place, have taken to themselves something of the arro- gance of the Pharisees, so that they believe that they may condemn the innocent and forgive the guilty. But the Lord looks not to the sen- tence of the priests, but to the way of life of those who are judged.

We read in Leviticus xiii and xiv about the lepers, where they are commanded to show themselves to the priests, and if they have leprosy they are then by the priest made un- clean. Not that the priest makes them lepers, and unclean. But since he understands concerning leprosy, and the lepers do not, he can tell who is clean, and who is unclean. As the priest there makes the leper clean or unclean, so here the bishop or the priest binds, or looses; not those who are guilty, or without blame, but in the fulfilment of his office he listens to their various sins, and understands who is to be bound, and who is to be loosed.

ORIGEN: Let him who binds or looses another be himself blameless: that he may be found worthy to bind or to loose in heaven. And to him who shall be able by his virtues to close the gates of hell, the keys of the kingdom of heaven are given as a reward. For when a person begins to practise every kind of virtue, he as it were opens to himself the gates of heaven; that is, the Lord opens it by His grace: so that the same virtue is found to be both the gate, and the key of the gate. It may be that each single virtue is the king- dom of heaven.

ADDITIONAL TO THE CATENA AUREA[3]

CYRIL OF ALEXANDRIA, *Fragments on Matthew*: *Simon Peter answered and said: Thou art the Christ the Son of the living God.* Peter did not say: Thou art Christ, or, a son of God, but, *The Christ the son of God.* For there are many Christs through grace, and they have received the dignity of adoption as sons of God. But One alone is there Who by nature is the Son of God. And therefore using the article, he said: *The Christ the Son of God.*

And by saying He was the Christ the Son of *the living God,* he makes known that He is Himself Life; and that death has no power over Him. For though His Body through dying was brought low, nevertheless it rose again: for it was not in the power of death to hold the Word that was in it in its bonds.

And the gates of hell shall not prevail against it. Just as by heaping wood on the flames a fire grows brighter, so also they who seek to destroy the Church by persecution lead it on to greater glory and power. If they cannot prevail against the Church, He says, much less can they prevail against Me. So be not troubled, Peter, when you hear that I must be delivered up to be crucified. Then He bestows another honour.

Upon this rock I will build my Church. *And I will give to thee the keys of the kingdom of heaven.* Consider how He reveals Himself as at once Lord of both heaven and earth. For He promises things which are above our nature, above even the nature of the angelic creation, and which it is befitting to attribute to the nature and glory that is above all things. First He says that the Church is His, and this though the Sacred Scriptures declare that it is subject to God rather than to any man. For Paul says that Christ has prepared Her for Himself, *without spot or blemish* (Eph. v. 27). He also professes that He is the Founder of it, adding to it that it shall be unshakeable: for the Lord is the source of its powers: and He places Peter over it as Pastor. Then He goes on:

And I will give to thee the keys of the kingdom of heaven. Words such as these no angel, nor any reasoning creature whatever, has power to utter. Language such as this is befitting but to God alone, Who holds power over heaven and earth. But it was already the time for *the gift* (Rom. v. 15), or the hour of the Resurrection, when He said: *Whose sins you shall forgive they are forgiven them; and whose sins you shall retain, they are retained.*

I. ST GAUDENTIUS, BISHOP OF BRESCIA

On Peter and Paul[4]

Venerable Bishop of Christ, and common father, the affection which has held me here, though I was about to leave, now compels me, though I would be excused, to address Your Charity once again on the subject of today's sermon. And therefore I shall according to my limited understanding speak to you for a little while in praise of the most blessed Apostles Peter and Paul; encouraged by their assistance whose Natal Day it is. For we should know that there are three birthdays bestowed by the Eternal Trinity on mankind. One is that of the body, which is common to all men. There are two which are spiritual, in proportion to the merit of each one's faith.

Our first birth is that in which we are brought forth from nothingness into the life of this world. Our second is that in which we are born again in Baptism, from sin and from errors, into the reality of charity. The third is that in which the most blessed martyrs who, because of their confession of Christ's Name, are born again of their torments into the kingdom of heaven.

This sequence first had place in Christ, Who was born of the Virgin, born again in the Jordan, and upon the gibbet of the Cross was baptized in the stream of His own precious Blood. For following on that Baptism which He had received for our sake in the Jordan, He said to His Apostles concerning His Passion: *I have a baptism wherewith I am to be baptized* (Lk. xii. 50). From this Baptism of His Passion He rose again to a life which no boundary will bring to a close: He returned to His kingdom, *and of his kingdom there shall be no end* (Lk. i. 33).

In the footsteps of this Master His faithful Disciples Peter and Paul have followed, and on this day all the churches of the whole world are celebrating with fitting honour the Birthday of their Passion. For on this day, in the City of Rome, the cruelty of Nero put them both to death, for the Name of Christ; and the justice of the Lord crowned them. Peter was crucified with his head to the earth,[5] protesting he was

unworthy to be crucified as his Lord was crucified. Paul was beheaded with the sword. Both are renowned; both were extraordinary men. They are the Two Lights of the world, the Pillars of the Faith, the Founders of the Church, Teachers of innocence, Models in all that relates to holiness and truth.

And we shall praise them worthily if we praise them with those divine testimonies by which Truth Itself has praised them. For to Peter who had confessed Him, the Lord said: *Blessed art thou, Simon Bar-Jona: because flesh and blood hath not revealed it to thee, but my Father who is in heaven. And I say to thee, Peter, Thou art Peter, and upon this rock I will build my church, and the gates of hell shall not prevail against it. And I will give to thee the keys of the kingdom of heaven* etc. And what did He say of Paul? *This man*, He said, *is to me a vessel of election, to carry my name into the whole world* (Acts ix. 5).

The Church is founded upon the one; the other by his teaching carried the precious myrrh of faith to the Gentiles, and became a *vessel of election*. Peter shone forth in signs and wonders. Paul is glorified in his teaching, and in the persecutions he suffered. Before this Peter was a fisherman, Paul a persecutor; but both became Fishers of men. For they spread the nets of their salutary teaching throughout the sea of this whole world. Peter was commanded to walk upon the waves (Mt. xiv. 29), Paul among the clouds:[6] when he was *caught up to the third heaven*. Both upheld by the power of faith took the first steps of a way that is pathless.

Whom to prefer to the other, I know not; I dare not: since the Lord ordained them equal in suffering through the same confession, joined them together in true fellowship, and bound them together by the bond of one mind; so that we may very rightly presume that of them also was it foretold by the prophetic Spirit: *Behold how good and pleasant it is for brethren to dwell together in unity* (Ps. cxxxii). Such were Moses and Aaron, of whom it is said that they were brothers. Such are the Prophets and Apostles, brothers in teaching, brothers in spirit. So in us are the interior man and the exterior man brothers: if they are of one mind.[7] Peter and Paul are truly brothers by blood also; since one faith makes them true brothers, by

the Communion of a special Blood· May I presume to say that they are also twin brothers, whom their Mother, through one confession, as from a fertile womb, brought forth unto the kingdom of heaven. For, *Blessed are they that suffer persecution for justice' sake: for theirs is the kingdom of heaven* (Mt. v. 10).

Let us then share with one another the memories of the Holy Apostles. Let us share in the fellowship of the Saints by faith, in good works, in our manner of life, in our words, so that by their prayers we may be helped to obtain all things whatsoever we ask for, by the grace of the Lord Jesus Christ. To Whom be all honour for ever and ever. Amen.

II. St Augustine, Bishop and Doctor

On the Natal Day of the Apostles Peter and Paul[8]

I. *The Rock upon which the Church is built is Christ Himself.* The passion of the most blessed Apostles Peter and Paul has consecrated for us this day. We are not speaking of some obscure martyrs. *Their* sound has gone forth into all the earth; and *their* words unto the ends of the world (Ps. xviii. 5). These martyrs had seen what they preached; they had followed Justice, confessing the Truth, dying for the Truth. Blessed Peter, First of the Apostles, fervent lover of Christ, who merited to hear: *And I say to thee: That thou art Peter.* For he had said: *Thou art the Christ the son of the living God.* And Christ said to him: *And I say to thee: That thou art Peter; and upon this rock I will build my Church.* Upon this rock I shall build my faith; the faith you confess. Upon what you have said: Thou art the Christ, the Son of the living God: I shall build

my Church. For thou art Peter. Peter from the rock (*petra*); not the rock from Peter. So Peter, because of the rock; as Christian, because of Christ.

Would you know after what rock (*petra*) Peter is called? Listen to Paul answering: *I would not have you ignorant, brethren,* the Apostle of Christ says, *I would not have you ignorant, that our fathers were all under the cloud, and all passed through the sea. And all in Moses were baptized, in the cloud, and in the sea. And all did eat the same spiritual food. And all drank the same spiritual drink; and they drank of the spiritual rock that followed them, and the rock was Christ* (I Cor. x. 1-4). From this rock Peter came.

II. *To Peter as representing the Church were given the keys of the kingdom of heaven. They were given* to one, as to the unity of the Church. *Christ first restores to life; the Church looses.* The Lord Jesus, as you know, before His passion selected His appointed Disciples, whom He called Apostles. Among them Peter alone has everywhere merited to represent completely the image and nature of the whole Church. Because he alone thus represented the person of the whole Church he came to hear the words: *And I will give to thee the keys of the kingdom of heaven.* It is not one man has received these keys, but the unity of the Church.

By this the pre-eminence of Peter is proclaimed: because he stood for the unity and universality of the Church itself, when to him was said, *I give to thee,* what was given was given to all. For that you may understand that the Church received the keys of the kingdom of heaven, hear what the Lord says in another place to all His Apostles: *Receive ye the Holy Ghost.* And then immediately following: *Whose sins you shall forgive, they are forgiven them; and whose sins you shall retain, they are retained* (Jn. xx. 22, 23). These words relate to the keys, of which it had been said: *Whatsoever thou shalt loose on earth, it shall be loosed also in heaven.*

But these last words He said to Peter. So that you may know that Peter then represented the whole Church, hear what is said to him, what is said to all the holy faithful. *If thy brother shall offend thee, go and rebuke him between thee and him alone. If he shall hear thee, then thou shalt gain thy brother. And if he will not hear thee, take with thee one or two more: that in the mouth of two or three witnesses every word may stand. And if he will not hear them: tell the Church.*

And if he will not hear the Church, let him be to thee as the heathen and the publican. Amen I say to you, whatsoever you shall bind on earth, shall be bound also in heaven; and whatsoever you shall loose upon earth, shall be loosed also in heaven (Mt. xviii. 15–18). The Dove binds, the Dove looses; the Building upon the rock binds and looses.

III. Let those who are bound be in fear; let those loosed be in fear. They who are loosed let them fear lest they be bound. And they who are bound let them pray that they may be loosed from their sins. *His own iniquities catch the wicked* (Prov. v. 22). And outside the Church nothing is loosed. To the man who was four days dead He says: *Lazarus, come forth.* And he came forth from the tomb, *bound feet and hands with winding bands* (Jn. xi. 43). The Lord awakens him to life, so that the one who was dead might come forth from the tomb; as He touches your heart, that confession of your sins may come forth. But he is still a little bound. So the Lord, after Lazarus had come forth from the tomb, says to His Disciples—to whom He had said: *Whatsoever you shall loose upon earth, shall be loosed also in heaven*—*Loose him, and let him go.* He Himself restores life; he looses by means of His Disciples.

The Strength of the Church and its weakness typified in Peter. And in like manner the strength of the Church is commended to us more particularly in Peter; following the Lord as He goes towards His Passion. And a certain weakness is also marked in him; for questioned by a maidservant, he denies the Lord. Behold of a sudden the lover is a liar. He finds out what he is; he who had thought too highly of himself. For he had said as you know: *Lord, I shall stay with you until death; and if it needs be that I should die, I shall lay down my life for you.* And the Lord said to his boldness: *You will lay down your life for me? Amen I say to you, before the cock crows, thou shalt deny me thrice* (Mt. xxvi. 33–5).

And it happened as the Physician had foretold. The sick man was not able to do what he believed he could do. And what happened? This is what is written; this is what the Gospel says: *And the Lord turning looked on Peter. And Peter going out, wept bitterly* (Lk. xxii. 61, 62). *Going out,* that is, confessing. He wept bitterly who had learned to love. Sweetness came after, in a love whose bitterness had died first, in grief.

IV. *To Peter as representing the Unity of the Church Christ commits His sheep. Why Peter was thrice asked of his love for Christ.* And after His Resurrection the Lord fittingly gave also to Peter the task of feeding His sheep. Not to Peter alone among the Disciples was given the task of feeding the Lord's sheep. But when Christ speaks to one, unity is commended to us: and it was given in the first place to Peter, because Peter is the First of the Apostles (Jn. xxi. 15–17).

Simon, son of John, says the Lord, *lovest thou me?* Peter answered: *I love thee.* And being asked again he again answers in the same way. Asked a third time, *Peter was grieved;* as though the Lord had not believed him. How could He not believe him, Who looked into his heart? And then after he had grieved he answers in this way: *Lord, thou knowest all things: Thou knowest that I love thee.* For You Who know all things are not ignorant of this one thing. Grieve not, Apostle! Answer once, answer again; answer for a third time. Let thy threefold confession triumph in love, as thy threefold presumption was defeated in fear. Let that be thrice loosed which you thrice bound. Undo by love what you bound by fear. And then the Lord, once, twice, and for the third time, entrusts His sheep to Peter.

V. *Donatists the dividers of the Lord's Flock.* Attend carefully, My Brethren. *Feed,* He says, *my lambs, feed my sheep.* Feed *My* sheep. Did He say, *your sheep?* Feed, good shepherd, the Lord's sheep; those that have the Lord's brand. For *was Paul crucified for you? Or were you baptized in the name of Peter or Paul?* (I Cor. i. 13). So therefore let you feed His sheep, those washed in His baptism, those marked with His Name, those redeemed by His Blood. *Feed,* He says, *my sheep.*

For heretics, wicked slaves and fugitive slaves, consider they are feeding their own sheep: distributing among themselves what they did not buy, making their own the petty gains of thievery. What else, I ask you, are they doing when they say: Unless I baptize you, you are still unclean; unless you receive my baptism, you will not be baptized? Have you never heard the words: *Cursed be the man that trusteth in man* (Jer. xvii. 5)? So therefore, Dearly Beloved, those whom Peter has baptized are Christ's sheep; and those Judas has baptized are Christ's sheep.

For look what the Bridegroom

says to His Beloved in the Canticle of Canticles, when the Spouse asked Him: *Show me, O thou whom my soul loveth, where thou feedest, where thou liest in the midday, lest I begin to wander after the flocks of my companions.* Shew me, She says, where thou feedest, where thou liest in the midday, in the splendour of truth, in the fervour of charity. Why are you fearful, O Beloved? What do you fear? Lest, She says, I become lost; that is, like one in the dark: as the Church is not; for the Church is not hidden. *A city seated on a mountain cannot be hid* (Mt. v. 14). And, through wandering may begin *to run after*, not thy flock, but, *the flocks of thy companions.* For heretics are called *companions. They went forth from us* (I Jn. ii. 19). Before they went forth they approached with us to a common table.

Well then, what does He say to her in answer? *If thou knowest not thyself*: the Bridegroom says, answering His Spouse: *If thou knowest not thyself, O fairest among women* (Cant. i. 7). O True One among heretics, *if thou knowest not thyself*: For so many things have been foretold of thee: In thy seed shall all nations be blessed (Gen. xxii. 18); The God of Gods, the Lord hath spoken, and He has called the earth, from the rising of the sun to the going down (Ps. xlix. 1): Ask of Me and I will give thee the Gentiles for thy inheritance, and the utmost parts of the earth for thy possession (Ps. ii. 8); And their sound hath gone forth into all the earth: and their words unto the ends of the world (Ps. xviii. 5). Of thee were these testimonies proclaimed.

If thou knowest not thyself, go forth. I do not drive thee forth: so that they

who remained may say of thee: *They went forth from us. Go forth, and follow after the steps of the flocks.* Not of the flock of which it was said: *There shall be one fold and one shepherd* (Jn. x. 16). *Go forth, and follow after the steps of the flocks, and feed thy kids*: not as Peter, *My sheep.* For the sheep entrusted to him Peter merited to be crowned with martyrdom; which is celebrated throughout the whole world by the solemnity of this day.

VI. *Paul from being a persecutor of Christ becomes His preacher.* Let Paul come from Saul, the lamb from the wolf; the enemy first, then the Apostle; the persecutor first, afterwards the preacher. Let him come. Let him receive his letter from the chiefs of the priests, that wherever he shall find Christians he may bring them bound to be punished. Let him receive it. Let him receive it. Let him set out for Damascus. Let him go, *breathing slaughter*, thirsting for blood. He that dwells on high shall laugh at him (Ps. ii. 4). For he went, as it is written: *breathing out threatenings and slaughter.* And, *he drew nigh to Damascus. Then* the Lord spoke from heaven: *Saul, Saul, why persecutest thou me?* I am here above, I am there below; here is the Head, there the Body.

Let us therefore not wonder, Brethren, that we belong to the Body of Christ. *Saul, Saul, why persecutest thou me? It is hard for thee to kick against the goad.* You but wound yourself: for My Church grows through persecutions. And he trembling and astonished says: *Who art thou, Lord?* And the Lord says: *I am Jesus of Nazareth whom thou persecutest.* And changed on the instant he now waits for a command. He puts away envy, and prepares to obey. He is told *what he must do.* And before Paul is baptized the Lord says to Ananias: *Go to that street, to that man named Saul. Baptize him; for this man is to me a vessel of election.*

A vessel must contain something; a vessel should not be an empty vessel. He must be filled. And with what if not with grace? But Ananias says in answer to our Lord Jesus Christ: *Lord I have heard by many of this man, how much evil he hath done to thy saints in Jerusalem. And here he hath authority from the chief priests to bind all that invoke thy name. And the Lord said to him. I will shew him how great things he must suffer for my name's sake* (Acts ix. 16). Ananias was frightened hearing the name of Saul: because of the evil reputation of the wolf, the timid sheep was afraid; even though it was in the care of the Shepherd.

VII. *Peter and Paul suffered for Christ.* And now the Lord shows him what things he must suffer for His Name's sake. For He tries him in labours. He tries him in bonds, in stripes, in prisons, in shipwrecks. He brought him to his passion; He led him to this day. One day of suffering for the two Apostles. But these two were one; even had they suffered on different days they were one. Peter died first. Paul followed. He was Saul in the beginning; afterwards Paul: for in the beginning he was proud; afterwards he was humble. Saul from Saul the persecutor of the holy David. The persecutor was cast down; the Preacher raised up. The name of pride changed to humility: for Paul means *little.* Consider, Your Charity, our

own speech. Do we not say every day: After a little while (*post paululum*) I shall see you. I shall do this or that, in a little while (*paulo post*). Therefore, what does Paul mean? Ask himself. *I am,* he says, *the least of the Apostles* (I Cor. xv. 9).

VIII. *The Day of the Martyrs is celebrated that we may be drawn to imitate them.* Let us celebrate this festival day, made sacred to us by the blood of the Apostles. Let us love their faith, their lives, their labours, their sufferings, their confession of Faith; what they have preached to us. For we profit by loving, not through celebrating these things with earthly pleasures. For what do the Martyrs seek of us? They have gained little if they are now seeking men's praise. If they are looking for praise from men, then they have not triumphed. But if they have triumphed, they seek nothing from us, for themselves. But they still seek for us.

Therefore let our way be directed in the sight of the Lord. It was a narrow way, a thorny way, a hard way. But trodden by the feet of so many and such great ones it has become an easy way. The Lord Himself first walked it. The Apostles passed fearless along it. Then came the Martyrs, young boys, women, girls. But Who walked with them? He Who said: *Without me you can do nothing.* Let us celebrate this festive day of the Saints who warred against error unto blood, and triumphed by the Lord's grace and assistance. And let us celebrate it by loving them; and let us love them by imitating them, so that imitating them we may merit to share their rewards, through Jesus Christ our Lord. Amen.

III. St Leo the Great, Pope and Doctor

The Natal Day of the Apostles Peter and Paul[9]

Synopsis:

I. How greatly the glory of Rome has increased through religion, by the ministry of the Apostles.

II. How the Roman Empire has served the Empire of Christ.

III. Why the chief See of the Church was established at Rome.

IV. How great the fortitude and love of Peter when beginning in Rome.

V. What were the labours of Peter before he came to Rome.

VI. Peter and Paul together, two illustrious shoots of the divine seed.

VII. How great should be our rejoicing upon their Feast Day.

The whole world is a sharer of all our holy solemnities, Most Dearly Beloved, and loyalty to the one faith requires of us, that whatever is remembered as done for the salvation of all men, should everywhere be celebrated with common rejoicings. But this day's Solemnity over and above the reverence it merits from all the world, is to be honoured with a special and particular exultation in our City: that where the glorious death of the chief Apostles took place, there above all should we rejoice on the day that commemorates their martyrdom.

For these are the men through whom the Light of the Gospel shone upon thee, Rome; and thou who wert the Mistress of error art become the Handmaid of Truth. These are thy holy Fathers, and thy true Shepherds, who founded thee, that thou mightest be brought into the heavenly kingdom. And far more happily and more perfectly than they by whose striving the first foundations of thy walls were laid; of whom the one who named thee defiled thee, with his brother's slaughter.[10]

It is these have raised thee to this glory, that being made a holy people, a chosen people, a royal and priestly people, and, through the Holy See of the Blessed Peter, Head of the world,[11] thy rule has spread wider far through heavenly faith, than ever by earthly domination. For though thou hast with manifold victories enlarged thy rule, so that it has spread over lands and sea, yet what thy warlike toil has subdued is less than what the Christian peace (*pax Christiana*) has conquered.

II. For the good and just and almighty God, Who has never denied His mercy to men, and has ever instructed all men in general in the knowledge of Himself, by means of His abundant gifts to them, with a yet greater love and with a deeper purpose has had compassion on the deliberate blindness of those who go astray, and upon their evil inclination towards what is worse, sending to us His own Co-Equal and Eternal Word. And the Word being made Flesh so united the divine nature to the human, that the favour of the Former to us has raised us to what is highest. So that the fruits of this ineffable favour might be spread throughout all mankind the divine providence made ready the empire of Rome, whose increase had reached to such an extent, that by means of it all the nations of the world were now joined together and become neighbours one with another.

For the divine plan needed this above all, that the many nations should be linked together under one power; for the preaching of the new life would unimpeded speedily reach those peoples whom the rule of one authority governed. But this authority, as yet not knowing the Author of its advancement, while it ruled over almost every nation was itself the slave of the errors of every nation, and because it rejected no falsehood appeared to itself to be the great support of religion. And so the more tenaciously it was held in bonds by the devil, the more wondrous was its deliverance through Christ.

III. For when the Twelve Apostles, after they had received from the Holy Ghost the power of speaking in every tongue, had taken upon themselves the task of teaching the Gospel to the world, and had apportioned among themselves the different parts of the earth, the most blessed Peter, the prince of the company of the Apostles, was sent to the chief place of the Roman Empire,[12] so that the light of truth which was being revealed for the salvation of all the nations, might more effectively be diffused throughout the whole world from its actual head. For at this time what nation was there that did not have some of its people in this city, or what peoples were there anywhere who were ignorant of what was known at Rome? It was here the notions of philosophers had to be fought, here the vanities of worldly wisdom must be answered, here the worship of demons had to be put down, here the blasphemy of all the idolatries was to be destroyed, here where, with the most thoroughgoing superstition, had been gathered together whatever had at any time been taught from among all the varieties of error.

IV. To this city therefore, You, O Most Blessed Apostle Peter, feared not to come, and while the Apostle Paul, the companion of your glory, was still engaged in the establishing of the other churches, you faced into this forest of roaring beasts, this deep and stormy ocean, with more firmness than when once you walked upon the sea. Nor did you fear Rome the Mistress of the world, you who had once trembled before the maidservant of the High Priest in the house of Caiphas. Was there less power in the Courts of Claudius than in those of Pilate, less cruelty in Nero than in the barbarity of the Jews?

It was the power of love therefore that overcame the causes of your fear: you did not think they should be feared whom you had taken to your heart to love. And you conceived this fruit of a fearless love when the love you professed for the Lord had become steadfast in the mystery of His thrice-repeated questioning (Jn. xxi. 15-17). And for this declaration of your soul nothing else was asked of you, but that you should feed the sheep of Him you loved, and give them the Food on which you had grown strong.

V. And your confidence had increased through so many signs and wonders, because of so many divine gifts, with so many proofs of your

own powers. You had already instructed the peoples who had believed from the Circumcision. You
had already founded the Church at
Antioch, where the dignity of the
name Christian had had its beginning. You had already instructed
men in the commandments of the
Gospel, teaching the countries of
Pontus, of Galatia, of Cappadocia,
Asia and Bithynia; and doubting
nothing of the outcome of your
labour, and knowing what time
remained to you, you bore the Sign
of Triumph of Christ's Cross against
the stronghold of Rome, whither by
divine predestination there had preceded you both the dignity of
government and the glory of your
Passion.

VI. To this City came your
blessed co-Apostle, *the vessel of
election*, and chosen Teacher of the
Gentiles, joining you at a time when
all innocence, all modesty, and every
human freedom suffered under the
rule of Nero, whose fury, inflamed
by excesses in every form of vice,
drove him headlong in a very torrent
of madness, so that he was the first
to make war against the Christian
name by the barbarity of a general
persecution. As though God's favour
to men would end by the slaughter
of His holy ones, to whom this very
thing was their greatest gain: that
contempt for this fleeting life should
lead to the reward of eternal joy!

Precious therefore, *in the sight of
God is the death of his saints* (Ps. cxv.
15). Nor can the religion founded
on the mystery of Christ's Cross be
destroyed by any kind of cruelty.
By persecution the Church is not
made less, but rather made greater;
and the fields of the Lord are clothed

with an ever richer harvest, as the
grains which fall singly to the
ground spring up multiplied. And
so it is that from these two illustrious shoots of the divine seed have
sprung up so great an offspring, as
the thousands of blessed martyrs
bear witness, who, emulous of the
triumphs of the Apostles, have gone
far and wide round about our city
in glorious blood-red throngs, and
crowned her as with a single
diadem, joined together from the
sacrifice of countless precious jewels.

VII. And because of this protecting host, divinely prepared for us,
Dearly Beloved, as an example of
patience, and for the confirmation
of our faith, there should be rejoicing everywhere in the commemoration of all the saints. But
rightly should we glory with a
greater joy in the supreme fidelity
of these Fathers whom God's grace
has exalted to so high a place among
all the members of His Church, so
that He has placed them as the twin
lights of the eye in that Body
Whose Head is Christ.

As to their merits and virtues,
which surpass the power of speech,
we ought to observe no difference,
no distinction; because the Lord has
made them equal in their election,[13]
alike in their labours, and comrades
in their end. And as we have learned
by experience, and as those before
us have confirmed, we believe and
trust, that amid all the labours of
this life, we are always helped in
obtaining the mercy of God by the
prayers of our special patrons: and
that the more we are weighed down
by our own sins, the more we are
uplifted by the merits of the
Apostles, through Jesus Christ our

Lord, to Whom with the Father and the Holy Ghost belong the same Majesty, the same Divinity, for ever and ever. Amen.

IV. St Leo the Great, Pope and Doctor

On the Natal Day of St Peter the Apostle[14]

Synopsis:

I. The Confession and the Supremacy of Peter.

II. What Christ bestowed on him.

III. He prayed for his faith; and gave him firmness of faith. He made him ruler of the whole Church.

I. Let us exult in the Lord, Beloved, and let us rejoice with spiritual rejoicing: Because the Only-begotten Son of God the Father, our Lord Jesus Christ, that He might penetrate us with the knowledge of the mysteries of His Divinity and of His plan for our salvation deigned to place over this City the Blessed Peter, Prince of the company of the Apostles; whose Solemnity this day, on which we recall the triumph of his martyrdom, is a pattern and a glory to all the world.

And this he obtained, Beloved, by that confession which God the Father inspired in his apostolic heart, and which, soaring above all the uncertainties of human opinion, received the firmness of a rock which no violence shall ever disturb. The Lord, as we learn from the Gospel narrative, had questioned all the Apostles as to whom men were saying He was. And the simple speech of the answers received is the measure of the obscurity of human understanding. But when He asks what is the belief of the Apostles, he becomes foremost in confessing the Lord who is first in apostolic dignity.

When he said: *Thou art the Christ the Son of the living God,* Jesus answers him: *Blessed art thou, Simon Bar-Jona: because flesh and blood hath not revealed it to thee, but my Father who is in heaven.* That is: You are blessed in that My Father has taught you, that earthly opinion has not led you astray, rather, that heavenly inspiration has been your Teacher, that it was not flesh and blood revealed Me to you, but He Whose Only-begotten I am.

And, He says, I say to you; that is: As My Father has made known to you My Divinity, so shall I make known to you your own high dignity. *That thou art Peter.* That is: As I am the inviolable Rock, as I am the *corner-stone,* as it is I Who *make both one* (Eph. ii. 14), so also are you a rock; for you are made firm from My power, and what relates to My authority over men is shared with you through your association with Me.

II. *Upon this rock I will build my church, and the gates of hell shall not prevail against it.* Upon this firmness, He says, I shall raise My Temple, and it will rise upon the steadfastness of this faith, and the summit of My Church will mingle with the heavens. The gates of hell shall not master this profession; nor the bonds of death bind it. For these words are the words of life, and as they raise those who confess them up to heaven, so they plunge those that deny them down to hell.

Because of this to the most blessed Peter was it said: *And I will give to thee the keys of the kingdom of heaven. And whatsoever thou shalt bind upon earth, it shall be bound also in heaven: and whatsoever thou shalt loose on earth, it shall be loosed also in heaven.* The power of His authority came also to the other Apostles; but not without purpose is that entrusted to one which was communicated to all. This power was entrusted in particular to Peter, for the reason that the authority of Peter is placed above that of all the rulers of the Church. Therefore the privilege of Peter (*privilegium Petri*) endures; everywhere judgement is given in accord with his rule of justice; nor shall there be too great severity nor too great laxity where nothing is loosed, and nothing bound, except where Peter has either bound or loosed.

III. As the Lord drew near to the time of His Passion, which was to trouble the constancy of His Disciples, He said: *Simon, Simon, behold Satan hath desired to have you, that he may sift you as wheat: But I have prayed for thee, that thy faith fail not: and thou, being once converted, confirm thy brethren* (Lk. xxii. 31, 32). The danger that arose from the trial of fear was common to all the Apostles, and all of them had equal need of the divine protection, since the devil desired to strike at all of them, to persecute all of them. And yet the Lord takes to Himself the special care of Peter, and prays especially for the faith of Peter, as though the

future state of the rest will be more secure, if the soul of their leader is not overcome. In Peter therefore the constancy of the others is secured, and the assistance of the divine grace is so ordered, that the firmness which Christ gives to Peter is passed through Peter to the other Apostles.

For after His resurrection, and after the keys of the kingdom had been given to the blessed Apostle Peter, in answer to his threefold profession of eternal love, with a mystical inwardness three times the Lord said to him: *Feed my sheep* (Jn. xxi. 17). And this beyond doubt he now does, and the devoted Pastor fulfils the command of his Lord, confirming us by his encouragement, and never ceasing to pray for us, that no temptation may overcome us. And if he bestows this tender care everywhere, to all the people of God, as we must believe, how much the more is it fitting that he should bestow his treasure on us his foster children, among whom he rests, upon the sacred couch of his blessed falling asleep, in that same body in which he ruled us in the flesh.

Since therefore, Beloved, we are able to see in our midst so great a divinely ordained guardian, let us fittingly and rightly rejoice in the dignity and in the merits of our Leader, giving thanks to the everlasting King, our Lord and Redeemer Jesus Christ, that He gave such power to him whom He made Ruler of His whole Church, to the praise and glory of His own Name, to Which be there glory and honour for ever and ever. Amen.

V. St Maximus, Bishop of Turin

On the Same Natal Day of the Holy Apostles Peter and Paul[15]

Argument: The power of Peter has gone forth into all the earth; and the words of the Epistles of Paul unto the ends of the world.

On the lame man cured by Peter; on Paul the vessel of election; and on the martyrdom of the two Apostles.

I. It is known to you all, Brethren, and well known to the whole world, that this is the Natal Day of the blessed Peter and Paul, and that such great devotion could not remain unknown to the whole world, since it is of these that the prophet David says: *Their sound hath gone forth into all the earth: and their words unto the end of the world* (Ps. xviii. 5). The wondrous power of Peter has gone forth into all the earth, and the words of the Epistles of Paul have reached unto the ends of the world.

For who has not heard that the blessed Apostle Peter gave back strength to the feet of the man who had been lame from his mother's womb, and who had for a long time sat at the gate of the Temple, which was called Beautiful; so that what nature had given him imperfect, the Apostle's grace had repaired? For when the lame man, asking for an alms, thought he was about to receive a little money from the Apostles, the Apostle Peter said to him: *Silver and gold I have none; but what I have, I give thee. In the name of Jesus Christ of Nazareth, arise, and walk* (Acts iii. 6).

Holy, blessed liberality, which gave health, not alms, to the one who asked for money. Blessed generosity, which *brought forth out of his treasury*, not gold, but healing! Blessed lame man who, expecting to receive money, receives instead the riches of a sound body! He received, given to him by the Apostles, that which no treasure could have purchased from the physicians. Peter's first sign therefore of his wondrous powers, was to set up again on the soles of his feet the man born lame.

We have told you often that Peter was named Peter (*petram*) by the Lord, where He said: *Thou art Peter; and upon this rock I will build my church.* If therefore Peter is the rock upon which the Church is built, rightly does he first heal feet, that as he holds firm the foundation of the Church, so in the case of this man he gives strength to the foundations of his members. Fittingly, I say, does he first cure the feet of a Christian, so that no longer anxious, no longer feeble, he may stand upon the rock of the Church, and now strong and robust may walk.

II. Where are the words of Paul not read? What place is there where they do not keep them in writing, hold them in their heart, observe them in their lives? This Paul who was called *a vessel of election.* A noble vessel, in which the precious teaching of Christ's commandments is stored. Noble vessel, from whose fulness the food of life is at all times distributed to the people, and remains full. Most fitting are the names of the Apostles: for the Rock and the Vessel are necessary to the

House of the Saviour. For a house is built up from the strength of rocks; and provided with vessels for its needs. The Rock sustains the people, lest they fall; the vessel holds them in safety, lest they be tempted.

How blessed their going forth from this life there is no one who does not know. For this in them is the first blessedness; that we know they both suffered on the same day, that is, that they whom one faith had joined in a common service, one faith crowned with the martyrs' crown. And though in their actual passion they differed, yet with equal virtue of holiness was it borne by both the one and the other. For Peter, like our Saviour, suffered the death of the Cross; nor even in the manner of his death was he separated from his loved Lord: for as he was made like to Him by faith, he became like to Him in his passion.

And of Paul it is said, that when the executioner struck his neck with the sword, milk rather than blood gushed forth, and that in a wondrous manner the holy Apostle, by the grace of his baptism, appeared in his very sacrifice shining and glorious, rather than covered with blood. And this happening in the holy Paul is not astonishing. For what wonder that the nourisher of the Church should abound in milk, since he has himself said to the Corinthians: *I gave you milk to drink, not meat* (I Cor. iii. 2).

This is that land full of promise which the Lord promised to our forefathers: *I will give you a land flowing with milk and honey* (Exod.

iii. 8). It was not said of this earth that is clothed with mud from the flowing streams that mingle with the clay, but of that land of Paul, and of those like Paul, which in a flowing stream yields what is pure and sweet. For the Epistles of Paul, are they not sweeter than honey, whiter than milk? These Epistles, do they not give nourishment like breasts for the salvation of the peoples of the Church? And so it is that from the throat of the Apostle milk flowed in place of blood. We read in his Epistle, *that flesh and blood cannot possess the kingdom of God* (I Cor. xv. 20). So Paul already possessed the kingdom of God, since he was without blood, which, it is said, prevents us from reigning there. And so Paul while still on earth is changed into the substance of the kingdom of heaven.

Therefore, dearest Brethren, as often as we commemorate the memory of the Martyrs, putting aside all worldly activities, let us without delay come together to the house of God, to honour them who obtained our salvation by shedding their blood for us; offering themselves as a sacred victim to the Lord, in atonement for our sins. And this especially because Almighty God has said to His holy ones: *He who honours you, honours me; and he who despises you, despises me* (Lk. x. 16). He therefore who honours the Martyrs, honours Christ. And he who despises these holy ones, despises our Lord, Who lives and reigns with the Father and the Holy Ghost world without end. Amen.

VI. The Venerable Bede, Priest and Doctor

The Birthdays of the Blessed Apostles Peter and Paul[16]

The Lesson of the holy Gospel you have just heard, Brethren, must the more earnestly be dwelt on, and kept in mind continually and without forgetfulness, the more it becomes plain to us that the great perfection of faith is here placed before us, and also the great strength of a perfect faith against all temptations. For if we would know how we ought to believe in Christ, what is clearer than that which Peter said to Him? *Thou art the Christ the Son of the living God.* Again, should you wish to learn how great is the strength of this faith, what is plainer to us than what the Lord says of the Church that is to be built upon it: *And the gates of hell shall not prevail against it?* These things however will be set out more fully in their own place. Returning now to explain in sequence the Sunday's lesson, let us look first at the scene where what is recorded took place.

Jesus Christ, it says, *came into the neighbourhood of Cesarea Philippi.* Philip, as Luke testifies, was the Tetrarch of the region of Iturea and the Trachonitis. He built a city there, in the place where the Jordan rises, close to the foot of Mount Lebanon, and to the north of Judea, and called it Cesarea Philippi; in memory of his own name jointly with that of Tiberius Caesar, under whom he reigned.

And coming into these parts Jesus asks His Disciples: *Whom do men say that the Son of man is?* He asks, not as ignorant of the beliefs of the Disciples and of outsiders; but He asks His Disciples what they think con-cerning Him so that He may bestow on their true confession of faith a fitting reward. For as Peter answered for them all, though all were asked together, so, when the Lord answers Peter, He answers all in Peter. He asks what others say of Him, so that the false ideas of those who err might be first set out, it would then be proved that the Disciples had received the truth of their Confession, not from the common belief, but through the mystery of the divine revelation.

Whom, He says, *do men say that the Son of man is?* Aptly does he speak of those as men who only know and speak of *the Son of man:* for they knew nothing of the secrets of His Divinity. For they who have come to grasp the mysteries of His divinity are rightly said to be something more than men, as the Apostle bears witness who says: *That eye hath not seen, nor ear heard, neither hath it entered into the heart of man, what things God hath prepared for them that love him* (I Cor. ii. 9, 10). Since he said this of *men,* that is, of those who come to know only through the human heart or eye or ear, he then adds of himself and of those like himself, who had transcended the common knowledge of mankind: *But to us God hath revealed them, by His Spirit.* Similar to this is what the Lord said to His Disciples after He had asked them whom did men say He was, and they had told Him of the different notions of different persons: *But whom do you say that I am?* As though setting them apart from the generality of men, and implying that they were become as gods, and sons of God, by adoption; according to the words of the Psalmist: *You are gods, and all of you sons of the most high* (lxxxi. 6).

Simon Peter answered and said: Thou art the Christ, the Son of the living God. He calls Him the *living God* to mark His difference from the false gods whom the Gentiles, led astray by various errors, had set up from men now dead, who had been just as themselves, or, with greater folly, from senseless matter, adoring what they had made; of whom the Psalmist says: *The idols of the gentiles are silver and gold, the works of men's hands. They have a mouth but they speak not* etc. (cxxxiv. 15).

Let Your Charity take note of what a wondrous difference there is between the manner of speaking of the Lord Himself and that of His faithful Disciple, when it is a question of the twofold nature of the same Lord and our Saviour. The Lord brings before us the lowliness of His assumed humanity, the Disciple the supreme perfection of the Eternal Divinity. The Lord Himself speaks of what is less, the Disciple of what is greater; concerning His Lord. The Lord speaks of what He has become for our sake; the Disciple of the Lord Who has made us. So also in the Gospel. There the Lord is wont more frequently to call Himself *Son of man* than *Son of God*: That He may remind us of the work of the Redemption He has undertaken for our sake. And we should the more humbly venerate the supreme glories of His Divinity, the more we remember that it was for our exaltation He came down to share the

lowliness of our humanity. For if among the mysteries of the Incarnation by which we were redeemed, we ever keep devoutly before our minds the power of the Divinity that created us, it will come to pass that we too shall merit with Peter the reward of heavenly blessedness.

Peter having confessed that Christ was the Son of the living God, let us now see what happens. Jesus answering, said to him: *Blessed art thou, Simon Bar-Jona.* It is certain therefore, that after a true confession of Christ the true rewards of blessedness await us. But let us consider carefully, what, or how great, is this name with which the Lord honours this perfect confessor of His own name: that we may merit to share it by also confessing His holy Name.

Blessed art thou, Simon Bar-Jona, He says. Bar-Jona in Syriac means in our tongue, *son of the dove*. Rightly is the Apostle Peter called, *son of the dove*, for the dove is a very simple creature, and Peter has followed the Lord with a prudent and pious simplicity, mindful of that precept of simplicity and truth he, with his fellow Disciples, had received from the same Master: *Be ye therefore wise as serpents, and simple as doves.* And also because the Holy Spirit descended in the form of a Dove, he is rightly called the son of the dove who has shown that he is filled with spiritual grace.

And with just praise does the Lord reward the one who loves and confesses Him, when He bears witness, that he is the son of the Holy Spirit who so strongly declares that the Lord is Himself the Son of the living God: though there is not a single person who believes would doubt that both the one and the other have place in a wholly different manner. For the Lord Christ is the Son of God by Nature; Peter, and with him the other elect, is a son of God through grace. Christ is the Son of the living God: being born of Him; Peter the son of the Holy Spirit: being re-born of Him. Christ is the Son of God before all time: for He is the Power of God, the Wisdom of God, Who says: *The Lord possessed me in the beginning of his ways, before he made anything from the beginning* (Prov. viii. 22). Peter is the son of the Holy Spirit from that moment in which, enlightened by Him, he received the grace of the knowledge of the Divinity. And because one is the Will and the Same is the Operation of the Holy Trinity, when He said, *Blessed art thou, Simon Bar-Jona,* rightly did He forthwith add:

Because flesh and blood hath not revealed it to thee, but my Father who is in heaven. The Father revealed to the son of the Dove, that one is the grace of the Father and the Holy Ghost, and the same is also the grace of the Son, which we shall prove to you from the clearest testimony of Holy Scripture. For the Apostle says of the Father: *God hath sent the Spirit of his Son into your hearts* (Gal. iv. 6). The Son says of the Holy Spirit: *When the Paraclete, whom I will send you from the Father* (Jn. xv. 26). The Apostle says of the Holy Spirit: *But all these things one and the same Spirit worketh, dividing to everyone according as he will* (I Cor. xii. 11). The Father therefore sends the Spirit; the Son sends the Spirit; the Spirit Himself *breatheth, where he wills* (Jn. iii. 8): because, truly, as I have said, one is the Will and

Operation of the Father and the Son and of the Holy Ghost. And so it is fittingly said, that the Father Who is in heaven has revealed to the son of the Dove the Mystery of Faith, Which flesh and blood could not have revealed to him.

By *flesh and blood* we rightly understand those who are inflated with the wisdom of the flesh, incapable of the simplicity of the dove, and therefore wholly averse to the wisdom of the Spirit. Of these was it said above, that, not knowing Who Christ was, some of them said He was John the Baptist, others that He was Elias, others Jeremias, or one of the prophets; and of these people the Apostle says: *The sensual man perceiveth not these things that are of the Spirit of God* (I Cor. ii).

And I say to thee: Thou art Peter; and upon this rock I will build my Church. Peter, who before was called Simon, receives from the Lord the name of Peter, because of the strength and constancy of his faith; for with a firm and tenacious soul he clung to Him of Whom it was written: *And the rock was Christ* (I Cor. x. 4). And upon this *Rock,* that is, upon the Lord Saviour, Who gave to him who knew Him, loved Him, and confessed Him, the privilege of sharing His Name; namely, that he should be called Peter from Petra (the *rock*), upon which the Church is built. For only through the faith and the love of Christ, through receiving the Sacraments of Christ, through keeping the commandments of Christ, can we come to share in the lot of the elect and to eternal life, as the Apostle testifies where he says: *For other foundation no man can lay, but that which is laid; which is Christ Jesus.*

And the gates of hell shall not prevail against it. The gates of hell are evil doctrines, which by seducing the unwary drag them down to hell. The gates of hell also are the torments and the blandishments of persecutors, which by terrifying or by softening the weak from the steadfastness of the faith open to them the way to eternal death. And the evil deeds of the believing, and their profane and idle talk, are also gates of hell, in as much as they point out to their applauders and followers the road to perdition. *So faith also, if it have not works, is dead in itself* (Jas. ii. 17); and, *Evil conversations corrupt good morals* (I Cor. xv. 33).

But many are *the gates of hell*, but no one among them will ever prevail against the Church which is founded upon *the rock*; for he who receives the faith of Christ with the inward love of his heart will make nothing of any danger whatever that may attack him from without. But whosoever, becoming corrupted in his heart, has betrayed either by denial or by act the faith of those who believe, this man cannot be regarded as having, with the Lord's help, built the house of his profession *upon a rock*, but as, in accord with the parable of another place in the Gospel, having built *upon sand*, without a foundation; that is, he does not follow Christ with a true and simple heart, but rather has put on an earthly, and, for that reason, a frail mask of Christianity. Then follows:

And I will give to thee the keys of the kingdom of heaven. He who with a devotion above all the rest confessed the kingdom of heaven has rightly had bestowed upon him

before others the keys of the heavenly kingdom: that it might be known to all, that without this faith, without this confession, no one can enter the kingdom of heaven. The keys of the kingdom designate the actual knowledge and power of discerning who are worthy to be received into the kingdom, and who should be excluded from the kingdom as unworthy. Accordingly, He goes on to say very clearly:

And whatsoever thou shalt bind upon earth, it shall be bound also in heaven: and whatsoever thou shalt loose on earth, it shall be loosed also in heaven. This power of binding and loosing, although it appears to be given to Peter alone, is we should nevertheless know beyond all doubt given to the other Apostles also, as the Lord Himself bears witness, Who, appearing among them after the triumph of His Passion and Resurrection, breathed upon them and said to all of them: *Receive ye the Holy Ghost. Whose sins you shall forgive, they are forgiven them; and whose sins you shall retain, they are retained* (Jn. xx. 22). And even now in every church this same office is committed to bishops and priests, so that they may carefully examine into cases of sinners, so that whosoever appear humble and truly repentant, these they may in mercy absolve from the fear of perpetual death. But those it knows are persisting in the sins they have committed, let it gently convey to such as these, that they remain liable to eternal punishment.

It was for this reason that the Lord on another occasion says of a brother who had been corrected once, twice, and for a third time, and yet does not mend his ways: *If he will not hear the Church, let him be to thee as the heathen and the publican* (Mt. xviii. 17). And for fear anyone might think it was a little thing to be condemned by the judgement of the Church, He immediately and fearfully adds: *Amen I say to you, whatsoever you shall bind upon earth, shall be bound also in heaven; and whatsoever you shall loose upon earth, shall be loosed also in heaven.*

To every church of the elect, therefore, authority is given to bind and to loose, according to the measure of sin or of repentance. But the blessed Peter, more particularly, who confessed Christ with true faith, and followed Him with true love, so received the keys of the kingdom, and the supremacy of judicial power, that all the faithful throughout the world may understand, that whosoever shall cut themselves off in any way from the unity of the faith, or from the unity of this fellowship, such persons can neither be absolved from the bonds of their sins, nor enter the gate of the heavenly kingdom.

Accordingly, Dearest Brethren, we have need to learn with all our heart the mysteries of the faith which it teaches us, and bring forth works that are worthy of our faith. It is necessary for us that, with all watchfulness, we avoid the many and subtle snares of the gates of hell, that we may, in the words of the Psalmist (ix. 15), be *lifted up from the gates of death*, and may deserve to *declare all thy praises in the gates of the daughter of Sion*; that is, to enter into the joys of the heavenly city.

Nor should we think that it is enough for salvation that in our works we are no worse than the mass of the careless and indifferent, or that in our faith we are, like so many others, uninstructed: for these as well as for the rest there is in Sacred Scripture but one and the same rule of living and of believing. And as often as the example of those others who have gone astray is brought before us, let us, *turning away our eyes that they may not behold vanity* (Ps. cxviii. 37), seek rather with our whole heart for what Truth Itself teaches us: following the example of the blessed Peter who, rejecting the falseness *of those who had gone astray* (II Pet. ii. 15), proclaimed with the unhesitating confession of the mouth the mystery of true faith he had learned, and held fast in the invincible love of his heart.

Of the faith of his confession we have learned here; in another place he testifies to the power of his singular love for Christ, Who, when some of the Disciples had left Him, said to the twelve: *Will you also go away?* (Jn. vi. 68). And Peter answered Him and said: *Lord, to whom shall we go? Thou hast the words of eternal life. And we have believed and have known, that thou art the Christ, the Son of God.*

Let us be earnest, therefore, My Brothers, in trying as best we can to take his example as our model, and then we also shall be worthy of being called *blessed*. The name Simon, that is, *obedience to Christ*, will then befit us also; and through the simplicity of *an unfeigned faith* (I. Tim. i. 5), and through the grace we receive from the Lord, we also shall be called sons of the Dove *of hosts*; and Christ, rejoicing in the spiritual increase of our soul, shall say to us: *How beautiful thou art, my love, how beautiful: thy eyes are dove's eyes* (Cant. iv. 1).

So shall it be that to us who heap upon the rock of faith, gold, silver, precious stones, that is, perfect works of virtue, the fires of tribulation shall bring no harm, and no storm of

temptation shall prevail against us, but rather, that made strong through trials, we shall merit to receive that crown of life He promised us before all ages Who with the Father, in the unity of the Holy Ghost, lives and reigns God for ever and ever. Amen.

NOTES

[1] The citations from Rhabanus Maurus in this portion of the *Catena Aurea* are drawn verbatim from the Sermon of the Venerable Bede, of an earlier century, on the subject of this Gospel: PL 94, Homily VI of this Feast. It is a slip all editions follow, including even Nicolai. Not wishing to assume the correction of the text we have simply put the name of the venerable English Father in parenthesis, after that of Rhabanus.

[2] Of this citation 'nothing is found in the work cited, or anywhere either in Latin or Greek; as Bellarmine notes in his *Tract. de Scriptoribus*', Nicolai, *in loco*, ed. Lyons, 1686. The words have a marked Cyrillian quality, and doubtless with much else of Cyril have been lost.

[3] PG 72, cols. 422–3. *Fragmenta* on Mt. xvi. 16, 18, collected from the Catenae of Corderius and Possinus. Also cols. 914–15 on Lk. xxii. 31.

[4] Bishop of Brescia, who accepted the See at the urging of his friend, Ambrose, Bishop of Milan; died 410. PL 20, col. 1993, Sermo 20. The Preacher opens addressing St Ambrose, who had invited him and pressed him to preach for the Feast.

[5] Cf. PL 20, col. 995, note *a*. Presumed to be taken from the Acts (Apocryphal) which were circulated under the name of Pope Linus.

But the fact is confirmed by frequent testimonies from the Fathers; Origen, Augustine, Prudentius, Chrysostom, and others. St Jerome says of Peter in his book of *Scriptores Eccles*: *He was crowned with martyrdom, affixed to a cross, with his head to the ground, and his feet pointing upwards; declaring he was unworthy to be crucified in the same way as His Lord.*

[6] Here the question arises: Do the words of Gaudentius, that Paul was bidden *to walk amid the clouds*, mean that Paul was *caught up to the third heaven* (II Cor. xii. 2) in his body, or in his spirit only? The words *walk in the clouds* seem to favour the first; confirmed by the parallel actuality of Peter walking on the waves here alluded to; which was bodily. A mystical beginning is also here hinted at.

[7] *Collations*, of Cassianus (contemporary of Gaudentius), xii. 11: 'This will come to pass when the flesh, ceasing to desire against the spirit, they have both agreed in desiring (chastity) and in virtue, and have begun to be leagued together and, in the phrase of the Psalmist, *to dwell together as brothers in unity.*'

[8] PL 38, col. 1348, Sermo 295.

[9] PL 54, col. 422, Sermo 82.

[10] Romulus (the founder and first king of Rome) murdered his brother Remus.

[11] Cf. PL 54, col. 423, footnote *a*. Here it is to be noted that though Peter and Paul are *the holy Fathers and true shepherds* of the Roman city, Leo says that the episcopal *See* (Seat) of Rome was given to Peter alone, and that it became *caput orbis*, that is, ruled the whole world; and from this it arises that his spiritual dominion was more widespread than ever was the earthly rule of imperial Rome.

[12] From the *Sacramentarium Romanum*, the most ancient of all, Tome II; from which it is evident that certain phrases of this sermon, and certain particular words, have been included in the Preface of the Natal Day of SS Peter and Paul.

[13] Cf. PL 54, col. 427, footnote *d*. Election to the *apostolate* is to be understood here: in this Peter and Paul were equals, for each was chosen by Christ as an Apostle. This is in no way prejudicial to the primacy of Peter, as Leo expressly states in Sermon 4, II.

[14] PL 54, col. 429, Sermo 83.

[15] PL 57, col. 671, Sermo 69. This sermon has been variously attributed to Ambrose, Augustine and Leo; but very plainly it is no work of theirs, and is now placed under the name of St Maximus of Turin.

[16] PL 94, col. 219, Sermo 16. A sermon of great perspicuity and witness.

SIXTH SUNDAY AFTER PENTECOST

I. St John Chrysostom: The Second Multiplication of the Loaves

II. St Augustine: Mystical Explanation of the Gospel

III. St Maximus: Mystical Exposition of the Loaves and Fishes

IV. The Venerable Bede: Explanation of the Gospel

THE GOSPEL OF THE SUNDAY

Mark viii. 1–9

At that time: when there was a great multitude with Jesus, and they had nothing to eat; calling his disciples together, he saith to them: I have compassion on the multitude, for behold they have now been with me three days, and have nothing to eat. And if I shall send them away fasting to their home, they will faint in the way; for some of them came from afar off.

And his disciples answered him: From whence can any one fill them with bread here in the wilderness? And he asked them: How many loaves have ye? Who said: Seven. And he commanded the multitude to sit down upon the ground. And taking the seven loaves, giving thanks, he broke, and gave to his disciples to set before them; and they set them before the people. And they had a few little fishes; and he blessed them, and commanded them to be set before them.

And they did eat and were filled; and they took up that which was left of the fragments, seven baskets. And they that had eaten were about four thousand; and he sent them away.

EXPOSITION FROM THE CATENA AUREA

V. 1. *When there was a great multi- tude, and had nothing to eat.*

THEOPHYLACTUS: Following on the miracle of the multiplication of the loaves and fishes which the Lord had wrought some time before, a fitting occasion now presenting itself, He is moved to work a similar miracle. Hence we have: *In those days when there was a great multitude,* *and had nothing to eat.* He did not in all circumstances work miracles to feed the people, lest they should follow Him for the sake of food. He works this wonder now only because He sees the multitude in danger. Hence we read: *If I shall send them fasting* etc.

BEDE: How it was that those who had come from afar off should wait for three days Matthew tells us more fully: *And going up into a mountain, he sat there. And there came to him great multitudes, having with them the dumb, the blind, the lame, the maimed, and many others: and they cast them down at his feet, and he healed them* (Mt. xv. 29, 30).

THEOPHYLACTUS: The Disciples did not yet understand Him; nor did they yet believe in His power, after the miracles He had wrought. So we read:

V. 4. *And his disciples answered him: From whence can any one etc.*

But the Lord did not rebuke them; teaching us that we should not be really angry with men who are ignorant and with those who do not understand, but that we should have compassion on their ignorance. Hence we read:

V. 5. *And he asked them: How many loaves have ye?*

REMIGIUS *on Matthew*: He did not ask them as though not knowing what they had; but that they might answer seven: for the fewer there were, the more would the miracle be spoken of, and the more known it would become. Then follows:

V. 6. *And he commanded the multitude to sit down upon the ground.*

In the previous feeding of the multitude they are said to have sat down *upon grass*, but here *upon the ground. And taking the seven loaves, giving thanks, he broke.* In that He gives thanks He left us an example; that we are to give thanks to Him for all the gifts He has bestowed on us from heaven. And we should note that the Lord did not give the bread to the people, but to His Disciples; and the Disciples gave it to the people. For we read: *And gave to his disciples to set before them.* And blessing, not alone the loaves, but also *the little fishes,* He commands that they be set before the people. For we read:

V. 7. *And they had a few little fishes; and he blessed them.*

BEDE: Therefore, in this lesson, we are to contemplate in the one and the same Redeemer the separate action of His Divinity and Humanity. And the error of Eutychus, which dared to lay down as Christian teaching that in Christ there is but one operation, must be driven from Christian lands. For who is there does not see in His having *compassion on the multitude,* the sympathy and pity of human tenderness; that He fed four thousand men with seven loaves and a few fishes, the effect of divine power?

V. 8. *And they did eat and were filled; and they took up . . .*

THEOPHYLACTUS: The multitude which had eaten, and were full fed, did not take away with them what remained of the loaves. The Disciples took up what was left, in baskets, as on the previous occasion. In which we learn, through this account, that we should be content with what suffices for our needs, and not seek for anything more. Then we are told the number of those who ate; where it is said:

V. 9. *And they that had eaten were about four thousand.*

Wherein we are to reflect that Christ sends no one away hungry;

since He wishes all should be nourished with His grace.

BEDE: The difference as Figures between this eating, and that of the five loaves and two fishes is this: that there the letter of the Old Testament, full of spiritual grace, is signified; here was shown the reality and grace of the New Testament, which is to be ministered to the faithful. And the multitude remains with the Lord for three days, for the healing of their sick, as Matthew tells us, when the Elect, with persevering earnestness, plead in the faith of the Holy Trinity for the forgiveness of their sins. Or, because they turn to the Lord in thought, word, and deed.

THEOPHYLACTUS: Or, those who remained with him for three days signify those who are baptized. For baptism is called *illumination*, and is administered by a threefold immersion.

GREGORY, *Morals*, I, 19: He does not wish them to go away hungry, lest they faint by the wayside. For men should receive the word of consolation through preaching, lest, hungering for the Food of truth, they perish in the hardships of this life.

AMBROSE: The good Lord, though He requires that men be zealous, will yet give them strength; and He will not send them away fasting, lest they *faint in the way*, that is, in the course of this life, or before they come to the Source of Life; that is, to the Father, and learn that Christ is from the Father, lest being told He was born of the Virgin, they may begin to believe that His power is not that

of God, but of man. The Lord Jesus therefore divides the food among them; and it is His will, as the Dispenser of all things, to give it to all, and He denies it to no one. But when He breaks the loaves to give them to His Disciples, if you do not put out your hands, that you may receive food, you will faint by the way; nor can you place the blame on Him who has had compassion on you, and apportions you food.

BEDE: They however who, after crimes, after robberies, after violence and murder, come to repent, come to the Lord from *afar off*. For the more anyone has gone astray in evil doing, the farther off has he strayed from Almighty God. They who believed from the Gentiles came *from afar off* to Christ; but the Jews, who had been taught about Him in the writings of the Law and the Prophets came from near at hand.

On the former occasion the multitude sat down upon green grass when they ate of the five loaves. Here they sit *upon the ground*. For in the Scripture of the Law they were commanded to crush the desires of the flesh; but in the New Testament we are commanded to abandon temporal things, and even earth itself.

THEOPHYLACTUS: The seven loaves are the seven spiritual words; for the number seven signifies the Holy Ghost, Who perfects all things. For our life is completed in a sevenfold number of days (or *ages*).

JEROME (*pseudo*): Or the seven loaves are the seven gifts of the Holy Spirit. The fragments of the loaves are the mystical understanding of these seven.

BEDE: That the Lord breaks the loaves signifies the making known to us of the seven sacraments. That He gives thanks shows how greatly He rejoices over the salvation of men. That He gives the loaves to His Disciples to set before the people means that He has given the gifts of spiritual knowledge to the Apostles; and that He wills that by their ministry the Food of spiritual life shall be distributed to the Church.

JEROME (*pseudo*): The *little fishes* He blessed are the books of the New Testament; for the Lord on rising from the dead asks for a piece of broiled fish. Or, in the little fishes we receive the saints whose faith, life and sufferings are contained in the writings of the New Testament, and who, caught up from the waves of this troubled world, have provided us with inward food through their example.

BEDE: The Apostles gather up what remains after the people are filled, because the higher precepts of perfection, to which the multitude cannot reach, relate to those whose way

of life is above that of most of the people of God. And yet we must keep in mind that the multitude is fed: for though they cannot leave all things, nor fulfil what is required of virgins, nevertheless, obeying the commandments of God's law, they attain to eternal life.

JEROME (*pseudo*): The seven baskets are *the Seven Churches*. The *four thousand* means the year of the New Dispensation, with its four seasons.[1] And fittingly are they four thousand, that through this number they might teach they had been fed with the food of the Gospels.

THEOPHYLACTUS: Or they are *four thousand*, that is, made perfect by the four virtues; and through this being stronger as it were they eat more and leave fewer fragments. For in this miracle seven baskets remain; in the miracle of the five loaves twelve basketfuls remained. For there were five thousand men, that is, those who were the servants of the five senses, and because of this they were unable to eat, and, being satisfied with a little, much remained over of the fragments.

I. ST JOHN CHRYSOSTOM, BISHOP AND DOCTOR

The Second Multiplication of the Loaves[2]

When, on the first occasion, the Lord was about to work this miracle, He first cured those who suffered from illness of the body. Here He does the same. For after He had healed the blind and the lame, He goes on to work the same miracle. But why did the Disciples on that occasion say to Him: *Send away the multitudes* (Mt. xiv. 15), while on this occasion, though three days had

now passed, they do not say it? It was either because they were now wiser men, or else because they saw that the people did not seem greatly troubled by hunger: for they were praising and glorifying God for what had taken place amongst them.

But see how on this occasion also He does not simply proceed at once to the miracle, but calls His Disciples to Him for this purpose. For the multitudes came to Him for healing; they did not dare to ask for bread. But He, kind and foreseeing, gives it to them even though they do not ask, and says to His Disciples: *I have compassion on the multitude, and shall not send them away fasting.* And lest they say that the people had come with food for the way, He says: They have now been with me three days; so that even had they brought some, it would now be consumed. He did not do this on the first day, or the second, but when everything was gone; so that when they were reduced by want they would acclaim the miracle with greater good will. And so He says, *Lest they faint in the way,* confirming that they were far from home, and that they had nothing.

But if you do not wish to send them away fasting, why do You not work a miracle? That by means of this question, and by the answer that followed, He might make His Disciples more alert; that they might show more faith; that they might come to Him and say: *Make* loaves. But they had not even seen the need of the question. Because of this, later, He said to them, as Mark tells us: *Are your hearts still so blinded; having eyes do you not see, and having ears do you hear not?* And if this were not the case, for what reason did He say these words to the Disciples, and show them that the multitudes were deserving of such a kindness, and add also that He was Himself moved with compassion for them? Matthew however says that a little afterwards He rebuked them sharply, in these words: *O ye of little faith. Do you not yet understand; neither do you remember the five loaves among the five thousand men, and how*

many baskets you took up, nor the seven loaves among four thousand men, and how many baskets you took up? (xvi. 8, 9). So the Evangelists are in accord with one another.

What then do the Disciples say? They are still crawling along the ground, though the Lord had done endless things to fix in their mind the remembrance of the first miracle, by question and by answer, by making them the ministers in what He did, by distributing the baskets among them; and they were still backward. Grasping nothing, the Disciples say: *Where should we have so many loaves in the desert?* For they thought He said this as though telling them to buy loaves. And quite foolishly. For the same reason had He said to them not so long ago: *Give you them to eat* (Mt. xiv. 16): to give them an opportunity of asking Himself for this favour. Now however He does not say, *Give you them to eat;* but what? *I have compassion on the multitude and will not send them away hungry;* actually moving them, and prompting them, to see that this food was to be sought from Himself. For the very words make this plain; that He was able not to send them away; and they also show His power. For the words, *I will not,* signify this.

And because they make mention of a multitude, and of the place, and the wilderness (for they say: *From whence can anyone fill them with bread in the wilderness?*), and since they had not grasped the meaning of Christ's words, He then goes on with His purpose, and says to them: *How many loaves have you? But they said: Seven, and a few little fishes.* This time they do not say: *But what are these among so many* (Jn. vi. 9), as they said before. And so, though they had not begun to grasp the whole matter, their minds are now a little more elevated. And He too, uplifting their minds by this, put the question in the same way as on the other occasion, that this might remind them of what He had done then.

And you, as you have seen their backwardness, now note here also their just spirit, and admire their truth, and how when writing of themselves afterwards they did not try to conceal their own stupidity, however great it was. For it was no light matter for them to have forgotten so speedily such a miracle, performed just a little while before; and it was for this they were rebuked. And I would like you to keep in mind their own personal austerity; how poorly they provided for the stomach, how they disciplined themselves to pay little attention to what they ate. For though they were in the desert, and were there for three days, they possessed but seven loaves.

The other things Christ ordered as on the former occasion. He bade them be seated, on the ground, and He multiplied the bread in the hands of the Disciples. *And he commanded the multitude to sit down upon the ground, and taking the seven loaves and the fishes, and giving thanks, he brake, and gave to his disciples; and the disciples gave to the people.* But the end of this miracle was not the same as the ending of the first. *And they did all eat,* it says, *and had their fill. And they took up seven baskets full of what remained of the fragments. And they that did eat, were four thousand men, beside women and children.* Why were there twelve basketfuls left when there were five thousand, while here,

where there were four thousand, only seven basketfuls of fragments remained over? Why are the fragments now so much fewer when the number of people was not so much less?

We must answer that either the baskets used this time were larger than before or else, lest the sameness of the miracle should cause the Disciples to forget it again, in order to stir up their memory by a difference, so that by this variation the memory of both this and the former miracle would remain in their minds. So the first time He made the number of baskets of fragments the same as the number of Disciples; and this time He made them equal to the number of the loaves, and in this reveals His ineffable power, and the ease with which He could use that power, in that He could both in this way and in the other way work miracles. For it was a matter of no small power to keep to the number exactly, both then and now: since there five thousand men ate, now four thousand: and leave neither more nor less fragments than the baskets would hold, though the number of the guests was unequal.

And what followed was like what followed on the previous occasion. For then, leaving the multitude, He withdrew by ship; and now He does the same; and John also speaks of this (vi. 17). For no other miracle had so roused the people to follow Him as the miracle of the loaves; and not alone to follow Him, but they also wished to make Him King. And to avoid all suspicion of desiring to be made King, immediately after the miracle, He quickly departs; and not on foot, lest they follow Him, but by boat.

And the Gospel goes on to tell us that, *when his disciples were come over the water, they had forgotten to take bread. Who said to them: Take heed and beware of the leaven of the Pharisees and Sadducees.* Why did He not say openly: 'Beware of their teaching'? He wishes of course to bring back to their mind the miracle that had taken place; for He knew they had already forgotten it. But it did not seem opportune to censure them openly then; though, as they gave Him occasion to do so, He made the reproof tolerable. And why did He not reprove them when they said, *Whence should we have so many loaves in the wilderness?* For then seemed a good time to correct them. He did not do so that He might not seem to be as it were rushing at the miracle. And besides He did not wish to correct them before the people, or make a display of His own authority. Now correction was more called for: that they should be so forgetful after two such miracles.

And so, after another miracle, He rebukes them; for He laid before them the thoughts they were thinking in their hearts. And what were they thinking? They were thinking: He says this *because we have taken no bread.* For they were still concerned about Judaic purifications, and about observances with regard to food. And so because of this He upbraids them very sharply, saying to them: *Why do ye think within yourselves, O ye of little faith, for that you have no bread. Do you not yet understand; neither do you remember?* Your heart is still blind; having eyes you see not; having ears you hear not. *Do you not remember the five loaves among five thousand men, and how many baskets you took up? Nor the seven loaves among four thousand men, and how many baskets you took up?*

You see here displeasure stretched to the utmost. In no other place is He seen to rebuke them in this manner. Why did He act so? That once again He might drive out of their minds their notions regarding foods. So, on the previous occasion, He said only: *Are you yet without understanding? Do you not understand?* But here, rebuking them fiercely, He says: *O ye of little faith.* For not everywhere is mildness to be used. As He allowed them to speak freely, so He corrects them in the same way; and in this change of manner He is seeking their welfare. For you see here both severity and great mildness. For, almost excusing Himself for correcting them, He says: Do you not recall to mind the five loaves among five thousand men, and how many baskets you filled? And the seven loaves among four thousand, and how many baskets you filled? He reminds them of the number who ate, as well as of how much remained; that at the same time He might both make them mindful of past events, and more attentive to future ones.

And to show us how efficacious His rebuke was, how it sharpened their torpid minds, hear what the Evangelist says. For when Jesus had finished speaking, and after rebuking them had added: *Why do you not understand that it was not concerning bread I said to you: Beware of the leaven of the Pharisees and Sadducees,* the Evangelist notes: *Then they understood that he said not that they should beware of the leaven of bread, but of the doctrine of the Pharisees and Sadducees;* although the Lord had not so interpreted these words. But see the good His rebuke did. It led them away from the Jewish observances, and from being heedless, as they were before, they became attentive to what He said to them. And He took them out of their littleness of faith, so that they were not afraid, nor apprehensive, when they had but a few loaves, nor concerned about hunger, but indifferent to all things.

And neither should we be always yielding to those subject to us; nor wish to be sheltered by those placed over us. For the human mind has need of either remedy. And it is in this way God orders all things, and now does this and now does that; and allows neither good things nor bad to continue permanently. For as it is now day, and now night, and now winter, and now summer, so within us we have now pleasure, now pain, now sickness, now health. And we should not wonder if we are sick; since we ought rather wonder that we are well. Nor let us be troubled should sorrow come; for since we are given happiness, it is reasonable that we should also have sorrow. For all things come to us in accord with nature, and with the order of things. Let us keep all these things in our mind, so that we may escape final punishment, and attain to everlasting blessings, through the grace and mercy of our Lord Jesus Christ, with Whom be there glory to the Father and to the Holy and Life-giving Spirit, for ever and ever. Amen.

II. St Augustine, Bishop and Doctor

Mystical Explanation of the Gospel[3]

1. *Feasts in Holy Scripture.* When we explain the Holy Scriptures to you, we are as it were breaking bread for you. Let you who are hungry receive it; and give forth from your heart the fulness of your praise. And you who are enriched with spiritual food, let you not be poor in virtue, or poor in good works. What I am giving you is not mine. What you eat, I eat; I live by what you live by. We have a common source of supply in heaven: for it is from there the Word of God comes.

2. *The Miracle of the Seven Loaves allegorically interpreted.* The seven loaves signify the sevenfold operation of the Holy Spirit. The four thousand men the Church founded on the Four Gospels. The seven baskets of fragments the perfection of the Church: for it is by this number that perfection is most frequently signified. Why else is it said that, *Seven times a day I shall praise thee* (Ps. cxviii. 164)? Does a man who has praised the Lord so often wander from the right way? What then does, *I shall praise thee seven times a day* mean, but that I shall never cease to praise Thee? For he who says *seven times* means at all times.

For the same reason the ages are said to roll forward in periods of seven days. What then does, *Seven times a day I shall praise thee* mean if not what is said in another place in the words: *His praise shall be always in my mouth* (Ps. xxxiii. 2)? It is with reference to this perfection that John writes to *the seven churches*

(Apoc. i. 4). The Apocalypse is the book of the holy Evangelist John; which he wrote to the seven churches. Be you the hungry. Recognize the baskets![4] For those fragments did not perish. And because you belong to the Church they nourish you also. As a minister of Christ I set them before you. And when you listen quietly, you are as it were sitting down. I am seated in my body; in my heart I am standing up, and ministering to you; with anxiety lest the vessel, not the food, give offence to any among you. You know of God's food; you have heard of it often. Your souls hunger for it; not your bodies.

3. *The Divine Secrets in those who were filled from the seven loaves.* We know that four thousand men were filled from the seven loaves. What could be more wondrous? And this was not all. Seven baskets were filled with the fragments that remained. O Mighty mysteries! They were wrought; and the works have spoken. For these works, if you understand them, are also words. And you are also part of the four thousand, because you live under the fourfold Gospel. The women and children were not included in the number. For it is written: *And they that did eat were four thousand men, beside women and children* (Mt. xv. 38). As though those who are without understanding, and the effeminate, are outside the number, Nevertheless let these also eat. Let them eat. Perhaps the children will grow up, and be children no more. Let the effeminate be reformed, and be sanctified. Let them eat. We hall distribute the food to them; we shall gladly minister to them.

But whoever they may be, God sees His guests, and if they have not reformed their lives, He Who invited them will also know whom to separate from the rest.

4. Who is invited to the Feast? You know, recall to mind, Beloved, the Gospel parable where the Lord went in to see His guests (Mt. xxii. 11). The Head of the family Who had invited them *saw there*, as it is written, a man who had not on a wedding garment. For the Spouse Who is *beautiful above the sons of men* had invited him to a wedding feast. This Spouse became repulsive for the sake of His repulsive Bride: that He might make Her beautiful. How has He Who was beautiful become repulsive? If I do not prove this I shall have blasphemed. That He is beautiful the prophet testifies, saying: *Thou art beautiful above the sons of men* (Ps. xliv. 3). That He is repulsive another prophet testifies to me, saying: *We have seen him; there is no beauty in him, nor comeliness; and his look was as it were hidden and despised* (Is. liii. 2, 3).

O prophet who said, *Thou art beautiful above the sons of men*, you are contradicted! Another prophet has come forward against you, and he says you speak falsely. We have seen him. What are you saying; *Beautiful above the sons of men?* We have seen him; there is no beauty in him, nor comeliness. Are these two prophets then at war over the Cornerstone of peace? Both spoke of Christ. Both spoke of the Cornerstone. Walls are joined at the corner. If they do not join, it is not a building; it is a ruin. The prophets agree; let us not dismiss them as in disagreement. More than that, let us see if we can learn more of their agreement; for they know nothing of discord.

O prophet who said, *Thou art beautiful above the sons of men,* where have you seen Him? Answer me, tell me where hast thou seen Him? *Being in the form of God, thought it not robbery to be equal to God.* I saw Him there. Do you doubt that He Who is equal to God is beautiful above the sons of men? You have given your answer. Let him answer who said: *We have seen him; there is no beauty in him, nor comeliness.* Tell us where you have seen Him? He begins from the other's words. Where the first left off, there the second begins. Where did the first end? *Who being in the form of God thought it not robbery to be equal with God.* Here is where he saw Him Who is *beautiful above the sons of men.* Tell us you, where have you seen him *without beauty or comeliness?* But *he emptied himself, taking the form of a servant, being made in the likeness of men, and in habit found as a man* (Phil. ii). See where I saw Him. They are both in perfect agreement; both at peace together. Who is more beautiful than God? Who more repulsive than the Crucified?

5. *The rejection of the guest without a wedding garment.* This Bridegroom therefore, *beautiful above the sons of men,* became repulsive that He might make His Spouse beautiful: to whom it was said: *O fairest among women* (Cant. i. 7); and of whom it is said: *Who is she that goeth up most fair* (iii. 6), enlightened, not dark with the colour of falsehood?

He then Who had invited His guests to a wedding feast found there a man not having on a wedding garment, and He said to him: *Friend, how camest thou in hither not having on a wedding garment? But he was silent.* For he had no answer to give. And the Master of the house Who had come in says: *Bind his hands and feet, and cast him into the exterior darkness: there shall be weeping and gnashing of teeth.*

For so small a fault so great a punishment! For it is great. Is it a small fault not to have on a wedding garment? It is small, but not to those who understand. How could He have been so angry, how could He have condemned him in this way, for not having on a wedding garment, and sent him, bound hand and feet, into exterior darkness, where there shall be weeping and gnashing of teeth, unless it was a great fault not to have on a wedding garment?

I am saying this to you because you also have been invited, through me; if He has invited you, He has invited you through us. You are all present at the feast; let you have on your wedding garment. I shall explain what it is, so that you all may have it; and should any one hear me who has not one, let him, before the Master of the house comes in to see His guests, be changed for the better; and let him receive a wedding garment: that he may sit down in security.

6. *The man cast forth a Figure of many.* He who was cast forth does not, Beloved, represent simply one man. Far from it. There are many. And the Lord Himself Who proposed the parable to us, the Bridegroom, the Preparer of the feast, He Who gives Life to the guests, has explained to us here in the same

place, in the parable itself, that this man does not merely represent one man, but many. I shall not go into this at length; I explain what is there; I break the bread and set it before you to eat. For the Lord says, when the man who had not on a wedding garment was sent forth into exterior darkness, He says, and goes on to say it immediately: *For many are called but few are chosen.* You cast forth *one* man, and you say that, *many are called but few are chosen.* Beyond doubt the Elect are not cast forth; they are *the few* who remained sitting there as guests. And there are *many* in that *one* man: for the *one* who had not on a wedding garment is the body of the wicked (*corpus malorum*).

7. The Wedding Garment is Charity. What is the wedding garment? Let us look for it in the Holy Scriptures. What is the meaning of a wedding garment? It is certain that it is something that good and bad do not possess in common. Let us find what that is and we shall have found out what a wedding garment is. Among the gifts of God what is there which good and the bad have not in common. That we are men, that we are not beasts, is a gift of God. But this is something that good and bad possess in common. That the light of heaven shines on us, that the rains fall from the clouds, that fountains run, that fields bear harvests, are gifts; but they are gifts shared in common by both good and bad.

Let us go to the marriage feast. We leave outside those not invited. Let us contemplate the guests; that is, the followers of Christ. Baptism is a gift of God. The good have it, and the bad have it. Both good and

bad together receive the Sacrament of the altar. Saul though an evil man prophesied; and raged against one who was holy and most just. And while he persecuted him, he prophesied. Are the good alone said to believe? *The devils also believe, and tremble* (Jas. ii. 19). What more shall I do? I have tried everything, and yet I have not found this wedding garment. I have emptied my satchel. I have considered everything, almost everything, but I have not yet come to the wedding garment.

The Apostle Paul in a certain place brings me a great satchel of wondrous things, and spreads them out before me. And I say to him: Show me if by chance I can find here this wedding garment. And he begins to reveal them to me one by one. *If I speak with the tongues of men and of angels, if I should have prophecy, and should know all mysteries, and all knowledge, and all faith, so that I could remove mountains. And if I should distribute all my goods to feed the poor, and deliver my body to be burned.*

Wondrous garments! Yet we have not here this wedding garment. Now bring us forth a wedding garment. O why, Apostle, will you keep us in suspense! Prophecy perhaps is a gift of God, one that good and bad have not in common? *If,* he answers, *I have not charity, I am nothing, it profiteth me nothing.* Here is your wedding garment! Put it on, O guests, that you may sit down with minds secure. Do not say to me: O we are too poor to possess such a garment! Put it on; be clothed with it. It is winter. Clothe the naked! Christ is naked; and whosoever has not a wedding garment, He will give him one. Run to Him; ask Him! He knows how to sanctify His faithful; He knows how to clothe His own who are naked.

Let you not fail in doing good works, that you may possess a wedding garment, and have no fear of the outer darkness, or of the binding of your members, of your hands and feet. For if they are wanting, what can you do when your hands are bound? Whither will you fly when your feet are bound? Hold fast to this wedding garment; put it on, and sit down secure when He shall come to see His guests. The Day of Judgement is near at hand. But He is giving us good time to prepare for it. He that was naked, let him be clothed in good time.

Turning then to the Lord our God, the Father Almighty, let us as best we can give thanks with all our hearts, beseeching Him that in His goodness He will graciously hear our prayers, and by His power drive evil from our thoughts and actions, increase our faith, guide our minds, grant us His holy inspirations, and bring us to joy without end through His Son our Lord and Saviour Jesus Christ. Amen.

III. St Maximus, Bishop

Mystical Exposition of the Loaves and Fishes[5]

Synopsis:
    I. The Twofold Operation in our Redeemer; against the error of Eutyches.
    II. The Mystical Explanation of the miracle of the multiplication of the Loaves and Fishes.

I. Our Lord Jesus Christ in many and various ways revealed to us in the Holy Scriptures, as also in His mysteries and sacraments, the sublimity of His Divinity and the tenderness of His Humanity: so that those who ask of Him shall receive, those who seek of Him shall find, and to those who knock it shall be opened to them. For all the wonders He wrought in this world, when clothed in our frail nature, He did for us. It was not without reason the Lord did these things, nor as it were idly and without purpose. Christ is the Word of God, Who speaks to men, not in words only, but also in deeds. And furthermore, this event which is read of in the holy Gospel today seeks for the one who will understand it; and when he has understood it, joy will fill his soul.

And in this reading from the Gospel we are to consider at the same time in our one and the same Redeemer, the separate activity of both His Divinity and His Humanity;[6] and we must detest with all our heart the error of Eutyches, who presumed to put forward as Catholic truth that in Christ there is but one sole operation. For in either case, he who says that He was only man will deny the glory of his Creator, and he who says that He is God only will deny the compassion of the Redeemer. For that the Lord had compassion on the multitude, lest they faint of hunger or through weariness of the long way to their homes, makes known to us that He possessed the tenderness and affection that belongs to human weakness; but that He fed four thousand men from seven loaves and a few fishes was we believe a work of divine power.

Let Your Sanctity therefore attend carefully to what is here put before us, so that with the assistance of your goodness we may explain what is the meaning of this so great and mysterious event; and why, as the Holy Scripture bears witness, and as the Gospel relates, God should reveal Himself in this way to His Disciples. For the Evangelist in today's lesson says: *When there was a great multitude with Jesus, and they had nothing to eat; calling his disciples together, he said to them: I have compassion on the multitude.* But let us enquire into what He says a little earlier. *In those days when there was a great multitude.* For earlier (Mt. xv) the Jews had come to the Saviour complaining that His Disciples *did not wash their hands when they ate bread.* And the Lord answered them, that it was rather the evil things that come forth from a man's heart that soiled a man. Then leaving them He came into the territory of the Gentiles, where a woman of Chanaan, who stands as the mother of the Gentiles, besought him on behalf of her daughter; that is, the Church. And she prayed to Him with such perseverance that at length she obtained what she prayed for. And after this He cured one who was deaf and dumb.

Therefore, in these days, when the multitude of people had flocked together, they had nothing to eat: for the Gentiles had not the Law, that is, the Five Books of Moses and the Prophets; nor the preaching of John: because the Gentiles came to the Redeemer, not through the Law, but through faith. And they persevered with Him for three days; that is, during the Birth, Passion, and Resurrection of the Lord; or in the Father, Son, and Holy Ghost. For to persevere means to remain steadfast in the praise of God, as the Lord Himself says: *He that shall persevere unto the end, he shall be saved* (Mt. x. 22).

The Lord therefore says: *They have nothing to eat,* because they have not the Law; *and I will not send them away fasting, lest they faint in the way*: so that they who believed through faith in Christ should be saved through the faith of Christ. *For some of them came from afar off.* For the Gentiles were far off from God, wandering among idols; and even now every one who sins is far off from God.

His Disciples say to Him: *From whence can any one fill them with bread here in the wilderness?* Unbelief still held the mind of the Disciples in its grip; until the mysteries would be revealed. And neither did they remember what He had wrought from the five loaves and the two fishes. *And Jesus asked them: How many loaves have you? They said: seven. And he commanded the multitude to sit down upon the ground. And taking the seven loaves, giving thanks, he broke, and gave to his disciples for to set before them. And they had a few little fishes; and he blessed them, and set them before them. And they did eat and were filled; and they took up that which was left seven baskets. And they that had eaten were about four thousand, beside children and women.* And we believe that the wonders of the Lord are seen most clearly even now. But let us seek through the gift of His grace to know what lies hidden in this mystery.

II. In the earlier account of the five loaves and two fishes He fed five thousand men; here He feeds four thousand men from seven loaves and a few fishes. There the Disciples suggest to the Lord, saying: *This is a desert place, and the hour is now past; send away the multitudes, that going into the towns they may buy themselves victuals* (Mt. xiv. 15). Here the Disciples are wholly silent. It is the Lord alone who is solicitous for them. Let us see why they are silent. Because they were not yet sent to preach to the Gentiles, but rather to the lost sheep of the house of Israel (Mt. x. 6). Therefore the first parable relates to the Jews, but this to the Gentiles. There, there were five loaves; that is, the Five Books of Moses. Here, there were seven; which stand for the sevenfold gifts of the Holy Spirit, according to the holy Isaias the prophet, who says: *The Spirit of wisdom and understanding, the Spirit of counsel and fortitude, the Spirit of knowledge and of godliness. And he shall be filled with the Spirit of the fear of the Lord* (Is. xi. 2).

There twelve baskets were filled with the Holy Spirit; here the *seven Churches*, or *the seven golden candlesticks* (Apoc. i. 4, 20). There they had two fishes, which stand for the Two Testaments, or one book of all the prophets, and the preaching of the holy John. Here an undefined number is spoken of, which are the gifts of grace, as the Apostle says: *To one, by the Spirit, is given the word of wisdom, to another the word of* knowledge, to another prophecy, to another diverse kinds of tongues, to another interpretation of speeches. But all these things one and the same Spirit worketh* (I Cor. xii. 8).

There the people sat on grass; here upon the ground. On both occasions the same manner of speech, the same grace, the same power, the one Divinity. There they sit on grass; that is, upon the dead works of the flesh—for *all flesh is grass*, as the prophet says (Is. xl). Here they sit upon the ground; that is, they tread down the things of earth. There five thousand are fed, and this number has reference to the Jews; for Peter, after the Resurrection of the Lord, lifted up his voice, and *the number who believed was made five thousand*. But here four thousand; which means that all peoples, from the four points of the heavens, are filled with the sevenfold grace of the Spirit unto Life eternal.

And so, Beloved, we who believe in our Lord Jesus Christ, not through the Law but by faith, who are redeemed, not by its works but by grace itself; who are filled, not from the five loaves, that is, from the Five Books of Moses, but by the sevenfold grace of the Holy Spirit, as the blessed Isaias had prophesied, saying: *The Spirit of wisdom, and of understanding, the Spirit of counsel, and of fortitude, the Spirit of knowledge, and of piety; And he shall be filled with the Spirit of the fear of the Lord* (Is. xi), let us continue in this grace of the Sevenfold Spirit, in which we were called, being filled with *the gift of the Holy Ghost* (Acts ii. 38) through our Lord Jesus Christ, Who lives and reigns in the Unity of the Holy Ghost God for ever and ever. Amen.

IV. The Venerable Bede, Priest/

Explanation of the Gospel[7]

MARK viii. 1–9

1. *In those days again, when there was a great multitude, and they had nothing to eat, calling his disciples together, he saith to them: I have compassion on the multitude, for behold they have now been with me etc.* And in this lesson we must consider in one and the same Redeemer the separate operation of His Divinity and of His Humanity. And the error of Eutyches, who dared to teach that in Christ there is but one operation, must be wholly driven forth from Christian lands. Who is there does not see that the Lord, in having compassion on the multitude lest they faint from want of food or from the weariness of the long journey home, was moved by the compassion of human pity, but that to feed four thousand men from seven loaves and a few fishes is a work of divine power?

Mystically, however, we are shown by this miracle that we cannot pass in safety along the road of this present life unless the grace of the Redeemer nourishes us by the food of His Word. As Figures there is however a difference between the meal given here, and that of the five thousand loaves and two fishes; because there the letter of the Old Testament, full of spiritual grace, is signified, but here the reality and grace of the New Testament, which is to be ministered to the faithful, was pointed out to us. Either meal took place upon a mountain (Jn. vi. 3), as the accounts of the other Evangelists make clear: for the Scriptures of either Testament,

rightly understood, declare to us the sublimity of the heavenly precepts and rewards. And each with unceasing voice proclaims the sublimity of Christ, *Who is the mountain of the house of the Lord on the top of the mountains* (Is. ii. 2). For He Who has uplifted the city built upon Himself, that is, the House of the Lord, the Church, to the sublimity of the works of mercy, and made it known to all the Gentiles, and, withdrawn from earthly delights, now nourishes it with the Bread of heaven, and kindles in it the desire for heavenly delights by means of this gift of Spiritual Food.

And if I send them away fasting to their homes, they will faint in the way. The Evangelist Matthew explains more fully why the multitude continued for three days with the Lord. He says: *Going up into a mountain he sat there. And there came to him great multitudes, having with them the dumb, the blind, the lame, the maimed, and many others: and they cast them down at his feet, and he healed them* (xv. 30). The multitude had therefore remained with the Lord for the healing of their sick; as each of the elect, shining in the faith of the Holy Trinity, makes urgent unceasing supplication to the Lord for the healing of the sicknesses of their soul, that is, for the forgiveness of their sins.

Again, the multitude remains for three days with the Lord when the multitude of the faithful, departing through repentance from the sins they have committed, turn to the

Lord in thought, word, and deed. These the Lord will not send fasting to their homes, lest they faint in the way; for those who are converted from sin faint in the way of this present life if they are sent away without the food of His holy teaching in their souls. Therefore lest they should grow weak on the journey of this earthly pilgrimage they must be fed with holy counsels.

2. We must therefore meditate deeply upon the sacred teaching that proceeds from the lips of Truth when He says: *For some of them came from afar off.* For it is such as have nothing to do with evil doing and carnal corruption who hasten to serve the Omnipotent God. He does not come from afar off who through innocence and integrity of soul was already close to God. Another, free of unchastity, stained by no evil, who has known only marriage, devotes himself to the works of the Spirit; neither does he come from afar off: for by reason of his service to God he does not wander far from Him after things forbidden. Then there are those who after the sins of the flesh, after having given false testimonies, after robberies, after inflicting grievous violence and injury upon others, after committing murders, turn to repentance and become converted to the service of Almighty God. Such as these come to God *from afar off.* For the more a man has strayed in doing what is evil, the further off he is from God.

Food is therefore given even to those who come from afar off; for the food of holy instruction must be offered to those who are converted from sin, that they may regain in God the strength they lost in evil

doing. The Jews however, those of them who believed in Christ, came to Him from close at hand; for they had learned of Him from the writings of the Law and of the Prophets. They however who believed from the Gentiles did truly come from afar off to Christ; for no sacred pages from the past had prepared them to believe in Him.

3. *And he asked them: How many loaves have you? Who said: Seven.* Fittingly do we find seven loaves set before us in the mystery of the New Testament, in which the sevenfold grace of the Holy Spirit is made known, to be believed by all the faithful; and being believed, it is given to them. Nor were these barley loaves that were put before them, as were the other five loaves, from which five thousand men were filled: lest the vital Food of grace be obscured, as under the Law, by corporeal rites. For the pith of the barley is enclosed in a very unyielding husk.

And he commanded the multitude to sit down upon the ground. In the former feeding of the multitude from five loaves the people sat upon green grass. Now that they are to be nourished from the seven loaves they are commanded *to sit down upon the ground.* For in the Scriptures of the Law we are commanded to restrain and to tread down the desires of the flesh. *For all flesh is as grass, and all the glory thereof as the flower of grass* (Ecclus. xiv. 18). But in the New Testament we are commanded to forsake all our temporal goods and even the world itself. And also because the mount on which the multitude was fed by the Lord's loaves signifies, as we have said, the sublimity of our Redeemer, there men sat upon grass, here upon the ground. For there the sublimity of Christ is obscured by carnal hope and desire, because of carnal men and the earthly Jerusalem; here however, putting away all carnal desiring, and with no grass intervening, the solidity of the Mount Itself, as the Foundation of our enduring hope, is the sustenance of the guests of the New Testament.

4. *And taking the seven loaves . . .* The Lord receiving the loaves began to give them to the Disciples, so that they, when they received them, might *set them before the people*: for in giving to the Apostles the gifts of spiritual understanding He wishes that the Food of Life should be distributed to the Church throughout the world by their ministry. That He broke the loaves which He gave to His Disciples signifies the revelation of the sacraments by which the world was to be nourished unto life everlasting. For since the Lord Himself says: *And no one knoweth the Son, but the Father; neither doth anyone know the Father, but the Son, and he to whom it shall please the Son to reveal him* (Mt. xi. 27), what does He mean if not that the Bread of Life is to be made known to us by Him, and that of ourselves we are unable to come to the knowledge of the inward things of God? And the prophet, grieving because of the miserable hunger of some of his people, cried out: *The little ones have asked for bread, and there was none to break it to them* (Lam. iv. 4). In other words he is saying that the uninstructed have looked for the Food of the Word of God, that being fed on It they might have the strength to do good works, but for want of teachers there was no one to open to them the hidden things of the Scriptures, and to lead them along the way of truth. And the Lord, receiving the loaves that He might break them, gives thanks, that He may show how greatly He rejoices over the salvation of mankind, and also to teach us that we should give thanks to God at all times; either when our bodies are fed with earthly bread, or when our souls are fed with heavenly grace from above.

5. *And they had a few little fishes.* If the Scriptures of the New Testament are indicated in the seven loaves, in the reading of which we find by the grace of the Holy Spirit the inward Food of the soul, what are we to understand by *the little fishes* which the Lord blessed, and also commanded to be set before the people, if not the saints of that time in which the Scriptures were composed, and whose faith and lives and sufferings are contained in the same Scriptures? They who were caught up from the troubled waves of this world, and sanctified with the divine blessing, and who have by the example of their lives and of their deaths provided us with inward food, lest we should perish in the course of our journey through this world.

6. *And they did eat and were filled.* They ate of the loaves and fishes of the Lord and were filled who, hearing the Word of the Lord, and meditating on His parables, rouse themselves and rise up from their sleep because of them, and hasten towards a better way of life. And with these things the words of the

psalmist fittingly accord, where he says: *The poor shall eat and shall be filled; and they shall praise the Lord that seek him: their hearts shall live for ever and ever* (Ps. xxi. 27); as though he said: The humble of heart will hear the word of God, and do it, and they will refer all the good they do, not to their own praise, but to the praise and glory of their heavenly Benefactor. And so justly, as being fed with the Bread of Life, they will attain to that eternal Life which is of the inward man. But those who hear the Word of God, and neglect It, He reproaches by the mouth of the prophet Micheas: *Thou shalt eat, but shalt not be filled* (vi. 14). For they eat and are not filled who hearing it taste the bread of the Word of the Lord, but not doing what they hear, they receive into the stomach of their memory nothing of that inward sweetness by which their soul would be strengthened.

7. *And they took up that which was left* . . . The Apostles gathered up what was left after the multitude had eaten. And they filled seven baskets with the remains of the fragments: for these symbolize the precepts of higher perfection, or rather, the exhortations or counsels which the common multitude of the faithful could not attain to; by observing and fulfilling them. Their fulfilment is rightly to be looked for from those who, because they are filled with greater graces by the Holy Spirit, surpass in loftiness of soul and good works the common turning of sinful

man to God in repentance. To such as these is it said: *If thou wilt be perfect, go sell all that thou hast* (Mt. xix. 21).

And so it was well said that the baskets in which the fragments of the Lord's Food were gathered up are seven in number; because of the sevenfold gifts of the Holy Ghost. For as baskets are usually woven from reeds and palm leaves they are aptly used to symbolize the saints. For reeds are usually found in water; the palm in the hands of the victor. And the elect are fittingly compared to reed baskets, since they plant the root of their heart in the Fountain of Life Itself, lest the love of eternity wither within them. And they are likened to baskets woven from palm leaves, since with a pure heart they keep ever before them the remembrance of eternal punishment.

And justly is it said of the multitude that though they could not partake of the fragments of the Lord's supper which remained, yet *they did eat, and were filled.* For there are those who, though unable *to leave all things,* or to take upon them what is laid down for virgins: *He that can take it, let him take it* (Mt. xix. 12, 21, 22), and other things of this kind, nevertheless, eating and drinking justice they are *filled;* when through obeying the commandments of the law of God they attain to eternal life, by the grace and favour of Jesus Christ our Lord, Who with the Father and the Holy Ghost lives and reigns God for ever. Amen.

NOTES

[1] Apocalypse i. 4. Also to the Gospels, which were yet to be written; also to the Four Cardinal Virtues, from which the others depend. Nicolai, *in loco*.

[2] PG 58, Homily 53–4.

[3] PL 38, col. 581, Sermo 95.

[4] The word (*agnoscite*) would be accompanied by a gesture indicating the Gospels, and the altar, where the fragments are preserved.

[5] PL 57, col. 741, Sermo 107.

[6] He here affirms the separate operations of the two natures, the divine and human, not *operatio confusa*. Against these errors Pope Agatho wrote (A.D. 680) his celebrated epistle, which was received with acclamation by the Third Council of Constantinople (6th Ecumenical), which declared that: '*Petrum per Agathonem locutum esse*' (Denz 288). 'Confounding', he said, 'the mystery of the holy Incarnation, in that as they say that one is the nature of the divinity and humanity of Christ, so they assert that as He has but one will He has but one operation. The Apostolic Church of Christ, the Mother of the spiritual empire founded by God, confesses that there is one Lord Jesus Christ, deriving from and possessing two natures, and She

defends that His two natures, the divine namely and the human, remain separate in Him, even after their inseparable union in Him. Consequently, following the rule of faith of the Holy Catholic and Apostolic Church She teaches and confesses that in Him there are also two natural operations.'

And Pope Leo the Great, in his famous *Epistle to Flavian* (Denz 143), in which also the Council of Chalcedon (A.D. 451) declared that Peter had spoken by the mouth of Leo, refuting the heretical teaching of Eutyches, writes of the divine and human operation in this way. Each form (nature) does, with the mutual participation of the other, that which is proper to it. The Word doing what belongs to the Word, and the Flesh carrying out what is proper to the Flesh: of whom one shines forth in miracles, the other succumbs to injuries. And as the Word does not depart from the equality of the Paternal Glory, so the Flesh does not separate Itself from the nature of our kind (13 June 449, *Ep. Lectis Dilectionis Tuae*, Patriarch of Constantinople).

[7] PL 92, col. 205, Liber II, Cap. VIII.

SEVENTH SUNDAY AFTER PENTECOST

I. St Ephraim: On the Various Places of Torment
and on the Judgement

II. St John Chrysostom: The Fountain of Alms

III. St John Chrysostom: The Judgement Day

IV. St John Chrysostom: Mutual Need

THE GOSPEL OF THE SUNDAY

Matthew vii. 15–21

At that time: Jesus said to his disciples: Beware of false prophets, who come to you in the clothing of sheep, but inwardly they are ravening wolves. By their fruits you shall know them. Do men gather grapes of thorns, or figs of thistles? Even so every good tree bringeth forth good fruit, and the evil tree bringeth forth evil fruit. A good tree cannot bring forth evil fruit, neither can an evil tree bring forth good fruit.

Every tree that bringeth not forth good fruit, shall be cut down, and shall be cast into the fire. Wherefore by their fruits you shall know them. Not every one that saith to me, Lord, Lord, shall enter into the kingdom of heaven: but he that doth the will of my Father who is in heaven, he shall enter into the kingdom of heaven.

EXPOSITION FROM THE CATENA AUREA

V. 15. *Beware of false prophets.*

CHRYSOSTOM, *Op. Imp.* 19: Earlier the Lord had told the Apostles they should not pray, give alms, or fast, before other men as hypocrites do. And that they may know that all these things can be done out of hypocrisy He says: *Beware of false prophets.*

AUGUSTINE, *Sermon on the Mount*, 2, 24, 78: When the Lord said that they

are few who enter the narrow gate and the strait way, lest heretics, who sometimes pride themselves on their fewness in numbers, should put themselves in this place, He immediately adds: *Beware of false prophets.*

CHRYSOSTOM, *Hom. 24 in Matt*: Because it is said that the gate is narrow, and that they are many who block the way that leads to it, He adds: *Beware of false prophets.* And so that in this they might exercise great caution He reminds them of what happened in their fathers' time, using the phrase, *false prophets.* For then such things happened.

CHRYSOSTOM, *Op. Imp. on Mt. Hom.* 19: What was written a little later; namely, that *the prophets and the Law prophesied until John* (Mt. xi. 13) was said because there would be no prophecy regarding Christ after He came. Prophets there were and are; but they do not prophecy of Christ, they interpret what was foretold of Christ by the ancients: that is, the Teachers of the Churches. Nor can any one interpret the meaning of prophecy unless through the Spirit of prophecy.

The Lord therefore, knowing that there would be false teachers, warns them of the various heresies to come, by saying: *Beware of false prophets.* And as these would not be obvious unbelievers, but persons cloaked with the name of Christian, He did not say: Look well at them, but, *Beware.* For where a thing is certain it is seen; that is, it may readily be seen. But when it is uncertain it is looked at, or watched carefully. And again He says, *Beware*: for to know whom to shun is a firm safeguard of security. He does not warn us to beware as though the devil will introduce heresies against God's will, and not by His permission. For since He will not choose His servants without trial, He permits them to be tempted. And as He wills that they should not suffer through ignorance He therefore warns them.

And so that no heretical teacher may say, that He did not say here they were the false prophets, but rather the teachers from both Gentiles and Jews, He goes on to add: *Who come to you in the clothing of sheep.* For Christians are spoken of as sheep; and the *sheep's clothing* is their outward pretence of Christianity and pretended religion. There is nothing that so menaces what is good as pretence. For evil that is hidden under the outward appearance of Good is not guarded against, since it is not known.

And that heretics may not here say that He is speaking of those who are true teachers, but also sinners, He adds this: *But inwardly they are ravening wolves.* Catholic teachers, though they may have been sinners, are not spoken of as *ravening wolves*, but as servants of the flesh: for they do not seek to destroy Christians. He therefore is manifestly speaking of heretical teachers: for it is to this end that they put on the garb of Christian; that they may rend Christians with the evil fangs of their seductions. And of these the Apostles said: *I know that after my departure, ravening wolves will enter in among you, not sparing the flock* (Acts xx. 29).

CHRYSOSTOM, *Hom.* 24 *in Matt*: Yet He seems to imply that the *false prophets* are not the heretics, but those who put on the cloak of virtue, while in heart they are corrupt. So He therefore says:

V. 16. *By their fruits you shall know them etc.*

For often you will find goodness of life among heretics; but among those I speak of this is never the case.

AUGUSTINE, *Sermon on the Mount*, 2, 24, *pars*. 80, 81: And for this reason it may rightly be asked: What fruits does He wish us to seek for? For many hold as fruit certain things that belong to the sheep's clothing, and in this way they are deceived by the wolves. As for example: fasting, alms, prayer, which they practise before men who seek to find favour with those to whom such things seem difficult. These practices therefore are not the fruits by which, He warns us, they are to be known. For such actions, done with a right intention, are part of the clothing of the sheep. When they are done with evil purpose, in deception, they clothe none other than wolves. But sheep must not for this hate their own clothing; because it sometimes conceals a wolf. What the fruits are by which we may know an evil tree the Apostle then teaches us: *The works of the flesh are manifest, which are fornication, uncleanness*. And what the fruits are by which we shall know a good tree, the same Apostle makes known to us, saying: *But the fruit of the Spirit is charity, joy, peace* (Gal. v. 19, 22).

CHRYSOSTOM, *Op. Imp*: The confession of his faith is also part of the fruits of man. For he who cries out according to God, with the voice of true humility, and true confession of faith, is a sheep. But he who utters blasphemies against the truth, and howls against God, is a wolf.

JEROME: And what is here said of false prophets can also be understood of all who say one thing in word and manner and another in deed. Yet it seems to be said more particularly of heretics, who are seen to clothe themselves with continence and fasting as with a sort of garb of piety, but inwardly their spirit is poisoned; and so the hearts of simpler brethren are deceived.

AUGUSTINE, *as above*, 2, 12, *par*. 41: But we can guess from their works whether they practise these outward things for a particular purpose. For when under certain trials these very things begin to be taken from them, or denied them, which they have either obtained or hoped to obtain under this veil, then of necessity it will appear whether it is a case of a wolf in sheep's clothing, or a sheep in its own clothing.

GREGORY: The hypocrite is also kept hidden through the peace the Church enjoys; and so he seems to our eyes clothed in the garb of true piety. But should a trial of faith arise, at once the ravening soul of the wolf throws off its sheep's clothing; showing by persecution how great is his hatred of the good.

CHRYSOSTOM, *in Hom*: Hypocrites are easily detected: for the way they are bidden to walk is painful to them. And a hypocrite does not readily choose what is painful. And so that you may not say that it is impossible to know them He gives us proof from human experience, saying: *Do men gather grapes of thorns, or figs of thistles?*

CHRYSOSTOM, *Op. Imp*: The grape contains within it the mystery of Christ. For as the cluster has many grapes joined by the wood of the stalk, so Christ has many faithful joined by the wood of the Cross. The fig however stands for the

Church, which holds the multitude of faithful in the sweet embrace of charity, as the fig contains so many seeds within its single covering.

The fig therefore stands for: charity in its sweetness, unity in its joining of many seeds. In the grape we have a figure of patience, in that it goes through the winepress; of joy, in that wine rejoices the heart of man; of sincerity, because it is unmixed with water; and of sweetness, in that it is delectable.

The thistles and thorns are heretics. As a thistle or a thorn has prickles on every side, so the servants of the devil, on whatever side you consider them, are filled with perversity. Such thorns and thistles can never bring forth the fruits of the Church. And what He has said under the figure of the fig and the grape, of the thistle and the thorn, He shows to be true in all cases, when He says:

V. 16. *Even so every good tree bringeth forth good fruit . . .*

AUGUSTINE, *as above*, 2, 23, *par.* 79: In this place we must be on our guard against those who say that the two trees refer to the two natures; the one of God, and the other which is not of God. These must be told that the two trees are no help to them. For it is clear to any one who reads what precedes this and what follows it that here He is speaking of mankind.

AUGUSTINE, *City of God*, 12, 4–5: The very natures of things displease the kind of men we have spoken of; as they do not value them because of their true usefulness. For it is not because of our gain, or loss, that a thing gives glory to its Maker, but

out of its own nature. All natures therefore are good in that they exist, and have therefore their own form of being, their own beauty, and a sort of harmony (peace) within themselves.

CHRYSOSTOM, *Hom.* 24: That no one may say that a bad tree does in fact bring forth bad fruit, but that it also brings forth good fruit, and so in face of its two sorts of fruit it is difficult to know it, He goes on to say:

V. 18. *A good tree cannot bring forth evil fruit, neither can an evil tree bring forth good fruit.*

AUGUSTINE, *as above*, 2, 24, 79: From this saying the Manicheans assert that neither can an evil soul be changed into something better, nor a good soul into a worse; as though it had been said that: A good tree cannot become bad, and a bad tree cannot become good. But this is what was said: *A good tree cannot bring forth evil fruit,* and vice versa. The tree is the soul, that is, the man himself; its fruits are the works it brings forth. An evil man cannot therefore bring forth good works, nor a good man evil. And so if a bad man wishes to bring forth good works let him first become good. As long as a man is evil he cannot bring forth good fruit. As it may happen that what was snow is not now snow, but it cannot happen that snow should be warm; so it can happen that he who was evil is not now evil, but it cannot happen that he who is evil does good. And though at times what he does is useful, this is not due to him, but to the providence of God that makes use of him.

RHABANUS: A man is called a good tree or bad as his own will is either good or bad. His fruits are his works, which cannot be good when they come from a bad will, nor bad from a good will.

AUGUSTINE, *Against Julian*, V, 38, 41: As it is plain that all evil deeds come forth from an evil will, as evil fruit of an evil tree, so from where can you say the evil will itself arises, unless you say that it arose in man from man himself, and that the evil will of an angel comes from the angel? And what were each of these two creatures before the evil will arose in them but a good work of God, a good and praiseworthy nature? See then how out of good evil arises; nor was there any other thing out of which it could arise save good. I am speaking of the evil will itself; for there was no evil before it, no evil works, which arise only from an evil will as from an evil tree. Nor could the evil will be said to arise from good in this way, because it was made good from the good God. For it was made from nothing, not from God. [The text of the work continues: For all that can sin is made from nothing. For if it were not from nothing it would by nature be from God whatever it was. If by nature from God it would possess the nature of God, and could not sin.]

JEROME: Let us ask of these heretics, who assert that there are two opposing natures, if, as they understand it, a good tree cannot bring forth evil fruit, how was it possible for Moses, a good tree, to sin at the waters of contradiction? Or how did Peter deny the Lord in His

Passion, saying: *I know not the man?* Or how it came about that the father-in-law of Moses, an evil tree, who did not believe in the God of Israel, should give good counsel?

CHRYSOSTOM, *Hom. in Mt*: Since He had not asked them to punish the false prophets (only to beware of them), He frightens those He speaks of with the punishment that will come to them from God, saying:

V. 19. *Every tree that bringeth not forth good fruit shall be cut down, and shall be cast into the fire.*

In these words the Jews seem to be referred to, and because of this He reminds them of the words of John the Baptist, threatening them with punishment in these same words. For he had spoken in this way to them, warning them of the *axe*, and of *the tree* that shall be *cut down*, and of *unquenchable fire*. If you consider this matter carefully you will see that here there are two punishments threatened: To be cut down, and to be cast into the fire; for he who is burned is also wholly cast out of the kingdom, which is the more grievous punishment. Many only fear hell. But I believe that the loss of glory is a more bitter torment than that of hell itself. For what evil great or small will not a father endure in order to see and delight in a son who is most dear to him? Let us think in the same way of that glory; for there is no son so sweet to a father as the peaceful rest from toil to the just, and *to be dissolved and to be with Christ*. Intolerable indeed is the pain of hell. But were there ten thousand hells, such pain would be as nothing to falling from that blessed glory, and to be hated by Christ.

GLOSS: From the foregoing parable He draws the conclusion, as some-thing plainly evident, to what He had just been saying: *Therefore by their fruits you shall know them* (v. 20).

I. ST EPHRAIM, CONFESSOR AND DOCTOR

On the Various Places of Torment and on the Judgement[1]

We know from the Gospel that there are various places of torment. For it has been revealed to us that there is *exterior darkness* (Mt. viii. 12), and so it follows that there is also interior darkness (cf. Mk. v). The fire of Gehenna is another place, the abode of weeping and gnashing of teeth (Mt. xxv. 30). Another place speaks of *the worm that dieth not* (Mk. ix. 43). We read in another place of *the pool of fire* (Apoc. xix. 20), and again of *tarturus*, of *unquenchable fire* (Mk. ix. 42, 44). The lower world of *destruction* and perdition are written of in precise terms (Mt. vii. 13; I Tim. vi. 9). The depths of the earth is another place. The hell where sinners are tormented, and *the depths of hell*, a more fearful place. The wretched souls of the damned are distributed throughout these places of punishment, each one according to the nature of his sins; fearfully or less fearfully, as it is written: *Each one is fast bound by the ropes of his own sins* (Prov. v. 22); and this is what is meant by the servant who is beaten with *many* stripes or *with few stripes* (Lk. xii. 47, 48). For just as there are differences of sin so also are there differences in their punishment.

They who foment enmities among themselves, if they should happen to pass from this life in that state, shall in that same hour undergo the inexorable condemnation of this Judge (Mt. v. 18), and as hateful to God they shall be cast into exterior darkness for having held as of no importance the precept of the Lord that says: *Love one another, and forgive one another, even to seventy times seven.* Let every sinner remember that he cannot live in security in this life, or free of anxiety; yet that we are never at any time to despair. For we have an Advocate with the Father, Jesus Christ (I Jn. ii. 1), and He is the propitiation for our sins; but not of the sins of those who live lives free from all concern and anxiety, lives of sloth, of sleeping, of living for pleasure, and laughter and drunkenness, but for the sins of those who grieve for their sins, who do penance for them, calling on Him in the day and in the night. It is these who shall receive the comfort of the Advocate.

But the sinner who is oblivious of his own sins, and who departs from his body in that state, upon him shall fall that anger which threatened Manasses; who cried: *Insupportable, O Lord, is the anger of Thy threatening against those who sin* (cf. 2 Paralip. xxxiii; Jer. x. 10). Woe to the fornicator, woe to the drunkard. Woe to the foul-tongued. Woe to those who drink with song and dance, with drums, with pipe and thabor, *but the works of the Lord they regard not, nor do you consider of the*

works of his hands (Is. v. 11, 12).
Woe to those who despise the words
of Holy Writ. Woe to gamblers,[2]
as often as they shall make themselves strangers to the Body and
Blood of the Lord Jesus Christ; as
the Holy Spirit admonishes us
through the blessed Apostles (Lk.
vi; Jas. iv). Woe to those who waste
the time of repentance in dissipation
and folly; for they shall seek for this
very time of repentance that they
wasted in vain, and they shall not
find it.

Woe to those who traffic with
sorcerers, and seek to learn from the
spirit of untruth; giving their minds
to the teaching of demons: for they
shall be condemned together with
them in the world to come. Woe
to those who bring forward false
accusations. Woe to those who
look for strange things, incantations,
divinations, the blood of infants,
amulets, dyes, protective oracles
inscribed on leaves, which bring instead disaster to the body, and damnation to the soul, and all similar
things.

Woe to those that deprive the
labourer of his wage (Jas. v. 4); for
he who deprives the labourer of his
wage is as one who sheds innocent
blood. Woe to those who give
judgement unjustly. Woe, I repeat,
to those who for a bribe justify the
wrong doer, and take away the right
of the just.

Woe to those who stain the holy
faith with heresies, or who give
place to heretics. Woe to those who
are afflicted with an incurable disease; such as are envy and malice.
But to what end need I name so
many sins instead of including all in
a few words? Woe to all who in
that dread hour shall be placed at the

left-hand side: for they shall be in
darkness, they shall tremble and
they shall weep bitter tears when
they hear that most fearful sentence:
Depart from me, you cursed. And
some shall hear again that most dole-
ful sentence: *The wicked shall be
turned into hell* (Ps. ix. 18). Others
will hear the words: *Amen I say to
you, I know you not, whence you are:
depart from me, all ye workers of
iniquity* (Lk. xiii. 27). Others, the
envious, will hear the words: *Take
what is thine, and go thy way* (Mt. xx.
14). And hearing what He says, the
dread word, *go,* they ask, whither?
There where they also shall be who
shall hear the words: *Depart from me,
ye cursed, into everlasting fire* (Mt.
xxv. 41).

Others will hear the command:
*Bind his hands and feet, and cast him
into exterior darkness.* Others shall
be gathered together like chaff to be
burned *in the furnace of fire* (Mt. xiii.
42). But just as there are many ways
of salvation, so are there also many
mansions in the kingdom of heaven.
And as there are many kinds of sin,
so are there various ways and places
of torment.

Whosoever has tears and compunction of heart let him now weep
with me. For I am mindful, my
blessed brethren, of that unhappy
separation, and I cannot support the
thought of it. In that terrible hour
men shall be separated, the one from
the other, in that last and most
sorrowful of all separations, and
many shall go on their way destitute
of all hope of ever returning. Who
is there so stony of heart who will
not from this time forward weep at
the thought of that hour? That
hour when bishops shall be separated
from their fellow bishops, kings from

kings, princes from princes, priests from other priests, deacons from the other deacons, hypodeacons (sub-deacons) and readers from their companions. Then shall they be separated who once were kings, and they shall cry as children, and they shall be driven forward like slaves. Then shall princes mourn, and the rich who were without pity, and pressed in on every side they shall look here, look there, and find no-where any one to help them. Then shall they be separated, to depart like captives into sorrow; where riches will not avail them, nor flatterers stand by them, there shall not be any place for mercy, for they had refused mercy to others; nor will they have sent mercy on before them, so that they might find it when they come, as the prophet says of such people: *They have slept their sleep; and all the men of riches have found nothing in their hands* (Ps. lxxv).

Then shall children be separated from their parents, and friends from friends. There in sorrow shall husband be separated from wife, because he has not kept his marriage bed undefiled. And they too shall be separated; they who though virgin in body were yet cruel and without mercy: *For judgement without mercy to him that hath not done mercy* (Jas. ii. 13). But I shall leave out many things here: for I am held by fear and trembling from speaking of them, and so I shall conclude in a few words.

Then at last they shall be driven forth from the Tribunal and led away by fierce angels, wretched and beaten, grinding their teeth, and turning back continuously to look once more if possible upon the just, and upon that joy from which they

are now for ever cut off. And they see that ineffable Light, they glimpse the beauty of paradise, and see there amid that joy those they knew and who were once their friends. They see the great and shining gifts which they have received from the King of Glory; they who have striven *lawfully for the mastery* (II Tim. ii. 5).

Soon they are led away, separated from all the just, and from those they knew, and hidden from the sight of God Himself, so that they can no longer look upon that joy or upon that true Light. And now they draw near to those punishments we have spoken of earlier, to be divided from one another among these various places, seeing themselves abandoned on every side, destitute of all hope, of all help, and of all intercession on their behalf by others, abandoned. For the judgements of God are just. *Thou art just, O Lord; and thy judgement is right* (Ps. cxviii. 137). Then crying and weeping most bitterly they will exclaim: O why did we spend our time in neglect and indifference? O why have we deceived ourselves? O how we have mocked at ourselves, hearing the divine Scriptures and mocking them? There God spoke to us, in the holy Scriptures, and we paid no heed to Him. Now we cry out to Him and He turns away His face from us. What has the end of the world brought us? Where is the father who begot us? Where is the mother who brought us into the world? Where are our children? Where are our friends? Where now are our riches? Where are our properties and our possessions? Where now the throngs of friends? The banquets? Where are the endless senseless races? Where are the kings and lords? How is it none of them can save us; none can bring us help? We are utterly abandoned, by God and by His holy ones. What shall we do? For there is no more time to repent. Prayer and intercession no longer avail; there is no help in tears. They no longer come who sold us oil: they who appear as the poor and the destitute.[3] Every festival is over. While we had time, and had the means, and when the oil-sellers were crying out, 'come and buy', we stopped our ears and refused to listen or to purchase their oil. Now we look for it and we do not find it. There is no more redemption for us unhappy ones; no more mercy. For we were not worthy. The judgement of God is just. We shall no more look up and see the company of the Saints. We shall look no more upon that True Light. We are bereft of everything; cut off from everyone.

What is there left for us to say? Farewell! Farewell all ye just! Farewell Apostles, Prophets, Martyrs. Farewell to the company of the holy Patriarchs. Farewell to the hosts of monks. Farewell, O precious and life-giving Cross! Farewell to the kingdom of heaven which is to be without end! Farewell to the spiritual Jerusalem; the mother of the Firstborn! (Gal. iv. 26). Farewell to the joy of paradise! Farewell to You Lady Mother of God; Mother of the Lover of Mankind! Farewell fathers and mothers, sons and daughters: we shall never see you again. And after that each one will go to the place of torment that was prepared for him because of his evil works; *where their worm dieth not, and the fire is not extinguished* (Mk. ix. 43).

You have heard me, my blessed brethren. I have fulfilled your request to me for knowledge of the judgement; I have fulfilled your desire. See now if you understand for what we are preparing ourselves? You have learned what they gain who are negligent, who are slothful, who scorn repentance. And you have heard for what reason they are mocked at who here on earth mocked at the commandments of God. You have learned how the evil one deceives the many, how he leads this world, wicked and rejoicing, astray. You have learned how those who laugh at the Scriptures are themselves laughed at. Let no one be led into error, dearly beloved. Let none of you be deceived, my blessed brethren. Beware of any one saying that they are but mere words; these that we speak to you of the judgement. Rather let us all firmly and carefully believe in Christ as He preaches to us of the resurrection of the dead, of judgement, of the rewards of the good and the wicked, according to the Holy Scriptures (Jn. v. and vi; I Cor. xv).

Rather, despising all earthly things, let us with earnest care give thought to rendering an account of these same things; and let us be resolved to go in fear of that Tribunal, and that in that dread and fearful day and hour we shall be prepared. For that is an hour to grieve over, one filled with anguish, and with pressure that shall shake the whole world. Of that day and hour the holy prophets and Apostles have spoken (Job xix. 20; Is. ii. 13, 30; I Cor. iii. 55; Mt. xxiv. 25; Lk. xii. 13; Apoc. iii). And of this day the Holy Scriptures cry out from end to end of the earth, through all the churches, in every place, and gives testimony to all men, and warns all men, saying to them: Take heed, Watch, Pray, Be sober, Show mercy, Be prepared, You know not the day nor the hour in which the Lord will come. Let all men therefore, as I have already said to you, cry out with tears and with grief, proclaiming that inevitable day.

Of that day the prophet Isaias has said: *Behold the Lord shall come, to lay waste the whole earth, and to destroy the sinners thereof out of it* (Is. xiii. 9). And the same prophet says again: *Behold thy saviour cometh: behold his reward is with him, and his work before him* (Is. lxii. 11). And another prophet cries out: *Behold the Lord cometh, and who shall endure the day of his coming? And who shall stand to see him?* (Mal. iii. 2). And another prophet cries to us: *Lord, I have heard thy hearing, and was afraid, and fear has entered into my bones* (Hab. iii. 1). And yet another prophet cries to us, in the person of the Lord, and says to us: *Revenge is mine, and I will repay them in due time* (Deut. xxxii. 35). And again: *I will deal vengeance to my enemies, and repay them that hate me. And there is no one can deliver out of my hand* (vv. 41, 39).

Of this day the prophet David has also spoken. *God shall come manifestly: our God shall come, and shall not keep silence. A fire shall burn before him; and a mighty tempest shall be round about him* (Ps. xlix. 3, 4). Of this day the Apostle Paul also speaks. *In the day when God shall judge the secrets of men by Jesus Christ, according to my Gospel* (Rom. ii. 16). And again he says: *See therefore how you walk circumspectly; not as unwise*; *It is a fearful thing to fall into the hands*

of the living God (Eph. v. 15; Heb. x. 31). And Peter, the Head and Summit of the Apostles, says of that day: *The day of the Lord shall come as a thief in the night, in which the heavens shall pass away with great violence, and the elements shall be melted with heat* (II Pet. iii. 10).

And why do I speak only of the prophets and Apostles? The Sovereign Lord Himself has given testimony to it in many places, saying: *Take heed to yourselves, lest your heart be overcharged, with surfeiting and drunkenness, and the cares of this life, and that day come upon you suddenly. For as a snare shall it come upon all that sit upon the face of the whole earth* (Lk. xxi. 34, 35). *Watch ye therefore, because at what hour you know not the Son of man will come* (Mt. xxiv. 43). *Strive to enter by the narrow way that leadeth to life* (Lk. xiii. 24).

Let us walk by this way, Brethren, that we may attain to the inheritance of eternal life. For he who enters in by this way will beyond doubt be the inheritor of eternal life. For this way is life. And though few there are who find it, yet let us, dear Brethren, not be deprived of it. Let none of us walk outside this way; lest we take the road to perdition; as was said by the prophet: *Lest the Lord be angry and you perish from the just way* (Ps. ii. 12). Let us listen to the Lord speaking to us. *I am the Light. I am the Good Shepherd. I am the Life. I am the Door. By me, if any man enter in, he shall be saved. I am the Way. He that followeth me walketh not in darkness, but shall have the light of life.*

Let us therefore follow Him on this blessed way which all have walked who have loved Christ. Its entrance is linked with tribulation and with torment; but there is blessed peace there. The gates of this way are narrow and forbidding; but its reward is joy. Its entry is strait, but the place of rest within is wide and spacious. The gates of this way are fasting, prayer, compunction, vigils, humility of soul, poverty of spirit, contempt of the flesh, care of the soul, sleeping on the ground, eating of dry food, lack of comfort, harshness, hunger, thirst, nakedness, mercy, tears, grieving, poverty, groanings, genuflexions, humiliations, persecutions, revilings from others, to be hated and not to hate, to hear evil and to render good for evil, to forgive debts to our debtors, to lay down our lives for our friends. Lastly, to shed our blood for Christ when the occasion calls for it. These are the narrow gates, and the strait way; these are the steps, the approaches, which lead to a most blessed reward, the Kingdom of Heaven itself, of which there will be no end.

Wide is the gate, and broad is the way that leads to destruction; whose steps are now joyous and gay, but beyond the gates they are sad; here they are sweet, there they are more bitter than gall; here the steps are quick, there they are slow and encumbered with pain. Here they seem as nothing, there they shall surround him like wild impenitent beasts attacking; as the prophet says: *In the evil day the iniquity of my heel shall encompass me* (Ps. xlviii. 6); that is, the evil of this life, that is, the wide gate and the broad ways of which the Apostle speaks, numbering them one by one; and of which are: fornication, adultery, shamelessness, idolatry, witchcraft, enmities, contentions, emulations, wraths,

quarrels, dissensions, sects, and such like (Gal. v. 20), which are the steps of *the wide way*. And akin to these is immoderate laughter, rioting, lute playing, spectacles, piping, dances, the baths, soft clothing, sumptuous eating, flattery, uproar, prolonged sleep, soft beds, varieties of food, an insatiable desire for food, fraternal hate, and what is worse than all this, impenitence, and never to recall to mind our departure from this life. These are the steps of that dangerous way along which so many now walk.

And such as these shall come to a fitting inn. They shall find hunger in place of delights, thirst for their drunkenness, pain for their repose, mourning in place of laughter, weeping for piping, the worm for their swollen bodies, grief for their ease and sloth of mind, for their witchcrafts association with the devil, for their gaming tables they shall be given over to the company of the demons, for their incantations and divinations they will be given over to the authors of these and other evil practices, exterior darkness, the gehenna of fire and similar things, which are the wages of Death, where he feeds his sheep, his own disciples, his own friends, who have entered in by the wide and broad gate, according to the saying of the holy prophet: *They are laid in hell like sheep: death shall feed upon them* (Ps. xlviii. 15).

But we, dearest Brethren, turning aside from this perilous and troubled way, let us listen to what Christ says to us. *Strive to enter by the narrow gate; for many, I say to you, shall seek to enter, and shall not be able* (Lk. xiii. 24). Many things such as these the Lord cries out to us, and many others also who have God within them.

Remembering these things the holy martyrs of God had no compassion on their own bodies, but submitted them to every kind of torment, rejoicing in the hope of their crowns. Some strove in the deserts, in mountains, and in caves, in fasting, in virginity, and they still strive, and not only men but women also, the weaker sex, and these entering in by the narrow gate, and by the strait way, have seized the kingdom of heaven. Who then will not be shamed when in that hour women shall be crowned and many men condemned? For there will be no more male and female. But each one shall receive his due reward, according to his labours.

Nor does this happen only in the deserts and in the mountains; much more does the multitude of those who shall be saved shine out in cities and towns and islands and in the churches. Each one in his own order who observes the commands of God: bishops, priests, deacons, and the other orders of the Church, kings, princes, rulers, governors, and those who live in palaces and castles. For the Lord God said there shall be no differences, but that there is one place that is above others: *Where there are two or three gathered together in my name*; that is, in the deserts, in the mountains and in caves, or in cities, towns or islands, or in any place of My dominion, *there am I in the midst of them* (Mt. xviii. 20) and with them, unto the consummation of the world, and then in the world to come I shall pasture them for all ages.

Dwelling within himself upon that tremendous judgement, and upon that Incorruptible Judge, the great and blessed David watered his couch with tears each night, and called upon the Lord, saying to Him: *Enter not into judgement with thy servant; for in thy sight no man shall be justified* (Ps. cxlii. 2). Enter not upon a reckoning with me; do not, Most kind Lord, pass judgement on me; for I am destitute of defence. And therefore I implore Thy goodness, Lord, *enter not into judgement with thy servant.* For if you will do this, there is not a man in Thy sight will be justified.

Behold, Brethren, the holy and blessed prophet David, beseeching the Lord because of that dread day and hour, and making ready for his defence. Let you also do this, Brethren and Beloved in Christ, before *that day or hour comes*, before *the wedding feast*, before *the Lord comes openly*, and comes upon us unawares. Let us come before His face with confession, with repentance, in prayer. Let us come before His face in fasting and in tears, and in hospitality. Let us come before His face, I say, before He comes openly to us, and find us unprepared. Let us not cease to pray without ceasing, doing penance, prepared for your meeting with the Lord, all alike, women as well as men, rich and poor, bond and free, old and young. Let no one say: I have sinned in many ways and so there is no hope of pardon for me. He who says this does not know that God is the God of the repentant; Who came into this world because of those who were sick; Who has said: *There shall be joy in heaven on one sinner doing penance*; Who has said: *I am not come to call the just, but sinners to repentance* (Mt. ix. 13).

This is true repentance; to cease from sin, and to hate it, according to

His words: *I have hated and abhorred iniquity; but I have loved thy law* (Ps. cxviii. 163); and to His words, saying: *I have sworn and am determined to keep the judgements of thy justice* (cxviii. 106). It is with joy therefore that God receives whoever comes to Him. Beware also of saying: I have not sinned. For he who says this is blind, groping with his hands, seducing himself, and knows not how Satan is seducing him, in word and deed, by hearing, by touch, by sight and in thought. For who has ever been able to glory that his heart was pure, and that all his senses were free of every stain? So there is no one among men who is wholly without sin save Him alone Who because of us took Flesh from the Holy Mary, Who is really and truly the Mother of God; Who *being rich became poor, for our sakes* (II Cor. viii. 9).

He alone is free from all stain of sin *Who takes away the sins of the world*; who will have all men be saved, and come to the knowledge of the truth (I Tim. ii. 4); Who wishes not the death of the sinner; Who is sweet and mild, and plenteous in mercy (Ps. lxxxvi. 5); Who is clement, good, the lover of souls, Almighty, the Saviour of all men, the Father of orphans, and the Judge of widows, Who is the God of the repentant, the Healer of souls and bodies, the Hope of the despairing, the Deliverer of those who are tossed to and fro in the tempest, the Help in every way of the destitute, the Way of life Which leads all to repentance, and rejects no one doing penance.

Let us fly to Him, Brethren; for as often as sinners have turned to Him they have been saved. And therefore let us not despair of our salvation, Dearest Brethren. We have sinned; let us repent. We have sinned a thousand times. Let us do penance a thousand times. The Lord rejoices in every good work; especially in a soul doing penance. For upon this He is wholly intent; receiving such as these with open tender arms, and calling to them He cries: Come to me, all ye that labour and are burdened, and I will refresh you, in the Heavenly City, where all My angels are refreshed with great joy. Come to me, all of you, to that ineffable and unending joy, to these delights *on which the angels desire to look* (I Pet. i. 2), and where are gathered the choirs, the hosts, of the blessed.

There they shall be received into the bosom of Abraham who here have borne tribulations, as the poor Lazarus was once received. There the treasury of My graces shall stand for ever open; there, in *that Jerusalem which is above; the mother of the firstborn* (Gal. iv. 26). There is the blessed land of the meek. Come to me, all of you, and I will refresh you. There where all things are at rest, and there is no discord, and all things are revealed. Where there is no tyrant, no oppressor, no sin, *no spot or blemish*, where there is *light inaccessible*, and joy that cannot be told.

Blessed are they that mourn. Mourn, do penance, be converted, and come to Me and I will refresh you; where there are waters of refreshment and a place of green grass, and wine that is prepared by the Lord of all things; to that blessed land of the meek, in which *I the True Vine, and my Father is the husbandman*, as you know (Jn. xv. 1).

Come to Me all you that labour and are burdened, and I will refresh you; where there is immortal life and the fount of every mercy. Come to me, all of you, and I will refresh you; where there is love alone, perennial joy, and everlasting happiness, where the light does not fade, nor the sun go down. Come to me, all you that labour and are burdened, and I will refresh you; where there is perfect life, and the fount of every good. Take My yoke upon you, and learn of Me, because I am meek and humble of heart, and you shall find rest for your souls; where there is ever the sound of festival days, and where the hidden treasures of wisdom and knowledge shall be revealed.

Come to Me, all of you, and I will refresh you; where there are wondrous gifts, and joy without compare, rest unchanging, happiness without end, unceasing melody, perpetual glory, unwearied giving of thanks, loving absorption in divine things, infinite riches, a kingdom without end, through all ages and ages, deeps of compassion, an ocean of mercy and kindness, which the human tongue cannot describe, but makes known only through figures. There shall be the myriads of the Angels, the multitudes of the First-born, the Thrones of the Apostles, the dignities of the prophets, the sceptre of the Patriarchs, the crowns of the Martyrs, the praises of the Just. And there is laid up the reward of every order, of every Power and Principality.

Come to Me all you that hunger and thirst after justice, and I will fill you with all that you desire, and which the eye has not seen, nor the ear heard, nor has it entered into the heart of man to conceive. These things have I prepared for those who love Me. These things I have prepared for those who have done penance for their wayward life. I have prepared them for the merciful; for the poor in spirit; for those who mourn in repentance. I have prepared them for the peacemakers. I have prepared them for those who suffer persecution, hate, reproaches, for My Name's sake.

Come to Me all you that labour; and shake off and cast from you the burden of your sins. For no one who comes to Me remains burdened, but casts off his evil way of life, and unlearns the conduct he had evilly learned from the devil, and learns of Me a new way of life. Those that deal in witchcraft, coming to Me they cast away their abject arts and learn the secrets of God in the knowledge of Him. The public farmers of taxes leaving their customs booths build churches. Persecutors ceasing from persecuting others suffer persecution themselves. Harlots ceasing from fornication have become lovers of continence and modesty. The Thief, putting an end to killing, putting away his life of robbery, received a true faith and became a dweller in paradise.

Come therefore to Me; for he who comes to Me I shall not cast forth. You have heard, Dearest Brethren, the perfect hope, the sweet promises, the words of the Saviour of our souls. Who has ever seen so kind a Father to His children? Who has seen so good a Physician? Come, therefore, let us adore and fall down before Him (Ps. xciv. 6), and let us confess our sins. Glory to His goodness! Glory to His loving kindness! Glory to His longanimity!

Glory to His care for us, to His tenderness! Glory to His words of pity! Glory to His Kingdom! Glory, honour, adoration to His Holy Name for ever and ever!

Again I say to you: I shall not cease from saying it: Let us not lie slothful in our sins lest we perish in our sloth. Let us not delay. Let us

not cease from crying out with tears to the Lord, in the day and in the night. For He is merciful, and *lieth not* (Tit. i. 2); the Defender of those that call upon him by day and by night. For He is the God of those who repent: to the Father, Son, and Holy Ghost be glory and honour throughout all ages. Amen.

II. ST JOHN CHRYSOSTOM, BISHOP AND DOCTOR

The Fountain of Alms[4]

And an angel of God coming unto Cornelius, said to him: Thy prayers and thy alms are ascended for a memorial in the sight of God (Acts x. 4).

Nothing equals the merit of almsgiving. It was said of Cornelius the centurion that *he was a just man*, and feared God with all his house, giving much alms to the people, and praying always to God. And his almsgiving opened for him the gates of heaven. So much was done, as the Scripture tells us, to bring Cornelius to believe, so that even an angel is sent to him, and the grace of the Spirit worked in him, and the chief of the Apostles is called to him, and he received a wondrous vision; for him nothing was left undone. How many other centurions were there, and rulers and kings, and none of them received what this man received. Hear all you who are in command; all you who stand close to kings. *A religious man*, Scripture says, *and fearing God*, and what is more, *with all his house*. So intent was he on this end that not alone did he order his own life justly, but saw to it that his household did the same. Not doing as we do: seeking that those subject to us fear us, not that they may be just. This man

feared God together with all his house.

Nothing equals the merit of almsgiving. Great is the power of this action, when it flows forth from untarnished sources. But when it comes from sources that are defiled, it is as if a fountain were to send forth mud. But when alms are given from our just gains, it is as if they flowed forth from a pure and limpid stream, one flowing from paradise, pleasant to the eye, pleasant to the touch; something cool and light given in the noonday heat. Such are alms. Beside this fountain grow, not poplars nor pines nor cypresses, but trees more rare and precious: the love of God, the praise of men, glory before God, the good will of all men, the wiping away of sins, great confidence in God, small esteem for riches.

By this fountain the tree of love is nourished; for nothing so nourishes love as to be compassionate towards others. It lifts its branches on high. More beautiful this than the fount of paradise; not divided into four streams, but *springing up into life everlasting* (Jn. iv. 14). Let Death light on this, and like a spark the fountain extinguishes it; for wherever it flows, such as these are its blessings. It extinguishes as though it were a spark a river of flame. This smothers *the worm* as though it were nothing (Mk. ix. 45). He that has this fountain of water shall not grind his teeth. For should a drop of this water fall upon chains it dissolves them; should it be poured upon furnaces, it extinguishes all of them.

As the fountain of paradise does not now give forth streams, now run dry—otherwise it would not be a fountain—but is ever springing up, so let our fountain give forth ever more generously of the stream of its alms, especially to those who stand in need, that it may remain a fountain. This makes cheerful the one who receives. This is almsgiving: to give forth, and not alone in a vigorous stream, but in an ever flowing stream. If you desire that God should rain upon you from as it were the fountains of His mercy, let you also have a fountain. Yet there is no comparison between the one and the other. If you open the gates of this fountain, such will be the gates of God's fountain that it overwhelms the deep. God but seeks from us an occasion, to pour forth blessings from His stores. When He spends, when He bestows, then He is rich, then He abounds. Great the mouth of this fountain; pure and limpid its stream. If you do not stop up this stream, neither will He prevent it from flowing.

Let no unfruitful tree stand by this fountain, to waste its moisture. Have you wealth? Then do not plant there the black poplar; for that is but luxury, conceit as it were. It consumes much and shows no return in itself, and spoils fruit. Neither let you plant the fir tree, nor the pine, nor any of these kinds, which consume moisture but bear no fruit: for such is the delight of rich clothing, beautiful to see, but profitable in nothing. Plant it around with young shoots of trees that bear fruit. Plant what you will, in the hands of the poor. There is no earth more fruitful than this. And though narrow the breadth of a hand, yet the tree planted there will rise to heaven itself; and stand firm. This is truly to plant. For what is planted on the earth will fade away, if not now then a hundred years from now. Why plant trees you will not enjoy? for before you can enjoy them death comes between, and snatches you away. But this tree, when you have gone from here, then will you eat its fruits.

If you plant a tree do not plant it in the stomach of a glutton, lest its fruit go down in waste. Plant it in a stomach that is narrowed with hunger, so that the fruit of it may ascend to heaven. Refresh the narrowed soul of the poor, lest your own generous heart grow straitened. Have you not seen how a tree that is watered too much begins to rot at the root; but grows well when watered in due measure? So you also; take care lest you water your own stomach above measure, so that it decays at the root. Give your drink to a thirsty man; that it may bear fruit. Trees that are watered with due measure the sun will not injure; but it withers those that are watered too much. Such is the nature of the sun. Excess anywhere is bad. So let us make an end of it: that we obtain what we long for.

It is said that fountains spring up in the highest places. Let us then be elevated of soul, and our alms shall flow forth quickly. A soul that is elevated cannot but be merciful, and one that is merciful not sublime. He therefore who rises above the love of money lifts himself above the root of evil. Springs are most often found in solitary places. Let us be retiring in our souls, and alms will spring up in us. And fountains, the more frequently they are made clean, the more abundantly they flow. So let it be with us; the more we give, the more our blessings will spring up. He who has a spring need not fear. And we who have within us a spring of almsgiving have nothing to fear.

For this spring is good to drink from; good for irrigating; for the needs of the house; it is useful for many things. There is nothing better to drink; it will not lead to insobriety. To possess such a spring is better than a fountain of gold. For richer than all gold-bearing land is the soul that yields this gold. It does not bring us into contact with the highest earthly orders of people; but it brings us to those above. Gold such as this is an adornment of the Church of God. From this gold is wrought the sword of the Spirit (Eph. vi. 7); the sword by which the dragon is slain. From such a spring as this come the stones that adorn the King's head.

Let us not neglect these riches; let us give alms generously, that we may be worthy of the love of God, by the grace and the mercies of His Son, to Whom together with the Father and the Holy Ghost be all praise, honour, and empire, throughout all ages. Amen.

III. St John Chrysostom, Bishop and Doctor

The Judgement Day[5]

For we must all be manifested before the judgement seat of Christ (II Cor. v. 10).

Let us listen to the voice of Paul telling us: *We must all stand before the judgement seat of Christ* (Rom. xiv. 10). And let us place before our mind a picture of that Tribunal, and let us think of ourselves as already present before it, and of the account of our lives that is to be demanded of us. I shall expound this more fully; for Paul, because he was here speaking of affliction, did not dwell long on the subject, as he did not wish to stress it too much, but having in a few words said that each shall receive according to his deeds, he passes on without delay.

Let us then imagine to ourselves that that day has now come; and let each one consider his own conscience, and imagine himself in the Presence of the Judge, and that all things are to be revealed and brought against us. For we are not alone to stand there, but we must also be revealed before all. Do you not burn with shame? Are you not in dread?

Description of the Last Judgement. But if it is not yet here in fact, but only supposed and pictured in our mind, and already our conscience almost faints, what shall we do when that day has really come, when the world shall be gathered together, when the angels and the archangels are present, and the thronging hosts, and there is a pressing together of all men, caught up in the clouds, and the host of all are arrayed and trembling? When the trumpets, one upon the other, speak in unceasing voices? And even if there were no hell, to be rejected before all that splendour, and to have to depart in shame and infamy, how dreadful a punishment? For even here, when the Emperor enters the city with his train, each one of us seeing his own poverty and insignificance, we feel dejection rather than pleasure at the scene, at having no share in all the glory about him, through not being near him. What will it be like then? Or do you think it a light punishment to have no place in that company, not to be admitted to a share in that mysterious glory, to be cast out far from that assembly of the Blessed, from those joys which no words of man can describe?

But when to this there is added darkness, and gnashing of teeth, and bonds that can never be untied, and the worm that dieth not, and inextinguishable fire, and torments, and being pressed in and shut away, and tongues that are for ever parched, like that of Dives, and when we lament there shall be no one to hear us, and when we weep and groan in our pain there will be no one to care, and when we turn our eyes in every direction there will be no one to comfort us: where shall we be among those thus held fast in this dreadful affliction?

Who more miserable than such souls? Who more to be pitied? For should we enter some prison, and see its inmates, some in squalor, some in chains, and suffering hunger, are we not moved to compassion, and filled with horror, and we resolve to do all we can so that we may never be thrown into such a place? How will it be then when we are led away to the torment chambers of hell? For there the bonds are not made of iron, but of fire that is never extinguished. Nor are those our fellow men who are placed over us to torment us, whom at times we may soften towards us, but angels whom you cannot ever look in the face, because of their anger at our past insults against their Master. Nor shall we as in this life ever see those who bring us money, or others who bring food, others words of comfort, or some consolation. But here all is without pardon; and though it might be Noah, or even Job, or Daniel (Ezech. xiv. 15) and he sees his own near ones tormented, he dare not aid them. For there all that compassion that arose from nature is extinguished. For as it can happen that there are good fathers and evil children, and contrarily, just children and evil parents, so that their joy may be pure, and free from the shadow of every sorrow, and so that those who earned the blessings of heaven may not be tormented by the urgency of pity, this very pity, I say, is extinguished, and they are enraged together with their Lord, on fire with wrath against their own blood. For if ordinary men, when they see their children worthless and bad, cut them off from themselves, and exclude them from the family, how much more will not the just do the same?

Therefore let no one hope for blessing if he has not wrought blessing, even though he has come from an endless line of just men: *Everyone shall receive the proper things of the body, according as he hath done, whether it be good or evil.* And here it seems to me that he is alluding to fornicators, and trying to pierce them with the fear of the chastisements to come, and not these alone, but all who are bound with any bond of evil doing.

Let us then also pay heed; and should you burn with the fire of passion, set against it this fire, and it will speedily be extinguished and leave you. And if you are about to give utterance to something that is injurious, think of the gnashing of teeth, and the fear of it will be a bridle to your tongue. And if you are designing to plunder another, hearken to the Voice of your heavenly Judge, commanding and saying: *Bind his hands and feet, and cast him into the exterior darkness* (Mt. xxii. 13), and you will do what will also cast out from you this evil design. If you are given to drunkenness, and cannot restrain yourself from it, hearken to what that rich man is saying: *Send Lazarus that he may dip the tip of his finger in water to cool my tongue; for I am tormented in this flame* (Lk. xvi. 24), and yet he does not get even this, and so you will hold yourself from this evil also. If you delight in delicacies and luxury, think of the torments there, and the straitness, and you will then not think so much of luxury. If you are harsh and cruel, recall to mind those virgins who, when their lamps had gone out, were not admitted to the bridal chamber, and then you will speedily put on a little humanity.

But if you pass your life in sloth and laziness? Then think of what happened to the *unprofitable servant* who hid his one talent, and you will

be more eager than fire itself (Mt. xxv. 30). It may be that the desire of your neighbours' possessions burns within you? Keep before your mind the worm that dieth not, and soon you will put away this disease; and you will fulfil besides all the other commandments of God: for He has laid nothing on us that is hard or impossible. Why does what He has laid on us seem so difficult to us? It is because of our own sluggishness. For just as when we labour with zeal, even what appears to be difficult will become light, so also if we labour with sloth, even what is tolerable seems hard.

Meditating upon all these things, let us not give our minds to delights, but to what is the end of delights. Here on earth it is excrement and obesity; hereafter it is fire and the worm. Think not of robberies and robbers, but of their end: here fear and cares and anxieties, there bonds that will never be undone. Nor of the lovers of glory and honours, but of what comes of it: here slavery and pretending, there unendurable loss and the perpetual torment of fire.

For if we speak in this way within our own souls, and through these reflections and meditations draw our minds away from evil thoughts and desires, soon we shall cast out from us the love of present things and kindle within us the love of things to come. Let us kindle this love within us, and let us make it blaze. For if the thought of them, though faint, can bring us such happiness, think, I beg of you, of the joy their unclouded possession will bring us.

Blessed and thrice blessed, and again thrice blessed, are they to whom it is given to enjoy those blessings; as they are wretched, and thrice wretched, who suffer the opposite evils. That we may not belong to the number of these, but to the first, let us give ourselves to the gaining of virtue, and through

this we shall come to those future joys, through the grace and loving kindness of our Lord Jesus Christ, to Whom with the Father and the Holy Ghost, be glory and empire, now and for ever. Amen.

IV. St John Chrysostom, Bishop and Doctor

Mutual Need[6]

He that had much, had nothing over; and he that had little, had no want (II Cor. viii. 15).

This happened with regard to the manna in the desert (Exod. xvi. 18). For they who gathered more, and they who gathered less, were found to have the same quantity: God by this means punishing their insatiable greed. And Paul says this, both that he may frighten the Corinthians, because of recent doings, and at the same time exhorting them that they must never allow themselves to be held fast by the desire to possess more, nor be grieved because of having less. It is a thing we see happening in our daily human circumstances; and not only with regard to the manna. For since we all have but one stomach to fill; since we all complete but one life, and clothe but one body, this abundance, this excess, will bring nothing more to the rich in his affluence, nor less to the poor in his poverty.

Why then should you fear poverty; why hunger after wealth? You will answer: I fear lest I should ever be forced to come to another man's door to ask for help. And I hear many making this same prayer, and saying: May I never come to this, that I shall stand in need of the help of men. And hearing men talk like this I laugh; for this is a childish fear. For there is no day, and, I

may also add, there is no thing in which some do not stand in need of the help of others. So words of this sort are the words of an unreflecting mind, of a mind swollen with arrogance, and not aware of the reality of things. Can you not see that we are all in need of each other? The soldier has need of the citizen, and the craftsman of the one who sells. The merchant has need of the farmer, the slave of the free, the master of the servant, the poor of the rich, the rich of the poor, he that has no work of the one who can give him alms, and he who gives alms of the one who receives them. For he who receives alms supplies something that is necessary, one of the greatest of our needs. For were there no needy, our salvation would in great part be undone, in that we would have no place where we might sow our wealth. From this it happens that the poor man, who appears to be the least useful, is in fact the most useful of all men.

But if it is a shameful thing to be in need of another's help, there is nothing for us but to die: for he cannot live who is afraid of this. But, you will say, I could not endure the superciliousness of others. And how can you accuse others of arrogance; denouncing yourself with the accusation? For to be unable to put up with someone else's arrogance, what is that but arrogance? And why are you afraid of things that are not worthy of notice? Why do you tremble at such things? Is it because of this you fear poverty? For if it happens that you are rich, you are more in need of others than are the poor and humble. For the more you come to possess, the more do you subject yourself to this prayer.

So you do not know what you are praying for when you pray for wealth, so that you shall never be in need of any man's help. This is just as if you should go to sea, where we have need of a ship, of sailors, and of endless equipment, and at the same time pray that we shall need none of them. For if you want to have absolutely no need of anyone, then pray for poverty; for then, if you do need anything, it will only be for food or for clothing. But if you are rich you will then have need of others, of lands, of houses, of expenditure, of personal dignity, of safeguard, of honour, of those who rule. And not alone of these latter but of all who serve them, or are subject to them, of those in the city, and those in the country, of those who buy, and of those who sell.

You see then that these are words of extreme foolishness. For if you think it is a dreadful thing to be in need of others, know that it is impossible not to be. If you desire to escape from the crowd, you may do this by fleeing to the untroubled harbour of poverty. Then, cut off from the multiple disquiet of affairs, do not think it a disgrace to be dependent on others: for this has been brought about by God's unspeakable wisdom. For if some of us have need of others, does not the necessity of our need draw us one to another?

If we were all self-sufficient, would we not be like the wild beasts? And so, by force and necessity, God makes us subject one to the other; and nevertheless each day we are in conflict with one another. And should this one curb be taken from us, who is there would be anxious for the friendship of his neighbour?

Let us then never think that this mutual need is a shameful thing, nor pray against it, nor say: Grant us to stand in need of no man's help. Rather, let us pray: Suffer us not when in need to refuse the help of those who can help us. For it is not the being in need of others that is a grave thing; it is the taking of what belongs to another. And till now we have never prayed for this; we have never said: Grant to me never to covet the goods of others. But to be in need: this seems something to be wholly shunned. Paul stood in need many times, and he was not ashamed of it, but regarded it as an adornment, and praises those who helped him, saying: *For once and twice you sent for my use* (Phil. iv. 16); and again: *I have taken from other churches, receiving wages of them for your ministry* (II Cor. xi. 8).

It is not therefore the mark of a noble free spirit, but rather of a weak and foolish soul, to be ashamed of this need we have of one another. For so has it pleased God to have others help us. Do not then push your philosophy beyond due measure. But again you will say: I cannot endure that man, of whom I have begged often; yet he never grants what I ask him for. And how will God bear you, by Whom you are often begged, and you never grant Him what He asks you for; asking too in things that concern your own salvation? *For Christ therefore*, it is said, *we are ambassadors, God as it were exhorting by us. For Christ, we beseech you, be reconciled to God* (II Cor. v. 20). Nevertheless I am His servant, you will say. What of that? For when you the servant are drunk with wine, while He the Master suffers hunger, and has not even the food His body needs, what meaning has the name of servant for you? And it will trouble you the more that you live in a three-storied house, while He is without shelter; that you lie on a soft bed, while He has no place whereon to lay His head.

But I *have* given, you say. Then you must not cease from doing this. For then only will you be excused from giving when you have no longer the wherewithal to give, and you yourself want for everything. But as long as you have anything, even though you have given a hundred times, and as long as there is still one who hungers, there is no excuse for you. But when you lock up your grain, and raise the price of it, and take a hand in the other evil practices of trading, what hope of salvation can you have? You have been commanded to give freely of your food to those who hunger. But some of you do not give it even at a just price. Christ emptied Himself of His glory, for your sake. But you do not think Him deserving of a little bread. While your dog is packed with food, Christ is weak with hunger. While your servant is surfeited with abundance, your Lord and his Lord goes without the food He needs. Are these the deeds of a friend? *Be reconciled to God.* For these are rather the actions of His enemies, of those

who are against Him. We should be ashamed of ourselves, because of all the benefits we have received from Him, and are yet to receive. And should a poor man come to us, and beg us for assistance, let us receive him with kindness of soul, comforting him and uplifting him with our words, that we in turn may receive the same from both God and man.

The Rule of Conduct regarding our Neighbour: For *all things therefore whatsoever you would that men should do to you, do you also to them.* This law contains nothing that is heavy, nothing tedious. What you would have done to you, it says, this let you do. Let the giving be mutual. The law does not say: *what you would not that men should do to* you; let you not do this! It says more. For this latter phrase would mean only to abstain from evil doing. But Christ's law is that we also do good; and in this the other law is contained.

Nor does the Lord say: Let you also wish them; but, *do you to them.* And what is the gain? *For this is the law of the prophets.* Do you wish that others should show mercy to you? Let you show mercy to them. Do you wish to be forgiven? Then let you also forgive. Do you wish to hear no evil spoken of you? Then do not speak evil of others. Do you wish to secure the approval and praise of others? Then bestow it yourself. Do you desire that no man shall rob you? Then rob no man. You see how He makes clear to us that virtue is a kind of natural good, and that we have little need of outward laws or teachers? For in that which we desire to receive or not to receive from our neighbour we impose a law upon ourselves. So if you do to another what you would not have done to yourself; or if you would have something done for you, but which you would not do for another, you are condemning yourself by your own standard, and you cannot be excused on the grounds that you did not know what you ought to have done.

Let us then, I beg of you, give serious thought to this, that we who lay down this law within our own minds, reading it so clearly and distinctly written within us, must always be to our neighbours as we would have them be to us, so that we may live in peace in this life, and may attain to the blessings of the life to come, through the grace and loving mercy of our Lord Jesus Christ to Whom with the Father and the Holy Ghost be there glory, honour and empire now and for ever world without end. Amen.

NOTES

[1] Vossio S. Eph., Tome I, Sermo 72.

[2] The Sixth Ecumenical Council (Constantinople III) decreed privation of Holy Communion against gamblers and drunkards. It also received the Apostolic Canons (No. 8) which quotes St Ephraim's words. Of gamblers St Basil says, in his Hexameron 8, 8, to his listeners: 'If', he says, 'I let you go, and bring our assembly to an end, there are those here who will run to the gambling table and to the dice, and there they will find cursing and fierce quarrelling and the beginnings of avarice. The spirit of evil will be there, inflaming the folly and madness of the players with the dotted bones. He turns over the same money, now to one, now to another. Now he gives victory to one man, and throws the loser into despair. Now he elates one, and depresses another. What use, I ask you, is it to fast in the body, while you give your soul over to every vice?'

[3] The Fathers speak everywhere of the poor as *olive trees*; i.e. as the source of spiritual wealth accruing to us permanently from almsgiving. Mercy and helping the poor and the afflicted are the supreme Christian good works.

[4] PG 60, col. 175, from Homily 22 in Acts x.

[5] PG 61, col. 471, Hom. 10 on II Cor. v. 10.

[6] PG 61, col. 520, Hom. 17 on II Cor. viii. 15.

EIGHTH SUNDAY AFTER PENTECOST

I. St Basil the Great: I Will Pull Down my Barns

II. St Gaudentius: The Unjust Steward

THE GOSPEL OF THE SUNDAY

Luke xvi. 1–9

At that time: Jesus spoke to his disciples the following parable. There was a certain rich man who had a steward: and the same was accused unto him, that he had wasted his goods. And he called him, and said to him: How is it that I hear this of thee? Give an account of thy stewardship: for now thou canst be a steward no longer. And the steward said within himself: What shall I do, because my lord taketh away from me the stewardship? To dig I am not able; to beg I am ashamed.

I know what I will do, that when I shall be removed from the stewardship, they may receive me into their houses. Therefore, calling together every one of his lord's debtors, he said to the first: How much dost thou owe my lord? But he said: An hundred barrels of oil. And he said to him: take thy bill and sit down quickly, and write fifty. Then he said to another: And how much dost thou owe? Who said: An hundred quarters of wheat. He said to him: Take thy bill, and write eighty. And the Lord commended the unjust steward, forasmuch as he had done wisely: for the children of this world are more prudent in their generation than the children of light. And I say to you: Make unto you friends of the mammon of iniquity; that when you shall fail, they may receive you into everlasting blessings.

Exposition from the Catena Aurea

V. 1. *There was a certain rich man who had a steward.*

BEDE: When He had in the course of three parables rebuked those who murmured because He received sinners, the Lord spoke a fourth parable, and a fifth: on the giving of alms, and on frugality; for it is in most fitting order that after He had preached on repentance (the Prodigal Son) He should preach on almsgiving. Hence we read: *And he said unto his disciples* etc.

CHRYSOSTOM (*Hom. of St Asterius*): There is a certain erroneous opinion inborn in mortal men that increases

320

evil doing and lessens good. It is the belief that whatever comes into our possession in this life we possess it as masters of it; and so when the chance arises we seize these things as ours by special right. The contrary is true. For we are not placed in this life as lords in our own houses, but as guests and strangers, brought hither whether we would or not, and at a time not of our choosing. He who is now rich in a moment is a beggar. Therefore, whoever you may be, know that you are but an administrator (*dispensator*) of things that are Another's, and that upon you has been bestowed but the right of their brief and passing use. Cast then from your soul the pride of dominion, and put on instead the modesty and humility of a steward. (Cf. PG 40, col. 179.)

BEDE: The steward is the manager of a farm (*villa*) and receives his title from the farm (*villicus*). An administrator (*dispensator*) however is the dispenser of the fruits of the property, of the money, and of all the master owns (Lk. xii. 32).

AMBROSE: From this we learn that we are not ourselves masters, but rather the stewards of Another's possessions.

THEOPHYLACTUS: And that when we do not administer wealth in accord with the will of the master, but abuse for our own pleasures what has been entrusted to us, we are unjust stewards. Hence: *And the same was accused unto him* etc.

CHRYSOSTOM, *as above*: Meanwhile he is removed from his stewardship. For we then read that:

V. 2. *And he called him and said to him etc.*

Daily the Lord cries out to us similar things, through the events of our life: showing us a man in the full possession of health at noon, and before evening he is lifeless; another dying at his evening meal, and so in various ways are we relieved of our stewardship. But a faithful dispenser, who is untroubled in his mind regarding his stewardship, desires with Paul rather *to be dissolved and to be with Christ* (Phil. i. 23). He however whose desires are earthly ones is troubled at the thought of his going forth. And so we read:

V. 3. *And the steward said within himself: What shall I do . . .*

To be feeble in action is the consequence of a life of sloth. Had he been accustomed to labour he would not now be fearful. But, if we take the parable allegorically, there is no time for labour after we have departed this life. The present life is the time for doing what was laid upon us to do; the future is our time of reward. If you have not laboured here, in vain do you make provision for the future; nor will it help you to beg. We have an example of this in the foolish virgins, who unwisely begged of the wise virgins, but came back without anything. Each one has put on his own manner of life as an inner garment; and it is not to be put off, or to be changed with another. The unjust steward however arranged for the cancelling of debts, contriving with his fellow servants a way out of the consequences of his own evil deeds. For we read:

V. 4. *I know what I will do, that when I shall be removed etc. . . .*

For as often as a man, seeing his own end approaching, lightens the burden of his own sins by some kind act to others, either by remitting the debts of a debtor, or by giving in abundance to the poor, bestowing the things of his master, he is making friends for himself of many who will give testimony of truth on his behalf before the judge, and not with words simply, but by making known his good deeds; and what is more, they will secure for him by their testimony an abode where he may find rest. But nothing is ours; all things are but part of the riches of God. Hence there follows:

V. 5. *Therefore calling together every one of his lord's debtors . . .*

BEDE: A barrel (*cadus*) in Greek is a measure containing three urns (an *urna* equals two gallons).

V. 6. *But he said: An hundred barrels of oil. And he said to him: Take thy bill . . . and write fifty;* that is, wiping out half the debt.

V. 7. *Then he said to another: And how much dost thou owe?*

A quarter (*corus*) contains thirty bushels. *Who said: An hundred quarters of wheat. He said . . . take thy bill and write eighty;* wiping out a fifth of the debt. It may be simply taken in this sense. Whoever relieves a poor man's need, either by supplying the half of it, or a fifth part of it, will be blessed with the rewards of mercy.

AUGUSTINE, *Questions on the Gospels* II, 34: That he told the debtor of the hundred barrels of oil to write down fifty, and of the hundred quarters of wheat to write eighty instead means, I believe, that what each Jew gave to the Priests and Levites should be given more abundantly in the Church of Christ: that where they gave a tenth, let these latter give the half, as Zacheus did of his goods; or at least, double the tenth, let them give a fifth so that they shall abound more in their giving than the Jews.

V. 8. *And the Lord commended the unjust steward . . .*

AUGUSTINE, *as above*: The steward whom the master deprived of his stewardship the Lord here praises, in that he made provision for himself for the future. So it is that the Lord commended him, *forasmuch as he had done wisely*. Nevertheless we are not to imitate him in all he did. For we should never practise any deceit against the Lord that from this deception we may give alms.

ORIGEN (*or* GEOMETER, *in Catena GP*): Although the Gentiles say that prudence is a virtue, and define it as, *the practical understanding of what is good, bad, or indifferent, the discernment of what we ought do and ought not do*, we should consider whether this description has one meaning or many. For we are told that the Lord *established the heavens by prudence* (Prov. iii. 19). And it is evident that because the Lord established the heavens by it that prudence is good. But we are also told in Genesis (iii. 1), according to the Septuagint, that the serpent was *the most subtle of all the beasts of the earth* (*serpens prudentissimus erat*), where prudence is not spoken of as a virtue but as craftiness, inclining its possessor towards evil. And so He perhaps used the word *commended*, not in the true sense of commendation, but used it in a lower sense; as when we say someone is to be commended in trivial and indifferent matters, or as a clash of wits or sharpness of understanding meets with approval because of the mental vigour displayed.

AUGUSTINE, *as above*: On the other hand these similitudes are recounted that we may understand that if he could be praised by the Lord who has acted deceitfully, how much more will they please the Lord who fulfil the good works He has commanded.

ORIGEN (*or* GEOMETER, *as above*): The children of this world also are not called wiser, but more prudent (Vulgate: *prudentiores*) than the children of light; and this not absolutely and simply, but, *in their generation*. For there follows: *For the children of this world are more prudent in their generation* etc.

BEDE: They are called *children of light*, and *children of this world* who are also called *the children of the kingdom*, and *the children of perdition* (Jn. xvii. 2). For the works a man does, of these he is known as their son.

THEOPHYLACTUS: By *the children of this world* he means those who give their minds to the pleasant things of this world. *The children of light* are those who out of divine love deal in spiritual riches. And in human affairs we find that we act in all things with prudence, and take great pains, so that when we withdraw

from active life we shall have a secure refuge. But in the management of divine things we do not look ahead and consider what may happen to us in the future life.

GREGORY, *Morals* xviii. 11, *in Job* xxvii. 19: That they may find something in their hand after death, before death let men place their riches in the hands of the poor. Accordingly we read:

V. 9. *And I say to you: Make unto you friends of the mammon of iniquity.*

AUGUSTINE, *Serm.* 35: What the Hebrews called *Mammon* we call riches. Therefore it is as if he said: *Make unto you friends of the riches of iniquity.* Now some persons, misunderstanding these words, seize what belongs to others and by this means give alms to the poor, and think that in doing this they do what is commanded. This notion must be corrected. Give alms out of your own just labours. For you shall not corrupt Christ your Judge. If from the plunder of a poor man you were to give anything to a judge, that he might give sentence in your favour, and if the judge were to do this, such is the force of justice, that you would be dissatisfied with yourself. Do not make a God for yourself after this fashion. For He is the Fountain of justice. Do not then give alms from the fruits of usury and interest. I am speaking to Christians to whom we give the Body of Christ. And if you have such money it is through evil doing you possess it. Let you no longer do evil. Zacheus said: *The half of my goods I give to feed the poor* (Lk. xix. 18). See how he runs to make friends by means of the mammon of iniquity. And lest he should be held wicked on other grounds he says: *And if I have wronged any man of any thing, I restore him fourfold.*

There is another interpretation also. The *mammon of iniquity* are all the riches of the world wherever they come from. For if you seek for true riches, they are those in which Job though naked abounded, when his heart was full towards God. For these others are called the riches of iniquity, because they are not true riches: for they are full of poverty, and ever liable to the risk of loss. For if they were true riches they would bring you security.

AUGUSTINE, *Questions on the Gospels* II, 34: Or they are called the riches of iniquity because they are riches only to the iniquitous, and to those who place their hopes in them, and the fulness of their happiness. But when they are possessed by the just they constitute a sum of money; but to those for whom riches are solely spiritual and heavenly they are not riches.

AMBROSE: Or, He said *the mammon of iniquity* because avarice corrupts our dispositions by the various entice-ments riches offer, so that we are willing to serve riches.

BASIL, *on Avarice*: Or should you inherit a patrimony you receive what has been amassed by unjust persons: for among many predeces-sors it must be that one will be found who has unjustly taken what was another's. But let us suppose your father has not taken anything unjustly; nevertheless whence do you receive the money? If you say,

'from myself', you are ignorant of God: not recognizing your Creator. If you say, 'from God', tell us for what reason you received it? Is not *the earth the Lord's and the fulness thereof* (Ps. xxiii. 1)? If then what is ours belongs to our common Lord, it will also belong to our fellow servants.

THEOPHYLACTUS: These therefore are called the riches of iniquity which the Lord has given to meet the needs of our brethren and fellow servants; but we hold them fast to ourselves. It became us that from the beginning we give all things to the poor. And though, through be-coming unjust stewards, we have held on unjustly to what was given to us to help others, we ought not continue in this cruelty, but should give to the poor, that they may receive us into everlasting dwellings. For there follows: *That when you shall fail they may receive you into everlasting dwellings.*

GREGORY, *Morals*, 21, 24: But if we through their good will obtain ever-lasting dwellings, we ought to con-sider that in giving we are making offerings to patrons, rather than bestowing gifts on the needy.

AUGUSTINE, *Sermo* 35: For who are they who shall possess everlasting dwellings but the saints of God? And who are they who shall be received by them into everlasting dwellings if not they who minister to their want; giving cheerfully whatever it is they stand in need of? They are the least of Christ's brethren, who have left all things, and have fol-lowed Him, and have distributed what they had among the poor, so that they may serve God without earthly ties, and lift once more as wings the shoulders now free of this world's burdens.

AUGUSTINE, *Questions on the Gospels* II, 34: We are not to regard as debtors of God those by whom we wish to be received into eternal tabernacles. For in this place the just and holy are signified, who bring those in there who shared with them their earthly possessions when they were in need.

AMBROSE: Or again: *Make unto you friends of the mammon of iniquity*; that by giving to the poor we may find favour with the angels and the other holy ones.

CHRYSOSTOM (*Hom. 33 to the People of Antioch*): Note that He did not say: That they may receive you into their own everlasting mansions. For it is not they who receive you. So when He said: *Make unto you friends*, He added, *of* (out of) *the mammon of iniquity*; showing us that their friendship alone will not obtain protection for us, unless we are accompanied by good works; unless we with a pure heart empty ourselves of riches unjustly gained. The giving of alms is therefore the most skilled of all the arts. For it does not build us houses of brick; but yields us eternal life. In each of the arts we need the assistance of others. But when we ought to show compassion we have need of nothing save our will alone.

CYRIL, *Catena GP*: In this way Christ has taught those who abound in riches to love greatly the friendship of the poor; and to lay up treasure for themselves in heaven. For He knew the sloth of the human soul; how they who are given to the pursuit of riches will not devote themselves to any work of charity for those in need.

I. ST BASIL, BISHOP AND DOCTOR

I Will Pull Down My Barns[1]

Trials are of two kinds. Either affliction will test our souls as gold is tried in a furnace, and make trial of us through patience, or the very prosperity of our lives will oftentimes, for many, be itself an occasion of trial and temptation. For it is equally difficult to keep the soul upright and undefeated in the midst of afflictions, as to keep oneself from insolence and pride in prosperity. We have an example of the first kind of trial in the blessed Job, that great and undefeated champion, who with unshaken courage and immovable purpose breasted every assault of the devil, as they came against him with the force of a torrent; and the more each attempt of the enemy appeared irresistible, the higher his patience rose superior to every trial. Of the second kind we have many examples besides this rich man of whom we have just read, who had much wealth, and hoped to have much more. And the most kind God did not in the beginning condemn him for his thankless soul; rather, each day He added new riches to what he already had, to see if, when his soul had at length attained satiety, it might then awaken to liberality and to kindness.

For He said: *The land of a certain*

*rich man brought forth plenty of fruits.
And he thought within himself, saying:
What shall I do, because I have no
room where to bestow my fruits? And
he said: This will I do: I will pull down
my barns, and I will build greater*
(Lk. xii. 16–18). Why then was the
land of this man so rich; he who
would do nothing of good with the
abundance that was coming to him?
That we might see more clearly the
forbearance of God, Whose goodness extends itself even to such
persons, since *He maketh his sun to
rise upon the good, and bad, and raineth
upon the just and the unjust* (Mt. v. 45).
But such goodness of God brings
greater chastisement upon the
wicked. He pours out His rains
upon the fields cultivated by avaricious hands. He gives us the sun that
warms the seed and multiplies it into
an abundance of fruit. And it is from
God such blessings are received;
fertile lands, a fitting climate, seeds
that are fruitful, the work of the
oxen, and all things else by which
the tilled earth becomes fruitful.

What kind of person is this man?
His nature is bitter; hating his own
kind; of an unyielding greed. This
was the return He was making His
Benefactor for those blessings. He
had no thought for those of his own
nature; it did not enter his mind to
give what remained over when his
barns were full to those who were
in need. He gave no heed to the
words that commanded: *Do not withhold from doing good who is able*
(Prov. iii. 27); and again: *Let not
mercy and truth leave thee* (iii. 3); and
also: *Deal thy bread to the hungry*
(Is. lviii. 7). He paid no heed to all
the prophets, to all the teachers, who
cried out to him. His barns were
near to bursting with the great

quantities of corn he had stowed
there; but his greedy heart was not
yet filled. For he was ever adding
new crops to the earlier ones; and
the mass swelling upwards through
yearly increase he found himself in
this predicament of avarice, that he
could not let go of the first yield,
nor find room to store the last.

So his deliberations were without
end, and his decisions kept changing.
What shall I do? Who cannot feel
compassion for a nature so obsessed? Wretched in his abundance,
miserable in his good fortune, and
yet more miserable for the blessings
to come. For him the earth does not
yield harvests, but sighs and groans;
not fruits in plenty, but cares, grief,
grave anxieties. He grieves like
those who are destitute. Is not this
what he cries who is in anguish
through want: *What shall I do?
Where shall I get food? Where shall
I find clothing?* This is what the
rich man is saying. Is not his heart
tormented; devoured with anxiety?
For what rejoices others brings pain
to the avaricious. He does not rejoice at his barns stuffed full. The
overflowing riches his barns cannot
hold torment his soul, lest perhaps
overflowing from his barns they
bring some of their blessing to
those in want.

2. To me his anguish of soul
seems to resemble that of those who
are given to the vice of gluttony, who
would rather burst themselves eating
than leave a crumb for the hungry.
Recall to mind your Benefactor, O
Man! Be mindful of yourself, who
you are, of what things have been
placed in your charge, from Whom
you receive them, and why you
were favoured above others. You

have been made a servant of the good God; an administrator for your fellow servant. Do not imagine that all these fruits were prepared for your stomach. Regard what you hold within your own hands as though it belonged to others. For a little while these things will give you pleasure; then flowing away from you they disappear, and then you must with exactness render an account of them. But you seek with bolts and bars to keep them all hidden, and you shut them up under seals, and watch them anxiously, and you think within yourself, *What shall I do?*

What shall I do? Offhand I would say: 'I shall fill the souls of the hungry. I shall open my barns, and I shall send for all who are in want. I shall be like Joseph (Gen. xlvii. 11) in proclaiming the love of my fellow man. I shall cry out with a mighty voice: "Come to me all of you who have need of bread; for of the abundance that divine love has given to me, let each of you take according to his need." '

You do not do this. Rather you are so in dread lest other men should have a share in the fruits you possess, that you take thought within your unworthy soul, not as to how you will give the poor what they hunger for, but how you, taking everything, may deprive all others of the help of them. They stood near him who would demand his soul of him (Lk. xii. 20); and he took thought within himself of food! That very night he was snatched away; when he had begun to imagine to himself the delights and the enjoyment of his possessions! It was permitted him to take thought of everything, to make known openly what was

in his mind, that he might receive a sentence worthy of his character.

3. Beware that the same does not happen to you! For to this end were these things written, that we avoid doing similar things. Imitate the earth, O Man, and let you also bear fruit, as it does, so that you may not be lower than the senseless creation. It nourishes its fruits, not for its own delight, but to serve you. And you, whatever fruits of beneficence you do yield, you gather up for yourself; for the grace of good works and their reward is returned to the giver. Have you given something to a person in need; what you have given becomes yours, and is returned to you with an increase. And as the wheat that falls to the earth brings increase to the one who has thrown it there, so the bread that you give to the hungry will later bring you a great gain. Therefore, let the end of your earthly tilling be the beginning of your heavenly sowing. *Sow for yourselves in justice* (Os. x. 12).

Why then are you anxious? Why do you torment yourself, striving to shut up riches behind bricks and mortar? *A good name is better than many riches* (Prov. xxii. 1). Should you desire riches because of the honour they bring you, consider how much more it honours you to be called the father of innumerable children than to have a purse filled with gold. And whether you will it or not you will leave the gold behind, while the glory that is born of good works you carry back to the Lord, where, standing before our common Judge all the people shall call you their nourisher and their benefactor, and give you those other names that signify kindness and

humanity. Do you not see those at
the theatre, at the public contests, at
the fights with beasts, those who
scatter their wealth for the sake of
applause from the common people
around them, of those whose very
appearance is abhorrent? And you
are mean and grasping in spending
the little by which you may attain
to such endless glory? The Lord
Himself shall praise you. The angels
shall praise you with Him, and all
who are gathered from the whole
world shall call you blessed. Eternal
glory, a crown of justice, the kingdom of heaven, these shall he
receive who was a just dispenser of
the things which perish.

Have you no anxiety, despising
the good things laid up for you in
hope, because of your eagerness for
the things of this present life? Come
then. Give out of your riches.
Become splendid and generous in
bestowing your riches on the needy.
Let it be said of you: *He hath distributed, he hath given to the poor; his
justice remaineth for ever and ever*
(Prov. xi. 26). Do not take advantage of those in want to sell dearly.
Beware of waiting for a famine before you open up your barns. For,
*He that hideth up corn, shall be cursed
among the people* (Prov. xi. 26). Do
not look to a famine to make money;
nor to the common want for your
private gain. Do not become a
dealer in human misery. Do not try
to make money out of the anger of
God. Do not torment the wounds of
the afflicted with your cruel whips.
You with your eyes ever on money,
do you never take a look at your
fellow man? You know well the
face of a coin, and you can tell a
true from a false one, but you know
not your brother in his time of need.

4. The bright glitter of gold delights you, but you never think of
with what groans, what execrations,
the poor pursue you. How can I
bring their sufferings before your
eyes? Consider one among them.
He stands there looking about him
in his miserable home. He sees no
money in his purse, nor any hope
of it. He looks at his clothes, his
poor tools, at the other few articles
that form the belongings of the
poor; in all they are worth but a few
coins. What will he do? His eyes
then come to rest upon his own little
ones, as if here he may, by taking
them to the market and exposing
them for sale, hold back that death
that now hangs over all of them.
Consider, I beg you, the anguished
struggle within him, between the
hunger that devours them and the
father's love. Hunger threatens
them with a miserable death. But
nature shudders; tells him rather to
die with his children. Now resolved
to act, now refusing. He at last
gives way; forced by want, and an
implacable hunger.

What thoughts now rise in the
mind of the father? Whom will he
first sell? Which of them will the
cornseller look at? Must it be my
eldest? But I must not put to shame
his rights as the eldest. Shall I
sacrifice my youngest? His tender
age torments me; unable yet to
understand this tragedy? He has the
face of both his mother and his
father; he is fit for study, for learning. O dread misery! On which of
them must I inflict this terrible
wrong? On which of them shall I
impose the life of a beast? How can
I forget my own nature? If I keep
them all with me, one by one I shall
see them die of hunger. If I sell

one, how shall I face the eyes of those left; I who am now guilty in their eyes of treachery and betrayal? How shall I remain in my house, deprived by my own act of my own children? How shall I come to the table, furnished at their price?

At length with tears the father goes, to sell the dearest loved among his children. But you do not bend before the face of such agony; no thought of nature enters your mind. Hunger drives this suffering creature, but you hold out, and play him, and prolong his agony. He offers as the price of food his heart's blood. Your hands that drag riches from the deeps of his pain not alone do not tremble in fear, but with them you haggle over the price. To gain more you offer less; by every trick you look to add to the unhappy man's affliction. Tears do not move you to pity; nor his groans of anguish soften your heart. You are immovable and implacable. Money fills your mind. You dream of it; sleeping and waking you hunger for it. Just as the insane see no reality, only the vision that torments them, so your soul, obsessed by avarice, sees all things as gold, all things as silver. You look more readily at gold than at the sun. You would change everything into gold, and this you try to do with all your power.

5. What scheme will you not set in motion for the sake of gold? For you wheat becomes gold, wine grows into gold, wool is woven into gold. All that is bought and sold, every human activity, brings you gold. Gold itself brings forth gold, when you multiply it at interest. And there is no sufficiency,

no end, to your rapacity. We sometimes let greedy children fill themselves with what they crave for, as satiety will bring disgust with what they were eager for. But it is not so with a miser. The more he is fed the more he hungers. *If riches abound, set not your heart upon them* (Ps. lxi. 11). You hold back what overflows, and you stop up every outlet. Then held back and grown stagnant what use do you make of them? They break through the banks that restrained them, and overflowing they destroy their owner's barns and level them flat like an overwhelming enemy. Will he build new ones, you ask? He is uncertain whether or not to leave the ruins to his successor. For were he cut off he would pass away more speedily than the new barns could be replaced by his greedy industry.

And so this man comes to an end that befits his own evil mind. You, if you will hear me, opening wide all the doors of your storehouses, give full outlet to your riches. And just as a wide stream is distributed through the fruitful earth by many channels, so let your riches flow, that by many ways they may reach the homes of the poor. Wells, when they are drawn from, flow forth in a purer and more abundant stream. Where they are in disuse they grow foul. And so do riches grow useless, left idle and unused in any place; but moved about, passing from one person to another, they serve the common advantage and bear fruit.

And what praise they would give you upon whom you had bestowed kindness! And this is something you must beware of despising. How great is the reward of the just judge in whom you have confidence! Keep ever before your mind the example of this rich man who, keeping firm hold of the possessions he already had, was also anxious about those to come to him, and, uncertain whether he would be alive to-morrow, he anticipated the morrow by sinning today. No one had yet come begging to him, and yet beforehand he shows himself unyielding. He had not yet gathered in his harvest, and already he has been condemned because of his greed with regard to it. The earth had brought forth fruits in plenty, the crops were standing thick in the fields, the grape hung heavy from the vines, the olive abundant and filled with richness, and every tree held forth its promise of precious fruit. He alone is neither joyous nor fruitful. He has not yet got hold of his harvest, and already he is envious of the hungry. And what dangers lie in wait for the fruits before he has gathered them in? For often they are struck by hail. And heat may wither them in his hands, or the rain bursting untimely from the clouds leave them worthless. Why then do you not pray to the Lord that He may bring His bounty to fulfilment? You rather make yourself still more unworthy of receiving before you receive what you hope for.

6. You speak to yourself in secret, but your words are weighed in heaven. And because of this you will receive an answer from there. And what do you say to yourself? *Soul, thou hast much goods laid up. Eat, drink, make good cheer* (Lk. xii. 19). What folly! Had you the soul of a pig what more could you say to it? Are you so beastlike, so ignorant of the delights of the soul, that you offer it only the pleasures of the body; that you destine for the soul what the pit will receive? If it has virtue, if it is full of good actions, if it is joined to God through the desire of Him, then indeed *it has much goods laid up*, and may rejoice with a joy that is worthy of the soul. But you, because you know no joy but earthly ones, and because your belly is your God, and you are wholly of the flesh, and the slave of your passions, you hear yourself called by a fitting name, and no man says this to you, but God says it to you: *Thou fool, this night do they require thy soul of thee; and whose shall these things be which thou hast provided?*

Better eternal punishment than this derision of your folly. The one who in a little while is to be snatched from this life and led away, what is he thinking of in his own mind? *I will pull down my barns.* You will do rightly. I would say the same myself. For well worthy of destruction are the barns of injustice. Tear down with your own hands what you have so unjustly built up. Destroy those granaries from which no one returns comforted. Throw down the roofs. Demolish the walls. Expose the withered corn to the sun. Lead from their prison the riches held fast in bonds. Open to the world the dark caves of mammon!

I will pull down my barns, and will build greater ones. And when you fill these up what next do you plan? Will you destroy these too, and build again? What more senseless than so to labour without end; diligently building, and diligently destroying again? You have barns ready if you want them: the houses of the poor. Lay up treasure for yourself in heaven (Mt. vi. 20). What you store there the moth will not consume, nor rust devour, nor thieves break in and steal.

When I have these new barns filled, you say, then I will distribute something to the poor. You have given yourself a long time to live. Take care that the appointed day does not, coming swift, forestall you. And promises of that sort are not very helpful; and an indication of a perverse heart rather than of kindness. For you promise, not that you will afterwards fulfil, but to relieve yourself of a present embarrassment. What keeps you from giving now? There are no hungry perhaps? Are your barns not full? Is the price not ready? Is the law of God not plain to you? The hungry are dying before your face. The naked are stiff with cold. The man in debt is held by the throat. And you, you put off your alms, till another day? Listen to Solomon's words: *Do not say: Go and come again: and tomorrow I will give to thee: when thou canst give now* (Prov. iii. 20); *Thou knowest not what the day to come may bring forth* (xxvii. 1).

What good counsel you are despising by shutting up your ears beforehand with avarice. And what thanks you should have offered to the most merciful God, how cheerful you should be, how joyful, because of the honour He has given you; namely, that you need not go knocking at the doors of other people, but that they must come knocking at yours! Instead you are sullen and repellent. You turn away from those you meet lest you be forced to let even a morsel escape your clutches. You have only one

phrase: 'I have nothing to give; I am a poor man.' You are indeed poor; and in need of every good. You are poor in love for your fellow man; poor in humanity; poor in faith in God; poor in the hope of eternity! Make your brothers sharers of your grain; and what may wither tomorrow, give to the needy today. For it is greed of the most horrible kind, to deny to the starving even what you must soon throw away!

7. Who am I injuring, you will say, when I keep what is mine for myself? And what, tell me, is yours? And from where have you brought it with you into this life? You act like someone who has secured a place at the theatre, and then excludes others from entering, claiming that the place was his which exists for the common use of all men. And such are the rich. For taking possession of the things which are for the common use of all, they count them as theirs because they hold them in possession. If each took only what was sufficient for his needs, and left what remained, there would be no rich and no poor. Did you not come forth naked from your mother's womb, and will you not return naked to the earth? How then are these things yours? If you say that this is so by chance, then you are a godless creature, ignorant of your Creator, and giving no thanks to your Benefactor. If you confess that they are from God, tell us then why it was you that received them. Or is God unjust, distributing among us in an unequal manner the necessities of life? Why are you rich, this other man poor? Is it not solely that you may earn the rewards of compassion, of good and faithful

administration, and that he may be honoured with the glorious rewards of patience?

But you, holding everything to your breast, in the unyielding grasp of greed, you believe are depriving no man of anything? Who has more than his share? He who is never content with enough. Who is the robber? He who seizes what belongs to another. Are you not a grasper of everything; are you not a robber? You who treat as absolutely yours what you received that you might dispense to others. He who strips another man of his clothing, is he not called a robber; and he who does not clothe the naked when he could, should he not be called the same? That bread you hold in your clutches, that belongs to the starving. That cloak you keep locked away in your wardrobe, that belongs to the naked. Those shoes that are going to waste with you, they belong to the barefooted. The silver you buried away, that belongs to the needy. Whomsoever you could have helped and did not, to so many have you been unjust.

8. These are fine words, he says, but gold is finer. The same thing happens to us as when chastity is preached to the unchaste. For these men, when woman is ill spoken of, roused by the reminder, are awakened again to evil desires. How then can I put before your eyes the suffer-ings of the poor, that you may know from what agony you gather in wealth? O how precious shall these words seem to you on the Day of judgement: *Come, ye blessed of my Father, possess you the kingdom prepared for you from the foundation of the world. For I was hungry, and you gave me to eat; I was thirsty, and you gave me to drink; naked, and you covered me* (Mt. xxv. 34-6)! And again, what horror and sweat of agony, and what darkness, will swallow you on hearing the words of condemnation: *Depart from me, you cursed, into everlasting fire, which was prepared for the devil and his angels. I was hungry, and you gave me not to eat: I was thirsty, and you gave me not to drink; naked, and you covered me not* (xxv. 41, 43)! For here a robber is not being condemned; but an unjust steward is being condemned.

I have spoken to you as best I could. For you who respond the blessings are ready that were promised you. For you who do not respond the sentence is already written; and I pray most earnestly that, reflecting upon this bitter counsel I am giving you, you may escape those penalties; that your riches may become instead the price of your redemption, and that you also may attain to those heavenly good things through His grace Who has called us all to His own heavenly kingdom. To Whom be glory and empire for ever and ever. Amen.

II. St Gaudentius, Bishop of Brescia

The Unjust Steward[2]

It is fitting that one who is given to sacred wisdom should at all times dwell upon the teachings of Wisdom, and apply all the power of his mind, all the keenness of his soul, to understanding them. And it is because of this that you who are acquainted with the teachings of worldly wisdom should learn of True Wisdom from its Sacred Writings, and not cease from searching into the hidden meanings of the words of Christ, Who is also known to you, from the teaching of the Apostle, as the Power of God and as the Wisdom of God.

Among the discourses of the Divine Law, whose explanation you are wont to look for from me, this also you have asked of me, that I might explain to you (in writing) the very difficult parable of the Unjust Steward, since none of our treatises seem to you to offer an adequate explanation. The explanation you wish to be given in writing so that you may have the manuscript of my reply on this chapter, which is as you confess so very obscure. Since you ask me to speak, or rather to write, I shall not be frightened to say what I understand here, within the limits of my mind, and saving what faith teaches us. But first, Beloved, let us have the words of this lesson. The blessed Luke, in the Book of his Gospel, relates that, *the Lord Jesus spoke a parable to his disciples: There was a certain rich man, who had a steward; and this man was accused unto him, that he had wasted his goods. And he called him and said to him: How is it that I hear this of thee? Give an account of thy stewardship: for now thou canst be steward no longer. And the steward said within himself: What shall I do, because my Lord hath taken away from me the stewardship? To dig I am not able; to beg I am ashamed. I know what I will do, that when I shall be removed from the stewardship, they may receive me into their houses. Therefore, calling together everyone of his lord's debtors, he said to the first: How much dost thou owe my Lord? And he said: An hundred barrels of oil. And he said to him: Take thy bill, and sit down quickly, and write fifty. Then he said to another: And how much dost thou owe? Who said: An hundred quarters of wheat. He said to him: Take thy bill, and write eighty. And the Lord commended the unjust steward, forasmuch as he had done wisely: for the children of this world are more prudent in their generation than the children of light. And I say to you: Make unto you friends of the mammon of iniquity; that when you shall fail, they may receive you into everlasting dwellings. He that is faithful in that which is least, is faithful also in that which is greater: and he that is unjust in that which is little, is unjust also in that which is greater. If then you have not been faithful in the unjust mammon; who will trust you with that which is the true? And if you have not been faithful in that which is another's; who will give you that which is your own? No man can serve two masters; for either he will hate the one, and love the other; or he will hold to the one, and despise the other. You cannot serve God and mammon* (Lk. xvi. 1–13).

It is the mark of a true teacher, in teaching his disciples, to put before them examples taken from events in the daily life of mankind, so that the listener who is well disposed may be aroused by the force of the parable to an eagerness to do good works; and the example of the parable will show him, should he hesitate, that the good work he proposes to do is both possible and necessary. And so the Lord Jesus, the True Teacher of the saving commandments of God, wishing at that time to encourage His Apostles, and after them all who would believe in Him everywhere, to the practice of almsgiving, puts before them the Parable of the Unjust Steward, so that by the example of this person He might make clear to us, that in this world nothing is really ours, but that instead we have been entrusted with the stewardship of the goods of our Lord, either to use them, with giving of thanks, according to our needs, or to distribute them to our fellow servants according as they have need, and that it is not lawful to misuse indiscriminately the means that have been committed to us, or to claim the right to extravagant expense and display; for we must render an account of our stewardship to the Lord when He comes.

Then at the end of the parable He adds: *And I say to you: Make unto you friends of the mammon of iniquity, that when you shall fail, they may receive you into everlasting dwellings;* that is, make the poor your friends, by means of those earthly possessions which the injustice of human greed claims as absolutely belonging to it; lest it be forced to bestow any part of it on the people of God. *Mammon* is a Syriac word for money or riches. *Make unto you therefore,* He says, *friends,* the poor, *from the mammon of iniquity; that when you fail,* that when you have given your substance for the needs of the poor and spent it all, *they may receive you into everlasting dwellings;* that is, our friends will obtain our salvation, since they are the same poor in whom Christ the Eternal Rewarder will confess that He has Himself received the kindnesses of our love for our fellow man. The poor themselves do not therefore receive us, but they receive us through Him Who is given to eat in them through

the good works of our faith and our obedience, into His eternal Kingdom.

For He says to us: *Come, ye blessed of my Father, possess you the kingdom prepared for you from the foundation of the world. For I was hungry and you gave me to eat; I was thirsty and you gave me to drink; I was a stranger and you took me in: naked, and you clothed me: sick, and you visited me: I was in prison, and you came to me* (Mt. xxv. 34). And to those who, modestly and reverently disclaiming, say to Him: Lord, when did we see thee in such need, and minister to Thee, He will answer: *Amen I say to you, as long as you did it to one of these my least brethren, you did it to me.* So let it therefore not seem absurd to anyone that they are said to receive us, on whose account we are received; for the Lord Jesus our Protector, Who is subject to no human need, Himself declares that in them He was hungry, in them He was thirsty, in them He was a stranger, naked, sick, imprisoned.

Therefore, He says, *make unto you friends of the mammon of iniquity; that when you shall fail, they may receive you into everlasting dwellings.* And a little later He adds: *If then you have not been faithful in the unjust mammon; who will trust you with that which is the true?* For who will believe that to a man who could not be faithful in the care of earthly riches, which are the most frequent source of iniquity, the true riches of heavenly things should then be entrusted; riches which justly and deservedly are to be the reward of the just and faithful steward? For, *glory and wealth shall be in his house, and his justice remaineth for ever and ever* (Ps. cxi. 3).

And to the Lord's discourse there

is then immediately added: *And if you have not been faithful in that which is another's, who will give you that which is your own?* (v. 12). For whatever is in this world does in truth not belong to us, who are commanded to live in this world *as strangers and pilgrims*, looking to the future for our reward (I Pet. ii. 11), so that each one of us, secure in the hope of salvation, may dare to confess to the Lord: *I am a stranger with thee, and a sojourner, as all my fathers were* (Ps. xxxviii. 13). For us who believe, our true and everlasting possession, our treasure, is where we know that our heart is also (Mt. vi. 21); where even now it is our joy to dwell with all our heart through faith: since as the blessed Paul has taught us, *our conversation is in heaven* (Phil. iii. 20). Ours therefore is *the kingdom of heaven*, as the Lord promises us, if we serve Him in lowliness of heart, and in mildness of spirit. For, *blessed are the poor in spirit: for theirs is the kingdom of heaven* (Mt. v. 3).

For no man can obtain this kingdom who was not a fit and faithful steward of that other patrimony of this world that was entrusted to him for a time. And so in another place the Lord said: *With what difficulty shall they who have money enter into the kingdom of God* (Mt. xix. 23). And at the end of this lesson He says: *You cannot serve God and mammon.* For the servants of Christ God, and His Disciples, should rather command money, not serve it: for fear that should money rule us, as long as we are obedient to the desire of it, we separate ourselves from the love of His service.

Therefore, according to the command of God the Creator of all

things, riches are to be distributed to those in need; for they are not ours, and no *covetous person* whatever may hold fast to them, without injustice and without disaster to his own soul. For according to the words of our Saviour, they hinder those who are attached to them from entering the kingdom of heaven; for *it is easier for a camel to pass through the eye of a needle, than for a rich man to enter into the kingdom of heaven* (Mt. xix. 24): for that rich man, namely, who is so swollen by the horror that is avarice that he is more monstrous than a camel. For money is a heavy burden; and the weight of avarice presses the souls of men who are held in the grip of it down to the earth, and will not suffer them either to rise up to higher things, or look upwards towards heaven; where is our true life. For the blessed Apostle teaches us that, *if you be risen with Christ, seek the things that are above; where Christ is sitting at the right hand of God. Mind the things that are above, not the things that are upon the earth. For you are dead; and your life is hid with Christ in God. When God shall appear, who is your life, then you shall also appear with him in glory* (Col. iii). And since strait and narrow is the way that leads to life, it does not permit those to enter upon it who are laden with the burdens of earthly riches. It is open to those who are free and unencumbered, disciplined by self-denial of every kind, and, if I may say so, who have become so spiritual, fine as thread, that they are even able to pass easily through the eye of this mystical needle.

This then is the meaning and purpose of this parable, which we should first obey, as we are commanded, as well as seek for its inward understanding, if we are able to perceive it; for *the kingdom of God is not in speech, but in power* (I Cor. iv. 20). For it is *not the hearers of the law are just before God, but the doers of the law shall be justified* (Rom. ii. 13). Nor can any one clearly grasp the inward knowledge of the divine utterances, as the Apostle solemnly assures us. *O the depth of the riches of the wisdom and the knowledge of God! How incomprehensible are his judgements, and how unsearchable his ways! For who hath known the mind of the Lord? Or who hath been his counsellor?* And in another place, where he was speaking of Adam and Eve (i.e. of man and wife) he perceived that within the divine discourse (Mt. xix. 5) there was a very great mystery, and that he was not able to speak fittingly with regard to it. *This is a great sacrament (mysterium); but I speak in Christ and in the Church* (Eph. v. 32).

And would you like to learn that we shall come to eternal life, not through knowing things hidden, but because of our good works? In the Gospel the Lord, replying to the question of a certain rich man, says to him: *If thou wilt enter into life, keep the commandments* (Mt. xix. 17). And although the man boasted that he had kept all of them, yet there was one commandment he could not then be brought to fulfil: that he should be compassionate to the poor, and make over all his wealth to heaven. *And when the young man had heard this word he went away sad.* And he had reason to be sad; for he could not possess the joy of having *treasure in heaven*, since he was himself possessed by the evil of avarice. Truly is *the desire of money the root of all evils*, as the Apostle laments

(I Tim. vi. 10); *which some coveting have erred from the faith, and have entangled themselves in many sorrows.* For he submits himself to a destructive error of faith, and entangles himself in many sorrows, who goes away from Christ out of love of earthly possessions, as this young man did: when he fled from His commandment, when sad and grieving he is led away by voluntary blindness from the sight of the Lord, to the punishments prepared for the avaricious, and for those who scorn Him. So rightly shall it be said to those placed on the left hand of fruitlessness: *Depart from me, you cursed, into everlasting fire which was prepared for the devil and his angels; because you showed no mercy to those in need, you showed none to me.*

I come now to what you so earnestly asked of me; and what I believe in this matter I shall tell you as briefly as I can; and without criticism of how any one else may interpret it, provided his explanation does not lessen in any way the tradition of the Apostolic Faith. I am of opinion that the Unjust Steward stands for the devil, who was sent into this world for the correction of mankind, so that we, flying from the malignant cruelty of this so evil steward, might run together towards the compassion of God, through Whose power and mercy we can be delivered from every assault: and seeing that the steward is also subject to the power of the Lord God, Who, as the Apostle teaches us, is *rich unto all that call upon him. For whosoever shall call upon the name of the Lord, shall be saved* (Rom. x. 12).

And the devil wasted the substance of his Lord when he sought the ruin of mankind; that is, our death, who are the possession of God, as the Son of God bears witness, repeating by the mouth of the prophet the words of His Father: *Ask of me, and I will give thee the Gentiles for thy inheritance, and the utmost parts of the earth for thy possession* (Ps. ii. 8). And again: *For the Lord had chosen Jacob unto himself: Israel for his own possession* (Ps. cxxxiv. 4). God seeing the insolence of the devil had become so great, that those he had been permitted to try, and solely for their correction, he had taken as his own, and put to death, now threatens him with expulsion, so that his cruelty is broken through fear of unending punishment. And this most wicked one, reckoning the death of man as his profit, is consumed with anxiety because the Lord is about to take away his power over others. And since he is unable to will what is good, and is ashamed to seek mercy through repentance, he thinks within himself how he may still have power over the debtors of his Lord (that is, over those involved in the debt of sin), not alone by open persecution, but also, under the pretext of benevolence, by deceiving them with smooth words, so that seduced by his false kindness they may more readily receive him into their houses since together with him they must be judged for ever.

The devil believes that this would be a great alleviation of his torments, to secure many sharers of the penalties inflicted on himself. For the enemy, full of guile, and troubled by the Coming, and by the threat of Christ, thought within his own poisonous mind how even those who fled from him when he was persecuting them, may yet follow him should he give up something to them. He hastens to try these new schemes, and with different kinds of temptations he tries to undo men; power over whom he well knows will be wholly taken from him at the end of the world. For after the coming of Christ the devil was inflamed with redoubled fury against mankind; *knowing that he hath but a short time* (Apoc. xii. 12), as was written of him. The debts of his fellow servants, which belong to his Lord, he promises falsely to remit himself, when he offers an empty forgiveness to those who sin either in belief or in work; when he persuades them that the sins which they who commit them know are grievous sins will not be regarded as sins. For they confess the amount of their debt, since they know in their hearts they cannot deny their debt to God; for their contempt of His faith, and for the good they have failed to do. For they who render to God what is God's are not God's debtors. And do not be surprised that he lies about the forgiveness of their debts to men whom he is trying even more cunningly to destroy by this very deceit, since he dared to promise Christ, the Creator of all things, the kingdoms of this world, impudently pretending they were his. *All these are mine*, he says, *and to whom I will I give them. If thou therefore will adore before me, all shall be thine* (Lk. iv. 6, 7).

O the indescribable patience of Christ, Who suffered the tempter to speak in this way, that He might show us, whose humanity He has taken upon Himself, the manner of fighting him, and of defeating him!

O the unbridled insolence of this liar the devil! He thinks Jesus is God, and yet tempts Him. He had reason to think that He was the Lord of all creation to Whom he lies that the kingdoms of the earth are his; and he promises that he will give possession of created things to Him by Whom he knew all things were made! For, as it was written: *He was a murderer from the beginning, and he stood not in the truth, because the truth is not in him* (Jn. viii. 44).

And now we come to the kinds of things of which there is question. The *wheat*, as we said before, is the Faith of Christ; the beginning of life for man. *For the bread of God is that which cometh down from heaven, and giveth life to the world* (Jn. vi. 33). And again He says: *He that believeth in me, although he be dead, shall live* (Jn. xi. 25). *Oil* stands for good works, and because the foolish virgins did not have any, the lamps of their souls were extinguished, and they remained shut out in the darkness from the Chamber of the Bridegroom (*heaven*). For our souls must not alone be virgin and untarnished; they must also ever carry in their vessels the oil of every good work: lest the lamp of faith go out for want of the oil of good works (Mt. xxv). *For even as the body without the spirit is dead; so also faith without good works is dead* (Jas. ii. 26).

The light of faith will then be steady and everlasting if it is nourished abundantly by the oil of good works. The devil therefore cheated mankind with false promises, so that they may disown their debt of faith and good works, until such time as they shall be thrust by the sentence of the Just Judge into the prison of hell; requiring of them that through torments they shall repay the last farthing (Mt. v. 25).

That he persuades them, in place of a hundred barrels of oil, that is, of good works, to write fifty, and forces them to alter the debt of a hundred quarters of wheat to eighty, is a more veiled deception, a far more subtle snare of the enemy: which is when he involves those now withdrawn from the worship of idols in the various errors of heretical teachings, lessening the sum of their saving faith, and when he trips up those now turned away from evil practices, and eager to walk in the way of good works, by the eager desire to make known their good works. For he tries to pervert both our faith and our good works from the centenary number, that is from the number that stands for perfection, and which stands at the right-hand side: perverting Apostolic Faith by the sinister interpretations of heretical teaching, and perverting the merit of our good works, of things done on the right-hand side, by leading us to a sinister way of life.

For how many has the devil not softened by his evil counsel, from the discipline of the right hand to the looseness of bodily pleasures? How many who were devout and eager in paying by good works the spiritual debts of religion has he not cheated of their heavenly reward, by infecting them with the desire of human glory, so that they may not receive the rewards promised to those on the right hand: for in their good works they now seek the good opinion of men rather than the praise and glory of God. And for this reason the Lord Christ the Son of God, warning His Disciples to be careful not to make known to men their uprightness, their alms, their fasting and praying, lest through the vain glory of the left-hand side *they may not have the reward* of the right hand, says to them: *Let not thy left hand know what they right hand doth* (Mt. vi. 3).

It is very plain to us then with what poisonous prudence this unjust steward alters the due debts of religion, transferring them from the right to the left-hand side of the account. And it was not without purpose that the Lord, to Whom we are indebted, suffered greater losses in His oil, by which our good works are signified, than in His wheat, placed before us as a figure of the Life-giving Faith. For he is less corrupted by the deceit of the devil who is led away from the true faith, than he who is led away from the practice of good works, as the Saviour bears witness: *And why do you call me, Lord, Lord; and do not the things which I say?* (Lk. vi. 46).

The Lord does not however praise him for goodness, nor for piety, nor for justice, but he praises the cunning, the artful prudence, of *the unjust steward*; He praised him because he had prepared his fraud with such subtle evil. He praises him menacingly, and at the same praises him for acting prudently. Menacingly, for by the very word *unjust* He condemns this most wicked prudence of the devil; He praises him as having acted *prudently*, while at the same time He prepares the minds of His listening Disciples against the subtle skill of his schemes, so that they may with all care, with all prudence, oppose this so cunning, this so evilly wise enemy. For *the serpent was more subtle than any of the beasts of the*

earth (Gen. iii. 1), and he slew the men who were first made by the poisoned bite of his seduction. The blessed Apostle making reference to the tortuous character of the serpent says: *We are not ignorant of his devices* (II Cor. ii. 11). And for the same reason the Saviour also says: *Be ye therefore wise as serpents and simple as doves* (Mt. x. 16). And the Apostle Paul conveyed the same to us in different words when he said: *In malice be children, and in sense be perfect* (I Cor. xiv. 20).

Christ bids us be prudent, but not venomous; wise, but not evil; and that putting off, like the snake, our old garment of sin, we are to be formed into a new man; protecting our Head, Which is Christ, with every care, and surrendering our members to be torn by the persecutors, that the Faith of Christ, the Head of our salvation and of our Life, may remain sound and unwounded.

Accordingly, Beloved, let us imitate the prudence of this unjust steward, but not his perfidy. Let us imitate his cunning, but not his wickedness. As he was skilled in injuring others by his evil deeds, so must we be prepared in salutary knowledge, instructed and armed with all prudence; having on us the breastplate of faith, the helmet of salvation, the sword of the Spirit, and the impregnable shield of justice, by means of which we can, as the Apostle exhorts us, *extinguish all the fiery darts of the most wicked one* (Eph. vi. 16, 17); lest while we are unawares he may pierce us with the darts of his evil promptings; lest being unarmed he may overcome us; lest being asleep he should slay us; lest though armed and watching he should still defeat us, because we are not accustomed to fighting him. For the unclean spirits, whom the Lord calls the children of this world, that is, the children of darkness, are oftentimes more prudent than the children of light, whom God, Who is Light, has deigned to call to be His children by adoption, being born again through the mysteries of the heavenly Baptism. Farewell, Beloved in Christ. Amen.

NOTES

[1] PG 31, Hom. 6 on Luke xii. 18. This celebrated discourse was delivered during the time of a terrible famine, when the rich who had corn, instead of helping the hungry, profited by the occasion to increase prices. The saint prayed that bread might fall from heaven upon the poor. But, says St Nazianzen (Oration 20), what was near to a miracle actually took place, and wrought the same effect; and he did this with the same faith. He opened the storehouses of the rich, which seemed shut the more tightly, the more want and hunger increased.

[2] PL 20, col. 971, Sermo 18. This wonderful exposition of this difficult parable was written as a letter by the holy bishop, the venerated friend of St Ambrose, in reply to a request made to him by one Serminium. It has the characteristic precision and holy discernment of all the sermons of St Gaudentius. It may well be regarded as a summary of sacred Tradition on this parable.

NINTH SUNDAY AFTER PENTECOST

I. St Augustine: Prayer for the Gift of Tears

II. St Gregory the Great: The End of Life

THE GOSPEL OF THE SUNDAY

Luke xix. 41-7

At that time: When Jesus drew near to Jerusalem, seeing the city, he wept over it saying: If thou also hadst known, and that in this thy day, the things that are to thy peace; but now they are hidden from thine eyes. For the days shall come upon thee; and thy enemies shall cast a trench about thee, and compass thee round, and straiten thee on every side, and beat thee flat to the ground, and thy children who are in thee: and they shall not leave in thee a stone upon a stone: because thou hast not known the time of thy visitation. And entering in to the temple, he began to cast out them that sold therein, and them that bought. Saying to them: It is written: My house is the house of prayer. But you have made it a den of thieves. And he was teaching daily in the temple. And the chief priests and the scribes and the rulers of the people sought to destroy him.

Exposition from the Catena Aurea

V. 41. *And when he drew near, seeing the city, he wept over it.* . . .

ORIGEN: All the Beatitudes of which Jesus spoke in the Gospel He confirms by His own example. Just as He had said: *Blessed are the meek*, He confirms this where He says: *Learn of me, because I am meek and humble of heart*. And just as He had said: *Blessed are ye that weep* (Lk. vi. 21), He also wept, over the city. So we read: *When he drew near*, etc.

CYRIL: For Christ Who wishes all men to be saved had compassion on these. And this would not have been very evident to us unless made so by some very human gesture. Tears shed however are a sign of sorrow.

GREGORY, *Hom*. 39 *on Gospel*: The compassionate Saviour weeps over the ruin of the faithless city, which the city itself did not know was to come. And so we have:

V. 42. *If thou also hadst known, and that in this thy day.*

Implying, you also would have wept, who now, not knowing what

341

threatens you, rejoice. Hence there follows: *And that in this thy day*, etc. For in that day in which she was giving herself to the delights of the body, she had (within her) the things which could have been for her peace. Why it was she held the delights of the present for her peace is made clear when He adds: *But now they are hidden from thine eyes.* For if the evils that threatened were not hidden from the eye of her heart, she would not have rejoiced in her present prosperity. For this reason He then adds the punishment which threatened it, when He says:

V. 43. *For the days shall come upon thee, and thy enemies . . .*

CYRIL: Or again: *If thou also hadst known . . .* The Jews were not worthy of perceiving the meaning of the divinely inspired Scriptures which speak of the mystery of Christ. For as often as Moses is read to them a veil is drawn over their heart, so that they may not see what has been fulfilled in Christ (II Cor. iii. 15); Who as the *Reality* scatters the shadows. And because they had taken no notice of the Truth, they have made themselves unworthy of the salvation that flows from Christ. And so there follows: *And that in this thy day.*

EUSEBIUS: Where He makes a reference to the fact that His Coming took place for the peace of the whole world. For to this end He came: that He might preach to far and near. But because they were unwilling to receive the peace that was announced to them, He hid it from them. So we read: *But now they are hidden from thine eyes.* And in this

way He foretells very clearly the siege that in a short while will come upon them, saying: *For the days shall come upon thee, and thy enemies shall cast a trench about thee.*

GREGORY: Here the Roman Emperors are referred to. For here is described that overthrow of the people of Jerusalem which was the work of the Roman rulers, Titus and Vespasian. And then follows: *And compass thee round, and straiten thee on every side.*

EUSEBIUS: How all these prophecies were fulfilled we may read in what Josephus has written, who though a Jew, yet each single incident he relates is in exact accord with what was foretold by Christ.

V. 44. *And beat thee flat to the ground, and thy children who . . .*

GREGORY: And this detail is also added: *And they shall not leave in thee a stone upon a stone.* This is testified to by the fact of the translation of the city; for the new city is now built where Christ was crucified, outside the gate, while the former Jerusalem, as it is called, was totally uprooted. And the crime for which this uprooting was the punishment is then added: *Because thou hast not known the time of thy visitation.*

THEOPHYLACTUS: That is, of My Coming. For I came to see and to save you. And had you known and believed in me, you might have been at peace with the Romans, and escaped all danger; as all who believed in Christ escaped.

ORIGEN: I do not deny that the former Jerusalem was destroyed because of the iniquity of its inhabitants. But I ask if this weeping does not perhaps relate to this your Jerusalem.[1] For if anyone should fall into sin after receiving the Mysteries of Truth he is wept over. No one of the Gentiles is wept over; but he who belonged to Jerusalem and has ceased to be.

GREGORY: For our Redeemer never ceases to weep through His Elect, when He sees those who from a good life have come to wicked ways. If these had known of the damnation that threatens them, they would, with the Elect, have wept over themselves. The corrupted soul has here its day, and takes its delight in the passing hour. To it things present are for its peace; since it rejoices only in temporal things. It turns away from seeing the things of the future which might trouble its present content. And so we have: *But now they are hidden from thine eyes.*

ORIGEN: Our Jerusalem is also wept over; for after sin enemies surround it (that is, evil spirits), and cast a trench about it, so that they may besiege it, and not leave a stone upon a stone; especially if after great self-denial, and after many years of chastity, should someone, seduced by the allurements of the flesh, and overcome, lose both patience and chastity. And should he commit fornication *they will not leave* in him *a stone upon a stone*; as Ezechiel says: *All his justice which he hath done shall not be remembered* (xviii. 24).

GREGORY: Or again: The spirits of evil besiege that soul going forth from the body which they caress

with delusive joys while it was occupied with the desires of the flesh. They cast a trench about it by bringing before the eyes of its mind the memory of all the evil it has done, and enclose it round about with the company of the damned, so that caught in this last extremity of life it sees itself ringed around with enemies, yet cannot find a way of escaping them; for it is no longer able to do good works, and those it might have done it despised. They also shut the soul in on all sides when they unroll before it all its sins, not alone of deed, but also of word and thought, so that the soul which before spread itself in evil in many directions, may now at the end be hemmed in from all of them as a punishment.

Then the soul is beaten flat to the ground, because of its state of guilt, when the body (which it believed to be its life) is now pressed hard to return to the dust. Then the children who are in it fall down in death, when the forbidden thoughts, which come only from it, are scattered in the final retribution of life. And these thoughts may also be signified by the stones. For when the corrupt mind adds one perverse thought to another it as it were places one stone upon another. But when the soul is led to its final punishment the whole structure of its thoughts is demolished.

Yet God visits the wicked soul at all times, through His teaching, and He sometimes visits it by means of chastisements, and sometimes through a miracle, that it may learn the truths it did not understand, and though still rejecting them may, moved by sorrow, return to Him; or may, overcome by His kindness, become ashamed of the evil it has done. But at the end of its life, it knew not *the time of its visitation*, it is delivered over to its enemies.

V. 45. *And entering into the temple, he began to cast them out.*

GREGORY: When He had recounted to them the evils that were to come, forthwith He entered the temple, to cast out from it those who bought and sold there, shewing us that the destruction of the people was in great part the fault of the priests. So we read: *And entering in He began,* etc.

AMBROSE: For God does not wish His Temple to be a place for buying and selling, but an abode of holiness. Neither does He intend the exercise of the sacerdotal ministry to be an act of religion that is bought, but rather a service freely given.

CYRIL: There were in the temple a great number of dealers, who sold the animals that, in accordance with the ritual of the Law, were to be slain as victims. Now the time was at hand for the shadows to end, and for the Reality of Christ to shine forth. Because of this Christ, Who together with the Father was worshipped in the Temple, commanded that abuses of the Law should be corrected, and that the Temple should become a House of Prayer. So there is added:

V. 46. *Saying to them: It is written: My house is a house of prayer.*

GREGORY: For they who resided in the Temple, in order to receive offerings, sought, there is no doubt, to injure those who gave them none.

THEOPHYLACTUS: The Lord did the same at the beginning of His preaching, as John relates, and here does it a second time; which made it a greater offence for the Jews: that they were not chastened after the first correction.

AUGUSTINE, *Questions on the Gospels, II, 48*: Mystically, you may understand as the Temple Christ Himself as man, or the Body united with Him, which is the Church. It was as Head of the Church He said: *Destroy this temple, and in three days I will build it up again* (Jn. ii. 19). The Temple of which He seems to have said in the same place: *Take these things hence*, means the Church united to Him: meaning that there would be those in the Church who would seek their own ends, or who would find there a place of refuge for the concealment of their wickednesses, rather than seek there the love of Christ, and, being pardoned through the confession of their sins, might reform their lives.

GREGORY: Our Redeemer does not withhold the words of His preaching from either the unworthy or the ungrateful. For this reason, after He had defended the authority of the divine law, by casting forth wrongdoers, He here makes known the gift of His grace. For there follows:

V. 47. *And He was teaching daily in the temple.*

CYRIL: It was but fitting that from what Christ had said and done they should adore Him as God; but the Jews, far from doing this, sought to kill him.

I. St Augustine, Bishop and Doctor

Prayer for the Gift of Tears[2]

1. O Lord Christ, Word of the Father, Who came into this world to save sinners, I beseech Thee, by the innermost depths of Thy mercy, cleanse my soul, perfect my actions, put in order my manner of life, take from me what is harmful to me, and what displeases Thee. Grant me what Thou knowest is pleasing to Thee, and profitable to me. Who but Thou alone canst make clean what was conceived of unclean seed? Thou art the Omnipotent God, Infinite in mercy, Who makest sinners just, and givest life to the dead; Who changest sinners, and they are sinners no more?

Take from me therefore whatever is displeasing to Thee; for Thy eyes can see my manifold imperfections. Stretch forth, I beseech Thee, the hand of Thy mercy, and take from me whatever in me offends the eyes of Thy goodness. In Thy hands, O Lord, are my health and my infirmity. Preserve me in the one; heal me in the other. Heal me, O Lord, and I shall be healed, save me, and I shall be saved: Thou Who dost heal the sick, and preserve those who are healed, Thou Who by Thy nod alone dost renew what is ruined and fallen. For if Thou wilt sow good seed in Thy field, there is need also to pluck from it the thorns of my sins by the hands of Thy mercy.

2. Most sweet, most kind, most loving, most dear, most precious, most desired, most lovable, most beautiful, pour out into my breast, I beg of Thee, the fulness of Thy sweetness and charity, so that I shall not think of or desire what is carnal or earthly, but rather love Thee alone, keep Thee alone within my heart, and upon my lips. Write with Thy finger upon my heart the precious remembrance of Thy sweet name, that no forgetfulness may ever from there erase it. Write Thy will and Thy law upon the tables of my heart, that always and everywhere I may have Thee and Thy holy precepts before my eyes, O Lord of unending sweetness.

Inflame my soul with the fire thou didst cast upon the earth, and willed it be enkindled (Lk. xii. 49), so that with welling tears I may offer Thee daily the sacrifice of *an afflicted spirit*, and of *a contrite heart* (Ps. l). Sweet Jesus, O good Jesus, since I long for it, and implore it of Thee with my whole soul, grant me Thy chaste and holy love, that it may fill me, hold me, possess me, completely. And grant me that visible sign of Thy love, a cleansing ever flowing fountain of tears, that these tears may also bear witness to Thy love in me, that they may show, that they may tell, how much my soul doth love Thee: that in the too great sweetness of Thy love it cannot withhold its tears.

3. I remember, O Lord, that good woman of whom Scripture speaks, who came to Thy House to implore of Thee a son, that after her prayers and tears *her face was no longer changed* (I Kgs. i. 18). But remembering her great virtue, her great constancy, I am afflicted with grief, overcome with shame: for I behold my miserable self lying prone upon

the ground. For if she so wept, and persevered in weeping, this woman who sought a son, how should not that soul lament, and cease not lamenting, which loves and desires God, and desires to come to Him; how it should not weep and mourn, day and night, loving only Christ? (Ps. xli. 4.)

Look upon me, and have pity upon me, for the griefs of my heart are multiplied. Grant me Thy heavenly consolation, and despise not this sinful soul for which also Thou didst die? Grant me, I beseech Thee, in Thy love, the inward tears that can dissolve the chains of my sins, and fill my soul for ever with Thy heavenly delight: so that I may merit to obtain, if not together with Thy true and perfect monks, whose steps I am unable to imitate, then at least with Thy devoted women, some little place within Thy kingdom?

4. There comes also to my mind the wondrous devotion of another woman, who with pious love sought Thee, lying in Thy tomb; who when Thy disciples departed from the tomb did not depart from it, but sad and grieving sat there, and long and sorely wept, and getting up again, in tears, searched with anxious eyes in every corner of the tomb, that somewhere she might see Him Whom she looked for with such fervent longing. Once and again had she entered and seen the tomb, but there is never enough to the soul that loves: for the crown of a good work is perseverance. And because she loved more than the others, and loving wept, and weeping sought, and seeking persevered, so did she merit to be the first of

them all to find Thee, to see Thee, to speak with Thee (Jn. xx. 11–17). And not this only, but the first to tell the Disciples themselves of Thy glorious Resurrection; Thou commanding her, and gently instructing her: *Go, tell my brethren that they go into Galilee, where they shall see me* (Mt. xxviii. 10).

If she then so wept, and continued weeping, the woman who looked for the Living with the dead, who with the hand of faith touched Thee not, how should not that soul mourn, and cease not from mourning, which believes in her heart, and confesses with her lips, that Thou art her Redeemer, ruling from heaven, and reigning everywhere? How ought not such a soul both weep and mourn, which loves Thee with all its heart, and longs with all its being to see Thee!

5. O Sole Refuge and Sole Hope of the unhappy, to Whom we can never pray without hope of mercy, for Thy sake, and for Thy Holy Name's sake, grant me this grace, that as often as I think of Thee, speak of Thee, write of Thee, read of Thee, preach of Thee, that as often as I remember Thee, stand before Thee, offer Thee sacrifice, prayers and praise, so often may I weep, the tears welling sweetly and abundantly in Thy sight, so that tears may be my bread by day and night. For Thou, King of Glory, and Teacher of all virtue, by word and by example, has taught us to weep and to mourn, saying: *Blessed are they that mourn: for they shall be comforted.* Thou didst weep for Thy dead friend, and Thou didst weep over the city that was to perish (Jn. xi. 35). I beseech Thee, O Good Jesus, through these most

blessed tears, and through all Thy tenderness, by which Thou didst wondrously come to our aid who were lost, grant me this grace of tears my soul so longs for, and now begs of Thee. For without Thy gift of it I cannot possess it.

By Thy Holy Spirit Who softens the hard hearts of sinners, and moves them to tears, grant me the grace of tears, as Thou didst grant it to my fathers, in whose steps I should follow: that I may bewail my whole life, as they bewailed themselves by day and night. By their prayers and merits who have pleased Thee, and most faithfully served Thee, have mercy on me Thy most pitiful and unworthy servant, and grant me the gift of tears. Water me from above, and water me from below, that day and night tears may be my bread. May I become in Thy sight, O my God, a sacrifice, rich and full of marrow, through the fires of Thy compunction. May I be wholly consumed on the altar of my own heart, and may I as a most acceptable holocaust, be received by Thee *as an odour of sweetness*.

Grant me a strengthening fountain, a clear fountain, in which this defiled holocaust may be continuously washed. For though by the help of Thy grace I have offered myself wholly to Thee, yet in many things I daily offend Thee, because of my great weakness. Grant to me, therefore, this gift of tears, O blessed and Lovable God, especially because of the great sweetness of Thy love, and also for a remembrance of Thy mercies.

Prepare this table before the face of Thy servant, and grant me this power with regard to it, that as often as I will I may be filled from it. Grant me, in Thy kindness and Thy goodness, that this Thy chalice (Ps. xxii), so good and so inebriating, may quench my thirst. Let my spirit long for Thee; let my soul burn with Thy love, forgetful of all vanity and of all misery.

Hear me, O My God; hear me, O light of my eyes, hear what I ask of Thee; and grant that I may ask of Thee what Thou wilt hear. Kind and gentle Lord, be not hard to me, because of my sins, but because of Thine own goodness receive the prayers of Thy servant, and grant me the answer to my prayer, the answer to my desire, through the prayers and merits of my Lady, Mary Virgin, and of all the Saints. Amen.

II. St Gregory, Pope and Doctor

Given to the People in the Basilica of the Blessed John called the Constantiniana On the End of Life[3]

Luke xix. 41–7

1. I desire, Brethren, if it is possible, to run briefly through the explanation of this short lesson of the holy Gospel, so that those who know how from the knowledge of a few things to reflect on many, may be given a fuller understanding of this. That the Lord, on this occasion of His weeping, described to us that overthrow of Jerusalem which took place under the Emperors Titus and Vespasian there is no one who has read the history of that disaster can doubt. For the Roman rulers

are here referred to when He says: *For the days shall come upon thee: and thy enemies shall cast a trench about thee, and compass thee round, and straiten thee on every side, and beat thee flat to the ground, and thy children who are in thee.*

That He also added: *They shall not leave in thee a stone upon a stone,* bears witness even to the very translation of the city itself, for the former Jerusalem, as we are told, was wholly destroyed, while the present city was constructed outside the gate, upon the site where our Lord had been crucified. He then adds the reason why this chastisement was inflicted on Jerusalem: *Because thou hast not known the time of thy visitation.* For the Creator of all things had deigned, through the mystery of His Incarnation, to visit it, but it had not concerned itself either with His love or with His fear for it. And because of this the prophet rebukes them, and even invokes the testimony of the birds of heaven against them, where he says: *The kite in the air hath known her time: the turtle and the swallow and the stork have observed the time of their coming: but my people have not known the judgement of the Lord* (Jer. viii. 7).

But first let us ask ourselves what is the meaning of the words: *Seeing the city, he wept over it, saying: If thou also hadst known?* The Redeemer did indeed weep beforehand over the destruction of that faithless city; and which the city itself did not know was to come upon it. And rightly does the weeping Lord say to it: *If thou also hadst known;* meaning, that you also would weep, you who now rejoice, since you know not what threatens you. And because of this He adds: *And that in this thy day, the things that are for thy peace.* For while it was giving itself over to the pleasures of the flesh, and saw nothing of the evils that were to come, it already possessed, and in its own day, the things that could have been for its peace. Why it held present things as the source of its peace is made clear, when He said: *Now they are hidden from thine eyes.* For if the evils that threatened it were not hidden from the eyes of its heart, it would not have rejoiced in its present good fortune. He then goes on to add the punishment which, as I said, threatened it from the Roman rulers.

2. And having described this, what the Lord then did is related. *Entering into the temple he began to cast out them that sold therein, and them that bought, saying to them: It is written: My house is a house of prayer, but you have made it a den of thieves.* That He recounted the evils that were to come, and straightaway went into the Temple to cast out those who bought and sold there, makes very evident to us that the destruction of the people was in great measure the fault of the priests. For by describing to us the disaster to come, and then scourging those who bought and sold (Jn. ii. 15) in the Temple, by doing this He shows us from where the disaster had taken root. And we know from the account of another Evangelist, that doves were sold in the temple (Mk. xi. 15). What does this symbolize but the gift of the Holy Ghost? But He drove from the Temple those who bought and sold there, because He is condemning those who gave the imposition of hands for money, and those who attempt to buy the gift of the Holy Spirit.

Of the Temple He goes on to say: *My house is a house of prayer: but you have made it a den of thieves.* For there is no doubt that those who remained sitting in the Temple to receive gifts, sought to do harm to those who gave them nothing. And so the House of prayer had become a den of thieves; for such men made it clear that they were there in the Temple, prepared to injure physically those who did not give them gifts, and indeed to destroy spiritually those who gave them.

But because our Redeemer did not deny the words of His preaching, either to the unworthy or to the ungrateful, after He had upheld the authority of His Teaching, by casting out the perverse, He reveals to them the gifts of His grace. For there is added: *And he was teaching daily in the temple.* We have run through these things, touching briefly on the simple record of what happened.

3. Because we now know that Jerusalem was overthrown, and changed for the better by its overthrow, and since we know the thieves were driven from the Temple, and the Temple itself uprooted, we ought from these outward happenings draw, inwardly, a certain similitude, and from these ruined structures of stone learn to fear the destruction of our own inward life and conduct.

Seeing the city he wept over it, saying: If thou also hadst known. He did this once; when He foretold the city would perish. In no way does our Redeemer cease from doing this, through His Elect, when He sees that some have departed from a just life to an evil way of living. And

He weeps for those who know not why He weeps; for those who in Solomon's words, *are glad when they have done evil, and rejoice in the most wicked things* (Prov. ii. 14). For if they but knew the hour of their own condemnation, which is close at hand, they would weep for themselves with the tears of the Elect. Well do the words that follow apply to the soul that will perish: *And that in this thy day the things that are for thy peace; but now they are hidden from thine eyes.*

The perverse soul which takes its joy in this passing hour has here its day. Here it finds the things that content it; for a while it takes its joy in earthly things, for a while it is puffed up with vanity, for a while it grows feeble through bodily pleasures, and then when it has lost its fear of the judgement to come, it has peace in its own day: to find it a grave stone of stumbling on that other day of its damnation. For there it shall be afflicted, while the just rejoice; all the things that now are for its peace, will then be changed into the bitterness of contention: for it will begin to rage within itself, for having closed its eyes from seeing the evils to come. For this reason He says to it: *But now they are hidden from thine eyes.* For the perverse soul that is given over to temporal things, and weakened by bodily pleasures, blinds itself to the evils that pursue it; for it turns from looking ahead at things to come, lest they trouble its present delight. And in abandoning itself to the allurements of this life, what else is it doing but hurrying with closed eyes towards the everlasting fire?

And because of this it was well

written, that: *In the day of good things
be not unmindful of evils* (Ecclus. xi.
27). And regarding this Paul says:
*And they that rejoice, as if they re-
joiced not* (I Cor. vii. 30); so that
should you rejoice in this present
world, let you so take your joy of it,
that the remembrance of the judgement to come is at the same time
never far from your mind. For in
the measure that the anxious soul is
penetrated with the fear of final
punishment, the more its present
delight is taken with moderation,
the more shall the wrath to come be
tempered. And because of this was
it written: *Blessed is the man that is
always fearful; but he that is hardened
of mind shall fall into evil* (Prov.
xxviii. 14). For the wrath of the
judgement to come will be the
harder to endure, the less it is now
feared, here in the midst of evil
doing.

4. Then we read: *For the days shall
come upon thee, and thy enemies shall
cast a trench about thee.* Who were ever
greater enemies of the human soul
than the spirits of evil, who caress
it with delusive joys while it gives
itself over to the lusts of the flesh, and
lay siege to it as it is about to leave
the body? They cast a trench about
it, when they bring before the eyes
of its mind the remembrance of the
sins it has committed; and they encompass it around by dragging it
into the company of the damned, so
that, held fast in this supreme hour
of its life, it then sees by what
enemies it is surrounded; and yet it
cannot find a way of escape: for it
may no longer do the good works
which, when it could do them, it
despised. Of such as these the words
that follow may still be truly under-

stood: *They shall compass thee round,
and straiten thee on every side.* The
spirits of evil straiten the soul on
every side when they unroll before
it its own iniquities, not alone of
deed, but also of word, and even of
thought, so that the soul that before
had spread itself out in many directions in wickedness, now at its end
is pressed in on every side in punishment.

Then there follows: *And beat thee
flat to the ground, and thy children who
are in thee.* Then the soul will be
thrown to the ground through the
knowledge of its own guilt, when
the body which it believed to be its
life is pressed hard to return to the
dust. Then shall its children fall
down in death, when the unlawful
thoughts that now come forth from
her are scattered in the final chastisement of life; as it was written: *In
that day all their thoughts shall perish*
(Ps. cxlv. 4). And these shameless
thoughts can also be understood as
stones. For there follows: *And they
shall not leave in thee a stone upon a
stone.* For the perverse soul, when it
adds to a perverse thought another
thought more perverse, what is it
doing but laying stone upon stone?
And as in the destroyed city not a
stone is left upon a stone, so when
the soul is led to final punishment
the whole structure of its thoughts
is demolished.

5. He adds the reason why these
things are suffered. *Because thou hast
not known the time of thy visitation.*
For the Omnipotent God is wont to
visit each soul in various ways. He
visits it continually by His commandments, sometimes with the
rod, sometimes by a true miracle,
that it may pay attention to the

truths it is ignoring. And should it still continue in pride and contempt, it is stung with anguish, that it may return to Him; or, overcome by His kindnesses, that it may be ashamed of the evil it had done. But when it was far from knowing the time of its visitation, at the end of its life it will be given over to those enemies, to whom it will be joined for ever by an eternal sentence of everlasting damnation; as it is written: *When thou goest with thy adversary to the prince, while thou art in the way, endeavour to be delivered from him: lest perhaps he draw thee to the judge, and the judge deliver thee to the exacter, and the exacter cast thee into prison* (Lk. xii. 58).

Our adversary *in the way* is the word of God, which in this present life is in conflict with our carnal desires. And from this adversary he is delivered who is humbly subject to His commandments. Otherwise the adversary will draw him before the Judge, and the Judge will deliver him to the exacter: for in the final judgement of the Judge a sinner will be held guilty if he has despised the word of the Lord. And the Judge will deliver him to the exacter; for He will permit the evil spirits to drag him to final punishment, to demand for torment the soul now driven from the body, and which of its own will had conspired with him in evil doing. The exacter *casts it into prison*; for it is thrust down to hell by the evil spirit, until the Day of Judgement comes; after which he also will be tormented in the fires of hell.

6. When He had finished with the destruction of the city, which we have used as a similitude of the soul

that is perishing, He goes on to say: *And entering into the temple he began to cast out them that sold therein, and them that bought.* As the Temple of God was in the city, so the life of Religious is now among the Christian people. And oftentimes many will put on the religious dress, and, while holding the state of sacred orders, drag the ministry of holy religion into the business of earthly trading. For they sell in the Temple, who give at a price that which belongs to certain persons as a right. To serve justice in return for money is to sell it. And *they buy in the Temple* who while refusing to render to their neighbour what is due to him, and while despising to do what they are bound by their office to do, with their master's possessions they buy themselves sin. To men like these was it well said: *My house is a house of prayer. But you have made it a den of thieves.* For it may sometimes happen that unprincipled men will have the care of some holy place, and where they ought to bring life to their fellow men by the merits of their prayers, they kill them rather by the sword of their wickedness.

7. The soul and conscience of the faithful is also the Temple and House of God. And should this bring forth wicked thoughts, for the injuring of our neighbour, these will as it were settle there like robbers in a cave, slaying one by one those that pass by, thrusting the swords of their malice into those who are without fault. The faithful soul is now no longer a house of prayer, but a den of thieves, when, scorning the innocence and simplicity of holiness, it tries to do what it can to injure its

neighbour. But since we are instructed without ceasing against all
such perversities of conduct, by the
words of the Redeemer throughout
the sacred pages, even now He is
doing what we are told He then did:
*And he was teaching daily in the
temple.* For Truth teaches daily in
the Temple when it carefully instructs the mind of the faithful: that
it may guard itself against these
evils.

And we shall know that we are
being truly formed by the words of
Truth if we have ever fearfully
before us the thought of our last
end; as another wise man has warned
us: *In all thy works remember thy last
end, and thou shalt never sin* (Ecclus.
vii. 40). And we ought to dwell
daily on what we have just heard
from the lips of our Redeemer: *And
that in this thy day, the things that are
to thy peace; but now they are hidden
from thine eyes.* For as long as the
Just Judge bears with us, and does
not put forth His hand to strike us,
and while we seem to have a certain time of freedom from anxiety
concerning the last judgement, we
should reflect upon the evil that
follows it, and reflecting grieve, and
grieving escape it; and keep ever
before us the sins we have committed, and recalling them weep
over them, and weeping over them
wipe them away.

Never let the joy of some passing
good fortune undo us, and neither
let any passing thing blind the eyes
of our soul, lest blinded by them
they may lead us to the eternal fire.
For if we consider carefully we shall
come to see the gravity of the reproach that proceeded from the
mouth of Truth, when He said to
the careless city, that gave not a

glance to the things that were to
come: *And that in this thy day, the
things that are to thy peace; but now
they are hidden from thine eyes.*

8. For we should ponder deeply
how fearful that hour will be of our
final dissolution, what dread of soul
shall be within us, how long the
memory of all our sins, what blot-
ting out of all past joy, what fear
and apprehension of our Judge?
Which of the things of this life
should delight us when, though
they will all pass away together, that
cannot pass away that there awaits
us? When that passes away forever
which we loved, and that begins
where grief never ends? Then will
the spirits of evil seek the fruits of
their labour in the soul that is going
forth. Then will they unfold the
record of the wickedness to which
they urged it, so that they may drag
it, now their partner, down to torment. But why speak only of the
perverse soul, when they also come
to prey upon the elect, as they go
forth, to find if they can something
in them that is theirs? One alone
was there among men Who with
untroubled speech said, before His
Passion: *I will not now speak many
things with you. For the prince of this
world cometh, and in me he hath not
anything* (Jn. xiv. 30). Because he
saw that He was a mortal man the
prince of this world had thought to
find in Him something of his own.
But He Who came into this world
without sin went forth from it free
of this world's corruption.

Not even Peter dares to say this of
himself against the prince of this
world. Peter who merited to hear
the words: *Whatsoever thou shalt
bind upon earth, it shall be bound also*

in heaven; and whatsoever thou shalt loose upon earth, it shall be loosed also in heaven. This Paul did not presume to; he who before he paid the debt of death had penetrated the secrets of the third heaven (II. Cor. xii. 2). And neither did John venture to say this; John who because of his singular love, *leaned on the breast* of the Redeemer at the Supper (Jn. xxi. 20). For when the prophet says: *For behold I was conceived in iniquities; and in sins did my mother conceive me* (Ps. l. 7), he who came into this world in guilt can not be without guilt in this world. And for this reason the same prophet says: *In thy sight no man living shall be justified* (Ps. cxlii. 2). And Solomon says: *For there is no just man upon earth, that doth good, and sinneth not* (Eccles. vii. 21). And for the same reason John also says: *If we say that we have no sin we deceive ourselves, and the truth is not in us* (I Jn. i. 8). And because of this James also says: *For in many things we all offend* (iii. 2). It is therefore very plain to us that all who are conceived of the delight of the flesh, beyond doubt, the prince of this world has something of his own in their thoughts or their words or in their actions.

But the prince of this world could not hold fast to them before this, nor afterwards snatch them away, because Christ had freed them from their debts, because He Who was without debt had paid for us the debt of death, that our debts might not hold us fast under the power of our enemy, because the Man Jesus Christ, the Mediator of God and men, had freely paid for us what He did not owe. For when He paid for us the unowed death of His Body,

He freed us from the death of the soul we owed. Therefore He says: *For the prince of this world cometh, and in me he hath not anything.* And so for this reason we should consider with anxiety, and ponder daily with many tears, how greedily, how fiercely, the prince of this world will come seeking what is his, upon that day of our going forth from here, since he came even to God dying in a Body upon the Cross, seeking something even from Him in Whom he could not find anything.

9. And what could we unhappy creatures say, what could we do, we who have committed endless sins, what could we say to our enemy, when he comes seeking us, and finds in us so much that is his, had we not this as our sure refuge, this as our firm hope: That we have become One with Him in Whom the prince of this world sought for something of his own, and could not find anything? For among the dead He alone is free (Ps. lxxxvii. 5).

It is true, and we do not deny it, we truly confess that the prince of this world has in us many things. Nevertheless, at the hour of our death he is unable to seize us, since we have become the members of Him in Whom *he hath not anything.* But what does it avail us to be joined by faith to our Redeemer if we separate ourselves from Him by our manner of life? He Himself says to us: *Not everyone that saith to me, Lord, Lord, shall enter into the kingdom of heaven* (Mt. vii. 21). We must therefore join good works to a true faith. Let us repent daily of the evil we have done; and let the good we do for the love of God and our neighbour abound more than our past offences; and let us never refuse to do to our brethren whatever good we can. For in no other way shall we become members of our Redeemer, unless by holding fast to God, and having compassion on our neighbour.

10. And as it happens that the hearts of those who listen are moved to love God and our neighbour more by example than by words, I shall try to tell Your Charity about a miracle that my son Epiphanius the deacon, who is here present, and who was born in Isauria (in Asia Minor), told me took place near Lycaonia (Greece). There lived, he says, in that place a certain monk of very venerable life named Martyrius, who on one occasion went to visit another monastery, ruled over by a holy abbot. And on his way he met a certain leper, whose members were all afflicted with elephantiasis, who was trying to return to his dwelling, but could not through weakness. His house, he said, was on the road along which Martyrius was going.

The man of God had compassion on the weakness of the poor leper, and so he spread his own cloak upon the ground, and, placing the leper upon it, wrapped him securely in the cloak, and lifting him upon his shoulders brought him along with him. And when they drew near the monastery gates the abbot of the monastery began to cry out with a great voice: 'Hurry, hurry, run quickly and open the gates. Brother Martyrius is coming, and bringing the Lord with him.'

As soon as Martyrius reached the entrance to the monastery, the man he thought was a leper leaped down from his shoulders, and Jesus Christ, True God and true man, appearing in that form in which the Redeemer of mankind was known to men, re-returned to heaven before the eyes of Marytrius. And as He was ascending He said to him: 'Martyrius, you were not ashamed of me on earth; I shall not be ashamed of you in heaven.'

And when the holy man went into the monastery the abbot said to him: 'Brother Martyrius, where is He you were carrying?' Martyrius answered: 'Had I known Who it was I would have held Him by the feet.' Then he told them that while he was carrying Him he had felt no weight. And it is not to be wondered at that he could not feel His weight Who upheld him who was carrying Him.

And from this account we should reflect upon the power of fraternal compassion, and on how closely the inward mercy of the heart unites us to Almighty God. For we then draw near to Him Who is above all things, when through compassion for our neighbour we renounce even our own selves. In material things no one can touch what is placed above him unless he reaches up. But in spiritual things it is certain that the more we lower ourselves through compassion, the more closely do we come to the things that are on high. See how it was not enough for our edification that the Redeemer of mankind should tell us what He will say at the Last Judgement: *As long as you did it to one of my least brethren, you did it to me* (Mt. xxv. 40), unless He also gave us, before the Judgement, a vision in Himself of what He had said, to show us that whoever does good now to those in need, does it in particular to Him for Whose sake he has done it. And the further anyone is from despising one who appears contemptible, the greater the reward he will receive.

For what in human flesh is more sublime than the Body of Christ, Which was exalted above the angels? And what in human flesh is more abject than the body of a leper, filled with running sores and giving off repulsive smells? But see how He appeared in a leper's flesh; and how He Who is to be revered above all men, does not disdain to be seen as *the most abject of men.* Why is this, if not that He might teach us who are slower of understanding, that whosoever is eager to come before Him Who is in heaven, let him not refuse to be humble on earth, nor to have compassion on his brethren who are abject or despised?

I had intended to speak briefly to Your Charity; but *the way of man is not his own* (Jer. x. 23), and *the word running swiftly* (Ps. cxlvii. 15) cannot be held back; and this He has so ordered of Whom we are speaking, Who lives and reigns with the Father in the Unity of the Holy Ghost for ever and ever. Amen.

NOTES

[1] That is, the soul mystically understood, which is a spiritual Jerusalem when it remains in justice, and abides in peace of conscience, but which is overthrown and destroyed when it departs from justice and falls into sin. Nicolai, note.

[2] PL 40, Book of Meditations I, Ch. 36, col. 930.

[3] PL 76, col. 1293, Homilia 39, On the Gospels. Nowhere has the theme of the Christian's approach to death, his trials and hopes, been spoken of with such authority, such precision, and with such holy wisdom, as in this explanation of the Gospel of Jesus weeping over Jerusalem. Here all men are taught, as Christ taught them.

TENTH SUNDAY AFTER PENTECOST

THE GOSPEL OF THE SUNDAY

Luke xviii. 9–14

At that time: Jesus said to some who trusted in themselves as just, and despised others, this parable. Two men went up into the temple to pray: the one a Pharisee, the other a publican. The Pharisee standing, prayed thus with himself: O God, I give thee thanks that I am not as the rest of men, extortioners, unjust, adulterers, as also is this publican. I fast twice in the week: I give tithes of all that I possess. And the publican, standing afar off, would not so much as lift up his eyes towards heaven; but struck his breast, saying: O God, be merciful to me a sinner.

And I say to you, this man went down into his house justified rather than the other: because every one that exalteth himself, shall be humbled: and he that humbleth himself, shall be exalted.

Exposition from the Catena Aurea

V. 9. *And to some who trusted in themselves as just,* . . .

Augustine, *Serm.* 36: Since faith is a gift given to the humble, not to the proud, He adds to what He had been saying a parable of humility, and against pride. So we read: *And to some,* etc., . . . *He spoke this parable.*

Theophylactus: Since pride more than any other feeling disturbs the minds of men, the Lord more frequently warns us against it. Pride is contempt of God. For as often as a man ascribes the good he does, not to God, but to himself, what is this but a denial of God?[1] So because of those who trust in themselves, not attributing all to God, and for this reason also despising others, He puts this parable before us; to show us that although a man draws near to God through justice, yet, if he becomes proud, this will cast him down to hell. Hence we have:

V. 10. *Two men went up into the temple to pray; the one a Pharisee* . . .

Greek Writer (*Asterius in Catena PG*): The lesson taught us in the previous parable, of the widow and

356

the judge, is that of perseverance in prayer. By means of the parable of the Publican and the Pharisee He teaches us *how* we are to direct our prayers to Him, so that our giving of ourselves to prayer may not be profitless. The Pharisee is condemned because he had prayed unwisely; for there follows:

V. 11. *The Pharisee, standing, prayed thus with himself; O God . . .*
THEOPHYLACTUS: By saying, *standing*, He indicates a conceited soul. For even from his demeanour it could be seen that he was proud.

BASIL: He says he prayed *with himself*, not as it were with God; for his sin of pride turned him in upon himself. For there follows: *I give thee thanks*. AUGUSTINE, *as above*: He is not reproved for giving thanks to God, but because he revealed no desire that anything might be added to himself. So you are already complete; you abound (in grace)? There is no need for you to say: *Forgive us our trespasses*. What then are we to think of the one who resists grace, if he is so rebuked who gives thanks with pride? Let those take notice who say: God made me a man; I make myself just. O worse and more detestable than the Pharisee, who proudly described himself as just, yet gave thanks to God for this.

THEOPHYLACTUS: Take note of the order of the prayer of the Pharisee. First he recounts the things he was not; then he tells us what he is. For he goes on: *I am not as the rest of men.*

AUGUSTINE: He should have at least said, 'as many men'. What does *the rest of men* mean, if not all others except himself? I, he says, am a just man; the rest of men are sinners.

GREGORY, *Morals* 23, 7: There are four forms in which every swelling of the arrogant is shown to us. When they think that the good in them is either from themselves, or, if they believe it is given from above, think they received it because of their own merits; or, certainly, when they boast of having what they have not; or, lastly, while holding others in contempt they desire to appear as though they alone possess that which they have. Because of this the Pharisee here attributes to himself alone the merits of his good works.

AUGUSTINE: Note that the proximity of the Publican was an occasion of greater pride for the Pharisee. For he goes on: *As also is this publican.* As though to say: I am unique; he is of the rest.

CHRYSOSTOM, *Sermon on Phar. and Publican*: It was not enough for him to hold all human nature in contempt; he must also attack the Publican. He would have sinned much less had he left the Publican alone. Now in the one sentence he attacks the absent, and wounds the only person present. We do not give thanks by speaking ill of others. When you give thanks to God, let Him alone be your thought. Do not let your mind turn to men; and do not condemn your neighbour.

BASIL: The proud man differs from the reviler only in his manner. The one uses reproaches against others; the other uplifts himself because of the inconsiderateness of his own mind.

CHRYSOSTOM: He who speaks ill of others does great harm to himself and to others. In the first place he makes the one who hears him worse than he was; for if he is a sinner, he becomes more content: finding a companion in sin. If he is a just man, he is uplifted in himself: because of others' sins he is led on to think more highly of himself. In the second place he injures the fellowship of the Church. For all who hear him will speak ill not only of the one who sinned, but will also impute calumnies to the Christian religion. Thirdly, he causes men to blaspheme the glory of God; for just as when we live justly the name of God is honoured, so when we live wickedly the name of God is dishonoured. Fourthly, he who is spoken ill of is shamed; and will become more hostile and reckless. Fifthly, he who speaks ill of others becomes liable to punishment for what he has said; which was also degrading to himself.

THEOPHYLACTUS: It is profitable to us, not alone *to decline from evil*, but also *to do good* (Ps. xxxvi. 27). And so when he said: *I am not as the . . . adulterers*, he adds, by way of contrast:

V. 12. *I fast twice in a week; I give tithes of all I possess.*

They called the week the *sabbath*, from the last day of rest. The Pharisees fasted on the second and fifth days of the week (Monday and Thursday). He therefore opposes fasting to the passion of adultery:

for lust is born from bodily delights. He sets the payment of *tithes* against, *extortioners and unjust*. For we read: *I give tithes*. So far do I shun extortion and injustice, that I also give away what is mine.

GREGORY, *Morals* 19, 17 (on Job xxix. 14): See how through pride he laid open the citadel of his heart to the enemies that lay in wait for him; and whom he had shut out in vain by prayer and fasting. In vain are all the remaining defences, as long as there is one place undefended where the enemy can enter.

AUGUSTINE: Examining his words you find he asks nothing of God. He came up to pray. He has no wish to ask God for anything. He wishes simply to praise himself; and insult the other man praying there. The conscience of the Publican holds him *afar off*; but his piety brings him near to God.

V. 13. *And the publican, standing afar off, would not . . .*

THEOPHYLACTUS: Though the Publican is said to stand he differed from the Pharisee both in word and in manner, and also in his contrite heart. For he was ashamed to lift up his eyes to heaven; regarding them as unworthy of the celestial vision: because they had preferred to look upon earthly things, and seek for them. And he also beat his breast. So we have: *But struck his breast*; as it were striking his heart because of its evil thoughts; and also as though awakening it from sleep. So he sought for nothing; only that God might be merciful to him. For there follows: *saying: O God be merciful to me a sinner.*

CHRYSOSTOM: He had heard the remark that, *I am not as this publican*, and he was not indignant, but rather moved to the heart. The one laid bare the wound; the other seeks a remedy. So therefore let no one put forward the poor excuse: I dare not, I am ashamed, I could not open my mouth. That kind of fear is from the devil. The devil wishes to close the approaches to God.

AUGUSTINE: What wonder then that God pardons what he confesses. He stood *afar off*; but he began to draw near to God, and the Lord began to draw near to him: *For the Lord is high, and looketh on the low* (Ps. cxxxvi. 7). And the publican would not *so much as lift up his eyes to heaven*; he did not look up, that he might be looked upon. Conscience pressed him down; hope uplifted him. He struck his breast; he sought to punish himself; and for this the Lord had mercy on the repentant. You heard the prideful accuser; you heard the humble accuser. Now hear the Judge speaking:

V. 14. *I say to you, this man went down into his house justified. . .*

CHRYSOSTOM: This present discourse puts before us two chariots, each with two charioteers. In one we have justice together with pride; in the other sin and humility. Yet see how the chariot of sin passes that of justice. Not by its own powers but by the power of its associate humility. The other is defeated, not by any weakness of justice, but through the weight and swelling of pride. For as humility by its excellence overcame the handicap of sin, and leaping forward reaches God;

so pride by its mass easily weighed down justice.

If therefore you give yourself earnestly to many good works, but take yourself for granted, you have lost all the purpose of your prayer. But should your conscience be laden with a thousand bundles of guilt, but you believe this only of yourself: that you are the lowest of men, you will obtain much confidence in God's presence.

And so He goes on to give the reason for this sentence; saying: *Every one that exalteth himself, shall be humbled; and he that humbleth himself shall be exalted.* The name *humility* is manifold in meaning. Humility is a certain moral excellence, according to the words: *A contrite and a humbled heart thou wilt not despise* (Ps. l. 17). There is a humility that comes from suffering, as we learn from the words: *The enemy hath persecuted my soul: he hath brought down my life to the earth* (Ps. cxliii. 3). There is the humility that comes from sin, and from pride, and from the insatiability of riches. For what is baser than those who cast themselves down before riches and power, and hold them as great things?

BASIL: It is possible also to be worthily uplifted; that is, when you do not dwell in thought on lowly things, but your mind is uplifted in virtue through greatness of soul. Such elevation of mind is conspicuous in affliction, or as a certain generous firmness in the midst of tribulations, a contempt for earthly things; a manner of life that belongs to heaven. And elevation of soul of this kind is seen to differ from the arrogance of pride as the fulness of a healthy body differs from the inflation of the flesh in dropsy.

CHRYSOSTOM: This prideful inflation can cast down, even from heaven itself, whoever is not watchful; while humility can uplift even a guilty man from the depths. For the one saved the Publican before the Pharisee, and led the Thief into Paradise before the Apostles; the other penetrated even among the spiritual Powers. And if humility alongside sin raced so fast that it passed justice joined to pride, if you yoked it to justice, how would it not go! With great confidence it will come to stand at the Divine Tribunal in the midst of the angels. And again, if pride joined to justice was able to cast this latter down, were pride joined to sin, to what deep Gehenna will it not thrust it down? I do not say this that we may neglect justice, but that we may avoid pride.

THEOPHYLACTUS: But someone may perhaps wonder why the Pharisee should be condemned for speaking a few words in praise of himself, while Job who said many is crowned with honour? For the reason that the Pharisee said such things while, for no reason, condemning others; Job on the other hand, though his friends urged him on, and affliction pressed hard upon him, was compelled to speak of his own virtues for the glory of God; lest men should cease from going forward in virtue.

BEDE: The Pharisee is a figure of the Jewish people, who boasted of their merits deriving from the Law. The Publican a figure of the Gentile, who though far from God confessed his sins: and of whom one goes away *humbled* because of his pride, the other because of his humble repentance merited to draw near *exalted*.

I. ST BASIL, BISHOP AND DOCTOR

On Humility[2]

1. O that man had remained in glory with God! For he would then possess, not the glory now imputed to him, but his own true glory, made great by the power of God, made luminous by the divine wisdom, made blessed by eternal life and its joys! But since he turned away from the desire of the divine glory, hoping for a greater, seeking eagerly for what he could not obtain, he lost what he should now possess. And now his surest salvation, the healing of his wound, his way of return to his beginning, is to be humble; not to think that he can ever of himself put on the cloak of glory, but that

he must seek it from God. In this way he will put right the false step taken; in this way he may return to the holy obedience he rejected.

But having overthrown man by the hope of false glory, the devil does not cease from tempting him with these very same delusions; devising countless snares for this purpose, proving to him that it is a great thing to amass riches, that by this means he may become great, and that he should be eager to obtain them: which in fact do not lead him to glory, but may rather lead him into great danger. For the amassing of riches is the beginning of avarice; and this amassing does not lead to any glory, rather it blinds men through folly, uplifts them to no purpose, and causes a sickness like an inflammation within the soul. A body that is swollen is neither healthy nor of use to any man; it is rather an unwholesome state, the beginning of danger for him, and a source of death. And this is what arrogance is to the soul.

This swelling up of the mind does not arise from money alone. It is not only because of their wealth, because of the elegance and richness of their dress that men become proud, nor because of their elaborate table, going far beyond what is needed, nor their excessive personal adornment, their splendid houses, splendidly furnished, their servants, their retinue of flatterers, but also because of their public office men become uplifted above what is natural. If the people have entrusted some dignity to any of them, if they have been thought worthy of some post of honour, or some distinction has been conferred upon them, they imagine that through this they have risen above the ordinary nature of man. They think that they now sit alone among the clouds, that the rest of men are but dust beneath their feet; holding themselves as superior to those who gave them their present dignity, they are contemptuous of those through whom they received their imagined glory. This shows how filled with folly they have become. For their glory is more fragile than a dream; their splendour more unsubstantial than a vision of the night: given them by the will of the people, and ended by the will of the people.

A senseless individual of this kind was that son of Solomon (Roboam, III Kgs. xii), young in years, and still younger in mind, who when the people were eager for a milder king, threatened them with one who was harsher, and by this threat lost his kingdom; and where he had hoped to reign with a more arrogant rule was cut down from the dignity he already possessed. The strength of his hand, his speed of foot, the beauty of his body, had made him insolent; things that an illness would destroy, and time consume. He did not remember that, *all flesh is grass, and all the glory thereof as the flower of the field. The grass is withered, and the flower is fallen* (Is. xl. 6, 7). Such was the arrogance of the giants of old, because of their size and strength (Gen. vi. 4); such also was the empty pride of Goliath who mocked at God (I Kgs. xvii. 4); and such also was Adonias, who gloried in his beauty (III Kgs. i. 5), and Absalom, who gloried in the beauty of his hair (II Kgs. xiv. 26).

2. Among the gifts given to men the greatest and most enduring seem to be wisdom and prudence, and these too have their vain uplifting, and their imagined unreal glory. If they who have them have not also the wisdom of God, all their gifts amount to nothing. For the evil which the devil worked against man turned against himself; without knowing it, what he contrived against man, he contrived against himself: for not only did he injure him whom he had hoped to separate from God, and from eternal life, but he betrayed himself, became an exile from God, and condemned to eternal death. The snare he laid for

the Lord caught him instead; he was crucified on the Cross he planned to crucify Him; and died the death by which he hoped the Lord would die.

And if the prince of this world, the first, the greatest, the invisible master of human wisdom, is caught in his own artifices, and brought down to utter ignominy, how much more will not his disciples and imitators be abased, no matter how clever they are: *For protesting themselves to be wise, they became fools* (Rom. i. 22). Pharaoh used guile to destroy Israel, and was caught unawares in a disaster he had never expected. And the child exposed to death at his order, was reared in secret in his own royal house (Jdgs. ix. 1); and after casting down the power of Egypt would lead Israel to deliverance. And Abimlach, the murderer, the natural son of Gideon, who slew the seventy lawful sons, and thought he had wisely planned to secure stable possession of the kingdom by slaying his accomplices also, was in turn crushed by them, and perished by a stone flung from the hand of a woman.

And the Jews took counsel against the Lord which was to be their own ruin, when they said: *If we let him alone so, all will believe in him; and the Romans will come, and take away our place and nation* (Jn. xi. 48) And after this plan of theirs, putting Christ to death, to as it were save their place and nation, by this very plan they came to disaster. For they were driven from their land, and cut off from their laws and from their worship of God. And so in a thousand ways we may learn how frail is the quality of human wisdom, how petty and lowly, rather than sublime and great.

3. Therefore no truly prudent man will think himself great because of his own wisdom, or because of the other things I have spoken of, but will attend rather to the excellent counsel of the blessed Anna, and the prophet Jeremias: *Let not the wise man glory in his wisdom, and let not the strong man glory in his strength, and let not the rich man glory in his riches* (Jer. ix. 23). But in what shall man glory: and in what is man great? *Let him that glorieth glory in this,* he said, *that he understandeth and knoweth me, that I am the Lord.* This is the grandeur of man, this his glory and greatness, truly to know Him Who *is* great, to cling to Him, and to seek for the glory of the Lord of glory. For the Apostle says to us: *He that glorieth, may glory in the Lord* (I Cor. i. 31) where he declares: *But of him are you in Christ Jesus, who of God is made unto us wisdom, and justice, and sanctification, and redemption: That, as it was written: He that glorieth, may glory in the Lord.*

This is complete and perfect glorying in God, when a man is uplifted, not because of his own justice, but because he knows he is empty of true glory, and made just only through his faith in Christ. In this Paul gloried, that he thought nothing of his own justice; that he sought that justice alone which comes through Christ, which is from God, *justice in faith* (Phil. iii. 9); and that he might know Him, and the power of His resurrection, and the sharing of His sufferings, and be made like Him in His death, if by any means he might himself *attain to the resurrection which is from the dead.* It is here that the whole toploftiness of arrogance falls down. Nothing is left to you to glory in, O man; whose true glorying and whose hope is in mortifying yourself in all things, and in seeking for that future life in Christ, of which we have already a foretaste when we live wholly in the love and in the grace of God.

And it is God *who worketh in you both to will and to accomplish, according to his good will* (Phil. ii. 13). And God has made known to us His own wisdom, through His Spirit, for our glory (I Cor. ii. 7, 10). And in all our efforts it is God who gives us strength. *I have laboured more abundantly than all they,* says Paul, *yet not I, but the grace of God with me* (I Cor. xv. 10). And God has delivered us from danger, and beyond all human expectation. *But we,* he says, *had in ourselves the answer of death, that we should not trust in ourselves, but in God, who raiseth the dead: who hath delivered and doth deliver us out of so great dangers: in whom we trust that he will yet also deliver us* (II Cor. i. 9, 10).

4. Why then, I ask you, are you full of pride, because of what you have, when you ought rather to give thanks to the Giver of what you have? *What hast thou that thou hast not received? And if thou hast received, why dost thou glory, as if thou hadst not received it?* (I Cor. iv. 7). You did not come to know God through your own excellence; but God looked upon you out of His own goodness. *But after you have known God, or rather are known by God* (Gal. iv. 9). You have not laid hold of Christ because of your virtue; but it is Christ Who through His Coming has laid hold of you. *I follow after,* he says, *if I may by any means apprehend, wherein I am also*

apprehended by Christ Jesus (Phil. iii. 12). *You have not chosen me; but I have chosen you* (Jn. xv. 16). And do you pride in this, and make the mercy of God a pretext for arrogance? Recognize yourself for what you are; another Adam cast forth from Paradise (Gen. iii. 24), another Saul abandoned by the Holy Spirit (I Kgs. xvi. 14), another Israel cut off from its holy root. *Thou standest,* he says, *by faith; be not highminded, but fear* (Rom. xi. 20).

Judgement is in accord with grace; and as you have used what was given you, so shall the Judge judge you. And if you do not even understand this: that you have been given grace; or should you through great stupidity believe that the grace is really your own virtue, you will do no better than the blessed Apostle Peter. For you cannot love the Lord more than he did who wished to die for Him. But since he spoke out of very great conceit when he said: *Although all shall be scandalized in thee, I will never be scandalized* (Mt. xxvi. 33), he was delivered over to human cowardice, and sank down to denial of Him; so that from his own fall he might learn to be compassionate to the weak and acquire discretion, and come to see clearly, that just as he had been raised up by the hand of Christ, when he was sinking in the sea, so when he was in danger of perishing in the storm of scandal, because of his own faithlessness, he was protected by the power of Christ; Who also foretold to him what was to happen, in these words: *Simon, Simon, behold Satan hath desired to have you, that he may sift you as wheat; but I have prayed for thee, that thy faith fail not; and thou, being once converted, confirm thy brethren* (Lk. xxii. 31, 32).

And Peter after he had been corrected in this way was greatly helped, and taught to put away his earlier boastfulness; and so learned consideration for those who are weak. And that Pharisee, overbearing, and swollen with pride in himself, not alone trusting in himself, but speaking ill of the publican, and this even in the presence of God, lost the glory of his uprightness, because of the sin of his arrogance. And it was not he went down justified, but the publican; because the publican had given glory to God the Holy, and had not presumed even to lift up his eyes, but prayed humbly for pardon, accusing himself even by his demeanour, beating his breast, and seeking for nothing save mercy.

Watch, therefore, be on your guard against grievous loss because of pride. This man forfeited his virtue because he was given over to pride. He lost his reward because he trusted in himself. He was placed lower than the sinful and the humble because he had exalted himself above him, and had not waited for the judgement of God, but had himself pronounced judgement. Let you beware of lifting yourself above any one; not even above those who are great sinners. For he who is guilty of many great sins, oftentimes will be delivered from them through humility. So never let you hold yourself as more virtuous than another, for fear that declared just by your own sentence, you may be condemned by the sentence of God. *Neither do I judge my own self. For I am not conscious to myself of anything; yet I am not hereby justified: but he that*

judgeth me, is the Lord (I Cor. iv. 3, 4).

5. Do you consider you have done some good action? Give thanks to God, and do not set yourself above your neighbour. *Let every one prove his own work, and so he shall have glory in himself only, and not in another* (Gal. vi. 4). For what have you profited your neighbour when you confessed your faith, when you suffered exile for Christ's name, when you laboured with fasting? The profit of your good work was not his but yours. Beware lest you fall down like the devil, who raising himself against men was cast down by a Man, and placed beneath the feet of the one he had trodden on. Such too was the calamity of Israel. For raging against the Gentiles as unclean, they became in very truth unclean themselves; while the Gentiles have become clean, their own justice has become like a menstruous rag (Is. lxiv. 6); while the wickedness and impiety of the Gentiles was wiped out through faith. In brief, keep before you the proverb: *God resisteth the proud, and giveth grace to the humble* (Jas. iv. 6). And keep at hand the words of the Lord: *Every one that humbleth himself shall be exalted; and he that exalteth himself shall be humbled* (Lk. xiv. 11).

Be not an unjust judge to yourself; and do not try yourself with favour. If you appear to have done something good, do not put that down to your favour, and consign your sins to oblivion; nor praise yourself for the good you did today, while pardoning yourself for your recent or past offences. But should the present uplift you, recall the past; and the foolish swelling of your pride will come down. And should you see your neighbour sin, beware of thinking only of his sin; think also of the good he has done, and continues to do, and keeping everything in mind, not looking at one thing only, very often you will find that he is better than yourself. For God will not examine man with partiality. *I come*, He says, *that I may gather together their works and their thoughts* (Is. lxvi. 18). Yet when He rebuked Josephat for the sins he had committed, He remembered also the good he had done. *But good works are found in thee* (II Paralip. xix. 3).

6. We should keep these and similar things before our minds as a safeguard against arrogance; humbling ourselves that we may be exalted, mindful of the Lord Who came down from heaven to our great lowliness, and was in turn raised up from lowliness to the sublimity that belonged to Him. All that the Lord has done, we shall find, is intended to instruct us in humility. As a Child He lay in a cave; and not in a bed, but in a manger. In the house of a carpenter, and of a poor mother, He was obedient to His mother and to her spouse. While being taught, He listened; learning what He had no need to learn. He asked questions, and, because of His wisdom, His questions instructed those who heard Him. He humbled Himself to John; that the Lord might be baptized by His servant. He resented no one who assailed Him; nor did He use against them the ineffable power that was His; but yielded as to higher power, and yielded to

temporal authority the power that belonged to it.

He stood as a criminal before the High Priests. He was led before a judge; and when He could have silenced His calumniators He bore their accusations in silence. He was spat upon by the lowest servants and by slaves, and delivered over to be put to death, and to the most shameful death known to men. And it was in this way He passed His life from birth to death. And after these humiliations He manifested His glory; sharing His glory with those who were the companions of His lowliness. Of these the first are the blessed Disciples, who poor and naked travelled the world, not with the words of wisdom, not with a multitude of followers, but solitary wanderers, destitute, journeying over land and sea, scourged with whips, stoned, persecuted, and in the end put to death. These are the Paternal divine lessons we have been taught. Let us return to them, that through humility we may also come to eternal glory, the true and perfect gift of Christ.

7. How are we to come to this saving humility, leaving behind us the deadly swelling of arrogance? By exercising ourselves in it in all things, and by keeping in mind that there is nothing which cannot be a danger to us. For the soul becomes like the things it gives itself to; and takes the character and appearance of what it does. Let your demeanour, your dress, your walking, your sitting down, the nature of your food, the quality of your bed, your house and what it contains, aim at simplicity. And let your speech, your singing, your manner with

your neighbour, let these things also be more in accord with humility than with vanity. In your words let there be no empty pretence, in your singing no excessive sweetness, in conversation be not ponderous or overbearing. In everything refrain from seeking to appear important. Be a help to your friends, kind to the ones who live with you, gentle to your servant, patient with those who are troublesome, loving towards the lowly, comforting to those in trouble, visiting those in affliction, never despising anyone, gracious in friendship, cheerful in answering others, courteous, approachable to everyone, never speaking your own praises, nor getting others to speak them, never taking part in unbecoming conversation, and concealing where you may whatever gifts you possess.

On the contrary, accuse yourself of your own faults (Prov. xviii. 17), and do not wait for others to find fault with you: that you may be like the just man who in the beginning of his speech is his own accuser (Job xxxi. 34); that you may be like Job who was not ashamed to confess his faults before the multitude in the city. Do not be heavy in rebuking; nor reproach another quickly or in heat (for this is a kind of arrogance), and do not find fault over little things, as though you yourself were wholly perfect. Give your help to those who have made a slip, helping them spiritually to restore them-

selves, as the Apostle warns us: *Considering thyself, lest thou also be tempted* (Gal. vi. 1).

Be as eager not to be glorified among men as others are to acquire glory among them, provided you remember the words of Christ, that he loses his reward with God who looks to be honoured before men, and does good that he may be seen by men. *For*, He says, *I say to you, they have received their reward.* So do not bring loss upon yourself, seeking to be esteemed by men. Since God is a great watcher of men, seek glory from God; for He gives a splendid reward. Have you attained to dignity, that men should stand about you, and show you respect? Then become like those subject to you; not as *having power*, as the Scripture says, *lording it over the clergy* (I Pet. v. 3); and not after the manner of earthly rulers. For he who would be first, the Lord has commanded him to be the servant of all (Mt. x. 44).

In brief then; follow after humility, as a lover of it. Love it, and it will glorify you. If you wish to travel to the true glory, this is the way, with the angels, and with God. And in the presence of the angels Christ will acknowledge you as His disciple; and He will give you glory if you have imitated His humility Who said: *Learn of me, because I am meek and humble of heart, and you shall find rest to your souls* (Mt. xi. 29): To Whom be glory and empire for ever and ever. Amen.

II. St Augustine, Bishop and Doctor

The Source of Prayer[3]

1. *Faith the Fountain of Prayer.* The Lesson of the holy Gospel today strengthens us both to pray and to believe, and to place our trust, not in ourselves, but in the Lord. What greater encouragement have we to

pray than the parable put before us earlier of the unjust judge? For this unjust judge, who was without fear of God, or regard for man, heard the petition of the widow who came to him; moved to this, not by compassion, but because he was overcome by her importunity. And if he gave ear who so hated to be importuned, how will He not hear Who exhorts us to ask of Him?

When the Lord had urged us, by this comparison with a contrary case, *that we ought always to pray, and not to faint* (Lk. xviii. 1), He added this also: *But yet the Son of man, when he cometh, shall he find, think you, faith on earth?* (v. 8). If faith fails prayer dies. For who will pray to Him in whom he does not believe? Because of this the blessed Apostle, when he exhorted us to pray, says: *For whosoever shall call upon the name of the Lord shall be saved* (Rom. x. 13).

And to show us that faith is the source of prayer, that the river cannot run when the fountain head is dry, he added this: *But how shall they call on him, in whom they have not believed?* Therefore, that we may pray, let us believe; and that the faith by which we pray may not fail, let us pray. Faith pours forth in prayer; and the prayer of faith poured forth obtains for us firmness in faith.

Faith, I repeat, pours forth in prayer; and prayer poured forth obtains constancy for faith itself. And lest faith should fail in time of temptation, the Lord says to us: *Watch and pray, lest ye enter into temptation. Watch and pray*, He says, *lest ye enter into temptation.* What does it mean, to enter into temptation, if not to depart from faith? As faith retires, temptation advances. That Your Charity may come to see more clearly that the Lord said, *Watch ye and pray, lest you enter into temptation,* in regard to our faith, lest it weaken and die, He also said, in the same place in the Gospel (Lk. xxii. 46, 31, 32): *This night Satan hath desired to sift you as wheat; but I have prayed for thee, that thy faith fail not.* He prays who watches; and should he not pray who is in danger?

But when the Lord said, *The Son of man, when he cometh, shall he find, think you, faith on earth,* He spoke of faith which is perfect. For this will scarce be found on earth. See how the Church of God is full. And who would come there were it not for faith? Who would not move mountains if they had perfect faith? Consider even the Apostles. Had they not great faith they would not, leaving all things, rejecting this world's hopes, have followed Him. And yet, had they had full faith, they would not have said to the Lord: *Lord, increase our faith* (Lk. xvii. 5). And consider that other man, when he presented his son to the Lord, that He might deliver him from an evil spirit—note his faith, though it was not full faith—and who when asked if he believed, said (with tears), *I do believe, Lord; help my unbelief* (Mk. ix. 23). *I believe*, he says, *I believe, Lord.* Therefore he had faith. But he added, *help my unbelief.* Therefore his faith was not perfect.

2. Faith the gift of the humble, not o the proud.

But because faith is given to the humble, not to the proud, He said to some who trusted in themselves as just, and despised others, this parable. Two men went up into the temple to pray: the one a Pharisee, the other a publican. The Pharisee said: O God, I give thee thanks that I am not as the rest of men. He should at least have said: As are many other men. What does *the rest of men* mean if not every one else but himself? I, he says, am the just man; all others are sinners. *I am not as the rest of men, unjust, extortioners, adulterers.* Do you see how the presence nearby of the Publican is an occasion for greater pride? *As,* he says, *also is this Publican.* I, he says, am unique; he belongs to the rest. I, he says, am in nothing like this man: because of my just deeds, by which I am not an unjust man. *I fast twice a week: I give tithes of all that I possess.*

But what did he ask of God? Search his words, and you will find nothing. He went up to pray. He had no desire to ask God for anything. He wished to praise himself. And it was not enough not to ask God for anything, but only to praise himself, he wished also to insult the other man praying there.

The publican standing afar off. And yet he began to draw near to God. The conscience of his heart held him *afar off*; his piety brought him close to God. *And the publican stood afar off.* But the Lord bent down to him from near at hand. For the Lord is on high; but he looketh on the lowly (Ps. cxxxvii. 6). But *the high,* as was this Pharisee, *he knoweth afar off*; but He does not forgive them.

Learn further of the humility of the publican. It matters little that he stood *afar off*; nor that he *would not so much as lift up his eyes towards heaven.* He did not look up, so that he might be *looked upon* (Ps. cxviii. 132). He did not dare to look up.

Conscience pressed him down; hope uplifted him.

And learn yet more about him. *He struck his breast.* He exacted punishment of himself; and for this the Lord spared the sinner confessing his sin. *He struck his breast, saying: O God, be merciful to me a sinner.* Hear how he prays. What wonder that God forgives him, when he accuses himself in this manner?

You have heard the case of the Pharisee and the publican. Now hear the sentence. You have heard the arrogant accuser. You have heard the accused; an humble man. Now hear the Judge. *Amen I say to you.* Truth is speaking; God is speaking; the Judge is speaking. *Amen I say to you, this publican went down into his house justified rather than the Pharisee.*

Tell us, Lord, the grounds of this sentence! I see the publican goes down from the Temple justified, not the Pharisee. But I want to know why? You want to know why? Hear why. *Because every one that exalteth himself, shall be humbled: and he that humbleth himself shall be exalted.* You have heard the sentence. Beware of the evil grounds of it. I shall say this in another way. You have heard the sentence. Beware of pride.

3. *Against the Pelagians.* Now let them see, let them hear and learn these things, these irreverent talkers, whoever they are, who presume upon their own strength; let them listen who say: God made me a man. I myself make myself a just man. O more perverse, more detestable, than the Pharisee! The Pharisee did indeed call himself a just man; yet he gave thanks to God for this. He

called himself a just man. But he gave thanks to God. *O God, I give thee thanks that I am not as the rest of men. O God, I give thee thanks!*

He gave thanks to God that he was not as the rest of men. And yet he was rejected as proud and conceited. Not because he gave thanks to God; but because he did not wish as it were for anything more to be added to him. *I give thee thanks that I am not as the rest of men, unjust.* You therefore are just. So you ask for nothing. So therefore you are perfect. So man's life on earth is not a warfare (Job. vii. 1). You are complete then? You abound already? There is no longer need for you to say: *Forgive us our trespasses.* If he is rebuked who gave thanks with such pride, what are we to say of one who impiously attacks God's grace?

4. *The Baptism of Christ necessary to Children.* And after this case was finished, and the sentence spoken, the little children then came to Him, or rather were brought to him, and placed before Him, *that He might touch them.* By whom should they be touched, if not by the Physician? These I take it were healthy. To whom should children be brought to be touched? To Whom? To the Saviour. If it is to the Saviour, then it is to save them. To Whom then, but to Him *Who came to seek and to save that which was lost* (Lk. xix. 10)? Where had these been lost? As to themselves personally, I know they are innocent. I wish to know of their guilt. From where did it come?

I learn from the Apostle. *Wherefore as by one man sin entered into this world. By one man,* he says, *sin entered into the world, and by sin death; and so death passed upon all men, in whom all have sinned* (Rom. v. 12). Therefore, let the children come; let them come to Him. Let the Lord be heard. *Suffer children to come to me* (v. 16). Let the little children come. Let the sick come to the Physician. Let the *lost* come to the Redeemer. Let them come to Him. Let no one prevent them. In the branch they had committed nothing; but in the root they had become lost.

Let the Lord bless both little and great (Ps. cxiii. 13). Let the Physician touch both little and big. We commend the need of the little ones to their elders. Speak you for those who cannot speak; ask for those who cry. And if you are true elders to them, be also their protectors. Protect those who cannot yet defend themselves. Their loss was a common loss; let their finding be one with another. We were lost together. Let our finding be together in Christ. In merit we differ one from another; but grace is common to all. In them there is nothing of evil; save what they draw from the common source. They have no evil; save what they draw from their birth. Let those not hinder them from salvation who have added so much to what they drew. He who is older in years, is older also in sin. But the grace of God wipes away what you have drawn; and wipes away what you have added. For where sin abounded grace has more abounded (Rom. v. 20).

Turning then to the Lord, let us beseech Him for ourselves, and for all people who are with us in the courts of the house of the Lord (Ps.

cxv. 19), that He may deign to watch over them, and protect them, through Jesus Christ our Lord. Amen.

III. The Venerable Bede: Priest and Doctor

Explanation of the Gospel[4]

He said to some who trusted in themselves as just. As the Lord had concluded the preceding parable of the unjust judge, in which He taught us, *that we ought always to pray and not to faint,* by saying that when the Judge shall come, it is with difficulty that *he will find faith on earth;* lest any one be satisfied with mere faith, or with mere knowledge or even by a simple confession of faith, He presently shows us very carefully by another parable, linked to the first, that it is not our protestations of faith that will be considered by God but our works. And among these works humility holds the chief place.

It was for this reason that a little earlier, when He compared faith to the tiny grain of mustard seed, which is minute indeed but ardent and burning when crushed, He added, concluding His discourse, the words: *So you also, when you have done all these things that are commanded you, say: we are unprofitable servants* (Lk. xvii. 10). In contrast to this are the proud, who, though they are far from doing all things that are commanded them, and do only a little of what is commanded, nevertheless, not alone do they dare to pride themselves upon their justice, but they also despise others; and so when they pray they are not heard, since their faith is without works.

Two men went up into the temple to pray. The publican praying humbly belongs to the members of the Church, to the members of that widow spoken of in the preceding verses, of whom it was said there: *And will not God revenge his elect who cry to him day and night?* The Pharisee throwing away his merits belongs to those upon whom that terrible sentence was pronounced at the end of the previous parable: *But yet the Son of Man, when he cometh, shall he find, think you, faith on earth?*

The Pharisee standing, prayed thus with himself. The pride of arrogant men is disclosed to us in four ways. When they think the good within them comes from themselves, or if they believe it is given to them from above, they consider that they receive it because of their merits. And most certainly when they boast of having what they have not, and lastly, when, despising others, they desire to appear as having in a unique way whatever it is they may have. The Pharisee here is seen to have fallen into this vice of boasting, and on this account he went down from the temple without righteousness, because he had placed himself above the publican who was praying there, and because he as it were attributed the merits of his good works to himself alone.

I fast twice in a week; I give tithes of all I possess. Ezechiel the prophet describes for us the vision he had seen of the living creatures of heaven (Ezech. i. 18). *And the whole body was full of eyes round about all four.* The bodies of the living creatures are described as full of eyes; because the action of the just is carefully considered from every side: looking forward with desire to the blessings to come, sagaciously avoiding what is evil. But it will happen to us, that while we are absorbed in certain things, we often neglect other things. And where we neglect there beyond any doubt we are not paying attention. Here the Pharisee is so wholly taken up with giving thanks to God, with making known his abstinence, with giving an account of his almsdeeds, that he has paid no attention to the safeguarding of humility. And what good is it if the whole city is carefully defended against the assaults of the enemy, if one way is left open by which they may enter?

And the publican, standing afar off, would not so much as lift up his eyes towards heaven; but struck his breast, saying: O God, be merciful to me a sinner. I say to you, this man went down into his house justified rather than the other. What hope of pardon have we not here for those who truly repent, when a publican confesses and weeps over the guilty state of his own soul; and though he comes a sinner to the Temple, he goes down from the Temple *justified*.

Mystically, however, the Pharisee stands for the Jewish people, which prided itself on its merits, which arose from the justifications of the Law. The publican stands for the Gentile, who, far from God, confesses his sins. Of these one because of pride goes away *humbled*, the other because of humble repentance merited to draw near to God, *exalted*.

Because every one that exalteth himself shall be humbled: and he that humbleth himself, shall be exalted. And this may well be understood of either people spoken of, or of any proud person, or of any humble person, as those other words also, that we read in another place: *Pride goeth before destruction; and the spirit is uplifted before a fall* (Prov. xvi. 18). And so let us, even from the words of the proud Pharisee, because of which he was humbled, take to ourselves that humility of soul, by means of which we shall be exalted. Just as he, dwelling on his own virtues, and upon the sins of those who were worse than him, exalted himself to his ruin, so we, having before our eyes our own sloth, but keeping before us also the virtues of those who are better than us, shall be humbled unto glory; in the measure that each one of us, bowed down and suppliant, prays *thus* within himself:

O Almighty God, have mercy on me Thy suppliant: for I am not as Thy innumerable servants, sublime in their contempt of the world, admirable in virtue, angelic in the glory of their chastity, as are also many of these who, after public offences, merited by their repentance to come to love Thee! And also, if I by the gift of Thy grace have done anything of good, in what measure I have done it I know not; or what penalty may be weighed by Thee in the scales against it, I know not!

In all this let us take note, that the Lord appearing among us in the Flesh confirmed by His example whatever He taught us by the words of His mouth. For He who said to us: *So let your light shine before men, that they may see your good works, and glorify your Father who is in heaven* (Mt. v. 16), also sought, *in all things that he began to do and to teach*, not His own glory, but the glory of His Father, Who with the Son and Holy Ghost liveth and reigneth God for ever and ever. Amen.

NOTES

[1] Cf. Book of Job, Ch. xxxi, vv. 27, 28.

[2] PG 31, col. 525, Homilia 20.

[3] PL 38, Sermo 115.

[4] PL 92, col. 551. Expositio in Lucae Evang. Lib. V.

INDEX

The following abbreviations have been used: Amb.: Ambrose; Aug.: Augustine; Chr.: Chrysostom; Clem. of A.: Clement of Alexandria; Cyl. of A.: Cyril of Alexandria; Cyp.: Cyprian; Eph.: Ephraim; Gaud.: Gaudentius; Gy. Gt.: Gregory the Great; Gy. Naz.: Gregory Nazianzen; Gy. Ny.: Gregory of Nyssa; Ir.: Irenaeus; Jus.: Justin; L. Gt.: Leo the Great; Max.: Maximus

184–5; repentance of, 210–11; prophesying day of judgement, 306; making ready his defence for this, 308

Devil, the: symbolized by unjust steward, 336; as tempter, 337–8; fall of, 364

Dionysius of Alexandria, 65; on missions of angels, 208

Dionysius of Rome, 65

Disciples: human love for Christ, 32; personal austerity of, 283. *See also* Apostles

Dives, torment of, 314, 315

Dominations, 204, 206, 209; men to be placed among, 207

Donatists, 60, 261 ˙

Dove: Holy Spirit in form of, 52–3, 70

Drunkenness, 318

Eating, delight in, 170. *See also* Gluttony

Elias, fasting of, 34

Envy, disasters brought by, 21–2

Ephraim, St, Confessor and Doctor: on the Mystery of the Eucharist, 121–3; on Charity and Forgiveness, 233–7; on the Various Places of Torment and on the Judgement, 302–11

Eucharist, the: in Prophecy, 111–13; mystery of, 121–3; Amb. on Sacrament of the Altar, 130–5; Chr. on the Memorial of Christ's Passion, 135–40; need to be worthy of, 137–9, 143–4, 145, 154; caution to priests, 139–40; Aug. on, 144–8; 148–51; Cyl. of A. on, 154–61

Eusebius of Palestine, 65

Eutyches, error of, 289, 292

Eve, the making of, 73–4

Evil: need to be at war with, 40; Christ weeps for those who do, 349–50; spirits of, enemies of the soul, 350, 351, 352

Eyes, as signifying all the senses, 179

Faith: nature of, 42; of Christians, Jus. on, 108–10; need to possess the eye of, 122; as the fountain of prayer, 366–7; as gift of the humble,

367–8; as grain of mustard seed, 370

Fasting, 45

Fig, as symbol of charity, 300

Fire, Holy Spirit as, 12–13, 18, 51, 53

Fish: miraculous draught of, 214 ff.; as possible symbol of martyrs, 221–2

Fishers of men, Apostles as, 223

Fishings, the two, 37–9

Flesh, the: of no value without the Spirit, 150–1; pleasures of, 166–7, 178, 183

Food: Clem. of A. on the Christian use of, 169–75

Forgiveness, 85; as neighbourly duty, 93; Eph. on, 233; need to show, 318

Frugality among Christians, 170–2

Gabriel, Archangel, 205

Gaudentius, St, Bishop of Brescia: on Peter and Paul, 257–9; on the Unjust Steward, 332–40

Gehenna, 230–1, 302, 360

Generosity, as sign of faith, 41–2

Gentiles: publican as figure of, 360; wickedness of, wiped out through faith, 364

Gideon, 13

Gluttony: avoidance of, 173; Chr. on, 312; Bas. on, 326–7

God: man's love of, 49; His place in the Trinity, 66–7, 68–9; works of Father and Son inseparable, 71–2; His part, as Father, in the Birth, Passion and Resurrection, 72–5; as beyond space, 75–6; incomprehensibility of, 76; similitude of, in man, 76–7; everything comes to us from, 362–3; various ways of visiting souls, 350–1

Gold. *See* Riches

Goliath, arrogance of, 361

Good: need to do, as well as having true faith, 353–4

Grace, forgiveness through, 34–5

Grape, symbolic meaning of, 300

Gregory the Great, St, Pope and Doctor: on the Holy Spirit, 48–56; on the Supper of God and the Soul, 180–9; on the Angelic Choirs,

42–5; The Redemption the Work of the Trinity, 45–8; on the Natal Day of the Apostles Peter and Paul, 264–7; on the Natal Day of St Peter the Apostle, 267–8

'Let us Consider One Another', Chr. on, 240–3

Life, eternal: Holy Spirit as, 13–14; way to, 306–7; need to kindle love of, within us, 315; blessed state of those enjoying, 315–16

Light, Holy Spirit as, 12

Loaves and fishes, second miracle of, 278 ff.; Chr. on, 281–5; Aug. on, 285–9; Max. on, 289–91; Bede on, 292–5

Love: of God, 55–6; of our neighbours, 55–6. *See also* Charity

Macedonians, 44

Malachy, on offering of sacrifice, 110–11

Mammon of iniquity, 323–4, 334

Man: created in God's image, 76–7; inseparable nature of memory, intellect and will in, 78; observance of chastity by, 153; fall of, 202, 203; to be placed in orders of angels, 207–8; likened to fish, 215; not great through his own wisdom, 362–3

Manna: the raining of, 126, 127, 129; as figure of Bread, 145

Martyrius, story of, 354

Mary, and the Virgin Birth, 74

Matthew, St: working of Holy Spirit on, 54; frugal eating of, 174

Maximianus, Bishop of Syracuse, 211

Maximus, St, Bishop of Turin: on the Natal Day of the Holy Apostles Peter and Paul, 269–70; Mystical Exposition of the Loaves and Fishes, 289–91

Melchisedech: as figure of the mystery of the Lord's sacrifice, 115; Amb. on the sacrifice of, 126–30

Mercy: praise of, 84 ff.; need to practise, 87–8, 318; of God, 90–1. *See also* Compassion

Michael, Archangel, 205

Money. *See* Riches

Moses, 362; fasting of, 34; and safeguarding of sacred mysteries, 63; and division of the waters, 128; and sweetening of the well, 128

Need, our, of one another, 316–19

Neighbour, love of, 234 ff.

Nets, of the Apostles: as figure of subtleties of discussion, 221

Noah: foreshadowing of the Passion by, 115

Obedience: fruits of, 156; required by Christ, 218

Oil, as figure of good works, 338

Origen, 65–6

Osee, on God's will, 111

Oxen, five yoke of: used as figure, 176–7, 182–3

Paraclete. *See* Holy Spirit

Pasch: Christ leads man away from the old, 136

Passion, the: made by Father and Son, 74

Pastor. *See* Priest

Patripassiani, heresy of, 72

Paul, St: on the gifts of the Spirit, 17; on the greatness of the Spirit, 18–19; on the fruit of the Spirit, 21; working of Holy Spirit on, 54; as authority on the Nativity, 73–4; on rash judgement, 91–2, 92–3; on the correction of one another, 98; on the Communion service, 118; on temporal things, 187–8; and orders of angels, 204; Gaud. on, 257–9; Aug. on, 259–63; Leo on, 264–7; Max. on, 269–70; Bede on, 271–6; on Day of Judgement, 306, 313

Peace: Aug. on nature of, 39–40; as inheritance of Christ, 40–2

Pelagians, 368–9

Pentecost: Aug. on the meaning of, 31–9; Christian, sacredness of, 42–3, 45

Pentecost Sunday, 1 ff.

Peter, St: recognition of Christ, Son of God, 32; his fear of Christ perishing, 33; denial of Christ, 54; courage after coming of Holy